ARIZONA'S HERITAGE
REVISED EDITION

ARIZONA'S HERITAGE
REVISED EDITION

JAY J. WAGONER

Gibbs M. Smith, Inc.
PEREGRINE SMITH BOOKS
Salt Lake City

First Edition printed 1977, 1978, 1979, 1980, 1981
Revised Edition 1983, printed 1982, 1983, 1984,
1985, 1986; revised again 1987

Designed by Richard A. Firmage
Cover design by Larry Winborg

Manufactured in the United States of America

Library of Congress Cataloging in Publication Data

Wagoner, Jay J   1923-
    Arizona's heritage.

    SUMMARY: A textbook tracing the history of Arizona
from prehistoric times to the present day.
    1. Arizona—History—Juvenile literature.
[1. Arizona—History] I. Title.
F811.3.W33   979.1   77-10778
ISBN 0-87905-028-4

INTRODUCTION

Arizona has an exciting history. The state has been inhabited for thousands of years. People of many origins and races have contributed to Arizona's rich heritage.

One of the earliest civilizations north of Mexico was developed by the prehistoric Hohokams in the Gila and Salt River valleys. Ruins of ancient Hohokam houses and irrigation canals can still be seen today.

The first Europeans in Arizona came from Spain. Spanish explorers crossed the area in the 1500s looking for gold. They were followed by missionaries, soldiers, and settlers. The Spaniards found Pimas, Papagos, Hopis, Yumas, and other Indians living here. The Navajos and Apaches entered Arizona at about the time the first Spaniards arrived.

American mountain men trapped for beaver along Arizona's streams in the 1820s and 1830s. At that time this region was a part of Mexico. In the 1840s the United States defeated Mexico in a war and was given the land north of the Gila River. Southern Arizona was purchased from Mexico in 1854.

Between 1863 and 1912 Arizona was a territory of the United States. During that era the grasslands were filled with cattle. Rich copper mines were opened. The Salt River Valley became a prosperous farming community. Railroads were built.

Arizona became a state in 1912. But it grew slowly until World War II. Then came one of the greatest migrations of people in the history of the world. An Arizona population of fewer than 500,000 in 1940 grew to 2.2 million by 1975. Two-thirds of Arizona's residents came from other states. Today's newcomers are the latest in a long line of pioneers dating back more than 11,000 years.

We gain many *values* from a study of Arizona's heritage. As we learn about the lives of other people, we share some of their experience. With this experience we can plan our future better. We may avoid some mistakes that others made and imitate ways of success.

History teaches us that change is always going on. A knowledge of historical change helps us to see where we are, where we have been, and where we might go. We can see that the future has already begun.

Arizona's Heritage was written to be read as a story. It can also be used as a resource book. The 29 chapters are grouped into 9 *units.* Each unit covers a major period of Arizona's history. Emphasis is placed on the economic and social life of people as well as political activities.

Each unit and chapter begins with an introduction to summarize important themes. The *chapters* are subdivided into *sections,* each covering a major concept. The main *topics* in each section are printed in bold face type. Some *key words* are in italics.

The *illustrations* in this book have been selected with care. Many of the maps were originally drawn for two of the author's books published by the University of Arizona Press. Hundreds of photographs were loaned by people all over the state. Most of these photos had never been published.

The illustrations are relevant. They tell something important or interesting about the story. Some of the photographs give us a view of different parts of the state. From others we get a feeling for an earlier way of life. We see people of the past and how they lived— their clothing, houses, transportation, or places of work and play. The portraits help us meet and understand persons who otherwise might be only names.

This book covers the full scope of Arizona's history and government. It would take many volumes, of course, to delve into each topic in full detail. Hopefully, the reader will want to know more about the people, places, and events which most interest him or her. The teacher's guide may be helpful in locating additional reading and audio-visual materials.

CONTENTS

THIS IS ARIZONA'S HERITAGE

UNIT ONE

ARIZONA'S LANDS AND FIRST PEOPLE

The Arizona story began when the sea covered everything. The state was then part of an ocean floor. It took millions of years for dry land to form. Pressure from inside the earth pushed up mountain ranges and plateaus. Volcanoes spouted hot lava. Rainwater formed rivers and cut deep canyons.

When the face of the earth was finally shaped, Arizona was a land of great variety. A high plateau in the northeast was separated from a low desert in the southwest by mountains.

Each of these three zones was the site of at least one prehistoric Indian culture. The Anasazi lived in cliff houses on the plateau. The desert Hohokam developed an irrigation system along the Gila and Salt rivers. The Mogollon lived in mountain villages in what is now eastern Arizona.

From tree ring studies, we know that there was a great drouth in Arizona from 1276 A.D. to 1299 A.D. This dry spell caused prehistoric Indian cultures to change or disappear. Some of Arizona's present-day Indian tribes — particularly the Pimas, Papagos, Hopis, and the Yuma-speaking groups — are probably descended from the earlier Indians.

1

GEOLOGY AND GEOGRAPHY OF ARIZONA

Arizona has one of the most varied landscapes of all the states. At higher altitudes there are forest-covered mountains with cold, pure streams. At lower elevations there is a dry desert where most of the people live. In the north, rivers have cut deep canyons through high plateaus. Some of these canyons are gigantic. Their cliffs of many colors tell the history of the earth since its creation.

KEY CONCEPTS

1. The land surface of Arizona has been changing for billions of years.
2. Arizona is a state with many contrasts in scenery and can be divided into three physiographic zones.
3. Arizona has a variety of climates.
4. All seven of the life zones can be identified in Arizona.
5. A rich variety of plant life is found in Arizona.
6. Few areas of the world have a greater variety of wildlife than Arizona.
7. All but about one-sixth of Arizona's land area is controlled by the federal and state governments.

This photograph of the Grand Canyon, taken at Grandview Point, shows the earth's strata (layers) that were formed during four geologic ages.

11

1

1. THE LAND SURFACE OF ARIZONA HAS BEEN CHANGING FOR BILLIONS OF YEARS

How old is the earth? It is at least four billion years old. Scientists say it began as a huge mass of gas. After millions of years, the gas cooled—first into a liquid, and then into a solid planet.

The earth has been changing constantly since it was formed. Dry land sank. Sea floors rose to become land. Earthquakes made cracks in the surface and buckled it. Volcanoes erupted, building up high peaks and spreading lava over the land. Wind and water wore away the earth's crust. All of these forces have been at work in Arizona.

Arizona is as old as creation. There is no better place to study the geologic history of the earth than the Grand Canyon of this state. For millions of years, the Colorado River has been cutting a gorge more than a mile deep. At the bottom of the canyon, scientists have discovered evidence of the first living organisms on earth. This evidence includes imprints in rock of sea life that resembled jelly fishes. Higher up, the varicolored layers of rock in the canyon walls reveal many changes in the earth since its beginning.

By studying the layers of the earth, historical geologists are able to tell what the earth was like at different times. These scientists have divided the past into "ages," each of which has a name: Precambrian (all geologic time up to 550 million years ago), Paleozoic (550 to 200 million years ago), Mesozoic (200 to 70 million years ago), and Cenozoic (the last 70 million years). Each of these ages can be split into shorter periods of time.

Land was built up by silt, volcanoes, and uplifts. During the *Precambrian Age*, much of Arizona was under water. Land was gradually built up in various ways. 1) Shallow seas washed in silt and laid down thousands of feet of mud. 2) The still-cooling interior of the

Descending the Grand Canyon.

earth pushed up piles of hot lava in some places. 3) And at least twice during the Precambrian Age, an uplifting of the earth in Arizona formed mountain ranges as high as those in the state today. After each upheaval, there followed a long period of erosion caused by wind and water. The mountains slowly eroded away to the level of the surrounding land.

Arizona remained under water for millions of years. During the *Paleozoic* ("older life") Age, Arizona was a low, flat area. Great inland seas once again poured in. One sea washed in from what is now Nevada in the northwest. Another sea came from Mexico into the southeast part of Arizona. Only two large islands of land remained above sea level. One of these was an area in the northeast near the present-day town of Window Rock. The second high spot was near Yuma in the southwest. Today, oddly enough, the Yuma area is the lowest part of the state.

The seas that covered Arizona in the Paleozoic Age left sediment that formed layers of sandstone, shale, and limestone. These stone formations are easily seen today. Millions of years of erosion have exposed the beautiful red sandstone of Canyon de Chelly and Oak Creek Canyon in northern Arizona. The Kaibab limestone that rims the Grand Canyon also was formed in Paleozoic times.

Fossils of sea life have been found in the Arizona limestone. As in the rest of the world, living things in Arizona during the Paleozoic Age all were in the water. There were crablike trilobites, clams and other shellfish, corals, sponges, and a fish which resembled a shark. Near the end of the Paleozoic Age, sea animals began to creep out of the water onto the banks. To survive on land, these ancestors of the dinosaurs and other reptiles gradually developed lungs and legs.

Dinosaurs roamed Arizona's swamps during the Age of Reptiles. The *Mesozoic* ("middle life") is known as the Age of Reptiles. During that time, ugly beasts roamed through the swampy "dinosaur belt" in northern

Shallow seas covered much of Arizona during prehistoric times.

Canyon de Chelly.

Trilobites found in the Grand Canyon.

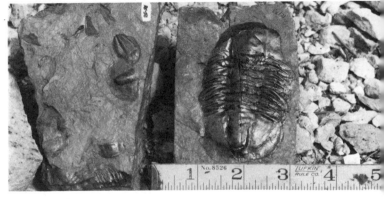

13

Arizona. The largest reptile, the long-necked *diplodocus*, browsed on plants and leaves. He had a small brain and was no match for the strong-jawed, meat-eating *tyrannosaurus*. The latter would stand on his hind legs to bite and claw the huge *diplodocus* to death.

Fossilized tracks of three-toed dinosaurs can be seen today on the Hopi Indian Reservation near Tuba City. Smaller reptiles also lived in Arizona. Remains of armored amphibians and primitive crocodiles, which were dug up near Chinle, have been shown in museums all over the world.

Many of Arizona's ore deposits and tourist attractions were created long ago. Besides being an age of strange animal life, the Mesozoic Age was also an exciting time for Arizona geology. The earth's crust shifted and cracked. In the Bisbee-Warren area of southern Arizona, for example, new openings in the surface, called "faults," were filled with copper deposited by the sea.

Great changes took place in other parts of the state too. At the beginning of the Mesozoic

Dinosaur Tracks near Moencopi Village, Coconino County.

Age, northeastern Arizona was part of a valley that stretched north into Utah and eastward across New Mexico into Texas. Streams in this valley often flooded and uprooted trees. Huge logs were washed downstream and buried under thousands of feet of silt. The trees had no chance to decay. Dissolved minerals in the groundwater seeped into the trunks, filling the wood cells with stone. The logs were thus petrified for all time and remained buried for millions of years. During the next geological age they were pushed up to the surface. Today, the Petrified Forest National Monument east of Holbrook is a popular tourist attraction.

Another big change occurred during the Mesozoic Age. Landfill was washed into northeastern Arizona from the Mogollon Highlands. The Highlands were created by an uplift of the earth in east-central Arizona. Rain swept tons of soil from the Mogollon mountains to the northeast lowlands. Some of the eroded material contained uranium that is now mined on the Navajo Reservation. The Navajos also have vast coal deposits left by a sea that entered Arizona from the north. This happened near the end of the Mesozoic Age.

An upheaval of mountains in California during that same Mesozoic Age was partly responsible for Arizona's dry desert climate today. Most of the clouds from the Pacific Ocean now dump their rain on the California coastal ranges and Sierra Madres before they reach Arizona.

Arizona's present shape and climate developed slowly. The Rocky Mountains, north and east of Arizona, were shoved up during the *Cenozoic* ("recent life") Age. At the same time, the northern section of Arizona was warped and pushed about. Great parts of the earth's inner layers were bent, folded, or cracked. There was widespread faulting at weak places in the earth's crust. Faulting occurred when one portion of the land was raised, while the earth immediately next to it was lowered. About 30 million years ago, the huge Colorado Plateau was raised to its

14

present height. Since then, the soft stone around the Petrified Forest has eroded away. The hard petrified logs—once 3,000 feet below sea level—now rest on a plain more than 5,400 feet in elevation.

Following this Cenozoic upheaval, the face of Arizona began to take its present shape. The inland seas disappeared along with the large reptiles. New forms of life appeared. The new plants, fish, birds, fresh water mollusks, and mammals tell us that the climate was similar to that of today, though more humid. Elephants and rhinoceroses roamed the San Pedro Valley in southeastern Arizona. Camels and antelopes lived in the Prescott area. Primitive horses galloped along the Tonto Rim.

During the Ice Age — from one million years ago down to 10,000 years ago—Arizona was much cooler than it is today. Four times, a huge ice cap covered most of North America, scooping out lakes like a giant bulldozer. The ice cap did not reach as far south as Arizona. However, the colder weather caused glaciers to form on the lofty San Francisco Peaks near present-day Flagstaff. The lower temperature and greater rainfall produced plenty of vegetation for animals in Arizona. The first humans, who arrived over 11,000 years ago, survived by hunting. They ate the bison, ground sloth, tapir, camel, and the huge mammoth which resembled a modern elephant.

Volcanic crater near Flagstaff.

Volcanic eruptions completed the topography of Arizona as it is today. The last active volcano was the 8,000-foot Sunset Crater near Flagstaff. In A.D. 1065 it spewed black lava over hundreds of square miles. There are other extinct volcanic mountains in the Flagstaff area. The highest are the San Francisco Peaks. In early times, there was also volcanic action in the White Mountains in eastern Arizona, the Chiricahuas in the southeast, and in other parts of the state. The peaks west of Tucson are an example of eroded ancient volcanoes.

The Petrified Forest where time and nature turned living trees to stone is located 20 miles east of Holbrook.

2. ARIZONA IS A STATE WITH MANY CONTRASTS IN SCENERY AND CAN BE DIVIDED INTO THREE PHYSIOGRAPHIC ZONES

Arizona's boundaries. Nearly 114,000 square miles in area, Arizona is the sixth largest state. At its widest points, Arizona spreads out 392 miles north-to-south and 338 miles east-to-west. It borders Mexico on the south and New Mexico on the east. California is across the Colorado River on the west and Utah to the north. The northwest corner touches the Las Vegas triangle of Nevada. The northeast corner is the only place in the United States where four states come together. These are Arizona, Utah, New Mexico, and Colorado.

Arizona is a land of variety. Within the state's boundaries is a land of great contrasts in elevation, rainfall, temperature, and vegetation. The elevation dips down to a low point of 125 feet above sea level south of Yuma. It zooms up to 12,670 feet on top of Humphreys Peak, one of the San Francisco Peaks. Rainfall varies from about 3 inches in the desert to over 30 inches per year in the highest mountains. Arizona sometimes has both the hottest and coldest temperatures in the nation on the same day. This variation in elevation, rainfall, and temperature has resulted in a wide assortment of plant and animal life. No other state, except California, can offer such a variety of climate and scenery.

The three physiographic zones. Tourists often think of two Arizonas — the north with its cool summers and the south with its warm winters. Geographers, however, recognize three main physical areas, called physiographic zones. These zones are: 1) the high, flat northeastern plateau; 2) a central mountain belt crossing the state diagonally from northwest to southeast; and 3) the low southwestern desert.

In area, the plateau zone is the largest. It covers 42 per cent of the state. The mountain zone comprises 28 per cent and the low desert region, 30 per cent.

The plateau zone is part of the high Colorado Plateau which extends beyond Arizona into the states of Utah, Colorado, and New Mexico. This zone is divided into sections by the deep canyons of the Colorado and Little Colorado rivers.

The Arizona Strip is the section north of the Grand Canyon which is linked historically with Mormon Utah. The best-known part of the Strip is the Kaibab National Forest. Within the bounds of this forest, which varies in elevation from 5,000 to 9,200 feet, are found beautiful aspens, firs, and spruces. By contrast, most of the plateau country west of the Kaibab is almost waterless and uninhabited. It is one of the loneliest parts of the nation. There are about 160 volcanic mountains in the area. The tallest is Mount Trumbull. Over 8,000 feet high, this isolated mountain is capped with ponderosa pine trees.

The plateau section south of the Grand Canyon. The lava-covered San Francisco plateau is dotted with old volcanic cones. The majestic San Francisco Peaks tower above the others. The Meteor Crater, another well-known landmark in the Flagstaff area, is not volcanic as was once believed. It was formed by a giant meteor which crashed against the earth thousands of years ago. The meteor broke up on impact, but a hard mass weighing nearly two million tons was buried 600 feet below the surface. The rim of solid rock that encircles Meteor Crater is almost a mile across. One can picture the huge size of this crater by imagining the Rose Bowl enlarged to seat 2½ million people.

The three physiographic zones of Arizona.

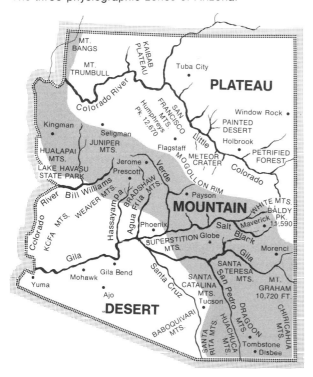

One of the largest ponderosa pine forests in the world is found about 7,000 feet high in the mountains around Flagstaff and along the Mogollon Rim. The Rim is a steep rock cliff that marks some 200 miles of the plateau's southern edge. Rain which falls north of the Rim drains into the Little Colorado River.

San Francisco Peaks near Flagstaff.

The ponderosa pine provides most of the wood for lumber mills in northern and eastern Arizona.

However, most of the water in the high, volcanic White Mountains—in the southeastern part of the plateau zone—flows westward into the Gila River system.

The Navajo section of the plateau zone. The Little Colorado River separates the high arid desert of northeastern Arizona from the rest of the plateau zone. This section is named for the Navajo Indian Reservation which covers much of it. Hundreds of dry, flat-topped hills, called mesas, are found there. One of the mesas is the site of the Hopi village of Oraibi. This is the oldest continuously-inhabited town in the United States. There are also many natural wonders in the Navajo section. These marvels include the Petrified Forest, the colorful rocks of the Painted Desert, and Monument Valley. The spectacular red sandstone pillars and buttes which rise above the plain in Monument Valley make this area a paradise for photographers. Many western movies have been filmed there—beginning in 1938 with the Oscar-winning "Stagecoach," starring John Wayne.

People on the plateau. The Navajo section of the plateau was the home of the early Anasazi Indians whose cliff houses can still be seen. In modern times, the Hopis and Navajos have lived there. The life-style of these latter Indians was influenced by the Spaniards, who taught them how to raise sheep and make silver jewelry. But there were no Spanish or Mexican settlements anywhere in the plateau zone. The first non-Indian people to settle there were Mormons from Utah. In the 1870s, Mormon pioneers built dams along the Little Colorado River and irrigated small farms.

The big migration of Anglo population started in the 1880s after the Atlantic and Pacific (now Santa Fe) Railroad was built across the northern part of the state. The main industries in which people are engaged today are lumbering, cattle and sheep raising, and tourism. Flagstaff, the largest city in the plateau zone, depends on all of these enterprises. It is also the most important trade center and the home of Northern Arizona University.

Navajos in the Monument Valley.

Aerial view of Flagstaff.

The mountain zone is roughly in the shape of an "S." Narrow and arid in the northwest, the mountain belt widens and increases in elevation across the middle of Arizona. It then turns into the southeast part of the state. Some geographers call the mountain zone the "Mexican Highland" because it extends south into Mexico. There it is called the Sierra Madres. The highland zone in Arizona is made up of about 30 different mountain ranges.

Most of the mountain ranges are between 25 to 75 miles long and 5 to 15 miles wide. The mountain tops are generally between 4,000 and 6,000 feet in elevation. But many peaks rise much higher. The highest peak in the mountain zone is Mount Graham in the Pinaleño range. It is 10,720 feet above sea level and

Superstition Mountains.

Bartlett Dam on the Verde River.

nearly 8,000 feet above the town of Safford in the Gila Valley. The Chiricahua Peak in southeastern Arizona is 9,795 feet high. Mount Wrightson in the Santa Ritas south of Tucson rises to 9,432 feet. Mount Lemmon in the Santa Catalinas north of Tucson has an elevation of 9,150 feet. Mount Bangs, at 8,012 feet, towers high above the Virgin Mountains range in the northwest corner of the state. A few peaks in the Bradshaws and other ranges near Prescott exceed 7,000 feet. The highest peak in the Superstitions east of Phoenix is closer to the average elevation. It is barely over 5,000 feet.

Drainage of the mountain zone. Most of the fertile valley basins between the mountain ranges are drained by tributaries of the Gila

River. In years past, the Gila and its main branch, the Salt River, cut deep channels through the mountains of eastern and central Arizona. The rivers roared out of the mountain canyons and fanned out on the desert plain. At one time, the 600-mile-long Gila spread out several miles wide in some places as it flowed gently across the western Arizona desert. Near sea level, the Gila joins the Colorado River only a short distance above the Gulf of California. Today, of course, most of the water is stored in beautiful man-made lakes behind dams on the Gila, Salt, and Verde rivers.

People in the mountain zone. The presence of mineral wealth—copper, silver, and gold—has determined the location of many cities and towns in the mountain zone. Bisbee, Tombstone, Morenci, Globe, and Jerome are some of the towns that were started near mines in the high country. Arizona's best grazing lands are also in the mountain zone. Grass-covered valleys began attracting ranchers as early as the 1870s. At the time when the first miners and ranchers arrived, they found that the Apache Indians controlled the mountain zone of eastern and central Arizona. The contest for "Apacheria" was a bloody episode in Arizona's history. Outnumbered and outgunned, the Apaches were eventually rounded up by the U.S. Army. They were confined to reservations in their homeland.

The low desert zone is in the southwest. This zone consists of broad, level valleys and plains which are bordered by mountains on two or more sides. The valleys are wider in the desert than in the mountain zone. They are seldom more than 2,000 feet in elevation.

Mountains in the desert zone are short, parallel ranges which rise sharply above the desert floor. They are rarely more than 4,000 feet above sea level. Most of the mountains look like great slabs of upended rock. They appear to be partially buried in the desert. In fact, they are. For millions of years, loose soil on the mountainsides has been washed down

Horses watering at the Salt River below Stewart Mountain Dam northeast of Phoenix. Below this point the water is diverted into canals at Granite Reef. The Salt River bed in Phoenix is usually dry.

The Granite Reef Diversion Dam on the Salt River.

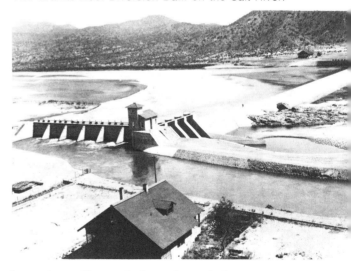

into the valleys. Only a few of the mountains support much vegetation today. Typical desert ranges are the Gila Bend Mountains (2,000 to 3,200 feet in elevation), the Estrellas (3,500 to 4,500 feet) southwest of Phoenix, and the Growler Mountains (2,000 to 3,300 feet) west of Ajo.

Several of the desert mountains are well-known because they are different in some way. The Baboquivari range is the highest. Few people have climbed the 7,730 foot Baboquivari Peak. But many have seen it as they look south from Kitt Peak in the Quinlan Mountains. Kitt Peak is the site of the nation's largest federally-supported observatory for research in optical astronomy.

The dry volcanic Kofa Mountains north of Yuma have been set aside as a preserve for bighorn sheep. The Kofas are treeless except for a freak of nature. The state's only known native palms are found there in Palm Canyon. The Tucson Mountains are famous for their dense forest of saguaro cactus. Also, two of Arizona's most popular tourist attractions— the Arizona-Sonora Desert Museum and Old Tucson — are located in the Tucson Mountains.

The valleys of the desert zone are not sandy wastes like the Sahara. For the most part, the valleys are river plains with deep, fertile soil. Only water is needed to convert dry desert land into lush farms. Irrigation has done this for Arizona.

People in the desert zone. The Hohokam Indians were the first people to dig canals and divert water from the desert rivers. For hundreds of years they farmed in the Gila and Salt River valleys. In later times, the Pima Indians, the Spaniards, and the Mexicans irrigated farms along the Santa Cruz, a tributary of the Gila. Other Pima farmers were living in villages along the Gila when Anglos began coming to Arizona in the 1800s. The first major Anglo irrigation project was started in the Salt River Valley in 1867. Ex-Confederate soldier Jack Swilling formed a canal company and was soon supplying water to farms in what is now East Phoenix. Today, more than half the people in the state live in the "Valley of the Sun," as the Phoenix metropolitan area is called.

Water is still the key to Arizona's progress. Where water flows, Arizona grows. Unfortunately, there is not enough surface water stored behind the dams to meet all the demands for farm, industrial, and home use. Ground water is being pumped faster than it can be replaced

An aerial photograph reveals the contrast between the desert and an irrigated citrus orchard.

Lightning flash before a storm.

by rainfall. Wells are drilled deeper and deeper as the water table drops. More water must be conserved or imported if Arizona is to continue growing at the present rate.

3. ARIZONA HAS A VARIETY OF CLIMATES

The range of temperatures in Arizona is extreme. The year-round mean temperature varies from about 75 degrees on the southern desert to about 45 degrees in the central mountain country. Arizona's hottest temperature was 127 degrees recorded in 1969 at two places, Parker and Fort Mojave (Mohave), both on the Colorado River. A low of 33 degrees below zero has been recorded at Maverick in the White Mountains and also at the Fort Valley experiment station northwest of Flagstaff. Maverick is consistently the state's coldest place. Mohawk, a desert town east of Yuma, is the warmest.

There is also a great variation in day and night temperatures in Arizona because of the dry air (low humidity). On the desert, summer days are hot because there are few clouds to deflect the sun's rays. But the night brings refreshing coolness because there are no clouds to keep daytime heat from rising.

Rainfall is infrequent and unreliable in most of Arizona. The average precipitation in Phoenix, for example, is less than 8 inches. The least amount recorded in Phoenix for one year was 2.85 inches in 1953. The greatest was 19.73 inches in 1905.

The spring months of April, May, and June are the driest time of the year in Arizona. During those months, the Pacific Ocean storms move farther north, where the clouds cannot get over the California mountain barrier. Arizona then has its maximum amount of sunshine and its lowest humidity of the year.

There are two rainy seasons. Gentle rains come in the winter months of December, January, and February. During this season, some clouds from the Pacific Ocean are able to get over the California coastal range and bring moisture to Arizona.

During the summer, usually around the first of July, a change occurs in the upper air circulation. The high winds—between 10,000 and 20,000 feet in elevation—shift from a westerly direction and begin to come in from the southeast. Arizona then gets its heaviest rainfall. The months of July, August, and September are the so-called "monsoon season." Great cumulus clouds float in from the Gulf of Mexico and bring late afternoon showers. In the desert, a rainstorm often follows a sandstorm. A cloudburst may drop several inches of rain in a few minutes. Torrents of water rush down washes. Severe damage is done to roads, poorly-located homes, or stalled automobiles. Streets are often flooded. Few Arizona towns have a sewer or drainage system that can handle the sudden runoff of a violent summer storm.

Another type of storm occurs in Arizona during late August or early September. At that time, tropical moisture comes in from the southwest—the Gulf of California or Mexico. The upper air flow then starts shifting back from a southeasterly to a westerly direction. In contrast to the short afternoon showers, the southwesterly tropical rains may fall on the desert or mountains anytime during the day or night.

The Rillito Creek flooded in 1965, washing out Swan Road in Tucson.

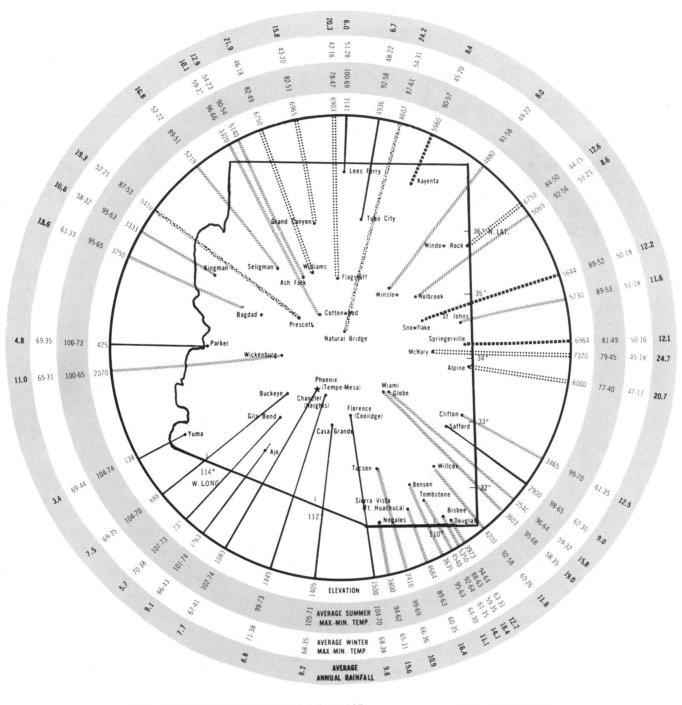

Hot desert climate. Average of coldest month above 32°F. Meager rainfall.

Hot steppe climate. Average of coldest month above 32°F. Slightly more rainfall than desert.

Cold steppe climate. Average of coldest month below 32°F. Slightly more rainfall than desert.

Cool highlands. Average of coldest month above 32°F. Adequate rainfall.

Cold highlands. Average of coldest month below 32°F. Adequate rainfall.

Elevation: Feet above sea level.
Rainfall: Inches.
Summer Averages: June, July and August.
Winter Averages: December, January and February.
(For cities with 20 years or more of temperature records.)
Basic Data: U.S. Dept. of Commerce, Weather Bureau.

INSTITUTE OF ATMOSPHERIC PHYSICS
The University of Arizona
Tucson, Arizona

Melting snow on McKay's Peak in the White Mountains near McNary.

Snowfall is another important climatic element in Arizona. The snow and winter rains provide most of the water that fills the man-made lakes. Snow, on rare occasions, has fallen in almost every part of the state—even in the desert. But the only areas that receive enough snow to remain on the ground are above 4,500 feet. The average annual snowfall in Flagstaff is 55 inches between December 1 and March 31. Heavier amounts fall at the Snow Bowl on the side of the San Francisco Peaks. Skiing is possible there during most of the winter. By contrast, mile-high Prescott gets only about 25 inches of snow each year.

Exceptionally heavy snowfalls rarely occur in Arizona. The record in Flagstaff came in January and February, 1949. At that time, 131.7 inches fell. Drifts measured up to 68 inches high. Under certain conditions, snows have been just as dangerous as summer cloudbursts. Heavy snows block highways and result in the starvation of cattle that are snowbound on isolated ranges. Sometimes, deep snowfall is melted too soon by warm rains in the mountains. This causes excessive runoff and flooding, as in both 1890 and 1891. In each of those years the flooded Salt River destroyed the Tempe railroad bridge. Today, of course, the dams control most of the flood waters so that they can be put to good use.

Climate control enabled Arizona's desert to grow in population. The evaporative cooler has been called "Arizona's sea." It provides the damp cooling effect that some Californians get from ocean breezes. Mass production of the cooler began in the 1940s—just in time for the comfort of thousands of people who migrated to Arizona after World War II.

Air conditioning (refrigeration) is more effective than the cooler in late summer when the humidity is higher—but also more expensive to operate. It was first used in Phoenix to refrigerate commercial buildings in 1931. Now, air conditioning equipment is standard for many homes and for most automobiles and public buildings.

Arizona's warm climate has many advantages. One is a long growing season. Arizona's farmers can produce lettuce and other winter vegetables. Refrigerated railroad cars, first developed in the 1890s, speed these products and citrus fruit to markets all over the nation. The climate also attracts a labor force for clean-air manufacturing—now Arizona's number one industry. Winter tourists, called "snowbirds," have faith in Arizona's warm desert climate and contribute greatly to the state's economy. Many people come to Arizona because someone in the family has arthritis, asthma, or some other ailment that is helped by warm, dry air. These families account for about one-fourth of the state's new residents each year.

Sun City, a fast-growing retirement community northwest of Phoenix.

4. ALL SEVEN LIFE ZONES CAN BE IDENTIFIED IN ARIZONA

"Ecology" is the science which deals with living things—humans, plants, and animals—and the environment in which they can best survive. This branch of science was developed by Clinton Hart Merriam in the mountains and deserts of Arizona. Merriam was one of the world's great naturalists. Financed by the Department of Agriculture, he worked in northern Arizona during the late summer and early autumn of 1889. Merriam tramped up and down the San Francisco Mountain. Twice he rode horseback across the arid Painted Desert. He even descended to

Hikers pass through five life zones between the rim of the Grand Canyon and the Colorado River.

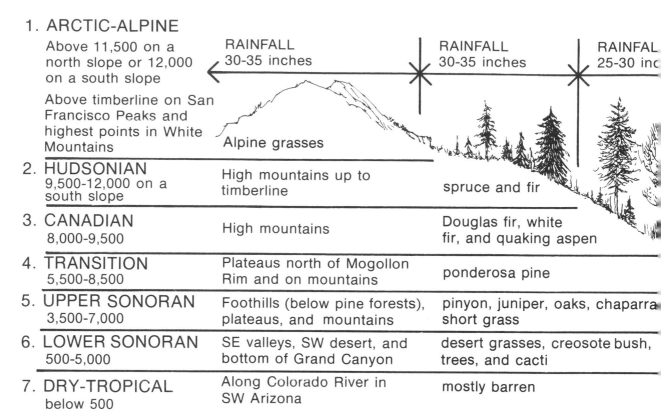

Zone	Elevation	Location	Vegetation
1. ARCTIC-ALPINE	Above 11,500 on a north slope or 12,000 on a south slope	Above timberline on San Francisco Peaks and highest points in White Mountains	Alpine grasses
2. HUDSONIAN	9,500-12,000 on a south slope	High mountains up to timberline	spruce and fir
3. CANADIAN	8,000-9,500	High mountains	Douglas fir, white fir, and quaking aspen
4. TRANSITION	5,500-8,500	Plateaus north of Mogollon Rim and on mountains	ponderosa pine
5. UPPER SONORAN	3,500-7,000	Foothills (below pine forests), plateaus, and mountains	pinyon, juniper, oaks, chaparral, short grass
6. LOWER SONORAN	500-5,000	SE valleys, SW desert, and bottom of Grand Canyon	desert grasses, creosote bush, trees, and cacti
7. DRY-TROPICAL	below 500	Along Colorado River in SW Arizona	mostly barren

RAINFALL 30-35 inches   RAINFALL 30-35 inches   RAINFALL 25-30 inc

Life zones in Arizona.

the bottom of the Grand Canyon. With the aid of assistants, Merriam collected hundreds of plant specimens and sketched pictures of animal life. He studied the effect of temperature on a great variety of plants and animals. From his research, Merriam formulated a theory of life zones. This theory helps to explain the great variety of plant and animal life in Arizona.

Merriam determined that a change of 1,000 feet in elevation had the same effect on plant life as a change of 300 to 500 miles in north-south latitude. There are seven life zones between the equator and the North Pole and seven corresponding zones in elevation. Traveling from arid Yuma, elevation 138 feet, to the top of snow-capped Humphreys Peak, 12,670 feet high, one would pass through all seven life zones. The difference in annual rainfall between these extremes is about 30 inches. The temperature drops 3½ to 5 degrees for every 1,000 feet rise in elevation.

5. A RICH VARIETY OF PLANT LIFE IS FOUND IN ARIZONA

Arizona has about 3,500 species of plants, classified into three main divisions: trees, grasses, and desert vegetation. Forests cover 33 per cent of the state; grasslands, 25 per cent; and the deserts, 42 per cent.

There are three types of forests: tall timber trees, pinyon-juniper, and chaparral. The main timber tree is the ponderosa pine, which grows 200 feet tall or higher. The lumber from it is both soft and durable. Ponderosa beams taken from an old 14th century building in the Hopi village of Walpi are still sound.

At elevations below the ponderosa pine, trees become smaller and usually are spaced farther apart. A good way to observe the change is to drive north from Flagstaff toward Cameron. Between these places, the annual rainfall drops from 20 inches to 6 inches. Large ponderosa pines at Flagstaff give way to smaller conifer trees—pinyons and junipers—

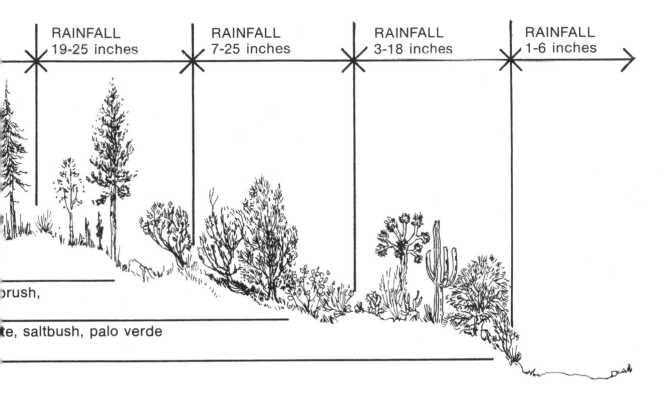

RAINFALL
19-25 inches

RAINFALL
7-25 inches

RAINFALL
3-18 inches

RAINFALL
1-6 inches

brush,

te, saltbush, palo verde

then to grasslands and finally to the northern desert at Cameron. The pinyon tree, a member of the pine family, is valuable for its nuts. Indians gather tons of these pinyon nuts in the early winter. There are several varieties of the juniper. The most common species is the Utah juniper, called "stringybark juniper." It makes good fence posts and firewood.

Pinyon, juniper, and grass country north of Flagstaff.

Chaparral, or brush thicket, is found on the slopes of mountains below the level of the ponderosa pine forests. A good example of chaparral country is the Tonto Basin, a rough, scrub oak-covered area south of Payson. The Kirkland Valley southwest of Prescott contains scrub oak. It also has other types of chaparral: manzanita, sumac, mountain mahogany, buckthorn, barberry, and Apache plume. In other areas closer to the desert, the jojoba grows. This chaparral shrub was called "coffee bush" by pioneers who ground up the jojoba nuts as a coffee substitute.

There are two types of Arizona grasslands which furnish forage for livestock: 1) Short grasses grow on the northern plateau where the annual rainfall is between 10 and 14 inches. They resemble the buffalo grass on the plains of North Texas. 2) The desert grasslands are found in southeastern Arizona between 3,000 and 4,500 feet in elevation. The largest solid grass areas are in Cochise County.

The valley floors in this county are covered with rolling seas of high grama and other varieties of desert grass. This is some of the best cattle country in the United States.

Deserts. Lower in elevation than the forests and grasslands is the third division of plant cover—the desert. The *northern desert*, also called the "high desert," usually receives less than 10 inches of rainfall. It is covered mainly by sagebrush. There are several species of sagebrush growing in northern Arizona. The "big sagebrush" — better known as the "purple sage" in Zane Grey's fiction books — grows three to six feet high. It is grazed by sheep, especially in the winter. Wildlife is usually scarce in the northern desert, except for jackrabbits, prairie dogs, and some deer and antelope along the fringes.

The southern desert is an extension of the Sonoran Desert of Mexico. Much of the southern desert is covered by creosote and salt bushes. Especially is this true on level, sandy terrain where rainfall is limited to 3 or 4 inches a year. The roughest terrain and higher levels of the desert are occupied by the palo verde tree and cacti. The palo verde is the state tree of Arizona. When young it has a smooth green bark which turns dark as the tree matures. The Indians make a porridge from ground palo verde seeds.

There are hundreds of varieties of cacti in the desert. Cacti come in all sizes, shapes, and colors. The largest is the saguaro, whose white blossom is the state flower. The saguaro needs hot weather and will not survive where the temperature stays below freezing for a day or more. It grows slowly, taking 15 years to reach a foot in height. The saguaro takes 150 years to reach full size, 35 to 50 feet tall. After a summer rain, a giant saguaro may store as much as a ton of water in the sponge-like pulp of its large fluted column and candelabra branches. Pima and Papago Indians harvest the fruit for food. They use the ribs of dead plants for house building and basket making. Small woodpeckers drill holes in the giant saguaros for nests. Hawks and vultures

Palo verde tree

Gila woodpecker

The barrel cactus can provide life-saving liquid when no water is available.

Papago Indians harvesting saguaro fruit.

Cactus wren in a cholla cactus.

Herbert Brown looks into elf owl's nest in a giant saguaro.

Elf owl in the hand of Herbert Brown.

roost on the taller cacti to get a commanding view of the country.

The barrel cactus which grows to a height of four to six feet can be a lifesaver. People wandering on the desert can get water by cutting off the top and crushing the interior pulp. Cactus candy is also made from this syrupy pulp. Ground squirrels love the rich seeds of the barrel cactus fruit. Somehow they manage to climb over the thorns to the top without harming their soft-padded feet. The fruit of another cactus, the prickly pear, is used for making delicious jams. The night-blooming cereus is also used for food. The Papagos eat the young shoots as greens. The large turnip-like tuber of the cereus tastes a little like egg-plant when sliced and fried in fat. Indians also relish the sweet, red fruit of the organ pipe cactus. It is eaten either fresh or dried.

The cholla, or jumping cactus, is the fierce touch-me-not of the desert. Its spines are stout and sharp as darning needles. The cholla spines easily pierce shoes. They are a problem to animals, especially sheep being driven out of the desert to cooler summer pastures. Many birds, however, like the thorny protection that

29

the cholla affords. The cactus wren—the Arizona state bird and the world's largest wren—prefers the cholla to any other nesting place.

The agave is a desert plant that is not a cactus but is often mistaken for one. Also known as the century plant or the mescal, the agave sends out thick leaves with a sharp barb on each leaf tip. The barb can be used as a needle. The leaf's fiber provides the thread. The early Indians used to go once a year to areas where the agave thrived. During the spring the large agave plants form a cabbage-like head as flowering begins. When the head of the agave is allowed to send up a flower stalk, it sometimes reaches 25 feet in height. The Indians, however, usually cut out the heart for baking on a pit fire until tender. When eaten raw it tastes like a potato. The stalk has a high water content. It can be used for quenching the thirst of desert travelers.

A great variety of plants may appear on the desert after a good rain. Indian wheat grass grows between the creosote bushes or cacti after a winter rain. Six-weeks and needle grama grasses often do well following a summer storm. In the springtime, countless wildflowers—whose seeds may have lain on the desert for years—sometimes burst forth in a dazzling display of beauty.

A pincushion cactus in bloom.

In most bottomlands where water collects after a rain, groves of mesquite and other trees can be found. Given deep soil and underground water, the mesquite tree may reach 30 or 40 feet in height and up to two feet in diameter. Mesquite is a problem today where it takes over grasslands which have been overgrazed. But it played an important part in early history. Mesquite beans, ground into meal, were a valuable source of food for Indians. Mesquite wood, which is strong and durable, was used by white settlers for roofs, bridges, corrals, fence posts, and fuel. Today, one of the largest growths of mesquite and salt cedar, another desert tree, is along the Gila River between Buckeye and Dateland. This green belt is supervised by the Bureau of Land Management. Biologists, hunters, and wildlife photographers consider this area to be one of the finest nesting places in the country for white-winged doves. At least 180 other species of migratory birds also find shelter in thickets along the Gila.

6. FEW AREAS OF THE WORLD HAVE A GREATER VARIETY OF WILDLIFE THAN ARIZONA

Arizona has a wide assortment of vertebrates: mammals, birds, fish, reptiles, and amphibians. The state has 60 per cent of all types of wildlife species found in North America. Most of them are harmless and more afraid of you than you are of them.

Arizona has nine species of "big game" mammals: elk (wapiti), antelope (pronghorn), mule deer, white tail deer, black bear, mountain lion, javalina, bighorn sheep, and the bison (buffalo).

The largest game animal is the elk, which is not the original native Merriam elk. The Merriam elk became extinct by 1900 because of uncontrolled hunting. The present herds of elk in Arizona are descendents of animals brought from Wyoming beginning in 1913. The elk herds today are found mainly in some of the national forests—Apache, Coconino, Sitgreaves, and Tonto. The Arizona Game and Fish Department issues just enough hunting permits each year to keep the elk from overbalancing the food supply.

The pronghorn antelope is another deer-like animal that nearly disappeared after the white man came to Arizona. The antelope once roamed over grasslands in nearly all parts of Arizona. Today they are found in the open grassy country in the northern and central areas. The mule deer is still found over most of the state and is divided into two classes: Rocky Mountain mule deer and desert mule deer. The mountain mule deer usually migrate to the lower chaparral country for the winter. Arizona's white-tailed deer is not so migratory. They stay at higher elevations in the mountains. The young are born in July and August, corresponding in time to the summer rainy season when browse food is abundant.

Arizona once had two species of the bear family: the grizzly and the black bear. It is believed that the last grizzly was killed in the White Mountains in 1916. Black bear are still plentiful. They are found in the mountain ranges of the north, east, and southeastern parts of the state. Today they are treated as game animals rather than as predators. Only a few bear hunting permits are issued each year. By state law, however, a rancher can still shoot a bear he suspects of killing his livestock.

Pronghorn antelope

Mule deer

J. W. Ellison with bear skins on ranch in eastern Arizona.

Elk herd

The mountain lion is another predator that is classified as a game animal. A member of the cat family, the lion lives in rough, mountainous areas all over the state and preys on elk, deer, javalina, and domesticated livestock. It considers the porcupine a delicacy. Arizona has one of the largest lion populations of any state.

The javalina, while not large in size, is classified as a big game mammal. A piglike animal which is also called a peccary, the javalina weighs 25 to 60 pounds. His habitat ranges from desert washes up to chaparral elevations. The javalina diet includes such things as prickly pear cactus, insects, roots, and mesquite beans. Not as ferocious as its reputation, the javalina runs in herds numbering up to 40. They are popular game for hunters.

The javalina and the lambs of the bighorn sheep are sometimes preyed upon by golden eagles. The bighorn sheep prefer isolation. They live mainly on the dry mountain ranges near the Colorado River. Two federal refuges are maintained for the sheep—the Kofa Desert Game Range of 600,000 acres north of Yuma and the Cabeza Prieta Game Range with 860,000 acres west of Ajo. Hunters prize the adult rams for their massive horns.

Peccary

Bighorn sheep

Mountain lion in the Gila National Forest.

Porcupine

Coatimundi

Kangaroo rat

Coyote

The bison, popularly known as the buffalo, is not native to Arizona. Herds totaling about 400 are maintained on two ranches. One is Houserock, north of the Grand Canyon, and the other, the Raymond Ranch, east of Flagstaff. The Game and Fish Department, despite some public opposition, has sponsored a controlled buffalo hunt once a year for a specified number of hunters.

Mammals which might be found almost anywhere in Arizona include the badger, the bobcat, the cottontail rabbit, the jackrabbit, the coyote, the gray fox, the kangaroo rat, the porcupine, the raccoon, the ringtail (in the raccoon family), and both striped and spotted skunks. Squirrels—the Abert, Kaibab, Arizona Gray, and Red—live in forested areas. Beavers are found along both desert and mountain streams which have cottonwood, willow, or aspen trees nearby. The long slender coatimundi, whose tail sticks straight up, is found in the high oak grasslands and canyons of southeastern Arizona. The coatimundis, as adept in trees as on the ground, travel in groups of forty or fifty. They feed on lizards, bird eggs, rodents, fruits, nuts, insects, and grasshoppers.

The coyote, whose name means "barking dog," is perhaps the most adaptable animal in the state. He lives anywhere—on the desert, in pine trees, or within city limits. Coyotes eat a wide variety of plants, small animals, insects, and carrion. They will scavenge in garbage cans for food. The coyote continues to multiply in numbers, despite all efforts to exterminate him by hunting, trapping, or poisoning.

Arizona's birds range in size from the small hummingbird to the Merrian wild turkey, the state's largest game bird. The wild turkey is found in pine forests of central Arizona. Listed as one of ten "big game" species in Arizona, it is being transplanted to mountains of southern Arizona—the Santa Catalina, Chiricahua, Graham, and Huachuca—where it thrived in earlier times. It is also found in the Arizona Strip.

Five species of quail once lived in Arizona. Two of these—the bobwhite and Benson's quail—are now extinct here. The soft-voiced Gambel's quail is abundant today in chaparral country below 4,000 feet in elevation. Gambel's quail are easily spotted by the chestnut crown and head plume that extends over the beak. The scaled quail is seen mainly in Cochise County. Mearn's quail are abundant in grassy, live-oak areas in years of good rainfall.

Two migratory doves, the white-winged and mourning, are popular game birds. The heavier white-winged dove comes north from Mexico for the summer. The mourning dove migrates south from as far away as Canada to spend the winter in Arizona.

The most comical Arizona desert bird is the chicken-sized roadrunner. Not sure that he is a bird, the roadrunner would rather run than fly. He frequently races cars along the roadside. A member of the cuckoo family, the roadrunner has an impressive foot-long tail. Unlike most birds, he eats lizards and snakes.

More than 60 species of fish now inhabit Arizona's waters. Less than half, 28, are native. There is only one native game fish, the beautiful yellow-golden Arizona trout. In its pure form it is found in Greenlee County in the headwaters of Eagle Creek, a tributary of the Gila River. Elsewhere in Arizona, the native trout is crossed with the imported rainbow trout. This hybrid and other planted imported trout species—brown, cutthroat, and eastern brook—are found mostly in the lakes and streams of timbered regions.

In warmer waters, the bigmouthed black bass is the most important sought-after game fish. Other warm water fish include the striped and smallmouthed bass, channel catfish, yellow perch, white crappie, walleye, green sunfish, and bluegill.

Arizona has several unique varieties of minnows. The Colorado squawfish is one of the world's largest, reaching five feet in length and one hundred pounds in weight. The smaller 16-inch, two-pound bonytail is a fun fish to catch in Arizona's rivers, but is too bony to eat. The Gila topminnow and the desert pupfish are among the smallest North American fish.

Roadrunner
Mourning dove

A happy fisherman with a huge catfish.
Crappie

Rattlesnake

Reptiles. Besides mammals and birds, Arizona's fauna includes nearly a hundred reptiles: 48 species of snakes, 44 species of lizards, and five species of turtles.

There are many varieties of *snakes* in Arizona. Some are rare and hard to find. Others, like the gopher snake, are found in most parts of the state. Known as the bull snake, the gopher snake is a real value to farmers. It devours mice, rats, and gophers which eat crops.

The only poisonous snakes in Arizona are the rattlesnakes and the coral snake. The diamond-backed rattler is the snake which has caused the most human deaths in Arizona. Its venom is injected into flesh through hollow fangs. The diamond-backed usually vibrates its tail and hisses before striking.

All other species of rattlesnakes in Arizona are also poisonous. One, the sidewinder, is small and has horns on its head. It moves by wiggling sideways in an "S" shape.

The coral snake has beautiful red, whitish-yellow, and black bands. The coral snake is shy and tries to avoid humans. It is unlikely to bite unless cornered or picked up. But the coral snake's venom can be deadly.

The king snake looks a lot like the coral snake. But the king snake is harmless to people. It kills other reptiles, including rattlesnakes, by squeezing them to death.

Many kinds of *lizards* are found in the deserts and mountains of Arizona. The Gila monster is the only poisonous lizard in the United States. The adult Gila monster is large and slow moving. Its back looks like a pattern of black and yellowish beads. The Gila monster minds its own business if left alone. It does not have fangs like a rattlesnake. The Gila monster has to bite and chew in its poison. This poison comes from glands in the animal's jaws. The Gila monster is now protected by law to keep it from becoming extinct.

The chuckwalla is another large lizard found in Arizona. It can change colors. The chuckwalla hides by wedging its body in a crevice and inflating it with air. Indians, who enjoyed the lizard's tender meat, used a pointed stick to puncture the chuckwalla's hide and pry it loose.

Chuckwalla

The flat-bodied horned lizard, called a horned toad, is also protected by Arizona law. Six of the seven American species of this small lizard are found in Arizona. When alarmed or angered, the horned toad can hold blood in its head and squirt it from the eyes. Gentle by nature, the horned toad is often made a pet by Arizona children.

Amphibians. There are 21 species of frogs and toads in Arizona, but only one specie of salamanders—the tiger salamander. The larvae of the salamander, called water dogs, are an excellent bass bait.

The bullfrog is not native to Arizona. It was imported from the southeastern part of the United States. Most of the toads are like those found in Mexico. The spadefoot toads become active with the summer rains. They seem to "explode" out of the ground and breed in temporary, rain-formed ponds. The Colorado River toad is both the largest and most poisonous. Its body length may reach six inches. The toxic skin secretion of the Colorado toad can be deadly to dogs that mouth it.

A mother horned toad with her young.

Colorado River toad

7. ALL BUT ABOUT ONE-SIXTH OF ARIZONA'S LAND AREA IS CONTROLLED BY THE FEDERAL AND STATE GOVERNMENTS

Only five states—Alaska, Texas, California, Montana, and New Mexico—are larger than Arizona in size. There are 72,688,000 acres of land in Arizona. But only about one-sixth of this land is in private hands. The remainder is owned by the federal government, Indian tribes, and the state.

Federal lands. More than 70 per cent of Arizona is either owned outright by the federal government or is held in trust for Indian tribes. The federal land includes seven national forests, comprising over 11 million acres. The Congress placed most of this land in forest reserves before Arizona became a state in 1912. The idea in removing these lands from private settlement was to preserve the timber and protect the watersheds. According to conservation-minded President Theodore Roosevelt, the public forest reserves accomplish "the greatest good for the greatest number of people in the long run."

The forest lands are now regulated scientifically by the Forest Service, a branch of the Department of Agriculture. This agency determines which trees should be cut for lumber and replaced with young trees. The Forest Service also limits the number of cattle and sheep on the forest ranges to prevent overgrazing and erosion. Recreational facilities are provided for campers.

Sheep grazing on the Coconino National Forest south of Flagstaff.

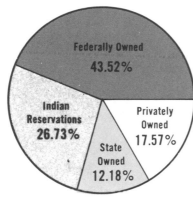

ARIZONA

LAND

OWNERSHIP

	Acres	% of Total
Federally Owned Lands . .	31,633,000	43.52%
Federal Trust Lands (Indian)	19,427,000	26.73
State Owned Land	8,857,000	12.18
Privately Owned Lands . .	12,771,100	17.57
TOTAL	72,688,000	100.00%

Land ownership chart.

Federal Land Includes Acreage In National Forests, As Follows

National Forest	Acres	National Forest	Acres
Apache	1,190,121	Prescott	1,247,572
Coconino	1,800,638	Sitgreaves	790,192
Coronado	1,721,329	Tonto	2,894,846
Kaibab	1,723,506	TOTAL	11,358,204

DISTRIBUTION OF ARIZONA LAND OWNERSHIP BY COUNTY

County	Federal Owned	Indian Reservations	State Owned	Privately Owned	Total Acreage
	(In Thousand Acres)				
Apache	646	4,552	695	1,258	7,151
Cochise	959	—	1,363	1,682	4,004
Coconino	4,907	4,402	1,034	1,544	11,887
Gila	1,794	1,149	30	67	3,040
Graham	1,215	991	504	240	2,950
Greenlee	988	—	143	68	1,199
Maricopa	3,750	252	465	1,438	5,905
Mohave	5,692	574	437	1,783	8,486
Navajo	621	4,197	343	1,182	6,343
Pima	1,806	2,480	921	707	5,914
Pinal	700	599	1,354	789	3,442
Santa Cruz	436	—	62	299	797
Yavapai	2,688	4	1,272	1,215	5,179
Yuma	5,431	227	234	499	6,391
TOTAL	31,633	19,427	8,857	12,771	72,688

Source: State Land Department; Arizona Department of Revenue; Office of Indian Affairs; and Federal Agencies, from "Arizona Agricultural Statistics, 1974."

Arizona land ownership map.

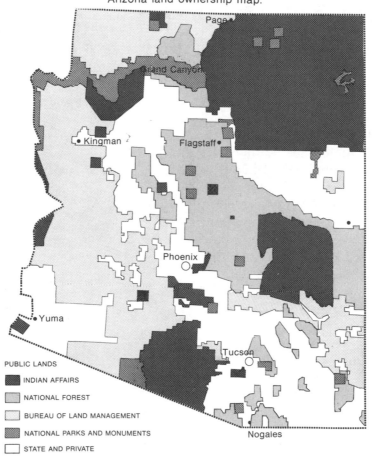

PUBLIC LANDS

INDIAN AFFAIRS

NATIONAL FOREST

BUREAU OF LAND MANAGEMENT

NATIONAL PARKS AND MONUMENTS

STATE AND PRIVATE

Contrast between grazed and ungrazed land in the desert northwest of Glendale.

The Bureau of Land Management, in the Department of Interior, administers over 12 million acres of federal land not in the national forests or set aside for some other purpose. One of the biggest jobs of the BLM is to regulate grazing lands leased to ranchers. Before the Taylor Grazing Act was passed in 1934, there was very little regulation and lessees were permitted to overstock the public domain. Too many cattle destroyed the rich grasslands and caused erosion of the soil.

Other agencies in the Department of Interior also control some federal land in the state. The National Park Service is in charge of the Grand Canyon National Park and other federal parks and monuments in Arizona. The Fish and Wildlife Service supervises several wildlife refuges.

Most military installations in Arizona are on federal land and under the Department of Defense.

A trout fisherman wades Oak Creek in the Coconino National Forest.

People enjoy boating on Lynx Lake in the Prescott National Forest.

Indian reservations cover nearly 27 per cent of Arizona's land area. Largest of the 19 reservations is the Navajo, which has nearly nine million acres. The smallest is the 85-acre Tonto-Apache Reservation near Payson.

State lands. The State of Arizona owns more than 9.6 million acres of desert, grass, and timber lands. Most of this land, which is administered by the State Land Commissioner, was acquired under the Enabling Act of 1910. By this law, Arizona was given four sections in each township (36 sections) for benefit of the state's public schools. In some cases these lands—sections 2, 16, 32, and 36—had already been homesteaded by pioneers or set aside for some other purpose. So the state selected "in lieu" lands. That is why there are large blocks of state-owned land, containing hundreds of square miles, near the national forests and Indian reservations. More than 90 per cent of the state lands are now under lease.

The major use of the state leased lands has been for livestock grazing.

The Arizona State Parks Board is in charge of some state property. This board maintains a number of recreational parks, camping grounds, and historic sites for public use. The largest, Lake Havasu State Park, contains over 13,000 acres along the Colorado River. One of the smallest, the Tombstone Courthouse, has about one acre.

Private lands. Nearly 13 million acres of land in Arizona are owned by individuals or corporations. The largest concentration of this land is in the central urban part of the state in the vicinities of Phoenix and Tucson. Most of the irrigated farming land in the Salt River, Gila, Santa Cruz, and other valleys is privately-owned. More than a million acres of this agricultural land is devoted to the production of cotton, vegetables, alfalfa, citrus, grains, and other crops.

39

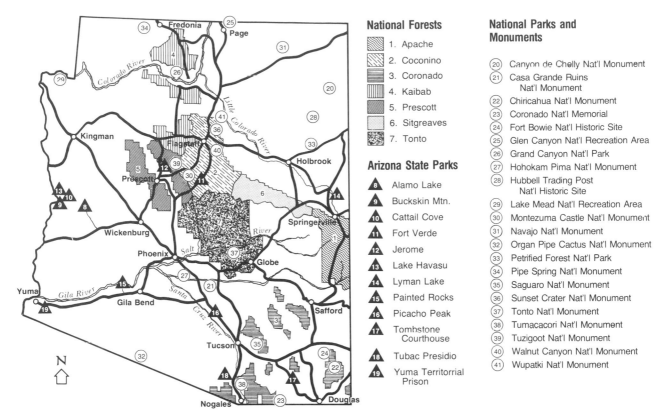

National Forests

1. Apache
2. Coconino
3. Coronado
4. Kaibab
5. Prescott
6. Sitgreaves
7. Tonto

Arizona State Parks

8. Alamo Lake
9. Buckskin Mtn.
10. Cattail Cove
11. Fort Verde
12. Jerome
13. Lake Havasu
14. Lyman Lake
15. Painted Rocks
16. Picacho Peak
17. Tombstone Courthouse
18. Tubac Presidio
19. Yuma Territorrial Prison

National Parks and Monuments

20. Canyon de Chelly Nat'l Monument
21. Casa Grande Ruins Nat'l Monument
22. Chiricahua Nat'l Monument
23. Coronado Nat'l Memorial
24. Fort Bowie Nat'l Historic Site
25. Glen Canyon Nat'l Recreation Area
26. Grand Canyon Nat'l Park
27. Hohokam Pima Nat'l Monument
28. Hubbell Trading Post Nat'l Historic Site
29. Lake Mead Nat'l Recreation Area
30. Montezuma Castle Nat'l Monument
31. Navajo Nat'l Monument
32. Organ Pipe Cactus Nat'l Monument
33. Petrified Forest Nat'l Park
34. Pipe Spring Nat'l Monument
35. Saguaro Nat'l Monument
36. Sunset Crater Nat'l Monument
37. Tonto Nat'l Monument
38. Tumacacori Nat'l Monument
39. Tuzigoot Nat'l Monument
40. Walnut Canyon Nat'l Monument
41. Wupatki Nat'l Monument

Arizona State Parks, National Forests, National Parks and Monuments.
Seven new state parks have been added to the list. Boyce Thompson Arboretum is a desert museum west of Superior. Catalina is a desert park north of Tucson. Dead Horse Ranch State Park is across the Verde River from Cottonwood. The Lost Dutchman State Park is northeast of Apache Junction. The McFarland State Historic Park is in Florence. The Patagonia Lake State Park is northeast of Nogales. The Riordan State Historic Park in Flagstaff features the 1904 homes of the Riordan brothers. Can you find these parks on an Arizona road map?

Cotton farming near Marana, 1979.

A citrus orchard in the Salt River Valley.

Irrigation ditch and cotton field in south Phoenix.

Irrigation water pumped by natural gas engine in Rainbow Valley.

On a land-ownership map of Arizona, several areas look like a checkerboard—especially in the northeast (south of the Navajo Reservation) and in the northwest (between Prescott and Kingman). About every other section is privately-owned land. The alternate sections are either state or BLM lands. There is a reason for this checkerboard pattern of ownership in the northern part of the state.

Most of the private sections once belonged to the Atlantic and Pacific Railroad. The federal government gave this railroad 40 square miles of land for each mile of track laid in Arizona. The odd-numbered sections — twenty on each side of the right-of-way went to the railroad. The federal government kept the even-numbered sections. Much of the railroad land was eventually bought by the big cattle companies. By buying the railroad land and leasing the alternate public domain sections, the companies were able to put together huge ranches. The most famous, of course, was the Aztec Land and Cattle Company, better-known as the Hashknife outfit, in the Holbrook area.

Diorama at the Arizona State Museum in Tucson. Hunters disabled the elephant by cutting tendons in its hind legs with stone knives. They then killed the animal with spears.

2

ANCIENT INDIANS OF ARIZONA

Indians lived in Arizona thousands of years before the Europeans came. For untold generations they called this region home and made a living here. They hunted animals, gathered wild foods, and eventually learned to farm. They survived with the materials at hand. Their food, clothing, and shelter were products of their environment. The Indians lived in harmony with nature, neither spoiling nor wasting it.

Unfortunately, the prehistoric Indians did not have a written language to record their daily activities. To learn about their cultures we must depend on material remains left at campsites, in caves, or in cliff dwellings. Modern scientific skills—such as tree-ring dating, the carbon 14 process, and archeomagnetism—have been used to fill in many parts of the story.

We do not have as much information on prehistoric life as we would like. But there is no doubt about one thing—the Indians were here first and are deserving of our study in their own right. Too often the story of the Indian is told only when he meets the white man—and then only from the white man's point of view.

KEY CONCEPTS

1. People have lived in Arizona for at least 11,000 years.

2. There were three main Indian cultures in prehistoric Arizona.

3. The Hohokam Indians built a civilization in the desert that lasted about 1,700 years.

4. The Anasazi Indian culture can be traced back nearly 2,000 years.

5. The Mogollon Indians developed a prehistoric culture in the mountains of eastern Arizona.

6. Other prehistoric Indians lived in northern Arizona and along the Colorado River.

2

1. PEOPLE HAVE LIVED IN ARIZONA FOR AT LEAST 11,000 YEARS

Elephant Hunters. Indians definitely were living in what is now Arizona 11,000 years ago—and probably much earlier. They were hunters and most likely came from Asia by way of Alaska in search of big game. A land bridge across the Bering Strait was opened after the fourth and last glacier began melting about 18,000 years ago.

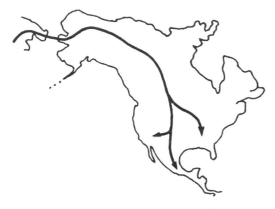

Route of early man from Asia into North America.

The first Indians found Arizona cooler and wetter than it is today. Land that is now desert was covered with dense vegetation and dotted with lakes and streams. Thick grass supported a variety of big animals. The largest were the mammoths and mastodons. These were prehistoric elephants which stood as high as 13 feet at the shoulder.

The nomadic Indians who stalked the giant beasts are called "elephant hunters." They usually waited for their prey at a watering place and worked together in killing it. The hunters used stone spearheads with a detachable foreshaft on each point. When the main shaft was removed, the wounded animal could not easily get the embedded point out of its body.

Two kill sites were discovered in Arizona and excavated in the 1950s. An extinct mam-

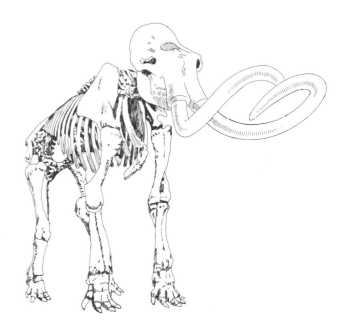

Skeleton of the imperial mammoth.

moth was uncovered in a sandy bank along Greenbush Creek near Naco by archaeologists from the University of Arizona. The remains of the huge Naco mammoth had eight stone spear points in its head and rib cage. It was covered with silt soon after its death and therefore was well-preserved.

Another kill site was found in the same vicinity. Nine elephants were unearthed at the Lehner Ranch on the west bank of the San Pedro River. The bones of a primitive horse, a bison, and a tapir (piglike animal) also were dug up at the Lehner site. The ashes from two fires—probably built to roast the meat—enabled scientists to date the killings at about 11,000 years ago.

Cochise people. Arizona's climate gradually dried up as the ice cap melted. With less vegetation to browse on, the big game animals disappeared. Descendants of the elephant hunters had to adjust to an environment with fewer resources. They hunted smaller animals and gathered wild berries, nuts, roots, and grains. A crude *metate* (stone) was developed for grinding seeds. About 2,000 B.C., the Arizona Indians learned from natives in Mexico how to cultivate corn or maize. Unlike modern

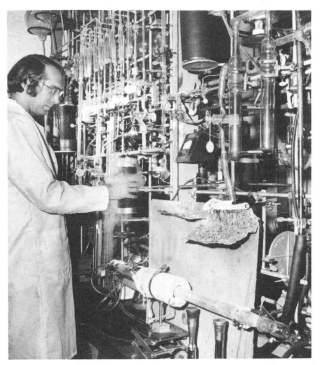

Carbon 14 laboratory at the University of Arizona.

corn, each kernal of this primitive variety was separately sheathed in a husk on the cob.

The early food gatherers and farmers were a link between the elephant hunters and later Indians of the Christian Era. They are called Cochise people because many of their remains have been found along creek banks in Cochise County.

Ventana Cave. A 10,000-year record of human habitation in Arizona was discovered in Ventana Cave, located on the Papago Indian Reservation west of Tucson. The floor of this cave was excavated in the 1940s. Archaeologists sifted through 15 feet of accumulated trash. From this material they were able to study how prehistoric man evolved through the stages of hunting, food gathering, and farming.

Near the bottom of the pile was a layer of debris dating back to 8,000 B.C. In this layer, the scientists found the bones of extinct animals, spear points, stone knives, and other

Carbon 14 process.

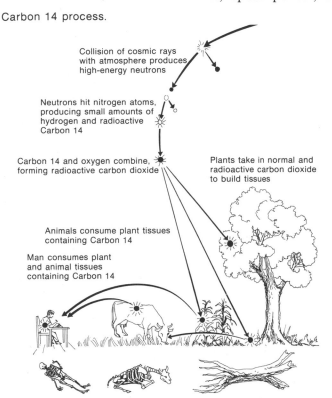

Collision of cosmic rays with atmosphere produces high-energy neutrons

Neutrons hit nitrogen atoms, producing small amounts of hydrogen and radioactive Carbon 14

Carbon 14 and oxygen combine, forming radioactive carbon dioxide

Plants take in normal and radioactive carbon dioxide to build tissues

Animals consume plant tissues containing Carbon 14

Man consumes plant and animal tissues containing Carbon 14

At death the radioactive Carbon 14 in plant and animal tissues is slowly decaying back into nitrogen. Since this progresses at a fixed rate, comparison of radioactivity between fossil and living specimens shows the elapsed time since death

Diorama showing herds of wild animals roaming Arizona 10,000 years ago.

objects left by hunters. On top of that were two layers containing stone tools and other remains belonging to the food-gathering Cochise people. A fourth layer higher up revealed Hohokam pottery and evidence of a corn-farming culture dating from about A.D. 1 to A.D. 1400. The fifth, or top layer contained modern Papago Indian arrowheads and other artifacts.

The Cochise and Hohokam peoples, who inhabited the cave at different times, probably were not related. The Papagos, however, very likely came from the Hohokams.

2. THERE WERE THREE MAJOR INDIAN CULTURES IN PREHISTORIC ARIZONA

The three main prehistoric tribal groups. The introduction of agriculture brought a cultural revolution to Arizona. The Indians were no longer completely dependent on nature. They could settle down in one place and control their food supply. The pro-duction of a surplus gave them leisure time to develop the civilizing arts. A higher civilization arose in three specific sections of Arizona.

The Hohokam occupied river valleys in the southern desert. The Anasazi were on the plateau in the Four Corners area. The Mogollon lived mainly in the mountain belt along the present Arizona-New Mexico border. Each group developed a life-style suitable for its own section. They intermingled with the others only after mastering the local environment. Archaeologists believe that the Mogollon are descended from the Cochise people. But they are uncertain about the origin of the Hohokam and the Anasazi.

Other prehistoric Indian groups in Arizona were the Sinagua, the Patayan, and the Salado. The Sinagua lived near the San Francisco Mountain north of present-day Flagstaff. The Patayan homeland was along the Colorado River and in the northwestern part of Arizona. The Salado people, who were of Anasazi origin, were in the Tonto Basin and other areas of east-central Arizona.

Ventana Cave.

Farming brought many changes in the lives of Indians. The security of a stable food supply made it possible for them to remain in one place. Diorama in the Arizona State Museum at Tucson.

3. THE HOHOKAM BUILT A CIVILIZATION IN THE DESERT THAT LASTED ABOUT 1,700 YEARS

The Hohokam were the first farmers in the Southwest with a knowledge of irrigation. They probably came from Mexico, bringing their own tools, pottery, and skills with them. Hohokam is a modern Pima Indian word that means "all used up" or "those who have vanished." It almost seems that the Hohokam wanted to be forgotten. Unlike many other Indians, the Hohokam did not bury the dead with their possessions. Instead, they cremated the dead and deliberately smashed their most beautiful artifacts—pottery, little statues, and ornaments.

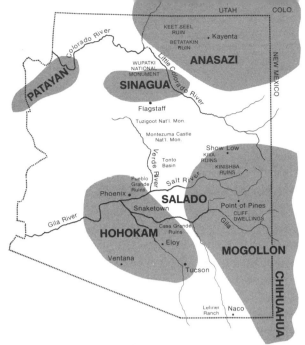

Location of prehistoric Indian cultures in Arizona.

The Hohokam settled in the desert valleys of central Arizona as early as 300 B.C. They grew corn to supplement a diet of mesquite beans, cactus fruits, deer, lizards, and rabbit meat. To water their fields, the Hohokam dug a system of gravity-fed canals along the Gila and Salt rivers. About 200 miles of these canals have been traced in the Salt River Valley. Some of the canals were 30 to 40 feet wide and 15 feet deep.

This irrigation system was a tremendous accomplishment for a primitive people who had no beasts of burden. The Hohokam had no earth-moving equipment other than stone or wooden tools for digging and baskets for hauling dirt. Modern engineers are amazed. When the present-day Grand Canal was built

This map by Charles O. Kemper shows similiarities between the Hohokam and modern Salt River Project canals.

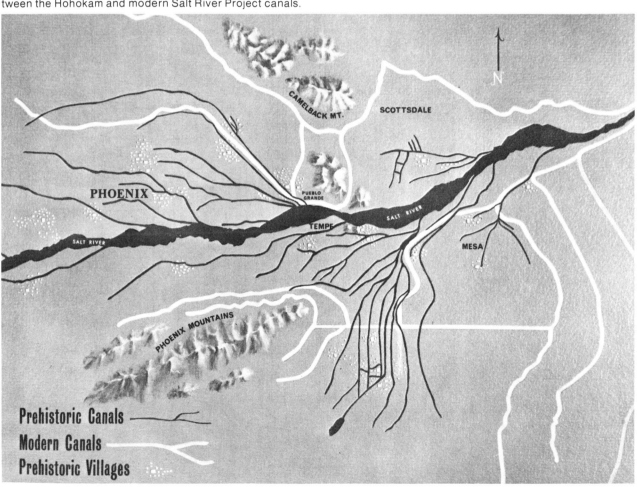

Prehistoric Canals
Modern Canals
Prehistoric Villages

Hohokam Indians building canals to bring life-giving water to the barren desert. From a painting by Charles O. Kemper.

A Hohokam etched shell from Snaketown.

through Phoenix, the surveyors followed an old Hohokam ditch. They couldn't gain an inch to the mile to improve the grade. The ancient Hohokam irrigation system was unequalled anywhere else in what is now the United States.

Permanent villages. What is more significant, irrigation farming made it possible for the Hohokam to settle in permanent villages and to develop crafts. With surplus food stored away in pithouses, they had time to learn new things. Potters made jars and bowls, some with 30-gallon capacity. A popular Hohokam design was a red, textile-weave pattern on a buff background. Some experts consider the Hohokam ceramic work the best done in Arizona at that time.

Another Hohokam craft was etching. Designs, usually of an animal such as a toad, were etched on sea shells. The technique was to first make the design on a shell with pitch. The shell was then soaked in a weak acid solution, which was probably the fermented juice of the saguaro cactus fruit. The unprotected part of the shell was eaten away by the acid, leaving the raised design. The Hohokam were three centuries ahead of European craftsmen, who later learned a similar etching process to decorate medieval armor.

49

Hohokam pottery from the Snaketown and Grewe sites.

Reconstructed framework of a Hohokam pithouse at Roosevelt.

Ball games. The Hohokam had time to play ball in a court excavated about five feet below ground level. This sport was learned from the Indians of Mexico. The object of the game was to get a rubber ball through twisted grass rings fastened on the sides of the court. There was little scoring. When a goal was made, the winning players could claim the jewelry and clothing of the spectators—if they could catch them!

Snaketown. The largest Hohokam village was Snaketown, located near the Gila River southwest of present-day Chandler. Thousands of houses were built at Snaketown during the town's 1,400-year existence. The people preferred the pithouse style. The pithouse was sunk at least a foot below the ground level for coolness in summer and warmth during the winter. The walls were constructed of poles and brush with mud

50

chinked in the cracks. The roof consisted of brush and mud piled on top of mesquite or cottonwood rafters. Since there were no windows, the house was dark inside. Tasks such as pottery-making, weaving, and corn-grinding were done outdoors under a ramada—a roof on poles with no sides.

Snaketown was excavated twice, in 1934 and 1964, and then covered. The chief archaeologist for both diggings was Dr. Emil W. Haury from the University of Arizona. He determined that irrigation was practiced at Snaketown as early as 300 B.C. Snaketown was abandoned between A.D. 1100 and 1200. The people congregated in other villages for greater safety. They began to build multi-storied apartment houses. The ruins of such fine structures as the four-story Casa Grande (big house) north of Coolidge and the Pueblo Grande in East Phoenix can be seen today.

The four-story Casa Grande had 11 rooms and was 40 feet high. Built about A.D. 1300, it

The main canal at Snaketown. A Pima Indian stands in a lateral canal.

Casa Grande Ruins near Coolidge.

A Hohokam ball game at Snaketown, from a painting by Peter Bianchi.

was America's first skyscraper. The Casa Grande served as a watchtower from which a sentinel could see outsiders approaching and warn field workers by smoke signal. The 25-inch-thick walls were constructed of wet caliche. This material is a cement-like clay with a high lime content that is found under the desert topsoil. The upper floors were supported by logs floated down the Gila River. The Casa Grande apartment house was used until about 1450 when it was mysteriously deserted along with the surrounding farm lands.

The Hohokam deserted the pueblos. For some reason the Hohokam villages were abandoned in the 15th century. No one knows what happened, but there are many theories. The farm land may have become waterlogged as the underground water table rose. Possibly the land was exhausted. After centuries of cultivation, it became laden with alkali brought in by irrigation water. Or perhaps the floods were to blame. Occasionally they washed out the brush, rock, and dirt dams. No one knows for certain what caused the departure of "the vanished ones." Whatever happened, it is very likely that the Hohokam remained in the desert country of southern Arizona and were the ancestors of the modern Pimas and Papagos.

A present-day farmer checks the flow of irrigation water on the Gila River tribal farms.

Is there a lesson in the Hohokam culture for our generation? The secret of their success was simple. They came to grips with nature, but did not abuse it. They survived in a harsh desert environment for at least 1,700 years. Considering our current problems — water shortage, shrinking open spaces, unplanned growth, and air pollution—will the present and future generations be able to match the Hohokam achievement?

4. THE ANASAZI INDIAN CULTURE CAN BE TRACED BACK NEARLY 2,000 YEARS

The Anasazi, whose name means "ancient ones," came to the Four Corners area in the first century after Christ. We know what they looked like and what they did because they buried their dead and placed personal possessions in the graves. The Anasazi were short, slender, long-headed, and broad-nosed. The men often wore a bob of hair on each temple and a braid down the back. Sometimes the top of the head was shaved to give a baldpate or wide part effect. The women had a reason for wearing a shorter hairdo than the men. They wove ropes from their hair, which they cut within two or three inches of the scalp.

Anasazi Inscription House burial.

Anasazi pottery from various sites in northern Arizona.

A student using a replica of an *atlatl* (spear thrower).

The Anasazi were excellent basketmakers. They used yucca fibers to make storage baskets for wild foods that were gathered. Before the bow and arrow came into use, the Anasazi hunted with the *atlatl*. This was a notched stick with which a spear could be hurled with great force.

After about A.D. 500, the Anasazi cultivated crops of corn, squash, and beans. They also domesticated the turkey. With a steady food supply, the Anasazi were able to settle down in one locality. They gave up their caves and built round pithouses, three to five feet deep. The pithouse had a cone-shaped roof made of poles. On one side of the one-room house there was always a small hole in the dirt or stone slab floor. This hole, called the "sipapu," represented the mythical place of emergence of the first people from the underworld. Once the Anasazi settled down in permanent homes, they learned to make pottery for cooking and

53

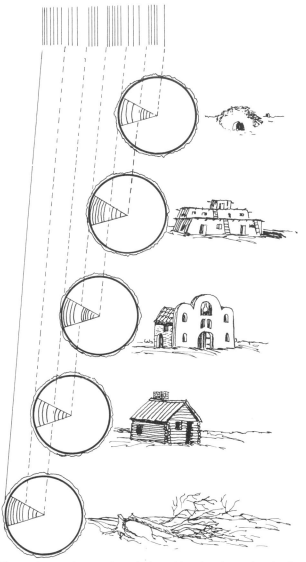

A.D. 1050. They began building large communal houses in cliff caves or on mesa tops. Unlike the Hohokam, who built villages in the open, the Anasazi tried to hide their apartment houses from view. They looked for out-of-the-way canyons which also had good farm land. Two impressive cliff dwellings can be seen today in the Navajo National Monument. Keet Seel (Navajo words meaning "broken pottery") originally had 350 rooms. Betatakin ("side hill house") had 200 rooms.

The great pueblos were abandoned in the last years of the 13th century. A 23-year drought (A.D. 1276 to 1299) probably caused the Anasazi to leave. They were dry farmers and could not produce crops without rainfall. Another problem was the soil. It was losing its fertility after centuries of farming. The Anasazi scattered. A few went eastward to what is now New Mexico. Others moved south to the land of the Salado or Hohokam. Some descendants of the Anasazi migrants moved back to the plateau home of their ancestors. The modern Hopis can trace their ancestry back to these returnees.

The Navajos, who occupy most of the old Anasazi stomping grounds, are not descended from any Arizona prehistoric Indian group. Like the Apaches, the Navajos are Athapascans and came from Canada in the 1500s.

Dr. A. E. Douglas studies tree rings in core sample taken from a ponderosa pine.

Illustrations of tree-ring dating (dendrochronology). By overlapping the wood samples, starting with a recently felled tree, the scientist can accurately determine the dates of the building of the blockhouse, the Spanish mission, the pueblo, and finally the prehistoric pit house.

other purposes. Their style was usually a white or gray pot with a black design for decoration.

After about A.D. 700, the Anasazi started the practice of artificially flattening the rear portion of the skull. It became the fashion to strap babies tightly against hard cradleboards. Their soft skulls were flattened and this deformity made their heads broader.

The Anasazi cliff dwellers. There was a big change in the Anasazi life-style after

Interior of Keet Seel.

5. THE MOGOLLON INDIANS DEVELOPED A PREHISTORIC CULTURE IN THE MOUNTAINS OF EASTERN ARIZONA

The Mogollon followed the Cochise seed-gatherers in eastern Arizona and southwestern New Mexico. They have been described as a drab and simple people in comparison to the Hohokam and Anasazi. Their contributions to the cultural history of Arizona and the Southwest were not great. But they did adjust successfully to their environment. Living in the mountains, the Mogollon subsisted mainly on the wild game which they hunted and the berries, roots, nuts, and seeds which they gathered. They did not rely on agriculture as heavily as did the Hohokam and Anasazi.

Yet, the round-headed, medium-built Mogollon were the first people in the Southwest to grow a good variety of corn, which they got from Mexican Indians. They were also the first to make pottery. They made brown and reddish pots by coiling a rope of clay into the desired shape. The sides were scraped before the pots were fired in a kiln.

The Mogollon lived in villages. A typical community had fewer than 20 homes that were usually built on the side of a mountain. Pithouse construction was used. The buildings were partly underground and were entered down a ramp on the east side. A large ceremonial and religious kiva was in the central part of the village. Social life in the village was based on the clan. A clan consisted of families with a common ancestry who tended to band together.

Several Mogollon villages have been excavated, including Point of Pines on the San Carlos Indian Reservation. The material goods uncovered at these sites were not very advanced. Some of the *metates* for grinding corn, for example, were no more than unshaped blocks of stone. Thin slabs of rock were used for tilling the soil. Awls for punching holes in wood and leather were made of bone. The Mogollon did excel in producing tubular stone smoking pipes, technically the most difficult to make. They also learned the art of basketmaking. In general, however, the Mogollon contributed little. In later years they borrowed new things and ideas from the Anasazi and Hohokam. After A.D. 700 they wove cloth from cotton fiber supplied by the Hohokam. From the Anasazi they learned to build stone and adobe surface houses.

Life-style. During the "golden age" of their "borrowed" culture — A.D. 1000 to 1200 — the Mogollon put surrealistic designs on their pottery. These pictures give us a glimpse of their life-style. The scenes show men picking bugs from corn plants, setting snares to catch birds, killing a deer with an *atlatl* or bow and arrow, and dancing. The men were shown wearing only a breech cloth. The women wore a fringed sash, sandals, and sometimes a blanket.

The Mogollon had few ornaments and may have painted themselves for decoration. At death the body was folded and placed in

Mogollon pottery.

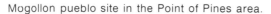

Mogollon pueblo site in the Point of Pines area.

a shallow grave. Only on rare occasions were personal possessions such as tools or pottery buried with the dead. During the golden age, however, the practice of burying the dead under house floors was not uncommon. In some areas, particularly the Mimbres Valley in New Mexico, the Mogollon left beautiful bowls and other pottery with the bodies. Many of the bowls had a hole punched in them. The reason for this custom is that each vessel was believed to house the spirit of the owner or the potter who made it. If the pot-

A Mogollon kiva at the Point of Pines site.

tery was buried with the dead owner it first had to be ceremoniously killed in the kiva and the spirit released through a "kill hole."

The Mogollon abandoned their mountain villages in Arizona and New Mexico about A.D. 1200. No one knows why they left, but archaeologists believe that they migrated to Chihuahua in Mexico. Traces of Mogollon culture began appearing there about the time of their mysterious departure from the Southwest. No modern Indian tribe in Arizona is descended from the Mogollon.

6. OTHER PREHISTORIC INDIANS LIVED IN NORTHERN ARIZONA AND ALONG THE COLORADO RIVER

Sinagua. A prehistoric people known as the Sinagua began farming near the San Francisco Peaks after A.D. 500. Sinagua is a name derived from the Spanish phrase meaning "without water." The name is appropriate. The Sinagua were dry farmers. They depended on rainfall to water crops, since there were few springs or wells in the area for irrigation. At first the Sinagua farmers lived in timber pit-houses. They covered the pithouse with grass or bark and banked it over with earth for protection against the weather.

For five centuries the Sinagua enjoyed peace and prosperity. Then disaster struck in late 1064 and early 1065. A volcano now known as Sunset Crater erupted. Streams of lava flowed down, covering eight hundred square miles with black ashes. The people were terrified and fled from their homes.

Eventually the Sinagua drifted back and had cause to rejoice. The soil had been enriched by the volcanic overflow. Word of the fertile fields soon spread. Other Indian groups moved in, bringing their customs and skills with them. There were Anasazi pueblo builders, Hohokam canal diggers, and Mogollon pottery makers—all of whom influenced the Sinagua culture.

Sinagua villages were built near Sunset Crater that reflected the new ways. One was Wupatki, a multi-room surface pueblo. At Wupatki, which is a Hopi word meaning "tall house," visitors can still see a Hohokam-type ball court and an open-air amphitheater that resembles a ceremonial Anasazi or Mogollon kiva.

Sinagua in the Verde Valley. The Wupatki pueblo and others in the Flagstaff area were deserted in the late 13th century. A long dry spell turned the area into a dust bowl. The Sinagua people moved south to the Verde Valley. There they adopted the Hohokam system of irrigation and built stone pueblos. Tuzigoot, on a hilltop near Clarkdale, was one population center. At one time, nearly a hundred families of mixed cultures lived there. Another stone apartment house was built in a cliff cave overlooking the Verde River. It was later named Montezuma Castle by Anglo settlers. They chose the name of the Aztec chief, falsely reasoning that the imposing cliff house had been constructed by his people.

Wupatki.

Montezuma Castle

Montezuma has 12-inch walls, curved to conform to the arc of the cave. The outside doors in the nineteen-room building appear to be low enough for pygmies, though the Sinagua men averaged five feet four inches in height. The openings were made small to keep the rooms warmer in winter. Also, a family could club an invader over the head as he stooped to enter a low door.

The 40 or 50 people who lived in the castle worked in the irrigated fields. They also killed wild game and gathered wild foods. Other activities included the weaving of cloth, mining salt, and firing a finely-polished red pottery. In general, the Sinagua seemed secure in their life-style.

Yet, about A.D. 1400 they suddenly left the Verde Valley. Why? Was it another drought? Disease? Water pollution? Scientists are at a loss to explain the sudden exodus. Whatever the reasons, the Sinaguans left their Verde Valley homes to the buzzards. Many of them probably went to the Hopi country.

Patayan. Along the Colorado River and in northwestern Arizona lived another prehistoric people. They are called Patayan, which

59

means "old people" or "ancient ones" in the language of the modern Yumas. Hakataya, the Yuma word for Colorado River, is another name used to describe them.

The Patayan farmed along the banks of the river. During flood seasons they went to the desert to hunt and to forage for edible plants. After the flood they returned to their fields and planted crops in the rich silt deposited by the river.

Most of the remains of Patayan civilization have been washed away or covered up by flood waters. But there is some archaeological material available. It is known, for example, that they began making a simple gray-brown pottery about A.D. 600. Shells for jewelry were brought from the Gulf of California. Patayan houses were usually made of tree trunks set in the ground and lashed together.

Archaeologists classify the Patayan into sub-groups. Two of these, the Cerbat and Cohonina, lived in the region west of Flagstaff and south of the Grand Canyon. There were also small sub-groups near present-day Prescott and Agua Fria.

By the time the Spaniards came in the 1500s, the Patayan had evolved into the modern Yuma-speaking tribes: the Yuma, Cocopah, Maricopa, Mojave, and the three Pais: Walapai, Yavapai, and Havasupai.

Salado. Distant cousins of the Anasazi, the Salado people are remembered for their beautiful polychrome pottery. They were also pueblo builders. Several of the Salado cliff houses can be seen today on the Tonto National Monument near the Roosevelt Dam.

The location of these pueblos near the junction of Tonto Creek and the Salt River was not chosen for convenience. The nearest spring was half a mile away. The cultivated fields on the flood plain of the Salt River were two or four miles from the cliffs. But the building sites were selected for safety as well as for homes and food storage. The Salado people felt threatened in the 14th century by an invasion of Anasazi. The latter were abandoning their homeland on the plateau because of drought.

The Salado people were spread out through the upper Gila and Salt River valleys. They mingled with both the Mogollon and Hohokam, sharing knowledge with them.

In one respect, the Salado were like the Hohokam, the Anasazi, the Mogollon, the Sinagua, and the Patayan. They all match the worldwide pattern of the rise and fall of ancient societies. Though obscured by time, their achievements have lent drama to Arizona's past.

UNIT TWO

THE SPANISH IN ARIZONA (1539-1821)

The Spanish were the first Europeans to make contact with the Indians of Arizona. For nearly three centuries they were the only non-Indians to enter the region.

Within 50 years after Columbus's first voyage in 1492, King Charles of Spain claimed the New World as far north as the Grand Canyon. Charles was the most powerful ruler in Europe. He regarded New Spain as his personal property. Gold and silver flowed into his coffers from two great Indian civilizations —the Aztec in Mexico and the Inca in Peru.

Mexico City, the Aztec capital, was conquered by Hernán Cortés. It became the Spanish base for further conquest. Spurred on by rumors of more wealth to the north, *conquistadores* (conquerors) swiftly expanded the frontier of New Spain north from Mexico City.

During the 1500s, Spanish explorers laid claim to most of what is now the American Southwest. They partially mapped this vast region and added something to the knowledge of the world. But the explorers were looking for riches and they found none. For that reason, the Spanish government never made much effort to develop the area north of the present international border—including Arizona.

The three g's—gold, God, and glory—were the main motives for expansion of New Spain. The Spanish greed for gold was only normal for human beings of any race. But it was not the gold seekers who built the Spanish empire. Before the end of the 1500s, more than 160,000 Spaniards lived in New Spain. The vast majority were merchants, ranchers, planters, miners, soldiers, or priests. These are the people who brought the Spanish culture, laws, religion, and language to the New World. They laid the foundation in Latin America for 18 Spanish-speaking republics.

Many younger sons of Spanish upper class families wanted land and adventure more than gold. They usually married Indian girls, since few Spanish women came to the New World. In fact, the whole Spanish system depended on the Indians. The natives were enslaved to work in the mines and to herd cattle on the ranches. Some of the Indians were branded. It is said that the first cowboy in this hemisphere wore a brand prior to the branding of the first cow.

The Spanish had a strong desire to convert the natives to the Roman Catholic faith. In Arizona the missionary was about the only contact that Arizona Indians had with the Spanish culture. After a few gold-seeking explorers hurried through in the 1500s, this section of the frontier was mainly in the hands of the churchmen. The only settlements of any size—Tubac and Tucson—were not founded until the final years of Spanish rule.

Hernán Cortés talks with ambassadors of Montezuma, the
Aztec chief.

Montezuma meets Cortés.

62

3

SPANISH EXPLORERS IN THE 1500s

Gold and silver from the mines of Mexico and Peru made Spain the wealthiest nation in Europe and fired the imagination of Spanish explorers.

In 1531 one of Cortés's lieutenants established a town at Culiacán, about halfway between Mexico City and present-day Arizona. It was from Culiacán that the first Spanish explorers came through Arizona seeking the legendary "Seven Cities of Cíbola."

Viceroy Antonio de Mendoza, the king's governor in Mexico, organized an expedition in 1539. He could not resist the opportunity to find out if rumors about the wealthy cities were true.

No gold was found by the exploring parties which crisscrossed Arizona in the 1500s. But the explorers brought back valuable information concerning the geography and the Indians on the northern frontier.

KEY CONCEPTS

1. Álvar Núñez Cabeza de Vaca was probably never in Arizona but had a great influence on its history.

2. Estevan, the black Moor who guided Fray Marcos de Niza, was the first non-Indian to step on Arizona soil.

3. Coronado led a great expedition across Arizona in 1540.

4. Antonio de Espejo discovered mines near Jerome in 1583.

5. Governor Oñate explored northern Arizona and the Colorado River.

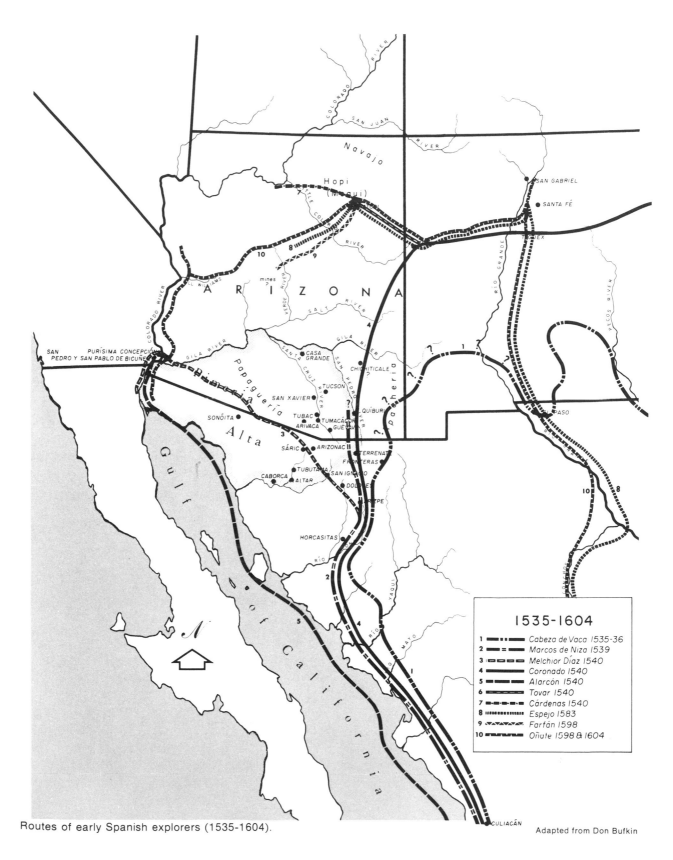

Routes of early Spanish explorers (1535-1604). Adapted from Don Bufkin

Map labels:

Navajo

COLORADO RIVER
SAN JUAN RIVER

Hopi
(Moqui)

SAN GABRIEL
SANTA FÉ

LITTLE COLORADO RIVER
ISLETA
TIGUEX

RIO GRANDE

PECOS RIVER

A R I Z O N A

10
8
9

BILL WILLIAMS RIVER
VERDE RIVER
SALT RIVER
GILA RIVER
mines

SAN PEDRO Y SAN PABLO DE BICUÑER
PURÍSIMA CONCEPCIÓN
COLORADO RIVER
GILA RIVER

Papaguería
Pimería

Alta

CASA GRANDE
SANTA CRUZ RIVER
SAN PEDRO RIVER
CHICHITICALE

EL PASO

TUCSON
SAN XAVIER
SONÓITA
TUBAC
ARIVACA
TUMACÁCORI
GUEVAVI
QUÍBURI

Papaguería

SÁRIC
ARIZONAC
TERRENATE
FRONTERAS
CABORCA
TUBUTAMA
SAN IGNACIO
ALTAR
DOLORES
COCÓSPERA

HORCASITAS

RÍO SONORA
RÍO YAQUI
RÍO MAYO
RÍO FUERTE
RÍO SINALOA

Gulf of California

N

CULIACÁN

10
8

1535-1604

1 - - - - Cabeza de Vaca 1535-36
2 - - Marcos de Niza 1539
3 □□□□ Melchior Díaz 1540
4 ——— Coronado 1540
5 - - - - Alarcón 1540
6 ======= Tovar 1540
7 -■-■-■- Cárdenas 1540
8 ▪▪▪▪▪ Espejo 1583
9 ▽▽▽▽▽ Farfán 1598
10 ◄◄◄◄ Oñate 1598 & 1604

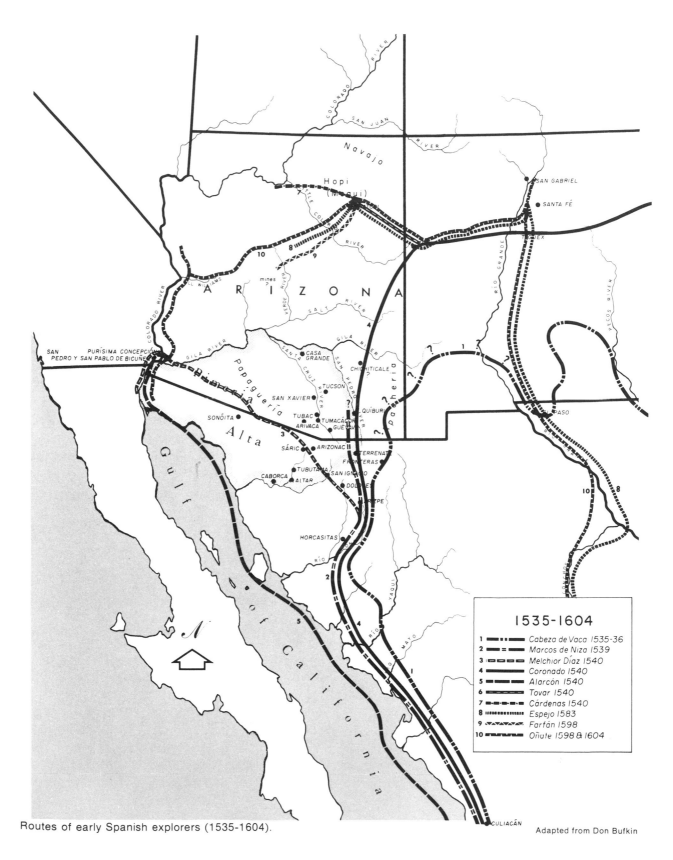

64

3

1. ÁLVAR NÚÑEZ CABEZA DE VACA WAS PROBABLY NEVER IN ARIZONA BUT HAD A GREAT INFLUENCE ON ITS HISTORY

Cabeza de Vaca and three weary companions arrived at Culiacán in 1536. They had just completed one of the most remarkable journeys in all history. They were survivors of the Narváez expedition that was driven out of Florida by Indians in 1528. Only a handful of the 242 men who left Florida in crude log boats survived a Gulf storm, disease, and unfriendly Indians on the coast of Texas.

Cabeza was enslaved. But he soon won fame as a medicine man and was given freedom to visit other tribes. Cabeza performed minor surgery and magically cured the sick by rattling a gourd and making the sign of a cross. Eventually he met three former companions: Castillo, Dorantes, and the latter's slave—a black Moor named Estevan.

Followed by crowds of Indians wanting medical attention, the four men slowly made their way across Texas and northern Mexico to Culiacán. The four castaways had endured eight years of hardship, most of it in slavery. Their journey from Florida via Texas covered more than 5,000 miles. Most of it was through country never before seen by non-Indians. Vaca's map of his route was vague. It is likely, however, that the man came only close enough to Arizona and New Mexico to hear rumors of rich cities in those areas.

Viceroy Mendoza interviewed the four heroes in Mexico City. Mendoza was impressed by their fantastic stories but didn't want to start a mad gold rush. He publicly denounced Vaca's reports while quietly organizing an expedition to explore the fabled region up north. Mendoza could not persuade Vaca to guide a scouting party. However, he was able to purchase Estevan for that purpose.

Sketch of Cabeza de Vaca and his companions crossing the desert.

Cabeza de Vaca returned to Spain and wrote a book about his experiences. He was rewarded with an appointment as governor of Paraguay in South America.

2. ESTEVAN, THE BLACK MOOR WHO GUIDED FRAY MARCOS DE NIZA, WAS THE FIRST NON-INDIAN TO STEP ON ARIZONA SOIL

Viceroy Mendoza made plans to conquer the legendary rich cities in the lands north of Mexico. He was cautious, however, and decided first to check out the rumors of riches with a small scouting party. Fray Marcos de Niza was selected in 1539 to head this advance group. His job was to make peace with the Indians along the way and send back any information he could get, especially about gold and silver. The 38-year old Fray Marcos was well-qualified for the assignment. He had served fearlessly among the Indians of Peru and Guatemala.

The Spanish in Arizona is the subject of this mural by Jay Datus in the state capitol. Only two figures represent definite persons—Estevan the Moor on the right and Fray Marcos de Niza next to him. A *conquistador* rides a horse and carries the banner of Spain. Priests work with the Indians.

Estevan was assigned to the advance group to guide. Fray Marcos sent him ahead on the trail with instructions to send back reports on the country. Since Estevan couldn't read or write, a simple system of communication was devised. He was to send an Indian courier back with a cross — the larger the cross, the more important the land. Fray Marcos must have been surprised several days later when he received a cross as high as a man. Estevan had heard about the legendary cities and urged the friar to hurry.

The giant Estevan was a showman. Once beyond the reach of Fray Marcos, he acted the part of a medicine man—a role Cabeza de Vaca had taught him. He carried a magic gourd filled with pebbles and adorned with red and white feathers. Bells jangled on his ankles and elbows. The Opata Indians of Sonora and the Pimas of Arizona were impressed by his performance. A horde of admiring natives, including a harem of Indian maidens, followed in his path. Estevan was treated like an oriental ruler until he got to Hawikuh, a Zuñi village in present-day New Mexico.

The Zuñi Indians were not impressed by his claims that he was a medicine man who could perform magical cures. Normally peaceful, the Zuñis filled Estevan's body with arrows and sent his escorts hurrying to tell Fray Marcos about the incident.

Fray Marcos tells of rich cities. Fray Marcos de Niza was naturally stunned by the bad news. In spite of the tragedy, the friar later claimed that he went ahead to view Hawikuh and erect a wooden cross on a hill at a safe distance. He took for granted that the Zuñi pueblo was one of the "Seven Cities of Cíbola." After a hasty retreat to Culiacán and Mexico City, he reported to Viceroy Mendoza and made a written report.

Using his imagination, he told the Viceroy about a city larger than Mexico City with buildings 10 stories high. He said the Indians decorated their doors with turquoise, used gold and silver utensils, and wore giant pearls, gold beads, and emeralds. Fray Marcos actually may have believed that these fantastic stories could be true. After all, he had observed the fabulous riches of the Incas in Peru. Whether he was lying or dreaming may never be known. One thing is certain—his exaggerated description of Cíbola, which means "buffalo cow," set Mexico City into a frenzy.

Fray Marcos de Niza

3. CORONADO LED A GREAT EXPEDITION ACROSS ARIZONA IN 1540

Coronado's background. Coronado was in many ways a typical Spanish adventurer in the New World. A younger son in a family of lesser nobles, he came to Mexico at the age of 25. His older brother, Gonzalo, had inherited most of the family estate in Spain. Two of his sisters were given endowments and sent to convents to become nuns. Another younger brother, Juan, made a good name for himself as a Spanish official in Costa Rica.

Francisco Coronado arrived in Mexico City with Viceroy Mendoza in 1535. Handsome and popular, Coronado married Doña Beatríz, a beautiful and wealthy heiress. For wedding gifts Beatríz's widowed mother gave the couple a mansion in Mexico City and half of a huge ranch south of the city.

Coronado rose fast in the Viceroy's favor. He was governor of New Galicia when Mendoza chose him to head the Cíbola expedition with the title of captain-general. Much of the expense for outfitting the expedition was borne by Mendoza and Coronado. It was a private venture. They intended to reap most of the profits. The king would get only the royal *quinto* (20 per cent).

Expedition organized. Recruiting was no problem—except for Marcos de Niza, who reluctantly agreed to go along as the guide. Lured by riches and glory, men of all walks of life clamored to join the expedition. Some 225 *caballeros* (horsemen) were selected. These men were young nobles in their twenties. Some of them wore coats of mail, but most of the men were only partially equipped with a breastplate or helmet.

February 22, 1540, must have been a glorious day for them. Members of the expedition assembled at the coastal town of Compostela and paraded before Viceroy Mendoza. The next day they moved out. Behind the *caballeros* were more than 60 foot soldiers carrying swords, long pikes, and shields. A thousand Indian allies armed with native weapons were next in the line of march. Then came Indian and Negro slaves. They tended the pack animals and herded thousands of cattle, sheep, and goats which would insure a food supply on the journey. This expeditionary force was the largest enterprise ever attempted by the Spanish in the New World.

Coronado stopped at Culiacán for a month. Leaving the main body of the army to proceed slowly, he pushed on through Sonora. With him was a vanguard of about one hundred men and a large body of Indian allies. Coronado followed the San Pedro Valley to a point just south of the present site of Benson. It was summertime and the *caballeros* were not wearing their armor, or "hot suits" as they were called. Besides, there was no need for armor. They were among a friendly Pima people called Sobaípuris.

From the San Pedro, Coronado traveled between mountain ranges to Eagle Pass, the opening between the Pinaleño and Santa Teresa mountains in modern-day Graham County. Here he saw a pueblo ruin called

Chichilticale, meaning "Red House." Fray Marcos de Niza had been wrong in his praises of this place and was now questioned on another point. He had reported that a sea could be seen from Chichilticale. Actually it was 10 days away. Coronado was disappointed, since he planned on getting supplies from three ships sent up the Gulf of California by Viceroy Mendoza.

First white man on the Colorado River. Captain Hernando de Alarcón commanded the ships. He anchored them at the mouth of the Colorado River. With 20 men Alarcón went up the river in boats. He visited a Yuman tribe and presented its members with gifts. Through an interpreter, Alarcón learned that Coronado had reached Cíbola. Failing to make contact with Coronado, the naval officer returned to Mexico. He had made history. Alarcón was the first white explorer to sail the Colorado River and to see the natives in that vicinity.

"Golden cities" a disappointment. Meanwhile, Coronado, short of supplies,

Coronado's expedition through Arizona. Painting by Frederic Remington.

Coronado Trail marker in eastern Arizona.

entered the rugged mountains of eastern Arizona. The expedition passed through the high country near present-day McNary. On July 7, 1540, the captain-general led his exhausted and half-starved treasure seekers to the mud and stone pueblo of Hawikuh. What a shock it was! Here they were at the end of the rainbow and there was no pot of gold.

Several hundred Zuñi warriors met the Spaniards at the edge of town. They drew lines on the ground with sacred cornmeal and ordered the Spaniards not to cross. The natives also made threatening gestures with their war clubs and bows-and-arrows. They showed no fear of the weary armored soldiers and strange horses. The situation was tense. And when the Indians tried to kill Coronado's interpreter, peace was out of the question.

"Santiagos y a ellos!" (St. James and at them!) That is what the angered soldiers shouted. With swords flashing in the desert sunlight, the Spaniards attacked. Hunger drove them on. During the battle, Coronado, in his gilded armor, was a special target. Twice he was knocked off his horse by rocks hurled from atop the pueblo. He also received an arrow wound in the leg.

In less than an hour the Zuñis were forced to abandon the pueblo, leaving their food supplies. The famished soldiers gorged themselves on beans, maize, and fowl—their first good meal in weeks! Even the long-sought gold and silver would have been less welcome at that moment.

In the weeks to follow, Coronado met with Indian chiefs from the other pueblos—there were six, not seven—and promised safety to the Indians. In August he wrote the sad news in a letter to Viceroy Mendoza. Fray Marcos, saddened by the whole affair, carried Coronado's message to Mexico City.

Visits to the Hopis and the Grand Canyon. Coronado discovered no gold, no silver, and no jewels. But he continued to search. It took him awhile to catch on to the Indian strategy. The natives got rid of the Spaniards by telling them of riches to be found "somewhere else."

Two side expeditions were important in the history of Arizona. Pedro de Tovar, led by Zuñi guides, took a small company of men to the Hopi villages. The Hopis at Awátovi were hostile. Like the Zuñis, they drew a cornmeal line and warned Tovar to stay away. Instead, he charged. Awátovi surrendered, as did all the other mesa-top villages.

Tovar was pleased to accept Hopi peace offerings of cotton cloth, cornmeal, and pinyon nuts. He was even more interested in what the Indians had to say about a great river and wealthy natives farther west. He hurried back to Hawikuh and reported this news to Coronado.

Coronado was excited. He was curious to find out if the "great river" had anything to do with the Strait of Anian—a legendary and non-existent waterway which was supposed to connect the Atlantic and Pacific oceans. Coronado sent his toughest officer, Captain Cárdenas, with 25 horsemen to look for the river. Cárdenas stopped by the Hopi villages, where he was well-received. The Hopis furnished him with guides and provisions.

Traveling over the plateau of northern

Coronado in full armor. Mural by Gerald Cassidy in the Santa Fe post office.

Arizona, Cárdenas unexpectedly came upon a canyon. To the Spaniards the stream at the bottom looked no more than six feet wide. They were surprised when the guides said it was actually a wide river. Cárdenas had discovered the Grand Canyon. But he was not impressed. He was seeking gold, not natural wonders. Unable to descend to the river, Cárdenas returned to Hawikuh.

Coronado in the Rio Grande Valley and at Gran Quivira. He took possession of Indian pueblos in the Albuquerque area. The severe winter of 1540 was spent in homes from which many of the natives had fled. The Rio Grande Indians, as had the Zuñis and Hopis, told the Spaniards of great wealth that could be found elsewhere. In fact, they had a slave—

a Texas plains native nicknamed "El Turco" — spin a tale about a rich land to the east called Gran Quivira. Coronado took the bait.

In the spring of 1541 the search for phantom gold began again. El Turco led the Spaniards on a wild goose chase across the Texas and Oklahoma panhandles. They finally came to a village of mud and straw huts near present-day Wichita, Kansas. The only metal in the village was a copper amulet* worn by the chief. Under questioning, El Turco confessed he had lied and was strangled. Dejected, the Spaniards returned to the New Mexican pueblos for another winter.

*An *amulet* is an ornament or charm worn for protection against evil.

In the spring of 1542 Coronado led his tattered army back across Arizona to Culiacán. Fewer than a hundred of the faithful were with him when he arrived in Mexico City to report to Viceroy Mendoza.

Coronado denounced as a failure. Coronado found no precious metals and no rich Indian civilizations to exploit—only natives who were willing to fight for their meager food supplies. His report was so discouraging, 40 years passed before another white man entered Arizona.

For later generations, however, the Coronado expedition was a success. They gained a knowledge of Southwestern geography and a description of the Indians. For this information Coronado gave up much of his fortune, two years of his young life, and his health. He died at the age of 44.

Today, the Coronado National Monument and the Coronado National Forest honor his memory.

Zuni Indians at Hawikuh. Mural by Gerald Cassidy in the Santa Fe post office.

4. ANTONIO DE ESPEJO DISCOVERED MINES NEAR JEROME IN 1583.

Antonio de Espejo was the next Spanish explorer in Arizona. He came from the east by way of the Rio Grande Valley of New Mexico.

Espejo was a well-to-do Mexican from the Santa Barbara mining district in Chihuahua. In 1582 he learned that the Franciscan priests in Santa Barbara were worried about three of their brothers in New Mexico. Volunteering to help, Espejo organized a small rescue party at his own expense. Reaching the pueblo villages near Albuquerque, Espejo discovered that the friars had been murdered.

Too late to save the missionaries, Espejo and his soldiers decided to make their fortunes. By March, 1583, they were in the Zuñi pueblos. Espejo was excited when he heard stories about rich mines to the west in present-day Arizona. With nine soldiers and 150

friendly Zuñis, he traveled first to the Hopi villages. The Hopis gave him blankets, tasseled towels, cotton *mantas* (shawls), and a large stock of blue and green ores. Espejo sent five men with the loot back to the Zuñi villages and continued his journey westward.

In the vicinity of Jerome, he discovered mines of unknown value. Espejo chose not to remain in the area because the Indians — according to the Hopis—were warlike. Fortunately for the Spaniards, the natives were frightened by the neighing of the white men's strange animals. The mountain-dwelling Indians fled from the horses and remained a respectable distance away.

Espejo hurried back to Mexico with his ore specimens. This ore and a story which Espejo had heard about a lake of gold northwest of Zuñi created a stir along the northern frontier. It was not until near the end of the century, however, that another explorer came into Arizona.

5. GOVERNOR OÑATE EXPLORED NORTHERN ARIZONA AND THE COLORADO RIVER

Governor Juan de Oñate of New Mexico traveled more within the present boundaries of Arizona than any previous explorer.

A wealthy man, he established the New Mexico colony in 1598 at his own expense. Oñate, whose wife was the granddaughter of Cortés, brought 400 men, 130 women, and a number of children to New Mexico. Governor Oñate was not satisfied with his remarkable success as a colonizer and turned to exploration. Within a period of six years, he made two notable treks into Arizona.

One attraction was Espejo's mines. In November, 1598, Oñate led an exploring party as far as the Hopi villages. But his soldiers and their horses suffered from the severe winter weather and a water shortage. Oñate wished to spare the entire group further hardship, so

Hopi village in Walpi.

he sent Captain Marcos Farfán with eight men to look for the mines. While the main party returned to Zuñi, Farfán located some rich silver ore in the vicinity of Prescott. Oñate was pleased when he heard about the mineral discovery, but never got around to developing the mines.

In 1604-1605 Oñate crossed northern Arizona and went down the Colorado River to the Gulf of California and back. His objective was to find the Pacific Ocean so that his colony in New Mexico could trade with Peru and China. Once again a Spanish explorer had to settle for rumors of gold, pearls, and distant seas—and also some strange tales.

One of Oñate's Franciscan diarists recorded some of the stories, unbelievable as they may seem. The Mojave Indians told the Spaniards about a great lake where the natives all wore gold bracelets. There was another account of a rich island of bald-headed men ruled by a fat woman with big feet. The Indians told about a tribe of one-legged people, some natives who slept in trees, and another people who slept under water. Supposedly there were Indians along the Colorado River who lived solely on the odor of food.

With Oñate's return to New Mexico, the first period of exploration in Arizona—1539 to 1605—came to a close. Nothing was found to attract colonizers—no gold, no pearls, and no ocean. Like Coronado and Espejo, Oñate succeeded only in making the region known to Europeans.

Governor Oñate was banished from New Mexico in 1609 and brought to trial on some thirty charges. He was convicted for cruelty to the Indians, concealing riches for his own use, and other offenses. Later the King of Spain pardoned Oñate after reviewing the enormous personal fortune he spent in settling New Mexico and exploring the Southwest.

During the 1600s the scene shifted from the explorers to the missionaries. Priests had accompanied the explorers to provide spiritual guidance for the soldiers, keep diaries of the journeys, and convert the natives. Now they were to have a bigger role.

Sketch of the Franciscan mission at Awátovi by Ross
Montgomery.

4

MISSIONARIES ON THE SPANISH FRONTIER (1629-1781)

Missionaries played an important role on the frontier of New Spain. From the beginning, priests accompanied the soldiers who explored the American Southwest. By education and training they were well-qualified to map and describe new lands. Priests wrote some of the best diaries on explorations in Arizona.

Furthermore, the missionary could go where the soldier was not always welcome. Though the missionary usually traveled with a small military escort, he often ventured out alone or with Indian guides.

The main goal of the missionaries, of course, was to win souls to Christ. But they were also a valuable asset to the Spanish government because of their influence with the Indians. Father Kino, for example, was said to be worth a whole company of soldiers in defense of settlements in Arizona and Sonora. He was able to enlist the support of the friendly Pimas against the Apaches.

Occasionally, however, the missionaries were victims of rebellions by the natives. Franciscan missionaries were killed during the 17th century while trying to convert the Indians in the Hopi villages. They were the first Christian martyrs to die on Arizona soil.

KEY CONCEPTS

1. The Hopis wanted nothing to do with Spanish rule and religion.
2. Padre Kino, the apostle of the Pimas, was Arizona's first successful missionary.
3. Spain sent some German missionaries to work with Indians on the frontier.
4. Discovery of silver near Nogales gave Arizona its name.
5. The Pima Rebellion of 1751 led to the founding of Arizona's first military base at Tubac.
6. The Jesuits continued to work in Arizona until 1767 when they were expelled by Charles III.
7. Fray Garcés was an ideal missionary and a remarkable explorer.

4

1. THE HOPIS WANTED NOTHING TO DO WITH SPANISH RULE AND RELIGION

Governor Oñate's New Mexico colony gradually expanded after his departure. Settlers began farming the Rio Grande valley. Missionaries spread out to bring Christianity to the natives.

The first attempt of the Franciscan friars to convert Indians in Arizona began in 1629. Three priests—Francisco Porras, Andrés Gutiérrez, and Cristóbal de la Concepcion—left comfortable churches in New Mexico to work among the Hopis. The Indians were at first hostile and it took a miracle to break the ice. Only after Porras healed a blind boy, did hundreds of Hopis become Christians. The medicine men were jealous and had Porras poisoned in 1633. There is no record of what happened to the other two friars.

Franciscans continued to come to the Hopi villages. By 1675 there were three missions and two sub-missions, called *visitas*. Then disaster struck in 1680. On August 9 the Pueblo Indians of New Mexico and Arizona revolted in unison. A medicine man named El Popé was the symbol of Indian discontent with Spanish rule. He had been imprisoned for witchcraft. After release from jail, he secretly made plans to kill all the Spaniards.

During the revolt, some 400 settlers were murdered. This number included 22 of 33 priests in the colony. At least three of the four missionaries on Arizona soil were killed. Fray Augustín de Santa Maria may have been enslaved at Oraibi and abused as an object of scorn and ridicule.

In 1692 Governor Diego de Vargas reconquered New Mexico. In November of that year he escorted two missionaries to the Hopi settlements with an army of 63 soldiers. Vargas wanted peace, not revenge, and chose not to punish the Hopis for the 1680 tragedy. When all the Hopi villages, except Oraibi,

Ruins of Awátovi.

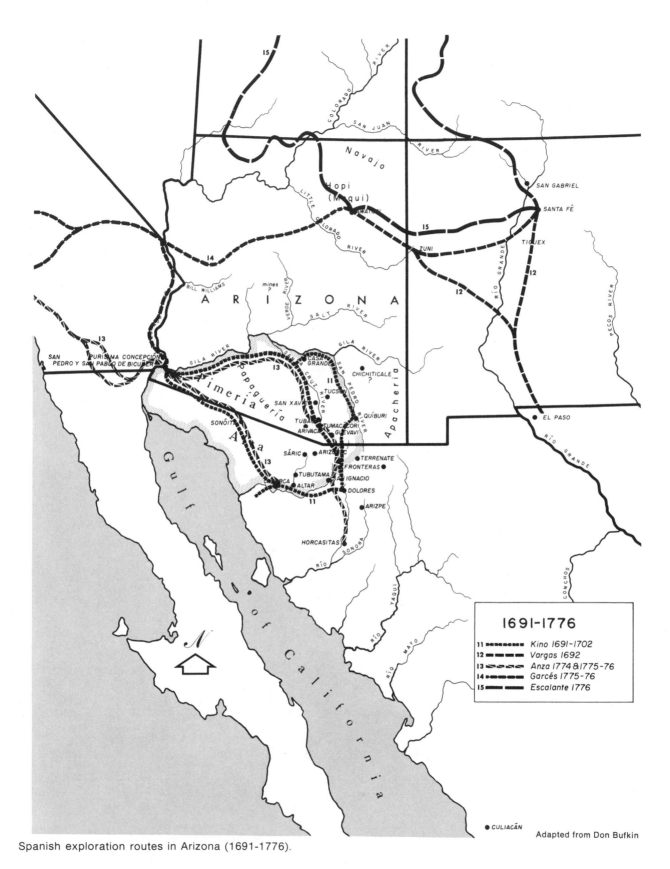

Spanish exploration routes in Arizona (1691-1776).

Adapted from Don Bufkin

promised to live in peace with the Spaniards, Vargas left without a fight.

The Hopis, however, preferred their own way of life and refused to cooperate with Spanish rulers. During the early 1700s they harbored Pueblo apostates*. These were runaway Indians from New Mexico who rejected their Christian faith and Spanish rule. In 1716 Governor Phelix Martinez sent an army to bring the apostates back to their homes in New Mexico. This force destroyed maize fields and killed several natives. But only a few apostates agreed to go back.

For the next century the Hopis remained defiant of Spanish authority. This Hopi independence was significant in Arizona history. It meant that Arizona would be colonized from the south, not from the east. Arizona was to develop as part of the province of Sonora, not New Mexico.

> *Apostates* are people who give up what they once believed.

Father Kino was Arizona's first cattleman. He brought livestock to the area for the Pimas. Mural at Tumacácori mission.

2. PADRE KINO, THE APOSTLE TO THE PIMAS, WAS ARIZONA'S FIRST SUCCESSFUL MISSIONARY

By any comparison, Father Eusebio Kino was one of the most important people in all Arizona history. Priest, explorer, rancher, astronomer, mapmaker, and defender of the frontier—he was all of these. From 1691, when he first entered the area, until his death in 1711, Kino was the outstanding figure in advancing the Spanish frontier into what is now Arizona.

Born in northern Italy in 1645, Kino was educated in Austrian and German schools. He decided to join the Society of Jesus while making a miraculous recovery from a serious illness. In 1687, six years after his arrival in Mexico, Kino was appointed a missionary to the Pimas. He established a mission at Dolores. This site, about 75 miles south of present-day Nogales, was his headquarters for some 24 years.

Father Kino. Painting by Frances O'Brien.

A young Papago girl at Bac kneels before the altar in prayer, as her ancestors did in Kino's time.

The Jesuit order, to which Kino belonged, had been establishing missions in Sonora since 1613. In the tradition of those who came before him. Kino extended the "rim of Christendom" northward along the Santa Cruz and San Pedro valleys to the Gila River.

Pimería Alta. The region in which Kino lived and worked was called Pimería Alta— "land of the Upper Pimas." There was no United States at that time and no State of Arizona. Pimería Alta included what is now southwestern Arizona and the northwestern part of the Mexican state of Sonora. The boundaries were the Altar River on the South, the San Pedro on the east, the Gila on the north, and the Colorado River and the Gulf of California on the west. The area south of the Altar River was called Pimería Baja— "land of the Lower Pimas."

Kino, the "apostle to the Pimas." A model missionary, Kino fully realized that the Pimas could best understand the gospel of love if they were assured a regular food supply. He believed in the "Give us this day our daily bread" part of the Lord's Prayer as well as "Hallowed be thy name." For that reason, he made each mission a complete community, teaching his Christian converts the best methods of crop production and animal husbandry. The cattle king of his day, Kino started the stock raising industry in Arizona.

Kino's missions. All of Kino's Arizona missions were in the Santa Cruz Valley. The first was established at the Indian village of Bac, near Tucson, in 1700 and named San Xavier del Bac. Farther south Kino built the Guevavi mission with a *visita* at Tumacácori in 1701. A *visita* was a temporary mission where a priest came at intervals to say mass and baptize converts.

When Kino was at Bac in 1692 he said there were 800 Indians eager for religious instruction. Seven years later he brought his superior, Father Visitor Antonio Leal, on a

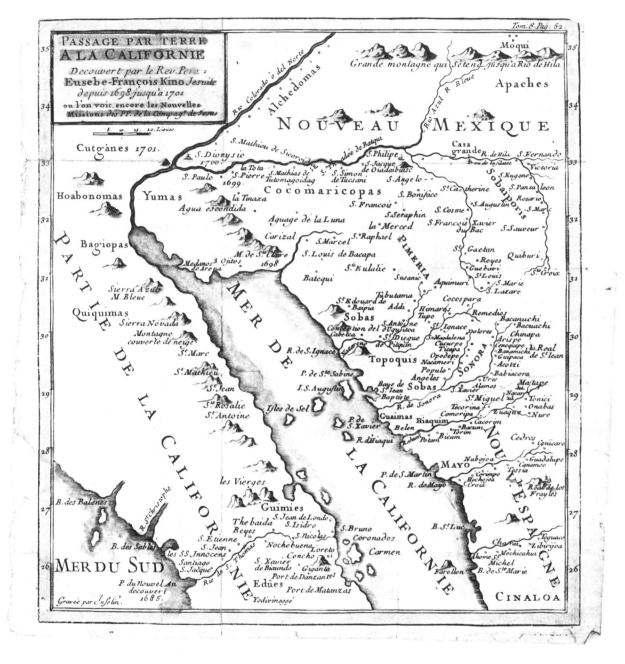

Map made by Father Kino in 1702.

tour of the Santa Cruz Valley. Leal was impressed by the fertile soil and the extensive grasslands suitable for cattle. He believed that the valley, served by a mission at Bac, could easily support 30,000 people. It would be an understatement to say that the modern growth of the Tucson area has fulfilled Leal's prophecy many times over. And it would be an oversight not to say that the Indians probably preferred it like it was before the white man came. There was running water in the streams then. Grass was knee deep before thousands of cattle overgrazed it in the late 19th century.

There seemed to be plenty of grass and water for cattle in 1700, however. In that year, Kino's Indian cowboys rounded up several hundred head at Dolores for the new mission of San Xavier. By late spring a good crop of wheat was ripening and a field of maize was planted. Only a church was needed to make San Xavier a full-fledged mission. The foundations were begun in late April. The exact location of Kino's church is not known. The present structure at San Xavier was built by Franciscans in the late 1700s.

One of the sorrows in Kino's optimistic life was that he could not be relieved at Dolores. He wanted to be the fulltime resident priest at San Xavier. Kino also regretted not having enough priests to establish missions on the San Pedro, Gila, and Colorado rivers. He urged the king to establish the New Kingdom of Navarre out of this region. The Apaches would be conquered and a trade route opened through Hopi country between Santa Fe and California. Unfortunately, most of Spain's money was committed to wars in Europe during the early 1700s. The empire was neglected.

Kino died as he had lived—with extreme humility and poverty. His deathbed consisted of two calfskins for a mattress, two Indian blankets for covers, and a pack saddle for a

pillow. Kino was buried in the chapel of a church in Magdalena, a town in Sonora south of Nogales. The burial place was forgotten for many years. There was great excitement, both in Mexico and in the United States, when the body was discovered in 1966.

Five years earlier, in 1961, the Arizona legislature bestowed a great honor on Kino. The members voted to have his statue placed in the capitol in Washington, D. C. The honor is evident by the fact that each state can have only two statues in the Statuary Hall collection.

3. SPAIN SENT SOME GERMAN MISSIONARIES TO WORK WITH INDIANS ON THE FRONTIER

Grazhoffer, Segesser, Stiger, Keller, Sedelmayr, Pauer, Pfefferkorn, and Middendorff—all have one thing in common. They were German Jesuit priests who served in Arizona.

For more than twenty years after Kino's death in 1711, Arizona was neglected by Spanish officials and missionaries alike. But in the 1730s, Spain recovered from wars in

An artist's rendition of Guevavi Mission, from historical sources.

Europe and again gave attention to Pimería Alta. Among the new padres were several recruited in the German states.

Father Johann Grazhoffer, a 42-year-old Austrian, was the first to arrive. He reached Guevavi on May 4, 1732, with a military escort. For the Pimas it was cause for celebration. They came in their best blankets and feathers to enjoy the occasion and to receive gifts. The new padre erected a Holy Cross and the soldiers fired their muskets. The Indians got into the act with races, dances, and singing.

There was one problem. Grazhoffer didn't leave when the festivities were over, as Kino used to do. He stayed as a resident missionary and exercised authority, speaking out against evils that he saw—polygamy and drinking orgies, in particular. The Pimas were unwilling to give up some of their native customs to become full-fledged Christians and resented Grazhoffer's scoldings. In 1733, the padre was given poison in his food. He died in the presence of Father Phelipe Segesser, the resident priest at San Xavier who had stopped by Guevavi on his way to Sonora.

Father Ignacio Keller and Father Jacobo Sedelmayr. These priests were the two best-known German Jesuits. Keller, like Kino, often preferred to travel alone. In 1736 he journeyed down the Santa Cruz Valley and observed the ancient Casa Grande near the Gila. The next year he noted a change in the San Pedro Valley since Kino's visits. The Apaches had forced some of Kino's Pima friends to desert their farming villages.

Sedelmayr spent five years exploring the Gila and Colorado rivers. On one trip in 1744 the busy padre preached a sermon against witchcraft at Casa Grande, visited forty-one Cocomaricopa villages along the Gila, and traveled north beyond the Bill Williams River. That was farther north than any Spaniard had ventured since Governor Oñate, 140 years earlier. The Indians along the Colorado gave him watermelons, squash, beans, and maize. They also furnished infor-mation about the Hopis. Neither Sedelmayr nor Keller, however, ever fulfilled an ambition to reach the Hopi villages.

San Agustín del Tucson. Bernardo Middendorff came to Arizona in 1756 as chaplain with a military expedition. He was assigned the task of building a head mission (*cabecera*) at San Agustín del Tucson for Indians near "A" Mountain. This mission was to exist only four months.

When Middendorff arrived in January, 1757, escorted by ten soldiers, there was no house and no church. Left to manage for himself, he built a brush hut for lodging. Mass was celebrated outdoors under a ramada. The German padre won the friendship of the natives with gifts of dried beef and gave them religious instruction through an interpreter.

On March 3, 1757, Middendorff wrote the first letter ever sent from Tucson. Writing in Latin, he asked the treasurer of the missions to send him wine for Mass and chocolate to trade for fresh meat. His meat supply had become rancid. He had nothing to eat but grain and the bird's eggs and wild fruits which the natives sometimes gave him.

Not all the natives had affection for the rustic little mission of San Agustín. In May it was attacked and destroyed. Middendorff, who can be called Tucson's first non-Indian pioneer, barely escaped with his life. He was helped by local Indians at San Xavier and soldiers from the Tubac presidio which was established in 1752.

4. DISCOVERY OF SILVER NEAR NO-GALES GAVE ARIZONA ITS NAME

In October, 1736, a notable event happened which gave Arizona its name. A Yaqui miner discovered some chunks of silver near Arissona, a Spanish mission *visita* southwest of Nogales. As news of the discovery spread, one of the first mining booms of the West got under way. Hundreds of hopeful Spanish prospectors rushed to the scene and began searching the hills. Silver, estimated at no less than 4,000 pounds in weight, was picked up in the form of large balls and slabs.

Captain Juan Bautista de Anza—father of the man with the same name who founded San Francisco in 1776—hastened to Arissona from the presidio of Terrenate. It was his job to protect the interests of the King of Spain. Under Spanish law, the king was entitled to one-fifth of any metal that was mined. But by the time Anza arrived, the miners had departed with their treasure.

The musical word "Arissona" was remembered by adventurers—first the Spaniards, then the Mexicans, and finally the Anglo-Americans—and eventually was adopted as the name of the 48th state. It is believed that the name is a softened spelling of two Papago words, *ali* (small) and *shonak* (place of the spring).

5. THE PIMA REBELLION OF 1751 LED TO THE FOUNDING OF ARIZONA'S FIRST MILITARY BASE AT TUBAC

The rush of impatient miners to Arissona created ill feelings with the Indians. During the 1740s, hardy Spanish frontiersmen searched for more balls of silver in the hills of Sonora and southern Arizona. This activity

Plan of the presidio of Tubac, drawn about 1765. It is the earliest known plat of an Arizona town.

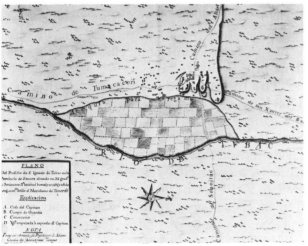

was just one more threat to the slow-paced lifestyle of the usually peaceful Pimas.

In Sáric, a few miles west of Arissona, there was an ambitious Pima leader named Luis Oacpicagigua. He was eager to drive out the white men and rule Pimería Alta himself. The Spaniards actually helped whet his appetite for power. As a reward for his help in fighting the rebellious Seris, Luis was appointed native governor with the title of captain-general. He began to undermine the missionaries, circulating stories about their cruelty. Once the few hundred Spaniards were driven out, he said, the Indians could have the loot from their missions, mines, and ranches.

The Pima Rebellion broke out on November 20, 1751. Under the ruse that Apaches were about to attack Sáric, Luis gave refuge in his home to some 20 Spaniards and faithful mission Indians. He then set fire to the house. The trapped occupants were either burned to death in the flames or were killed trying to escape. The rebellion soon spread. Bands of Pimas and Papagos began putting the torch to Spanish possessions. In the course of a few days, two Jesuit priests and more than a hundred miners, settlers, and herdsmen were murdered.

The missions and ranches of the Santa Cruz Valley did not escape the killing and plundering. Father Francisco Pauer of San Xavier and Father Joseph Garrucho of Guevavi had guessed trouble was coming and were safe at the Terrenate presidio. But their mission properties were destroyed. And at Arivaca, the rebels attacked the Spanish *visita* and farms, killing 11 Spaniards and a number of loyal Indians.

Spanish soldiers from the presidio of Terrenate were ordered to the field by Governor Diego Ortiz Parrilla of Sonora and Sinaloa. After three months, Luis was cornered in the Catalina Mountains north of Tucson and forced to negotiate for peace.

Presidio of Tubac. After putting down the Pima Rebellion of 1751, the Spaniards made preparations to prevent future uprisings.

Two new military garrisons were established in 1752—one on the Altar River in Sonora and the other at Tubac, until then a *visita* of Guevavi.

Tubac became the first Spanish military post in Arizona when fifty soldiers were assigned there. The commander was Captain Tomás de Belderrain, an officer who knew the country and had proven himself in the recent uprising. Very soon a settlement grew up around the fort. Evidently the people felt relatively safe. The first white women to touch Arizona soil arrived in 1752.

Tubac continued to grow. By 1757 it had a population of more than 400 counting the soldiers. Except for brief stretches when the whites were driven away by raiding Apaches, Tubac has been inhabited continuously. President Gerald Ford gave recognition to the town's significant place in history when he held a conference there in October, 1974, with President Luis Echeverria of Mexico.

6. THE JESUITS CONTINUED TO WORK IN ARIZONA UNTIL 1767 WHEN THEY WERE EXPELLED BY CHARLES III

No missionary worked harder than Father Alphonso Espinosa, the resident priest at San Xavier del Bac from 1756 to 1765. He was escorted to Bac by Juan Antonio de Mendoza, the Spanish governor of Sinaloa-Sonora. Mendoza was determined that all the natives of Bac and Tucson—the "gateway to the Gila" —should become Christians.

Rebellion at San Xavier. Jabanimó, or "Crow's Head," the old chief of the Gila Pimas, wanted no part of Christian salvation. He advised the people at Bac and Tucson not to be converted. Espinosa played into the chief's hand by trying to purify the traditional wine feast that followed the cactus fruit harvest. As a priest, he wanted to stop the Indians from getting intoxicated. He proposed doing away with the drinking and native elements of the festival. It would be put on the church calendar as a Christian celebration. The natives resisted this change.

Jabanimó saw his opportunity to close down the mission. With his own warriors and some of the San Xavier converts, he raided the mission house and the huts of loyal natives. Espinosa escaped to Tubac where the news had reached Ensign Juan María de Oliva. The Tubac soldiers rode to Bac and put the lingering rebels to flight.

The Gila Expedition. Governor Mendoza led an expedition of soldiers from Terrenate to punish Jabanimó. The rebels were tracked to the Gila River and downstream to the vicinity of the present-day town of Gila Bend. The Pimas, no match for the better-armed soldiers, were routed with a loss of 15 killed.

Mendoza then returned to San Xavier and laid the first stone for Espinosa's church. It was also at this time that Mendoza gave his chaplain and cartographer*, Father Middendorff, the job of starting the San Agustín del Tucson mission. Middendorff was with him on the Gila expedition and later wrote an account of it.

A new San Xavier del Bac. Espinosa built a church west of the present "White Dove of the Desert." The building was eighty-five feet long and twenty feet wide. The 20-foot ceiling was spanned by combining two 10-foot beams, called *vigas*, with a post for support in the center. Later the church was torn down and the *vigas*, which were hewn from mesquite wood, were used in the convento wing of the present church where resident priests live today.

The Indian settlement of Tucson. After 1762 Espinosa had the responsibility of assisting a new *ranchería* at Tucson—then called San José del Tucson. Several hundred new residents were living there. They were Pimas who were escorted by soldiers from the San Pedro Valley where Apaches raided their homes. Espinosa introduced cattle and sheep

*cartographer: map maker

84

in the new Tucson settlement. But the Indians would have nothing to do with livestock. They preferred to work in their irrigated fields and then migrate to the foothills to gather wild foods or to hunt after the end of the harvest season.

In 1765 the hard-working Espinosa, then in ill-health, was replaced by a younger priest. Twenty-six-year-old José Neve served two years at San Xavier.

Jesuits expelled. King Charles III of Spain expelled all Jesuits from the New World in 1767. More than fifty Jesuit priests in Sonora-Sinaloa—including Espinosa and Neve—were confined in a warehouse in the seaport of Guaymas. They were transported down the coast by ship to San Blas and then marched overland to Vera Cruz for deportation to Spain. Neve and Espinosa were not among the 20 priests who died on the march. Neve died in a Cadiz, Spain, hospital at the age of 34. Espinosa lived his last seventeen years in a monastery at El Yuste in western Spain.

Why did Charles III expel the Jesuits from

King Carlos (Charles) III of Spain. Original painting in the Prado Museum at Madrid.

the New World? A new king, he wanted to streamline the colonial government and make it operate more directly under his personal rule. He may have thought that the Society of Jesus was more an international than a Spanish society. It was said that the Jesuits had grown too powerful and independent of the king's authority. Whatever his reasons, Charles III was an autocratic king and didn't have to explain his actions to anyone.

7. FRAY GARCES WAS AN IDEAL MISSIONARY AND A REMARKABLE EXPLORER

Gray-robed Franciscan priests replaced the black-robed Jesuits in 1767. The most famous of the Franciscans, Fray Francisco Garcés, was given a rude welcoming at San Xavier. Apaches swooped down on the mission late in 1768 to pillage and destroy a part of Espinosa's adobe church. At that time, San Xavier was the northernmost outpost in Arizona and the least defended. The small garrison of troops at Tubac was barely large enough to protect Tubac settlers and their families. Garcés was assigned only two soldier escorts for protection.

Apache raids continued. Garcés reported one attack in February 1769, while most of the San Xavier villagers were away gathering agave hearts. "The attack was over in a matter of minutes," he wrote to the Viceroy, "the time it took to make off with the livestock, which was most of what we had."

Despite the dangers, Garcés eagerly began his work of restoring the mission and winning souls. He also worked with the Indians in Tucson. After building a tiny brush hut in the Pima village, he made frequent visits to Tucson. Evidently Garcés had a sense of humor. He invited his soldier friend, Captain Juan Bautista de Anza at Tubac, to visit and stay in the "captain's room."

Thirty years of age and a native of the Spanish province of Aragon, Garcés was well-suited by temperament for his work. He appreciated Indian customs. He would sit cross-legged with Indians for hours and eat their food with gusto*, saying it was good for the stomach. Though Garcés was young, the Indians lovingly called him "Old Man."

Garcés, a restless explorer. Within six months after his arrival, Garcés visited villages on the Gila and explored most of southwestern Arizona. By the time he returned to the Gila in 1770 he was speaking the Pima language fluently. There was an epidemic of measles that year. He cared for the sick and baptized many Indians. The Gila Pimas were eager for his teachings and tried to detain him when it was time for him to move on.

Always in search of converts, Garcés used a visual aid to help explain the plan of salvation. He carried a linen print with the Virgin Mary holding the child Jesus on one side and a picture of a lost soul on the other.

In 1771 Garcés was authorized to look for an overland route to California and to locate desirable mission sites. With only three Indian guides, and a horse to carry supplies, Garcés traveled west over Kino's old border trail, the dry *Camino del Diablo* (Devil's Highway). Welcomed by the Yumas on the Colorado River, he ventured out over the Yuma desert and back. This exploration convinced the Spanish authorities that an overland route could be opened to California.

For the next decade, Garcés helped organize two expeditions to California that were headed by Captain Anza. Garcés also established missions near the Yuma crossing on the Colorado.

Garcés visited the Hopis. On July 4, 1776, he was in the village of Oraibi, the oldest continuously inhabited community on the North American continent. His Hopi hosts feared that the Spaniards wished to conquer and humiliate them. They made the priest feel unwelcome. After only two days at Oraibi, Garcés was packing his mule and preparing to leave town. As he adjusted the load, he was

*gusto: enthusiastic enjoyment

thinking about how the Hopis would not invite him into their homes or accept his gifts of tobacco and shells. And he thought about the night before, when he huddled in a dark corner of the village.

"As soon as day broke," he wrote in his diary for July 4, "I heard singing and dancing in the streets. The Indians passed by the place where I was, and only then did I see that some of them were painted red, with feathers and other decorations on the head, beating the sound of the dance on a kind of drum with two small sticks, to which the flute played in accompaniment. Many persons on the streets and the housetops kept time to the music.

"The sun having now risen," he continued, "I saw coming nigh unto me a great multitude of people, the sight of which caused me some fear of losing my life. There came forward four Indians who appeared to be leaders. The tallest of them asked me with a grimace, 'For what hast thou come here? Get thee gone without delay—back to thy land!'

"I made them a sign to be seated," Garcés wrote, "but they would not.

Fray Garcés

Oraibi is the oldest continuously occupied town in the United States.

"I arose with the Santo Cristo in my hand and spoke—partly in Yuma, partly in Yavapai, and partly in Spanish—with the aid of signs. I explained to them my route, naming the Indian tribes whom I had seen, those who had kissed el Cristo. I told them all of these had been good to me and that I also loved the Hopis, and for that reason I came to say to them that God is in the sky, and that the man whom they saw on the cross was the image of God, Jesus Christ, who is good."

But when an old man responded, "No! No!," Garcés decided it was time to leave.

Realizing that he had failed as a missionary to the Hopis, Garcés could at least take satisfaction in other things. As he rode out of town on his mule he passed a peach orchard and saw flocks of sheep, samples of European culture which the Hopis had accepted without embracing the religion or authority of the Spanish king.

During his absence from San Xavier, Garcés had proved that a Spanish trade route could be laid out between the West Coast and Santa Fe across Hopi country. He covered the entire distance except for the section east of Oraibi which Spanish explorers had traveled many times since the 1540s. Garcés did not know as he left Oraibi that another Franciscan, Fray Escalante, was at that moment preparing for a journey westward from the Zuñi pueblo into present-day Arizona.

From Oraibi, Garcés retraced his route back to the Mojave villages and down the Colorado River to the Yumas where he arrived on August 27. Three weeks later he was back at San Xavier del Bac. In the wilderness almost continuously for 11 months, he had traveled more than 2,000 miles.

Just before Garcés reached San Xavier he was pleased to see Lieutenant Juan María de Oliva and his soldiers camped at Tucson. Garcés had often complained in letters to the viceroy in Mexico City that San Xavier needed more military protection. In 1775 the Tucson site was selected to replace the presidio at Tubac. Lieutenant Oliva moved the troops the following year.

Juan Bautista de Anza, commander of the presidio at Tubac, led two expeditions to California and founded San Francisco in 1776. Drawing based on an oil painting by Fray Orsi.

5

THE INDIANS OF ARIZONA AND THE LAST YEARS OF SPANISH RULE

The frontier of New Spain covered a vast region stretching from Texas to California. This area was largely arid and occupied by nomadic or semi-nomadic Indians. In contrast to the great cities, cattle ranches, and mining districts farther south, little effort was made to colonize the northern frontier. Spain tried to control the Indians by establishing missions and presidios.

Fearing a British or Russian takeover of California, Spanish officials tried to open an overland supply route from Mexico. This hope was ended by an uprising of Yuma Indians, who controlled the Colorado crossing.

Beginning in the 1770s, the Spanish military authorities concentrated on exterminating the Apaches. Failing in that, they adopted a peace policy that brought some settlement and prosperity to southern Arizona. Apaches were encouraged to settle near presidios in return for free rations.

KEY CONCEPTS

1. The Spanish were concerned mainly with three Indian groups: the Pimas, Yumas, and Apaches.

2. Juan Bautista de Anza opened an overland route to California and founded San Francisco.

3. The Yuma Massacre ended the career of Father Garcés and forced the Spanish to abandon the overland route to California.

4. The Tucson presidio was established in 1776 for defense against the Apaches.

5. The Spanish government pacified the Apaches with free rations.

6. The last thirty years of Spanish rule was the "golden age."

5

1. THE SPANISH WERE CONCERNED WITH THREE INDIAN GROUPS: PIMAS, YUMAS, AND APACHES

The word "Pima" is the white man's word for a tribe of Indians who were living in Sonora and southern Arizona when the Spanish arrived. The Pimas called themselves *o-odham,* which simply means "people." There were three major groups of Upper Pimas who lived between the Gila River on the north and the Altar River in Mexico on the south. Each adjusted to the desert environment in its own way.

1) River Pimas. These people lived along the streams. They were essentially flood plain farmers—relying on the rivers to widen during the flood season to water their crops. They also hunted and gathered wild plants. When Kino visited Arizona several times in the 1690s, he found the river Pimas living in the valleys of the Gila, the Santa Cruz, and the San Pedro.

With rare exceptions, the Spaniards had friendly relations with the river Pimas. Colonel Anza visited the Gila Pimas several times between 1774 and 1776. He said they had good crops at Uturitac and at Vah Ki, located about where Interstate 10 now crosses the Gila River.

"The fields of wheat are so large," he wrote, "that one cannot see the ends because they are so long. Their width is also great, embracing the whole width of the valley on either side, and their fields of maize are of corresponding size."

Wheat, first brought to Arizona by Father Kino, was the principal crop harvested in the summer. But the Pimas also planted maize and corn, using only a pointed stick to make a hole for seed. For cloth the Indians planted cotton. They also raised sheep from which they sheared wool for spinning and weaving. Castilian hens, another Spanish contribution, were kept in the Pima villages.

A River Pima village.

Physically, the Pimas were described as dark, robust, and sometimes fat. The men wore either cotton breeches or a light blanket gathered up and tied. The male hair style in the 1700s seemed peculiar to Spanish observers. It consisted of long hair twisted into a crestlike crown held in place by a woolen cord. Feathers, sticks, and other ornaments were inserted into the hair crown for decoration. The Pima women covered themselves with cloth or deerskin. They wore their hair hanging down their backs. In front it was cut in bangs at eyebrow level.

2) The "two village Papagos" were a second group of Upper Pimas. In the winter they gathered wild food and hunted near permanent springs in the mountain foothills. In the summer they moved to flat land to grow crops of maize, beans, and squash. The Papagos dammed arroyos with brush to spread rain water over their fields. In Kino's time, the Papagos—a word which means "bean eaters"—lived in the same vicinity of their present reservations west of Tucson. They have been less disturbed by the white man than almost any Arizona Indian group.

The Papagos were usually friendly with the Spaniards. But on occasion they would rebel. Captain Anza reported one uprising. "I attacked them personally on May 10, 1760," he wrote, "and took the lives of Ciprian, their captain, and nine others." Anza said that all the rest surrendered and promised to remain at peace.

3) The "sand Papagos." These Indians lived in the driest of desert regions. They were nomads who had no fixed places to live. Their livelihood was based on hunting, gathering, and trading. In season they were at the head of the Gulf of California gathering shellfish. They traded shells and salt to the Yuma Indians along the Colorado River for pottery and farm crops. At other times, the sand Papagos went inland to live on desert products, locusts, lizards, and small animals. Kino met up with the sand Papagos in his travels along the present international border. He instructed them in the Word of God. As a separate group, the sand Papagos disappeared in the 20th century.

The Yumas. The Yumas along the Colorado River were described by most Spaniards in the 1770s as being better looking but less industrious than the Pimas. The men daubed their naked bodies with red and black paint and kept warm in cool weather by carrying firebrands. De Anza thought the unusual hair style of the Yuma men was worth mentioning in one of his reports. He said they encased their hair in mud and sprinkled it with powder having a silver luster. They sometimes slept sitting up in order not to disturb the hairdo. The men put on a ferocious appearance by piercing the cartilage of the nose and inserting a feather or sprig of a palm.

Yuma women went barefooted like the men. They wore skirts that covered the body from the waist to the thighs or knees. The skirt was made from the inner bark of willows or cottonwood. It was divided into two pieces, the shorter part in front.

Unlike the Pimas, the Yumas did not irrigate farmland. They waited for floods to recede each year. Then they planted crops of wheat, maize, beans, calabashes, and muskmelons in the rich silt deposited along the banks of the river. Ripe melons were buried in the sands for cooling and were "in season" almost year-round.

The Spaniards sought the goodwill of the Yumas because these Indians controlled the ford across the Colorado.

The Apaches. The Spanish classified the Apaches of Arizona and New Mexico into five principal tribes. Three of these were in Arizona—the Chiricahuas, Gileños, and Tontos. The Chiricahuas lived in southeastern Arizona. Gileños liked the mountains of eastern Arizona. The Tontos were in central Arizona, northeast of present-day Phoenix.

These tribal groups broke up into bands. The smaller bands were united by kinship and controlled by a chief, at least in wartime. When convenient, the Apaches preferred to be independent and to roam about at will.

The Apaches were physically robust, agile, untiring, and always in harmony with the environment. They were constantly moving in search of new game and wild foods for subsistence. The Apaches had a new source of food when the Spaniards brought in horses, cattle, and sheep. The Indians could now survive by hit-and-run raids to drive off the livestock and plunder the settlements. They were not primarily interested in killing people. It was to their advantage to have the settlers producing the grains and stock that they wanted.

When chased, the Indians sometimes lured their pursuers into ambush. More often they fled swiftly across rugged mountains or waterless deserts to a secluded camp to avoid capture. The frontier Spaniards were also a hardy breed. But after years of bloody effort, they were unable to crush the Apaches.

2. JUAN BAUTISTA DE ANZA OPENED AN OVERLAND ROUTE TO CALIFORNIA AND FOUNDED SAN FRANCISCO

Juan Bautista de Anza was only 25 in 1760 when he was appointed commander at Tubac

A Spanish soldier wore a leather jacket and carried a heavy bullhide shield.

army on the Sonoran frontier.

Like his father, Anza dreamed of finding a land route to California. In 1772 he offered to lead an expedition at his own expense. One reason for an overland route was to supply colonies in California from Sonora. Another objective was to establish a presidio for their protection. In this venture, Anza had the enthusiastic support of Fray Garcés.

Anza's first expedition to California. Viceroy Bucareli in Mexico City approved the project. On January 8, 1774, the first of two Anza expeditions got under way from Tubac. The caravan included twenty volunteer soldiers, Indian interpreters, muleteers, a carpenter, and a large herd of horses and cattle. Anza took a long route to reach the Colorado River. He went south to the Sonora missions in the Altar Valley and then northwest over the *Camino del Diablo* to the Yuma crossing.

Anza lingered on the Colorado to win the friendship of Chief Olleyquotequiebe (the Wheezer), better known as Palma. This man's good will was needed, since the Yumas controlled the river ford. Anza got off on the right foot when he presented Palma with a silver medal embossed with a likeness of Charles III. The Yumas cheered as Anza strung the gift on a red ribbon and placed it around Palma's neck.

Garcés guided the expedition across the desert and through the mountains of California to San Gabriel. He then returned to the Yuma area while Anza went north to Monterey and back. During Anza's absence, the Colorado River rose and the Yumas built rafts to help the caravan to the Arizona side.

"In all my life," Anza wrote in his diary, "I have never crossed another river with greater confidence...Even though the craft might have capsized, I had close to me more than five hundred persons ready to rescue me."

Anza followed the shorter Gila route back to Tubac. After reporting to Viceroy Bucareli in Mexico City, he was promoted to lieutenant-colonel and received permission to lead a

—a presidio that was established earlier by his father. The younger Anza was born at the presidio of Fronteras, located in Mexico south of present-day Douglas, Arizona. He was the third generation of his family to serve in the

colonizing expedition to the San Francisco Bay Area.

Anza's colonizing expedition to California. Anza recruited settlers and soldiers and began his second expedition at the presidio of Horcasitas — near present-day Hermosillo, Mexico. Tubac was reached on October 23, 1775. Anza was disappointed to learn that the Apaches had raided the corrals at Tubac. Many of the good horses he planned on using for the remainder of the trip were driven off. But he replaced as many as possible and moved on down the Santa Cruz Valley.

The caravan included 240 persons, a majority of whom were women and children. All but one of the 30 soldiers had his wife with him and most of the colonists had their families. There were three priests. Fray Garcés and Fray Tomás Eixarch went as far as Yuma. Fray Pedro Font continued all the way to California as the diarist and chaplain. Colonel

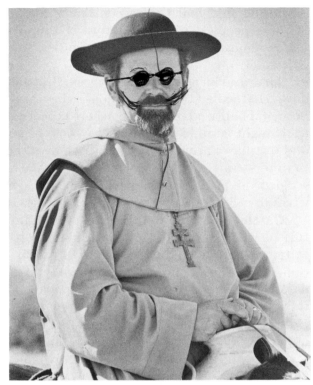

Fray Pedro Font as portrayed by Father Fox in the bicentennial re-enactment of the Anza expedition in 1975.

Diorama of the Anza expedition crossing the sand dunes west of the Colorado River in 1774.

Anza not only had the responsibility for all of these people, but also for tons of supplies and a thousand head of horses, mules, and cattle.

The caravan slowly moved to the Gila and down that valley to the Colorado. Babies were born and baptized. Families gathered together each night around campfires to cook beans and tortillas. Father Font kept watch over the manners and morals of the colonists. He scolded the jealous soldiers who forbade their wives to talk to anybody or to attend Mass.

Cattle meandered into the brush and turned wild. Horses died from drinking salty water or were abandoned because of exhaustion. Saddles grew hard and feet heavy. The desert alkali dust caused eyes to smart and throats to burn. The emigrants grew tired. But no one turned back. If Colonel Anza grew impatient, he did not show it in his diary.

Anza's meeting with Palma on November 28, 1775, was another festive event. The Yumas treated their guests with 3,000 watermelons and helped them across the river. They were rewarded with beads and tobacco. Palma was given a gala outfit which Viceroy Bucareli sent to him. It consisted of a decorated jacket with yellow front, blue trousers, a gold-braided blue cape, and a cap of black velvet adorned with imitation jewels and a palmlike crest. The chief's new clothes and the gifts which the other Yumas received made the river crossing a happy occasion for all. Fray Eixarch remained with the Yumas while Garcés did some exploring.

The colonists reached the Bay Area in June 1776. After picking out a site for the presidio of San Francisco, Anza turned his command over to Lieutenant José Moraga. He then made the journey back to the Yuma crossing in 10 days.

Chief Palma and three other Indians went with Anza to Mexico City. They must have been impressed by the hero's welcome

Bicentennial re-enactment of the Anza expedition crossing the Colorado River.

The Anza expedition reaches the San Francisco Bay.

given Colonel Anza. Anza pleaded with Viceroy Bucareli for missions and a presidio at the Yuma crossing. He and Garcés had laid the groundwork for friendly relations with the Yumas. But the Spanish government delayed doing anything until 1780. By that time relations with the Yumas took a turn for the worse.

While in Mexico City, the Yuma chief was baptized in the famous Cathedral of Mexico as Salvador Carlos Antonio Palma — a big name for one of Arizona's most powerful men in 1776.

Colonel Anza was soon appointed Governor of New Mexico and left the Arizona scene.

3. THE YUMA MASSACRE ENDED THE CAREER OF FATHER GARCÉS AND FORCED THE SPANISH TO ABANDON THE OVERLAND ROUTE TO CALIFORNIA

The Yuma Indians wanted missions. When none were established, they began to ridicule Chief Palma. Twice the big chief went personally to Sonora to plead for missionaries. His visits came to the attention of the man who was in charge of all frontier military defenses, Commander-General Teodoro de Croix. At long last, Croix gave Father Garcés the go-ahead.

Yuma's first mission settlements. In August 1779, Garcés and Father Juan Díaz went to the Yuma crossing area with a small military escort. A worse time could not have been chosen. The summer was abnormally dry and hot. The Yumas were hostile. Instead of receiving lavish gifts, they had to provide subsistence* for the holy fathers.

Díaz went to Arispe in Sonora to appeal to Croix for aid. The commander-general decided on two hybrid-type* establishments in the Yuma country. Each would have two missionaries, about ten soldiers, 10 families of colonists, and a half dozen laborers.

The two mission-presidio-colony settlements got under way in the fall of 1780. Garcés and Father Juan Berreneche were located across the Colorado River on Mission Hill— opposite the present site of the Yuma territorial prison. Díaz and Father Matias Moreno were in charge of a second mission upstream called San Pedro y San Pablo.

The Yumas had good cause to rebel. Not all the soldiers and colonists were as kind to the Yumas as the friars. They made fun of the natives for their primitive method of planting—punching a hole in the soil with a stick for the seeds. They crowded the Indians out of the missions and took the best farmland.

The soldiers overused the whipping post and the stocks, hurting the Indians' pride. Worst of all, the Spaniards grazed their horses and livestock on mesquite beans, a valuable food source which the Yumas ground into flour. The Yumas became more and more hostile. Even Chief Palma turned against the Spaniards and began plotting to drive the white men out.

The Yumas were given one more reason to rebel in June 1781. A large party of Cali-

*subsistence: minimum food to sustain life
*hybrid-type: composed of differing elements

fornia-bound soldiers and their families stopped at the Yuma crossing to rest. They let their livestock browse on the mesquite beans. Their commander, the arrogant* Captain Javier Fernando de Rivera, ordered several Indians whipped for stealing Spanish property. In some instances the Yumas were retrieving their own horses. Fortunately, Rivera did one thing right. He sent the families and some soldiers on to San Gabriel with the animals able to travel. But then he camped on an Indian field near the present site of downtown Yuma.

The Yuma Massacre. On July 17, 1781, the Yumas rose in rebellion. One mob of Indians attacked the San Pedro y San Pablo mission. They killed Father Díaz and Father Moreno, beheading the latter with an ax. Most of the men at this mission were murdered. For some reason, all the women and children were spared and later put to work, but not mistreated.

A few hours after the first attack, the Yumas surrounded the church on Mission Hill where Garcés was giving Mass. The people who took refuge in the church were not harmed on the first day of the rebellion. But all the white men working in the fields were killed and homes were ransacked. The next morning the aroused Indians massacred the Rivera party on the Arizona side of the river. They then returned to Mission Hill.

While waiting for death, the survivors in the church sang hymns and Father Berreneche offered Mass. Before the Indians arrived, the Spaniards decided to try escaping. The more vicious of the Yumas searched for Garcés and Berreneche. The two priests were finally found drinking chocolate in the home of friendly Indians. After the two men were clubbed to death, pious Yumas reverently buried their bodies and planted flowers on the graves.

*An *arrogant* person pays little attention to the feelings of others.

Bronze marker honoring Father Garcés.

Altogether about 50 Spanish men were murdered in the Yuma revolt. Troops came from Sonora and were able to trade blankets, beads, and tobacco for the release of 48 captives. But the Yumas were never punished for their crimes. They remained hostile and blocked the overland route to California.

Without control of the Yuma crossing, the Spaniards had to supply the California colony by sea from Mexico. The Yuma massacre did not bring the mission era to a close. It did end the career of the last dynamic pioneer priest, Father Garcés.

The Spaniards adopted a new Indian policy. In 1786 the viceroy in Mexico City gave top priority to the conquest of the Apaches. All Spanish contact with the Yumas ceased. The dream of Kino and Garcés for a northern trail between Santa Fe and California was also dropped. The Hopi and Navajo continued their time-honored religions and customs, little affected by Spanish contact. For the remainder of the Spanish period—to 1821—all efforts to maintain an outpost of civilization in Arizona were concentrated in the Santa Cruz Valley.

4. THE TUCSON PRESIDIO WAS ESTABLISHED IN 1776 FOR DEFENSE AGAINST APACHES

The presidio for the protection of the Santa Cruz Valley was moved from Tubac to Tucson in 1776. This change was part of a master plan for defense against the Apaches. The main provision in this plan—set forth in the Royal Regulations of 1772—was a realignment of 15 forts stretching from Texas to Tubac. This huge task was given to Colonel Hugo O'Conor, a red-headed Irishman long in the Spanish service. Starting in Texas, O'Conor worked his way to Arizona.

On August 20, 1775, he inspected the Tucson area with Father Garcés. A site was selected for the future Royal Presidio of San Agustín on the east side of the Santa Cruz River. The Indian village was on the west side at the base of "A" Mountain. O'Conor said the Tucson site was better than Tubac because it was well-situated to defend San Xavier and to protect Anza's overland route to California.

At the time the troops were finally moved to Tucson, Colonel Anza was busy with his second expedition to California. In his absence, Lieutenant Juan María de Oliva was in charge. Oliva, though illiterate, had risen through the ranks since coming to Tubac in 1752. He was a veteran of many Indian battles with the Apaches.

Unfortunately, Anza took some of the best troops to California, leaving Oliva's garrison undermanned and ill-equipped. He had only 15 usable muskets and carbines, 22 swords, and 10 arrow-proof jackets made of six-ply leather. There were only six lances. The lance

Royal presidio of Tucson as it looked about 1790.

A Spanish musket, called an *escopeta*.

was considered the most effective weapon in fighting Apaches.

Captain Don Pedro de Allande. The first permanent commander of the Tucson presidio, Captain Allande, arrived in 1777. He directed the construction of a temporary palisade* of logs. The permanent presidio with adobe walls was not completed until 1783. Meanwhile, Allande fought Apaches and helped Charles III raise money for the American colonies fighting for independence. The donation of Tucson's soldiers and settlers was 459 pesos. At that time, four pesos would buy a beef animal. An excellent riding horse could be bought for seven pesos. Spanish Sonora as a whole gave 22,420 pesos.

The May Day Apache Attack on Tucson. By the 1780s the Apaches were getting bolder. On May 1, 1782, several hundred warriors attacked the unfinished Tucson presidio. Fortunately, not all the soldiers were inside. While the Indians concentrated on the open entrance of the fort, a lieutenant fired on them from a nearby rooftop. His Indian servant also diverted a few attackers with his bow and arrows.

Two other soldiers happened to be on the opposite side of the Santa Cruz. They defended the bridge and kept the Apaches from attacking the Pima village. Captain Allande received a severe leg wound making a valiant stand with about 20 soldiers inside the entrance of the stockade. He later claimed to have killed two Apaches with his own hands after being wounded.

In the face of superior Spanish firepower, the Apaches sheathed their arrows and departed, even though their casualties were light. The May Day assault on the presidio was not typical of the Apaches. Their usual style was to raid a settlement to get livestock or goods of economic value.

Spanish troops invade Apache country. Allande led several campaigns to harass the Apaches in the Gila country. In 1784 he cooperated with troops from other presidios in a mass invasion of Apachería, as the homeland of the Apaches was called. The Indians

A Spanish cavalry pistol.

*palisade: fence of stakes pointed at top

were impressed by the presence of Spanish troops, but did not stop raiding the Spanish settlements. The Apaches used guerrilla* tactics and refused to fight the Spaniards in open battle to determine power in European style.

Tubac got some protection in 1784 when a company of Pima allies was formed. Pimas continued to serve in this capacity for the remainder of the Spanish period. Later, a few Spanish soldiers were added to the old Tubac presidio.

*a *guerrilla* is a warrior who makes surprise attacks.

5. THE SPANISH GOVERNMENT PACIFIED THE APACHES WITH FREE RATIONS

There was no peace on the frontier until Viceroy Bernardo de Galvez in Mexico City adopted a new Indian policy in 1786. The objective was still to exterminate warring Apaches. But the Indians were encouraged to settle down in permanent settlements near the presidios and become dependent on the Spaniards. Offered gifts to surrender, the Indians were to be supplied with food rations and all the liquor they could drink. As part of the program to weaken their native culture, they were given firearms of inferior quality. In his instructions to military officers, Galvez said the bow and arrow in the hands of the Indians was actually more deadly than 18th century Spanish firearms.

Vigorous campaigns against the Apaches in 1788 brought some success. Apache bands began to surrender and settle near the presidios. The first settlement at Tucson began in 1793 when the Aravaipa Apaches agreed to move from the San Pedro Valley. Chief Nautil Nilché showed his sincerity by presenting six sets of enemy Apache ears to the Tucson presidio commander, José Ignacio Moraga.

Tumacácori as it looked in the 1920s.

The chief was given a new suit of clothes. His people received supplies of meat, corn, tobacco, and candy.

There was no town council in Tucson or state legislature in the capital of Sonora at Arispe to debate the merits of the 1786 peace-at-a-price policy. It seemed to be working, but an outspoken Franciscan priest tried to get it changed. Father Diego Bringas said the free hand-outs made the Indian weak and dependent. He pointed out that Indians were picking up the white man's vices of gambling, cussing, and alcoholism. Bringas argued that the money could be better spent for farming implements and missionaries to teach the Indians moral virtues and how to support themselves.

The Spanish government admitted the ration system was expensive and corruptive. But it helped to bring peace and prosperity to the frontier during the last 30 years of New Spain. The Indians were still on the dole when Mexican revolutionaries overthrew Spanish rule in 1821.

6. THE LAST THIRTY YEARS OF SPANISH RULE WAS THE "GOLDEN AGE"

During the period of peace, 1790 to 1821, the settlements in southern Arizona began to prosper. More gold and silver mines were opened than in previous years of Spanish occupation. Ranchers brought in herds of cattle to stock the ranges, mainly in the Santa Cruz Valley.

Tucson and Tubac began to grow. New settlers applied for land grants near these towns. The first Spanish land grant in Arizona

San Xavier Mission.

Two-story Franciscan convento in Tucson as it looked in the 1890s. It was built about 1800.

was given to Torbio Otero in 1789 at Tubac. One of the best-known settlers in Tucson was Reyes Pacheco who was granted land near the presidio in 1802. Under the Spanish law, any settler on land within five miles of a presidio was obliged to give military service against the Apaches whenever there was a shortage of troops. In return, he was exempted from paying the personal tax to the government and church. The Spanish government had a monopoly on tobacco and raised some money from a tobacco tax. Tubac also had a sales tax.

Tucson was the center of population of northern Sonora, as it is today of southern Arizona. When Father Garcés arrived in the Tucson area in 1768 there were no Spanish settlers. By 1804 there were 37. The total population—settlers, soldiers, and Indians—was 1,015.

Most of the people were engaged in farming and the livestock industry. Wheat, corn, beans, and vegetables were the main crops. Cotton was raised only by the Indians and woven into cloth for their own use. Dependent Apaches were being fed from a herd of nearly 4,000 cattle. Surplus hides were sold at Arispe, the state capital. Both the settlers and soldiers went to Arispe to buy merchandise. There was also a presidio store and a private merchant in Tucson. Four men operated pack trains.

Very little was manufactured locally. Some soap was made in Tucson and San Xavier. There was a lime mine north of town which supplied what was needed for local construction. Captain José de Zúñiga, the presidio commander in 1804, called for more growth. He said Tucson could support woolen and cotton weavers, a leather tanner, a shoemaker, and a saddlemaker. Zúñiga's observations were compiled in a report to Governor Alejo García Conde at Arispe.

Beautiful mission churches. New church construction was symbolic of the peace that prevailed during the golden age. At Tumacácori, which had become an independent mission, a large church with a domed

The architecture of modern Los Arcos Mall in Scottsdale shows many Spanish influences.

roof was built during the 1800s. At San Xavier, Franciscans erected the beautiful "White Dove in the Desert." This church still stands. It is one of the most beautiful and best preserved Spanish missions in North America, thanks to Papago Indians and priests who cared for it in later times.

The original cost of San Xavier was estimated at 40,000 pesos, a huge sum in those days. An ornate* church was constructed for two reasons—to serve Christian Pimas in the San Xavier village and to attract, by its loveliness, the unconverted Papagos and Gila Pimas beyond the frontier. The Franciscans also built a two-story *convento*. This building was a home for missionaries near the base of "A" Mountain in Tucson.

ornate: highly decorated.

UNIT THREE

ARIZONA UNDER MEXICAN RULE (1821-1854)

On September 16, 1810, Father Miguel Hidalgo called upon the masses of Mexican people to revolt and throw off the yoke of Spain. Hidalgo was killed and the rebellion failed because the upper class leaders of New Spain remained loyal to the king.

Mexico won independence in 1821 by a palace revolt. This time, the colonial upper classes took the lead in seizing control of the king's government in Mexico City.

In Tucson a new flag was raised over the presidio. The commander, Captain José Romero, took the oath of allegiance to the new government of Mexico.

Arizona was not part of the Republic of Mexico very long. The unsettled area north of the Gila River, including the present site of Phoenix, was turned over to the United States in 1848, following the Mexican War.

The United States got the region south of the Gila, including Tucson, in 1854. The Gadsden Purchase of that year filled in the now-familiar profile of the United States. In 1856 American troops arrived in Tucson to take official possession of the Gadsden Purchase.

Mexico and the United States, 1821.

6

MEXICAN ARIZONA AND THE APACHE CONQUEST

After Mexico won its independence, there was much work to be done. Leaders of the new nation in Mexico City drew up a constitution and organized a republic. Unfortunately, the nation split into political factions and the government was very unstable. As a result, the frontier regions, including Arizona, were neglected.

The Apaches waited to see if the new government would continue the Spanish peace policy. When their free rations were cut off, the Indians went on the warpath again. By 1835, Arizona was nearly deserted except for settlements at Tucson and Tubac. Spanish missions were abandoned. Mexican stockmen let their cattle roam wild over huge ranches.

KEY CONCEPTS

1. Isolated settlers in Arizona were not much involved in Mexican politics.
2. The Arizona missions were deserted and some of their lands sold at public auction.
3. There were many large Mexican cattle ranches in southern Arizona.
4. The Apaches took to the warpath again.

6

1. ISOLATED SETTLERS IN ARIZONA WERE NOT INVOLVED IN MEXICAN POLITICS.

First mayors of Tucson. An Arizona "first" happened on January 1, 1825, four years after Mexico got its independence from Spain. José Leon was sworn in as the first constitutional mayor of Tucson. The National Republican Congress in Mexico City limited mayors to a one year term. So Leon was replaced in 1826 by Ignacio Pacheco.

Mayor Pacheco's descendants in Arizona today possess land deeds and registered cattle brands dating back to the early 1800s. Pacheco lived in Tucson during the entire period of Mexican rule. He was there in 1856 when American troops arrived to take possession of the Gadsden Purchase.

The State of Occidente. Mexico was divided into states by the Congress in 1824. The settled area of southern Arizona was part of *El Estado Libre de Occidente* (The Free State of the West). Occidente also included the present Mexican states of Sonora and Sinaloa.

The state capital was at Fuerte where a one-house legislature of eleven members convened. Sinaloa had six representatives and Sonora only five. None were from Arizona. Sinaloa and Sonora were too different in geography and problems to continue as one state very long. In 1831 they were separated and Arizona became a part of Sonora.

Two political factions in Sonora

El Estado Libre de Occidente—the Free State of the West —was created by the Constitutional Act of the Mexican Federation of January 31, 1824, and consisted of present-day Sinaloa, Sonora, and southern Arizona. On August 28, 1826, the capital of Occidente was moved from Fuerte to Casolá because of an uprising by the Yaqui Indians.

Los Estados Unidos de Mexico
1826
(THE UNITED STATES OF MEXICO)

Legend
- NATIONAL CAPITAL
- CAPITAL OF STATE OF OCCIDENTE
- 1826 MEXICAN TOWN now in Arizona

drawn by Don Bufkin

Romero expedition at Tucson in 1823. Diorama at Arizona Historical Society in Tucson.

fought a long, bloody civil war. The *centralists* favored a strong central government in Mexico City. The *federalists,* on the other hand, wanted powers to be divided between the national government and the states. The leader of each faction served several times as governor of Sonora. José Cosme Urrea, the federalist leader, was born in Tucson in 1797. He fought as a Mexican general in the battle of the Alamo in Texas. Manuel Gándara, the centralist, operated the Calabasas ranch near Tubac in the early 1850s.

Tucson presidio commanders. Arizona was isolated from the Sonoran civil war and state politics. The few residents in the Arizona part of Sonora were more interested in who was presidio commander at Tucson. This officer could help them more in their daily struggle for survival. Three men occupied the position during the Mexican era—José Romero (1821-30), Antonio Comaduran (1830-53), and Hilarión García (1853-56). They were good soldiers but were never given enough men to stop Apache raids.

Romero was the "Mexican Anza." In May, 1823, he went overland to California. In his party were ten soldiers and a Dominican padre named Felix Caballero. Bypassing the unfriendly Yumas, Romero crossed the Colorado River near its mouth. Indians in that vicinity helped the Mexicans cross the river, but then stole most of their baggage. On the return trip, Romero tried to locate a route north of the Yuma crossing. He got lost in the Mojave Desert and had to return to the Pacific coast. Finally, Romero arrived back in Tucson in December, 1825.

Little social progress was possible in Sonora. Political turmoil and Apache raids held up progress during the short time that Arizona was a part of Mexico. Except for minor efforts in a few places like Hermosillo, no public schools were started in Sonora. Most children in this state grew to adulthood without learning to read or write. The mestizo class—people with mixed Spanish and Indian blood—increased in numbers. But mestizos had little opportunity to improve themselves.

Calabasas ranch in 1854. Sketch by Charles Schuchard.

Public health conditions were bad and unsanitary conditions led to epidemics. Public administration also left much to be desired. Half the copper coins in Sonora were said to be counterfeited. Taxes were levied by the legislature but not collected. Severe penalties, including death, failed to halt robberies and assaults committed by people other than Apaches.

2. THE ARIZONA MISSIONS WERE DESERTED AND SOME OF THEIR LANDS SOLD AT PUBLIC AUCTION

Missions abandoned. The Spanish put great faith in the mission system as a means of controlling frontier Indians. But the missions all but disappeared during the Mexican period. The Congress in Mexico City forced all priests to take an oath of loyalty to the new republic or leave Mexico. All foreign missionaries were sent back to their homeland.

San Xavier del Bac was without a resident priest for years. The chapel and mission build-ings were used as barns, stables, and barracks. Tumacácori was abandoned after Father Ramón Liberós was taken away and expelled to his native Spain. Liberós completed the Tumacácori church before his forced departure.

Abandoned mission lands sold. In 1834 the Mexican Congress claimed all abandoned mission lands. Ten years later, the mission farm land at Tumacácori and the adjacent stock ranch of Calabasas were sold at public sale for $500 to Francisco Aguilar. Actually Aguilar was a stand-in for his brother-in-law, ex-Governor Gándara, who put the ranch into operation. The old Calabasas church was converted into a ranch house. Mexican herdsmen were soon tending thousands of sheep and goats on the old mission lands.

Apaches attack the Gándara ranch. A large band of Apaches attacked the ranch in April, 1854, only to meet with one of their rare reverses. An Apache woman revealed the Indian plan to Colonel García, the Tucson presidio commander. On the day of the attack, García was waiting with 60 Mexican soldiers and 40 friendly Apaches. Only a few shots were fired. The raiding Apaches were all killed by the lances of the ranch defenders. One observer said the Apaches' ears were cut off.

"It looked first like a string of dried apples 2½ to 3 feet long," he said, "but on close inspection they were the ears of the dead foe."

The Apaches were more successful in later raids. The ranch had to be abandoned in 1856, a few months before the arrival of American troops to take possession of the Gadsden Purchase.

3. THERE WERE MANY LARGE MEXICAN CATTLE RANCHES IN SOUTHERN ARIZONA

The cattle industry got a good start in Arizona during the last years of Spanish rule.

After Mexican independence in 1821, stock raisers continued to drive their vast herds northward. *El rancho grande* well describes the Mexican ranches in the 1820s. A typical government land grant consisted of four *sitios,* amounting to more than 27 square miles. A *ranchero* was also allowed to occupy and buy surrounding lands known as "overplus."

Most of the land grants were in the valleys of the Santa Cruz, San Pedro, and their tributaries. The biggest operators in the Santa Cruz Valley were two brothers, Tomás and Ignacio Ortiz. They selected the Canoa ranch south of Tucson and went to Arispe to claim it. They paid $250—about $9 per square mile. The Ortiz brothers also owned the Arivaca ranch west of present-day Nogales. They inherited the Arivaca from their father who bought it for $747 in 1812 when he was a resident of Tucson.

Spanish and Mexican Land Grants as confirmed by U.S. courts.

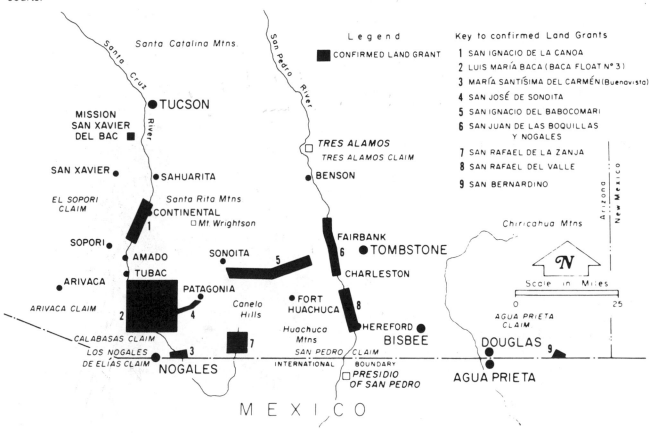

San Rafael de la Zanja ranch. Cattle have grazed on this southern Arizona ranch since the 1820s. They were wild during the 1830s and 1840s.

Mr. and Mrs. Juan Elías

There were two large Mexican land grants along the present international border east of Nogales. The Tuvera family occupied the Buenavista. Ramon Romeros acquired the San Rafael de la Zanja in 1825. He bought it as a range for livestock belonging to residents of the Mexican town of Santa Cruz.

The Leon Herreras family grazed cattle on the Sonoita grant west of the present-day town of Patagonia. Herreras started ranching in the Tubac area, but there wasn't enough pasture land for his big herd. He picked out new grasslands along the Sonoita Creek and was issued a title by the Republic of Mexico in 1825.

Farther east along the San Pedro and its tributaries were the vast holdings of the Elías Gonzalez family—the Boquillas, San Rafael del Valle, Babocomari, and other grants.

In the extreme southeastern part of Arizona, the Pérez family controlled the vast San Bernardino land grant. This ranch was occupied in the 1820s by thousands of cattle, horses, and mules. But in the 1830s the

110

Pedro Aguirre

Apaches went on the warpath and forced the owners to desert the San Bernardino. The livestock were left to roam wild.

Mexican ranches abandoned. Ortiz, Tuvera, Romeros, Herreras, Elías Gonzalez, Pérez—these and other Mexicans were Arizona's first big cattlemen.

Most of their ranches were carved out of the public domain between 1821 and 1833. Nearly all of them were deserted in the late 1830s and 1840s because of Apache raids. The Mexican ranchers moved to Tucson, Tubac, or to towns and ranches south of the present international border.

The abandoned cattle reverted to a wild state. U. S. soldiers, who observed these wild animals during the Mexican War, described

San Bernardino ranch east of Douglas. John Slaughter, the famous sheriff of Cochise, owned this ranch from 1884 until his death in 1922.

them as "mealy-nosed" because their faces were covered with coarse hair. They were all colors—black, brown, blue, and red—though black predominated. Their trim horns were white. The long-legged wild cattle were quick, restless, and easily excited. They moved with a high, elastic trot, sniffing the air and frequently looking around for danger.

Mexican ranchers in later years. After the Gadsden Purchase of 1854, there were many Mexican stockmen who operated big spreads in Arizona. Among them were Sabino Otero, Teofilo Otero, Bernabe Robles, Jesus Robles, Manuel Amado, Juan Elías, Pedro Aguirre, and Yjinio Aguirre.

Mexican-American ranching heritage. Most of the American cowboy's language, equipment, and methods are of Spanish-Mexican origin. From the Mexican cowboy, called *vaquero*, came the horned saddle, roping techniques, and branding. Even the term "ten gallon hat" comes from a mistranslation

Sketch of a Mexican vaquero roping a longhorn.

Felix Ruelas. This picture was taken at his first ranch near Patagonia about 1880. He had just ridden a race on the horse shown in the photo.

112

of *su sombrero galoneado,* which means a fancy-braided hat.

The very language of the range is Spanish. Such terms include bronco, lasso from *lazo,* lariat from *la reata,* rodeo, corral, *remuda,* stampede from *estampida,* and *rancho.* The Mexican expression *dale vuelta,* meaning to twist a rope about the horn of a saddle, became "dolly welter" or simply "dolly."

4. THE APACHES TOOK TO THE WARPATH AGAIN

During the 1820s, the Apaches waited to see how they would be treated by the Mexican republic. Ignored by the new government, they took to the warpath again.

Beginning in 1831, the Apaches in eastern Arizona and western New Mexico followed their plunder trails into Sonora and Chihuahua. They stole livestock, burned and looted buildings, carried off women and children, and left a trail of blood. Most ranches and settlements on the frontier had to be abandoned.

State governors and presidio commanders pleaded with the central government in Mexico City for help. They asked for a well-equipped army to stop the Apache raids. But little assistance was given. The Sonora frontier was regarded as a kind of wasteland by President Santa Anna and the other Mexican leaders.

In desperation, the governors offered bounties for Apache scalps. The bounty system attracted some of the worst Mexican and American renegades. To collect bounties, ranging up to $100 per head of hair, the scalp-hunters brought in hundreds of scalps—some of them belonging to innocent Mexicans and peaceful Indians. The only result of this system was to increase the hatred of the Apaches for the whites, both Mexican and American.

The Apache raids continued throughout the period of Mexican rule. No growth or progress was possible in Arizona after the 1820s.

Mountain man with his ponies.

7

THE MOUNTAIN MEN

In 1806, a young American explorer named Zebulon Pike was arrested in what is now southern Colorado for trespassing on Spanish territory. He was escorted to Chihuahua by way of Santa Fe and detained for a year. After his release, Pike wrote a report that excited new and widespread American interest in the Spanish Southwest. Among other things, he mentioned the high prices that people in Santa Fe paid for goods.

After Mexico got its independence from Spain in 1821, the attitude toward Americans changed. Traders and trappers from the States were welcomed by the isolated residents of Santa Fe. The Mexicans were eager to exchange silver and gold bullion, mules, beaver furs, and Indian blankets for manufactured goods.

A pioneer in the Santa Fe trade was William Becknell. In 1821 he got together a pack train in Missouri and led it nearly 800 miles through Indian country to Santa Fe. The goods were sold to Mexicans for a handsome profit. Becknell then organized the first of the great wagon caravans to Santa Fe. A party of 81 men transported $30,000 worth of merchandise in 25 wagons and brought back $180,000 in gold and silver in addition to $10,000 in furs.

Becknell did more than bring back bags of money. He opened up the Santa Fe Trail for all who followed. The volume of trade over this trail was never very large, but it furnished the means by which American pioneers entered the Southwest. Many of the early arrivals were fur trappers, better known as "mountain men."

The mountain men fanned out along the streams of the Mexican Southwest. In their search for beaver, the trappers became the first American explorers in this region. Between 1824 and 1832, there were hundreds of these pathfinders along the Gila, Salt, Verde, San Pedro, Colorado, San Francisco, and other rivers in Arizona.

Among the more famous mountain men who touched Arizona soil were Sylvester and James Ohio Pattie, Jedediah Smith, "Old Bill" Williams, Pauline Weaver, Kit Carson, Miguel Robidoux, "Pegleg" Smith, Ewing Young, David E. Jackson, Milton Sublette, Ceran St. Vrain, Felix Aubrey, and Antoine Leroux.

KEY CONCEPTS

1. The fur trade helped open up the West.
2. James Ohio Pattie made a permanent imprint on Arizona history.
3. Jedediah Smith twice visited the Mojaves in Arizona.
4. "Old Bill" Williams was a master trapper.
5. Pauline Weaver made Arizona history as a trapper, guide, prospector, and scout.
6. No mountain man in the United States was more famous than Kit Carson.

7

1. THE FUR TRADE HELPED OPEN UP THE WEST

For hundreds of years there was a demand for beaver furs. Hairs from the soft underfur made the finest felt. The felt was made into tall-crowned beaver hats which were popular in the East and in Europe.

The beaver lives in wooded areas along the banks of streams and lakes where he has the bark and leaves of trees for food. A large animal, the beaver weighs between 30 and 40 pounds, though often much more. The fur pelt from a full-grown beaver weighs up to two pounds.

The beaver was as much at home in the desert rivers of the Southwest as in colder waters farther north. The fur of the desert river beaver was lighter in color and worthless from early spring to late fall. But it was only slightly inferior to that of the northern beaver during the remainder of the year. The Mexicans called the beaver *castor*. Sometimes the word *nutria* was used, though that literally means otter.

To catch the beaver, mountain men used a strong steel trap with a five foot chain. The trap was placed in three or four inches of water close to the bank and chained to a strong stick. The bait—a sweet-smelling secretion from the musk gland of beaver—was dropped on a twig above the trap.

After the beaver was trapped and drowned, the skin was carefully removed and dried on a willow hoop. The cured pelts were packed in bundles by means of a crude press. Bundles

The United States and New Spain in 1819.

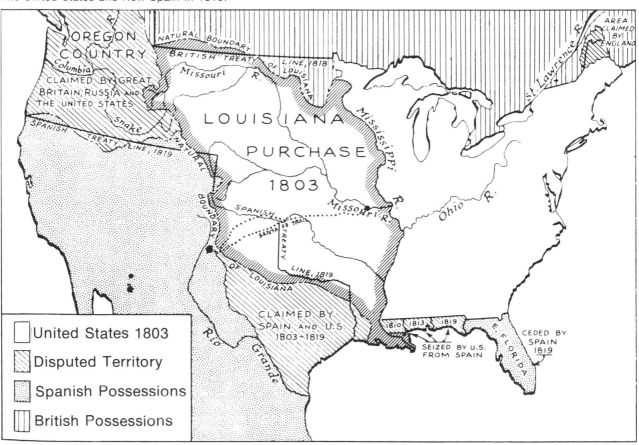

United States 1803
Disputed Territory
Spanish Possessions
British Possessions

Mountain men setting traps for beaver. Watercolor by Alfred Jacob Miller.

The beaver pelt was used to make felt for men's hats.

Beavers built dams creating ponds in which they built their lodges.

were tied with green buckskin thongs which shrank while drying and tightened around the bundle like an iron band.

The mountain man was daring, carefree, and independent. He loved adventure. To travel and see new places, he would leave a home with comforts and security. The mountain man stayed alive in the wilderness by adopting Indian ways and learning Indian skills. He stood, walked, rode, and wore his hair like the natives and sometimes took an Indian girl for his wife. In hostile Indian country the trapper had to keep his wits about him to stay alive. Only a few mountain men had much formal education, but they were well-trained in the knowledge of frontier life.

The trusted weapon of the mountain man was his small-bore, long-barreled rifle. He carried flints, a hickory ramrod, a powder horn, and a bullet pouch. He made his own bullets. The rest of his equipment consisted of a short-handled axe or tomahawk, a keen-

A typical mountain man. Sketch by Frederic Remington.

Mountain man.

edged skinning knife, a few blankets, and cooking gear. Except for a scant supply of flour, salt, tea, and coffee, he lived off the country. His costume was unique. It was an adaptation of Indian materials to the white man's way of dress. For transportation the mountain man relied mainly on the horse and pack mules.

Taos and Santa Fe, New Mexico, became headquarters for American as well as Mexican and Indian fur trappers in the Southwest. Supplies were purchased in these towns and trapping parties were organized. Pelts were brought there for sale to Santa Fe traders returning to Missouri.

The mountain men often evaded the regulations of Mexican authorities in the towns. It was a common practice for one person in a party to buy the expensive Mexican trapping license. All the others sold their pelts through him at the market place.

2. JAMES OHIO PATTIE MADE A PERMANENT IMPRINT ON ARIZONA HISTORY

Few of the mountain men kept accurate records or diaries of their wanderings. James Ohio Pattie, however, wrote the story of his experiences in Arizona after his fur trapping days were over. Many details of his *Personal Narrative* are vague, but the book is one of the first authentic accounts describing the Southwest at the dawn of American civilization.

Pattie was only 20 when he arrived at Santa Fe in 1824. He was with his father, Sylvester, and a caravan of traders and trappers from Missouri. At first the Mexican officials would not give the Americans permission to trap in Mexican territory. But fortune soon smiled on them as the result of an exciting experience. While waiting in Santa Fe, they helped a Mexican force rescue the beautiful daughter of a former governor from some Comanche Indians. For his personal bravery, the young Pattie won both the affection of the girl, called Jacova, and the trapping license.

First Anglo-Americans touch Arizona soil. The Patties joined a company of 14 men which was the first known group of Americans to enter Arizona. From the headwaters of the Gila River in New Mexico, this expedition went downstream early in 1825. By the time the men reached the juncture of the Salt and Gila, southwest of modern Phoenix, they were cold and hungry.

Retracing their steps, they stopped to trap along the San Pedro River. After getting a lot of beavers, the party was about ready to break camp when Indians crept in at night and stampeded their grazing horses. The stranded trappers hid the heavy bundles of furs, then returned to New Mexico on foot to get more horses and supplies. They came back to the cache site, only to find that the pelts had been removed. The trappers had little to show for months of danger and hardship.

James Ohio Pattie returned to Arizona. For several months the Patties worked at the Santa Rita copper mines near present-day Silver City, New Mexico. Sylvester was content to stay there, but James was restless. He joined a company of Arizona-bound French trappers headed by Miguel Robidoux. Only Pattie, Robidoux, and one other trapper survived an Indian attack at the fork of the Salt and Gila. The three survivors joined the Ewing Young party then in the vicinity.

Pattie accompanied his new party, more than 30 trappers, up the Salt River. At the Verde junction the company split. Pattie's group continued up the Salt to the White

A party of mountain men. Painting by William Henry Jackson.

Mountains. The second went up the Verde. The groups reunited and followed the Salt and Gila westward to the Colorado. The Yumas were friendly, but the Mojaves upstream attacked the trappers as they slept. Two men were killed.

After getting all the beaver pelts they could pack, the Ewing Young party began the long trip home. They suffered great hardship crossing northern Arizona. By the time the half-starved trappers reached the Zuñi villages, they had eaten all the dogs. They arrived in Santa Fe during the summer of 1826 only to have Governor Manuel Armijo seize all their furs. He charged that the Americans had been trapping without a license.

The Patties went to California. After a trading expedition to Chihuahua and Sonora, the young Pattie and his father joined another company of trappers. They started for the

Routes followed by Jedediah Smith.

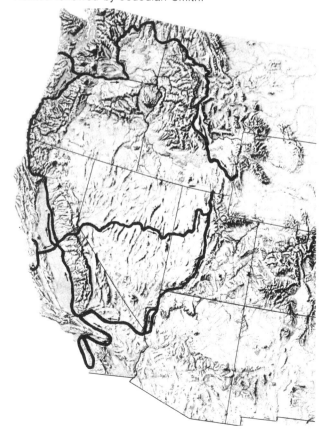

Colorado River in the fall of 1827. The Patties and six other men reached the river. There the trappers were forced to improvise when Indians stole their horses. They hollowed out cottonwood dugout boats and floated their furs down river to the Gulf of California. After hiding their furs in that area they struck out across the desert to San Diego.

The whole party was clamped into a Mexican jail. Sylvester died in solitary confinement. James secured the release of the rest of the party as a reward for his services as an amateur doctor. Having some knowledge of a crude technique for smallpox vaccination, James was sent throughout California by Mexican Governor José María Echeandía.

Pattie returned to his Kentucky home. In 1830 Pattie finally was granted a passport and sailed from Monterey for San Blas, Mexico. He went overland to Vera Cruz and took a stagecoach to New Orleans. By autumn he was back at the home of his grandparents in Kentucky. After the publication of his remarkable narrative in 1831, he apparently disappeared into oblivion. But in six exciting, action-packed years, James Ohio Pattie carved out a permanent niche for himself in the history of Arizona and the Southwest.

3. JEDEDIAH SMITH TWICE VISITED THE MOJAVES IN ARIZONA

The Patties reached California by the overland Gila route. Another American mountain man got there first. He was Jedediah Strong Smith who took the central route through Utah and northwestern Arizona in 1826.

Smith was a rarity among fur trappers. He received a good education as a youth in New York and was an outspoken Christian. He saw more of the West than any man of his time. Smith survived some of the worst disasters of fur trapping history, only to be killed by Comanches while searching for water to supply a wagon train on the Santa Fe Trail. His

Jedediah Smith. From a sketch made by a friend, from memory, after Smith's death.

journals and maps, unfortunately, were destroyed in a St. Louis fire and never published.

Contact with the Mojaves. Twice he came down from what is now Utah by way of the Virgin River into northwestern Arizona. In 1826, Smith and his party of trappers rested for two weeks in the Mojave villages en route westward.

He described the Mojave men as tall and powerfully built, wearing nothing but a loin cloth. The women were short and stout with plump, friendly faces. They wore only a skirt, fashioned from strips of bark, below the waist.

After trading for food and some better horses, Smith's party went on to the San Gabriel mission. They used the same trail Garcés had traveled in 1776.

Mojave massacre. In 1827, Smith unsuspectingly led nineteen men into a massacre in the Mojave country. The Indians appeared to be friendly, but made a surprise attack on the trappers while they were crossing the Colorado on rafts. In a few minutes ten of them fell dead from the poisoned arrows and war clubs of the Mojaves. Smith heroically marched the survivors across the hot California desert to safety. The Mojave massacre was just one more hair-raising event in the life of Jedediah Smith. He was involved in at least two other massacres and had a crippling fight with a grizzly bear—all in a short life span of 33 years.

4. "OLD BILL" WILLIAMS WAS A MASTER TRAPPER

William Shirley "Old Bill" Williams has a mountain, a stream, and a town named after him in Arizona. Born in North Carolina in 1787, he grew up in what was then a wild and woolly St. Louis, Missouri. Reared a Methodist, Williams became a missionary to the Osage Indians. He married an Osage girl, who bore him two daughters, and developed an admiration for Indian superstitions and ceremonials. After the death of his wife, Williams turned to hunting and trapping.

His first entrance into Arizona was in 1826. He came with Ceran St. Vrain on an expedition down the Gila. In the next few years Williams wandered across northern Arizona from the Little Colorado River to the Grand Canyon and the Colorado River. Mysterious and unpredictable, "Old Bill" preferred to go alone. An Indian of the Ute tribe, with whom he lived for awhile, said he was as solitary as "the eagle in the heavens or the panther in the mountains."

A good trapper, Williams would show up at Taos or some other rendezvous point in the Rockies with a big bundle of furs. Then he would gamble and drink away his profits. Unfortunately, there are more eyewitness accounts of his sprees at the trading posts than of his work along the streams.

Another trapper, Antoine Leroux, told how he came across Williams in 1837 sitting alone on the river in northwestern Arizona that now bears his name. Williams told him that he had gone westward from New Mexico through the land of the Apaches to the Bill Williams fork. After visiting with Leroux,

Williams went downstream to trap. The next year he showed up unexpectedly at a rendezvous in Wyoming. No wonder he was regarded with a certain air of mystery.

What manner of man was Bill Williams? He was six feet one inch in height, lean but tough, and redhaired. His weather-beaten face had been deeply marked by smallpox. He was a dead shot with his rifle, though he shot with a double wobble. Williams couldn't hold the gun steady, but like many good shooters he squeezed the trigger on his muzzle-loading, long-barreled, flintlock rifle just as it swept across the target.

His walk was peculiar. He staggered like a drunk but never seemed to tire. Even when well past middle age, he could run along streams all day with half-a-dozen five-pound beaver traps on his back. Though an excellent horseman, he used short Mexican stirrups which made him lean forward and look like a hunchback. His buckskin pants were worn so that his legs were bare below the knee.

In other respects, Williams was like the Indian. He didn't consider it necessary to cook meat. He believed in dreams to foretell the future. Williams said that when he died his soul would be reincarnated in the form of a buck elk.

5. PAULINE WEAVER MADE ARIZONA HISTORY AS A TRAPPER, GUIDE, PROSPECTOR, AND SCOUT

Another "lone wolf" mountain man was Pauline Weaver. He came to Arizona about 1830. His activities were largely confined to this area until his death in 1867.

Weaver was born in Tennessee in 1800. His mother was the daughter of a prosperous chief of the Cherokees. He was named Paulino, later changed to Pauline. The spelling didn't matter, since Weaver never learned to read and write. As late as 1864, he signed a mining claim notice in Yavapai County with an "X."

Weaver, the trapper. At an early age,

Weaver was employed in the Northwest by the Hudson Bay Fur Company. But he soon grew tired of the cold winters. Weaver trapped in the Rockies for a few years and then came to Arizona. He found the beaver more plentiful in the Southwest, although the pelts were of inferior quality.

Like Old Bill Williams, he remained aloof from organized companies of trappers. Roaming alone in search of beaver, he became familiar with the geography of Arizona. Later he was able to offer his service as a negotiator with the Yavapai Indians. Weaver worked as a guide and scout for soldiers, explorers, and prospectors.

Weaver, the miner and guide. Though not a miner, he discovered gold placers along the Colorado and Gila rivers. In 1863 he guided the Abraham Peeples party from Yuma to the mining area south of Prescott, better known as the Weaver District. Here the richest placer deposit ever found in Arizona was discovered.

Later life. Near the end of his life, Weaver fell out with the Yavapai Indians. For his own safety, he attached himself to the troops at Fort Whipple, near Prescott. He was later

Sketch of Kit Carson as a young man.

assigned to Camp Lincoln on the Verde. Refusing to live at the post, Weaver pitched his tent among the willows on the river bottom. It was here that he died on June 21, 1867.

His body was buried at Fort Whipple and later moved to the presidio cemetery in San Francisco. In 1929 it was brought back to Prescott. Sharlot Hall, a famous pioneer historian, collected pennies from Arizona school children to defray the cost. A large granite boulder marks the grave on the grounds of the territorial Governor's Mansion at Prescott.

Part of the bronze plaque reads thus: "He was born, lived, and died on the frontier of the country, always in the ever advancing westward move of civilization and was the first settler on the site of Prescott."

6. NO MOUNTAIN MAN IN THE UNITED STATES WAS MORE FAMOUS THAN KIT CARSON

Christopher "Kit" Carson was born in Missouri in 1809. At age 16 he was apprenticed in a saddle and harness shop in the town of Franklin. After about a year he ran away to lead a more exciting life in the Far West. While Kit was en route to Santa Fe, his ex-employer ran an insulting advertisement in the Franklin newspaper. A reward of one cent was offered for the boy's return. The idea was to show what a worthless apprentice Kit seemed to be. During the next 40 years, however, Kit Carson became the most admired trapper, guide, and scout in America.

Carson became a mountain man. Physically undersized and too poor to provide his own outfit for trading and trapping, Carson spent three years in Mexico doing menial tasks. During that time he became an expert rifleman and learned enough Spanish to serve as an interpreter. His big opportunity came in 1829. He joined a party of 40 trappers organized by the veteran Ewing Young for an expedition into Arizona.

After the company trapped along the Salt and Verde, about half the group was sent back to New Mexico with the furs. The rest of the company, including Carson, set out for the Colorado River and the west coast. They trapped along the beaver streams in northern California. On the return trip they worked along the banks of the Colorado and Gila.

By the time the men arrived at the Santa Rita copper mines in the fall of 1830, they were packing ten thousand pounds of beaver pelts. Young had no Mexican trapping permit, so he cached the furs and went to Santa Fe to get a license to trade with the Indians in the vicinity of Santa Rita. This way he was able to sell his beaver skins in the capital city without interference from Governor Armijo.

Carson's later career. Kit Carson started out on the 1829-30 expedition as an apprentice trapper. He returned a full-fledged mountain man. Carson experienced near-starvation. He fought with unfriendly Indians, both along the Salt River and in California. His firsthand knowledge of the geography of the Southwest served him well as a guide in this region during the Mexican War. Prior to this war he trapped throughout the Rockies and guided three exploring expeditions for John Charles Frémont. It was Frémont who made Carson a famous figure in American history.

Kit Carson

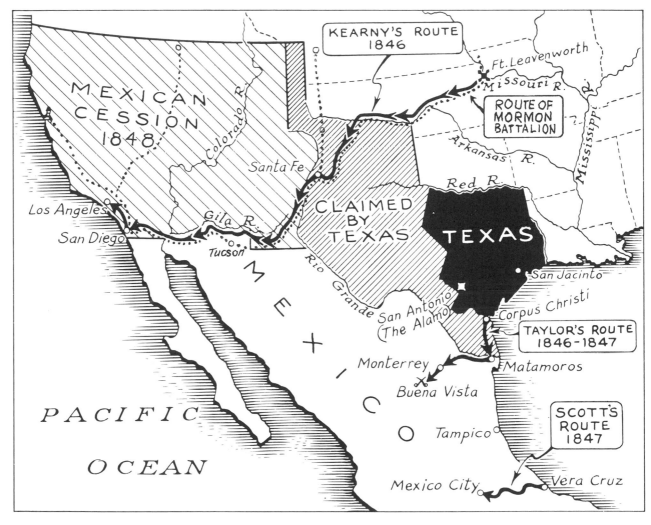

The Mexican War, 1846-1848.

8

MEXICAN WAR, BOUNDARY PROBLEMS, AND THE GADSDEN PURCHASE

American settlers had been pushing westward since colonial times. By the 1840s one thing was clear. The United States was about to extend its western boundary all the way to the Pacific Ocean.

Congress took a giant step in that direction by annexing Texas in 1845. President James K. Polk hoped to buy California and other Mexican territory, including Arizona, in the Southwest. For this purpose he sent John Slidell to Mexico City to make an offer. The Mexican government, still angry over the loss of Texas, refused to talk to Slidell and continued feverish preparations for a possible war.

The desire of American expansionists for more Mexican land was only one cause for the Mexican War. Unpaid debts owed by Mexico to American citizens was another. The Texas boundary dispute, of course, was the spark that set off the war. President Polk asked Congress to declare war when Mexican troops crossed the Rio Grande, which was the boundary according to the United States.

American war strategy centered on California and the more populated cities of Mexico. Commodore J. D. Sloat landed naval forces at Monterey and proclaimed California part of the United States. Commodore Robert F. Stockton and General John C. Frémont were already in California. They cooperated in wresting that province from Mexican control. Two military expeditions crossed Arizona en route to California—General Stephen W. Kearny's "Army of the West" and the Mor-

mon Battalion.

General Zachary Taylor invaded northern Mexico and defeated an untrained Mexican army several times larger than his own. General Winfield Scott landed on the east coast of Mexico. He took Vera Cruz and marched inland to Mexico City. Despite a gallant defense, the city fell in September, 1847. Faced with the loss of their capital city, the Mexicans were ready for peace. Nearly half of Mexico's territory was given up by the treaty signed in 1848.

In 1854 the United States added the Gadsden Purchase to complete the now familiar profile of the United States, except for Alaska and Hawaii.

KEY CONCEPTS

1. Kearny's army occupied New Mexico and rode across Arizona on the way to California.
2. The Mormon Battalion was the second major military group to make a trek across Arizona during the Mexican War.
3. Arizona north of the Gila River became a part of the United States in 1848.
4. Thousands of "forty-niners" took the southern route to California.
5. Surveying the Mexican boundary proved to be a difficult task.
6. The Gadsden Purchase filled in the now familiar profile of the United States.

8

1. KEARNY'S ARMY OCCUPIED NEW MEXICO AND RODE ACROSS ARIZONA ON THE WAY TO CALIFORNIA

Congress declared war on Mexico on May 12, 1846. Colonel Stephen W. Kearny was instructed to occupy New Mexico. He was also to cooperate with a naval force in the conquest of California.

An officer with many years service among the Indians in the West, Colonel Kearny was well-qualified for his assignment. He put together a military force at Fort Leavenworth on the Missouri River. The "Army of the West," as it was called, consisted of a great variety of troops—300 regular dragoons, 800 mounted Missouri volunteers, and an assortment of frontier-hardened infantry recruits.

The men were sent ahead in small detachments. They followed the Santa Fe Trail to Bent's Fort, a trading post in what is now southeastern Colorado. When Kearny arrived he found that his 1,657-man army had a large group of Santa Fe traders under its protection. Their million dollars worth of merchandise, packed in some 400 wagons, proved to be a helpful lure in breaking down Mexican resistance to American occupation of Santa Fe.

American conquest of New Mexico. Kearny paved the way for an easy conquest of New Mexico. On July 31 he dispatched a proclamation to Governor Manuel Armijo promising civil and religious liberties to the people. Kearny also sent Captain Philip St. George Cooke and James W. McGoffin, a jovial Kentucky Irishman and influential trader, to Santa Fe for secret talks with Governor Armijo. Before the American army arrived, Armijo deserted his people and rode south to Chihuahua with a troop of Mexican dragoons.

On August 18 Kearny entered the old mud village of Santa Fe without firing a shot or spilling a drop of blood. Four days later he

General Stephen W. Kearny

issued a proclamation claiming the whole of New Mexico, including Arizona, for the United States.

With the help of Colonel Alexander W. Doniphan of the first regiment of Missouri volunteers, Kearny drew up a code of laws—a hodgepodge based on the laws of Mexico, Missouri, and Texas. He also set up a civil government with Charles Bent as governor. Bent was gruesomely beheaded by Taos Indian rebels several months after Kearny's departure for California on September 25, 1846.

Treaty with the Navajos. Before leaving New Mexico, Kearny, who was promoted to general, instructed Colonel Doniphan to make a treaty with the Navajos. These Indians did not understand why they should stop raiding Mexican settlements when Americans themselves were waging war against Mexico. Doniphan took his summer-clad citizen-soldiers into the rugged snow-covered Navajo country.

Though uncomfortable without proper clothing, the Missouri volunteers rounded up

126

about 500 natives for a council near present-day Gallup, New Mexico. The treaty, signed by 14 chiefs on November 22, was worthless. The troops were hardly out of sight when the Navajo warriors resumed their raids, not only on Mexicans but also on the Zuñi Indians.

Kearny's journey through Arizona. Kearny left Santa Fe with 300 mounted soldiers. South of Albuquerque he met Kit Carson. The ex-mountain man was carrying dispatches to inform President Polk that the war in California was over. Carson reluctantly turned his messages over to another courier and agreed to guide Kearny to the coast. Since the rugged but quicker Gila route was chosen, Kearny sent his wagons and 200 dragoons back to Santa Fe. He moved on with 100 picked men. Supplies were carried on pack mules. There was nothing to slow down the army except two 12-pound howitzers.

The Kearny expedition, though primarily military, was in part scientific as well. Two good diarists—Colonel William H. Emory and Dr. John S. Griffin—kept notes on the ecology of the Gila Valley. Captain Henry Smith Turner, the adjutant, also recorded his observations. He was especially impressed with the Pima Indians, who produced all the necessities of life in abundance and by their own work.

"The old chief," Turner wrote, "exhibits more of human kindness in his face, air, and manner than I have ever seen in any other single individual."

General Kearny traded with the Pimas for cornmeal, flour, beans, pumpkins, and melons. He was also able to get cattle from the Maricopas downstream from the Pima villages. The Army of the West did not lack for food in its winding journey down the Gila to the Colorado. It was a long trip and every mile was recorded on a viameter attached to a howitzer wheel.

Near the Yuma crossing an incident occurred which tried Kearny's patience. His orders were to befriend the Mexican citizens and make them loyal to the United States. A

Kearny's Army of the West moving slowly down the Gila. Sketch by John Mix Stanley in 1846.

camp of Mexicans with 500 horses was discovered a few miles north of the Gila. As it turned out, the drovers were taking the horses to Sonora for the Mexican army. Kearny, however, felt obligated to accept their story. They claimed to be merely herding the horses to Sonoran markets for some wealthy Californians. The herdsmen must have been surprised when they were released and permitted to go unmolested.

The war in California was not really over. Kearny arrived in time for some action. About a third of his small force fell before Mexican lancers near San Diego. The remainder were saved by the timely arrival of Commodore Stockton's troops. After this skirmish, Kearny cooperated in putting down the last resistance. On January 13, 1847, General Andres Pico surrendered his army near the site of modern Hollywood.

Kearny, Arizona, is named after the commander of the Army of the West. The town was started on the Gila River in 1958 by the Kennecott Copper Company.

2. THE MORMON BATTALION WAS THE SECOND MAJOR MILITARY GROUP TO TRAVEL ACROSS ARIZONA DURING THE MEXICAN WAR

Led by one of Kearny's officers, Captain Philip St. George Cooke, the Mormon Battalion blazed the first practical wagon trail over the southern Arizona desert.

The battalion was organized mainly in Iowa by Brigham Young, head of the Latter-day Saints Church. Persecuted Mormons wanted to demonstrate their patriotism. They also saw a chance to learn more about the West, with the idea of founding settlements later. The group that left Council Bluffs in July, 1846, was an untrained outfit numbering about 500 men, 25 women, and some children.

Cooke assumed command after the battalion reached Santa Fe. He culled out the men unfit for service and sent them with most of the women and children to Pueblo in present-day Colorado. On October 19 the remaining 397 men—later cut to 340—and five women set out from Santa Fe to California. They arrived at Warner's Ranch near San Diego on January 21, 1847, after one of the most remarkable journeys in history.

Cooke's wagon road. Cooke's route was farther south than the dangerous Gila Trail taken by Kearny's mule train. After leaving the Rio Grande the battalion was guided by Pauline Weaver and Antoine Leroux. They dipped south of the present Mexican border and then turned northwest. Passing through the abandoned San Bernardino Ranch, the battalion reached the San Pedro River. The valley was grazed by wild cattle which the Mormons killed for meat as they tirelessly whacked their way over the rough hills of southeastern Arizona.

Battle with the bulls. On December 11 the battalion was attacked by a herd of wild bulls. The animals gored the mules, damaged the wagons, and injured some of the men. The "battle" lasted several hours because the bulls were hard to kill. Private Henry Standage,

Philip St. George Cooke as a general in the Union Army during the Civil War.

The Mormon Battalion reaching a stream on its march across the Arizona desert.

who later lived in Mesa, Arizona, wrote in his diary that "they would run off with half a dozen balls in them unless they were shot in the heart." Several dozen bulls were killed with musket fire, however, before Cooke was able to reorganize the wagon train and move on toward Tucson.

Mormon Battalion in Tucson. The Tucson presidio commander, Antonio Comadurán, deserted Tucson when he received word that Cooke was coming. All but about a hundred civilians fled south with his army to the San Xavier mission.

On December 17, 1846, the Mormon Battalion entered Tucson without firing a shot and raised the Stars and Stripes over an Arizona town for the first time. The soldiers experienced another first—tortillas and pomegranates—which the friendly Tucson residents provided. The tortillas were made from local flour. Nearly every Tucson home had a burro flour mill, called *molino*. A blindfolded burro went round and round turning a rough stone that could grind a half-bushel of wheat each day.

Cooke took only the grain and provisions that he needed and wrote letters of apology to Comadurán and Governor Gándara of Sonora. He ended his letter to the Governor by saying he hoped his wagon road would be useful to citizens of both Mexico and the United States.

It is interesting that Lieutenant George Stoneman paid for the Tucson supplies with U. S. War Department drafts. These were written in English and were redeemable only in the United States.

Tucson to Yuma. From Tucson the battalion went to the Pima villages and then cut across the Gila Bend country. Once back on the river, Cooke decided to float some of the supplies downstream to lighten the loads. A barge was made from two wagons lashed together between dry cottonwood logs. Lieutenant Stoneman insisted he could pole this boat to the Colorado Junction, about 70 miles away. He set sail with about 2,500 pounds of food and tools. The desert sailor reached the destination, but sand bars forced him to discard precious supplies along the way.

Meanwhile, Cooke's exhausted battalion arrived at the Yuma crossing with the rickety wagons. Three weeks later they were in San Diego. The war over, they were assigned to garrison duty in several towns until they were discharged on July 16, 1847.

The wagon road which the Mormon Battalion made across Arizona was later used by hundreds of emigrant wagon trains. The value of having the Cooke route within the boundaries of the United States was also mentioned many times by people who argued for the Gadsden Purchase of 1854.

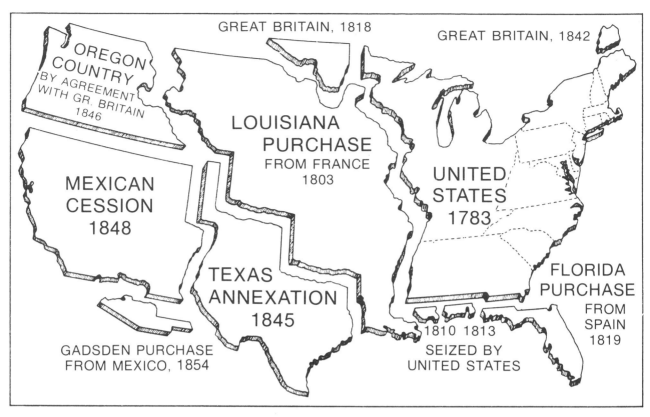

Territorial Growth of the United States.

3. ARIZONA NORTH OF THE GILA RIVER BECAME A PART OF THE UNITED STATES IN 1848

Treaty of Guadalupe Hidalgo. General Winfield Scott's American troops entered Mexico City as conquerors on September 14, 1847. The peace terms were signed in Guadalupe Hidalgo, a small town outside the Mexican capital, early in 1848.

Mexico gave up all claims to Texas and recognized the Rio Grande as the boundary. Mexico also gave up over a half million square miles of land. Included was all of Arizona north of the Gila River. The remainder of the Mexican Cession* gave the United States most

---

*The *Mexican Cession* was the land that Mexico gave up to the United States in 1848.

of New Mexico and all of California, Nevada, and Utah in addition to parts of Wyoming and Colorado.

In effect, Mexico was forced by war to sell this real estate for less than President Polk offered for it in 1845. The United States paid Mexico $15 million outright. This country also agreed to pay Mexico's debts to American citizens, amounting to nearly $3,250,000.

Article VIII of the treaty had to do with property rights and citizenship in the lands transferred to the United States. All legal Mexican titles to property were to be recognized by the United States. Any person living in the Mexican Cession, at the time the treaty was signed, could choose either Mexican or United States citizenship. Those who made no choice were automatically considered to be citizens of the United States after one year.

4. THOUSANDS OF "FORTY-NINERS" TOOK THE SOUTHERN ROUTE TO CALIFORNIA

In January, 1848,—just two weeks before Mexico signed away California—gold was discovered in the Sacramento Valley. The news reached the East in the fall and a gold mania* swept the country. The greatest rush of gold seekers was in 1849.

Thousands of the "Forty-niners" followed the Santa Fe Trail and Cooke's wagon road

*mania: excessive excitement, craze

Boundary controversy of 1848 and the Gadsden Purchase of 1854.

through Mexican territory to California. Soon the desert between Tucson and the Colorado was strewn with skeletons of horses and oxen, abandoned baggage, and the graves of those who perished of sickness or thirst. Large caravans usually suffered little mishap but smaller parties were often less fortunate.

The Oatman Massacre. A notorious incident occurred on February 18, 1851, about 100 miles east of Fort Yuma. Royse Oatman, his wife, and seven children were attacked by Yavapais. Six of the Oatmans were murdered and a son, Lorenzo, was left for dead.

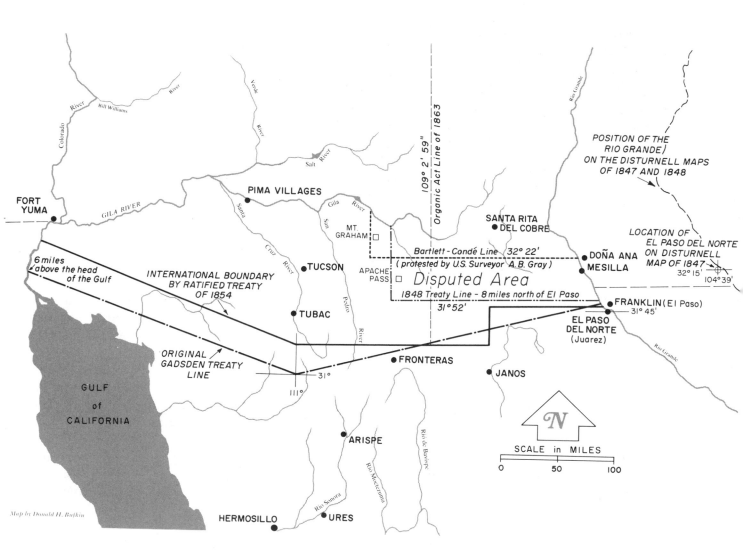

Olive Oatman

John Russell Bartlett

Two teenage sisters, Olive and Mary Ann, were taken into captivity and forced into slavery. They were traded to the Mojaves for horses and blankets. The girls were tatooed on the chin with five vertical blue lines. Mary Ann starved to death, but Olive was turned over to a Fort Yuma carpenter in 1856 and reunited with her brother Lorenzo.

5. SURVEYING THE MEXICAN BOUNDARY PROVED TO BE A DIFFICULT TASK

The boundary line spelled out in the Treaty of Guadalupe Hidalgo seemed simple enough. Two commissioners, one from each country, would work together in surveying and marking the boundary. The task proved to be more difficult, however, than anyone anticipated. Politics and an inaccurate map complicated the job. An inexperienced American boundary commissioner made the survey almost impossible.

John R. Bartlett. Most of the controversy revolved around Boundary Commissioner John R. Bartlett of Rhode Island. He was a Whig, like President Zachary Taylor, but otherwise had no qualification for the job. His inexperience was apparent from the moment he first met with his Mexican counterpart, General Pedro García Condé, at El Paso in 1850.

A compromise had to be made on the boundary because the Disturnell map was inaccurate. This map was designated by the treaty as the final authority. But El Paso, a key city in the survey, was located in the wrong place on the map. Instead of insisting on a correct map and survey, Bartlett conceded a strip of land west of El Paso that was 35 miles wide and 175 miles long. The surveyor, A. B. Gray, refused to sign the 1850 Bartlett-Condé agreement. Congress opposed it and, in 1852, refused to vote Bartlett any more money.

Bartlett gave little attention to supervising the boundary survey. Most of his time was spent on unnecessary jaunts. He traveled in style in a mule-drawn ambulance with military escort. His first trip to Arizona was in September 1851—not to survey the Gila River boundary, but to return a 14-year-old Mexican girl to her family in Santa Cruz, Sonora.

Inez Gonzales had been kidnapped by Apaches and sold to traders in New Mexico. She was doing menial work as a slave near the Santa Rita copper mines when Bartlett rescued her in June, 1851. Condé, the Mexican commissioner, was going to Santa Cruz and was willing to return Inez to her family. But Bartlett went to considerable trouble and tax-payers' expense to deliver the señorita in person. En route to Sonora he saw the wild Mexican cattle and mustangs on the deserted Babocomari Ranch.

From Santa Cruz Bartlett took his military escort on a whirlwind tour of Magdalena, Hermosillo, and other Mexican cities—supposedly in search of mules and supplies. He then went by sea to San Diego. Not until May 1852, almost a year after he left New Mexico with Inez, did he return to the Gila River. In his absence, two efficient engineers—Andrew B. Gray and Lieutenant Amiel Whipple—had stayed on the job to survey the Gila boundary to within sixty miles of the Colorado River.

Once again Bartlett left the survey party and took off. He stopped long enough in Tucson to sketch a picture. Continuing on through

Bartlett's sketch of Tucson in 1852.

Tubac and the deserted Calabasas Ranch, he reached El Paso by way of Chihuahua. When Congress refused to give him any more money, Bartlett moved the boundary commission to San Antonio. There he sold the animals and field equipment. The survey work was completed in December 1853, by a new commissioner, General Robert B. Campbell of South Carolina. By that time the United States was about ready to negotiate the Gadsden Purchase and do the survey all over again.

As a boundary commissioner, Bartlett was a failure. But as an artist he left later generations with an image of Arizona and the Southwest in the early 1850s. His original sketches were found in the basement of Brown University in 1963 and reproduced in book form.

President Antonio López de Santa Anna

6. THE GADSDEN PURCHASE FILLED IN THE NOW FAMILIAR PROFILE OF THE UNITED STATES

A second Mexican War nearly erupted in the early 1850s over the so-called Mesilla Strip. This was the disputed land that Bartlett conceded to Mexico. Troops were sent into the strip by both Governor William Carr Lane of the New Mexico territory and Governor Angél Trias of the Mexican state of Chihuahua. Any little incident would have started a war.

President Franklin Pierce knew that the boundary errors in the hastily-drawn Treaty of Guadalupe Hidalgo had to be corrected. He was also influenced by Secretary of War Jefferson Davis who favored buying more land from Mexico for a southern railroad route to California. In 1853 the President sent James Gadsden, a South Carolina railroad promoter, to Mexico City with five different offers.

The first offer was $50 million for a huge stretch of land from the Pacific Ocean to the Gulf of Mexico—including all of Lower California, a sea outlet on the Gulf of California, and a large slice off the northern states of

Juan Nepomuceno Almonte

William H. Emory as a general in the Civil War.

Sonora, Chihuahua, Coahuila, Nueva León, and Tamaulipas.

The other offers were for lesser amounts of land. The smallest offer was $15 million for a railroad route and an outlet on the Gulf of California. The United States also wanted to be released from Article XI of the 1848 treaty. This article made the United States responsible for all Indian raids into Mexico. The article was too difficult to enforce.

Dictator Santa Anna was back in power and needed money. But he refused to give up any land except for a transcontinental railroad. He wanted to keep Mexico's land bridge to Lower California. The original Gadsden treaty, signed December 30, 1853, was later changed by the U.S. Senate—both the amount offered and the boundary line.

The original line ran southwest from El Paso to a point south of Nogales and then northwest to a point six miles up the Colorado River. The United States was to give Mexico

Boundary marker erected by Emory's survey crew in 1855. Sketch by J. Ross Browne in 1864.

$15 million outright and pay a total of about $5 million to American citizens who had claims against the Mexican government.

President Pierce was disappointed. He wanted more land. But the Senate was divided. In general, pro-slavery southerners favored the Gadsden treaty. Anti-slavery northerners were opposed.

A compromise was reached. The amount of territory was reduced by 9,000 square miles and the southern boundary of Arizona and New Mexico was set as it is today. The purchase was reduced to a total of $10 million. The Mexican minister to Washington, D.C., Juan Almonte, was a skilled diplomat and had a strong voice in working out the compromise. He was most anxious to prevent another war.

The Gadsden Purchase Treaty was ratified by both nations on June 30, 1854. The United States made a good bargain. Some 29,670 square miles of land were added, most of it in Arizona.

The eastern section of the boundary was surveyed by Commissioner William Emory, an efficient army officer, and his Mexican counterpart, Commissioner José Salazar y Larregui. The western line from the Colorado River to a point near Nogales was surveyed by Lieutenant Nathaniel Michler and Francisco Jiménez. The latter was escorted by troops commanded by Captain Hilarión García, remembered in Arizona history as the last Mexican commander of the Tucson presidio. All the survey work was completed by October 1855.

Mexican soldiers remained in Tucson, the principal settlement in the Gadsden Purchase, until March 10, 1856. In November a detachment of United States dragoons arrived to raise the American flag and take formal possession of the only section of Arizona which had been previously settled by non-Indians.

UNIT FOUR

ARIZONA AS PART OF THE TERRITORY OF NEW MEXICO (1850-1863)

Arizona became part of the United States by two treaties: the Treaty of Guadalupe Hidalgo in 1848 and the Gadsden Purchase in 1854.

From 1850 to 1863 part or all of Arizona was an isolated portion of the Territory of New Mexico. There were only a few settlers. They lived in what is now southern Arizona. That region was aptly described as a "paradise for devils." The people had almost no law enforcement to keep outlaws in check. They had little military protection against raiding Apaches. Every man went armed, and administered justice to suit himself.

Considering the obstacles in the 1850s, the constructive work done by pioneers—miners, ranchers, merchants, surveyors, stage drivers, road builders, and soldiers—seems remarkable.

All progress came to a halt when the Civil War erupted in the East. Troops were ordered to abandon the military posts and report to forts along the Rio Grande or in California. Apaches seized the opportunity to regain their old stomping grounds from the whites. Most miners and ranchers fled for safety. The Anglo-American style of life all but disappeared in Arizona for awhile.

Southern Arizona and New Mexico were occupied by Confederate troops until Union forces drove them out. Finally, in 1863, the Territory of Arizona was created. The first capital was temporarily located at Fort Whipple early the next year.

Beale expedition watering the animals.

9

ARIZONA IN THE 1850s

Arizona was a neglected part of the Territory of New Mexico during the 1850s and had almost no government. But there was a lot of economic activity.

Pioneers developed silver mines in southern Arizona. There was a gold rush east of Yuma along the Gila River. Transportation routes were surveyed. Steamboats operated on the Colorado River. Stagecoaches carried mail and passengers, giving Arizona communication with the rest of the country. Army posts were established to protect settlers and travelers. Several towns grew as trade centers to supply the mines and ranches.

KEY CONCEPTS

1. Arizona had almost no government in the 1850s.
2. Northern Arizona and the Colorado River were explored for transportation routes in the 1850s.
3. Southern Arizona was an important link in transcontinental travel.
4. The need for transportation on the Colorado River was solved by ferries and steamboats.
5. Tubac and Tucson were the population centers of Arizona.
6. Towns grew up in the Yuma area during the 1850s.
7. Army posts were built to protect settlers and travelers.

9

1. ARIZONA HAD ALMOST NO GOVERNMENT IN THE 1850s

Northern Arizona was unsettled. During the 1850s the only two settlements north of the Gila were military posts. Fort Defiance was established in 1851 as a base from which the army could control the Navajos. Fort Mohave was built on the Colorado in 1859 to protect California-bound emigrants crossing northern Arizona.

The territorial legislature in Santa Fe extended seven New Mexico counties westward to the Colorado River. But these counties were no more than lines on the map.

Southern Arizona was settled first. Like the Spaniards and Mexicans before them, the American pioneers were attracted to southern Arizona. In 1855 the New Mexico legislature added the Gadsden Purchase lands to Doña Ana County. The county seat was far away at Mesilla on the Rio Grande River. It was this area—southern Arizona and southern New Mexico—that was known as "Arizona" in the 1850s.

Arizona pioneers got the attention of Washington D.C. Two conventions were held in 1856, one in Tucson and one in Mesilla. Both groups asked Congress to organize Arizona as a territory separate from New Mexico. The assembled citizens argued that their local needs were ignored by officials in distant Santa Fe. They said that Arizona had no laws, no courts, no vote, and no representation in any legislative body.

The pioneers continued to hold mass meetings and sign petitions. They elected first Nathan Cook and then Sylvester Mowry to speak for them in Washington, D. C.

In December 1857, President James Buchanan recommended that Arizona should have a separate territorial government. He said that American citizens, mines, farms, and mail routes needed to be protected. But by 1860, ten bills to create Arizona as a separate territory had been defeated in Congress. Some of these bills were introduced for the Arizona settlers by Miguel Otero. He was the New Mexico territorial delegate to Congress from Santa Fe.

Unofficial "Territory of Arizona." Finally, the inhabitants of "no man's land" took matters into their own hands. They held a convention at Tucson in April 1860. Delegates from 13 towns in the Gadsden Purchase region drew up a temporary constitution for the "Territory of Arizona."

The capital was to be at Mesilla. Dr. Lewis S. Owings of that town was elected governor. Most of the offices in the temporary government were filled by southern sympathizers. After the Civil War started in 1861, they helped the Confederate States to organize Arizona as a territory.

Counties created by the territorial legislature of New Mexico in 1852.

Miguel Otero

Dr. Lewis S. Owings

2. NORTHERN ARIZONA AND THE COLORADO RIVER WERE EXPLORED FOR TRANSPORTATION ROUTES IN THE 1850s

During the 1850s the United States government took an interest in the real estate acquired "sight unseen" from Mexico. The Army Corps of Topographical Engineers was given the task of looking for navigable streams and good routes for wagons and railroads.

Captain Lorenzo Sitgreaves. The first American military man to lead an expedition across northern Arizona was Captain Sitgreaves. In 1851 he took a survey party of 20 men, escorted by 30 soldiers, along the 35th parallel route. That is the route of the Santa Fe Railroad today. The going was rough. The guide, ex-mountain man Antoine Leroux, was wounded by a Mojave arrow. So was Dr. S. W. Woodhouse. The Yumas also attacked the expedition as the men marched down the Colorado.

One by one the pack mules gave out from exhaustion and were butchered for food. By the time the expedition reached the Yuma crossing, the men were in a deplorable condition. They rested several days before pushing on to San Diego.

Sitgreaves National Forest, Mount Sitgreaves, and Sitgreaves Pass are named after Arizona's first U. S. Army explorer.

François Xavier Aubry. A Santa Fe trader, Aubry made two round trips between Santa Fe and San Francisco in 1852 and 1854. Each time he drove large flocks of sheep to California by way of Tucson and explored northern Arizona for possible railroad and wagon roads on the return trip. He was convinced that a railroad could be built along the 35th parallel route. His private diaries were studied in Washington, D. C., and stirred the government to make further exploration.

Lieutenant Amiel W. Whipple. A second military survey along the 35th parallel route was made by Whipple in 1853-1854. His recommendations, published by the government in *Pacific Railroad Reports* in 1856, were enthusiastic. He said a railroad could be built through the passes of the various mountain ranges. Whipple was also one of the first to realize that northern Arizona was adaptable to settlement. It is only proper that Whipple Valley and Fort Whipple should be named after him.

Lieutenant Joseph Christmas Ives. Whipple's chief assistant, Lieutenant Ives, was chosen to chart the Colorado River's course. He also led an overland expedition to explore the Grand Canyon country.

Ives invited another member of the Whipple party, Heinrich Baldwin Möllhausen, to join the expedition. Möllhausen was a German artist-naturalist. Though not a great painter, he was able to draw sketches of the terrain and of Indians whose culture was still almost untouched by the white man.

General Amiel W. Whipple. Promoted to general during the Civil War, Whipple was killed in the Battle of Chancellorsville, 1863.

Sketch of Mojave Indians crossing the Colorado River in Whipple's Railroad Report.

The *Explorer*.

Diorama of Beale's camel expedition.

In 1858, Ives charted the Colorado on the river steamer *Explorer* and discovered that the Black Canyon was the head of navigation. He then sent the steamboat back to Fort Yuma and switched to mule transportation. Guided by a Mojave chief named Iritaba, the Ives party reached the Lower Granite Gorge and descended. They were the first white men of record to reach the floor of the canyon. Returning to the rim, Ives said farewell to Iritaba. He traveled east to Fort Defiance and on to Santa Fe.

Lieutenant Edward Fitzgerald Beale.

In 1857, Lieutenant Beale was selected by Secretary of War Jefferson Davis to build the first wagon road across northern Arizona. Beale had the challenge of combining a camel experiment with road building. Davis hoped that camels might solve the army's transportation problems in the arid West.

Lieutenant Edward F. Beale. Disguised as a Mexican, Beale rode across Mexico with dispatches telling of the discovery of gold in California.

On the first of two trips, Beale looked for terrain that was passable for wagons. About two dozen camels were assigned to this survey expedition along the 35th parallel route. The animals were handled by Hadji Ali, better known as Hi Jolly, and other imported camel drivers. Beale had nothing but praise for the camels. He said they carried heavy loads over long distances without water and arrived in good shape. But there was one problem. The strange, bad-smelling beasts frightened the pack mules and wagon teams, causing them to panic.

Nothing ever came of "Operation Camel," though it was a romantic episode in the history of Arizona. Hi Jolly later worked in Arizona as an army scout and married a Tucson girl named Gertrude Serna. His grave near Quartzsite, Arizona, is appropriately marked with a pyramid-shaped stone monument topped with a copper camel.

Monument on grave of Hi Jolly at Quartzsite.

In 1859 Beale's work crew smoothed out the wagon road, built some temporary bridges, and located water sources along the way. The road was used by many emigrant parties going to California.

3. SOUTHERN ARIZONA WAS AN IMPORTANT LINK IN TRANS-CONTINENTAL TRAVEL

There were two possible transcontinental railroad routes through Arizona—the 35th parallel in the north and the 32nd parallel in southern Arizona.

Southern Arizona railroad surveys. Lieutenant John G. Parke was assigned by the Department of War to learn more about the 32nd parallel route. In 1854 and 1855 he surveyed alternative routes between El Paso and the Pima villages. Instead of following Cooke's wagon road south into what is now Sonora, Parke's crew located shortcuts through passes in southeastern Arizona. Parke said the 32nd parallel route had the advantage of level terrain. The greatest drawback was the lack of timber and water.

Parke was a general in the Union Army during the Civil War and later was appointed superintendent at West Point.

Andrew Belcher Gray was employed by the Texas Western Railroad Company to survey a route across southern Arizona. Gray had only 19 men in his survey crew, but they were nearly all hardy Texas Rangers. Among them was Peter R. Brady, who settled in Arizona after the railroad survey was completed and became prominent in business and politics. The artist, a German named Charles Schuchard, made Tucson his home.

Gray recommended that the Texas Western company build a railroad from El Paso through Apache Pass, Tucson, the Pima villages, Fort Yuma, and on to Los Angeles. But no rails were laid. It was a California company, the Southern Pacific, that finally built a railroad through southern Arizona between 1877 and 1881.

General John G. Parke

Andrew B. Gray

Leach wagon road. The first wagon road across southern Arizona was built in 1858 by Jesse B. Leach, a civilian with a government contract from the Department of Interior. The road ran from El Paso to Fort Yuma, missing the settlements of Tucson and Tubac. Leach chose to follow Parke's railroad survey route down the San Pedro Valley. The road then turned westward along the Gila River through Maricopa Wells to Yuma.

The roadbed was 18 feet wide on straight stretches and 25 feet wide on curves. Improvements consisted mainly of clearing away brush, boulders, and timber. Wells and water tanks were constructed along the way for travelers. Part of the Leach road was soon used by the stage lines.

San Antonio and San Diego Mail Line. The first mail and passenger line that operated

Advertisement of the San Antonio and San Diego mail and passenger line.

OVERLAND TO THE PACIFIC.

The San Antonio and San Diego Mail-Line.

This Line, which has been in successful operation since July, 1857, is ticketing PASSENGERS through to San Diego and San Francisco, and also to all intermediate stations. Passengers and Express matter forwarded in NEW COACHES, drawn by six mules, over the entire length of our Line, excepting the Colorado Desert of one hundred miles, which we cross on mule-back. Passengers GUARANTEED in their tickets to ride in Coaches, excepting the one hundred miles above stated.

Passengers ticketed through, from NEW-ORLEANS, to the following points, via SAN ANTONIO:

To Fort Clark,	Fare, $52.	To Fort Bliss,	Fare, $100.
" Hudson,	" 60.	" La Mesilla,	" 105.
" Port Lancaster,	" 70.	" Fort Fillmore,	" 105.
" Davis,	" 90.	" Tucson,	" 135.
" Quitman,	" 100.	" Fort Yuma,	" 162.
" Birchville,	" 100.	" San Diego,	" 190.
" San Elizario,	" 100.	" Los Angelos,	" 190.
" El Paso,	" 100.	" San Francisco,	200.

The Coaches of our Line leave semi-monthly from each end, on the 9th and 24th of each month, at 6 o'clock A.M.

across Arizona was started in July 1857. It ran from San Antonio, Texas, to San Diego, California, and was called the "Jackass Mail" line. Mules were often used to pull the coaches. Passengers had to ride muleback in some of the desert country.

The largest station between El Paso and San Diego was at Maricopa Wells. Like some of the other station stops, it had a brush corral and an adobe hut. The majority of the stations were merely camping places.

Traveling by day and camping at night, or vice versa, was a slow and uncomfortable routine. The San Antonio and San Diego Mail Line made forty trips during the year that it was in operation across Arizona. No one was pleased with the service, but the line blazed the trail for the more ambitious Butterfield company.

The Butterfield Overland Mail. This was the first dependable, well-organized transcontinental stage line. It ran from the railroad terminal near St. Louis to San Francisco over the "Oxbow Route," so-called because it dipped south through Texas and the Territory of New Mexico. The line began operation on September 16, 1858, with a government contract to carry passengers and mail. Service was provided twice weekly in each direction on a twenty-five day schedule.

Stations were built about every 20 miles and stocked with fresh horses or mules, extra coaches, expensive hay and corn, and food. Most of the Arizona stations were built of adobe and enclosed with a wall for protection against Indian attack.

Fancy Concord stagecoaches were used mainly near the eastern and western terminals. The Concord had an oval-shaped body resting on straps slung between the front and rear axles. This type of suspension let the coach roll rather than bounce over bumps. In the Southwest desert country, the specially-built lightweight "Celerity Wagon" was used. It was pulled by mules and had wooden seats that could be folded down to provide beds for the passengers.

Concord coach used on the Butterfield stage line.

Maricopa Wells stage station in 1870.

John Butterfield's instructions to his drivers was "Remember boys, nothing on God's earth can stop the U. S. Mail!" During the line's existence, the mail was late only three times at the terminals. This was a remarkable record considering the obstacles and dangers. A total of 168 people, for example, met violent deaths as a result of Indian attacks and other causes.

The first Butterfield stage arrived in Tucson on October 2, 1858. On board was a *New York Herald* reporter named Waterman L. Ormsby. During his brief stop, Ormsby observed that Tucson consisted of a few adobe houses. Most of the people were Mexicans, though a handful of Americans ran a few stores and were elected to the town offices. William Buckley was in charge of the Butterfield operations.

In March 1861, a month before the Civil War started, the Butterfield line was shifted north through Utah. But for a brief time, southern Arizona—still a part of the Territory of New Mexico—was an important link in the greatest overland stage venture ever undertaken.

4. THE NEED FOR TRANPORTATION ON THE COLORADO RIVER WAS SOLVED BY FERRIES AND STEAMBOATS

The Yuma crossing. Thousands of California-bound gold seekers crossed the Colorado at the Yuma ford. Operators of ferry boats grew rich. In 1850 Able B. Lincoln grossed $60,000 in three months. A band of murdering scalp hunters led by John Glanton saw how well he was doing. They forced Lincoln into a partnership and began mistreating the Yumas who ran a competing boat. Glanton set the Indian ferry adrift and beat up their chief. At the first opportunity the Yumas got revenge. They killed 11 white ferrymen, including Lincoln, and threw their bodies on a fire. Only three men who were away cutting willow poles survived.

A new company of California ferrymen, led by Louis J. F. Jaeger, soon arrived to reopen business. They welcomed the arrival of United States troops commanded by Major Samuel P. Heintzelman to protect the crossing. In 1852 Fort Yuma was established as a permanent post on the California side of the river.

Louis J. F. Jaeger and Chief Pascual of the Yumas.

Steamboats on the Colorado. Troops at the crossing were supplied by boat from California. Supplies were poled upstream on flatboats from a schooner anchored near the mouth of the Colorado. In 1852 the first steamboat began navigating the river. The *Uncle Sam* was a 65-foot-long sidewheeler and carried 32 tons of freight. When the *Uncle Sam* went aground in 1853, Fort Yuma's provisions were brought in by mule team from San Diego.

New steamboats were soon assembled—the *General Jesup* and two sternwheelers, the *Colorado* and the *Explorer*. The latter was used by Lieutenant Ives to explore the Colorado in 1858. The boats were gradually made bigger. The *Cocopah* was 140 feet long and carried a hundred tons. The *Mojave*, launched in 1863, was shorter but had a capacity of nearly 193 tons.

Steam navigation on the Colorado River was difficult. The channel changed constantly because of shifting sand. The river spread out in places so that not even the most experienced pilot could determine its true course. Fifteen miles a day was the most a steamboat could make going upstream. Yet, land transportation along the river was even slower. When Fort Mohave was built in 1859, it was supplied by steamboat.

An 1854 sketch of Fort Yuma. The steamer was the *General Jesup.*

The *Cocopah* was launched in 1859. The Southern Pacific Railroad bridge in the background was built at Yuma in 1877.

Southern Arizona in 1860.

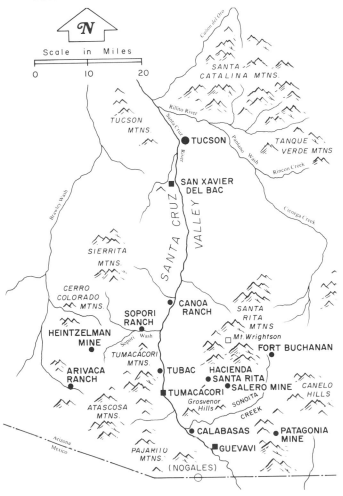

5. TUBAC AND TUCSON WERE THE POPULATION CENTERS OF ARIZONA

There were few people in Arizona during the 1850s. The principal towns—Tubac, Tucson, and Colorado City—were all south of the Gila. The short-lived gold rush town of Gila City came into existence in 1859. There were three military posts—Fort Buchanan, Fort Defiance, and Fort Mohave. Another post was located on the California side of the Colorado.

Tubac mining boom. The Tubac area was the site of Arizona's first mining boom during the American period. Easterners—still thinking about the California gold strike—eagerly invested in corporations to develop Arizona mines. The Sonora Exploring and Mining Company was the biggest. It was organized in Cincinnati with Major Sam Heintzelman as president and Charles D. Poston as general manager with the title of "colonel." These men met in 1854 when Heintzelman was commander at Fort Yuma. Poston came by with ore samples which he and Herman Ehrenberg had discovered in the Tubac area.

Poston recruited miners and bought supplies in San Antonio in 1856. He established the company headquarters in the old Spanish presidio of Tubac. The buildings were in bad shape, but still habitable. Tubac grew fast. Mexicans came in great numbers. Some were skilled miners. Others came to cultivate farms. Traders arrived with goods from Sonora, New

Tubac in 1857 with the Santa Rita Mountains in the background.

Mexico, and California. By 1860 a thousand people were living along the Santa Cruz in the Tubac vicinity.

The company prospered. The richest silver ore came from the Heintzelman mine west of Tubac. Ore was smelted and sent to Guaymas for shipment to San Francisco. The first ore sent to the East was hauled by Santiago Hubbell, a trader from New Mexico. Hubbell arrived at Tubac in 1857 with supplies loaded on 12 large wagons, each pulled by 12 mules. Among other things, he delivered the first mine machinery ever brought into Arizona. While he was encamped at Tubac, Poston contracted with him to have ore in rawhide bags transported to Kansas City.

Poston acted as "the government" of Tubac. He got into trouble with the church by marrying young eloping couples from Sonora. He married them for nothing, gave them a certificate stamped with a seal made from a Mexican peso, and threw in a free feast.

Poston solved the problem of money exchange in Tubac by having pasteboard bills, known as *boletas,* printed in New York. The *boletas* were paid to the company's miners on Saturday and circulated as currency. Not many natives could read, so the value of the bills was indicated by pictures of animals. A pig was one bit, or 12½ cents. A calf was worth two bits, or 25 cents; a rooster, 50 cents; a horse, one dollar; a bull five dollars; and a lion ten dollars.

Charles D. Poston, called the "Father of Arizona" for his efforts in getting Congress to create the Territory of Arizona.

Not everyone in Tubac was illiterate*. Arizona's first newspaper began publication there on March 3, 1859. The *Weekly Arizonian,* edited by Edward E. Cross, was a neat four-page, four-column journal. It was full of advertisements for Eastern goods, local gossip, Indian raids, and mining activities. Cross opposed separate territorial status for Arizona and was challenged to a duel by Sylvester Mowry. The July 8 contest with Burnside rifles at 40 paces turned out to be bloodless. Both men were bad shots. Mowry later bought the *Arizonian* and moved the press to Tucson.

Mowry first came to Arizona as an army officer at Fort Yuma. After resigning his commission, he developed the old Patagonia mine into a big producer. Mowry was also a big stockholder in several mining and land companies. Prior to the Civil War he was the most zealous spokesman for the creation of a separate territory of Arizona.

The Civil War ended the Tubac boom. Troops were withdrawn from Fort Buchanan and other posts in Arizona. The Apaches went on the warpath. By the end of 1861, most American and Mexican miners had departed. Tubac was a ghost town.

*illiterate: unable to read or write.

Sylvester Mowry

Tubac as sketched by J. Ross Browne in 1864.

Tucson in the 1850s. Tucson grew in the 1850s because it was a center of trade with Sonora and the Southwest. The stage line and mining activity in southern Arizona contributed to Tucson's growth. The census of 1860 showed 650 people living in Tucson. This was nearly 10 percent of the total population of 6,482 in the area now known as Arizona. The total included 2,421 whites, 4,040 Indians, and 21 Blacks.

Forty-niners, boundary and railroad surveyors, stage travelers, and soldiers—all described Tucson in the 1850s as a one-story adobe Mexican town. The residents of Tucson were mainly Mexican, but most of the well-to-do men were Anglo-American merchants. Mark Aldrich had possessions valued at $52,000; Charles Trumbull Hayden, $20,000; Palatine Robinson, $12,800; and John G. Capron, $12,000.

Mark Aldrich was the first Anglo-American to open a store in Tucson and to become involved in civic affairs. A native of Illinois,

where he served in the legislature with Abraham Lincoln, Aldrich was chosen *alcalde** of Tucson. In this job he had to deal with the horse thieves and other evildoers who swarmed into town. Since there was no jail, Aldrich sentenced offenders to be flogged at a whipping post in the public plaza. His constable, a muscular Mexican, would administer half the lashes and Aldrich would ask the culprit to return the next day for the remainder. Before the appointed time, the man was far away, as it was intended he would be.

Solomon Warner was the first Tucson merchant to stock his shelves with American goods. He arrived from Fort Yuma in March 1856, with his merchandise packed on the backs of 13 mules. Before long, Warner's General Store was the shopping center for southern Arizona. Prices were high for goods brought from San Francisco. Other prominent

*The *alcalde* (a Spanish word) was both a mayor and a judge.

148

Mark Aldrich   Solomon Warner

businessmen in Tucson were Hiram S. Stevens, Sam Hughes, John B. "Pie" Allen, and Charles H. Meyer.

6. TOWNS GREW UP IN THE YUMA AREA DURING THE 1850s

Early Yuma had other names. Colorado City was the first Anglo-American town to be located where Yuma stands today. Charles Poston is called the "father of Yuma" since he surveyed the first townsite in 1854.

The town grew slowly. The first Anglo-American store in what is now Arizona was established there in 1854 by George F. "Colonel" Hooper and partner. They maintained a well-stocked store near the steamboat landing. The 1860 census showed Hooper's wealth to be $9,000. Only Louis Jaeger at $55,000 and steamboat operator George A. Johnson at $16,000 were doing better.

Arizona City, as Colorado City was called by 1858, was described as a flourishing little town containing some half-dozen respectable adobe houses. There were two stores, two saloons, and a post office. The Colorado Ferry, the Butterfield Overland Mail depot, two blacksmith shops, and Sarah Bowman's Inn were located downstream.

A flood in 1862 wiped out all of Arizona City except two buildings. After the waters subsided, the town was rebuilt and became a thriving commercial center. The population in 1864 was 151. The name was changed to Yuma by the territorial legislature in 1873.

Gila City boomed for a short time. Gila City was Arizona's first wild and wicked gold-rush town. In 1858 a Texan named Jacob Snively discovered gold placers* about 20 miles up the Gila from Arizona City. Within a year, about a thousand people rushed in to pan the coarse gold found in alluvial deposits near the stream.

The center of activity was Gila City, a village of tents and brush shanties. Merchants rushed there with barrels of whiskey, billiard tables, and ready-made clothing. Traders crowded in with high priced food—flour was a dollar a pound and beans fifty cents a pound. Gamblers came with cards and monte tables. It is said that Gila City had everything but a church and a jail.

By 1859 the bonanza was over. An estimated two million dollars worth of gold had been panned. Anything that was left of Gila City was destroyed by the 1862 flood.

7. ARMY POSTS WERE BUILT TO PROTECT SETTLERS AND TRAVELERS

Fort Buchanan. The first American troops were sent to southern Arizona in 1856 under the command of Major Enoch Steen. The next year Fort Buchanan was built in the Sonoita Valley east of Tubac. Experience with summer heat at Fort Yuma no doubt influenced the selection of a cooler site. Unfortunately, fever-spreading mosquitos were bad during the rainy season.

The danger of malaria and bad living quarters made for low morale at Fort Buchanan. Walls of the barracks were made of decaying timbers set upright and chinked with mud. During the wet weather the mud roofs served little purpose except to give dirty showers to the unhappy occupants.

*A *placer* is a deposit of sand or gravel containing minerals.

149

Captain Richard S. Ewell   Lieutenant George Bascom

While Fort Buchanan was under construction, Captain Richard S. Ewell led troops to the Apache country. He was ordered to cooperate with other cavalry units to break up Apache bands. Indian crops were destroyed and about 20 warriors killed. But the Apaches were not crushed.

In 1858 Ewell tried the treaty approach. He and an Indian agent, Dr. Michael Steck, met with some 300 Pinal Apaches at Cañon del Oro northeast of Tucson. The Pinals were given goods and corn for signing a peace treaty. Apache raids continued, however, especially into Sonora. The Apaches often bypassed American settlers as long as plundering was good in Mexico.

Relations with the Apaches were worsened by the "Bascom Affair" at Apache Pass. Lieutenant George Bascom, a young officer fresh out of West Point, arranged a meeting in his tent with Cochise, chief of the Chiricahuas. Without any proof, Bascom accused the chief of kidnapping Feliz Martinez. This boy, later known as Mickey Free, was rancher John Ward's twelve-year-old foster son. Cochise fled from Bascom's tent and later tried to trade some white captives for Indian friends held by the lieutenant. Turned down, Cochise tortured and killed several whites. Bascom retaliated by hanging the Indian captives. Nothing constructive came out of this "tragedy at Apache Pass." But much fear and hatred was generated.

Entrance to the Cochise Stronghold in southeastern Arizona.

Mickey Free as a government scout and interpreter.

After the Civil War erupted in 1861, soldiers were ordered to abandon military posts in Arizona, including Fort Buchanan. Bands of Apaches and lawless whites began roaming the countryside. Mines and ranches were deserted by the pioneers. Once again, Tucson became a refuge for the survivors.

Fort Defiance. This was the first United States military post in what is now Arizona. It was built on Bonito Creek, north of present-day Window Rock in 1851 to keep the Navajos in check.

Since their first contact with the Navajos in 1846, American troops had been trying to quiet these Indians by peaceful means. Treaty after treaty proved to be worthless scraps of paper. After each agreement, Navajo raids on settlements in New Mexico grew more bold. What the military leaders failed to see was that the political unit of the Navajos was the clan—not the tribe. A treaty was binding only on the individual Indians who signed it. Besides, when the military expeditions sent against them handed out gifts, the Navajos mistook the army's generosity as a sign of weakness.

Fort Defiance in 1852.

Things changed when Colonel Edwin Vose Sumner was appointed commander in New Mexico. His strategy was to impress the Navajos with a display of force. Fort Defiance was built in the heart of Navajo country. Actually it was a fort in name only. Located in a narrow canyon, it was easily attacked from three sides. There was no stockade. Soldiers called it "Hell's Gate" because it was so isolated. But the mere presence of a military post in the Navajo heartland was effective—for awhile.

In 1858, however, the Navajos boldly attacked the post herd, killing two soldiers and wounding five. They drove off 62 mules and three horses. On April 30, 1860, the warriors made a surprise attack on the fort itself. A small force of 150 infantrymen held off the Indians and forced them to retreat.

Then Fort Defiance became a beehive of activity. Colonel Thomas T. Fauntleroy brought 3,000 troops from New Mexico to

Edwin Vose Sumner

punish the Navajos. Little was accomplished, though the Indians did sign another treaty. Meanwhile, 1,500 soldiers were assigned to Fort Defiance which was constructed for about 250. For housing, the men built "dugouts," half below and half above the ground.

Fort Defiance was abandoned after the outbreak of the Civil War in April 1861. The Navajos thought the white man was admitting defeat by leaving. They resumed their raids up and down the Rio Grande Valley.

Fort Mojave (Mohave). This fort was established in 1859. It was located where Beale's wagon road crossed the Colorado River, a few miles north of the present Interstate 40 (highway 66).

The fort was built to protect California-bound travelers from the Mojave Indians. The Mojaves had lived for centuries along the Colorado and resented the intrusion of the Anglo-Americans.

The nation's attention was focused on the Mojaves in 1858 when they attacked a party of white migrants preparing to cross the Colorado. News of the tragedy soon spread after survivors returned to Albuquerque and told the story. The Department of War gave orders that a military post be established at Beale's crossing.

Colonel William Hoffman, a West Point classmate of Robert E. Lee, was chosen to locate a site. In 1858 Hoffman led a small force overland from California. After fighting a skirmish with the Indians near the crossing, he returned to the coast for more soldiers. Infantry troops were transported by boat from San Francisco and San Diego to Fort Yuma. From this point the troopers had a tough 18-day march along the banks of the Colorado. One of their guides was Joseph Reddeford Walker, a famous old mountain man.

The Mojaves were overawed by the size of Hoffman's expedition. Iritaba, Kairook, and four other chiefs agreed to a council at which 500 Indians appeared. After the Mojaves promised to live in peace, Hoffman returned to California, leaving Major L. A. Armistead in charge of the new post.

The living quarters were constructed of cottonwood logs chinked with mud. Food rations were bad. Bread, baked in San Francisco, was hard and stale by the time it arrived at the post. The post trader, Peter R. Brady, did a lively business selling crackers at 40 cents a pound. Brady also published the *Mohave Dog Star*. This news sheet might be called northern Arizona's first publication.

In May, 1861, Fort Mojave was abandoned and burned down. It was feared that the Confederates planned to take over the Arizona posts. The soldiers at Fort Mojave were transferred back to California. The fort was reoccupied by Union troops in 1863 and remained in existence until 1890.

Fort Mohave

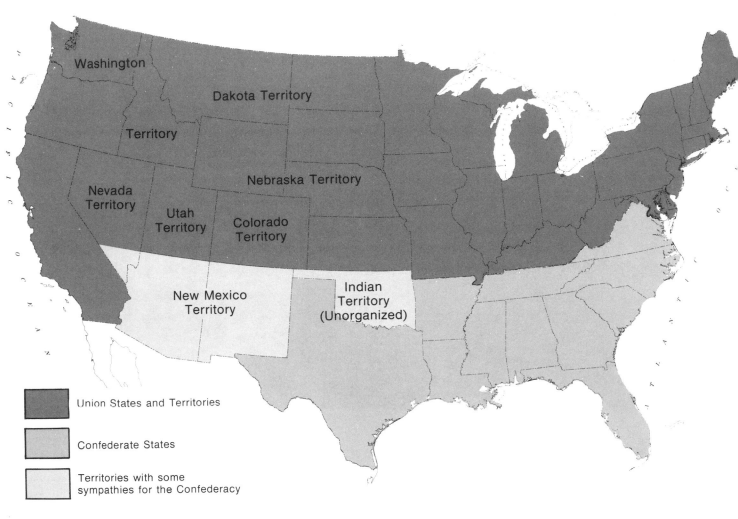

Washington

Dakota Territory

Territory

Nevada
Territory

Nebraska Territory

Utah
Territory

Colorado
Territory

New Mexico
Territory

Indian
Territory
(Unorganized)

Union States and Territories

Confederate States

Territories with some
sympathies for the Confederacy

A divided Union in 1861.

10

THE CIVIL WAR ERA

The story of the Civil War in Arizona involves three main trends: 1) the struggle between the North and South for control of the Southwest, 2) a conflict between the Indians and the whites, and 3) the beginning of territorial government.

Confederate President Jefferson Davis wanted to annex the Territory of New Mexico, which included Arizona until 1863. This territory was rich in minerals. It was the connecting link between Confederate Texas and the California coast.

In 1861 the Texas Volunteers succeeded in occupying southern New Mexico and Arizona. Many career officers in the United States Army defected to the South and received higher ranks. Among these officers were Captain Richard S. Ewell, who was at Fort Buchanan before the war. Another was Major Henry H. Sibley. He was given the rank of brigadier general and placed in command of the South's Army of New Mexico.

Once aroused, the North drove the Confederate troops out of the Southwest. Union army regulars were assisted by volunteers from Colorado, California, and New Mexico. The Confederate dream of a pathway to the Pacific coast was shattered by the summer of 1862.

Many Indians saw an opportunity in the white men's Civil War to reconquer what they had lost. They attacked outlying settlements and roads with fury. Both Confederate and Union army officers struck back with Indian extermination* orders. The Navajos in Arizona and the Mescalero Apaches in New Mexico were forced to go to the Bosque Redondo Reservation in present-day New Mexico.

There were two Arizonas during the Civil War. The Confederate Territory of Arizona was created in 1861 by Colonel John R. Baylor. It stretched across the southern parts of the present states of Arizona and New Mexico with the capital at Mesilla on the Rio Grande. The Union Territory of Arizona was taken from the western half of New Mexico in 1863. Except for the loss of Pah Ute County (where Las Vegas is located) to Nevada, the boundaries are the same today.

*extermination: killing off.

KEY CONCEPTS

1. Confederate control over the Territory of New Mexico was brief.
2. The California Volunteers ran the Confederates out of Arizona.
3. Colonel (later General) Carleton brought law and order to Arizona.
4. The Apaches and the Navajos tried to hold on to their homelands.
5. Gold discoveries attracted miners to Arizona.
6. Congress created the Territory of Arizona in 1863.

10

1. CONFEDERATE CONTROL OVER THE TERRITORY OF NEW MEXICO WAS BRIEF

The military struggle for New Mexico began in July 1861. Lieutenant Colonel John R. Baylor led a "flying squad" of 300 daredevil Texans to Mesilla. This town was occupied on July 25. A few days later, Baylor's mounted rifle regiment caught federal troops fleeing from Fort Fillmore. Major Isaac Lynde, in an act of cowardice, surrendered his entire command without a fight at San Augustine Pass.

Confederate Territory of Arizona. Baylor returned to Mesilla. On August 1 he proclaimed himself military governor of the "Confederate Territory of Arizona." This territory stretched from Texas to California. It included the southern parts of the present states of Arizona and New Mexico.

Before Baylor's Territory of Arizona was a week old, a mass meeting was held in Tucson. The people voted to secede from the Union. They elected Granville H. Oury as territorial

Lt. Col. John R. Baylor   Granville H. Oury

delegate to the Confederate Congress in Richmond, Virginia. Arizona was officially made a Confederate territory on February 14, 1862—exactly 50 years before Arizona statehood day.

Why did so many people in Arizona side with the South? For one reason, many residents of Tucson came from southern states. They also resented the way Arizona was abandoned to the Apaches and to the lawless whites. This happened when Union troops were ordered away from Fort Buchanan and Fort Breckenridge in July. The people were willing to accept protection from any government.

Territories of New Mexico and Arizona during the Civil War.

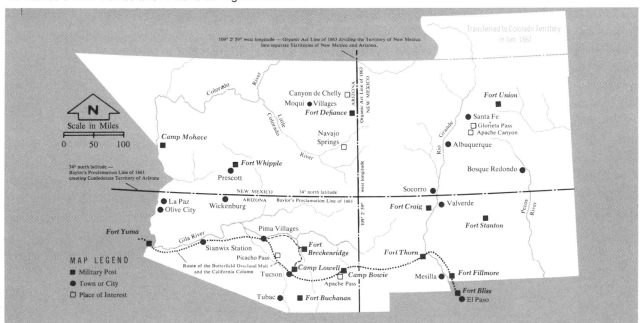

Confederate invasion fails. In February 1862, General Henry H. Sibley led a large army of Texas Volunteers to Mesilla and up the Rio Grande Valley. At Valverde he defeated Union troops under Colonel R. S. Canby.

The tables were turned at Glorieta Pass, the "Gettysburg of the West," on March 28. More than 1,300 Colorado Volunteers, known as "Pike Peakers," attacked the Confederates like demons. A flanking movement on the Texas rear guard was led by Major J. M. Chivington, a Bible-pounding preacher turned soldier. The Confederate supply wagons were burned. Hundreds of horses and mules were bayoneted. After this defeat, the Confederates retreated down the Rio Grande and back into Texas.

2. THE CALIFORNIA VOLUNTEERS RAN THE CONFEDERATES OUT OF ARIZONA

Confederates occupy Tucson. Before General Sibley started his ill-fated march up the Rio Grande, he sent a company of mounted troops under Captain Sherod Hunter to take possession of Tucson. Hunter's "Arizona Volunteers" received a friendly welcome as they rode into town on February 28, 1862.

He gave Union sympathizers the choice of swearing allegiance to the Confederate States or leaving the territory. Solomon Warner, Estevan Ochoa, Peter Brady, and Sam Hughes were among the Tucson leaders who left town. They refused to take an oath to support the Confederacy.

Captain Hunter's operations along the Gila. Hunter took the supplies he needed at Tucson and led a detachment to the Pima villages. There he arrested Ammi M. White, a miller. White had been buying grain, forage, and other supplies for Union troops coming from California. Hunter took 1,500 sacks of wheat from White. He gave them to the Indians, since he did not have any wagons in which to haul the grain away.

Hunter sent out raiding parties to destroy

Grist mill and home of Ammi White near the Pima villages.

the old Butterfield stage stations where the Union was storing hay for future use. Rebel scouts got within a few miles of Fort Yuma where the California Volunteers—better known as the California Column—intended to launch a drive into Arizona.

Before leaving Los Angeles, Colonel James H. Carleton sent Captain William McCleave to scout the Confederates. McCleave and nine picked men walked into a trap at the Pima villages. Captain Hunter, posing as the miller, was able to get the Yankees inside and take them prisoners. Hunter assigned Lieutenant Jack Swilling to escort McCleave and White to Mesilla.

Skirmish at Stanwix Station. California troops under Captain William P. Calloway were sent to rescue McCleave but arrived too late. On the way, Calloway's soldiers came across Confederates destroying hay at Stanwix Station, about 80 miles east of Yuma.

James H. Carleton

Shots were exchanged and a California private was wounded before the rebels retreated. This encounter at Stanwix Station was not a battle of the size of a Gettysburg or Bull Run. But it was the westernmost skirmish between soldiers during the Civil War.

Battle of Picacho Peak. From the Pima villages, Calloway sent two lieutenants with cavalrymen to capture Confederates still in the vicinity. At Picacho Peak, about 45 miles northwest of Tucson, Lieutenant James Barrett caught up with the Confederates. A fierce battle was fought on April 15, 1862, that lasted only a few minutes. Barrett and two Union privates were killed and three others wounded. No Confederates were killed but two were wounded and three captured. The remaining Confederates escaped to Tucson.

Union troops move into Tucson. When the main body of the California Volunteers began arriving at the Pima villages, they built a military post and named it Fort Barrett in memory of the dead lieutenant. Fort Breckenridge on the San Pedro was reoccupied and named Fort Stanford in honor of the California governor.

The California troops moved into Tucson on May 20, 1862, without a shot being fired. Hunter had departed two weeks earlier, realizing that his small force was no match for the 1,800-man California Column. Colonel Carleton delayed his entrance into Tucson until June 7. He wanted an artillery unit to get there first and fire a salute when he arrived. A short time later, Carleton was promoted to brigadier general.

3. COLONEL (LATER GENERAL) CARLETON BROUGHT LAW AND ORDER TO ARIZONA

Colonel Carleton appointed himself as military governor of Arizona and declared martial law. Trials were conducted by a military commission since there were no civil courts. All citizens of legal age were required to take an oath of allegiance to the United States and have a legitimate job. Carleton ordered the arrest of nine Tucson desperadoes, some of them murderers, and sent them to Fort Yuma for imprisonment. Gambling houses and saloons were taxed and the money was used for the care of sick and wounded soldiers.

Carleton arrested and imprisoned about 20 persons accused of being Confederate sympathizers. The most notable was Sylvester Mowry. A board of officers in Tucson listened to witnesses who testified against him. The board reached the opinion that Mowry had helped Hunter's troops and corresponded with Confederate leaders. Carleton agreed and ordered Mowry confined at Fort Yuma.

Mowry insisted he was innocent. He was released after Carleton's superior, General George Wright, investigated the case and found no grounds for holding him. Carleton was convinced of Mowry's guilt, however, and ordered him arrested if he returned to Arizona. In July, 1864, Mowry's rich Patagonia silver mine property was sold at public auction for a mere $2,000. A federal court in 1868 awarded Mowry $40,000 for damages, but his reputation was never completely redeemed.

Headquarters and smelter of the Mowry mine.

4. THE APACHES AND THE NAVAJOS TRIED TO HOLD ON TO THEIR HOMELANDS

Carleton took time to bring law and order to southern Arizona. But he was mainly occupied with preparations for the next leg of his march to the Rio Grande. Because of the scarcity of water, the California Column was divided into sections. These smaller groups marched along the old Butterfield route several days apart. The first detachment reached the Rio Grande in time to raise the flag on July 4.

Battle of Apache Pass. The biggest battle of the Civil War in Arizona was fought on July 15, 1862, at Apache Pass. The second detachment of 126 California Volunteers was ambushed by Apaches led by Mangas Coloradas and Cochise. As the soldiers approached a spring of water, the Indians fired on them from behind the rocks along the rim of the canyon.

After stubborn resistance, the Apaches were finally dislodged by bursting howitzer shells. The "Battle of Apache Pass" was a victory for the troops since they lost only two killed and three wounded. Estimates of Apache losses vary from 10 to 68.

The battle focused attention on the importance of controlling the strategic Apache Pass. General Carleton gave orders for the establishment of Fort Bowie there. For years this post protected travelers, wagon trains, stagecoaches, and cattle herders passing through the Apache danger zone.

Carleton's Indian policy. The last units of the California Column reached the Rio Grande by mid-August. Carleton soon replaced Colonel Edward R. S. Canby in command of the Department of New Mexico. With the Confederate soldiers gone, he concentrated on trying to control the Indians.

Several expeditions were launched against the Apaches. Many lives were lost, but by the end of the Civil War the Apaches were still not conquered. Carleton's greatest success was with the Mescalero Apaches in New Mexico

and the Navajos. Both groups were rounded up and confined to the Bosque Redondo Reservation.

Navajos confined at Bosque Redondo. The Navajo campaign was led by Colonel Kit Carson. To stop raids up and down the Rio Grande Valley, Carson gave the Navajos an ultimatum—surrender and go to Bosque Redondo or every male Navajo adult would be killed. With the help of Ute Indian scouts, Carson's New Mexico Volunteers tracked down the holdouts. Sheep were slaughtered and crops destroyed. By November 1863, the only Navajos who had not surrendered or had been killed were in Canyon de Chelly.

This canyon was regarded as a stronghold that was impossible to take, even in the summertime. But Carson chose to strike in midwinter. A detachment of soldiers marched through the canyon from each end. The Navajos threw rocks on the soldiers from high ledges, yelling and cursing in both Navajo and Spanish.

The immediate results of the canyon marches were not significant. But the spirit of the Navajo was broken. In January 1865, Carleton reported that 8,354 Navajos had taken the "long walk"—400 miles—to the Bosque Redondo Reservation in the Pecos Valley.

Fort Bowie in the 1880s.

New Mexico did not prove to be a good country for the Navajos. They quarreled with the Mescalero Apaches, their traditional enemies. A smallpox epidemic took hundreds of lives. They suffered crop failures caused by cutworms and bad irrigation practices. There were no wild berries or roots to gather as in their homeland. Before long the Navajos were wards of the federal government, depending on rations to survive.

After four years of dismal failure, the Bosque Redondo Reservation was investigated by the Department of War. In 1868 the Navajos agreed to a peace treaty and were permitted to return to a defined portion of their former lands. A Navajo agency was set up at Fort Defiance and the federal government provided the Indians with liberal assistance to get them back on their feet again.

5. GOLD DISCOVERIES ATTRACTED MINERS TO ARIZONA

La Paz gold rush. The danger of Indian attack during the Civil War did not stop prospectors from searching northern Arizona hills for precious metals. In 1862 Pauline Weaver and others discovered gold placers along the Colorado north of Yuma. People flocked to the spot and a new town, named La Paz, was born. The boom lasted two years during which time more than $2 million worth of gold was produced. La Paz began to decline in 1864 when the gold became too difficult to extract. At the height of its prosperity, the town had a population of 1,500, living in tents and brush houses.

Walker Mining District south of Prescott. In the year 1863 there was great mining activity around present-day Prescott and Wickenburg. Captain Joseph R. Walker led a party of more than 30 hardy frontiersmen to this area. These men fanned out along the Hassayampa panning gold. A lot of gold ore was also picked up in the mountains. Jack Swilling, who joined the Walker party after a tour of duty in the Confederate Army, sent two specimens of pure gold to General Carleton. Anticipating more discoveries, Carleton established Fort Whipple with a small garrison to protect the miners.

The Abraham H. Peeples party was guided from California to the Prescott region by Pauline Weaver. They struck gold in Weaver's Gulch and in the nearby mountains. Nugget gold was found just below the surface on Rich Mountain. Within a few months the prospectors were able to gather thousands of dollars worth of gold. They were able to force out the metal using only knives.

Wickenburg's Vulture Mine. More miners poured into Arizona to investigate reports of the Walker and Weaver discoveries. The richest deposit of gold was the Vulture mine, discovered in 1863 by Henry Wickenburg. Ore was hauled ten miles from the mine to the Hassayampa River for processing. The town of Wickenburg grew up along the river. The population of 200 included about 80 miners who worked for Wickenburg, merchants and saloon keepers with high-priced goods, and the usual hangers-on: gamblers and gunmen.

The "vast gold fields," about which General Carleton wrote to officials in Washington, proved to be a mirage. But the discovery of gold was one reason that Congress created Arizona as a territory separate from New Mexico in 1863.

Vulture mine.

6. CONGRESS CREATED THE TERRITORY OF ARIZONA IN 1863

Organic Act passed. Arizona's undeveloped mineral wealth was the main reason Congress passed the Organic Act. Ohio Congressman James M. Ashley introduced the bill and got it through the House of Representatives. Two of the biggest mining companies in the Tubac area were chartered in his state of Ohio. Ashley was impressed by what these companies had already done in Arizona. He listened carefully to everything Charles Poston, William Wrightson from Cincinnati, and Sam Heintzelman had to say about Arizona's future. All of these men were in Washington, D. C., lobbying for the Ashley bill at the time it was passed by the Senate and sent to the President.

There was strong opposition to the Organic Act in both the House and Senate. Opponents argued that Arizona didn't have enough people to justify the expense of a territorial government. They quoted 1860 census figures, showing fewer than 2,500 whites, mostly of Mexican origin, in Arizona.

But this point was countered in a very dramatic way by Delegate to Congress John S. Watts from Santa Fe. In a House debate he held up a large specimen of rich silver ore from the Heintzelman mine for all to see. Watts said that millions of dollars worth of Arizona silver could be put into circulation. All the miners needed to develop the mines was protection.

Carleton and Canby smoothed the way for the Organic Act. They drove the Confederates out of the Territory of New Mexico in 1862, giving Congress a territory to split and organize.

Territorial officers. The first territorial officers for the Territory of Arizona were appointed by President Lincoln. He chose two "lame duck" congressmen who had been defeated in the November 1862 elections. Ohio ex-Congressman John A. Gurley headed the slate as governor. His illness delayed the departure of the new officers for Arizona.

John A. Gurley

When Gurley died at his home in Cincinnati in August 1863, Lincoln promoted Maine ex-Congressman John N. Goodwin from chief justice of the Arizona Supreme Court to governor.

Richard C. McCormick of New York was appointed secretary. He had been a war correspondent and chief clerk in the Department of Agriculture. William F. Turner of Iowa became chief justice. The associate judges were William T. Howell of Michigan and Joseph P. Allyn of Connecticut.

The other officers were: District Attorney Almon Gage, of New York; Surveyor-General Levi Bashford, of Wisconsin; United States Marshal Milton B. Duffield, of New York; and Superintendent of Indian Affairs Charles D. Poston, of Kentucky and Arizona.

These men made their way to Arizona in two parties. Poston, Duffield, and the latter's deputy marshal took the stagecoach to California and entered Arizona from the west. Governor Goodwin's party traveled over the Santa Fe Trail to Santa Fe. Until then, their exact destination in Arizona was not known.

General Carleton suggested that the capital should be located near the new Walker gold diggings. After listening to Carleton, everyone in Goodwin's party was "gold struck." It did not take long to decide that Fort Whipple, near the mines, would be a good temporary capital for Arizona.

161

Some of the first officials of the Territory of Arizona. Seated (left to right): Associate Justice Joseph P. Allyn, Governor John N. Goodwin, and Secretary Richard C. McCormick. Standing (left to right): the Governor's private secretary, Henry W. Fleury; U.S. Marshall Milton B. Duffield; and U.S. District Attorney Almon P. Gage.

Marker at Navajo Springs where the first territorial officials took the oath of office.

Ceremony at Navajo Springs. Escorted by troops provided by General Carleton, the Goodwin party traveled along the 35th parallel route. Sometime on December 27, 1863, they crossed the western boundary of New Mexico. To make certain they were in Arizona, the party traveled two more days. The heavily-loaded wagon creaked to a halt beside a waterhole called Navajo Springs, just south of the town of Navajo on Interstate 40.

There, on a snowy afternoon on December 29, 1863, the Territory of Arizona was formally established. Oaths of office were taken and Secretary McCormick delivered a stirring oration. On January 22, 1864, Governor Goodwin's caravan pulled into Fort Whipple. Arizona was a territory at last.

162

UNIT FIVE

THE TERRITORY OF ARIZONA (1863-1912)

February 24, 1863! On that day President Abraham Lincoln signed the Organic Act which made Arizona a territory separate from New Mexico.

February 14, 1912! On that day President William Howard Taft signed the proclamation admitting Arizona into the Union.

Between those historic events Arizona's non-Indian population grew from about 4,000 to more than 200,000. The new residents built towns, developed mines, irrigated farms, and filled the open ranges with livestock. Two railroads were built across the territory. At the beginning of the territorial period there was not even a stagecoach to ride. By 1912 Arizonans owned more than 1,800 automo-

biles. Airplanes were beginning to fly over the territory.

While Arizona was a territory waiting for statehood it was administered by 16 governors appointed by the president. The people elected 25 different legislatures. The territory was represented in Washington, D. C., by a delegate to Congress who had no vote. Twelve different men were elected to this position, beginning with Charles D. Poston.

Arizona was part of the Territory of New Mexico from 1850 to 1863 and a territory in its own right until 1912—a total of 62 years. No other territory, including Hawaii and Alaska, was "stateless" for so long.

PROCLAMATION.

TO THE PEOPLE OF ARIZONA:

I, JOHN N. GOODWIN, having been appointed by the President of the United States, and duly qualified, as Governor of the TERRITORY OF ARIZONA, do hereby announce that by virtue of the powers with which I am invested by an Act of the Congress of the United States, providing a temporary government for the Territory, I shall this day proceed to organize said government. The provisions of the Act, and all laws and enactments established thereby, will be enforced by the proper Territorial officers from and after this date.

A preliminary census will forthwith be taken, and thereafter the Judicial Districts will be formed, and an election of members of the Legislative Assembly, and the other officers, provided by the Act, be ordered.

I invoke the aid and co-operation of all citizens of the Territory in my efforts to establish a government whereby the security of life and property will be maintained throughout its limits, and its varied resources be rapidly and successfully developed.

The seat of government will for the present be at or near Fort Whipple

JOHN N. GOODWIN.

By the Governor:

RICHARD C. M'CORMICK,

Secretary of the Territory.

Navajo Spring

FORT WHIPPLE, ARIZONA

December 29th 1863—

Proclamation establishing the territorial government of Arizona.

11

TERRITORIAL GOVERNMENT ESTABLISHED

What was Arizona like in 1864? It was one of the least known and most thinly-populated areas in the United States. About half of the 4,573 non-Indians lived in the Tucson vicinity. Most of these settlers were of Mexican origin.

There were scattered settlements south of Tucson in the Santa Cruz and Sonoita valleys. A few people lived along the Colorado River—mostly at Arizona City (Yuma) and La Paz. Several parties of gold seekers were mining near Wickenburg. Other miners were combing the hills in northwestern Arizona for precious metals. Add some widely-spaced and under-manned military posts—that was it!

In 1864 Arizona had all the earmarks of becoming a mineral empire. Governor John N. Goodwin had that in mind when he located the capital at Prescott. Gold diggings in the Walker Mining District were nearby. The first territorial legislature in 1864 passed laws to protect mining claims and to encourage mine development. The need for food in the mining areas gave agriculture a start in the Salt River Valley in the late 1860s.

The population grew slowly to 9,658 in 1870. This figure included 9,581 whites, 26 Blacks, and 20 Chinese.

In 1880 the census takers counted 41,574 non-Indians in Arizona, including about a hundred Blacks and more than a thousand Chinese. By that time the territorial legislature had divided the four original counties into seven. Pima County was still the largest, with nearly 20,000 people. Maricopa County had grown to almost 5,700 and Yavapai to more than 5,000. Apache County had 3,500; Yuma, 3,200; Pinal, over 3,000; and Mohave, 1,200.

KEY CONCEPTS

1. Governor Goodwin organized the territorial government in 1864.
2. The First Legislative Assembly worked on problems facing the territory.
3. Counties were created by the territorial legislatures.
4. Governor Safford was the "father of the Arizona public schools."
5. Arizona had elections and political parties in territorial days.
6. Tucson was the Mexican-American stronghold in territorial days.

11

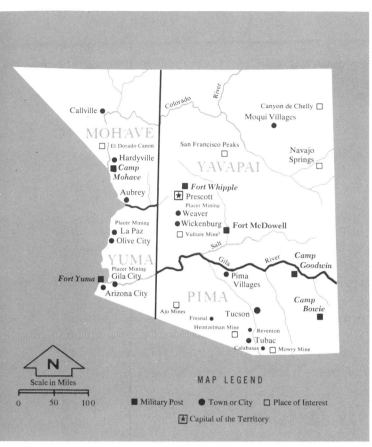

Arizona in 1865.

1. GOVERNOR GOODWIN ORGANIZED THE TERRITORIAL GOVERNMENT IN 1864

When Governor John N. Goodwin arrived at Fort Whipple on January 22, 1864, he found no government, no laws, no office buildings, no civilian mail service, and no railroads. The Army had almost no control over unfriendly Apaches. There were miners and trappers who called no place home. Some Confederate sympathizers wanted the new territorial government to fail. And even some of the new officials were more interested in striking it rich than in their jobs.

These were the conditions under which Governor Goodwin began his duties in 1864.

Governor John N. Goodwin

Capital located at Prescott. After his arrival at Fort Whipple, Governor Goodwin spent several months touring Arizona with a military escort. He visited mines and traveled through the Salt River Valley. While at Tucson on May 11 he appointed William S. Oury, a southerner, as mayor.

Goodwin considered several possible locations for the territorial capital. He finally picked a mile-high spot in the pines on Granite Creek. The brand-new town was named after William H. Prescott, the historian. The Army moved Fort Whipple from its original location in Chino Valley to a site near Prescott.

By July 4, some 232 lots had been sold in the capital city. The first one sold for $175 and was soon occupied by the corner store of "J. Goldwater & Brother." The highest-priced lot went to Richard C. McCormick for $245. McCormick had a wood-frame office built on the lot for his newspaper, the *Arizona Miner*.

Goldwater's store in Prescott was built in 1878. It was one of the first brick buildings in Arizona.

Two territorial buildings were constructed out of rough-hewn logs. One of them, an 11-room "Governor's Mansion" is preserved today as the Sharlot Hall Museum.

A log capitol on Gurley Street was not completed when the first legislature assembled on September 26, 1864. The walls were not yet chinked with mud. Cool autumn breezes whistled through the cracks. Tallow candles were used for lighting because there were no windows, only shutters. The seats and tables were made of rough boards. There were no cuspidors, usually found in legislative halls in those days. But that didn't matter. The floors were dirt.

Territorial court system organized.
Governor Goodwin busily organized the territorial government. In April he divided Arizona into three judicial districts. Each judge was later assigned a town—Tucson, La Paz, or Prescott—where he presided over trials.

Once a year, the three district judges met together as the territorial supreme court. In this capacity they heard appeals from their own district courts. The number of judges—and the number of districts—was increased to four in 1891 and to five in 1905.

In 1864 courtrooms were not elegant. Judge William T. Howell, who presided at Tucson, left Arizona before a year was out. He told Governor Goodwin that he would not act as judge in a district where two out of three people were barefooted, where court was held in an adobe shack with an earthen floor, and a dry goods box was used as the rostrum.

Judge William T. Howell

Judge Charles G. W. French was Chief Justice of the Arizona Supreme Court from 1876 to 1884.

Census of 1864. Before an election could be held, a census had to be taken. U. S. Marshal Milton B. Duffield and his assistants went to every settlement, mining district, and ranch in the territory. The 4,573 people who were questioned came from nearly every state then in the Union and from many foreign countries, particularly Mexico. Indians were not counted, but nearly 800 soldiers at the forts were included in the total. About half of the territory's residents lived around Tucson. Most of the people in that vicinity were of Mexican origin.

The following figures were submitted by Marshal Duffield: First District (total of 2,377)—Tucson (1,568), Mowry Mine (145), women and children at the Mowry Mine (107), Apache Pass (74), Cerro Colorado Mine (45), Pima Villages (29), San Pedro (6), Raventon

Governor's Mansion in Prescott, built in 1864.

and Calabasas (183), San Xavier (112), and Fresnal (91).

Second District (total of 1,157)—La Paz (352), Arizona City (151), Fort Mojave (120), La Laguna (113), El Dorado Canon (90), San Francisco District (62), New Water (61), Hughes Mines (54), Castle Dome and Potato (32), Hardy's Landing (32), Olive City (19), Mineral City (16), Los Pasos (14), Plomoso Placers (14), Apache Chief Mine (8), Picacho Mine (7), Salizar Mine (5), Scottie Mine (4), and Apache Wide West (3).

The total of the more sparsely settled Third District was 1,039 persons.

Governor Goodwin called Arizona's first election. On July 18, 1864, members of the First Legislative Assembly and a delegate to Congress were elected. The Assembly consisted of a nine-member Council and an 18-member House of Representatives.

Charles D. Poston, already known as the "Father of Arizona," defeated five opponents for the delegate to Congress seat. He received 514 votes to 226 for Charles Lieb, his closest rival. After the election, Poston departed for Washington, D. C. He took a long route by way of Panama. This trip cost the nation's taxpayers $7,000.

At the second delegate to Congress election in September, 1865, Governor Goodwin was elected. He received 717 votes to 381 for Judge Joseph P. Allyn and 206 for Poston.

a legislator. They escorted him to a creek and scrubbed him with soap and water and a horse brush. A hand-me-down suit and a trip to the barber shop gave him all the dignity he needed in frontier Arizona. Ten years after his first experience as a lawmaker, McCrackin discovered a rich silver mine in Mohave County where a peak is named after him.

Only two members, Francisco S. Leon and Jesus M. Elías, were born in the territory. They spoke only Spanish. Another Mexican-American—José M. Redondo, a well-to-do rancher in the Yuma area—was not eligible to serve. He was born in Mexico and had not yet been granted United States citizenship.

Two Tucson lawyers were elevated to leadership positions. The Council chose Coles Bashford, formerly governor of Wisconsin, for its president. House members elected W. Claude Jones as speaker. Jones was a Confederate sympathizer who had taken an active part in the secession convention at Mesilla in 1861.

The first legislature at work. The first territorial legislature did not have to start from scratch. Judge William T. Howell, with the assistance of Coles Bashford, had compiled a basic code of laws before the legislature convened. The Howell Code, with some amendments and changes, was adopted by the legislature.

Coles Bashford

2. THE FIRST LEGISLATIVE ASSEMBLY WORKED ON PROBLEMS FACING THE TERRITORY

The first territorial legislature began convening at Prescott on September 26, 1864. The mining interests were well-represented. Nearly half of the legislators were either miners or mining engineers.

One of the miners was Jackson McCrackin, who came to Arizona with the Walker party in 1863. The story was told that his friends thought he should go to Prescott looking like

The code dealt with such things as mining claims, water rights, property ownership, crimes, jury trials, posses, gambling licenses, and a poll tax. Howell was well-paid for his work—$2,500 in addition to his salary. By comparison, the legislators received only $3 a day for a 40-day session.

The problem of transportation quickly got the Assembly's attention. The territorial government could not afford to build the needed roads. So the legislature authorized six toll roads. One of them, the Santa Maria Toll Road, ran west from Prescott to steamboat landings on the Colorado River. It became one of the most used roads in the territory, even though tolls were high. The charge was four cents a mile for a wagon or 2½ cents a mile for a rider on horseback.

The Assembly sent a pile of requests to Congress for federal aid. They asked for

weekly mail service between all the major towns. The only mail line in 1864 was a military express that ran from Los Angeles through Tucson to Mesilla. Delegate to Congress Poston was successful in getting several of the mail routes approved. By the end of 1865, mail routes connected Prescott with Los Angeles, Santa Fe, and Tubac.

Congress turned down the Assembly's requests for money to solve the Indian problem. The legislators agreed with Governor Goodwin's idea that the Indians should be placed on reservations. As a start, they asked for $150,000 to place the Yumas, Yavapais, Mohaves, and Hualapais on the Colorado River Indian Reservation. Congress set aside 75,000 acres for a reservation but voted no money to settle Indians there until 1867.

The Arizona Volunteers. A request for $250,000 in federal funds to send volunteer

Prescott in 1868.

rangers into war against the Apaches was rejected by Congress. The territorial government proceeded on its own. Five companies of Arizona Volunteers were mustered into service in 1866 to fight Apaches. Most of the 350 men were Mexicans or friendly Pimas and Maricopas. Their 11 officers were mainly Anglo-Americans.

The volunteers were ill-equipped. Some were even barefooted. They were never paid the $100 bonus promised when they enlisted. After enduring months of hardship pursuing Apaches, the Arizona Volunteers were given one reward—a "thank you" from the third legislature in 1866 for a job well done.

Divorces. The first territorial legislature began the practice of granting divorces. A law was passed to annul the marriage of John G. Capron, a member of the House, and his wife. Capron was a pony express mail carrier in the 1850s and later ran a stagecoach line. The legislature also divorced Elliott Coues, a doctor at Fort Whipple, from his wife.

Later territorial legislatures continued this practice. In 1873 the seventh legislature passed an act divorcing Governor A. P. K. Safford from his wife Jennie. In 1879 the tenth legislature passed the Omnibus Divorce Bill which released 15 couples from the bonds of matrimony. Among them was Secretary of the Territory John J. Gosper. It seems that Gosper had left his wife in Nebraska and wanted to remarry in Arizona. Congress stopped this legislative practice in the 1880s.

The "capital on wheels." A number of bills were introduced in the first legislature to move the capital away from Prescott. Among the new places proposed was La Paz on the Colorado River. Another was Walnut Grove, population 40, on the lower Hassayampa River. A site for a new town near the juncture of the Verde and Salt Rivers, to be called Aztlan, was suggested too. All these bills were turned down by a vote of 9 to 8 in the House. In 1867, however, the capital was moved to Tucson. It was moved back to Prescott in 1877 and finally to Phoenix in 1889.

3. COUNTIES WERE CREATED BY THE TERRITORIAL LEGISLATURES

The first legislature divided Arizona into four counties. Each was named for an Indian tribe which lived in the area. Yuma County was in the southwest part of the territory and La Paz was its first county seat. Pima was south of the Gila River with Tucson the county seat. Mohave was along the Colorado River in the northwest. Mohave City was the first county seat. Yavapai took in the vast northeast part of the state. Prescott was designated as county seat. All the original counties have been split to form other counties.

Pah Ute County. The second legislature in 1865 created Pah Ute County from the northern part of Mohave. First Callville and then the little Mormon community of St. Thomas served as the county seat. The new county of Pah Ute was recommended by Acting Governor Richard C. McCormick because farmers were rapidly settling there along the Colorado River.

Pah Ute became Arizona's "lost colony" in 1866. Congress gave the portion west of the Colorado to the State of Nevada. The legislature in 1871 restored what was left of Pah Ute County to Mohave. Today, the sites of Callville and St. Thomas are submerged under Lake Mead. The "lost county" is now better known for another town—the gambling town of Las Vegas.

Yavapai is called the "mother of counties." Territorial legislatures took parts of Yavapai to form Maricopa County in 1871, Apache in 1879, and Coconino in 1891. The boundaries of Pinal County have been changed since it was formed in 1875 from parts of Yavapai, Maricopa, and Pima counties.

Gila, Graham, and Cochise counties were created in 1891 and Santa Cruz in 1899. Cochise and Santa Cruz were carved out of Pima County. Greenlee, the fourteenth, was organized in 1909. The voters in Yuma County voted in favor of creating a fifteenth county out of the northern part of that county in 1982.

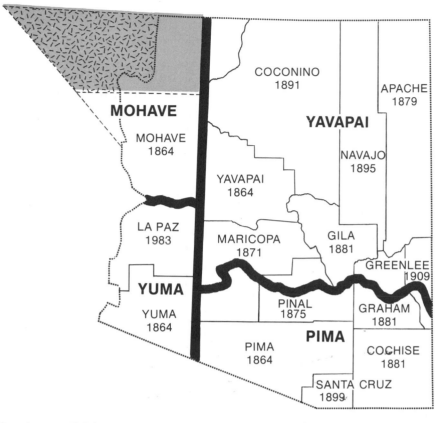

Legend

Boundaries of the four original Counties (1864)
Present County boundaries
Year of original organization is shown under the County name.

Congress gave this section of the Arizona Territory to Nevada in 1866. (All of shaded area was the county of Pah Ute.)

(All of shaded area was the county of Pah Ute.)

Which part of Yuma County was split off in 1982 to form a fifteenth county? What is the new county name?

County map of Arizona.

Tombstone Courthouse.

Isaac Polhamus, steamboat captain.

There have been many county seat changes. In 1871, for example, the Sixth Legislative Assembly decided La Paz was becoming a ghost town and moved the Yuma County seat to more prosperous Arizona City. County Sheriff O. Frank Townsend put the records and property on the steamboat *Nina*

Tilden, commanded by Isaac Polhamus, and transported them downstream. This was a unique way of moving a desert county seat.

The Mohave County seat was changed the most often. Starting out at Mohave City, it was moved to Hardyville in 1867, Cerbat in 1873, Mineral Park in 1877, and finally to Kingman in 1887. The location of the Mohave County seat tells the early economic story of that county. Steamboating was most important at first. Then came mining and finally the Atlantic and Pacific (Santa Fe) Railroad.

4. GOVERNOR SAFFORD WAS THE "FATHER OF THE ARIZONA PUBLIC SCHOOLS"

First private schools. The first territorial legislature provided for a system of public schools, but no school taxes were levied. The legislature gave $250 to Arizona's first educational institution—the San Xavier mission school. The money was used for books, paper, and furniture.

The county seat towns of Prescott, La Paz, and Mohave were each offered $250 and Tucson $500. The catch was that each town had to raise an equal amount. Only Prescott qualified for the grant. S. C. Rogers got the $250 for his private school by matching it with contributions from people in the Prescott community.

School districts created. The Fourth Legislative Assembly in 1867 passed a bill creating school districts in Arizona. Each county board of supervisors could set up a district where at least 100 people lived in a four-square-mile area. The first district organized under this law was Tucson Public School District Number 1 in 1867. The Pima County supervisors named a three-member board of education: John B. "Pie" Allen, Francisco S. León, and William S. Oury. The board rented an old adobe building for a schoolhouse. Augustus Brichta, a New Yorker, was employed as Tucson's first tax-supported public schoolteacher. Brichta's school had money for only one term of six months in 1868. Approximately sixty Mexican boys were in attendance.

In 1869 the Sisters of St. Joseph opened a private academy for girls in Tucson. The school was sponsored by Mexican-American mothers.

Anson P. K. Safford is known as the "Father of the Arizona Public Schools." He took office in 1869 as the third territorial governor. At that time there were no public schools operating in Arizona. With some difficulty he persuaded the sixth legislature to pass the school law of 1871. This law provided for both territorial and county school taxes. Schools were required to remain open "for at least three months each year." A uniform system of textbooks was adopted. The law also listed the required subjects: spelling, reading, grammar, arithmetic, geography, and physiology.

After this law was passed, Governor Safford visited nearly every settlement in the territory and encouraged the people to organize public schools.

The first public school under the 1871 law was opened in Tucson in March 1872 for boys. The teacher was John Spring, a well-educated Swiss immigrant. A Civil War veteran, Spring came to Arizona with the U. S. Army in 1866. His school was a one-room adobe building on the corner of McCormick and Meyer streets. The crude furniture and equipment included splintery desks and benches, two brooms, and a sprinkling pot for the dirt floor. The parents brought in some ash whipping sticks and urged

The first school in Prescott, 1865.

Governor A. P. K. Safford (sitting in rocker) and his household.

the teacher to use them liberally. Spring had his hands full in the little one-room school—especially when the enrollment reached 138.

The first public school for girls was opened in an old brewery building in Tucson in 1873. The teacher was Mrs. Josephine Brawley Hughes. She was the wife of Louis C. Hughes, publisher of the *Arizona Star* and later a territorial governor.

The people of Prescott voted bonds and built a two-story brick schoolhouse in 1876. The school was divided into grades. Several teachers taught under the direction of Principal Moses Sherman. It was the best-equipped school in the territory and the pride of the town. Sherman, a native of Vermont, had been persuaded by Governor Safford to come to Prescott to teach. In 1879 another governor, John C. Frémont, appointed Sherman to be the first fulltime superintendent of public instruction for Arizona.

The Ehrenberg school. Safford's enthusiasm for education resulted in new schools all over the territory. Some of the buildings were not exactly planned as schools. In Ehrenberg, for example, an abandoned saloon was the school room where Mary Elizabeth Post taught for five months in 1872. Sometimes prospectors, who had been used to visiting the saloon, would wander in, only to be embarrassed. Miss Post came to Arizona from San Diego at the urging of John Capron. By the

1870s Capron operated a stage line between San Diego and Mesilla, New Mexico. Miss Post rode the stagecoach to Yuma and went upstream by steamboat to Ehrenberg. Later she taught for nearly 40 years in Yuma.

The first school in Phoenix was held in the courthouse in 1871. The first teacher, J. R. Darroche, did not have to move far to his next job. In 1872 he was appointed county recorder. The first schoolhouse in Phoenix was built in 1873. Constructed of adobe, it was located on Center (now Central Avenue) between Monroe and Van Buren streets.

Miss Ellen Shaver, from Wisconsin, was the first teacher in the new building. She had 35 students—24 girls and 11 boys. In 1875 Miss Shaver married John Y. T. Smith of Camp McDowell. One of the teachers who followed her in the adobe schoolhouse was Miss Carrie G. Hancock. She was the sister of Captain William Hancock, the man who surveyed the original townsite of Phoenix.

The first schoolhouse in Phoenix, built in 1873.

The early Benson school bus had only four horse power.

Josephine Brawley (Mrs. Louis C.) Hughes in her later years. She was Arizona's first woman public schoolteacher.

The Prescott High School freshman class in 1897. Classes were held in the old territorial capitol building.

Governor Safford labored for good tax-supported schools throughout his administration. In his last message to the ninth legislature in 1877, Safford was pleased to report progress. He said that about half of nearly 3,000 children of school age in Arizona had learned to read and write.

5. ARIZONA HAD ELECTIONS AND POLITICAL PARTIES IN TERRITORIAL DAYS

Governors. Sixteen different men served as governor while Arizona was a territory. The governor was appointed, not elected. Every president from Lincoln through Taft, with the exception of Garfield, appointed at least one territorial governor. All but three of the governors were Republican. Democratic President Grover Cleveland appointed Zulick, Hughes, and Franklin.

TERRITORIAL GOVERNORS OF ARIZONA
(with dates of term, political party,
and president by whom appointed).

A. P. K. Safford
1869-1877
Republican
Grant

John P. Hoyt
1877-1878
Republican
Hayes

John C. Frémont
1878-1882
Republican
Hayes

Frederick A. Tritle
1882-1885
Republican
Arthur

Conrad Meyer Zulick
1885-1889
Democrat
Cleveland

Lewis Wolfley
1889-1890
Republican
B. Harrison

John N. Irwin
1890-1892
Republican
B. Harrison

Nathan O. Murphy
1892-1893
Republican
B. Harrison
and 1898-1902 McKinley

John N. Goodwin
1863-1866
Republican
Lincoln

Richard C. McCormick
1866-1869
Republican
A. Johnson

Louis C. Hughes
1893-1896
Democrat
Cleveland

Benjamin Franklin
1896-1897
Democrat
Cleveland

▷Myron H. McCord
1897-1898
Republican
McKinley

✗Alexander O. Brodie
1902-1905
Republican
T. Roosevelt

Granville H. Oury
1880, 1882
Democrat

Curtis C. Bean
1884
Republican

⚘Joseph H. Kibbey
1905-1909
Republican
T. Roosevelt

⚘Richard E. Sloan
1909-1912
Republican
Taft

Marcus A. Smith
1886, 1888, 1890, 1892,
1896, 1900, 1904, 1906
Democrat

Nathan O. Murphy
1894
Republican

ARIZONA'S DELEGATES TO CONGRESS
(with dates of election and political affiliation).

John F. Wilson
1898, 1902
Democrat

Ralph H. Cameron
1908
Republican

Charles D. Poston
1864
Union (Democrat)

John N. Goodwin
1865
Independent (Republican)

Coles Bashford
1866
Independent (Republican)

Richard C. McCormick
1868, 1870, 1872
Independent (Republican)

Hiram S. Stevens
1874, 1876
Independent (Democrat)

John G. Campbell
1878
Independent (Democrat)

Elections. Just as today, Arizona had elections in territorial days. The greatest interest centered around the race for a delegate to Congress. But the people also voted on candidates for county offices and for the territorial legislature.

Legislature. The Legislative Assembly consisted of two houses—a Council and a House of Representatives. In 1878 Congress enlarged the Council from 9 to 12. The number of assemblymen, as members of the House were called, was increased from 18 to 24.

The legislators were elected for two-year terms. But they met only once during that time and were limited to a two-month regular session. Altogether there were 25 territorial legislatures. The first met in 1864 and the last in 1909. The Democratic Party usually had a majority in the legislature.

A delegate to Congress. A delegate to Congress was elected to represent the Territory of Arizona in Washington, D. C. He could speak in the U. S. House of Representatives but had no vote. Twelve different men were elected to fill the delegate position while Arizona was a territory.

Two delegates stand out—Richard C. McCormick, a New York Republican, and Marcus A. Smith, a Kentucky Democrat. McCormick was a leader in the organization of the territory. Smith fought for statehood in the last part of the territorial period.

Richard C. McCormick. McCormick was appointed the first secretary and the second governor of the Territory of Arizona. He was then elected to three terms as delegate to Congress. Though physically small, the red-haired, energetic McCormick was long on brains, personality, and political savvy*.

As secretary, McCormick helped Governor Goodwin win the delegate to Congress seat in 1865 so he could move up to governor. McCormick understood the power of the press. In Prescott he published the *Arizona Miner*. After the capital was moved to Tucson in 1867, he started the *Citizen*.

savvy: understanding

The *Arizona Citizen* building.

As governor, McCormick clearly saw what the function of a frontier government ought to be—to protect property and maintain law and order so that economic development can take place. McCormick soon realized, however, that the territorial governor didn't have as much power as the delegate to Congress. A persuasive delegate could lobby for federal funds requested by the territorial legislature. McCormick wanted to speak for more military protection, reservations for the Indians, better postal service, and higher salaries for territorial officials.

In his six years as delegate, McCormick persuaded Congress to pass several bills. Most important was a law that extended the military telegraph from San Diego into Arizona. He also got the legislature a much-needed salary increase—from $3 to $6 a day while in session.

In the early days of the territory, McCormick and other politicians tried to achieve unity by not using political labels. The first six delegates to Congress ran as non-partisan "Independents." In reality, Goodwin, Bashford, and McCormick were Republicans. Poston, Hiram S. Stevens, and John G. Campbell were Democrats. Campbell, a Yavapai County stockraiser, actually served illegally as delegate since he was still a citizen of Scotland.

In 1880 party lines were drawn for the first time in Arizona. Organization of the Republican Party was started by the Republican Club in Prescott. The club first called a Yavapai County convention and then a territorial convention in Phoenix. The Phoenix convention nominated Madison W. Stewart for delegate to Congress. He was a Pima County businessman and Speaker of the House in the territorial legislature.

The Democrats, who had been holding territorial conventions since 1868, chose Granville H. Oury as their candidate for delegate in 1880. Oury had experience as a lawmaker in both the New Mexico and Arizona territorial legislatures. He was also a delegate to the Confederate Congress during the Civil

War. When the Democrats adjourned their 1880 convention in Phoenix, they held a torchlight rally. Oury, Delegate Campbell, and Morris Goldwater (Barry's uncle) spoke to about 200 Phoenix residents.

After a hard-fought campaign, Oury won with 4,095 votes to 3,606 for Stewart. He was reelected in 1882.

Marcus Aurelius Smith. Smith, a Tombstone lawyer, was elected delegate to Congress in 1886. A physically small man, like McCormick, he succeeded in one ambition where the latter failed. He became one of Arizona's first U. S. senators when statehood was achieved.

Smith, a staunch Democrat, spent nearly a quarter of a century working for statehood. He was elected eight times between 1886 and 1906. A forceful speaker, he could appear to be all things to all people. His enemies called him "Marcus Octopus Smith."

Smith was finally defeated in 1908. Republican Ralph Cameron was the delegate to Congress at the time Arizona became a state.

Something to crow about! *The Flagstaff Gem,* a Democratic newspaper, was happy that Marcus Smith defeated Republican N. O. Murphy for Delegate to Congress in 1900.

"Cameron and Statehood" was a winning slogan in 1908. Here he campaigns in front of the Yuma Theatre.

6. TUCSON WAS THE MEXICAN-AMERICAN STRONGHOLD IN TERRITORIAL DAYS

Until the 1870s Mexican-Americans were a majority in Arizona. But unlike the Spanish-speaking residents of New Mexico, they did not hold political power. Most of the Mexican people in Arizona before 1880 were immigrants who held transient jobs on farms and ranches. By the 1880s they were working in mines, smelters, and on the railroads. Mexicans were paid lower wages than Anglo-Americans for the same jobs.

Anglos held firm control over Arizona throughout the territorial period, 1863-1912. No one with a Spanish surname served in an important territorial office. Only a few Mexican-Americans were able to win seats in the legislature, mainly in the years before 1880. Most of the Mexican-American winners were well-to-do businessmen from Tucson— Jesús M. Elías, Francisco S. León, Juan Elías, Estevan Ochoa, and Mariano Samaniego. Add the names of Yuma rancher José M. Redondo and Ramón Romano of Tubac and the short list of Mexican-American legislators is complete.

Anglo fear of Mexican-American domination of Arizona was an important theme in territorial politics. Tucson, the population center, was denied the capital—except from 1867 to 1877—partly because it was the only part of Arizona where Mexican-Americans were politically strong at the local level.

Estevan Ochoa

177

Until about 1880 the Anglo and Mexican-American upper classes in Tucson enjoyed political and social equality. A shortage of Anglo women was one reason for harmony. Prominent merchants—like Sam Hughes and Hiram Stevens—married into Mexican families. Before the arrival of the railroad, trade was mainly with Sonora. Tucson businessmen had good relations with Mexican merchants and freighters. The peso was the most-circulated money until the 1870s.

But the railroad ended the days of mutual interests and cooperation. Merchants no longer were dependent on goods from Mexico. The railroad brought both merchandise and more Anglos into the territory. By the 1890s Mexican-American community leaders were forming organizations to fight discrimination.

The Alianza-Hispano-Americana (Spanish-American Alliance) was organized in 1894. It was one of the first Mexican defense associations on the American continent. Some 49 persons were listed as *Alianza* founders, but Carlos Velasco and Mariano Samaniego were credited with the idea.

Velasco had a law degree from the University of Sonora. A street in Hermosillo bears the family name. After coming to Tucson in the late 1870s he founded an outstanding Spanish language newspaper called *El Fronterizo*. Some of Velasco's descendants still live in Tucson today.

Carlos Velasco

Mr. and Mrs. Mariano Samaniego

Sam Hughes, his wife, and baby.

Some Tucson members of the *Alianza Hispano-Americana.*

Samaniego was born in Sonora where his family was socially prominent. He graduated from St. Louis University and served as an interpreter for the Confederate Army in Texas during the Civil War. After reaching Tucson in 1869 he started a stage line and entered territorial politics.

The years following the formation of *Alianza* were the "golden age" for Tucson's Mexican politicians. Samaniego was elected to another term in the legislature. He also served as chairman of the Pima County board of supervisors and as delegate to the Democratic national convention. Nabor Pacheco

was elected sheriff. By the time of statehood, however, the power of the *Alianza* had declined. It was the 1930s before Mexican leaders—including the sons of Samaniego and Velasco—got back into politics.

"Dutchy," a Chiricahua Apache Indian scout for the army.

12

ANGLO-APACHE RELATIONS (1865-1886)

The Apache economy was built on hunting, gathering, and raiding. To Anglo-American pioneers, this system was wrong. They thought of the Indian as an obstacle to progress that must be removed.

The Indians naturally resented the invasion of their homeland by outsiders—first the Spaniards and Mexicans and then the Anglo-Americans. Peaceful tribes such as the Pimas and Papagos learned to live with the whites on their lands. But the Apache fought for his right to lead his own way of life on his own land. He fought with merciless fury and cunning. Apachería with its rugged mountains was ideal for hit-and-run warfare. Apache warriors descended upon settlements to capture livestock, to burn, and to kill. They then retreated into their strongholds where the soldiers couldn't reach them.

The Army played an important role on the Arizona frontier. Army engineers built roads. Cavalry and infantry units protected settlements, wagon trains, and Colorado River crossings. Life was tedious and dangerous for soldiers assigned to duty in Arizona. Aside from military drill and camp chores, their main job was to chase marauding Indians.

One by one the Apache bands were defeated and forced on reservations. Confinement to a restricted area often brought more discontent, more rebellions, and more military campaigns to bring order. Not until Geronimo surrendered in 1886 and was shipped off to Florida, did Apaches accept their fate and fight no more.

KEY CONCEPTS

1. The Camp Grant Massacre was a low point in Anglo-Apache relations.
2. President Grant's peace commissioners put most of the Apaches on reservations.
3. General Crook forced all Tonto Basin Apaches to live on reservations.
4. John P. Clum, a young Indian agent, was respected by the Apache Indians.
5. The Indian Bureau made a mistake in concentrating all of the Western Apaches at San Carlos.

12

1. THE CAMP GRANT MASSACRE WAS A LOW POINT IN ANGLO-APACHE RELATIONS

Between 1865 and 1870, United States troops in Arizona were attached to the military Department of California. General John S. Mason, and commanding officers who followed him, increased the number of forts to 18.

General Stoneman appeased the Apaches. In 1870 a separate military Department of Arizona was created with General George Stoneman in command. Like Mason, he was criticized for giving food rations to the Apaches. But Stoneman had instructions to follow President Grant's Indian peace policy of "moral suasion* and kindness." The Indians were to be put on reservations as soon as possible. Meanwhile, most of the 2,000 troops in Arizona were occupied building roads and improving the military posts rather than chasing Apaches.

Moral suasion is the act of persuading people, without using force, to do what is expected of them.

General George Stoneman

There was public outcry at the government's soft-on-Apaches policy. Indians continued to raid up and down the Santa Cruz Valley. A rancher was killed near Tubac and a woman kidnapped. An Apache raiding party drove off livestock from the San Xavier mission. The Tucson *Citizen* published a story blaming Aravaipa Indians near Camp Grant for the San Xavier raid.

The *Aravaipa Apaches* did not want to live on Stoneman's White Mountain Reservation. They were given permission to live near Camp Grant on their old home lands in Aravaipa Canyon near the San Pedro River. Plans had been made for them to farm, gather hay for Camp Grant, and work for neighboring ranchers. Every second or third day Lieutenant Royal Whitman counted the Aravaipas and gave them rations. The Indians seemed contented.

The Camp Grant Massacre. The Tucson people were angry at the Army as well as at the Apaches. General Stoneman was carrying out orders to appease the Apaches. He refused to give the Santa Cruz Valley settlers any more military protection. Left to their own devices, leaders in Tucson organized an expedition to attack the Aravaipa Apache camp.

On April 28, 1871, some 148 men—94 Papagos, 48 Mexicans, and 6 Anglo-Americans—gathered outside Tucson. The leaders were William S. Oury, who was a former mayor, and two Elías brothers, Juan and Jesus María. The Elías brothers belonged to a prominent Tucson family which had been run out of the Tubac area by Apache raiders. At least three members of the Elías family were killed by Apaches. Both Juan and Jesus María Elías had a burning desire for revenge.

With guns, ammunition, and grub supplied by Sam Hughes, the expedition traveled on foot and by night. About daybreak on Sunday morning, April 30, they reached Camp Grant and split into two groups. The Papagos attacked the sleeping Indians in the Aravaipa camp with clubs. The Mexicans and Americans waited on nearby bluffs and shot down

William S. Oury

Eskiminzin, chief of the Aravaipa Apaches. His group was attacked during the Camp Grant massacre.

any Apaches who managed to escape from their wickiups.

The assault was so swift and fierce, approximately a hundred were dead within a few minutes. All but eight were women and children since most of the men were away hunting in the hills. About 30 of the Apache children were spared and turned over to the Papagos as slaves.

The trial of "The United States versus Sidney R. DeLong and others." President Grant was naturally shocked by the brutal massacre. Calling it "purely murder," he threatened to declare martial law if the perpetrators were not arrested and brought to trial. About a hundred were indicted. Only one, Sidney R. DeLong, was tried before Judge John Titus in Tucson. It was agreed before the trial started that the fate of DeLong would be that of the others. The trial was a farce, a judicial circus just to satisfy the government in Washington. The jury found DeLong and others not guilty.

It was almost impossible at that time to convict a person for killing an Apache. Even Judge Titus was convinced the Oury expedition was legal and justifiable. The United States government, he said, did not give the Papago, Mexican, and American residents protection from Apache raids and murders.

They had "a right to protect themselves and employ a force large enough for that purpose," Titus told the jury.

The Camp Grant Massacre has been called one of the bloodiest incidents in the white man's long and shameful relationship with the American Indian. By any standard of decent human conduct, it was one of the saddest days in Arizona history.

2. PRESIDENT GRANT'S PEACE COMMISSIONERS PUT MOST OF THE APACHES ON RESERVATIONS

The Camp Grant Massacre focused national attention on the Territory of Arizona. General Stoneman was blamed—by both those who sympathized with the Apaches and those who hated them—for the Army's ineffectiveness in dealing with the Apaches. He was replaced by General George Crook.

Vincent Colyer. President Grant sent Vincent Colyer to Arizona as a "peace commissioner." Colyer was a Quaker and Grant's principal adviser on Indian matters. He was sent to Arizona because of his sympathy for the Indians. His job was to make treaties with the Apaches and get them on reservations.

The territorial newspapers were hostile to Colyer and called for a strong military campaign against the Apaches. The peace commissioner proceeded with his work, however, and persuaded about 4,000 Apaches to go on reservations. When he departed in October 1871, all the major Apache tribes were on reservations except the Chiricahuas.

General O. O. Howard, the second peace commissioner. General Howard arrived at Yuma in March 1872. Howard, a one-armed Civil War hero, was known as "the Christian general." He was met at Yuma by C. H. Cook, a successful missionary to the Pimas, and was guided to central Arizona. Howard talked with General Crook at Fort McDowell and then held a nine-day conference with Apaches at Camp Grant. He arranged for the return of the captive Aravaipa Apache children from the Tucson residents who had adopted them after the Camp Grant Massacre. Howard also established the San Carlos reservation along the Gila River.

General Howard met with Cochise. The most dramatic event of Howard's visit in Arizona was a meeting with Cochise. He was led to the meeting by Tom Jeffords, a former superintendent of the Butterfield stage line who had sealed his friendship with Cochise by an Apache blood ceremony. Jeffords was probably the only white man who could have convinced Cochise to meet with Howard in October 1872.

At the parley in the Dragoon Mountains, Cochise agreed to a treaty. He promised permanent peace in return for the Chiricahua Reservation in southeastern Arizona. Jeffords was appointed as Indian agent. "Hereafter," Cochise said in his native tongue, "the white man and the Indian are to drink of the same water and eat the same bread."

Before Howard left Arizona in November he abolished Colyer's temporary "feeding post" reservations. All the Apaches were concentrated on three reservations: the White Mountain with its San Carlos subdivision, the Camp Verde, and the Chiricahua.

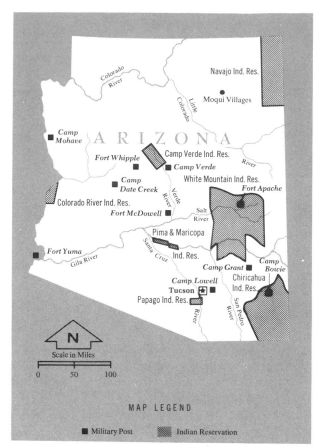

Arizona Indian Reservations and Main Military Posts—1874.

3. GENERAL CROOK FORCED ALL TONTO BASIN APACHES TO LIVE ON RESERVATIONS

After General Howard made peace with Cochise, General George W. Crook was permitted to take the field against the Apaches and Yavapais who were not on reservations. While waiting for his chance, Crook trained an unusual but efficient army. It was made up of small, fast-moving units. Apache scouts were hired as trackers and paid regular Army wages. Crook himself wore a weather-beaten canvas suit with a Japanese summer hat—not one symbol of his high rank—and rode a mule.

Battle of Skull Cave. Crook's first campaign was aimed at encircling Indians in the Tonto Basin area. The first major encounter was the "Battle of Skull Cave" in December,

General Crook on his mule near Fort Bowie in 1885.

"Skull Cave," where Apaches were killed by ricocheted bullets in 1872.

1872. The Indians hid in a cave on a cliff near the Salt River and twice refused to surrender. The soldiers discovered that rifle bullets fired at the slanted ceiling of the cave would ricochet down on the Indians. When all the shooting was over, the troops found piles of dead bodies in the cave. Some seventy-five Indians died. Only eighteen women and children lived long enough to leave the Salt River Canyon as captives.

Battle of Turret Peak. Next came the battle of Turret Peak in March 1873. Crook's forces caught up with Apaches who murdered three people near Wickenburg. One of these victims, George Taylor, was an 18-year-old British immigrant. He was severely tortured—rolled in cactus, his ears and eyelids cut away, and his body stuck with burning splinters. The Apaches who committed this crime also ran away with stolen horses and cattle.

Crook, with the help of his Indian scouts, tracked the renegades to Turret Peak, north of the Verde Valley. Crawling up the mountain on their stomachs at night, the soldiers charged the Apaches as the sun rose. Some of the Apaches were so panic-stricken they jumped down a steep precipice and were dashed to death.

The Skull Cave and Turret Peak battles broke the resistance of the Tonto Apaches. In both instances, raiders were caught by surprise after attacks on white settlements. They suffered great losses in strongholds considered impregnable.

By April 1873, the holdout Apaches began to assemble near Camp Verde. In return for food and protection they agreed to remain on reservations.

Roads and telegraph. Crook then gave attention to building first-class wagon roads to connect the military posts. And he brought in the first long telegraph line. It ran from San Diego via Fort Yuma to Maricopa Wells. One branch went to Fort Whipple and Prescott. Connecting lines were built later to other forts.

Crook was popular with the people. Before leaving Arizona in 1875, he was honored by Governor Safford and a large banquet crowd at Hatz's Hall in Prescott.

4. JOHN P. CLUM, A YOUNG INDIAN AGENT, WAS RESPECTED BY THE APACHE INDIANS

Contrary to common belief, there were many whites who treated the Apaches as human beings. Tom Jeffords did much for the Chiricahuas while he was agent. General Crook was fair with Indians who lived peacefully. He offered to help them become self-supporting by buying all the corn and hay they could produce. Another man who stands out is John P. Clum.

Clum trusted the Apaches. Clum was only 23 in 1874 when the Indian Bureau appointed him agent at San Carlos. A member of the Dutch Reformed Church, he was determined that Apaches would get a square deal. He soon earned the respect of the Apaches at the agency.

A small body of Indian police was organized to replace supervision by soldiers. The Apaches were given their own court. Clum had each band of Apaches elect a representative to meet with him as a council. More impor-

tant, he persuaded the Apaches to turn in their guns. An Indian who wanted to go hunting could check out a rifle. Clum forbade the manufacture of tiswin, an alcoholic drink. He found work for the Indians, principally in constructing agency buildings and living quarters. The Apaches liked Clum and trusted him.

The Indian Bureau's removal policy. Clum's fault was arrogance. He thought he could control all the Apaches without military help. During his three years at San Carlos, the Indian population grew to about 5,000. The Bureau of Indian Affairs tried to concentrate all the western Apaches on one reservation. Clum cooperated in this "removal policy."

The Camp Verde and most of the Fort Apache Indians were moved to San Carlos in 1875. During the next two years, Clum and his Indian police personally escorted the Chiricahuas to San Carlos. He also moved Victorio's Apaches from Warm Springs, New Mexico.

Indian agent John P. Clum with Apaches at San Carlos in 1875.

Apache girl getting water.

Apache boys playing a hoop game at San Carlos.

186

In 1877 Clum suggested that the Army be ordered out of Arizona. He said the presence of troops made the Indians edgy. Clum claimed he could take care of all the Apaches with Indian police. When the Indian Bureau turned him down, he resigned and rode away from San Carlos to become a newspaperman in Tucson and Tombstone.

5. THE INDIAN BUREAU MADE A MISTAKE IN CONCENTRATING ALL THE WESTERN APACHES AT SAN CARLOS

Before he left Arizona in 1875, General George Crook protested against the herding of many different Apache tribes into one reservation. The Indians themselves resented it too. They were restless and unsettled. Some were removed from reservations which Crook and Howard promised would be theirs forever. At San Carlos they were overcrowded and often were shorted on rations. Some of the tribes were supicious and hostile toward each other. The Chiricahuas, for example, made fun of men in other tribes who worked, calling them "squaws."

The Warm Springs Apaches, who were blood brothers of the Chiricahuas, were especially unhappy at San Carlos. In September 1877, they slipped away with Victorio. They were able to live at their old reservation for awhile. But the Army brought most of the tribe back to San Carlos in 1878. Victorio refused to go. After two years of plundering*, he and his band were killed by Mexican soldiers and Indian scouts.

Geronimo on the warpath. Geronimo and his Chiricahua followers were troublemakers for a dozen years. After Cochise died in 1874 they left the Chiricahua Reservation to raid in Mexico. Now and then they went to the Warm Springs Reservation for rations and rest. Geronimo was arrested there in 1877 by Agent Clum and brought to San Carlos in chains. Clum kept him in the guardhouse, but the Indian Bureau ordered him released.

Geronimo and his renegades slipped away in 1878 for a year and a half and departed again in 1881. Many other Chiricahuas and Warm Springs Apaches also left for Mexico in 1881 and 1882. During that time the Army was busy putting down a revolt of White Mountain Apaches.

plundering: taking something by force or theft.

Victorio

The village of San Carlos in the 1880s, on the Apache reservation of the same name.

Ration day at San Carlos, 1886.

Council between Geronimo and General Crook.

The White Mountain Apache Revolt.
These Indians were stirred up by Nock-ay-del-klinne, a medicine man. He had learned about Christianity at a school in Santa Fe and was impressed by the story of resurrection. Nock-ay-del-klinne started his own religion and taught his fanatic followers a kind of ghost dance. He claimed power to bring two dead chiefs to life, once all the whites were driven away.

After Nock-ay-del-klinne was killed trying to escape from soldiers who arrested him, many White Mountain Apaches went on the war path. They killed white ranchers in Pleasant Valley north of Globe and drove away stock. Cavalry troops from Fort McDowell finally ended Apache resistance at the Big Dry Wash on July 17, 1882. This battle, in the southeast corner of present-day Coconino County, was the last major action between the military and Apaches on Arizona soil.

Crook returned to Arizona.
With the Chiricahuas in Mexico and the White Mountain Reservation Apaches in a bad mood, General Crook was reassigned to Arizona in September 1882. He listened to Indian grievances. Considering the way they were cheated on rations, Crook thought the Apaches had been very patient.

Corrupt government contractors were bribing Indian agents to sign for more food than was delivered. General Crook hoped to make the Apaches independent of these grafters. He let them scatter to the more fertile lands on the reservation so they could farm and become self-supporting.

Meanwhile, Geronimo, Juh, and Nachez led the Chiricahuas in raids north and south of the border. Not until January 1884, did the combined pressure of American and Mexican soldiers force all the Apaches to surrender and return to San Carlos. Geronimo was angry because all the horses and cattle stolen in Mexico were taken away. He waited for a chance to escape again and looked for an incident to convince his followers to leave with him. That incident came in May 1885.

In violation of a reservation rule, the Chiricahuas made some tiswin and drank it. Fearing punishment, 42 men fled to Sonora, taking 90 women and children with them. On the way they left a trail of death and burning ranches. More than 400 Chiricahuas and Warm Springs Apaches refused to join the renegades, and remained at peace.

By an 1882 treaty with Mexico, the American troops could pursue outlaws across the border. So Crook stationed himself at Fort

Bowie and sent cavalry and Indian scouts into Mexico to chase Geronimo. Finally, Geronimo agreed to meet with Crook just south of the border on March 25, 1886. He agreed to surrender his band on condition they could return to the reservation after two years imprisonment in the East.

While Crook was returning to Fort Bowie, however, Geronimo and a small group of his warriors bought some mescal from a traveling peddler and got drunk. They then took off for their hideouts in Mexico. The remaining Apaches were taken to Fort Bowie and later shipped to Fort Marion, Florida.

General Miles captured Geronimo. General Crook resigned his Arizona command in disgust and was replaced by General Nelson Miles. For better communication, Miles set up an expensive heliograph system. Messages were sent by mirrors from station to station until they got to the destination.

General Nelson A. Miles

Soldiers signal with the heliograph at the Fort Bowie station.

Miles selected a picked force of about a hundred soldiers and Indian scouts to track down Geronimo. Late in August, Lieutenant Charles B. Gatewood met with Geronimo under a flag of truce and secured his promise to meet with Miles. The final surrender took place on September 4 in Skeleton Canyon near the border. The Indians were taken to Bowie Station and put on a Southern Pacific train for exile in Florida.

The peaceful Chiricahuas on the reservation were taken to Holbrook and also sent by train to Florida.

Geronimo's later life. The Chiricahuas were never permitted to return to Arizona. In 1894 they were settled at Fort Sill in the Indian Territory of Oklahoma. Geronimo became a Christian and confessed his many bloody deeds committed on the plunder trail. He urged his people to give up dancing and other worldly amusements and to repent of their sins.

Geronimo was in demand as a showman. The War Department permitted him to attend expositions, including the St. Louis World's Fair. He made money selling souvenir bows and arrows and pictures of himself. In 1905 Geronimo rode with Quanah Parker and other Indians in President Theodore Roosevelt's inaugural parade. He died at Fort Sill in 1909.

Movies, novels, and television have made Geronimo a famous American. His name was popularized during World War II by paratroopers who yelled "Geronimo" after they jumped from an airplane.

Nachez and Geronimo at Fort Bowie.

Washington Street in Phoenix, 1890s. The old Maricopa
County courthouse is in the background.

13

ARIZONA TERRITORY BEFORE 1900

By the time Governor Safford left office in 1877, the Territory of Arizona showed all the signs of a prosperous future. The Indians had been pacified, though outbreaks occurred after that date. The Southern Pacific Railroad was coming in from the West. Bonanza silver mines were being discovered by prospectors. Hundreds of ranchers were filling up the free open range lands. The Salt River Valley was developing as a major agricultural area. Mormon families from Utah were beginning to settle in valleys all over the territory. Many immigrants were coming to northern Arizona—one reason that the territorial capital was moved back to Prescott from Tucson in 1877.

In the same year the territorial prison was completed and partly filled. Arizona had its share of lawbreakers. As an example, a former Missouri streetcar conductor forged Spanish documents in the 1880s and nearly pulled off the biggest land swindle in history.

In the 1880s and 1890s Arizona continued to prosper and entered a new cultural era. Mines near Tombstone and Superior made silver supreme for awhile. The completion of two railroads across the state marked a boom in Arizona's economy and population. A higher state of civilization was symbolized by more and better schools. In 1885 the territorial legislature established a university and two colleges.

Political changes were in the making too. The capital was moved to Phoenix in 1889. The people began to clamor for statehood and held constitutional conventions in 1891 and 1893. Arizonans were ready to participate in affairs of the nation. Young men eagerly volunteered to fight in the Spanish-American War in 1898. For the first time, Arizona— though still a territory—was part of the United States when the country entered a war with a foreign nation.

KEY CONCEPTS

1. The Salt River Valley became Arizona's main agricultural area.
2. Mormon settlers from Utah established many farming communities in Arizona.
3. John Wesley Powell explored the Colorado River.
4. The so-called "thieving thirteenth" legislature accomplished many things of lasting value for Arizona.
5. The capital was moved to Phoenix in 1889.
6. Claims to Spanish and Mexican land grants held back the development of Arizona.
7. Arizona Rough Riders fought in the Spanish-American War.

13

1. THE SALT RIVER VALLEY BECAME ARIZONA'S MAIN AGRICULTURAL AREA

Fort McDowell was established in 1865. It was located on the Verde River a few miles northeast of the future site of Phoenix. Soldiers at the fort cleared some desert land. They planted and irrigated a grain crop.

John Y. T. Smith. Civilians were paid to cut wild hay for the Army's horses at Fort McDowell. One of the men who cut tall grass along the Salt River was John Y. T. Smith. He lived in a tent for awhile near present-day Sky Harbor Airport in Phoenix.

Smith laid out a road to Fort McDowell. He hauled hay over the road in wagons. Smith did not claim any land, however, or plant any crops.

Why did farmers come to the Salt River Valley? The high cost of grain and vegetables led to the settlement of the Salt River Valley. Food and feed were expensive because they had to be freighted in from Mexico or California.

Local farm products were needed. Jack Swilling, an ex-Confederate soldier, had great faith in the future of the Salt River Valley as a farming area. After Swilling saw the old Hohokam canals he began planning a modern irrigation canal.

The Swilling Ditch Company. In 1867 Swilling went to Wickenburg and drummed

Jack Swilling

up enthusiasm. He returned with more than a dozen hard-working men with teams. The Swilling Ditch Company was organized and began digging a ditch on the north side of the Salt River near Tempe. They hit bedrock at that location and moved about a mile west. By March 1868, the Swilling ditch was completed and water was flowing to freshly-cleared land.

The first crops were planted by Frenchy Sawyer and Charles L. Adams on farms in the vicinity of 24th Street and Van Buren in present-day Phoenix. By summer, crops of barley and pumpkins dotted the area. The word spread quickly to mining camps at Wickenburg, La Paz, Weaverville, and Lynx Creek. Columbus Gray and his California-bound family were at Maricopa Wells when they heard of the Salt River Valley. They came up to look the place over and never left. Soon canal companies were digging ditches from both sides of the river.

Map of Phoenix area in 1870.

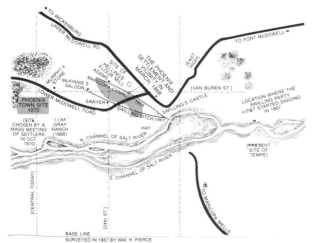

Painting of the legendary Phoenix bird by Paul Coze in the Phoenix Air Terminal.

Captain William A. Hancock, the "father of Phoenix."

The name of Phoenix was given to the little settlement that grew up near Swilling's ditch. The name was suggested by Darrell "Lord" Duppa, one of the men who came from Wickenburg with Swilling. He said that a new city was about to rise over the old Hohokam ruins—just like the legendary Phoenix bird, consumed by fire, rose from its own ashes.

Mill City and Punkinsville were other names for the Phoenix settlement. William B. Hellings and partners built a flour mill. It was located near what is now 30th Street and Fillmore in East Phoenix. The expensive mill machinery was brought by boat from San Francisco to Ehrenberg in 1870. Freight teams hauled it from the Colorado by way of Wickenburg.

Hellings produced 12,000 pounds of good flour every day. He fed the by-products, bran and shorts, to hogs. Soon he had the first meat packing business in Arizona. Hellings sold tons of smoked hams, sausage, bacon, and lard to stores all over the territory. He also operated an inn, the beginning of East Van Buren's motel row, and the "Marble Front" Store. In the 1880s the Hayden flour mill in Tempe took away much of the business and the Hellings mill closed.

Phoenix townsite surveyed. The population of the Salt River Valley was 240 in 1870. In that year, the Salt River Valley Town Association was organized by prominent pioneers to select a townsite. They chose two quarter sections of higher land where downtown Phoenix is located today. The land had little value for farming. William Hancock was employed to survey the townsite and divide it into blocks and lots. Mexican laborers cleared the town plaza and the wide streets of desert growth. Sixty-three lots were sold in December for an average price of $40.

Maricopa County was created in 1871 by the 6th Legislative Assembly meeting in Tucson. The first county-wide election on May 1, 1871, was very exciting. Voters chose a county seat and the first set of county officials. The election resulted in bloodshed when one candidate for sheriff killed his rival following a violent argument.

The contest for the county seat was close. The new "Phoenix Townsite" won out over Mill City, much to Jack Swilling's disgust. Supporters of both towns were guilty of "dirty tricks." Votes were bought with cheap whiskey. Wagon loads of Indians, not eligible to vote, were taken to two or three polling places to cast ballots.

This adobe store was the first building erected on the townsite of Phoenix. It was built by William Hancock in 1871 on the northwest corner of First Street and Washington.

Phoenix grew fast in the 1870s. The population was 1,708 in 1880. The people had a regular stagecoach line. Freighting companies traveled up and down the valley. They supplied the needs of farmers and hauled away hay, grain, and flour to mining camps and other settlements. The first newspaper, the *Salt River Herald*, was established in 1878 and the *Gazette* in 1880.

Everybody came to town on Sunday. Some people attended one of the town's churches. Others came for fun and games. Horse races on what is now Central Avenue were a popular pastime. Farm workers sometimes invested their money in gambling games such as 7-up, casino, faro, monte, draw poker, and "tiger."

Phoenix had its first crime wave in the summer of 1879 when unemployed railroad workers wandered into town from Casa Grande. The Southern Pacific Railroad had temporarily halted construction because of hot weather. Workers were laid off.

After two prominent Phoenix residents were murdered, the citizens administered justice frontier style. Two prisoners accused of murder were taken from jail and lynched. Other rowdies were ordered to leave town.

The Southern Pacific tracks reached Tucson in 1880. But Phoenix had to be satisfied with a stage line to the Maricopa station until 1887. On July 4 of that year, the first steam locomotive of the Maricopa and Phoenix Railroad Company arrived in Phoenix.

Press used by the *Salt River Herald* after 1878.

Washington Street in Phoenix, 1872.

Arizona, 1879

2. MORMON SETTLERS FROM UTAH ESTABLISHED MANY FARMING COMMUNITIES IN ARIZONA

Jacob Hamblin was one of the most important pioneers in northern Arizona. Sometimes called the "Saint in Buckskin," Hamblin was a Mormon missionary and explorer who lived near St. George, Utah. He

194

was the first American missionary to go among the Hopis and Navajos. To reach the Hopis in the late 1850s, he crossed the Colorado northeast of the site known today as Lee's Ferry. Hamblin was the first white man to travel that route since Father Escalante's expedition across Arizona from New Mexico to Utah in 1776.

In 1858 Hamblin discovered Pipe Spring in the dry country north of the Grand Canyon. The Mormons built a fort there in the 1870s and called it Windsor Castle. They ran livestock in the area and made butter and cheese. Today Pipe Spring is set aside as a national monument to preserve an example of how the pioneers protected themselves and developed home enterprises.

In 1864 Hamblin guided Anson Call and a party of Mormons to the Colorado River where Callville was founded. Brigham Young, the head of the Latter-day Saints (Mormon) Church in Salt Lake City, wanted a place to land converts to the church coming from Atlantic coast ports. He also hoped to cut down the high cost of transportation in supplying goods to southern Utah. That section was to be connected by road to a steamboat landing on the Colorado.

The Union Pacific Railroad, however, solved many of Utah's transportation problems. Mormons could come safely westward by railway without fear of persecution. The railroad cut freighting costs in half. Callville

Fort at Pipe Spring, known as Windsor Castle. The fort is now part of the Pipe Spring National Monument.

was abandoned in 1869. The sites of Callville and another nearby Mormon town, St. Thomas, are now submerged beneath Lake Mead behind Hoover Dam.

Hamblin was a big help to the famous Major John Wesley Powell. He guided Powell and his men in their survey of the region north of the Grand Canyon. Powell and Hamblin made a peace treaty with the Shivwits. These Indians admitted to having killed three of Powell's men. In 1871 the two explorers went to Fort Defiance, where Hamblin negotiated a treaty between the Navajos and Mormons. The Navajos agreed to stop raiding Mormon cattle and horses in southern Utah.

In 1873 Hamblin blazed a wagon road from southern Utah to the Little Colorado and up that river toward its headwaters. Many Mormon settlements soon sprang up along this new trail. Hamblin moved his family to Arizona in 1879 and settled in the vicinity of Springerville. He died in 1886 and was buried at Alpine, southeast of Springerville. By that time there were dozens of Mormon settlements in Arizona.

Mormon colonies along the Little Colorado River. In 1876 Brigham Young sent 200 families to colonize in Arizona along the Little Colorado River. The Saints were to live by the United Order. That meant they were one great family, working together and sharing the products of their labor. Traveling in four groups along the Hamblin wagon road, they crossed

Jacob Hamblin

the icy Colorado at Lee's Ferry. They traveled by way of the Hopi village of Moenkopi. The first families reached Sunset Crossing on the Little Colorado on March 23.

Within a week four colonies were founded. They were Allen's Camp, Obed, Ballenger's Camp or Brigham City, and Sunset. All the settlements eventually failed except Allen's Camp. It became St. Joseph in 1878, in honor of the prophet Joseph Smith, and then Joseph City. The Mormons built a fort of cottonwood logs, the start of the oldest Mormon colony in Arizona. After they learned there was no Indian danger, the colonists began constructing stone homes away from the fort.

The Mormons planned to dam the river and irrigate crops. They did not know about the torrents that swept down the Little Colorado in flood season. By 1894 seven dams were constructed and washed out. The first one was a joint venture with the Obed colony. It was finished in less than six weeks.

On June 6 the Saints began watering vegetable gardens, a 60-acre corn field, and 50 acres of wheat. But a flood on July 19 washed out both settlements. The total value for the harvest in 1876 was $20. To tide them over, 4,000 pounds of flour was hauled in by wagon from Utah. This was the first and last time St. Joseph was forced to seek outside aid. Payment for the flour was made within two years. More dams were built and washed out. Finally, in 1939, one was built which has withstood the floods.

Many other Mormon towns were founded in Arizona. More pioneers from Utah and families from the abandoned Little Colorado settlements were directed to new places. Among the Mormon towns in northern Arizona are Woodruff, Pine, Heber, Shumway, Taylor, Snowflake, Springerville, Eagar, and St. Johns. The most important Mormon settlements in the Upper Gila Valley were Pima (Smithville) and Thatcher.

The Mormons also maintained missions among the Hopis at Moenkopi and Tuba City. The word "Tuba" was the Anglo way of saying

the name of Tivi, a Hopi chief. Hamblin won Tivi's friendship and took him to Utah on a visit in 1870.

There are two Mormon towns north of the Grand Canyon. Littlefield, in the extreme northwest corner of the state was founded by Henry W. Miller in 1864 on the Virgin River. The settlement, called "Beaver Dams" at first, was flooded out in 1867. It started again 10 years later. The name Littlefield was adopted because the postal department turned down the name Beaver Dams. Fredonia, considered the northernmost town in Arizona, was located in 1865 on Kanab Creek by Mormons who moved south from Kanab, Utah—supposedly so they could practice polygamy free of federal laws. Fredonia is close to Pipe Spring where the Deseret Telegraph line, Arizona's first, began operating in 1871.

Lehi. In 1877 a Mormon colony was established at Lehi on the south side of the Salt River—north of present-day downtown Mesa. Eighty-four Lehi pioneers, consisting of several large families, assembled a wagon train at St. George, Utah. Their instructions from Brigham Young were to settle in a place "in the far south" that impressed them. The colonists had a difficult journey through sparsely-settled Nevada and northwestern Arizona.

Led by Daniel Webster Jones, they passed through the little hamlet of Phoenix and continued upstream to the McDowell crossing. On the day of their arrival, March 6, 1877, they began constructing a four-mile irrigation canal. With the help of friendly Pima Indians, the Mormons completed the project in time for summer planting. For protection they built an enclosure called Fort Utah.

St. David. By August, dissension arose. About half the Lehi colony left to settle in the San Pedro Valley. Despite Indian scares and a problem with malaria fever, the settlement, called St. David, survived.

Mesa. The second group of Mormon pioneers who settled in the Salt River Valley left Utah in September 1877. They followed Jacob Hamblin's Old Mormon Wagon Road. After stopping at the Little Colorado River settlements, the Mormons reached Fort Utah on February 14, 1878. They were encouraged by Charles T. Hayden, then a resident of Tempe, to remain in the valley.

They camped upstream from the Lehi colony and began digging the Mesa Canal. Enduring the hot summer sun, dust storms, rattlesnakes, and the many hardships of frontier life, they finished the canal. The Mormons then moved from the river camp to the new townsite of Mesa.

John Wesley Powell and Tau-Gu, Paiute chief, overlooking the Virgin River near Cedar, Utah, 1873.

School in the Mormon community of Strawberry, 1898.

3. JOHN WESLEY POWELL EXPLORED THE COLORADO RIVER.

Lake Powell in northern Arizona was named after John Wesley Powell. He was a Union Army officer who had lost his right arm in the Battle of Shiloh during the Civil War. Major Powell became famous as the first man to explore the wilderness area at the bottom of the Grand Canyon.

In 1869 he led a ten-man party through the dangerous rapids of the Colorado River. The Powell expedition was an exciting adventure which turned up something new at every bend of the river.

Powell started with four heavy wooden boats. Each was built to stand the rough, rocky rapids. One boat, however, was whipped against a boulder by the fierce current. It broke in two. In some places the rapids were too steep to navigate. The boats had to be let down by rope.

When the last rapids were reached, three of the men refused to go on. They left the river and climbed out of the canyon. Unfortunately, these men were killed by Shivwits Indians before they could reach Mormon settlements. Meanwhile, Powell and the remaining men shot the last rapids on the Colorado. Near the mouth of the Virgin River they were picked up by Mormon colonists.

Two years later, Powell made another trip down the Colorado. As on the first exploration, he kept a journal about his exciting experiences and the fascinating geology of the Grand Canyon. His story and scientific observations were later published. The full title was *Exploration of the Colorado River of the West and Its Tributaries.*

Powell's interest in the West led him to several important jobs. He was the founder and first director of the Bureau of Ethnology. In this position he enthusiastically undertook a detailed study of American Indians and their languages. Powell was also the second director of the United States Geological Survey.

4. THE SO-CALLED "THIEVING THIRTEENTH" LEGISLATURE ACCOMPLISHED MANY THINGS OF LASTING VALUE FOR ARIZONA

Of all the 25 territorial legislatures, none was more colorful than the one which convened in Prescott in 1885. It is sometimes called the "bloody thirteenth" because of several fights in the legislative halls and in neighborhood saloons. More often the legislature is labeled the "thieving thirteenth" because of its extravagant expenditures.

The 13th legislature overspent. Operating expenses exceeded the legal limit of $4,000 by nearly $47,000 in the 1885 session. An excess of nearly $24,000 was paid to legislative helpers. The number of people hired was over the legal limit by 51 clerks, 4 pages, and 8 janitors. Some clerks later testified before a grand jury that their only duty was to sign the payroll.

Another thing provoked the secretary of the territory, H. M. Van Arman, who had to pay the bills. He thought the lawmakers requested $4,000 more in travel allowances than they were entitled to have. The biggest requests came from five Pima County legislators who claimed $330 each—fifteen cents a mile for 2,200 miles of travel to and from Prescott. They took a Southern Pacific train to Los Angeles and returned on the Atlantic and Pacific (Santa Fe) via Needles, California to Ash Fork. From that junction they reached Prescott by stage.

The Pima legislators intended to take a stagecoach north from Maricopa via Phoenix to Prescott. But the Salt River was flooding and the U.S. marshal at Tucson told them the road was impassable. Representative John S. Armstrong of Mesa said they made a wise decision to take the long way around. He crossed the Salt and said he would have drowned except for the swimming ability of his horse.

Good work of the 13th legislature. With all its faults, the 13th Legislative Assembly in 1885 accomplished much. The lawmakers created public institutions that are still a credit to Arizona.

In his message to the legislature, Governor Frederick A. Tritle recommended that a university be built. Most legislators liked the idea of building more institutions. Here was a chance to take home a political plum. In earlier years some towns depended on a nearby fort and military spending to bolster the town's economy. But now that the Apaches were almost quieted, the people needed something else to keep the money rolling in. They dreamed of a branch railroad or a money-spending territorial institution. By 1885 the larger towns were rivals for new sources of revenue. At the time, the two big prizes were considered to be the capital and the insane asylum. A university and a teachers' college were rated as spoils of lesser importance.

The lawmakers traded and made deals. When the politicking was over and the smoke-

Prisoners build a new wall at the territorial prison which was established at Yuma in 1875. Between 1907 and 1910 the convicts were moved to the new prison at Florence.

filled rooms aired, the capital was still at Prescott and the prison at Yuma. Phoenix got the desired insane asylum with an appropriation of $100,000. Tempe was given the normal school for teachers, now Arizona State University, and $5,000 to spend. Tucson wanted the capital but had to settle for the university and a $25,000 grant, one-fourth the amount provided for the insane asylum.

Other spoils were voted to please different sections of the territory. Yuma was promised a new levee along the Colorado River. Florence received a $12,000 bridge over the Gila. The latter project turned out to be a complete waste of money. Flood waters cut a new channel, leaving the bridge "high and dry" in the desert.

Tempe was pleased with the teachers' college. Charles Trumbull Hayden, a prominent Tempe businessman, believed that one of frontier Arizona's greatest needs was for teachers. Politically alert, he helped John S. Armstrong, one of his employees, win election to the territorial house in 1885. Early in the session, Armstrong thought he had a chance to get the insane asylum for Tempe. He took the dusty, two-day stage trip from

Prescott to inform his boss. The elder Hayden sent him back to the capital with instructions to get the normal school. He did.

The law gave Tempe only 60 days to secure a school site of 20 acres. Fortunately, George and Martha Wilson sold their 20-acre cattle pasture for a meager $500. This was a personal sacrifice for the Wilsons, since they were people of modest means. Wilson, however, was employed as caretaker of buildings and grounds at the new college. He held this job for 25 years.

First building of the Tempe Normal School (now Arizona State University).

Old Main, the first building at the University of Arizona, in the late 1890s.

Councilman C. C. Stephens

Tucson got the university. Many Tucson residents were disappointed in not getting the capital. Councilman C. C. Stephens tried to explain his failure to get the capital to one enraged audience. He was greeted with a shower of ripe eggs, rotting vegetables, and, reportedly, a dead cat.

On the other hand, the *Arizona Daily Star* expressed the viewpoint of more enlightened citizens. "It will not only add to the importance of our city," the *Star* said of the university, "but bring hither several hundred students from abroad who would live here at least 10 months of the year."

Today, of course, the University of Arizona pours millions of dollars into the Tucson community.

Tucson in 1892. The University of Arizona is in the distance on the right side.

Railroads were built to Phoenix and Prescott. The creation of a university and other institutions was only part of the good work done by the 13th Legislative Assembly.

Two branch railroads were authorized to connect Prescott and Phoenix to main lines. Maricopa County was authorized to sell $200,000 in bonds to connect Phoenix with the Southern Pacific at Maricopa. Yavapai County was authorized to sell $292,000 in bonds to connect Prescott with the Atlantic and Pacific.

The Maricopa and Phoenix Railroad was completed through the Gila Indian Reservation and Tempe. It reached Phoenix on July 4, 1887. The last spike was driven by Captain William A. Hancock, the "father of Phoenix." For the first time, Phoenix was free from total dependence on animal-drawn stagecoaches and wagons for transportation.

Governor Tritle took the lead in organizing the Prescott and Arizona Central Railroad. He wanted cheaper transportation for the United Verde Copper Company in which he had an interest. It cost too much to haul copper ore in wagons—pulled by 14-mule teams—from rugged country around Jerome to the Atlantic and Pacific main line. The branch line was completed from Prescott Junction (now Seligman) into Prescott on

January 1, 1887. Two antique locomotives —
the "Governor Frederick A. Tritle" and the
"Pueblo"—pulled into town with whistles
blowing. A hundred gun salute was fired at
nearby Fort Whipple. Governor Zulick drove
a golden spike into the last wooden tie. After
speeches and band music, about two hundred
sightseers rode the train to Seven Mile House
and back.

The Arizona Central was short-lived. It
was forced out of business by the Santa Fe,
Prescott, and Phoenix Railroad. The new line
ran through Congress, the site of a rich gold
mine, and Wickenburg. It reached Phoenix on
February 28, 1895.

Passengers on a Santa Fe, Prescott, and Phoenix train.

The "Governor Frederick A. Tritle" engine in Prescott,
1887.

DeForest Porter

5. THE CAPITAL WAS MOVED TO PHOENIX IN 1889

The 15th Legislative Assembly passed a
law to move the capital from Prescott to
Phoenix, effective on February 4, 1889.

On January 29 the legislators boarded a
train for a joyous junket to the new capital.
Scorning the quicker Black Canyon Stage,
they used their free railroad passes and traveled in royal style via Los Angeles. At Maricopa, their two Pullman cars were switched to
the Maricopa and Phoenix Railroad. Phoenix
Mayor DeForest Porter happily picked up the
entertainment tab for the entire trip and presented each official with a shining silk hat.

**The legislature reconvened in Phoe-
nix's brand-new city hall.** John J. Gardiner,
the contractor, worked his crew day and night
for six weeks to finish the second floor before
the "refreshed" lawmakers arrived. The territorial government occupied the Phoenix City
Hall for 12 years.

The 15th legislature chose three commissioners to obtain a site for a capitol building.
The land where the capitol still stands was
donated to the territory. The original structure was built of Arizona stone—gray granite
for the ground floor and a porous, volcanic
stone called tufa for the upper stories. The
capitol was not completed until 1901. It was
first occupied by the 21st Legislative Assembly and Governor Nathan O. Murphy.

**In 1889 Phoenix was a flourishing
trade center.** The population was about

201

The old city hall in Phoenix. This building was the territorial capitol in the 1890s.

Washington Street in Phoenix in 1890.

Arizona Capitol, 1903.

3,000. The city hall was located on Washington Street, the main boulevard. There were trolley cars on the streets and good roads running in every direction. Phoenix was lighted by gas and electricity. It had four banks, two ice plants, and good hotels.

There were three daily newspapers: the *Republican, Gazette,* and *Herald.* The town had three public elementary schools with a total of 450 students. The people were thinking about a high school—but that was six years away. Plans were being started, however, for an Indian school north of town. The Territorial Insane Asylum was a couple of miles east on the road to Tempe.

6. CLAIMS TO SPANISH AND MEXICAN LAND GRANTS HELD BACK THE DEVELOPMENT OF ARIZONA

Little value was placed on the lands in southern Arizona until the Apaches were settled on reservations in the 1870s and 1880s. Then another obstacle to settlement developed. When Anglo-American pioneers began moving into the Santa Cruz, San Pedro, and other valleys, they found the choice sites were in the hands of absentee owners. Speculators, many of them from California, had sought out heirs to Spanish and Mexican land grants. They bought the titles for a song.

The Gadsden Purchase Treaty of 1854. By this treaty the United States agreed to recognize all valid Mexican titles to land grants — providing the titles were properly recorded in the archives* of Mexico or Spain. By the 1850s most of the land grants in Arizona were abandoned. Little value was placed on them by either the original grantees or their Mexican heirs.

No time limit was set in the treaty to confirm or reject the Mexican titles. The investigations of titles in Mexico and Spain, surveys of the grants, and court hearings were not completed until 1904 — fifty years after the Gadsden Purchase was made.

archives: place where public records are kept.

202

Sabino Otero (left) and Charles Poston in 1888. Otero was heir to a Spanish land grant in the Tubac area going back to 1789. Poston gave testimony in several land grant hearings.

Congress created a special Court of Private Land Claims in 1891 to handle claims for land grants. There was one unusual thing about this court. Its decisions had to be based on Spanish and Mexican laws. The court met in Tucson to hear cases involving 17 land grant claims in Arizona. Many of these cases were appealed to the U. S. Supreme Court.

All of the legal work was finally completed in 1904. Titles to 116,540 acres of 837,680 acres claimed in Arizona were confirmed. These totals do not include two 100,000 acre Baca Float grants and the fraudulent 10½ million acre James Addison Reavis claim.

The Baca Float land grants. Two land grants in Arizona—Baca Float No. 3 and Baca Float No. 5—were not occupied in Spanish or Mexican times. In 1860 Congress authorized the heirs of Don Luis María Baca to select five 100,000 acre non-mineral grants in the Territory of New Mexico. The territory at that time included Arizona and part of Colorado.

That is the way Congress solved the problem of two legal claims to a 500,000 acre land grant at Las Vegas, New Mexico. A large group of Mexican settlers held on to the Las Vegas grant. The Baca heirs chose two 100,000 acre tracts in what is now New Mexico. Baca No. 3 was selected in the Santa Cruz Valley north of Nogales. Baca No. 4 is now in southeastern Colorado. Baca No. 5 was located northwest of Prescott.

Baca Float land grants and two fraudulent claims.

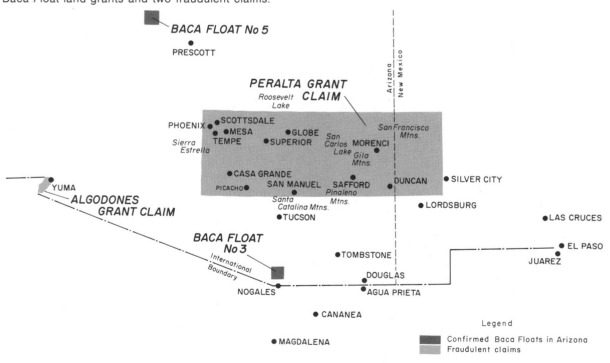

Henry O. Flipper surveyed several land grants. He was the first Black graduate of West Point.

A survey party on the San Rafael de la Zanja. Surveying the old Mexican land grants was no easy task. The grants were often made for indefinite amounts of land.

Baca Float No. 5 is the only land in northern Arizona that can be classified as a Spanish or Mexican land grant.

The Peralta-Reavis land grant fraud. Property rights in the Salt and Gila valleys were threatened in 1883. James Addison Reavis almost pulled off the most gigantic swindle of all time.

What Reavis did was to invent a Spanish aristocrat named Peralta. Forged documents showed that the king of Spain gave Peralta a land grant in 1748 along with the title of Baron of the Colorados. Reavis established connections between himself and the fictitious Peralta family.

First there was a forged deed to the Peralta land grant. Reavis explained how he got this document from George Willing, a mine developer from the East. Willing was actually in and out of Arizona several times after 1864. He supposedly purchased the deed from a descendant of Baron Peralta—a poverty-stricken Mexican named Miguel Peralta. In reality, Miguel never existed except as a name in the forged papers. Willing could not contradict Reavis's "big lie." He died in Prescott the day after he recorded the deed in the Yavapai County courthouse in March 1874.

Baroness of Arizona. Besides Willing, there was another real character in the plot—this one a Cinderella-like creation of Reavis' fertile imagination. To strengthen his phony claim, he found a Mexican orphan girl and had her educated. He eventually married her, giving her the title of Baroness of Arizona.

For a man who forged documents in Spain and Mexico, it was an easy task to change church birth records in California to make his bride the last surviving descendant of the Peralta family. Before this alteration and other false documents were revealed, Reavis and his lady were to make a deep imprint on Arizona history.

Size of the Peralta claim. The barony which they sought was no ordinary land claim. It was a large rectangle of land, stretching from present-day Sun City in the northwest corner to a point south of Silver City, New Mexico, in the southeast. In addition to Phoenix, it included the towns of Tempe, Mesa, Globe, Clifton, Solomonville, Casa Grande, and Florence. The Southern Pacific Railroad crossed the southwest corner. The rich Silver King mine was located within its bounds.

People were frightened, even though the huge claim had not been validated in any court. What was the little man to do when the Southern Pacific Railroad paid Reavis $50,000 for a quitclaim deed? The rich Silver King mine owners gave him $25,000. And the *Arizona Gazette* editor, who was urging people to fight for their rights, was one of the first to buy a deed from Reavis.

Dozens of ordinary people began to pay varying amounts for deeds to their homes, farms, mines, businesses, and even schools.

James Addison Reavis, alias the "Baron of Arizona."

The "Baroness of Arizona."

With his big income, Reavis and his baroness were able to live in courtly style. They had homes in St. Louis; Washington, D.C.; Madrid, Spain; and Chihuahua City, Mexico.

Peralta fraud revealed. Meanwhile, the surveyor general's office carefully investigated the claim. In 1889 Royal A. Johnson released his exposé of the fraudulent Peralta grant. He disclosed several forgeries. The people of Phoenix showed their appreciation by holding a celebration in Johnson's honor.

It was 1895, however, before the Court of Private Land Claims, meeting in Santa Fe, decreed the Reavis claim a fraud. The court declared that he secretly planted forged documents into the archives of Madrid, Seville,

and Guadalajara and into the church records of San Bernardino and San Salvador in California.

Reavis was arrested and charged with conspiracy to defraud the government. He was fined $5,000 and sentenced to two years in prison.

7. ARIZONA ROUGH RIDERS FOUGHT IN THE SPANISH-AMERICAN WAR

When the United States declared war on Spain in 1898, Arizona's young men were eager to volunteer. Governor Myron H. McCord easily raised two companies of cavalry troops. He placed Major Alexander O. Brodie in command. Brodie was a West Point graduate who had served under General Crook in the Apache campaign. He was also a former head of the Arizona National Guard. Captain William O. "Buckey" O'Neill, then the mayor of Prescott, was in charge of Company A. Captain James H. McClintock, a Phoenix newspaperman, commanded Company B.

The flag for the Arizona troops was made by Phoenix women who were members of the Relief Corps of the Grand Army of the Republic. Lacking the proper cord, the ladies decorated the top of the flag with ribbons and sent it to the volunteers at Whipple Barracks. The Arizona banner was the first American flag to fly on Cuban soil. It was carried by the conquering army into Santiago. Today it is displayed in the capitol building in Phoenix—tattered, weather-beaten, and bullet-ridden.

Major Alexander O. Brodie

Governor Myron H. McCord addresses a crowd in Prescott on May 4, 1898. He presented a flag made by Phoenix women to two companies of Arizona Volunteers.

Col. Theodore Roosevelt and Lieut. John C. Greenway.

After the recruits reached San Antonio they became part of the First United States Volunteer Cavalry, better known as the Rough Riders. Though led by a doctor and sponsored by a dude, the Rough Riders gained a measure of fame achieved by few military units. Colonel Leonard Wood, the doctor, served in Arizona during the Apache wars. He admired the type of cowboys, ranchers, and miners who joined the Rough Riders in Arizona. The principle organizer of the unit was glory-hungry Theodore Roosevelt, who resigned as Assistant Secretary of the Navy to serve as a lieutenant colonel.

The Rough Riders completed a short period of training near San Antonio and were then ordered to Tampa, Florida. Fearing that they might be left behind, the Rough Riders rushed aboard a ship which had been assigned to a New York regiment. After waiting for a week in the troop transport, they departed for Cuba singing their war song, "There'll be a Hot Time in the Old Town Tonight."

Horses were left behind because of a lack of ships. So the First Cavalry became known as "Wood's Weary Walkers."

The Arizonans landed near Santiago on June 22 and fought through the thick of the Cuban campaign. Major Brodie, who was wounded at Las Guásimas, was promoted to lieutenant colonel. He served as Colonel Roosevelt's second in command. After the war, when Roosevelt became President, Brodie was appointed governor of the Territory of Arizona.

"Buckey" O'Neill. Captain O'Neill was killed near San Juan Hill in Cuba. Instead of hugging the ground, he carelessly stood up as Spanish soldiers fired from entrenchments on the hill. Just before a sniper shot him, O'Neill supposedly told his sergeant, who had pleaded with him to lie down, "The Spanish bullet isn't molded that will kill me."

Colonel Roosevelt, who later led the famous charge up San Juan Hill, said that O'Neill was a serious loss to the Rough Riders since he was the idol of the Arizona men. Buckey's body was buried on the battlefield where he fell. Later it was moved to Arlington Cemetery outside Washington, D. C.

Buckey O'Neill was one of the most colorful pioneers in Arizona history. Though a lawyer by training, he worked as a typesetter for the Phoenix *Herald* after he came to Arizona in 1879. The next year, O'Neill joined the silver rush to Tombstone. He soon became a reporter for the *Epitaph* at the time Wyatt Earp and his brothers were policing the town.

Later O'Neill worked as a circuit-court reporter and then started his own newspaper, *Hoof and Horn*. This publication was primarily a stockmen's publication. O'Neill offered a $100 reward for the capture of any rustler

Captain William O. "Buckey" O'Neill

"Buckey" O'Neill monument in Prescott.

who stole cattle with a brand advertised in his paper.

After a term as probate judge, O'Neill was elected sheriff of Yavapai County in 1888. In this job he gained fame by tracking down four train robbers and bringing three of them to jail in Prescott. The robbers were Hashknife cowboys. They took $7,000 in cash and valuables from an Atlantic and Pacific train which stopped for water at the Canyon Diablo station between Winslow and Flagstaff. O'Neill and a small posse trailed the outlaws into Utah and captured them after a gun battle.

He was returning the robbers on a train via New Mexico when one of the captives jumped off in a tunnel. The escapee was later arrested in Texas and brought to Prescott for trial. Two weeks before the train robbery in March 1889, the 15th Legislative Assembly in Phoenix established the death penalty for the crime of train robbery at gunpoint. But all four of the outlaws pleaded guilty in return for 25 year sentences at the Yuma prison.

O'Neill was not so helpful to the railroads in his next job as Yavapai County tax assessor. But he did win the hearts of the people. He increased the valuation on Atlantic and Pacific land in the county. There was a lot of this railroad land. The federal government gave the Atlantic and Pacific forty square miles for every mile of railroad built in Arizona.

In 1894 and 1896 "the people's candidate" ran for delegate to Congress on the Populist ticket. He ran third both times, but polled a large vote considering he was a third party candidate.

When the war started, O'Neill was mayor of Prescott and captain of a militia unit. The bronze equestrian O'Neill statue in front of the Yavapai County courthouse is a fitting tribute to the memory of all the Rough Riders.

The Rough Riders were not the only troops raised in Arizona during the Spanish-American War. Governor McCord resigned to serve as colonel in the First Territorial Infantry Regiment. Like Teddy Roosevelt, he had no military experience. But he had political pull with President McKinley. Three companies of Arizona volunteers trained at Fort Hamilton, near Lexington, Kentucky, with units from the other territories. The regiment was not sent overseas but lost more men from typhoid fever than many units left on the battlefield in Cuba.

Arizona also had about fifty infantry soldiers in the Philippine campaign following the Spanish-American war. The Arizonans were in a company commanded by former Rough Riders J. E. Campbell and A. H. Stanton. A future state governor, Rawghlie C. Stanford, was a sergeant.

The town of Pearce before it became a ghost town.

14

LIFE IN TERRITORIAL DAYS

During the early territorial days, Arizona was a frontier—a land of mining camps, army posts, lonely ranches, and scattered villages.

The coming of the railroads in the early 1880s brought many changes. Arizona's isolation from the rest of the country was ended. Travelers were no longer completely dependent on rickety stagecoaches for transportation. Throngs of people in all walks of life began migrating to Arizona to make their homes. More women and more families moved to the territory. Churches began to compete with saloons and gambling halls for the attention of sinners. Eastern styles of clothing, foods, and architecture began to fuse with the Spanish and Mexican heritage.

By the end of the century, many towns had broad clean streets, good water systems, newspapers, rental libraries, gas or electric lights, trolley lines, and excellent schools. Annual festivals and celebrations were becoming traditional as people developed a spirit of community pride. The general store was still the pioneers' main shopping center, but specialty stores were beginning to open.

Medical care improved greatly during territorial days. At first the only doctors and hospitals were on the military posts. Only 22 doctors were listed in the 1870 census, and most of them practiced medicine only part time. Civilian hospitals, beginning in 1880 with St. Mary's in Tucson, were gradually built in larger towns. There were enough MDs in 1892 to form the Arizona Medical Association. This group got the legislature to set higher qualifications for doctors and to pass health laws.

Arizona is one of the few states that can boast of three large ethnic minorities: Indians, Mexican-Americans, and Blacks. It was during the territorial period when black pioneers first came to Arizona in any great number.

KEY CONCEPTS

1. Most of Arizona's towns were founded during the territorial period.
2. People in the territorial towns tried to solve their water, sanitation, and cooling problems.
3. Electricity brought changes in lighting, communication and transportation.
4. Saloons and gambling halls did a thriving business in territorial Arizona.
5. Religious groups helped to civilize the Arizona frontier.
6. People had fun in the frontier towns.
7. Black pioneers helped to build Arizona.

14

1. MOST OF ARIZONA'S TOWNS WERE FOUNDED DURING THE TERRITORIAL PERIOD

New towns were started for a variety of reasons. Some grew and prospered. Others became ghost towns.

Mining towns. Many towns grew up in mining districts—Tombstone, Bisbee, Globe, Clifton, Morenci, Jerome, Wickenburg, and many others.

Other towns were started as farming communities—notably Phoenix, Chandler, Safford, Florence, and most of the Mormon towns. Gila Bend was an agricultural town as well as a stage stop.

Railroad towns. Some towns sprang into existence along transportation routes. Yuma was located where the Colorado River was crossed by Forty-niners, stagecoaches, and the Southern Pacific Railroad. A lot of stations along the Southern Pacific became important towns—Casa Grande, Benson, and Willcox, in particular. After 1880 the location of Gila Bend shifted from the deserted stage station on the Gila to the new railroad depot.

Duncan was a stop on the Arizona and New Mexico Railroad which connected Clifton to Lordsburg on the Southern Pacific. A number of new towns also grew up along the Atlantic and Pacific route. Holbrook, Winslow, Ash Fork, Seligman (first called Prescott Junction), and Kingman are all railroad towns. A combination of the railroad, livestock, and the lumber industry gave Flagstaff and Williams a start.

Some of the railheads became important cowtowns where ranchers corralled their cattle for shipment to Eastern or California markets. Willcox, Holbrook, and Seligman all fit into that category.

Arizona towns have a great variety of names. Some are of Spanish origin: Agua Caliente (hot water), Aguila (eagle), Casa Grande (great house), Concho (shell), Ganado

Main Street in Florence, 1896. First settled 30 years earlier, the town's prosperity depended on farming.

(cattle), Marana (impassable), Nogales (walnuts), Picacho (peak or point), and Sierra Vista (mountain view). Ajo is the Spanish word for garlic, but it also sounds similar to the Papago word for paint. The Papagos used the copper ores as a source of red paint to decorate their bodies.

Names derived from Indian words are common. Tucson comes from "Chuk Shon," the Papago name for Sentinel Peak. It means "black base," referring to the fact that the base of the peak, known as "A" Mountain, is darker than the summit. Tubac is Papago or Pima. The "tu" means "not known" and the "bac is the word for "house" or "ruin." Sonoita is a Papago word meaning "place where the corn will grow."

Moenkopi is Hopi for "place of running water." The "Orai" in the Hopi name Oraibi refers to a particular rock and the "bi" means "the place of." Chinle is Navajo for "at the mouth of the canyon." Many towns as well as most of the counties are named after Arizona Indian tribes. In most cases, however, these names are not what the Indians called themselves.

Many towns were given unusual names: Ash Fork, Buckeye, Flagstaff, Oracle, Show Low, Snowflake (named after its two Mormon founders, Erastus Snow and William J. Flake), and Tombstone. Among the ghost towns with uncommon names were Bumble Bee, Christmas, Chloride, Crown King, Gunsight, and Paradise.

Ghost towns. Besides the territorial towns which have grown and prospered, Arizona has at least 130 ghost towns. Some of these—like Jerome, Oatman, and Paradise—still have life left. Most of them have only a few buildings or mounds of adobe dirt to show where miners or stage station operators once lived and worked.

Congress City in Yavapai County, for example, was the site of a celebrated gold mine. In 1900 the town had a mill, hospital, homes, boardinghouses, Chinese and Mexican restaurants, Catholic and Presbyterian churches, a three-teacher adobe school, saloons, telegraph and telephone connections to the outside world, and its own electric light plant. President William McKinley visited the town of Congress in 1901. He was greeted underground by miners waving U.S. flags. Today only a few buildings, in various stages of ruin, remain.

Pearce in Cochise County had a similar history. A silver and gold discovery in 1894 eventually brought 1,500 people to the town. The mine closed in the 1930s. A once prosperous business district is now reduced to a post office and a combination country store and museum. Other mining towns in Cochise County—Gleeson, Courtland, Paradise, Dos Cabezas, and Charlestown—went through the same cycle of boom and bust.

Ehrenberg had a population of 233 in 1870. Steamboat freight was unloaded there for shipment to Prescott. Ehrenberg quickly became a ghost town after the railroad was built to Yuma in 1877.

2. PEOPLE IN THE TERRITORIAL TOWNS TRIED TO SOLVE THEIR WATER, SANITATION, AND COOLING PROBLEMS

Water for drinking and bathing was often hard to find in the frontier towns of Arizona. In Tucson, for example, alkali usually got into the wells after a few years. Water was hauled from springs by enterprising Mexicans who sold it for five cents a pail. At that price, and with soap selling for 50 cents a bar, bathing was considered a luxury. Travelers sometimes stopped at a barber shop or hotel and paid a dollar for a bath in a tin washtub. It was not until 1879 that the town of Tucson granted a franchise to T. J. Jeffords and Associates to supply water from artesian wells.

Water was piped into Tucson in 1885. It contained vegetative matter, however, and had a disagreeable odor. The *Citizen* expressed the complaints of the town's residents: "The water was a little too thick for navigation, and rather thin for real estate, and totally unfit for use."

Tombstone was ahead of Tucson in supplying drinkable water. In 1882 a waterworks was completed at a cost of a half million dollars. The water came from the high Huachuca Mountains, twenty-one miles away. It was stored in a reservoir cut in solid rock and brought to Tombstone through a seven-inch wrought iron pipe. The new system was designed not only to furnish water for drinking and bathing, but to give enough pressure—160 pounds per square inch—to put out fires. The Tombstone business district had been destroyed twice by fire in 1881 and 1882.

Phoenix got its drinking water from wells during territorial days. The first water company was formed in 1880 by John J. Gardiner, who also owned a flour mill at Second Street and Adams. A rival company, which took over in the 1890s, was given the first franchise issued by the Phoenix city council. This company used riveted steel pipes that leaked. A water line to the state hospital on Van Buren Street had to be abandoned because of the

An early Phoenix water line. A waterboy carries a bucket and tin cup for the workers.

poor pipes. In 1907 the city took over the waterworks. Water was still pumped from wells, even after some Verde River water was brought in through a redwood pipeline beginning in 1922.

Very few towns in territorial Arizona had a pure water supply. Water from shallow wells was usually contaminated by nearby privies which were dug without sealed vaults. This lack of sanitation caused frequent typhoid fever epidemics like the one in 1905. To kill typhoid germs, the Prescott city council that year urged everyone to boil all water obtained from the city's well. After Bisbee had 150 cases of typhoid, a modern sewer system was installed in 1906.

Sanitation problems in the towns. A sewerage disposal system was not the sole solution for every town.

Yuma had several epidemics of typhoid fever after the territorial prison was completed in 1876. Wastes from the prison were discharged into the Gila River, upstream from where Yuma residents got their water supply.

Phoenix was criticized by the Arizona Medical Association in 1895 for dumping its sewage into the Salt River. This practice contaminated the water supply of rural families downstream.

Some Phoenix residents got their water from the town's irrigation ditch, even though good well water was available. Water in the ditch was polluted by livestock, by people who bathed in it at night, and by saloonkeepers who washed their spittoons in it.

Phoenix newspapers often complained about the filth that littered the town's drainage ditches and dusty streets. One paper got sarcastic in the early 1880s. "If you have any broken bottles, old boots, worn gunny sacks... throw them in the streets. They are comfortable to travel over, and besides, give the town a good reputation."

Chinese laundries were singled out by the press as another Phoenix health hazard. The laundrymen ran their dirty wash water over the ground, creating a stench that wafted over the town every night.

Other towns also had to cope with filthy conditions. More than one visitor to Tucson wrote about the dead carcasses of animals, manure piles, and garbage heaps that often served as landmarks for giving directions.

Filth in the towns attracted vermin of every description. In Prescott, the *Weekly Miner* reported in 1875 that a hundred rats were killed under a restaurant building that was razed.

The territorial legislature became concerned with sanitary matters. In 1877 a law was passed to prohibit hogs from running loose within any town or village. Another law in 1889 made every constable a sanitary inspector. He was given the power to force property owners to either remove filth or garbage at least one mile from the city limits or pay a fine.

Beating the heat. Sanitation is a problem that most growing communities anywhere must face. Coping with extreme heat was a more unusual Arizona problem.

In the desert country, both the Mexicans and Anglos built houses with thick adobe walls. When lumber was available, a wide porch was built to shade the walls. During the hot summer days water was sprinkled on the dirt floor. The doors were closed to trap the cool air inside. By evening, however, the sun-heated adobe houses were hot.

Nearly everyone slept outdoors in a cot or hammock. As people became more prosperous, they added screened sleeping rooms to their desert homes. Most hotels provided a sleeping porch for their guests. The fancy Hotel Adams, built in Phoenix by J. C. Adams in the late 1890s, had a sleeping roof. The men slept on one side and the women on the other. A solid 12-foot board fence separated the two sections.

In territorial days, most Yuma homes were built of adobe and had a shaded porch.

A typical home in Yuma.

Outside sleeping area at a home in Florence in the 1890s.

Adams supposedly developed the first air conditioning system in Arizona. It consisted of seven or eight large pans spaced around the lobby. Each pan contained a huge block of ice with an electric fan blowing over it. Air conditioning as we know it today did not come into general use until the 1930s.

Ice-making companies began operating in Tucson and Phoenix in 1879. At 10 cents a pound, however, the ice was too expensive for many people to enjoy. Most small towns, of course, were beyond the reach of the ice wagons.

Most families used an outdoor "desert refrigerator" to preserve perishable foods. It was a homemade device that operated on the same principle as a modern evaporative water cooler. A wooden frame was built and covered with burlap on all sides. The burlap was kept damp by water dripping from a container on top. Obliging breezes furnished the "fan." It was surprising how well this desert refrigerator kept milk, butter, and meat from spoiling in hot weather.

A desert refrigerator.

A Tucson family wearing the normal Anglo clothing of the period.

Clothing. The Mexican people adapted to the hot climate better than most Anglos from the East. In their homes the Mexican women wore short-sleeved muslin or calico gowns. By contrast, fashion-conscious American housewives sweltered in long-sleeved dresses with high ruffled collars.

For men, wool "California pants" without cuffs were popular. Wool was a preferred material because it absorbed the perspiration. For dress, the men bought dark wool suits with a matching vest. They wore either boots or shoes with leather spats. Hats came in all sizes and shapes. The wide-brimmed sombrero was most popular with the Mexicans. Many of the Mexican men wore sandals and clothes made from lightweight materials to beat the heat.

Many Arizonans who could afford it, left for the summer. Businessmen annually put their wives and children on the stagecoach or train and sent them to the seashore or mountains. Some farmers in the Salt River Valley would load their wagons and go camping in the high country after harvesting their grain crops. Those who stayed to sweat it out tried nearly everything to stay cool. Children went swimming in the canals or the river.

3. ELECTRICITY BROUGHT CHANGES IN LIGHTING, COMMUNICATION, AND TOWN TRANSPORTATION

In the early days, candles or rags dipped in a saucer of grease furnished light for homes and stores. Kerosene (coal oil) lamps were used during most of the territorial period. These lamps were smoky and sometimes dangerous. Six exploded in one week in Phoenix. One started a fire at the Bijou Theater when a spectator accidentally knocked it off the chandelier.

Gas lighting for streets and stores was an improvement. In 1886 a gas plant was built in Phoenix by Hutchlon Ohnick, whose Japanese name was Hachiro Onuki. He came to the United States to visit the Centennial Exhibition in Philadelphia in 1876. He stayed to take part in the Nevada gold rush and the Tombstone silver strike. Ohnick and two partners raised $50,000 capital and started the Phoenix Illuminating Gas and Electric Company. Gas was manufactured from crude petroleum. Ohnick installed the gas pipes and fixtures in time to illuminate the stores of Phoenix during the 1886 Christmas season. His biggest customer was the Capital Saloon which installed new bronze chandeliers and fancy lamps.

Electric lighting. In 1889 Ohnick was employed by the Phoenix Electric Company. This company had a 25-year franchise from the City of Phoenix to operate an electric plant and distribution system. Little did Ohnick know that someday this company—now known as Arizona Public Service—would be serving half a million gas and electric customers in 11 of the state's 14 counties.

Electricity generated. From the beginning, steam engines were used to generate electricity. Water power was also used extensively after the first large hydroelectric plant in the nation began operating at Niagara Falls in 1895.

The Childs plant, on the Verde River about 70 miles north of Phoenix, was one of the first hydroelectric plants in Arizona. Lew Turner, a Yavapai County cattleman, formed the Arizona Power Company and began producing power at Childs in 1910. The company's Irving plant on Fossil Creek began operating in 1915. The water for both plants came from Fossil Springs which gushed out 20,000 gallons of water per minute.

Turner sold electricity to Prescott, Mayer, mining camps in the area, and the Verde smelter and mine at Jerome. Transmission lines were also run to the Salt River Valley. In the 1920s a Phoenix population of more than 40,000 got 70 percent of its electricity from the Childs and Irving stations. Arizona Public Service got the plants by merger in 1952 and still uses the facilities to generate electricity for the Strawberry-Pine-Payson area.

Telephones. The telephone was invented by Alexander Graham Bell in 1876. Five years later the first commercial switchboard in Arizona was installed in Tucson. The small exchange was located in the stage station and post office building on Congress Street. Postmaster Charles H. Lord was president of the

Lee Quin's store in downtown Tucson had both an electric and a kerosene lamp.

Electric plant under construction in Phoenix in 1902. The plant was located at 2nd Avenue and Buchanan.

Arizona Telephone Company. In 1888 the telephone exchange was moved to the second floor of the City Hall—a frame building resembling a Dutch windmill. It was called Bell Tower because Tucson's fire bell was located on the third floor. Charlie Hoff, the new manager of the exchange, had the job of ringing the bell when a fire was reported.

In Phoenix, the first two telephones were connected in 1882 by S. D. Lount between his home and his ice factory. Only private phones of this type existed in Phoenix until a switchboard exchange was installed in 1891 by Sunset Telephone and Telegraph Company. Like other towns in the territory, Phoenix never had one unified phone system.

As late as 1912 Phoenix residents had to buy phones from both the Consolidated and Overland companies if they wanted to talk to all phone subscribers in town. Each company had its own telephone book. Consolidated leased facilities from the Sunset company for a short time. In 1908 Consolidated established the first long distance service between Phoenix and Tucson. The Overland Company installed an automatic dial system in Phoenix in 1910—the first in Arizona and one of the first in the nation.

Many of the telephone companies were of the home-grown variety. The Prescott Elec-

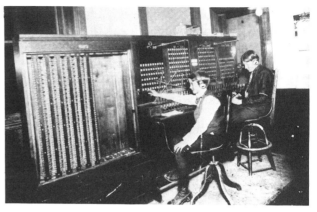

Prescott Electric Company switchboard in 1900. Operators dreaded rainstorms. Lightning that hit open wires around town would crack their eardrums.

tric Company owned by Frank Wright was a good example. The company sold electricity and operated a telephone exchange for a small number of subscribers. Wright did some unusual things, at least by modern standards. On one occasion he hired a two-man orchestra to play music for an hour to some 50 telephone customers. This might be called one of the first commercial broadcasts in America. Wright's company also installed a free phone on a tree in the town plaza.

Prescott, like Phoenix, was well-equipped with "hello" lines. The Sunset company had most of the business. Both the Sunset and Wright's company played an important role in alerting volunteer fire fighting hose teams. Together they helped save the town on July 4, 1900, when a great fire raced up Whiskey Row on Montezuma Street.

Mountain States Telephone and Telegraph Company finally succeeded in consolidating all the independent telephone companies in Arizona. A Colorado-chartered company, Mountain States started its Arizona operations at Bisbee-Douglas. The company expanded to give Arizona one uniform telephone system. Reliable Bell System equipment was installed in nearly every town and village. The Arizona phone system was connected with Bell's national and international long distance network.

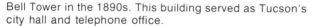

Bell Tower in the 1890s. This building served as Tucson's city hall and telephone office.

A Phoenix telephone installer in the early 1900s. He carried phones over his shoulders and tools around his waist.

All of these changes took a few years, but the Arizona mergers were completed in June, 1912—just four months after Arizona became a state. At that time there were 6,051 telephones in Arizona. On the centennial of the telephone in 1976, the company had 1.4 million phones in operation in the state.

Streetcar lines. At least five territorial towns in Arizona had electric trolleys — Douglas, Bisbee-Warren, Prescott, Phoenix, and Tucson. Some of the lines started out as mule or horse-drawn streetcars.

Phoenix's first horse cars began operating in 1887 on Grand Avenue. The cars had open sides. Two long seats, back to back, ran the full length of the car. Mules later pulled cars along another track on Washington Street. In 1893 the first electric street railway was launched. Electric trolleys then carried passengers between downtown Phoenix and Eastlake Park on 16th Street. Service was later extended to the capitol, Brill Street, the Indian School, and Glendale.

In June, 1913, the streetcar drivers in Phoenix went on strike for higher wages. Policemen rode the cars, which were operated by substitute drivers, to prevent trouble.

More than once, however, they were plastered with rotten eggs and lemons by strike sympathizers.

The Tucson Street Railway began operating horse and mule cars between the Southern Pacific depot and the University of Arizona campus in 1898. The line was later extended south to 17th Street. Pranksters at the University sometimes removed the lightweight cars from the track at night and parked them on the campus.

In 1905 the company decided to electrify. It became the Tucson Rapid Transit Company. The whole town turned out to celebrate on June 1, 1906, when the first electric car made its maiden trip. It was called "Izzer" because of the sound it made. The new line had a few problems at first, including an occasional power failure. More than once the cars slid off the end of the tracks when students greased the rails. The Tucson streetcars served the Tucson public until 1930.

Prescott had electric streetcars along Gurley Street to Fort Whipple between 1905 and 1915. Called the Prescott and Mount Union Railway, the line was patronized mainly by soldiers at the fort and school children. After the Prescott railway went out of business, one of the cars was sold to the Tucson Rapid Transit. Later the same car

A "strike" on the Tucson Street Railway line.

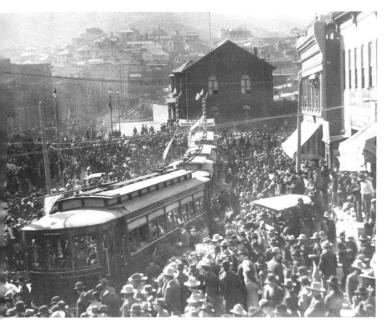

Bisbee residents celebrated the opening of the Warren-Bisbee Street Railway in 1908.

Charley Loeb's Saloon in Tucson.

Gamblers playing faro in Morenci, 1895.

saw service in Bisbee. Some of the old rails were used to construct the bank vaults of the Bank of Arizona in Prescott.

4. SALOONS AND GAMBLING HALLS DID A THRIVING BUSINESS IN TERRITORIAL ARIZONA

In territorial days nearly every town had at least one saloon, if not a whole row of them. The saloon was the frontier social center for many cowboys, miners, businessmen, politicians, and professional men.

It was claimed that Tombstone in its heyday had more than 160 saloons and liquor stores to serve a population of only 6,000. Prescott's Montezuma Street was called "Whiskey Row" because saloons outnumbered other businesses. Phoenix had its First Street, one section of which was paved with empty beer bottles planted neck down in the ground. Most of the settlements in the territory were "wide open," though some town councils tried to regulate saloons. In Jerome, for example, the number of saloons was

limited after a fire destroyed the town in 1898.

In the 1890s more than 600 saloons and seven wholesale whiskey dealers operated in the territory. Whiskey was imported from the states, though beer was made in local breweries. The largest was the red-brick Arcade Brewery in Phoenix. Brewery Gulch in Bisbee got its name from the adobe brewery once operated by Al Sieber, the famous Indian scout.

Some of the earliest saloons were no more than a tent with a rough board for a bar. There were also fancy places such as the

Crystal Palace in Tombstone, the Fashion in Jerome, the Stope in Prescott, the Gold Coin in Globe, the Blue Goose in Clifton, and many others. These saloons often had velvet drapes, expensive glassware, and a polished wood bar with heavy brass rails. Occasionally there was a mirror large enough for a man to see his image from hat and moustache to boots.

The Congress Hall Saloon in Tucson even had a large mineral collection. Legislators congregated at the Congress Hall when the capital was in Tucson. Many social functions were held there — including a festive ball honoring territorial Governor McCormick.

The Congress Hall, like many saloons in the territory, operated a gambling casino for its patrons. Keno, a game resembling bingo, was a favorite. Craps was a popular quick-action game that required only a pair of dice and a simple knowledge of such terms as "snake eyes," "Little Joe," and "big train." Tables were provided for card games: poker, faro, and an Aztec game called "monte" that was played with a 40-card deck. Chusu, another Aztec invention, required a table with a hollow center around which eight balls rotated. Gamblers bet on where the balls would land.

There was some honest gambling. But most of the saloon owners made the games of chance as crooked as they could and still attract customers. Roulette wheels were rigged so the operator could stop the marble where he wanted it. Loaded dice were used. Card sharks often marked or trimmed the corners of important cards. The losers were the cowboys, soldiers, and wagon freighters who came in with their wages or the prospectors who brought their gold dust.

Opposition to saloons developed as the territory grew and received the civilizing influences of churches and schools. In 1907 the territorial legislature made gambling illegal in Arizona. In 1914 the people voted to close the saloons.

5. RELIGIOUS GROUPS HELPED TO CIVILIZE THE ARIZONA FRONTIER

The Catholic faith was the only non-Indian religion in Arizona in Spanish and Mexican times. The Catholic Church continued to have many believers, including most Mexican-Americans, after the United States took over Arizona.

In 1868 Father Jean Baptiste Salpointe was appointed Vicar Apostolic (missionary bishop) in Arizona. He recruited priests in France and trained them in Tucson for assignment to parishes in the territory. Salpointe also built the famous San Augustín Cathedral in Tucson. In 1870 he brought in nuns from St. Louis to establish St. Joseph's Academy for girls. Ten years later the sisters also opened Tucson's St. Mary's Hospital, the first general hospital in the territory.

Papago Indian children, shown in front of San Xavier mission, were taught by Catholic nuns.

Bishop Salpointe

219

Protestants. Before railroads were built across Arizona in the early 1880s, Protestant missionary boards in the East had difficulty finding ministers to serve in isolated Arizona. A handful of churches in the 1870s competed with several hundred saloons for the attention of sinners. By the mid-1880s, however, there were at least 25 Protestant churches in Arizona.

The Methodists were first on the scene with traveling preachers. Beginning with Reverend J. L. Dyer in 1868, they spoke wherever people would assemble to worship. The first Protestant congregation in the territory was the Prescott Methodist Episcopal Church South, organized in 1871.

The *Presbyterians* were the most active Protestant group in working among the Indians. In 1870 Charles Cook started the Sacaton Indian agency and opened a school for the Pimas. Cook later founded the Tucson Indian Training School which operated for seventy-five years before it was closed in 1960.

The First Presbyterian Church of Phoenix was organized in this "tabernacle" in June, 1879. The framework of the church was built of cottonwood, the roof of willow, and the walls of ocotillo cactus stems. Reverend William Meyer (left) directed the construction work.

Presbyterian Indian School for Pimas.

The *Baptists* got off to a good start in 1875 when J. C. Bristow, a fire-and-brimstone evangelist, began preaching in the Prescott area. Bristow preached his first Arizona sermon under a cottonwood tree at Camp Verde. In 1880 the Reverend R. A. Windes of Chicago organized the Lone Star Baptist Church of Prescott. His small congregation had only one Bible and one hymn book. However, as Windes said, "They sang with enthusiasm and volume, but not much tune."

Another colorful frontier Baptist preacher was the Reverend Uriah Gregory, founder of the first Baptist church in Tucson. A bearded and distinguished looking man, he worked side by side with Mexican bricklayers in building the church.

The *Episcopalians* also sent out some effective missionary priests. Young two-fisted Endicott Peabody was the most famous, though he was not in Arizona very long. He was still in seminary school near Boston when invited by a Tombstone resident from Massachusetts to preach in the rip-roaring boom town. Arriving in Tombstone on a stagecoach early in 1882, the muscular 200-pound Peabody had to conduct services in the district courtroom for a short time. But St. Paul's Episcopal Church—the oldest Protestant church in Arizona still in use—was completed in July, 1882. Peabody returned to Massachusetts. He founded Groton Academy which Franklin D. Roosevelt attended as a boy. In

Interior of St. Paul's Episcopal Church in Tombstone.

220

1937 Peabody gave the benediction at President Roosevelt's second inaugural.

The Protestant churches often worked together on civic projects. In Tombstone they joined with the fraternal organizations — Masonic Lodge, Odd Fellows, and Grand Army of the Republic—to start a new cemetery. Some did not want their loved ones buried at Boot Hill. This plot was fast filling up with deceased gamblers, outlaws, and other seamy characters.

Judaism. Considering their small numbers, the Jewish settlers made a strong impact on the economic and cultural growth of the Arizona Territory. At least four Jewish pioneers—Herman Ehrenberg, Isador Solomon, Joe Mayer, and Jacob Isaacson — gave their names to towns.

David Abraham built wagon roads and was one of the first to discover copper in Arizona. Dr. Herman Bendell served as Superintendent of Indian Affairs for the territory during President Grant's administration. Selim Franklin, as a member of the territorial legislature, led the fight for the bill that created the University of Arizona. Most of the Jewish pioneers were merchants.

There were fewer than 50 people of Hebrew faith scattered over Arizona during the 1870s. Since there were no rabbis, the men held informal Sabbath services in private homes. In Tucson, Samuel Drachman, a Russian Jew, led the prayers and songs during the High Holy Days. He also presided over Hebrew weddings. Morris Goldwater performed the same duties in Prescott.

The first two Hebrew congregations to organize in Arizona were Temple Emmanu-El at Tucson and Temple Beth Israel at Phoenix.

Latter-day Saints. Brigham Young, the Mormon leader, planned an empire in the West for his people where they would be free from persecution. In 1849 Mormon pioneers in Utah organized the State of Deseret. This vast region extended from Idaho to the Gila River in Arizona. Congress was asked to admit the State of Deseret into the Union. The Mormon proposal was turned down. But Brigham Young went ahead and sent colonies of Mormons from Utah throughout the West.

Dozens of Mormon settlements were established in Arizona after 1876. Religion was the most important thing in the lives of the colonists. The bishop was not only the highest religious authority in a settlement, called a ward, he also supervised the farms and social activities. Wards were combined into "Stakes of Zion," each under a president.

The Mormons lived, worked, and prayed together. They were the closest-knit religious group in Arizona.

Fourteen Army chaplains served in Arizona during territorial days. They were stationed at military posts but also visited troops who did not have a chaplain. Some of the chaplains also mingled with civilians in towns near the forts. In fact, Alexander Gilmore at Fort Whipple was known in Prescott as the "marrying parson" after his arrival in 1870. He was a Methodist.

The most famous Army chaplain was Winfield Scott, a Baptist, who was assigned to Fort Huachuca in 1882. After his army service, he was the first chairman of the Scottsdale board of education. Scott was also a member of the House from Maricopa County in the 20th Legislative Assembly in 1889. Two towns are named after him — Scottsdale, Arizona, and Winfield, Kansas.

I.E. Solomon's store in Solomonville.

Winfield Scott

221

The Jerome hose cart team of 1899. The young man out front is Thomas E. Campbell. He was the fire chief, hose team captain, and a future governor of Arizona.

4th of July celebrants in Tucson.

6. PEOPLE HAD FUN IN THE FRONTIER TOWNS

Life in frontier Arizona was not all work and no play. Holidays and festivals were always fun times—especially the Fourth of July. Most towns planned events for everybody on these occasions.

Fourth of July celebrations. The program usually included contests for the young: foot races, sack races, burro races, and the always popular scramble for the greased pig. Tugs of war, bronco riding, and trap shooting contests were sometimes scheduled.

A special event in most northern Arizona towns was the hose race. Each team in the hose race pulled a two-wheeled cart with a reel of hose to a fire hydrant, hooked up the hose, and turned on the water. The team with the fastest time won. The rivalry between

teams from Jerome and Prescott was especially keen in the early 1900s. Both towns had been destroyed by fire and realized the importance of speed in putting out a fire.

The hard rock drilling contest was an important event in mining towns. One man would hold a steel drill while his partner wielded a sledge hammer to drive it into a block of stone. There was danger involved. Once in awhile the hammer man would miss the center of the drill and smash the hand of the holder. Mining companies made the risk worthwhile by offering big prizes. The winners of an $800 prize in Bisbee in the early 1900s drilled a record hole of forty-six and three-fourths inches.

The hilly town of Bisbee also had the distinction of introducing coaster racing—better known as the soap box derby today—to the United States. In 1911 the boys of Bisbee between the ages of 10 and 14, borrowed wheelbarrow wheels from mining companies to make their coasters. On the Fourth of July the boys started a minute apart down a three-mile dirt road that had 17 dangerous curves. The three boys with the fastest times received cash prizes. Coaster racing became an annual tradition in Bisbee.

Most towns had parades on the Fourth of July. In 1879 Tucson residents saw a parade that was half a mile long. It was led by Pinckney R. Tully, a well-known merchant, and a snappy brass band. Then came school children with banners saying "Our Free Schools—the Century's Honor." They were followed by horse-drawn carriages decorated in red, white, and blue. The most applause was reserved for a float carrying lovely ladies representing the States of the Union and the Territory of Arizona.

During the afternoon a baseball game between Congress Street and Main Street dwellers was played at Military Plaza. In the evening the military band from Fort Lowell played a concert of patriotic music at Levin's Park. A speaker read the Declaration of Independence.

222

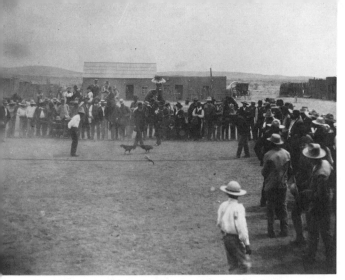

Cockfights were a popular pastime in Tombstone.

San Juan's Day. Two of the favorite Mexican holidays were Cinco de Mayo and the Fiesta de San Juan. The 1883 San Juan's festival in Phoenix was typical. Some 1,500 people bought huge glasses of lemonade at the booths, gambled, or danced to the music of a six-piece band. Most of the spectators at the bull fight jeered. Some of the bulls were ferocious, but their horns were sawed off.

In the afternoon the Mexicans celebrated the *corriendo de gallo.* A rooster was buried in the ground, except for the head. The object of the contest was for a horseback rider to pull the rooster from the ground as he sped by on a running horse. Many grabs were made before one rider pulled the bird out. All the other participants then rushed at the winner and tugged at the rooster until it was dismembered.

Sports. *Baseball* was not as well organized in territorial days as it is today. There were a few semi-pro leagues. Athletic clubs fielded teams in some towns. But most games were of the pick-up variety. In Jerome the young miners and merchants would pile on wagons and ride downhill to a flat spot near the Verde River. There a diamond was marked off. Mine companies, however, soon realized the importance of providing entertainment for their employees and began to promote organized baseball. After statehood, both Jerome and nearby Clarkdale won the state baseball championship.

Tombstone baseball team, 1887.

Football became a sport in high schools and colleges in the 1890s. The Phoenix Union High School team was organized in 1898 and played four games—two with Phoenix Indian School and two with Tempe Normal Teachers' College (now ASU). The Phoenix Union team won three and tied one. The last game with the Indian School ended in a 5 to 5 tie. A touchdown counted five points then.

The players wore canvas suits. At first they had no headgear and no protective pads. Special handgrips were attached to the trousers of linemen. Backfield men could grab these grips and be pulled for extra yardage. There was no coach, and practice consisted mainly of running long distances to get in shape.

There was lots of gouging, slugging, kicking, and biting in the pileups. The game was divided into two 30-minute halves with no time-outs. A player could not re-enter the game once he left. Teams were penalized for forward passing over the line of scrimmage. A play was not dead until the runner could no longer move, or until he said "down."

The Phoenix Indians used a play known as the "revolving wedge." All the players stood up around the center. As they moved down field they whirled in a compact mass like a cyclone.

The football game between Phoenix Union and the Indian School always drew a good crowd.

The theater was a popular form of entertainment in the towns. Tucson Mexicans enjoyed night plays performed outdoors in the park. A favorite in the 1870s was *Elena y Jorge*. The beautiful Elena had a wicked uncle who wanted to sell her for gold. But the plot ends happily when her true lover, the handsome Jorge, wins her hand.

Traveling troupes came to the fancy saloons and theaters to perform. By the 1880s Tombstone had several theaters. Some had large auditoriums with theater boxes, chandeliers, curtains, and footlights. Schieffelin Hall—named after the man who discovered silver at Tombstone—was the largest and best-known theater between El Paso and San Francisco. With a seating capacity of 700, it was the largest adobe building in the United States. Plays, operas, musicals, and lectures were booked at the Schieffelin Hall.

Many miners and cowboys preferred the famous Bird Cage Theater in Tombstone which opened in 1881. The entertainment was not highbrow. Girl dancers, comedians, and variety shows were well-received. The ever popular stage play, *Uncle Tom's Cabin,* was performed at the Bird Cage in 1882. A drunken cowboy got too involved and shot the bloodhound that was pursuing Eliza, a runaway black slave, as she crossed the icy Ohio River.

Most of the towns had local entertainers—glee clubs, brass bands, and amateur actors. John P. Clum, the former Indian agent, performed in several plays in Tombstone.

The Bird Cage Theater (theatre) stands today as one of Tombstone's most authentic tourist attractions.

The first moving pictures came to Arizona towns in the 1890s. They were shown wherever a paying crowd could be gathered. Charles M. Clark, a Jerome telegrapher, bought an interest in the first projector from a traveling man who gambled away all his money. Clark took the projector and films to Ash Fork, Kingman, and all the towns in northern Arizona. A favorite film was the Corbett-Courtney prize fight. To make the show longer, Clark sometimes ran several rounds of the film on the reverse side. At Fort Apache one soldier said, "Gee, look at Corbett work his right hand." Actually it was Corbett's left hand pounding away.

Mexican musicians in Tucson.

7. BLACK PIONEERS HELPED TO BUILD ARIZONA

Black pioneers, cowboys, and soldiers played a big part in developing the West. The idea persists, however, that only white men and Indians were on the frontier. Western movies, television shows, and novels have kept this myth going.

The first big westward migration of Blacks to the West came from the southern states after the Civil War. Black cowboys tended huge herds of longhorns on ranches in Texas. Other Blacks settled in the plains states or in the Indian Territory (Oklahoma) where some married Indian women. Eventually, the more venturesome ones drifted westward into Arizona.

Black migration came slowly. There were only 21 Blacks in Arizona in 1860 and 26 in 1870. The census reports showed that the Black population gradually increased during territorial days: 155 (1880); 1,357 (1890); 1,848 (1900); and 2,009 (1910).

Not long out of slavery, the first Blacks worked at jobs they had learned in the South: cooks, barbers, laborers, drivers, maids, table waiters, and porters. Before long, however, they were on the scene as cowpunchers, cavalrymen, merchants, gold prospectors, stagecoach drivers, and musicians.

Charley Embers was typical of some of the early Blacks. He came from California in the 1860s. Before moving to Tucson, Embers cooked for a mining camp at Ajo. He then took a job unloading freight at the Maricopa Wells stage station. Like many pioneers, both Black and Anglo, Embers married a Sonoran girl of Mexican descent.

Ben McClendon was one of the first Black prospectors. A runaway slave, he came to Yuma in 1862. The next year McClendon joined the Abraham Peeples party and was in on the rich gold discoveries in the Prescott area. In 1864 Ben discovered a gold mine but never revealed its location. He would hang around Wickenburg until his money was spent and then disappear in the hills. A few days later, the town residents would see him returning with his burro loaded with ore. The rocks were smashed and the gold washed out. Then the cycle of spend-and-more-mining was repeated. On one trip Ben never returned. His body was found near his dead burro about four miles from Wickenburg. To this day no one has located the "Nigger Ben Mine," as it was called.

William Neal was one of the most well-to-do Blacks in territorial days. Born in the Oklahoma Indian Territory of a Black father and a Cherokee mother, he also had an Indian name, "Bear Sitting Down." But in a long life of hard work, he seldom sat down except on a horse or wagon. Before coming to Arizona in 1878, "Curley Bill" Neal traveled with William "Buffalo Bill" Cody when the latter was a U.S. Army scout. Through the years Buffalo Bill visited his friend many times in Arizona.

Neal got his start in Tucson as a hotel cook. He soon became a transportation magnate. Acquiring property along Pennington Street in downtown Tucson, he hauled freight and passengers. With wagons and mules purchased in Kansas City, Neal supplied fuel wood to the copper smelters. He transported ore from the mines at Mammoth. For a time Neal also carried the mail between Tucson and Oracle.

In 1895 Curley Bill and his young wife, Ann, opened the Mountain View Hotel in Oracle. Arizonans went there in the summer time to enjoy the cool, crisp air of the Santa Catalina Mountains. Eastern visitors came in the winter. They took Neal's stage line from Tucson to Oracle. Mrs. Neal was a gracious hostess and kept the hotel patrons occupied with picnics, parties, horseback riding, and other activities. Curley Bill died in 1936, but his wife continued to operate the Mountain View until her death in 1950.

Mountain View Hotel.

A CHARMING RESORT.

The New Mountain View Hotel at Oracle Open Next Month.

MR. AND MRS. WILLIAM NEAL, PROPRIETORS.

Tucson's Favorite Mountain Resort and Health Sanitarium— Unexcelled for Summer and Winter Residences.

One of the most laudable undertakings and one that should be fully appreciated by the people of this city and county, is the erection and luxurious furnishing of the Mountain View Hotel, at Oracle, by Mr. Wm. Neal.

It is an enterprise that was born of necessity, and cannot fail to be both profitable and advantageous. Oracle has long been noted for its natural beauty and magnificent location, and all that has heretofore been needed was the handiwork of man in the way of suitable accommodations for the comfort of those who sought its shady nooks in summer time. This has at last been cold water service. Bath rooms have also been provided. Every room on the lower floor is also furnished with excellent fire places, and those on the upper have been provided with stoves.

In the parlor a first-class piano and other musical instruments will be placed for the enjoyment of the guests, and the furniture of all the rooms will be of squared oak, solid, substantial and artistic. Instead of ordinary carpets, art squares will be laid on the floors of all the rooms, this being preferred because of their easily permitting the cleaning of the floors every day, if necessary.

The interior finish of the building is

Oracle is situated at an altitude of 5000 feet above the level of the sea, and is a health resort with climatic conditions unsurpassed, being especially beneficial to those who are afflicted with pulmonary troubles. The summer days are bright and comfortable for a period of seven months in the year, and the winters are mild and pleasant, but little snow falling.

Mr. and Mrs. Neal have been residents of Tucson for the past seventeen years, where for all that time Mr. Neal has been a prominent figure in business circles. He is one of the foremost and most progressive citizens we have, true as steel, and a man whose word is as good as his bond. It is fortunate, indeed, that this charming resort at Oracle will be conducted by such enterprising people, and it is safe to state that no more enjoyable, comfortable and excellent hotel will be found anywhere than will be the Mountain View Hotel.

Mrs. Neal is a charming lady, and she will assume the sole management of the resort, and it will be opened to the public on February 1st. The structure was begun in June, 1894, and will be fully equipped by the beginning of next month. Mrs. Neal will conduct the place in a first-class manner and on the best of principles. It cannot but be a most successful enterprise, because it is something that has long been wanted, and not only the people of this county, but visitors from elsewhere will patronize it. It is a delightful place, and will repay an extended visit or permanent residence in every way.

For particulars concerning rates, and all further information concerning the hotel, write to Mrs. William Neal, P. O. Box 95, Tucson, or call at the Opera Corral Stables, Tucson, Arizona.

This article on the Neal resort in Oracle was in the *Arizona Daily Citizen* (Tucson), January 1, 1895. Inset: Mrs. William Neal.

Black cowboys. William Neal ran thousands of cattle on the 3-N Ranch at Oracle. Most Black cattlemen in territorial Arizona, however, worked as cowboys.

John Swain was one of the Black cowboys who punched cattle for John Slaughter on the San Bernardino Ranch in southeastern Arizona. Known as "Sweeney" and "Little John," he was born a slave on the Slaughter ranch near San Antonio, Texas. Given his freedom after the Civil War, he chose to remain with Slaughter. Swain helped drive huge herds of longhorns from Texas. He tracked and shot rustlers. One of his jobs was to protect his boss on trips into Mexico to recover stolen cattle.

In later years "Sweeney" lived in a shack on the outskirts of Tombstone. His time was occupied with a vegetable garden. Swain's ambition was to live long enough to ride a bronco on his 100th birthday. If it pitched him into the next world, he said, that would be all right. Swain missed his 100th by only a few months. He died in 1945 and is buried in the Boothill cemetery.

Some of the Black cowboys went by only a first name. Jim was another cowpuncher who came from Texas with John Slaughter. A giant of a man, he once fought John L. Sullivan, the famous heavyweight boxing champion. In 1884 Sullivan was in Tombstone and offered $500 to any man who would face him for two rounds. Jim volunteered, and a match was set on the stage of Schiefflin Hall.

Sullivan looked like a runt in the ring with Jim. But he was a master of boxing science. The spectators, mostly miners, cheered when Jim took a roundhouse swing that caught Sullivan on the head and staggered him. The great John L. then went to work and quickly knocked out his strong but unskilled opponent. Oldtimers around Tombstone talked about the fight for years.

Sweeney and Jim were real live cowboys. There were dozens like them who played an important part in the history of the Arizona cattle industry.

John ''Sweeney'' Swain. Born a slave in Texas, Swain came to Arizona in 1879. He was a top cowhand on John Slaughter's ranch in Cochise County.

Nat Love, a Black cowboy in Arizona during the 1870's, was born a slave in Tennessee. He gave up cowpunching to become a Pullman porter.

''Arizona Joe'' was the hero of a fictional story in an 1887 western magazine. There were many hard working Black cowboys on the frontier. It is unfortunate that most modern western movies and TV shows have excluded them.

Buffalo soldiers. After the Civil War, the U.S. Army was reorganized to include Black units. Two of the 10 cavalry regiments—the 9th and 10th — and two of 45 infantry regiments—the 24th and 25th—were all Black with white officers. The Black troops were assigned to the western frontier. They were called "buffalo soldiers" by the Indians because of their short, curly hair.

In 1885, when Geronimo's Chiricahuas were on the loose, the 10th Cavalry was transferred from Texas to the Department of Arizona. Twelve companies — 696 enlisted men with 38 white officers—followed the Southern Pacific railroad tracks into Arizona. At Bowie Station the regiment split up. Colonel Benjamin Grierson established headquarters at Whipple Barracks. Companies were stationed at Fort Grant, Thomas, Apache, and Verde.

The buffalo soldiers joined other cavalry units in searching the mountains of southeastern Arizona for Geronimo. Many were assigned by General Crook to guard waterholes along the border. Others chased the Chiricahuas in Mexico. After Geronimo surrendered to General Miles, the 10th Cavalry got the unwelcomed job of rounding up more than 400 peaceful Chiricahuas at Fort Apache. The Apaches were put on the train at Holbrook and sent to Fort Marion. Florida.

Frederic Remington, the greatest artist of the frontier West, accompanied a unit of the 10th Cavalry on patrol in Arizona in 1888. Rising above the race prejudice that was so common at the time, Remington said that the buffalo soldiers were not only good fighters but also "charming men with whom to serve."

The Black infantry soldiers also made their mark on Arizona history. Two Black soldiers of the 24th Infantry regiment—Sergeant Benjamin Brown and Corporal Isaiah Mays—were awarded the Congressional Medal of Honor in 1890. On May 11, 1889, they were part of a small detachment under Major J. W. Wham en route from Fort Grant to Fort Thomas. Their job was to guard the Army payroll—$26,000 in gold and silver. The payroll was robbed by a gang of Gila Valley farmers and stockmen. The robbers fired down from a rocky ledge, forcing the soldiers to retreat to a dry creek bed and leave the money wagon unattended.

"Buffalo soldiers" of Troop A, 10th Cavalry stand ready for inspection at Fort Apache in 1887.

The Wham payroll robbery was reenacted the day after the ambush.

Booker T. Washington visited Phoenix in 1911. Washington was the founder of Tuskegee Institute in Alabama. He wanted Blacks to improve themselves by learning trades and practical skills.

In the fight that followed, eight soldiers were wounded. Brown and Mays were singled out for special courage. They continued to fight after receiving severe wounds. Mays crawled and walked two miles to a ranch house to get help. But aid arrived too late. The robbers had broken the wooden strongbox and made off with the money. Suspects were later arrested and tried. Defended by a capable lawyer, Marcus A. Smith, they were freed.

Booker T. Washington, the famous Black educator and ex-slave, visited Phoenix in 1911. He spoke at a patriotic rally in Eastlake Park in honor of President Lincoln's proclamation freeing slaves. Two bands played, one Indian and one Black. Washington said Phoenix was a melting pot. He was impressed by the way different races got along. During the three-day celebration there were baseball games between Black and Mexican teams. Washington said he witnessed a foot race in which an Indian, a white, and a Mexican took part. The timekeeper was Black.

Washington observed that all the restaurants in Phoenix, except two, were run by Chinese. Most of the truck gardens in the suburbs were controlled by Chinese. At that time the Japanese were just beginning to come into Arizona. Washington said he was pleasantly surprised to see the Chinese farmers delivering vegetables in horse-drawn wagons. He expected to see them pulling two-wheeled carts. There were many Chinese merchants too. They made calculations with the abacus*.

Washington could not help but note the sad plight of the Indians. "I saw hundreds of them standing about on street corners in their picturesque Indian costumes," he later wrote. "They idly watch the strange spectacle of a new civilization pouring into this new country, sweeping away their primitive life."

Washington was happy to see Phoenix Blacks moving into a variety of occupations. The Home Kitchen restaurant had a Black owner. One of three wholesale fruit merchants in the city was Black. The Blacks had almost a monopoly on the barber trade.

Washington did not suggest that there was no racial prejudice in Arizona. But he said Arizona was a new country where all the races existed in harmony and had equal opportunities.

*The *abacus* is a frame with beads that slide back and forth on wires for doing arithmetic.

Railroads were important to the lumber industry. In the
early 1880s, sawmills made wood ties for the railroads.
Later, logs and lumber were hauled by trains such as the
one shown here.

15

ECONOMIC ACTIVITIES

Most of Arizona's present industries were started in territorial days. After the Civil War, hundreds of ranchers occupied the free public lands and raised Texas longhorns. Gradually purebred cattle were introduced and ranching methods were modernized. The sheep industry was centered in northern Arizona. Sheepmen started bringing their livestock to the Salt River Valley for winter pasturing, as did many cattlemen.

Mining developed rapidly in the territorial period too. High silver prices and bonanza mine discoveries in the 1870s near Tombstone and present-day Superior made silver supreme for awhile. During the 1880s, Phelps Dodge and other eastern corporations were buying up copper mines for large-scale development in later years. Miners had trouble organizing and lost several strikes at the copper mines in the early 1900s.

The Salt River Valley became Arizona's main agricultural area during territorial days. It supplied food for the miners and feed for livestock. Cotton raising was also started in the early 1900s.

The development of farms, ranches, and mines created a demand for better transportation. In the early 1880s Arizona was connected to the coasts by two railroads. Branch rail lines and dirt wagon roads soon connected the major mining districts and agricultural communities to the main lines. Automobiles were introduced in Arizona near the end of the territorial period.

There was little manufacturing, except for local needs, in territorial times. Lumbering was Arizona's first major manufacturing industry. Lumbermen got a good start by sawing railroad ties for the Atlantic and Pacific Railroad.

KEY CONCEPTS

1. Mining became an important industry in territorial days.
2. The Arizona cattle industry depended on vast areas of public land.
3. Northern Arizona was the center of the sheep industry.
4. The ostrich industry thrived in Arizona for twenty years.
5. The cotton industry got started in the early 20th century.
6. Lumbering was Arizona's first major manufacturing industry.
7. Most of Arizona's labor unions were organized in territorial days.
8. The growth of Arizona depended on good transportation.

15

1. MINING BECAME AN IMPORTANT INDUSTRY IN TERRITORIAL DAYS

Mining in the 1850s and 1860s. After the Gadsden Purchase in 1854, American prospectors rushed into southern Arizona. Rich silver mines near Tubac and Patagonia were opened by enterprising men like Sylvester Mowry and Charles Poston.

During the Civil War, placer gold was discovered at La Paz along the Colorado River. Prospectors were also led into the gold mining districts of central Arizona by Pauline Weaver and Joseph Walker. The biggest find was Henry Wickenburg's Vulture mine.

In the 1870s many silver mines were opened. Among the richest was the famous McCracken mine in Mohave County which was discovered in 1874. It was one of Arizona's typical surface-rich silver mines. In a few years it was producing an estimated $200,000 worth of silver a month. The ore was packed on burros to a stamping mill on the Big Sandy River eight miles away.

The rich Tip Top and Peck mines in the Bradshaw Mountains south of Prescott also began producing in the 1870s.

The most famous silver strike was at Tombstone. It came 20 years after Frederick Brunkow discovered the first mine in that region in 1857 west of present-day Tombstone. Brunkow, an engineer for the Sonora Exploring and Mining Company at Tubac, was killed by an employee. Brunkow's mine never produced much silver.

In 1877 Ed Schieffelin located a rich float at Tombstone. He took samples of the ore to show his brother, Albert, who was working at the McCracken mine. The assayer there, a mining engineer named Richard K. Gird, was impressed. He accompanied the Schieffelin brothers to the silver discovery. Northeast of modern Tombstone they located the rich Lucky Cuss and Toughnut silver deposits.

By 1879 one of the maddest mining rushes in American history was underway. The next year the Schieffelins sold their interests for $600,000 to a syndicate* of Eastern capitalists. By that time, the new town of Tombstone was booming. The mines were producing $5 million a year. Most of the Tombstone mines were abandoned after 1888, however, because of underground flooding below 500 feet. Attempts to pump out this water ended in failure.

*syndicate: group of persons carrying on a business.

A Wells Fargo guard protects a pile of gold ingots from the smelter at Wickenburg.

Dick Gird, Al Schieffelin, and Ed Schieffelin.

232

Another famous silver strike was the Silver King. It was located in the Pinal Mountains northwest of Superior. A rancher named Charles G. Mason and four of his neighbors discovered the mine in 1875. Within two years, James M. Barney, a Yuma merchant, bought out all the partners except Ben Regan. The Silver King Mining Company was organized to step up production. By the 1920s some $6,500,000 worth of silver had been mined—most of it before the government quit buying silver in 1893.

An overproduction of silver in the West caused the market price to drop. The government had a problem because it had promised to pay one ounce of gold for sixteen ounces of silver, the set rate. Large government purchases of silver were draining the U.S. Treasury's gold reserves. So President Cleveland had Congress repeal the Sherman Silver Purchase Act of 1890. This action stopped the flow of silver into the treasury.

After 1893 most silver miners went after gold. Among the richest gold mines developed in the 1890s were the Congress and Octave in Yavapai County. The King of Arizona and La Fortuna in Yuma County were also rich finds.

Copper mining. Before the 1880s, gold and silver were the only metals mined in quantity in Arizona. Until the railroads were built into Arizona, high transportation costs made copper mining unprofitable. Besides, there was little demand for copper until the electric motor, telephone, and electric lights were invented.

Some rich copper ore from Ajo, however, was shipped to Wales for smelting as early as 1855. And copper mining was started in the Clifton-Morenci area in the 1870s. Transportation was a problem in the rugged country of eastern Arizona. The copper ore had to be shipped in wagons to Kansas City, 1200 miles away. That was a long haul, even after a smelter was built at Clifton to reduce the ore. The smelter was owned by the Lesinsky brothers, Henry and Charles.

The Lesinskys also built a narrow gauge railroad—the first in Arizona—from Clifton to the Longfellow mine about five miles uphill. Mules pulled empty cars up to the mine and rode back on top of the ore. The Lesinskys later replaced the mules with small locomotives. The most famous was "Little Emma." This steam engine was driven and kept in good repair by Hank Arbuckle. He would not have traded jobs with anyone.

Typical ore wagons used at the Silver King mine.

Minority groups were often employed in the mines and paid low wages. Mexicans and Chinese are seen in this group.

Locomotives used at Clifton.

In 1882 the Lesinskys sold out to a syndicate from Scotland. This group organized the Arizona Copper Company, Limited. The Arizona company nearly went out of business in the early 1890s when the price of copper was down to 10 cents a pound. Fortunately, James Colquhoun, later president of the company, developed a method of leaching copper ores with sulphuric acid. With this process the company could make a profit from low-grade as well as high-grade ores.

In 1875 William Church organized the Detroit Copper Company at Morenci. Twenty years later, Phelps Dodge and Company of New York bought Church's company. Phelps Dodge had acquired its first Arizona copper mine, the Copper Queen at Bisbee, in 1881. Dr. James Douglas, later president of Phelps

Dodge, and other geologists soon found more rich copper deposits in the Bisbee area.

From 1880 to about 1910, copper mines in Arizona were of the "bonanza" or high-grade type. In this category were the Copper Queen at Bisbee, the Clifton-Morenci mines, the Old Dominion at Globe, and the United Verde at Jerome.

When most of the bonanzas were mined out, copper companies were forced to mine low-grade ores, called "porphyries." The copper in this low-grade ore is scattered through a rock mass. To show the contrast, in 1910 an average of 50 pounds of pure copper was smelted from a ton of high-grade ore. Today's ore yields only about 10 pounds of copper a ton. To stay in business, modern copper companies have developed better mechanical and chemical ways to process the ore.

Interior view of the Arizona Copper Company's smelter at Clifton in the early 1900s.

An early Arizona cattle ranch near Ft. Grant.

2. THE ARIZONA CATTLE INDUSTRY DEPENDED ON VAST AREAS OF PUBLIC LAND

During the 1850s large herds of Texas cattle were driven across Arizona to California markets. There were so many, in fact, that prices dropped from a high of $500 a head in 1849 to $6 a head in 1855.

Very few cattle were raised in Arizona before the 1870s. Bill Kirkland was the first American from the States to begin ranching in Arizona. In 1857 he brought 200 head of Mexican cattle to the old Canoa Ranch south of Tucson. Some stock was driven in during the late 1850s to supply the stage stations and the solders garrisoned at Fort Buchanan and Fort Breckenridge. Arizona ranching in the 1850s was on a small scale.

With the outbreak of the Civil War all progress stopped. Pete Kitchen was able to keep his ranch going north of Nogales. The Pimas and Papagos had a few beef animals. But other than that, the only cattle in Arizona in the mid-1860s were three small herds near Prescott. One of these was John P. Osborn's dairy herd. Osborn was the grand-father of Sidney Osborn, governor of Arizona in the 1940s.

Hundreds of ranchers filled up the free open range lands in the 1870s and 1880s. They were attracted by the abundance of grasses and the mild climate. One of the most successful pioneer ranchers was Henry Hooker. He got his start by driving in large herds of Texas longhorns to supply beef to the Army posts and Indian reservations. Hooker homesteaded in the Sulphur Springs Valley in southeastern Arizona. In a few years he controlled all the surrounding public grazing lands—an estimated 800 square miles.

Henry C. Hooker

235

Henry Hooker's ranch house near Fort Grant in southeastern Arizona.

Windmill and water tank in a big pasture near Sonoita, Arizona.

Overstocking of the grasslands. In 1877 Governor A. P. K. Safford reported that stock raising had become one of Arizona's leading industries. Unfortunately, many of the grasslands were soon overstocked. Rangeland which nature had stocked with a few hundred game animals, was overrun with thousands of cattle and sheep.

Vegetative destruction and erosion began in the 1880s. Valleys once covered with high rich grasses were taken over by scattered groves of mesquite, sage, and greasewood. A severe drouth in 1885 and another in the early 1890s caused a grass shortage. Thousands of cattle died. Cattlemen were forced to sell their steers at greatly reduced prices to avoid further losses.

The destruction of many grasslands resulted in changes in the Arizona cattle industry. Most cattlemen turned their ranches into breeding operations. They cut the size of their herds by concentrating on the raising of calves. Yearlings were sold for fattening in feeder lots. Some were pastured in the Midwest or in the Salt River Valley. Stockmen also followed Hooker's example in introducing purebred cattle, particularly Herefords. Unprofitable scrubs were removed from the ranges. Small cattle companies consolidated, giving them more capital to make ranch improvements. Steam pumps and windmills were installed and dirt reservoirs constructed.

Cattle feeding became an important industry in the Salt River Valley. In the fall of 1888, Colonel Hooker drove 12,000 young steers from Graham County to the Hatch Ranch to fatten on alfalfa. The same year, Walter Vail shipped seventeen carloads of cattle from his huge Empire Ranch near Sonoita to pasture on farms near Tempe. It was the 1890s, however, before grain and cottonseed products became cheaply available. The feeding business was then conducted on a large scale in the Phoenix area.

Cattle industry in northern Arizona. The first large cattle outfit in the Flagstaff area was the Moroni Cattle Company. It was started in 1882 by John W. Young, son of the Mormon leader Brigham Young. The Mormons first came to the area to supply the Atlantic and Pacific with railroad ties. In 1883 Young joined with several eastern businessmen to form the Arizona Cattle Company. At one time the A One, as the ranch was called, ran 16,000 head of cattle northwest of Flagstaff.

Holbrook became a center of ranching activity in the 1880s. Many ranches were started in that vicinity after the railroad was built. The largest outfit was the Aztec Land

and Cattle Company. Better known by its brand, the hashknife, this company built up a ranch stretching along the railroad from Holbrook almost to Flagstaff. It used both the free public domain and the railroad land it bought from the Atlantic and Pacific. The United States had given the railroad 40 square miles in alternate sections for every mile of track laid.

The Aztec Company was incorporated in 1884. Eventually the company ran 60,000 head of cattle. When rustling became a problem, black-hatted Texas gunmen were imported to protect the livestock. The thievery was not stopped, however, until Burt Mossman was hired in 1897 to manage the herds. He personally escorted to jail three neighboring ranchers he caught butchering Hashknife cattle. With the help of sheriffs and civic leaders he was able to send a large number of rustlers to the territorial prison at Yuma. In 1901 Governor Murphy appointed him captain of the Arizona Rangers to clean up crime in the territory.

Branding was especially important in Arizona because of the open range system of grazing. The vast public domain was roamed by cattle of many different owners. When disputes arose, the brand was the only proof of ownership. Cattlemen worked together in spring and fall roundups. Each calf was branded like the mother cow.

Beginning in 1887 all ranchers were required by territorial law to register their brands and earmarks. At first a cattleman recorded his brand at the county courthouse. He also burned the monogram on a piece of tanned leather. Starting in 1897 brands had to be registered in the *Territorial Brand Book*. At one time there were 17,000 brands listed. With so many on the book, it became difficult to devise a new brand.

The brand language involves some plain geometry: box, circle, diamond, bar, triangle, or cross. The hearts are still popular. The old Empire Ranch heart brand is the most famous. There are numerous character brands:

rocking chair, umbrella, tepee, half moon, coffee pot, anvil, violin, and many interesting Mexican designs. The pair of dice brand has geographical significance. It is used in Paradise Valley. Initials are commonly used. One rancher used the ICU brand. Some cowpoke with a sense of humor caught one of the calves and added a number to make the brand read ICU2. One of the humorous brands was recorded by a heavy-set cattleman. He used 2FAT.

Brands advertised in the *Hoof and Horn magazine*.

There is a trick to branding properly. The first essential is a proper iron. If the iron is too narrow and sharp it cuts and goes in too deep. A fairly wide brand holds the heat better. Some cattlemen use a "running iron" and simply draw the brand on a calf. When the branding iron is cherry red, it doesn't have to be held against the calf very long. With a little salve or grease spread over the brand, the burn is healed in a week or ten days.

Typical cowboys in territorial days.

Branding a calf.

The cowboy, fact and fiction. Branding was a hot, dirty job. In fact, very little of the cowboy's work was romantic. His was a life of loneliness and drudgery. He worked long hours, and often seven days a week. He dug holes for fence posts, repaired fences, cleaned corrals, cared for injured or sick stock, shoed horses, fixed windmills, hauled salt, and even milked cows. Most of the early day cowboys were drifters with very little education. Their pay was low.

But the cowboy—not his rancher boss—has become the folk hero of the cattle industry. Through Western short stories and novels the cowboy has been pictured as a noble outdoorsman who protects the weak and fights against wrongs. He was big-hearted, free, and happy-go-lucky.

The American image of the cowboy closely resembles the hero of Owen Wister's *The Virginian*, the most famous of cowboy novels. The Virginian typified the mythical cowboy. He was a slim young giant, quiet with strangers, and a practical joker. He loved his horse dearly and defended frail women. Though fast with the gun, he preferred not to use it. He was a man of action who bowed to no one. His life was a simple struggle of good versus evil, with no shading in between.

Sheep on the Navajo Reservation.

3. NORTHERN ARIZONA WAS THE CENTER OF THE SHEEP INDUSTRY

The Navajo and Hopi Indians had a few sheep in the 1850s. About the only other sheep in Arizona at that time were on their way to California. Thousands were driven from the Rio Grande Valley in New Mexico and from Mexico.

In 1855, for example, John Abel drove 10,000 sheep from Chihuahua via Tucson to the coast. Arizona was then open country with no highways or fenced ranches for sheepherders to worry about. But there were other obstacles. The Abel party was attacked by Apaches led by Mangas Coloradas. The Indians ran off sheep and horses. They also poisoned water holes. At the Yuma crossing the sheep had to be ferried across the Colorado River. Despite his heavy losses, Abel reached coastal markets and made a handsome profit.

Manuel Candelaria was the first white man to establish himself in the sheep business in Arizona. In the 1860s he drove a flock from New Mexico to a ranch site near present-day Concho in Apache County. Manuel and his sons prospered as sheep raisers. They raised the fine Merino breed. Juan Candelaria, the

eldest son, became one of the wealthiest men in the county.

Sheep raising became a major enterprise in Arizona after the Civil War. In the 1860s, 1870s, and early 1880s sheep were raised mainly for the wool. Getting the wool to eastern markets was a problem, however. Some of it was transported by steamer from the Colorado River around Cape Horn to Boston, the leading wool market.

Many sheep were driven to Arizona in the early 1870s after a severe drouth hit California. The incoming flocks carried alfilaria seed in their wool. The "filaree," as it is called, started growing in Arizona. Today it is one of the most valued plants on the state's ranges.

Flagstaff became the center of the sheep industry in the northern part of the territory. In 1875 John Clark brought 3,000 head from California. He established a ranch south of Flagstaff in an area now known as Clark Valley. More sheep were brought in from Nevada by William Ashurst. He was the father of Henry Fountain Ashurst, who was one of Arizona's first U.S. senators.

The three Daggs brothers — J. F., W. A., and P. P. — ran sheep along Silver Creek in Apache County before moving to Flagstaff.

239

The Daggs operation stressed both quantity and quality. At one time the brothers owned 50,000 head. In 1882 they bought sixty-two purebred Merino rams in Vermont to improve their flocks. The Daggs sheep won many first prizes at fairs.

Sheep drives. In the 1880s sheepmen in northern Arizona started a new practice. When the frosts bit the high mountain areas in late October, the sheep were started on a long trek down to winter pastures in the Salt or Gila valleys. The sheep spread out and slowly ate their way through the public grazing lands. They sometimes took as long as two months to reach the valleys.

Cattlemen protested, especially in the spring when the sheep were driven back to northern grasslands. On the way they ate a lot of forage just as it was beginning to make good feed for the cattle. This problem was partly solved in the early 1900s. The Forest Service marked off driveways through the national forests. Sheepmen then had to take their sheep over these designated routes. They were required to move their sheep at least five miles a day. This prevented dawdling and kept the sheep from eating up nearby pastures.

Most sheepmen do not use the forest driveways today. They go by truck or train to save time and cut losses from poisonous weeds or other causes.

The Graham-Tewksbury feud. By the mid-1880s the Daggs brothers were unable to find enough grazing land north of the Mogollon Rim. Most of the good private land and the water holes were controlled by the Hashknife outfit. The Hashknife cowboys had orders to run all sheep and herders off the company's ranges.

Unable to compete with the Hashknife, the Daggs brothers decided to drive a flock of their sheep into the Tonto Basin south of the rim. This decision got them involved in the bloody feud going on between two rancher factions led by the Graham and Tewksbury families.

In earlier years, the Grahams and Tewksburys were friends. They even rustled cattle together. But then they began quarreling over stolen cattle. Court records in St. Johns and Prescott reveal that each family accused the other of stealing its livestock.

The decision of the Daggs brothers to move sheep into the Tonto Basin did not start the Graham-Tewksbury feud. It kept the trouble going, however. The Grahams and other cattlemen were determined to keep sheep off the Tonto ranges. The Tewksburys, on the other hand, sided with the sheepmen.

Hashknife cowboys—some of them former outlaws from New Mexico and Texas—ambushed the Daggs sheep herders before they got to the Rim. A Basque herder was shot down and beheaded. Two Indian herdsmen were more fortunate. They escaped to the Tewksbury cabin for safety. The cowboys drove most of the sheep over a cliff and clubbed the rest to death. P. P. Daggs said the slaughter cost him $90,000.

Following the murder of the Basque herder and the loss of the sheep, the Daggs brothers gave up any hope of grazing sheep in the Tonto Basin.

The Graham-Tewksbury feud, however, went until only one male member of each family was left. The feud ended in 1892 when Tom Graham, who had moved to Tempe, was ambushed while taking a load of grain to town. Ed Tewksbury was charged with murder and sent to prison. After 2½ years behind bars, he was tried again and released on a technicality.

Thomas H. Graham   Edwin Tewksbury

4. THE OSTRICH INDUSTRY THRIVED IN ARIZONA FOR TWENTY YEARS

In the early 1900s ostrich farms thrived near Phoenix and Yuma. There was a good market for ostrich feathers. Every woman in fashion had one or more ostrich plumes in her hat. Ostrich feathers were also used to make boas (a type of scarf) and feather dusters.

The ostrich business in the United States started with a pair of birds at the Centennial Exposition in Philadelphia in 1876. A firm in Pasadena, California bought the birds and imported more from South Africa.

The first ostriches in Arizona were brought by train from California in 1887. Josiah Harbert wanted to raise them on his alfalfa farm in north Phoenix. The birds arrived during the sweltering heat of August.

A crowd of people gathered at the railroad depot to see the strange birds. To satisfy public curiosity, Harbert left his small flock on exhibit in downtown Phoenix for awhile. He then hired a man with a high-sided horsedrawn wagon to transport the ostriches to his farm.

The driver took precautions to prevent the birds from escaping. He put an old sack over the head of each ostrich. A tarpaulin was tied over the top of the wagon. Unfortunately, all but three birds suffocated before the wagon reached the Harbert farm. One of the survivors ate a piece of barbed wire and soon died. However, an adult male and a female chick did well. The ostrich industry was started in Arizona.

By 1905 six ostrich farms were operating near Phoenix. There were also small troops, as the flocks were called, scattered over the valley. The first ostrich farmers made money by selling chicks. Watson S. Pickrell's Tempe Ostrich Company, for example, sold six-month-old chicks for $100 each. Mature four-year-old birds sold for $800 a pair and more. Ostriches brought a higher price than cattle and ate less.

The main objective of the ostrich industry was to produce feathers. The feathers were plucked every eight months. Each bird yielded 1½ to two pounds a year. With the market price at $20 to $30 a pound, ostrich farming was highly profitable. By 1912 a store at First Street and Adams in Phoenix was buying $250,000 worth of feathers a year.

Cowboys became ostrichboys. To protect themselves against the big 300-pound, eight-feet-tall birds, an ostrichboy carried a shepherd's staff. With this tool he could hook the

Nona Marshall proudly wears an ostrich feather in her bonnet.

An ostrichboy at work.

An incubated ostrich chick is helped out of its shell.

neck of an ostrich and bend it down to the ground, rendering the bird harmless. Ostriches were not always easy to catch, however. They were capable of taking 25-foot strides and running 60 miles per hour.

On the bigger ostrich farms, eggs were gathered from the pastures by wagonloads for incubation. The eggs provided a delicious food, too. One ostrich egg was equal to more than 30 hen eggs. A big joke on ostrich ranches was to ask an unsuspecting breakfast guest, "Do you want one egg or two?"

Dr. A. J. Chandler bought out a Buckeye ranch and hired a crew to drive the birds to Chandler. But the ostriches did not know they were supposed to act like cattle. They lit out in all directions. What should have been a one-day drive turned out to be a week-long circus. It took that long to corral all the runaway ostriches.

There was a brief market for ostrich feathers in the early 1920s. They were used to clothe kewpie dolls.

5. THE COTTON INDUSTRY GOT STARTED IN THE EARLY 20th CENTURY

Arizona may be the oldest cotton-producing area in the United States. When Christopher Columbus sailed into the New World in 1492, the people of Arizona were already growing cotton and weaving it into cloth. The Pima Indians not only grew cotton for fiber, they also ground the cotton seeds with mesquite beans to make flour. Sometimes, cotton seeds, which are rich in protein, were dried and eaten without grinding.

Cotton as a commercial crop got a late start in Arizona. Most of the cotton grown before statehood in 1912 was for experimental purposes. It is believed that the first cotton raised by Anglo-Americans in Arizona was in 1873. John Osborn planted a five-acre patch near Phoenix. The lint was combed by hand and used mainly for making bed comforters. Osborn gave the cotton he had left to friends. They used it, unginned, to fill mattresses.

To encourage agriculture, the territorial legislature in 1883 authorized the governor to pay $500 to the person who raised the greatest amount of cotton on any five acres. Governor Tritle awarded the money to Felix G. Hardwick who produced 3,390 pounds of cotton on the Larsen ranch south of Tempe.

In spite of the success of these early patches, cotton cultivation was not continued. The price of short staple cotton was too low. There was more profit at the time in grain and alfalfa.

Long staple cotton. Egyptian cotton finally gave the Arizona cotton industry a start. After years of experimenting, the Department of Agriculture developed a good American-Egyptian long staple variety. It was called "Yuma" in honor of the experimental station where seed selection and testing began in 1902. A few acres of Yuma cotton were planted in the Salt River Valley in 1911. The new variety was given a boost by the American Thread Company which paid 28 cents a pound for the lint. This was double the price paid for other cotton in the United States.

In 1912 a group of Mesa farmers planted more than 300 acres with Yuma cotton. The seed was supplied by the Department of Agriculture. The average lint yield was a profitable 400 pounds per acre. The cotton industry

"Pima" long staple cotton arriving at the gin.

was born—in the same year that Arizona became a state.

By 1913 there was great interest in cotton farming. About 4,000 acres of Yuma cotton was planted that year. Small cotton gins were installed in Phoenix, Mesa, Chandler, and Glendale. By 1917 cotton was the leading industry of the Salt River Valley.

Meanwhile, a superior variety of cotton called "Pima" was developed at Sacaton, on the Pima Reservation, by the Department of Agriculture. The Pima cotton evolved from years of careful experiments with the Yuma variety. The average length of the Pima fiber was one and 11/16 inches—the longest in the world. The first production on a large scale was undertaken in fields south of Tempe.

6. LUMBERING WAS ARIZONA'S FIRST MAJOR MANUFACTURING INDUSTRY

Tucson had a sawmill in 1857. Mills were built in other towns to supply timbers to the mines. In 1867 a Curtis steam sawmill was operating in Prescott.

Edward E. Ayers built Arizona's first large commercial sawmill near Flagstaff in 1882. The mill turned out railroad ties for the Atlantic and Pacific. Before entering into a contract with the railroad, Ayers came to Arizona from Chicago to look over the forests. The A and P had halted construction at Winslow in 1881 until a bridge across Canyon Diablo could be completed. From Winslow, Ayers was provided with an Army ambulance, wagons, and a military escort to the Flagstaff area. He quickly decided that there was an ample timber supply there.

Ayers raised $200,000 in capital and built a sawmill about a mile from the original site of Flagstaff. This mill had a daily capacity of 150,000 board feet. Ayers employed D. M. Riordan, an Indian agent on the Navajo Reservation, as manager. The Ayers Lumber Company soon expanded its operations. Lumber was supplied to growing towns in the territory. Ties and telegraph poles were sold to the Mexican Central Railroad. Lumber yards were opened in Los Angeles, Albuquerque, and other towns outside the territory. A box factory was started.

Edward E. Ayers talks to sawmill workers during a lunch break.

Ayers moved back to Chicago, selling his company to Riordan. In 1887 Riordan incorporated under the name Arizona Lumber and Timber Company.

Arizona was not a manufacturing state until the 1940s. In territorial days there were only a few manufacturing enterprises to supply local needs. These included flour mills, meat packing plants, cotton gins, leather tanneries, explosives works, canneries, and brick factories. There were some domestic manufactures such as brooms, copper and silver jewelry, saddles, and hats.

Not until World War II did Eastern investors recognize that Arizona was an ideal place for light industries. By that time Arizona had adequate transportation and available skilled labor.

7. MOST OF ARIZONA'S LABOR UNIONS WERE ORGANIZED IN TERRITORIAL DAYS

Railroad brotherhoods. The first effective labor unions in Arizona were organized by the skilled railroad workers. In 1900 engineers and trainmen at Douglas formed Arizona's first lodge of Railroad Brotherhoods. Guided by their national organizations, the railroad unions quickly gained strength and political influence throughout the territory.

They had success in gaining their objectives of increased wages, seniority rights, and improved railroad safety practices. They got the 22nd Legislative Assembly in 1903 to pass a law forbidding railroads to work trainmen for more than sixteen consecutive hours.

Mine unions grew more slowly. In the early days, mining was on a small scale. The owner worked alongside his hired miners. The worker could talk to his boss at lunch or supper and iron out common problems.

This personal kind of relationship ended in the 1880s and 1890s. Corporations developed big, mechanized mines with hundreds of employees. Mine bosses who came in contact with miners were not owners. They were hirelings of nameless stockholders and had no power to solve the miners' problems. The miners began to feel the need to communicate with the corporation. But most early efforts to organize failed. Strikes at Clifton-Morenci, Globe, Bisbee, and other places did more harm than good.

Globe miners unionized. The Western Federation of Miners tried to organize the mine workers. The first local of this union to survive was started in 1896. The Globe union was formed in protest to a wage cut and the employment of Mexicans at the Old Dominion Mine. The white miners were prejudiced against Mexicans and Chinese because these groups usually worked for lower wages.

Instead of striking, the miners presented their demands to the mine superintendent. He was told to grant the demands or be escorted out of town. The Old Dominion owners reacted to the threat by closing the mine down. The union was able to survive this lockout and to grow. Before long Globe was labelled as the "center of labor agitation in the territory."

Clifton-Morenci Strike. A law passed by the territorial legislature in 1903 resulted in a mine strike at Clifton-Morenci. The legal working day for miners was set at eight hours instead of 10. The law didn't say if daily wages were to be cut. The miners said no. The operators said yes. The companies at Clifton-

Morenci had been paying $2.50 for a 10-hour day. James Douglas of the Detroit Copper Company and James Colquhoun of the Arizona Copper Company offered a compromise—$2.25, which was nine hours pay for eight hours work.

Some of the 1,500 miners refused this offer and went on strike. Many of the strike leaders were foreign-born agitators who wanted to loot company stores and blow up the railroad bridges. Representatives of the Western Federation of Miners Union from Denver spoke against violence. But they had little influence with the strikers.

When mobs formed on the streets and threatened to become violent, Acting Governor Isaac C. Stoddard sent in the Arizona Rangers. He also asked President Theodore Roosevelt for federal troops. Before the soldiers arrived, a large group of armed miners seized the Detroit Company's mill. They disarmed the sheriff's deputies who were guarding it. But the strike failed.

The companies got a court injunction to restrain the workers from interfering with their mine property. Agitators were arrested.

Newspapers in the territory expressed opposition to lawlessness in any form. However, they tended to blame the companies for much of the labor trouble. The papers generally criticized the practice of hiring foreign-born workers.

At least one newspaper, *Our Mineral Wealth* of Mohave County, thought the companies could pay higher wages. "Their pluck-me stores get back nearly all they pay out," said the paper, "yet they buck and snort around like they were in the last throes of poverty." Miners in the company towns had to buy nearly everything at company stores. Prices were usually high.

The Clifton-Morenci strike of 1903 showed that the miners and corporations were still not communicating. There was no real effort by either side to sit down and discuss problems. The miners were not organized into an effective union.

The Western Federation of Miners. This union was controlled for a long time by the radical IWWs (Industrial Workers of the World). But Charles Moyer broke with the IWW and took the miners' union into the American Federation of Labor in 1911. The AF of L group became known as the International Union of Mine, Mill, and Smelter Workers. The membership grew rapidly.

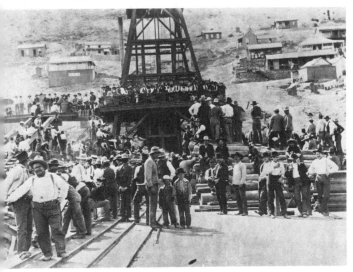

Mass meeting of miners during Morenci labor strike of 1903.

Arizona National Guard at Morenci during mine strike, 1903.

Other unions in territorial days attracted less attention. There were strong unions in the printing and building trades. The barbers, bartenders, gas and steam fitters, boilermakers, and other skilled workers were organized. No progress was made in unionizing agricultural and livestock workers. Most of the field hands were foreign-born Mexicans who had to work for low wages or starve. And the cowboys had a tradition of independence and loyalty to the "old man," as a ranch owner was called.

The Arizona State Federation of Labor was formed in January, 1912—less than a month before statehood. It was organized by 47 delegates representing practically every union in Arizona except the Railroad Brotherhoods.

8. ARIZONA'S GROWTH DEPENDED ON GOOD TRANSPORTATION

Stagecoaches lost out to the railroads. When Arizona became a territory in 1863, there was no public transportation. The Butterfield Overland Mail line had been abandoned at the outbreak of the Civil War. Tucson, the major community, remained isolated during the war.

A few horseback mail routes and stagecoach lines began operating in the 1860s. In 1866 the Santa Fe Stage Company offered stage service between the capital at Prescott and Santa Fe with connections to Denver and Kansas City. The next year this line was extended from Prescott to Tucson. In 1868 the Arizona Stage Company gave both Prescott and Tucson mail and passenger service to California. The Arizona Company stages ran via Wickenburg, Ehrenberg, and La Paz. Each town had a company agent. Joseph Goldwater had the job at La Paz.

Hundreds of small stage lines were started in the 1870s and 1880s to serve the needs of towns and mining districts. Many of the drivers and coaches came from California where the railroads were fast displacing stage lines.

A stagecoach at Naco, Arizona about 1900. The canvas sides could be dropped for protection against the sun or rain.

Arizona Railroads in 1887.

The stagecoach business in Arizona picked up for awhile after railroads were built across

246

the territory in the early 1880s. The Southern Pacific and Santa Fe lines brought hundreds of people into Arizona who needed transportation to places not on the railroad. But the stage companies fought a losing battle in the 1890s and early 1900s. Branch rail lines and smaller railroads were eventually built into remote areas. By the time of statehood in 1912, the stagecoach was almost a relic of Arizona's colorful past.

Travel on stagecoaches was slow and uncomfortable. Five miles an hour was the average speed. The term "stagecoach" was used loosely. Not every stage line used the classical Concord coach always seen in western movies. Buckboards, buggies, and home-created vehicles were more typical. In most coaches, the passengers sat on hard seats and were crowded like sardines. Many discomforts had to be endured. The roads were rough and dusty. There was always the odor of foul-smelling cigar smoke and unbathed traveling companions. Stage holdups were frequent, especially on lines that carried Wells Fargo payroll boxes and mail.

Stage stops were famous for bad food. The usual fare was jerky or salt pork, stale bread, bad coffee, and beans. A Chicago reporter, A. H. Noon, wrote in 1879 about a traveling salesman, called a drummer, who refused to eat the beans at one Arizona stage stop. When the drummer demanded something better, a local man wearing a slouch hat, cowhide boots and western clothes, thrust a Colt's revolver in his face and said, "Stranger, eat them beans!" And he did.

Wagon freighting was an important business in territorial days. Before railroads crossed Arizona in the early 1880s, all goods from the States were hauled in by wagons. Albert Steinfeld, a pioneer merchant in Tucson, said it took him 60 to 90 days to get merchandise from San Francisco in the 1870s. Shipments came either overland or by boat to the Colorado River and by wagon the rest of the way. Freight from eastern points was shipped to the railroad terminals in Kansas or Colorado and from there by ox or mule team to Tucson. It took from four to six months time. A merchant had to plan on three stocks of goods: one on hand, one in transit, and one with instructions to ship.

Freight was hauled in huge high-sided wagons pulled by mule teams. It was not uncommon to see 20 to 30 mules hitched to a tandem of three of four wagons. Some of the lead wagons had wheels eight feet in diameter and the capacity of half a railroad car. Mules were more expensive than oxen but were faster and needed less water. The smartest pair was put in front and the strongest span, called the wheeler mules, was next to the wagon.

20 Mule Team Freighters

Albert Steinfeld

247

Horse-drawn freighters.

The driver rode the left wheeler mule. Instead of a double handful of reins, he guided the team by a jerkline—a single rein running to the bit of the left lead mule. A steady pull meant move to the left. A number of jerks and the animals swung to the right. A wagon driver had to have great skill to drive a team of 20-odd mules over a mountain road with sharp curves. In addition to the jerkline, he manipulated the brakes of the wagon by another rope. This system was difficult when the heavy wagons snaked going down hill. Usually the drivers had one or more helpers, called "swampers," to handle the brakes and other chores.

The teamsters were tough, rugged men. Their language was coarse and profane, but easily understood by balky mules. They often drank heavily and could be found in the saloon at the end of a dusty trip.

Some drivers owned their rigs. But most of them worked for freighting companies. Dozens of companies did a thriving business serving the towns and mines of the territory. Every major town had freight depots, wagon and harness shops, blacksmiths, and big corrals for the mules. Wagon builders opened shops in Yuma, Prescott, Phoenix, and Tucson.

The completion of two major rail lines across the territory actually helped the wagon freighting business. Long-haul freighting was ended, but wagons were needed between outlying areas and the railroads. Even Phoenix and Prescott depended on wagon freight until branch railroads connected them to main lines.

Beginning in the late 1880s, Mormons worked as freighters hauling government supplies from the railhead at Holbrook to Fort Apache or the Indian agency at Whiteriver. The round trip of 180 miles was made in eight days in good weather. A freight outfit on that run usually consisted of two coupled wagons pulled by four or six horses. The wagons were Studebakers, Bains, or Schutlers. They were ordered from the middle west by mercantile companies with government contracts. The covered wagon, so familiar in western movies, was a necessity to protect perishable goods. Freight ran the gamut from barbed wire, hay, and machines to clothing, flour, canned goods, and "U-needa-biscuit" frosted cookies.

Wagons were not replaced by trucks in Arizona until after World War I. Truck transportation was ushered in along with improved roads.

Dr. Hiram Fenner in his steam Locomobile, the first "horseless carriage" in the territory.

248

Sometimes road conditions left a bit to be desired. Grand Avenue in Phoenix after the 1905 Cave Creek flood.

The automobile. Dr. Hiram Fenner's 1899 Locomobile was the first horseless carriage in the Territory of Arizona. He had it shipped from Boston by rail. When the City of Tucson required that all cars be licensed in 1905, Dr. Fenner received License Number One.

The earliest horseless carriages—whether electric, steam or gasoline-powered—were little more than amusing playthings. Gradually, however, eastern auto makers produced cars that were more powerful, dependable, and cheaper. Soon people were traveling on dusty wagon roads in nearly every part of the territory. At the time of statehood in 1912 there were 1,852 automobiles in Arizona.

In the beginning, the "gas buggies" were sold as a sideline by bicycle stores and wagon makers. Druggists put in a stock of gasoline and motor oil. Livery stables were converted into garages and blacksmiths learned how to repair broken parts. Edward Rudolph, the original Ford dealer in Phoenix, was probably the first to handle cars in great volume.

Once cars were accepted as a means of transportation, roads became a problem. The territorial wagon routes were not built for automobiles. In 1904 some 60 motorists organized an association and local chambers of commerce began to promote better roads.

Automobiles on Washington Street in Phoenix, 1904.

The need for highways was demonstrated in 1910. In that year the American Automobile Association sponsored A. L. Westgard to look for a transcontinental automobile route. The only usable roads he could find from northern New Mexico into Arizona led him to Springerville. There he made a good impression on a merchant named Gustav Becker who was to become known as the "Father of Good Roads" in Arizona.

From Springerville Westgard drove his Pathfinder over an old road to Fort Apache and then to Globe. From there he found his way to Phoenix and then to Yuma and Los Angeles. Westgard made two more trips through Arizona. The second time he drove a Saurer truck and carried six 16-foot planks to get across washes, mud puddles, and sandy areas.

Westgard's pioneering efforts stimulated an interest in better roads. Shortly after statehood, Becker promoted the first Ocean-to-Ocean Highway Convention. It was held in Springerville. To celebrate the occasion the Round Valley Rodeo was inaugurated. The rodeo was held in the middle of the street in front of Becker's store.

Auto races. In 1911 the businessmen in Phoenix and other towns organized a Los Angeles to Phoenix auto race to promote a national highway. Each town along the way put up a purse for the first racer to enter the city. Local auto enthusiasts used their teams, wagons, and shovels to smooth out the road in their areas. Signs were posted to keep the drivers on the right course.

250

Famous driver Barney Oldfield in the 1912 Los Angeles to Phoenix race.

Harvey Herrick, in a National, won the race in 20 hours and 23 minutes. He picked up the lion's share of the winnings—$900 in El Centro and Yuma alone. Roger Stearns, in a Stoddard-Dayton, was leading the race coming into El Centro. But he was a Good Samaritan and stopped to help a driver and mechanic whose Maxwell had turned over and pinned them down. After the race, another mechanic's wrist was broken by a "kick-back" while cranking a Lexington racer at Ehrenberg on the way back to California. Blood poisoning developed and the hand had to be amputated.

The Los Angeles-Phoenix race became an annual event in connection with the Arizona State Fair.

A. L. Westgard is greeted by the people of Ehrenberg, 1910.

President William McKinley (second from left) toured Arizona by train in May, 1901. Here he stops at Tucson. Four months later, McKinley was assassinated in New York.

16

BEGINNING OF THE 20th CENTURY (1900-1912)

By the beginning of the 20th century, Arizona was getting close to statehood. The population of the territory in 1900 was over 122,000. In January 1901, the territorial legislature convened in a brand new capitol to hear Governor Nathan O. Murphy's address. The following May, President William McKinley rolled into Phoenix on a Southern Pacific train. McKinley toured the new capitol and visited with the peaceful natives at the Phoenix Indian School. He took a side trip to see how gold was mined at the Congress Mine northwest of Phoenix. For a brief moment, the nation's attention was focused on Arizona.

Most Easterners were not yet willing to accept Arizona as an equal in the family of States. But statehood was just a matter of time. Arizona was making rapid economic and social progress. During the first decade of the 20th century, the Arizona Rangers rounded up outlaws who were using Arizona as a hiding place. People in the Salt River Valley took advantage of federal funds to build Roosevelt Dam. When completed in 1911, this dam gave farmers a dependable water supply for irrigation. It also provided electricity.

The Laguna Dam on the Colorado was built to divert water to about 130,000 acres. Sheep raisers were doing well in the northern part of the territory and the cattle industry was prosperous all over the territory. Lumbering was an important industry. By 1910 the territory had 2,000 miles of steam railways. Perhaps more important, Arizona was leading all states and territories in the production of copper.

Banks in the territory were sound and had large deposits. There were more than 60 newspapers and magazines. The territory was proud of a good public school system, a university, and two teachers' colleges. The institutions—a prison, insane asylum, industrial school, and a home for the aged and infirm pioneers—were functioning well.

By almost any standard, Arizona was ready for statehood. On February 14, 1912, Arizona's star—the 48th—was added to the United States flag.

KEY CONCEPTS

1. The Arizona Rangers helped to establish law and order in the territory.
2. Theodore Roosevelt Dam gave the Salt River Valley a dependable water supply.
3. Arizona voters were opposed to joint-statehood with New Mexico.
4. A big majority of delegates at the Arizona Constitutional Convention were Democrats.
5. The progressive constitution was rejected by President Taft.
6. Arizona was admitted into the Union as the 48th state.

Southeastern Arizona in 1903.

1. THE ARIZONA RANGERS HELPED TO ESTABLISH LAW AND ORDER IN THE TERRITORY

The Arizona Rangers were a territorial police force established by the legislature in 1901. During their brief existence, seven and one-half years, a total of only 107 men served as Rangers. But they were men who became a legend in their own time.

Reasons for the Rangers. The Ranger company was organized to prevent cattle stealing and to rid the territory of outlaws. By the turn of the century, rustling near the Mexican border was forcing many cattlemen

out of business. Only the big cattle ranches could afford range riders to drive rustler gangs away.

Another problem was train robberies. A Southern Pacific train was held up at Cochise Station in 1899. A Benson-bound train from Nogales was robbed at Fairbank in 1900. These crimes frightened the railroads into joining cattlemen and miners in seeking a ranger force.

Captain Burt Mossman. There were only 14 men in the first group of Arizona Rangers—a captain, a sergeant, and 12 privates. Governor Murphy appointed Burt Mossman captain. Mossman had gained experience dealing with rustlers when he was foreman of the huge Hashknife ranch near Holbrook. In 1901 he was in the butcher business in Bisbee's Brewery Gulch.

Mossman selected Rangers who were good ropers, riders, shooters, and trailers. They had to be in good physical shape and needed a general knowledge of the country. There was no uniform, though they tended to dress alike. After the first year, the Rangers wore a five-pointed star that was sometimes concealed under a vest or jacket.

The first headquarters of the Rangers was at Bisbee. This town was near the Mexican border where most of the outlawry was centered. The Rangers cooperated with the *Rurales*, a Mexican patrol of soldiers, to rid the border country of bandits and smugglers.

Burton C. Mossman, the first captain of the Arizona Rangers.

A group of Arizona Rangers.

Colonel Emilio Kosterlitski, commander of the Mexican *Rurales*.

The first big assignment of the Rangers, however, was in eastern Arizona. The mountains of this area were a robbers' roost for the Black Jack Christian gang and other outlaws. They would hide out in the Blue River wilderness country after leaving a trail of robberies, murders, and cattle thefts in New Mexico and Texas. The Rangers took a train to Clifton, unloaded their horses, and joined a Graham County posse headed by Sheriff James V. Parks. They found the worst of the outlaws and arrested them.

The next target was Augustine Chacón, a ruthless killer who once confessed to having killed 15 Americans and 37 Mexicans. In 1897 he dug his way out of an adobe jail in Solomonville and escaped. His hanging was scheduled in 10 days. Mossman personally traced down Chacón in Mexico. Posing as an escapee from the Tucson jail, the Ranger captain got acquainted with the outlaw. He arrested

Chacón and forced him to ride handcuffed and with a rope around his neck into Arizona. This time Chacón was hanged by Sheriff Parks in Solomonville.

Wild and woolly Douglas. The second captain of the Arizona Rangers was Thomas H. Rynning. He was a Rough Rider friend of Governor Brodie. After Rynning took over, the size of the force was increased to 26 men. The headquarters was moved to Douglas. In 1902 Douglas was one of the toughest towns in the West. The saloons, dance halls, and gambling joints were visited by cattle rustlers and known killers. The Cowboy Saloon and other dives were run by men who boasted of notches on their six-shooters.

The Rangers slowly cleaned out Douglas and turned their attention elsewhere. Nearly 1,800 arrests of all kinds were made in the territory during two years' time.

The hanging of Augustine Chacón.

Thomas H. Rynning, the second captain of the Arizona Rangers.

Arizona Rangers at the Morenci mine strike in 1903.

Arizona Ranger John Redmond looking for cattle thieves at Pusch's Steam Pump Ranch, 1908.

Harry Wheeler, the last captain of the Arizona Rangers and later sheriff of Cochise County.

A shoot out. The Rangers were sometimes forced to shoot it out with desperadoes. On one occasion, for example, Sergeant Harry Wheeler shot a robber named Bostwick in the Palace Saloon on Congress Street in Tucson. Bostwick had the saloon patrons lined up against the wall when Wheeler walked through the swinging doors. The robber fired first, but he was brought down by two shots from the Ranger's quick gun.

Arizona Rangers abolished. Wheeler was the third and last captain of the Rangers. With Douglas tamed, he moved the headquarters to Naco, another border town. In 1909 the 21st Legislative Assembly abolished the Rangers. Governor Kibbey wanted to keep the Rangers and vetoed the bill. But it was passed again over his veto.

In bringing law and order to Arizona, the Rangers stayed out of politics—only to fall victim of a political war between a Republican governor and a Democratic legislature.

2. THEODORE ROOSEVELT DAM GAVE THE SALT RIVER VALLEY A DEPENDABLE WATER SUPPLY

The Salt River Valley today has rich fields of alfalfa and cotton, green lawns, swimming pools, and a big city population. It is hard to imagine that farmers in the "Valley of the Sun" were once troubled by an uncertain water supply—alternating disasters of flood and drought. By the end of the 1880s, there was need for a huge storage dam upstream. A dam would make it possible to store water in wet seasons for use in drier years.

The great flood of 1891. Water was plentiful. It just needed to be controlled. This was emphasized by the great flood in February 1891. The Salt River overflowed its banks. At some places below the Verde junction the Salt was eight miles wide. The Tempe railroad bridge was washed out, cutting Phoenix off from rail transportation. The flood waters gouged a new channel into a low section of Phoenix, forcing people to evacuate. Houses were damaged as far north as Jackson Street.

Later in the 1890s there was a long drought in the valley. The normal flow of the Salt River could not fill all the canals that had been built. Armed, desperate men patrolled the canals to protect their water

An armed man guards a canal to protect water rights during a dry season.

The Salt River flood of 1891 washed out the Tempe railroad bridge. Phoenix was without train service for several months.

rights. At least a third of the farmland was forced out of cultivation. Livestock died. Orchards became firewood. Families packed and left, expecting Phoenix to die. Then the rains came. A flash flood destroyed the dirt diversion dams. The water rushed on to the Gulf of California. It was wasted for all purposes except to dramatize the need for water control.

Roosevelt Dam site selected. A huge storage dam in the mountains upstream was the obvious way to insure a permanent and dependable water supply. A committee was appointed by the Maricopa County Board of Supervisors back in 1889 to locate a good site for a dam. The committee chairman was the county surveyor, W. M. "Billy" Breckenridge, who had ridden with Cochise County Sheriff John Behan during Tombstone's wilder days. An ideal spot was found in the Salt River just below its confluence with Tonto Creek. But it was 1911 before Roosevelt Dam was completed on the site selected by Breckenridge's committee.

First come, first served water rights. Before the dam was built, the courts ordered that water be distributed in times of shortage on the basis of "prior appropriation." Farmers who had been using the water longest were served first. This system was based on Spanish law. It was applied in the Salt River Valley in 1892 in the famous "Kibbey decision." Judge Joseph H. Kibbey, later governor, decided that water belonged to the land where it was first used. The water, Kibbey said, did not belong to the canal companies to sell wherever they chose.

The Newlands Reclamation Act. This law was passed by Congress in 1902. The act provided federal funds for irrigation projects in desert lands of the West. It made Roosevelt Dam possible. But before a federal loan could be obtained, there had to be an organization to sign a contract for the money and repay it.

The Salt River Valley Water Users' Association was formed in February 1903. By July, some 4,000 landowners were members of the association. They pledged 200,000 acres as

The Salt River Valley in 1902.

The Salt River Valley
in 1902

security for a federal loan. Each acre represented a share of stock in the association. John P. Orme was elected the first president of the Salt River Valley Water Users' Association.

In October, Louis C. Hill, an engineer for the U. S. Reclamation Service, arrived in the valley. He started plans for what was to be the world's highest dam.

Construction of Roosevelt Dam. Much preliminary work had to be done. Some 112 miles of access roads were built. The most important was Roosevelt Road, now called Apache Trail, from Mesa. Most of the construction machinery and supplies were hauled over this narrow, dangerous route in freight wagons pulled by 20-mule teams. Other roads ran to Globe and to a sawmill. A cement mill was built near the dam site.

Electricity was generated at an auxiliary dam that was built 20 miles up the Salt River. A 500-foot tunnel was dug through solid rock to divert the river around the main dam site. Hot springs in the tunnel raised the temperature to as much as 130 degrees. The heat made work difficult.

Roosevelt Road (now Apache Trail) in 1905.

Italian stone cutters near Roosevelt Dam.

Indian worker at the Roosevelt Dam construction site.

A mill was built on the hill near Roosevelt Dam to convert clay and limestone deposits into cement.

The town of Roosevelt in 1906.

Site of Roosevelt Dam as construction began.

Roosevelt Dam under construction.

The town of Roosevelt was built for construction workers. People who moved in did so with the understanding that the town site would be under water once the dam was completed. The town was unusual for frontier Arizona in other ways too. No saloons or gambling halls were permitted. A school, meeting hall, daily stage and mail service, and telephone connections with Globe and Phoenix were provided.

A better location for Roosevelt Dam could not have been chosen. It is an arched dam built between steep canyon walls on a tough sandstone foundation. Some 343,000 cubic yards of native stone and 338,000 barrels of cement were used in the world's largest masonry dam. The 284-foot dam is 170 feet thick at the base and tapers to a 16-foot roadway at the top. Including spillways, it stretches more than a thousand feet across the mouth of the canyon.

The first stone was laid in 1906 and the dam was completed on February 5, 1911. It cost $10 million. But the Salt River Project repaid every dollar to the federal government by 1955.

The dam was dedicated by ex-President Theodore Roosevelt on March 18, 1911. People made the rough trip to the site on horseback, in buggies, on bicycles, and in automobiles.

Theodore Roosevelt at the Roosevelt Dam dedication on March 18, 1911.

Roosevelt Dam

3. ARIZONA VOTERS WERE OPPOSED TO JOINT-STATEHOOD WITH NEW MEXICO

Arizonans began to clamor for statehood in the 1890s. They held constitutional conventions in Phoenix in 1891 and 1893. Delegate Marcus Smith got a statehood bill passed by the U. S. House in 1892 and again in 1893. Statehood was delayed, however, by the U. S. Senate. Many senators, including Albert J. Beveridge—the powerful chairman of the Committee on Territories—still thought of the Southwest as a "great American desert." The

Eastern Republicans also feared that Arizona and New Mexico would send four Democratic senators to Washington.

By the early 1900s, however, it was only a matter of time before Arizona and New Mexico were admitted as states. Beveridge and other opponents then tried to combine the two territories into one huge, Texas-like state. A joint statehood bill passed the House in 1904. It was supported by President Theodore Roosevelt. The name of the super state was to be Arizona. But the capital would be in Santa Fe.

In 1905, Tempe was a small farming community.

Arizonans, both Democrats and Republicans, opposed joint statehood. Petitions were circulated against it. Almost every club, church, and organization in the territory worked against joint statehood. The feeling of the people was indicated at the territorial fair in Phoenix. It took only 30 minutes of work in the grandstand to get 3,200 signatures.

Arizona also got support from many leading politicians. J. W. Babcock, the former chairman of the Republican National Committee, argued against joint statehood. In an article written for a national magazine, he said that Congress promised Arizona separate statehood in the 1863 Organic Act.

Another Arizona friend, U. S. Senator Joseph B. Foraker of Ohio, introduced an amendment—written by Marcus Smith—to the joint statehood bill in 1906. The Foraker Amendment was passed. It permitted the voters of Arizona and New Mexico to vote on

the question of joint statehood. Either territory could stop Arizona and New Mexico from being combined.

As it turned out, Arizonans voted against joint statehood 16,265 votes to 3,141. New Mexico, on the other hand, favored it by a big margin.

4. A BIG MAJORITY OF DELEGATES AT THE ARIZONA CONSTITUTIONAL CONVENTION WERE DEMOCRATS

The Arizona statehood bill, called the Enabling Act, was passed by Congress and signed by President William Howard Taft on June 20, 1910.

The Enabling Act provided for a constitutional convention. Delegates were to be nominated by county party conventions—not by direct primary. Governor Richard E. Sloan

262

A Flag Day Dream. Congress passed Enabling Acts for both Arizona and New Mexico in 1910. New Mexico became the 47th state in 1911. Arizona was admitted into the Union as the 48th state in 1912.

Members of the constitutional convention in 1910.

called for an election on September 12 for the choosing of 52 delegates.

It was an overwhelming victory for the Democratic Party and its progressive platform. The Democrats elected 41 delegates, most of whom were pledged to support the initiative, referendum, recall, and direct primary. All of these measures would give the people a bigger voice in government.

5. THE PROGRESSIVE CONSTITUTION WAS TURNED DOWN BY PRESIDENT TAFT

The constitutional convention convened at the capitol in Phoenix on October 10, 1910. Judge A. C. Baker, a Phoenix lawyer, served as temporary president. There was some discussion over seating. It was decided that the delegates would select seats in the order that the names of their respective counties were drawn from a hat. Some members had trouble adjusting to the swivel chairs. One leaned too far back and sprawled on the floor. E. W. Coker of Florence, who weighed 350 pounds, had difficulty rising from his chair to make motions.

The Democratic majority elected George W. P. Hunt of Globe as president. On the next to the last day of the convention, Morris Goldwater, another Democrat, was elected vice-president. It seemed desirable to have a substitute in event the president should be incapacitated after the convention adjourned. Someone had to be in charge to set up an election so the people might vote on the constitution.

All clerks and other employees were appointed and received $5 a day—a dollar a day more than the delegates were paid. Goldwater jokingly offered to resign as delegate from Yavapai County to take a job as an attaché. Miss Ethel Ming, a clerk, reminded him that "the delegates get big chunks of honor" which was worth something.

Once organized, the convention operated much like a legislature. The members introduced "propositions" which were assigned to committees. If approved, a proposition was debated in the "committee of the whole." The latter was simply the entire convention acting in an informal way to speed up action. To become part of the constitution, a proposition had to be approved by a formal vote and referred to the Committee on Style, Revision, and Compilation. This committee was headed by Michael Cunniff, a Harvard-educated former editor of the *World's Work* magazine.

Initiative, referendum, and recall.
Some of the propositions submitted by delegates were approved. Others were not. The three most controversial provisions included in the constitution were the initiative, referendum, and recall. In vain, the conservative delegates argued that President Taft would veto the constitution if these measures—especially the recall of judges measure—were not removed. Labor unions, which had a strong influence with the progressive majority, insisted on the recall of judges. This way, they could remove judges from office who abused their power to stop strikes by issuing injunctions.

Other popular reforms of the day did not pass. Prohibition and woman suffrage propositions were defeated.

About 3,200 women signed a petition asking that the sale of intoxicating liquors be forbidden. The delegates were reminded that the people in Safford voted 4 to 1 in favor of prohibition in that town. But a proposition to submit the question of prohibition to all the voters in the territory was defeated 33 to 15.

The delegates also voted down a woman suffrage proposition 30 to 19. Dozens of petitions—one from Gila County was 10 feet long—did no good. A special postcard also failed to influence the delegates. The card had a picture

Cartoon in the *Arizona Republican,* October 9, 1910. Many people feared that Arizona would lose its chance for statehood because of the populist constitution.

George W. P. Hunt presiding over the constitutional convention.

Morris Goldwater (uncle of U.S. Senator Barry Goldwater).

PHOENIX, ARIZONA, SUNDAY MORNING, OCTOBER 9, 1910.

THE BIG QUESTION

WILL IT DROP THE BONE FOR THE SHADOW?
(With Apologies to Aesop.)

of a drunk opposite a young mother. The caption was: "This man can vote. This woman can not."

Segregation. The question of segregation of blacks and whites in the schools caused another heated debate. The fight for segregation was led by Dr. B. B. Moeur of Tempe. He was chairman of the Committee on Education and a future governor. Most of the delegates, however, had a strong feeling for tolerance and racial equality. They voted against making school segregation compulsory.

The most basic work of the convention was to establish the machinery of state government. The delegates put their faith in a powerful legislature. The *governor* was given little power. Most of the top executive officers were to be elected. They were independent and had no responsibility to the governor. Experience with territorial governors, who were political appointees of the president, caused the delegates to distrust the executive branch.

Most political scientists today think that the office of governor should have been given more power. That is what Richard E. Sloan, the last territorial governor, recommended. Sloan said there should be no elective state commissions or boards. He favored electing only three executive officers: the governor, attorney general, and auditor. With a short ballot, the people could find out about all the candidates. They could hold the governor—who would appoint most executive officers like the president does—responsible for his administration. Sloan also favored limiting the governor to one four-year or six-year term.

A *bicameral** legislature* was established. The Senate had 19 members and the House of Representatives 35. Each of the fourteen counties had at least one senator. Five counties (Cochise, Maricopa, Pima, Gila, and Yavapai) were given one extra senator because they cast the largest number of votes for delegate to Congress at the last election.

*bicameral: consisting of two legislative chambers or houses.

The convention delegates apportioned House membership in favor of the Democrats. The four safely-Democratic counties at that time—Mohave, Yuma, Yavapai, and Graham—were given 14 representatives for a combined population of 38,056 people. By contrast, the five possible Republican counties in 1910—Pima, Santa Cruz, Coconino, Apache, and Navajo—were given only 13 representatives for 58,411 people.

But not all Democrats were satisfied. Delegate Sidney Osborn, a future governor from Phoenix, was not pleased. Osborn said it was unfair for Cochise County to have one more representative than Maricopa County. The population of each was about the same, 34,500.

The legislature was limited by the constitution to a 60-day session every other year. Members had to be 25 years of age. The pay was set at $7 per day.

Voters approve the constitution. The constitutional convention finished its work on December 9, 1910. All the Democrats signed it except E. E. Ellinwood of Cochise and A. M. Tuthill of Graham. All the Republicans refused to sign it except John Langdon of Gila County. An election was called for February 9, 1911. The voters were to ratify or reject the constitution.

Governor Sloan, Delegate to Congress Ralph H. Cameron, and others warned that President Taft would not approve the constitution. But the Arizona Statehood League headed by Hunt worked hard for its adoption. The people approved the constitution 12,584 to 3,920. Only 49 per cent of the registered voters, however, cast a ballot. Many were undecided and did not vote.

President Taft delayed Arizona statehood. Congress passed a joint resolution giving Arizona statehood. As expected, Taft vetoed it on August 11, 1911. He said he could not accept the Arizona constitution with the recall provision in it.

The nation debated Taft's veto. Former President Teddy Roosevelt wrote about it in the *Outlook* magazine. Roosevelt favored Arizona statehood, even with the recall. He preferred that judges be removed by the legislature rather than the people. But he said that each state should be able to decide for itself how to remove bad judges.

Arizonans decided to comply with President Taft's wishes. At an election on December 12, 1911, the voters removed the recall from the constitution. The vote was 14,963 to 1,980.

The scorn of many Arizonans for Taft's veto was expressed in a poem published in the Florence *Blade-Tribune*, a Democratic paper:

> We will tolerate your gall
> And surrender our recall
> Till safe within the statehood stall,
> Billy Taft, Billy Taft
>
> Then we'll fairly drive you daft
> With the ring of our horse-laugh
> Billy Taft, Billy Taft
>
> As we joyously re-install
> By the vote of one and all,
> That ever-glorious recall,
> Billy Taft, Billy Taft.

President Taft opposed the recall provision in the Arizona constitution. Cartoon in the *Washington Evening Star,* April 11, 1911.

And that is the way it happened. After Arizona became a state, the people voted to put the recall of judges provision back in the constitution. In the presidential election of 1912, Taft ran fourth in Arizona. Woodrow Wilson, Teddy Roosevelt, and Eugene V. Debs all received more votes.

Election of public officials. There was no election of state officers in 1912. That was done in December 1911. George W. P. Hunt was elected the state's first governor, defeating Judge Edmund W. Wells of Prescott. The two U. S. Senate seats were won by Marcus A. Smith of Tombstone and Henry Fountain Ashurst of Prescott.

Sheriff Carl Hayden of Maricopa County easily won Arizona's only seat in the U. S. House. Hayden was to serve longer in Congress than any person in American history. After seven terms in the House, he was elected to seven six-year terms in the U. S. Senate—a total of 57 years between 1912 and 1969. At the time of his retirement in 1969, Hayden was president *pro tempore* of the U. S. Senate. That position made him third in line for the presidency.

Henry Fountain Ashurst   Carl Hayden

6. ARIZONA WAS ADMITTED INTO THE UNION AS THE 48th STATE

Valentine's Day, February 14, 1912! On that day President Taft signed the proclamation admitting Arizona to the Union. He wrote

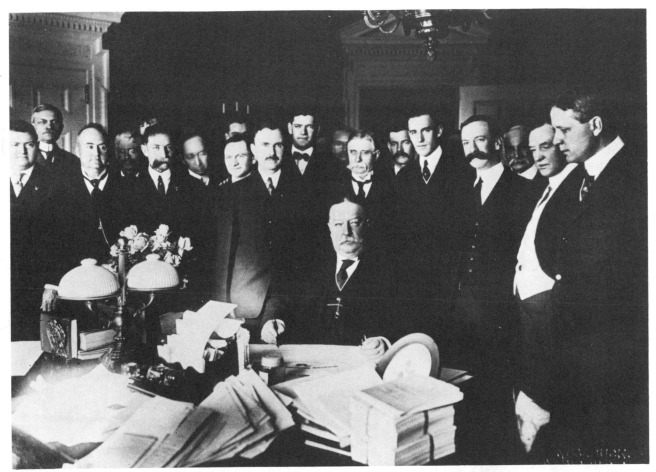

President Taft signing the Arizona statehood bill in 1912.

Cartoon in the *Arizona Gazette* on the fourth anniversary of Governor Hunt's economy walk.

Governor Hunt On His Famous Economy Walk to the Capitol. He Uses An Auto Now and It Costs the Taxpayers $300.00 a Month

his name at 10:02½ A.M. and handed the golden pen to Delegate to Congress Ralph Cameron.

When the good news reached Phoenix by telegraph at 8:55 A.M. Arizona time, steam whistles were blown. People took to the streets to celebrate. Soon the whole state knew. In Tucson, a holiday was declared at the University of Arizona for the 254 students. Bisbee began its celebration by exploding dynamite on top of the Copper Queen Mountain.

People in Phoenix were still shouting when Governor-elect Hunt appeared in the lobby of the Ford Hotel at 11:15 A.M. He walked to the capitol. His purpose was to set an example of thrift for everyone. Dressed in a brown suit with a carnation in the lapel, Hunt smiled and doffed his woolly hat as drivers in touring cars stopped to offer him a ride. As soon as the governor reached the capitol, his walking days were over. Thereafter he was chauffeured in a $3,000 automobile that cost the taxpayers $300 a month.

Following Hunt's inaugural and speech, there was a parade in downtown Phoenix. William Jennings Bryan, "the silver-tongued orator," spoke for two hours to a big crowd at the city plaza. The crowning event of the day was the inaugural ball held on the pavement in front of the Hotel Adams. A brass band from the Indian School played for a jubilant crowd.

The next morning, Governor Hunt was at his desk in the capitol at 6:30 A.M. Most Arizonans thought the "baby state" was in good hands.

Governor Hunt delivers his inaugural speech on February 14, 1912.

Parade in front of the old city hall in Phoenix on February 14, 1912—the day Arizona was admitted into the Union.

UNIT SIX

EARLY STATEHOOD ERA (1912-1945)

As a state after 1912, Arizona became more involved in the mainstream of American history. The generations of Arizonans between 1912 and 1945 participated in two world wars. They witnessed a period of rapid change in between those wars.

The 1920s was a decade of prosperity for most people—a time when the automobile, radio, movies, and electrical appliances became a reality for many families. The 1930s brought the Great Depression. Money was scarce. Many people were out of work. America and Arizona had experienced depressions before, but none so long or so serious.

The coming of World War II brought new economic activity. The federal government dumped millions of dollars into air bases and new defense plants located in Arizona. Farmers planted more cotton and got higher prices. The copper mines operated at full capacity. The war effort brought the United States, including Arizona, out of the depression.

A 1916 Franklin car, in front of a Tucson filling station, is filled with a gallon of gas for a mileage test. This model averaged 40.3 miles per gallon.

17

BORDER TROUBLES, WORLD WAR I, AND THE 1920s

During the first years of statehood, foreign events were important to Arizona. After the Mexican people overthrew President Porfirio Díaz, revolution followed revolution. Rebel forces fought government soldiers as far north as the border towns across the line from Arizona. U. S. troops were stationed in Douglas, Naco, and Nogales to protect American citizens.

Then, just five years after statehood, the United States entered World War I. It was a patriotic war. Americans dreamed of saving the world for democracy. President Wilson wanted a League of Nations to keep the world at peace. Arizona's senators, Smith and Ashurst, supported this idea, but it was voted down in the U. S. Senate. Most Americans wanted to return to isolation and the carefree pre-war days. Instead of ideals, the public was interested in material things. People wanted to get rich quickly and have a good time.

There was a short depression in 1920 and 1921. Then in 1922 business began to prosper. Industries developed rapidly as cars, radios, electrical appliances, silk stockings, cosmetics, and many other products came into common use. Arizona had very little manufacturing in the 1920s except for copper smelting and lumber milling. But the state had the same economic ups and downs that the rest of the nation experienced.

With money in their pockets and more leisure time than ever before, Americans looked for entertainment. Businesses that catered to leisure time activities enjoyed a boom. Radios, movies, magazines, and chain newspapers spread the same news, songs, jokes, and ideas throughout the country. The culture of Arizona and every other state became less unusual as people adopted nationwide styles and fads.

KEY CONCEPTS

1. There were many problems along the Mexican border.
2. The people of Arizona can be proud of the state's record in World War I.
3. Arizona's industries underwent many changes between 1912 and 1930.
4. The decade of the 1920s was fast-moving and brought many changes for Arizona.

17

1. THERE WERE MANY PROBLEMS ALONG THE MEXICAN BORDER

The outbreak of the Mexican Revolution in 1910 brought much excitement and some bloodshed to Arizona. Fighting between Mexican armies raged for years. Lives of Americans were endangered in the border towns of Douglas, Naco, and Nogales. The border at that time was an informal thing. People wandered back and forth from both sides. There was always danger that violence in Mexico would spread to the American side.

Douglas. In 1911, for example, bullets flew wildly into Douglas. Revolutionists under Tucson-born Martin "Red" Lopez had Mexican federal troops cornered across the border in Agua Prieta. American officers of the First U. S. Cavalry, then stationed in Douglas, observed the hopeless plight of the Federalists and persuaded them to surrender to Lopez.

In 1915 Pancho Villa, the Mexican outlaw, fought a battle in Agua Prieta with Mexican government troops.

Naco was another battle-scarred border town. In 1914 Pancho Villa's bandit army engaged President Carranza's federal troops at Naco, Sonora. Americans tried to protect their homes with sandbags. But every house in town had bullet holes. Some buildings were hit as many as fifty times.

One day when Mexican troops were firing into a section of Naco, Arizona, Sheriff Harry Wheeler rode out between the lines with a white handkerchief on a stick. Both sides stopped firing until Wheeler explained the situation. Apologies were offered and the line of fire was changed.

The Naco battle attracted the curious. Dozens of sightseers came from Bisbee by automobile to visit with American soldiers and observe the Mexican Revolution firsthand.

Nogales, Arizona, also felt the effects of the Mexican Revolution. Villa captured Nogales, Sonora, in 1915. When his men

Francisco "Pancho" Villa

Pancho Villa's men at Nogales.

threatened to cross the border, American infantry soldiers were deployed along International Street by Colonel William Sage. Lying in a prone shooting position, the Americans were ordered to return the fire of any of Villa's soldiers who fired on them. A number

272

of Villistas were killed by the American sharpshooters during a tense 30-minute standoff.

Late in August, 1918, Nogales again became an international battleground. This time there were civilians and soldiers fighting on both sides. The trouble supposedly started when a Mexican ammunition smuggler was shot while crawling under a border fence. Citizens began taking potshots at each other across the border.

When Mexican and American troops arrived on the scene, they also exchanged fire. An American captain was killed while leading Black cavalry across the border. After four bloody days, an armistice was arranged by Governor Hunt and Governor Plutarco Calles of Sonora. Seventy to 80 Mexicans, including the mayor of Nogales, Sonora, and more than 30 Americans were killed.

Pancho Villa was one of the losers in the revolution to overthrow dictator-President Porfirio Díaz. At one time, Villa was one of Venustiano Carranza's lieutenants. But when Carranza became president of Mexico, Villa revolted against him. He blamed the United States for helping Carranza gain power and wanted revenge. Early in 1916 Villa led his bandits in raids along the border. At Columbus, New Mexico, they killed 17 Americans.

President Wilson sent General John J. Pershing into Mexico with an army to capture Villa dead or alive. One of the American units involved was the Black 10th Cavalry from Fort Huachuca. Pershing's expedition did not succeed in its aim. Wilson recalled Pershing in February, 1917, leaving the Mexicans to deal with Villa.

Meanwhile, in 1916, the 1st Arizona Infantry of the Arizona National Guard was mobilized. After they left for the border at Douglas, rumors spread that Villa might blow up Roosevelt Dam or rob a Phoenix bank. Home Guards units were quickly organized and trained in Phoenix, Tempe, and Mesa. About 400 men drilled and practiced shooting with rifles furnished by a local bank. Women were given instruction by trained nurses. But after about

eight months, the Villa scare disappeared along with the Guards. Many of the Guards got some valuable training, however, for service in the Army during World War I.

The U. S. Border Patrol. Until 1924 the border was patrolled by a handful of cowboys, ex-Rangers, and outdoorsmen known as the Mounted Guard. In that year, Congress created the United States Border Patrol. One of its main purposes was to stop illegal entries of foreign citizens into the United States. This was no easy task. More than a million Mexicans immigrated, legally or illegally, into the United States between 1910 and 1930.

Chinese were smuggled in. There was no legal way they could immigrate to the United States after Congress passed the Chinese Exclusion Act in 1882.

In the late 1920s the Mexicans in Sonora and Sinaloa decided the Chinese owned too many restaurants and stores. The two Mexican states decided to get rid of the "celestials." Chinese businesses were boycotted. The merchants were arrested and fined. One grocer, for example, was fined for keeping a cat while other Chinese storekeepers were fined for not having cats to keep down the mice. Forced out of Sonora and Sinaloa, the Chinese fled to the United States in great numbers.

Chinese aliens climb under the border fence near Nogales. Many Chinese were forced out of Mexico. They had to enter the United States illegally.

Smuggling rings—made up of Mexicans, Chinese, and some Americans—charged a fee for delivering the Chinese to designated interior towns in Arizona. Tucson, Phoenix, Globe, Florence, Prescott, Flagstaff, and other places had Chinese populations that could find jobs for the immigrants. The Chinese had well-concealed hideouts. Trapdoors opened to underground tunnels leading from one building to another. About the only Chinese who were caught wanted to return to China. They knew that the United States government would ship them home free in a style they couldn't afford themselves.

The Border Patrol had its hands full dealing with liquor smugglers until prohibition was repealed in 1933. The Patrol was also responsible for supervising a multimillion dollar trans-border commerce.

2. THE PEOPLE OF ARIZONA CAN BE PROUD OF THE STATE'S RECORD IN WORLD WAR I

Arizona contributed a larger percent of soldiers and sailors per capita than any state in the Union. More than 12,000 men were drafted or enlisted after America entered the war on April 6, 1917. Arizona and Rhode Island were the states with the lowest percent of men rejected for failure to meet physical requirements. The 158th Infantry—an Arizona National Guard unit commanded by

The last draftees in Pinal County during World War I.

Colonel A. M. Tuthill, a medical doctor—was assigned to the 40th Division and sent to France. After the war, the 158th, Arizona's pride, was selected as President Wilson's special honor guard in Paris.

Draft evasion. The only famous attempt at draft evasion in Arizona was made by John and Tom Power. They refused to come down from their cabin high in the Galiuro Mountains to register for the draft at Safford. A posse of four lawmen rode from Safford to arrest the brothers. The lawmen surrounded the cabin at daybreak on February 10, 1918. But the Powers resisted. In the gunfight that followed, the brothers' father was killed. Frank McBride and two deputies were also shot dead. Only U. S. Marshal Frank Haynes escaped to spread word of the shootings.

The Power boys fled south into Mexico with about 3,000 pursuers on their heels. They surrendered to a U. S. Cavalry patrol to escape a lynching. At Safford the Power brothers were put in cages so that long lines of curious onlookers could see them. Convicted of murder in a trial at Clifton, they were sentenced to life imprisonment. The Powers served 42 years before being paroled in 1960. They were responsible for the largest manhunt in the state, the longest prison terms served, and the reinstatement of the death penalty by voters in 1918.

Frank Luke, Jr. One of America's greatest aviation heroes was Frank Luke, Jr. Known as the "Balloon Buster from Arizona," he was the first American airman to receive the Congressional Medal of Honor. In his short but gallant career he destroyed 14 German observation balloons and four airplanes in the skies above France.

Luke was an athlete at Phoenix Union High School where he graduated in 1917. After pilot training he was assigned to combat duty and decided to specialize in shooting down balloons. This was one of the most dangerous jobs for a pilot. It required swooping down near the earth and exposing the airplane to accurate ground attack. The balloons were

Lieutenant Frank Luke, Jr.

Frank Luke's last stand. Drawing by Clayton Knight when he visited Luke Air Force Base in 1951.

expensive and of great military value in directing artillery fire against enemy troops. The Germans protected the balloons with pursuit planes. They also had anti-aircraft guns, long-range machine guns, and special mortars that shot up aerial bombs called "onions."

On September 29, 1918, Luke shot down three balloons and machine gunned German troops. Pursued by German planes and wounded by ground fire, he made a forced landing in his Spad XIII behind German lines. Refusing to surrender, Luke died defending himself with a pistol.

Two other Arizona pilots entered the select circle of American air aces. Lieutenant Ralph O'Neill of Nogales shot down five planes. Major Reed Chambers of Fort Huachuca had seven planes to his credit.

Indians in World War I. Mathew B. Juan, a Pima Indian, was the first of 321 Arizona men killed in World War I. Like many Arizona Indians, he showed his patriotism by enlisting.

The navy was the favorite branch of service for the Indians. Many had lived on the desert all their lives. They saw the ocean for the first time during the war.

The home front. On the home front Arizona also contributed greatly to the war effort. A Council of Defense was appointed by the governor. This council coordinated the state's civilian war activities with those of the national government. Indians, older boys, and alien workers from Mexico were recruited for farm labor. People were encouraged to buy war bonds and conserve food.

There was a great surge of patriotism during World War I. Arizonans went along with the nation in staging big Liberty Day parades on October 24, 1917. Every economic, ethnic, and age group was encouraged to participate. In the Phoenix parade a Mexican delegation from *Liga Protectora Latina* carried both American and Mexican flags. Pretty señoritas dropped flowers along the parade route. Mayor Dick of Chinatown rode in a Packard.

An Indian band, a Girls' Loyalty League from the high school, Civil War veterans, and

The *Liga Protectora Latina* was organized in Phoenix in 1914 to protect the rights of Mexican-Americans. The leader was Pedro G. de la Lama. At its 1918 Tucson convention, the *Liga* urged its members to buy U.S. Liberty Bonds, save food, and keep peace between capital and labor because "it will help win the war."

many others marched or rode in the parade. Signs on parade trucks—such as "Buy a Bond and Drop a Bomb on the Kaiser's Roof"—told what it was all about. After the parade Vice President Thomas R. Marshall and Congressman Carl Hayden spoke to a large crowd at the old Central School in downtown Phoenix.

Arizonans were expected to buy bonds according to their wealth. Many bought $100 bonds and joined the "100% American Club."

School children in Chandler bought $1,155 in thrift stamps with money they earned themselves. Albert Steinfeld of Tucson led the big buyers in that city's 4th Liberty Loan Drive with a $25,000 purchase. Names of bond buyers were published for all to read.

Volunteer speakers, known as "Four Minute Men," were organized, with George Stoneman as state chairman. Their purpose was to sell the war and keep people informed. The

A patriotic World War I parade in Tucson on "American Sunday," April 1, 1917.

Movie advertisement in *The Arizona Republican,* April 5, 1918.

speakers went wherever there was an audience. They handed out red-white-and-blue pamphlets.

Patriotic movies were shown in movie houses. In April, 1918, for example, the Hip Theater in Phoenix ran "The Kaiser, the Beast of Berlin." This film was one of the best "Hang the Kaiser" movies. In commenting on it, a reporter for the *Arizona Republican* said that "no American, unless his blood be made of ice water, can remain in his chair as this smashing story unfolds."

"Food will win the war" signs were seen everywhere. Arizonans helped America save the extra food needed for our allies in Europe. Thousands of Arizona housewives signed pledge cards. They promised to cooperate with Food Administrator Herbert Hoover's "wheatless" and "meatless" days. Cornmeal was much in demand in Arizona grocery stores as a substitute for wheat bread.

The Council of Defense encouraged more production of milo, kaffir corn, and feterita. These grains were formerly used for livestock forage. Under war necessity they were found to make good bread. Demonstrations for preparing "war bread" and other Hoover substitute food recipes were given at the state fair and to women's groups. Many restaurants in the state quit using wheat products. In May, 1918, bread cards were issued. Each person was limited to six pounds of wheat flour a month. That is as close as the nation got to rationing in World War I.

Public officials in Arizona attempted to enforce the 1917 Espionage Act. This law provided penalties for aiding the enemy. U. S. Marshal J. P. Dillon raided the Metal Mine Workers' Union house in Phoenix. He confiscated IWW propaganda literature and books on sabotage. But no arrests were made.

Several pro-Germans were accused of making disloyal statements. They were brought before the grand jury in Tucson. None were indicted, however.

Peace. "The armistice has been signed," said the Phoenix newspaper employee. He was phoning the engineer at the waterworks. "Let her go," he yelled. And the engineer let go with a loud blast from the fire whistle to inform the whole town. The big whistle at the gas plant took up the joy scream. Soon steam

Newspaper headline reporting the end of World War I.

THE ARIZONA REPUBLICAN
AN INDEPENDENT PROGRESSIVE JOURNAL

TWENTY-NINTH YEAR | 14 PAGES | PHOENIX, ARIZONA, MONDAY MORNING, NOVEMBER 11, 1918 | 10 PAGES | VOL. XXIX., NO. 172

HUNS SIGN ARMISTICE
WORLD WAR IS OVER!

WASHINGTON, NOV. 11--By Associated Press--Armistice terms have been signed by Germany, the State Department announced at 2:45 o'clock this morning. There was no announcement as to whether hostilities had ceased or the hour at which they

Armistice Day parade in Flagstaff on November 11, 1918.

Members of the 158th Infantry as they detrained at El Paso on their way home after World War I; May, 1919.

whistles at the cotton gin, at the Arizona Eastern and the Santa Fe railroad shops, and in every locomotive in the yards let go with all the steam in their boilers.

The armistice was signed in Europe on November 11 before noon, but it was much earlier in Arizona. The news reached Phoenix over the Associated Press wire at 12:45 A.M. when most people were in bed. But they were up in a hurry.

Church bells rang. Guns and revolvers were fired. People filled the streets of downtown Phoenix. Cars fell in line and a parade a mile long rounded the streets of the city. It was a joyful night. The great war was over, and the boys were coming home.

The celebration scene in Phoenix was duplicated in every other town when the good news arrived.

A Spanish flu epidemic took its toll during the winter of 1918-1919. Throughout the world an estimated 22 million died. The disease killed 550,000 in the United States. Starting with a soldier in Massachusetts, the flu virus spread across the country like wildfire. It reached northern Arizona in October. Some 600 students in the Northern Arizona Normal School at Flagstaff were put under quarantine with the discovery of about 50 cases of influenza. Winslow had several hundred people down with the flu almost overnight.

Isolated cases soon appeared in southern Arizona. Pool halls were closed down in Bisbee and Douglas. The authorities did not want crowds to gather. That was to become the pattern for all of Arizona.

As the Spanish flu virus spread across Arizona at an alarming rate, public gatherings were forbidden. Schools, churches, and movie theaters were closed. The state fair was cancelled in November. In Winslow, Jerome, and other towns, school houses were turned into hospitals. Phoenix and Tucson looked like mass holdup scenes when adults were required to wear gauze masks while on the street. People in both towns who did not comply were arrested and fined. In the public effort to keep the flu from spreading, even handshaking was discouraged.

The peaks of deaths in Phoenix and Tucson, the two largest cities, came in November and January. Schools were opened after Christmas only to be closed again for most of January. An absolute quarantine was placed on every house with a flu victim. In Phoenix, a 50-man special police squad was hastily organized to enforce the quarantine. By the end of January the epidemic was over. The virus somehow changed form. It began attacking pigs and chickens.

3. ARIZONA'S INDUSTRIES UNDERWENT MANY CHANGES BETWEEN 1912 AND 1930

During World War I the prices paid for Arizona cotton, copper, cattle, and lumber soared to new high points. There was also a big market for Arizona horses and mules. World War I was not a fully-motorized war like World War II.

Cotton. In the years after Arizona became a state in 1912, cotton farming in this area was in the process of changing from a curiosity to the major source of farm income. The war gave the industry a big boost. Extra long staple Pima cotton was very much in demand in 1917 when the United States entered the war. It was needed for cotton cord in automobile tires. The Pima fiber was also found to be a good substitute for scarce linen in the manufacture of fabric to cover airplanes. As the price of long staple cotton went up to about a dollar a pound, the acreage planted to this crop increased rapidly.

Oddly enough, Arizona's first real cotton king was not a farmer at all. He was Paul W. Litchfield, an official of the Goodyear Tire and Rubber Company. Late in 1916 Litchfield bought 24,000 acres in the Salt River Valley. Part of the land was south of Chandler. The remainder was west of Phoenix where Litchfield Park and Goodyear are located today.

Litchfield brought his cousin, a New York fruit farmer named Kenneth McMickin, to Arizona to direct Goodyear's Southwest Cotton Company. McMickin cleared 6,000 acres of desert land. Extra-long staple cotton was planted in 1917. Wells were drilled and irrigation ditches dug. McMickin soon became a cotton expert and the recognized "father of the cotton industry" in Arizona. The Goodyear company expanded. More land was brought under cultivation. Twenty-four cotton gins were built.

Boom and bust. Other tire companies—Firestone, Fisk, and Dunlop—entered the race to buy Arizona's long staple cotton on a contract basis. These companies injected a new sparkle into a struggling cotton industry. The price went sky high in 1919. The next year nearly every farmer in Arizona turned to cotton. Alfalfa, the number one crop in the state, was plowed under. Dairy cows were sold. Mer-

chants bought farms. The banks eagerly provided money for cotton growers. New lands were developed along the Santa Cruz south of Tucson. Land prices doubled. In 1920 a record 230,000 acres were planted to cotton—about 180,000 of which was long staple.

Then came the crash. The military no longer needed cotton so government contracts were cancelled. Imported cotton from Egypt

Chandler in the 1920s.

Salt River Valley alfalfa hay en route to market.

Wagonloads of cotton at a Phoenix gin on Washington St.

279

was available. Much of the 1920 crop couldn't even be sold. Loans were unpaid. To help the farmers, the state legislature in 1921 formed the Arizona Pima Cotton Growers Association. Instead of dumping the 1920 surplus on the market, this organization shipped a trainload to New Bedford, Massachusetts for storage. With a "spot" supply near the mills, the surplus was sold by 1922. But low prices wiped out most small contract farmers.

New spinning techniques lessened the demand for long staple cotton. Short staples could be woven into strong cords for tires. In 1924 Pima long staple was planted on only 9,000 acres of the 178,000 acres in cotton in Arizona.

Goodyear led the way in mechanizing cotton farming. The change came during the 1920s. During World War I the Goodyear farms had nearly 1,200 mules at work. By 1929 most of the mules had been replaced by 36 tractors. The all-purpose tricycle type of tractor was introduced in 1924. After 1932 most tractors and other farm vehicles had rubber tires. For several years Litchfield Park was the center for Goodyear's tractor tire testing. Truck and automobile tires were also tested there.

Poverty to riches in the cotton industry. Arizona has many large cotton farms. But many of the farmers started on a small scale. Diwan Singh was one of the more colorful pioneers. Born in India, he immigrated to America in 1906. Singh was a common laborer when he drifted into Casa Grande in 1924. He wanted to farm but was penniless. The only land he could get had hard, alkali soil. But with a horse and a mule he plowed 80 acres and planted cotton. Singh did well. In 1932 he was able to buy the first Caterpillar tractor in the Casa Grande area. By the 1940s he was farming 9,000 acres of land.

Other crops. Agriculture became more diversified in the 1920s. Arizona farmers profited by a change in American eating habits. Health-conscious people shifted away from cereals to vegetables, fruits, and dairy pro-

ducts. The climate in the Salt River Valley and Yuma area proved to be ideal for the head lettuce industry—mild winters and little rainfall but lots of irrigation water. The market for Arizona lettuce was good. The crop was harvested between December and April when much of the country and Canada had freezing weather. Many farmers in the 1920s also started producing cantaloupes, carrots, cabbage, citrus fruit, dates, pecans, and other specialty food crops. Cotton, however, was to remain the number one agricultural crop.

Mining industry. Copper mining underwent many changes in the early years of statehood. By the time of World War I high grade underground copper mines were about exhausted. The Magma mine near Superior was the only rich ore bonanza remaining.

The open pit mine, so common today, was developed when underground mining of low grade ores became unprofitable. Steam shovels were first introduced for strip mining at the Ajo pit in 1917. The next year steam shovel operations were started at Sacramento Hill near Bisbee. In the 1920s the shovels were lifting ore into long lines of railroad cars. The trains rolled around great looping spirals to the smelters.

Trucks were tried for hauling at smaller mines before World War I. They had become quite common as freight carriers in the towns.

This well dressed truck driver must have doubled as a stove salesman in the 1920s.

Jerome in 1914. This booming town had 15,000 people in the 1920s.

But the early solid-tired, clumsy trucks frequently broke down and were not powerful enough for the rugged mining conditions of those days. They were abandoned temporarily in favor of the old reliable mule-pulled wagons. It was not long, however, before improved trucks replaced wagons and teams permanently.

Mining became more of a manufacturing industry. New methods for processing a great volume of low-grade ore at a profit were developed. One process supposedly was discovered by a washwoman. In washing a miner's greasy overalls she noticed that oil and sulfide minerals (copper, zinc, and lead) stuck together and floated on the water.

Oil was the first of many reagents used by scientists in the "flotation process." This method of removing copper from ore was perfected by Dr. Louis Ricketts at the Inspiration mine near Superior in 1915. The ore is first crushed. It is then put in a cast iron drum with water and steel balls. When the drums are rotated the ore is ground into dust as fine as flour. The copper is then separated from the waste materials in the flotation tanks.

Arizona's copper industry has always been affected by national and international conditions. When German submarines closed the shipping lanes in 1914, the copper industry lost almost half its market. The price was already down to 13 cents a pound because of overproduction. Most of the Arizona mines were temporarily shut down. But when American industry got into full war production in 1915 there was a great demand for copper. By 1916 the price was up to 27 cents a pound. Then came the post-war depression of 1921. Copper prices fell to 12 cents. Once again most of the mines closed until prosperity returned.

The copper industry did well during most of the 1920s. The American public went on a buying spree. The age of installment buying was launched. Everybody in the country was

Appliances on display at Bisbee in 1929.

Trucks did not replace all freight wagons in the 1920s. These two "hay burners" earned their keep by delivering electrical refrigerators.

urged to buy on credit. Clever advertising helped to sell the automobile, radio, refrigerator, vacuum cleaner, washing machine, and toaster. Copper was used in all of these items. But then came the 1929 stock market crash and the Great Depression of the 1930s.

There was no longer a big demand for copper. The mines cut back on production as prices dropped. Fortunately, all the big Arizona copper corporations were soundly financed and organized. None went bankrupt. When World War II broke out in Europe in 1939 the copper industry began booming again.

Lumbering. Arizona's livestock, tourist, and lumbering industries had the same economic ups and downs as cotton and copper between 1912 and 1945.

Lumbering expanded from the Flagstaff area into the White Mountains. Lumberman Tom Pollock built his own railroad. Named the Apache Railway, it ran from Holbrook to the new town of Cooley. In 1923 he sold out to W. M. Cady and James G. McNary, an El Paso banker.

The Cady Lumber Company had sawed up all the available trees near McNary, Louisiana. The company needed new timber and was attracted to the forests of Arizona. In 1924 Cady moved about 800 people, mostly Blacks, from Louisiana to the town of Cooley which was renamed McNary. Three special trains were needed to transfer the families and all their household goods and logging equipment.

An almost completely new town was built around the company store. The isolated little lumber town thrived. During the depression years of the 1930s there was no one on public welfare or relief of any kind. By the 1970s McNary was a model integrated community. It was one-third Black with the remainder Mexican-Americans, Navajo and Apache Indians, and some whites.

Apache Railway log train.

4. THE DECADE OF THE 1920s WAS FAST-MOVING AND BROUGHT MANY CHANGES FOR ARIZONA

Automobiles. The impact of the automobile on American life was tremendous. It did much to create the booming prosperity of the 1920s. Millions of people were employed in the manufacture, sales, and servicing of automobiles. The auto manufacturers became important buyers of raw materials—including Arizona's copper and cotton. New businesses opened. Filling stations, garages, tourist cabins, and drive-ins were built. Countless new roads ribboned out to meet the demand of motorists for smoother, faster highways.

In 1912 there were 1,852 motor vehicles in Arizona. The number registered increased to 34,619 in 1920 and to nearly 123,000 in 1929. The latter figure included about 13,000 trucks and other commercial vehicles. There were over 400 buses and taxis in Arizona by the end of the 1920s. The last horse-drawn cab in Phoenix went out of business in 1917. For years, foot weary pedestrians could find Jim "Slim" Cooper's horse and buggy cab in front of Doyle's cigar stand. But he finally gave in to the gasoline age and bought a Buick 6 in 1917.

Highways. The Arizona highway system got a slow start. A highway department headed by an engineer was created by the last territorial legislature in 1909. But the people were not convinced that an expensive highway system was needed. Arizona was a big area and there were not many people to pay taxes. Only $250,000 was appropriated in 1912 by the state legislature for roads. And 75 per cent of this amount went to the counties. This small-scale approach to road building was continued for many years. It resulted in a patchwork highway system. The only improved roads in the 1920s were near the thickly settled communities.

Highway funds came from a variety of sources. The property tax was used until 1933. A gasoline tax was levied after 1921. Some federal funds were available too after Congress passed the Federal-Aid Act of 1916. Arizona's

A truck used in the early 1920s.

Ford garage in Yuma in the early 1920s.

Arizona road conditions map, 1930.

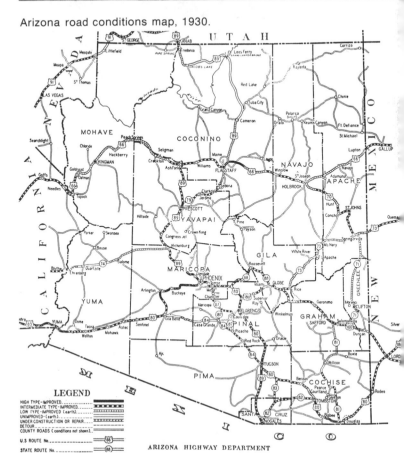

ARIZONA HIGHWAY DEPARTMENT

283

This highway between Phoenix and Tempe was the heaviest traveled road in Arizona during the 1920s.

Dirt loading pit used in the early 1930s during construction work on Highway 66 east of Holbrook.

A Maricopa County concrete farm-to-market road near Chandler, 1928.

primary roads became part of the national highway system in 1925. Connected with roads of adjacent states, they became U. S. Highways.

Maricopa County set an example for the rest of the state. Between 1920 and 1923 more than 300 miles of concrete farm-to-market roads were constructed. Maricopa financed the county project—the biggest in the nation—by borrowing $8,500,000 through the sale of bonds. Unfortunately, it was necessary to stretch the money. Roads had to be built too narrow, only 16 feet wide.

By 1929 the state highway system included 2,150 miles of roads. About 85 percent of this mileage, however, was gravel-surfaced and suitable for only a few cars per day. Only 138 miles were paved with concrete. Another 72 miles had asphalt surfacing. The first paved

Black and white front cover of the first *Arizona Highways* magazine, April 1925. Early editions of the magazine featured highway construction topics and travel articles.

Pulling an automobile out of the sand near Silverbell. Arizona highways were bad in 1920s.

highways ran from Phoenix to Buckeye, Phoenix to Florence junction, north and south of Tucson, between Tombstone and Douglas, and near Safford.

Motoring in Arizona in the 1920s was not always a pleasure. Not only was there little pavement, but the high pressure tires were easily punctured. The engines were low-powered. A motorist going very far was advised to carry a tool box, at least two spare tires, a tow rope, emergency gaskets, extra spark plugs, a box of wheel cup grease, an oil can, and a tire repair kit. Most of the cars were open, with only a canvas top.

Radio. The most exciting and influential invention of the 1920s was the radio. It added a richness to the daily lives of most Americans. Radio found an immediate and enthusiastic reception in Arizona. It was 1930, however, before national network broadcasts were received on a regular basis.

The first American commercial station was KDKA of Pittsburgh in 1920. Soon air waves were filled with the squawking of hundreds of big and little stations all over the country. In 1927 Congress created the Federal Radio Commission—renamed Federal Communications Commission in 1934—to bring order to the air waves. Stations were licensed by the federal government and assigned frequencies. Many stations joined one of two rival national networks. NBC was founded in 1926 and CBS the following year.

The first amateur experimental station in Arizona was 6BBH. It went on the air in 1921. A young Barry Goldwater, later to become a U. S. Senator, was one of several radio operators involved in 6BBH. Most of the receiving sets in the early 1920s were crystal sets built by amateurs. There were no speakers, only headphones. After several changes in call letters, 6BBH became KOY.

KFAD of Phoenix—later changed to KTAR—was Arizona's first licensed commercial station. Its first broadcast was on June 22, 1922. Started by the MacArthur brothers as a 1000-watt station, it eventually was owned by the Electrical Equipment Company of Phoenix and the *Arizona Republic* newspaper. Arizona's next two stations were located in Tucson. KTUC was started in 1926 and KVOA (now KCUB) in 1929.

October 23, 1924, was a big day for Arizonans with radio receiving sets. They heard a speech given by President Calvin Coolidge in Washington, D. C. Some 28 radio stations across the land picked up the speech over telephone lines and broadcast it. People in Tucson put on their earphones and heard the speech over WBAP Fort Worth. Other listeners tuned in KHJ Los Angeles. The *Tucson Citizen* called the radio speech a climax to a "week of wonders." A few days earlier, Tucson residents saw the navy dirigible Shenandoah, the first of its type to cross and recross the continent.

Not many people owned radio sets in the 1920s. In 1929 only 16 per cent of the families in Phoenix had a radio. By comparison, 93 per cent had electricity in their homes. About 66 per cent owned an automobile and 22 per cent had an electric washer. Only two per cent had an electric refrigerator. The census of 1930 revealed that 18.1 per cent of Arizona's 106,630 families had a radio.

Public listening areas were set up with loudspeakers. University and Encanto parks in Phoenix were favorite listening spots for the younger people who could not have "radio

THE ARIZONA REPUBLICAN

Covers All the State

THE STATE'S GREATEST NEWSPAPER

INDEPENDENT · JUST · PROGRESSIVE

Today 24 Pages

38TH YEAR, NO. 125. PHOENIX, ARIZONA.

FRIDAY MORNING, SEPTEMBER 23, 1927

TUNNEY SCORES DECISIVE VICTORY

Arizona Accepts Governors' Proposal

Gene Takes Count Of 9 But Rallies To Victory

Water Pact May Result From Move

Arizona Delegates Take Step In Order To Solve Colorado River Problem

RESERVATIONS

If Conference Fails, Arizona's Plan Of Acceptance Will Be Withdrawn In Full

(Exclusive Republican Dispatch)
DENVER, Colo., Sept. 22.—Arizona's Colorado River commission today agreed to accept the upper basin state governors' proposal for the allocation of water, with the reservation that if negotiations at the present conference on Colorado river problems fail, the

Millionaire Gets Two Year Term In Big Oil Swindle

Arizona Is Gaining In State Favor

(Exclusive Republican Dispatch)
DENVER, Colo., Sept 22.—The conditional acceptance by Arizona of the governors' proposal

Tucson Will Greet Paris Flyer Today

Delegation Of Phoenix Citizens Will Join Old Pueblo In Greeting Famed Aviator

SPECIAL TRAIN

Gold Spot Special To Carry More Than 500 Phoenicians To Lindbergh Celebration

HEADED by Acting Governor James H. Kerby, Mayor Frank Jefferson and Capt. H. B. Watkins, secretary of the Phoenix Chamber of Commerce, approximately 500 persons are expected to take the Gold Spot special this morning, leaving the Union station

Phoenix Hears The Fight Returns

KUNSELMAN PHOTO

Dempsey Floors Champion In Seventh Round With Two-Fisted Attack To Head

DISPUTE COUNT

Ringside Fans Claim Tunney Given Long Count When Jack Failed To Take Corner

BY ALAN J. GOULD
(Associated Press Sports Editor)
SOLDIERS' FIELD, CHICAGO, Sept. 22.—Gene Tunney, the man of destiny, is still heavyweight champion of the world, but his crown was perilously close to being toppled from his head tonight by the gallant thrust of the old warrior, Jack Dempsey, in the greatest comeback of all time.

On September 23, 1927 the *Arizona Republican* reported Tunney's victory and the visit of Lindbergh to Tucson.

parties" at home. An estimated 10,000 excited boxing fans crowded Phoenix's Central Avenue in September 1927 to hear a broadcast of the Dempsey-Tunney fight. *The Arizona Republic* used a public address system to share the fight with the cheering, rain-dampened crowd. Radio owners who stayed home heard the fight broadcast over KFAD.

"Arizona on NBC Parade." That was the program for June 8, 1930 when KTAR was welcomed as the newest member of the NBC network. Tunes from the New York musical "Whoopee," sung by Mary McCoy, were featured. Arizonans all over the state heard the finest performers in the land—without fading and without static. U. S. Senators Ashurst and Hayden and Congressman Lewis Douglas also spoke over the national hookup.

"It has been hard to convince the rest of the world there is an Arizona," Hayden said,

"but Arizona is very much alive, progressive, and striding on to new achievements and new triumphs."

Aviation. After the historic flight of Orville Wright in 1903, the airplane was used primarily for stunts and amusement. The first airplane flight in Arizona took place in Phoenix on February 12, 1910. Charles K. Hamilton, a barnstorming "Man-Bird," flew a bamboo and silk contraption at the state fairgrounds. He beat a Studebaker car in a five-mile race, only to lose the next day.

Hamilton shipped his plane by rail to Tucson where he thrilled another crowd on February 19. He reached an altitude of 900 feet and a speed of 40 miles per hour. Tickets were sold for the spectacle. To prevent gate crashing, the pilot was required to take off and land his flimsy, awkward plane in a very small field surrounded by a board fence. He

Charles Hamilton at Tucson, 1910.

Charles Hamilton's plane in flight at Tucson in 1910.

Cal Rodgers and his Vin Fiz Flyer.

Katherine Stinson delivered the first airmail to Tucson.

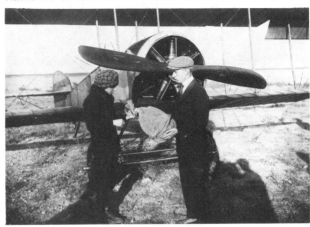

received about $2,000 for the Tucson appearance. Hamilton turned down a $4,000 offer to perform at the small town of Patagonia and went on to El Paso.

Two transcontinental flyers going in opposite directions landed in Tucson on November 1, 1911. Cal P. Rodgers, six-foot four-inch ex-football player, and Robert G. Fowler were trying to win a $50,000 prize. The prize was offered by newspaper publisher William Randolph Hearst for the first pilot to complete a coast-to-coast flight in 30 days.

Rodgers flew the "Vin Fiz Flyer," a biplane named after the new grape drink he was advertising for Armour's. A Vin Fiz train with mechanics, spare parts, and free pop accompanied him all the way from New York. It took Rodgers 49 days to reach Pasadena, California. In Arizona he made overnight stops at Willcox and Maricopa. In Phoenix, Rodgers

landed at the fairgrounds when a crowd at the circus grounds would not clear enough space for him to come down safely. Fowler was 149 trouble-plagued days flying from San Francisco to Florida.

In 1915 Katherine Stinson, a 19-year-old woman flyer, thrilled Tucson fair crowds. She did loop-the-loops and a death-dip. The latter was a steep power dive toward the crowd. On November 5 Miss Stinson flew a sack of air mail from the fairgrounds on South 6th Avenue and dropped it on a vacant lot behind the downtown post office. This was the first "official" air mail flight in Arizona. The U. S. Post Office Department, going along with the stunt, had already designated the 6th Avenue route as U. S. Mail Route Number 668001.

In 1919 the City of Tucson built the

Charles Lindbergh at Tucson in 1927.

nation's first municipal airport on the Nogales highway south of town. In 1927 a new airport, named Davis-Monthan, was established. It was dedicated by Charles A. Lindbergh—four months after his historic solo flight across the Atlantic Ocean. More than 12,000 people were at the new airport when Lindbergh landed his famous silver-tinted monoplane, the Spirit of St. Louis. Another large crowd greeted him later in the day at the University of Arizona football stadium. Lindbergh returned to Arizona many times. In 1928 he chose a route through Kingman and Winslow for Transcontinental Air Transport Company's coast-to-coast airline. In 1929 he was a passenger on T.A.T.s first flight. At the stops, another famous pilot, Amelia Earhart, also got a lot of attention.

Commercial air service in Arizona began in 1927. Jack Frye, president of Aero Corporation, flew a Fokker monoplane on a tri-weekly schedule from Los Angeles to Phoenix and on to Tucson. The flight took seven hours and 10

minutes. The Aero Corporation was reorganized as Standard Airlines. In 1930 it was sold to Western Air Express (WAE), a line that flew between Los Angeles and Salt Lake City. WAE and TAT later merged to form TWA.

There were other pioneer airlines in Arizona. One of the most interesting was Scenic Airways. During 1928 this airline carried more than 5,000 passengers to view the Grand Canyon in Ford tri-motored planes which were called "the gooses." Scenic also built a $150,000 airport in Phoenix. The City of Phoenix got possession of this airport, the present Sky Harbor, in 1935.

The first air mail in the East was delivered in 1911. But Congress did not authorize transcontinental air mail contracts until 1930. TWA got the central route through Winslow. American Airways got the southern route but needed the help of Standard Airlines to carry the mail between Los Angeles and El Paso. This southern route went through Phoenix, Tucson, and Douglas. Each of the four Arizona cities on air

A Fokker tri-motor plane used by Aero Corporation on commercial flights between Los Angeles and Tucson by way of Phoenix.

Air mail delivery announced in the *Arizona Republican*, October, 15, 1930.

mail routes staged celebrations on the first day of service, October 15, 1930.

Phoenix postmaster, James H. McClintock, brought 15,000 air mail letters to Sky Harbor in an old horse-drawn stagecoach. In Tucson the first 1911 air mail flight was reenacted with the original cast. *Tucson Citizen* publisher Frank H. Hitchcock handed an air mail letter to Earle Ovington, a passenger on the trimotored Fokker plane. As the U. S. postmaster general in 1911, Hitchcock had started the first air mail service. Ovington was the first government air mail pilot.

Motion pictures. Crude movie projectors were invented in the late 1890s. The first movie to tell a connected story was *The Great Train Robbery*, produced in 1903. This breathless melodrama and other early "flickers" were shown all over the country in vacant storerooms. The first theaters were called nickelo-

deons because the price of admission was usually a nickel. During World War I the first full-length movies were made. After the war, "picture show" theaters were built in most towns that did not already have them.

All the early films were "silents." That is why large audiences at the Elks theater in Phoenix in 1913 were thrilled by the *kinetophone* invented by Thomas Edison. "Movies that talk are here," said the *Arizona Republican*. The *kinetophone* was really two machines—a film projector and a phonograph that ran in unison. The new invention was at the Elks for six days in November 1913. At a special matinee for school children, all kinds of movies were shown—comedies, educational films, and Shakespearean drama.

It was 1927, however, before a movie was made that synchronized voice, music, and other sounds on the same film. The first "talkie," *The Jazz Singer*, starring Al Jolson, was shown in Arizona theaters in the late 1920s. By that time the making of motion pictures was the nation's fourth largest industry. Great elaborate movie palaces were built all over the country.

Phoenix alone had seven movie theaters in 1929 with a total seating capacity of 6,000. Phoenix residents celebrated the opening of the fancy Orpheum Theater on January 5, 1929. Hollywood star Richard Arlen was there. Governor Phillips spoke briefly at the dedication. Gene Redewill's orchestra played. More than 5,000 applicants for tickets were turned away from the first movie, *Give and Take*.

Orpheum Theatre under construction in Phoenix, 1928.

A good seat in the balcony at the Grand Theatre in Douglas cost 10 cents. The theatre is now preserved as a national historic site.

Lubin films were shown in a tent theatre in Tucson. The price was right.

The Cisco Kid was the first cowboy film star to carry two six-guns.

First-nighters at the Orpheum marveled at the electric fountains, Mayan idols, art work, and the ceiling with its sky effect of rolling clouds and blinking stars.

The first movies were made in the East. But the producers began to move west. In 1912 Cecil B. De Mille was looking for a location to produce a western film for the Lasky company. He might have chosen Flagstaff except for a bad snowstorm that was raging when his train stopped there. Instead, he went on to the coast and helped to establish the film industry in Hollywood.

Tucson was the site of the first movies produced in Arizona. In 1912 the Lubin company of Philadelphia made six pictures in Tucson in 100 days. All these pictures were "one-reeler" silent films, 12 to 15 minutes in length. Viewers followed the conversations by reading the print at the bottom of the film. The Lubin studio was a rented home on Stone Avenue in downtown Tucson. But all the Lubin films made use of Arizona scenery, activities, and buildings—especially the San Xavier mission. Director Romaine Fielding produced one movie, *The Sleeper*, which stirred the world of cinema.

It was the story of a luckless old prospector who made a fabulous strike near Tucson. Hundreds of people came in by wagon, horseback, or train to join in the gold rush. About 400 Tucson residents worked as extras. Dressed in their roughest clothes, carrying packs and mining tools, they boarded a borrowed Southern Pacific train which chugged into the depot.

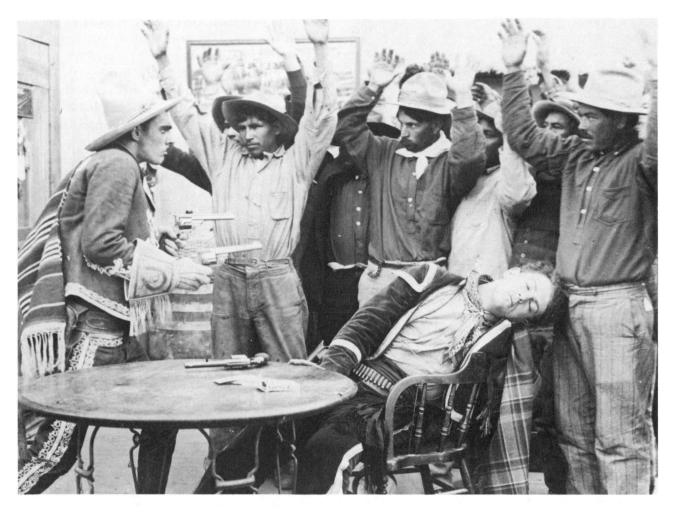

The Cisco Kid (Herbert Stanley Dunn) in a silent film scene made in Tucson in 1913.

They jumped off en masse and ran for the "gold fields."

Between 1913 and 1915 the Eclair company of New York made silent "Cisco Kid" one-reelers in and around Tucson. The original Cisco Kid was Herbert Stanley Dunn, the first film cowboy to use two guns. The studio was a deserted adobe house at Main and Congress streets. Many of the scenes were shot in the Catalinas and other nearby mountains. Warner Baxter was the most famous "talking" Cisco Kid. He did filming in the Tucson vicinity in 1933.

Between 1912 and 1933 at least six major movies were filmed in southern Arizona. Superstar Douglas Fairbanks made *Heading*

South in Tucson in 1917. The next year *Light of Western Stars* was filmed at La Osa Ranch on the Mexican border near Sasabe. This movie was based on a novel written by Zane Grey who lived near Payson. Several movies were also based on western novels written by Harold Bell Wright of Tucson. Part of *The Mine with the Iron Door* was filmed in Cañada del Oro, a scenic canyon between Tucson and Oracle.

In 1925 Warner Baxter did *Son of His Father* at La Osa. Arizonans were angry at the publicity release for this film. It was reported that Baxter and company had to ride 18 miles on pack mules to reach the location, subsisted on food supplies dropped from an airplane,

Silent movie star Tom Mix.

and were constantly in danger of attack by Mexican bandits. The film's producers apologized and held a party for the state's residents at the old Blue Moon Ballroom on Miracle Mile in Tucson.

Tom Mix was the greatest cowboy star of silent westerns. During the 1920s he made a few of his 300 movies in the Prescott and Grand Canyon areas. Mix got his start in Prescott where he was the national rodeo champion in 1909. A great showman and stuntman, he was the hero of millions of people who saw him in silent films. But he had a high-pitched voice which was not suitable for "talkies." Mix spent a lot of time in Arizona after his movie career was over. A speeder, he was killed when his Cord convertible turned over on the highway south of Florence in 1940. Tom Mix Wash was named after him.

The prohibition experiment. The people voted to make Arizona a "dry" state in 1914. At that time there were 354 saloons in the state. Saloon owners were ordered to close their doors on January 1, 1915. At the 1916 election, every county in the state voted against amending the Arizona constitution to permit local option. In 1920 the 18th "prohibition" amendment was added to the U. S. Constitution and the whole nation went "dry." Prohibition, however, was not easy to enforce. People who wanted to drink did so in spite of the Constitution.

As in the rest of the country, Arizona moonshiners operated illegal stills. Bootleggers peddled the illegal whiskey and sometimes sold smuggled Mexican tequila too. Despite hundreds of arrests, it was estimated that Tucson alone had 150 bootleggers in the mid-1920s. Almost every town in the state had the same problem.

By the end of the 1920s a majority of the American people had decided that the prohibition experiment was a failure. The 21st amendment, which repealed prohibition, was ratified by the states in 1933. The problem of controlling the liquor business was turned back to the individual states. Arizona voters had already repealed the prohibition amendment in the state constitution in 1932 and were ready to go "wet." A few states chose to remain "dry" or give the people in each community a choice.

Ku Klux Klan. The 6th state legislature in 1923 passed a law making it a misdemeanor to wear a mask in public. The law was aimed at the Ku Klux Klan. The KKK was a secret organization whose members wore hoods and white sheets. The Klan was fairly active in Arizona during the early 1920s. It organized first in the urban areas of Phoenix and Tucson before spreading out to the smaller towns.

In a campaign speech at Nogales in 1924, ex-Governor Hunt pointed out the groups of citizens the Klan usually opposed: Catholics, Jews, Mormons, and Negroes. In Arizona the Klan claimed to be working mainly for better

Law officers raid a bootlegger's whiskey still in 1929.

law enforcement. The Klan's methods, however, were usually outside the law. In 1922, for example, the Klan flogged a Lehi school principal after he was freed of charges brought against him. A "K" was branded with acid on each cheek and his forehead. The Klan was secretly active in the recall of Pinal County Superior Court Judge Stephen H. Abbey in June, 1924. Abbey's opponents said he was too lenient in sentencing convicted criminals.

The Arizona Grand Dragon, as the chief of the Klan was called, made the KKK official by incorporating it as a non-profit organization in 1925 and again in 1927. But by that time the Klan seemed to have faded away. There was actually no more activity after the defeat of most Klan-supported candidates in 1924. Both political parties had strong anti-Klan planks in their 1924 platforms.

In 1933 gasoline was 16 cents a gallon for regular. Oil was
15 cents a quart at this downtown Phoenix service station.

18

ARIZONA IN THE DEPRESSION OF THE 1930s

The prosperity of the 1920s turned suddenly to depression in the 1930s. There was widespread unemployment. Business activity was slow. For many people the basic necessities of food, clothing, shelter, and fuel were hard to obtain. No depression in history struck so hard or remained so long.

What caused the depression? This question has puzzled the best minds for years. How to overcome it was an immediate problem for everyone in the nation. Until the 1930s most Americans believed that government should keep hands off the economy and business. The severity of the depression brought a change in their thinking. Just as they looked to government for leadership during World War I, so now they expected government to solve the riddle of the depression.

In Arizona the depression struck hardest in the mines and on the cotton farms. The prices of copper and cotton fell rapidly. Arizona's climate attracted large numbers of transients out of work. The need for relief was great. Private groups, public charities, and state and national governments waged war on the depression. Somehow life went on. The state slowly recovered.

KEY CONCEPTS

1. The Great Depression of the 1930s was statewide, nationwide, and worldwide.
2. Many banks failed but the Valley National Bank came out of the depression stronger than ever.
3. The burden of relief was on local programs from 1929 to 1933.
4. The New Deal was a national effort to overcome the depression.
5. The Indians got a New Deal in 1934.
6. Despite the depression, life went on and some progress was made.

18

1. THE GREAT DEPRESSION OF THE 1930s WAS STATEWIDE, NATIONWIDE, AND WORLDWIDE

The 1930s depression was more severe, lasted longer, and affected more people than any economic decline in history. By 1932 there were 15 million Americans unemployed. Thousands of banks failed. People lost their savings. Farm prices dropped. Mines and factories closed down. Foreign trade came to a standstill. Charity soup kitchens opened in the cities. Many jobless people became hoboes. They roamed the country looking for work.

The causes of the Great Depression were complex. Economists are still arguing about them. *Overproduction* by both farm and factory was a major cause. More was produced than the consumers could afford to buy. The reason for that is explained as follows: Too much income went to a few wealthy people. Their income was either held as idle capital in the bank or invested to produce even more surplus goods. Not enough income was going into wages and salaries to increase the buying power of workers.

Too much credit was another depression cause. The "easy money" policy of the banks promoted speculation. It also led consumers to buy goods on the installment plan. By 1929 many consumers were deep in debt. They had to stop spending. When they did, there was a sudden drop in sales of automobiles, radios, and other goods. Then factories had to close down and there were more unemployed people.

Too much speculation was another major cause. Thousands of people gambled on the stock market in the 1920s. Hoping to get rich quickly, they borrowed money to buy corporation stocks. The big demand for stocks raised their price up higher than they were worth. The bottom finally fell out of the stock market on October 29, 1929. In panic everyone tried to sell. As stock prices fell, some people lost everything they had. The Wall Street stock market crash signalled the beginning of the depression.

The depression in Arizona. Statistics show that the Great Depression jolted the Arizona economy. The state's industries had made great progress during the 1920s. But the 1930s depression was disastrous to all of them.

Mining was hit hard. When eastern factories shut down, the copper markets began to disappear. With little demand for copper, the price fell from 18 cents a pound in 1929 to 5½ cents in 1932. At this price the mines could not operate at a profit. Many companies closed down their mines and laid off miners. Some of the unemployed men tried to make a living by prospecting for gold.

The mines that continued to produce copper, cut wages to reduce expenses. Total production of copper tumbled from 830 million pounds in 1929 to 182 million pounds in 1932. The federal government tried to help by putting a four cent import duty on copper. The mines began to recover by 1936. But prosperity never returned until World War II.

Farmers all over the country struggled with low prices, interest payments, and taxes on their land. The cotton growers were hurt the most by the depression in Arizona. In 1928 they planted 153,000 acres in short staple cotton and got 19 cents a pound for the crop. A low point was reached in 1932. Only 91,000 acres were seeded. And the price dropped to 6 cents a pound. During the same time period, long staple Pima cotton acreage was reduced by more than half. The price received for Pima cotton fell from 36 cents to 14 cents a pound.

Orange and grapefruit growers also saw their products go way down in price.

Cattlemen and sheepmen had a similar experience. Wool prices dropped from 36 cents a pound in 1929 to 9 cents in 1933. Beef went down from 9 cents a pound to 3 cents. The price got so low, some cattlemen gave their animals away. The Yavapai County Cattle Growers in Prescott supplied the Salvation Army in Prescott with beef for the poor.

Cultivation of a grapefruit orchard in the Salt River Valley in 1937.

Statistics tell the story of what happened to *Arizona's three main sources of income* during the darkest days of the Great Depression:

	Mining Prod.	Farm Prod.	Livestock Prod.	Total
	(millions of dollars)			
1929	$155.7	$41.8	$25.5	$223.0
1930	79.7	29.1	23.5	132.3
1931	40.6	16.9	19.0	76.5
1932	14.7	13.8	14.7	43.2

The tourist industry and private construction also fell off during the depression. There was almost no home building in Arizona between 1932 and 1935.

School and population trends were weather vanes for the depression. School enrollment decreased as worker's families moved out of Arizona. Migrant children were in and out of the schools. Arizona's population increased only 30 per cent during the 1930s and actually declined in the early part of the decade. By contrast, the Arizona population grew by 63 per cent in the 1920s.

2. MANY BANKS FAILED, BUT THE VALLEY NATIONAL BANK CAME OUT OF THE DEPRESSION STRONGER THAN EVER

When economic conditions went from bad to worse, banks all over the country took a beating. In Arizona the per capita income slipped to $271 in 1932. People were forced to use up their savings. They took their money out of the bank. As a result, bank deposits in Arizona dropped from $93 million in 1929 to $45 million in 1932.

This large withdrawal of deposits combined with uncollectable loans to put some banks out of business. Four banks in Arizona closed their doors in 1930, four more in 1931, and five in 1932. Many small banks merged with others rather than close. The First National Bank of Prescott, for example, was absorbed by the Valley Bank.

Walter Bimson was a good banker. He also collected many fine paintings.

297

Walter Bimson, the new president of Valley Bank, had reason to worry during the early morning hours of March 2, 1933. Over the telephone came word that Governor James Rolph of California had temporarily closed all banks in that state. The California and Arizona banks were closely linked.

Bimson feared that the California banks would start withdrawing their deposits from Arizona banks. He arranged a meeting with Governor B. B. Moeur and persuaded the Governor to proclaim a three-day holiday for Arizona banks. On the same day, the legislature, acting with unusual speed, legalized Moeur's action. A possible epidemic of bank runs and failures was prevented by Governor Moeur's bank holiday.

A national bank holiday was declared by President Franklin Roosevelt on March 6, 1933. In a radio "fireside chat," he explained that all banks were being examined. Sound ones could reopen. Soon most banks in the country were back in business. Only four banks in Arizona—located in Florence, Scottsdale, Springerville, and Wickenburg—did not reopen. A short time later, Congress set up the FDIC (Federal Deposit Insurance Corporation) to protect bank deposits. Public confidence in banks was restored.

The Valley National Bank was Arizona's most successful financial institution during the 1930s. This bank's share of loans made in Arizona rose from 17 percent in 1932 to nearly 53 percent in 1940. Bimson made Valley Bank a "people's bank" by stressing small installment loans. To do this he had the help of two federal agencies—the RFC and the FHA.

In 1933 Bimson secured much-needed credit by getting a $840,000 loan from RFC (Reconstruction Finance Corporation). The RFC was a federal lending agency established during the administration of President Herbert Hoover. With new money to lend, Bimson conducted a vigorous advertising campaign. The key slogan was this bold statement: "Yes, Mr. Jones, We Will Gladly Make That Loan!" Needless to say, the bank had a lot of customers.

Congress helped both the banks and the depressed construction industry by creating the FHA (Federal Housing Administration) in 1934. The FHA partially guaranteed bank loans for home improvements and new housing construction. When the FHA law went into effect, Valley Bank employees in Phoenix rang doorbells. They talked to people about new porches, plumbing repairs, and cooling systems. Within one week after FHA started, about 700 loans were set up in Phoenix alone. On August 30 Carl Bimson, Walter's brother, made one of the first FHA loans in the nation. The money was borrowed by a young couple with a new baby. They got the loan to add a room to their house.

The Valley Bank continued to grow at a fantastic rate during the 1940s. By the end

Gila Valley Bank in I. E. Solomon's store in Solomonville. This small bank was the beginning of the Valley National Bank.

Walter Bimson was honored at Luke Air Force Base in 1942.

of World War II it accounted for 72 cents of every dollar loaned in the state. Nearly 14,000 loans, totaling almost $4 million, were made during the war to GIs stationed in Arizona. The Valley Bank set up a plan called the "300 Club." Any aviation cadet who finished pilot training could get a $300 loan by simply signing his name three times. A specific amount was then deducted from his paycheck and remitted to the bank each month.

In 1945 the Valley National Bank entered the charmed circle of America's "100 Largest Banks." It was 76th in size among the 15,000 banks in the United States. This was a rare feat for a bank that started in 1899 in the corner in I. E. Solomon's general store in Solomonville.

3. THE BURDEN OF RELIEF WAS ON LOCAL PROGRAMS FROM 1929 TO 1933

Few people looked to government for help in the early years of the depression. Poverty-stricken families stopped buying. Old clothes were remade and mended. Entertainment was centered in the home. The pioneer practices of "make it over," "make it do," "wear it out," and "eat it up" were repeated in many households. It was expected that each family would try to take care of its own problems. One of the biggest tasks in Arizona, however, was to

take care of transients who were attracted to the mild climate. Churches and private charities did what they could.

Dozens of private and public groups organized to help the needy, both resident and transient. In 1930, for example, the Phoenix Board of Public Charities was given $3,000 by the city commission to start a municipal woodyard. On opening night in November, 60 men were fed and 50 were housed in clean, warm quarters on South 9th Street and Jefferson. The men chopped wood for four hours each morning in return for housing and food.

Phil Tovrea of Phoenix headed a committee in 1931 to solicit unmarketable surplus food from farmers and grocers. Tovrea was connected with the meat packing industry. He pledged 1,000 pounds of meat daily for the unemployed. The Arizona Cotton Growers' Association agreed not to import any cotton-pickers from Mexico in 1931.

The next year, some 2,000 Phoenix high school and junior college students took part in a three-day "Create-a-Job" campaign. These "minute men and women of '32" contacted everybody in Phoenix. They listed all the odd jobs available. An estimated 12,000 days of work were found in the Madison and Creighton school districts alone.

In Tucson an Emergency Relief Committee was headed by Harold Bell Wright, the writer. This group, and another called Organ-

Cotton pickers from Texas, Oklahoma, and Arkansas pose for this picture near Phoenix in 1932.

Harold Bell Wright at work near his desert foothills cabin.

ized Charities of Tucson, raised money to assist several thousand unemployed local residents. In the month of March 1932, nearly 40 tons of food were distributed. The unemployed earned the food by working on public projects.

Groups of college students at the University of Arizona rented small houses and shared expenses. At Flagstaff, college students were permitted to pay their tuition fees with hay, oats, or turnips instead of cash. The college dairy made good use of these fees.

The state legislature took action to provide some relief for the needy. A sales tax was enacted to raise money. A State Welfare Board was given 96 percent of all revenue from the state luxury tax and 10 percent of the gasoline tax.

Each county set up a board of public welfare. These county boards distributed both state and federal relief funds. For the first time in history, President Hoover's administration made some federal emergency relief money available to the states in July 1932. The county welfare boards, however, shouldered the primary relief burden during the early years of the depression. The task was too great for them. By 1933 Arizona gave up all pretense of self-reliance and eagerly sought federal aid. Governor Moeur asked President Roosevelt's New Deal administration for every federal relief program available.

4. THE NEW DEAL WAS A NATIONAL EFFORT TO OVERCOME THE DEPRESSION

Despite piecemeal local programs and Hoover's efforts, the depression grew worse. Democrat Franklin Roosevelt took office in March 1933. He took a *trial-and-error approach* to the nation's problems. "Try something," he said. "If it fails, try another."

The first task was to care for jobless people. At first the New Deal gave money to the states. This money was handed out as direct relief. But the unemployed wanted jobs, not charity.

The next New Deal relief programs were "make work" projects such as leaf raking and picking up litter in parks. Critics called this kind of work "boondoggling."

Finally, however, programs were designed to provide socially useful work. Most of them were best known by the initials of their three word titles.

The PWA (Public Works Administration) stimulated employment through contracts with private industry. It continued, on a bigger scale, the emergency program of public work started by President Hoover. A large part of Arizona's PWA funds was spent on the completion of Boulder (Hoover) Dam. Several archaeological projects were undertaken at Wupatki, Montezuma Castle, Tuzigoot, and Tumacácori. Many of the buildings at the University of Arizona and other schools were built by private contractors with some PWA funds.

The WPA (Works Progress Administration) was created in 1935. It was based on the belief that everyone has the right to useful work and the self-respect that goes with earning a living. The WPA soon became the nation's chief relief agency. WPA workers improved the state highway system. They also constructed school buildings, post offices, libraries, the National Guard armory in Phoenix, water systems, sidewalks, bridges, and municipal facilities. One of the bigger WPA

A WPA Mexican music concert in Phoenix.

jobs was the state fairgrounds project. Workmen built a racetrack, grandstand, and several exhibit halls.

The WPA employed people in all walks of life—both manual and white-collar workers. People with talents were given a chance to practice their skills. One of the interesting WPA programs was the Federal Writers Project. Under the direction of Ross Santee, Arizona researchers and writers gathered data all over the state and prepared a *State Guide*. The Federal Music Project presented some 1,250 concerts during its existence in Arizona.

Jobs were given to long-idle actors, artists, and teachers.

The NYA (National Youth Administration) was a division of the WPA. Many students in Arizona colleges and high schools were given part-time work. The NYA made it possible for many of these young people to continue their education.

The CCC (Civilian Conservation Corps) was one of the most popular of the federal relief programs. It was designed to give work and vocational training to young men between the ages of 18 and 25. At the same time, the

CCC promoted a nationwide program of conservation. Some 1,500 camps were built, mainly in forested areas. The men lived under army discipline. They were supervised by the federal agency to which they were assigned. The pay was $30 a month. Out of this amount, $22 to $25 a month was sent home to parents or dependents. The men also received food, clothing, shelter, medical attention, and education.

The CCC started in 1933. In three years there were 9,000 corpsmen at more than 40 camps in Arizona. The camps were divided among the Forest Service, Soil Conservation Service, Bureau of Reclamation, Division of Grazing of the Department of Interior, and the National Park Service.

One of the first jobs of the Forest Service men was to eradicate twig-blight disease. This fungus threatened to destroy the state's huge ponderosa pine forests. The only known way to combat the disease was to remove infected twigs and trees. Many forest lands were replanted and mountain roads constructed.

The CCC restored range lands. Check dams were built in eroded gullies. Overgrazed land was reseeded in grass and fenced off.

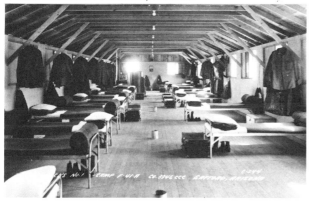

CCC enrollee moves rocks on a sled to a check dam construction site, 1935.

A CCC barracks at Safford, Arizona.

CCC men leaving for work, 1935.

Flood detention check dams built near Bisbee, 1936.

Thousands of visitors at Colossal Cave have walked along stone and concrete trails, built by the CCC, to see the beautiful crystal formations.

A typical CCC camp in Arizona.

Stock ponds were constructed. CCC men near Yuma and Tempe cleaned out irrigation systems and lined canals with concrete. The CCC built a trail in the Grand Canyon and a scenic road in the Petrified Forest. Tucson Mountain Park was reseeded with native grasses and fenced. New trails and guard rails were built in Colossal Cave near Tucson.

Other New Deal agencies. The New Deal tried to give relief to the jobless. But there were other measures passed to help industries recover. Arizona farmers, for example, began receiving subsidies under the first AAA (Agricultural Adjustment Act) in 1933. Farmers in Maricopa County were paid $125,000 that year to take 9,000 acres out of cultivation. The New Deal hoped to raise farm prices by creating scarcity.

Many aspects of the New Deal were of lasting value for Arizona. This is true of reforms in banking and housing. Many of the construction projects are still in use. Conservation was given a big boost. However, it was not the three R's of the New Deal — relief, recovery, and reform — which brought the

United States out of the depression. It was a fourth R — rearmament — that ended hard times. The outbreak of the war in Europe in 1939 led to a demand for American goods. The products of Arizona's basic industries were needed. Once again prices rose. A prosperity began in Arizona which has not let up since for any long period of time.

5. THE INDIANS GOT A NEW DEAL IN 1934

Background. Most of Arizona's Indians were put on reservations between 1859 and 1916. The reservation system may have made it possible for the Arizona Indians to survive. For one reason, part of their land was saved from Anglo-American settlement. Also, the larger tribes were able to preserve much of their native culture on the reservations. Finally, after a long period of mistreatment and hardships, the Indian population began to increase—despite the white man's bullets, booze, and bacteria.

A Pima Indian girl. Reservation Indians were able to hold on to much of their native culture.

Tom Torlino before he went to Carlisle Indian School.

Tom Torlino three years after he arrived at Carlisle Indian School.

But the reservation system had many flaws. The Indians were segregated from the rest of society. In a sense, the reservations were like open air prisons without walls. The Indians, somehow, were expected to become part of the mainstream of American life while being isolated from it. The policy of the federal government was to eliminate Indian lifestyles, religions, and languages.

Schools became a principal means for changing Indian ways of living. School attendance was made compulsory in the 1890s. Many Indian children were taken from their homes—sometimes by force if the parents objected—and placed in boarding schools. All instruction was in English. Every attempt was made in these schools to make the Indian youths speak, think, act, look, and be like the dominant non-Indian population.

The Dawes Act was passed by Congress in 1887. Its purpose was to turn the Indians into farmers and taxpayers. Tribal lands was divided into 160 acre family farms. The government sold the surplus. In this way, the American Indians were dispossessed of over 90 million acres of land.

Fortunately for Arizona Indians, only about 3 per cent of the reservations in this state were allotted to individuals. Only the San Xavier, Salt River, Gila River, San Carlos, Colorado River, and a small part of the Navajo reservations were divided into family farms. The remaining 97 per cent of Indian-owned land in Arizona is held by tribes in individual shares.

Boarding schools and individual land ownership were only two methods used by the government to turn the Indian away from his native culture. In 1896 all male Indians were ordered to wear their hair short like urban Anglo-Americans. After 1900, native religions were discouraged.

Citizenship. In 1924 all native-born Indians were given American citizenship. But this act of Congress was no real victory for Indians. Having citizenship changed their lives very little. By the 1920s most Indians lived in extreme poverty. On the reservations they were controlled by federal bureaucrats. The "Indian problem," as it was called by non-Indians, was investigated by the U. S. Senate between 1926 and 1933. The Senate's findings resulted in an "Indian New Deal."

The Johnson-O'Malley Act of 1934. This was the first New Deal law passed to help the Indians. Among other things, this law provided funds for school districts willing to educate Indians. Before the Johnson-O'Malley bill was enacted, Indian children could not attend public schools. The legal reason was simple. The reservation Indians are exempt from state and local property taxes, including school taxes. But since 1939 the State of Arizona has contracted for Johnson-O'Malley money each year. As a result, Indian boys and girls are in public schools all over the state.

Apache dancers going under a ceremonial *tipi* at girl's puberty rite near Bylas, 1937.

Papagos working on a federal project in the 1930s. They are building a check dam and water reservoir.

Mabel Anton, a Papago judge.

The Indian Reorganization Act (IRA) of 1934. This law was the most important New Deal act for Arizona Indians. They were encouraged by IRA to continue their tribal organization. Indians were allowed to adopt their own tribal constitutions, hire lawyers, and form business corporations. They were given the right to practice their own native religions and tribal customs.

The IRA also made the secretary of interior responsible for preventing erosion and overgrazing on the reservations. Nearly 2,000 Indians were soon employed in the Indian division of the CCC. They built check dams to stop erosion and conserve water supplies, constructed reservoirs and truck trails, and reseeded thousands of acres on the reservations.

Tribal government. Each Arizona tribe—except the Navajos and Prescott Yavapais—adopted a constitution and set up an elective tribal government. The Indians used the U. S. Constitution as a model. Legislative and executive branches—usually a council and tribal chairman—were provided. In later years, nearly every reservation organized a police force and tribal courts with Indian judges. These courts handle only misdemeanors and offenses against tribal law. The more serious crimes are tried in state or federal courts.

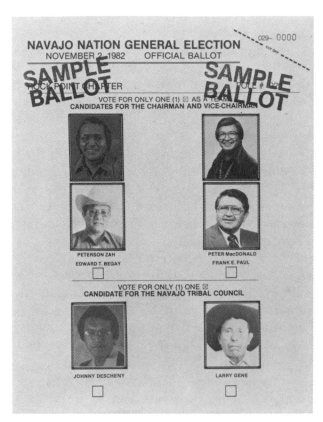

NAVAJO NATION GENERAL ELECTION
NOVEMBER 2, 1982   OFFICIAL BALLOT

029- 0000

ROCK POINT CHAPTER

VOTE FOR ONLY ONE (1) ⊠ AS A TEAM
CANDIDATES FOR THE CHAIRMAN AND VICE-CHAIRMAN

PETERSON ZAH
EDWARD T. BEGAY
☐

PETER MacDONALD
FRANK E. PAUL
☐

VOTE FOR ONLY (1) ONE ⊠
CANDIDATE FOR THE NAVAJO TRIBAL COUNCIL

JOHNNY DESCHENY
☐

LARRY GENE
☐

Navajo tribal ballot. Like other Indian tribes, the Navajos elect their own tribal officials. They also take part in county, state, and federal elections.

Navajo Tribal Chairman Peter McDonald, seated at podium, conducts a session of the Navajo Tribal Council.

The Navajos, the largest tribe in the United States, have no constitution. The tribal council follows a code of guidelines in conducting the tribe's extensive government and business operations. Every four years the Navajos elect 74 council members. The tribal chairman and vice chairman are elected at large. Other tribes follow a similar procedure.

Self-government was not an easy thing for the Indians at first because they had no training. For several generations they were forced to be dependent on the federal government for rations and direction. Strong tribal leaders did not begin to emerge before the 1950s and 1960s. Until then, officials in the BIA (Bureau of Indian Affairs) really ran the new tribal governments.

The policy of John Collier, who was the Commissioner of Indian Affairs from 1933 to 1945, was to allow the Indians to remain Indians. During his tenure, some boarding schools were closed and replaced by community day schools. An Indian Arts and Crafts Board was created to work for the preservation of native culture.

6. DESPITE THE DEPRESSION, LIFE WENT ON AND SOME PROGRESS WAS MADE

Life went on in the 1930s. Not all was gloom and doom. There were still "picture shows," though it was more of a luxury to see one. Drug stores continued to sell fountain drinks, chocolate bars, and magazines. Students were still transported to school in motor buses. Free baseball games gained more spectators and competition improved. As always, young people courted and married. But they had fewer children.

People still drove automobiles, the difference being that they kept them longer. Auto dealers did a good business in 1936, however. Many World War I veterans bought cars when they were finally paid a bonus for war service. The average bonus was about $600. Newspapers stayed in business, though they often

The 1934 state champion Funk Jewelers softball team of Phoenix that reached the national semifinals in Chicago. Paul Fannin (top row, third from right) was a pitcher. He was later elected governor and U.S. Senator.

Before natural gas was piped into Phoenix in 1934, gas had to be manufactured. It was stored in huge pressure tanks like the Hortonsphere at 5th Street and Sheridan.

Employees of the Central Arizona Light and Power Company advertise the coming of natural gas to Phoenix.

lost circulation or had to cut down the size of the paper.

Arizona had some "firsts" in the 1930s. The first natural gas pipe line from Texas via Douglas reached Tucson in 1933 and Phoenix in 1934. The Arizona Highway Patrol was established. Evaporative coolers came into general use.

At a special election in 1933, Mrs. Isabella Greenway—the first woman to seek high office in Arizona—was elected to Congress as a Democrat. She replaced Lewis Douglas who resigned to be Director of the Budget under President Roosevelt.

At the same election, Arizonans voted to substitute the lethal* gas chamber for the gallows. The 1930 hanging of Eva Dugan—the first and last woman to be hanged in Arizona—was one reason for the change. A heavy woman, her head was snapped from her body as she plunged through the trap.

The Arizona Highway Patrol was created by the 10th state legislature in 1931. The law provided for a superintendent, a chief clerk, and a patrolman for each of the 14 counties. By 1938 there were 42 patrolmen, one for every 3,500 registered vehicles.

The primary function of the patrol in the beginning was to increase the registration of motor vehicles. The patrol was designed as a revenue-producing agency and paid its own way for awhile. Hundreds of out-of-state car owners were forced to buy Arizona plates. Citations were issued to many people who had bought cheaper pleasure car license plates for commercial vehicles.

Within a month after the Highway Patrol was started, more than 17,000 drivers in Maricopa County alone applied for an operator's license at the assessor's office. At least that number had been driving illegally without a driver's license.

Gradually the patrol was able to give more attention to enforcement of traffic laws.

*lethal: capable of causing death

Safety programs and auto inspections became important duties of the Highway Patrol by 1937.

Room coolers were first used in Arizona in the 1930s. The first ones were homemade wooden boxes installed in windows. On one side, charcoal was packed between chicken wire. In the opposite side was a hole one foot in diameter. The box was placed in a window with the hole facing the room. A garden hose hung at the top of the box dripped water into the charcoal. An electric fan was placed in the box to draw air through the charcoal. By 1935 Phoenix had 1,500 of these window coolers—sometimes called "swamp cooler" or "wet air cooler." A year later, the Central Arizona Light and Power Company counted about 5,000. People in other Arizona desert towns also took part in the cooler epidemic.

Improvements were added to the coolers. Excelsior was used instead of charcoal. The hose was replaced by copper tubing and the fan by a blower. Most new houses, beginning in 1937, had provision for cooler ducts.

Oscar C. Palmer began the assembly line production of coolers in Phoenix in the 1930s. The Goettl brothers also started manufacturing coolers about the same time. By the 1950s Phoenix was the "Cooler Capital of the World."

Air conditioning. The first refrigerated air conditioning in the state was installed in Phoenix in 1929. Hotel Westward Ho, the Mountain States Telephone Company office, and the Orpheum Theater led the way. Before long, other hotels, theaters, and businesses had to install some kind of cooling system to attract customers.

In 1937 Dr. Willis Carrier—who invented air conditioning in 1902—designed air conditioning equipment for the Magma Copper Mine near Superior. The rock temperature at the 4,000 foot level was lowered from 140 degrees to 93 degrees. This was the first use of air conditioning to cool a mine shaft in North America.

Early coolers were homemade affairs.

Oscar Palmer (far right) stands beside his father in this 1913 photo of the Phoenix Sheet Metals Company shop. As a teenager, Oscar made his experimental coolers in this shop.

Refrigeration units for the home were not efficient until the late 1940s. The earlier units sat in a living room like a piece of furniture. They took heat from the air in front and dumped it out the back side.

Frank Lloyd Wright, one of the world's greatest architects, first visited Arizona in the late 1920s. Wright was a consultant for awhile on the Arizona Biltmore designed by Albert Chase McArthur. Attracted to the desert, the famous architect returned to Arizona with his students in 1936. Together they built Taliesen West on Wright's property in Paradise Valley. From this workshop, and Wright's other home in Wisconsin, came architectural designs for some of the world's most famous buildings.

Wright believed that a building should be built of native materials and blend with the

The beautiful Arizona Biltmore in Phoenix, designed by architect Albert Chase McArthur. The walls were built of specially cast concrete blocks.

An interior view of Taliesen West. A bust of Frank Lloyd Wright is on the right.

Old Tucson

The wedding scene in *Arizona*, filmed at Old Tucson.

environment. He preferred the use of native trees and plants for landscaping around desert homes. Today, people in water-short areas of Arizona are learning to appreciate both the beauty and necessity of what Wright was saying in the 1930s.

Old Tucson was built in 1939 by Columbia Pictures. It cost $500,000 and was constructed for the shooting of a film called *Arizona*. The adobe village is a replica of an Arizona town as it might have appeared in the

1860s. The man most responsible for bringing Columbia Pictures to Tucson was Nick Hall. He was the manager of the Santa Rita Hotel in Tucson and a member of Governor Jones's Moving Picture Commission.

The movie *Arizona* was based on Clarence Buddington Kelland's thrilling novel that first appeared in the *Saturday Evening Post*. Kelland was a popular New England writer who moved to Phoenix in a trailer in the 1930s. He embellished the pioneer history of Arizona in a thrilling story. His heroine was Phoebe Titus. She was stranded in Old Tucson when her father died. Phoebe baked pies for a living. She also ran a freighting business and survived an Indian attack. The story is made doubly attractive by a tender romance between Phoebe and Peter Muncie. The whole town turns out for their wedding. Jean Arthur and William Holden had the starring roles.

Since 1940 hundreds of western movie and TV films have been produced at Old Tucson. John Wayne has probably made more films there than any other star. The first was *Tall in the Saddle* in 1944.

Mae West was popular with moviegoers in the 1930s. Here she visits with U.S. Senator Henry F. Ashurst.

Walter Brennan backs up John Wayne in a scene from *Rio Bravo*. This movie was filmed at Old Tucson's Mexican plaza area in 1958.

Bill Mauldin drawing a Willie and Joe cartoon during World
. Mauldin attended Phoenix Union High School.

19

ARIZONA DURING WORLD WAR II

While Americans were busy fighting the depression in the 1930s, Europe and Asia were moving toward war. In 1931 the military leaders of Japan invaded Chinese territory. Four years later, dictator Mussolini of Italy took over Ethiopia. Adolf Hitler gobbled up Austria and Czechoslovakia. On September 1, 1939, his Nazi troops smashed into Poland. World War II officially began two days later, when Great Britain and France declared war on Germany.

The United States sympathized with Britain, France, and their allies. President Roosevelt gave these countries all the material aid possible short of war. Our economy was partly on a war footing when the Japanese made a sneak attack on Pearl Harbor on December 7, 1941. For the United States the war lasted from that infamous day until 1945. Fighting ended in Europe on May 8 and the Japanese signed surrender terms on September 2, 1945.

Arizona, like all the other states in the Union, fully cooperated in the national war effort. In turn, Arizona was affected by the war. Family life was disrupted. Employment patterns changed. Arizona was called upon to furnish men and women for the armed forces.

Arizona's copper mines and cotton farms prospered. New defense plants and military bases brought many people to the state. The expenditure of huge sums of money by the federal government led to full employment and to prosperity. No other event has changed Arizona so much or so quickly as World War II. Modern Arizona came fully into being as a result.

KEY CONCEPTS

1. The *USS Arizona* was sunk at Pearl Harbor.
2. Arizona men and women served on many war fronts.
3. Thousands of pilots and other military personnel were trained in Arizona.
4. Arizona's minority groups made a good record during World War II.
5. World War II defense contracts gave manufacturing its first big boost in Arizona.
6. The relocation of Japanese-Americans was a serious mistake and a sad experience.
7. Several prisoner-of-war camps were located in Arizona.

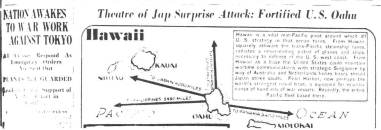

The Arizona Daily Star

An Independent NEWSpaper
Printing the News
Impartially

VOL. 100   NO. 342   Entered as second-class matter, Post Office, Tucson, Arizona   TUCSON, ARIZONA, MONDAY MORNING, DECEMBER 8, 1941   TEN PAGES   PRICE FIVE CENTS

JAP BOMBS SMASH AT HAWAII BEFORE TOKYO DECLARES WAR

NATION AWAKES TO WAR WORK AGAINST TOKYO

All Classes Respond As Emergency Orders Are Sent Out

PLANTS ARE GUARDED

Leaders Urge Support of U. S. All Out in Conflict

Theatre of Jap Surprise Attack: Fortified U.S. Oahu

Hawaii is a vital mid-Pacific pivot around which all U. S. strategy in that ocean turns. From Hawaii, squarely athwart the trans-Pacific steamship lanes, radiates a never-ending patrol of planes and ships, necessary to defense of the U. S. west coast. From Hawaii as a base the United States could maintain wartime communications with strategic Singapore by way of Australia and Netherlands Indies bases should Japan strike south. Pearl Harbor, now perhaps the world's strongest naval base, is equipped for maintenance of hundreds of war vessels. Recently, the entire Pacific fleet based there.

LEADERS MEET TO MAP POLICY OF U. S. IN WAR

President Will Address Congress Today in Special Message

PHILIPPINES BOMBED

No Great Damage There Is Reported by General MacArthur

WASHINGTON, Dec. 7—(P)—The White House announced...

HUNDREDS ARE KILLED AND DAMAGE IS HEAVY IN SURPRISE ASSAULT

U. S. Army Transport is Sunk in Action East of Honolulu and Wake Island is Reported Captured by Enemy Forces

BY THE ASSOCIATED PRESS

Japanese warplanes made a deadly assault on Honolulu and Pearl Harbor Sunday in the first surprise attacks against American possessions in the Pacific.

The *Arizona Daily Star* (Tucson) headline, December 8, 1941.

1. THE USS ARIZONA WAS SUNK AT PEARL HARBOR

The *USS Arizona* was the hardest hit of 94 American ships at Pearl Harbor. Two torpedoes and seven bombs struck the giant battleship before it sank. About 1,400 of the ship's crew of 1,553 were aboard on that fatal Sunday of December 7, 1941. A total of 1,177 officers and men were killed. Of that number, 1,102 died below deck, and remain entombed forever in the sunken vessel.

Only nine Arizonans were members of the crew, and eight of them are within the ship. Dr. Daniel J. Condon, a native of Ajo, was the only Arizonan who survived. He was ashore at the time of the Japanese attack. Dr. Condon was the ship's junior medical officer. After the war he became the Maricopa County medical examiner.

The history of the *USS Arizona* goes back to 1913, when Congress authorized its construction. The 32,000-ton battleship was launched at the Brooklyn Naval Yard in 1915. It was christened by a pretty high school girl from Prescott, Miss Esther Ross. With Governor Hunt looking on, she cracked two bottles

The anchor of the U.S.S. Arizona now rests on the east mall of the State Capitol. A large crowd attended the dedication of the anchor memorial on December 7, 1976, the 35th anniversary of the Pearl Harbor attack.

over the ship's bow. One was filled with water from Roosevelt Lake. Hundreds of Arizona girls and prominent women wanted to do the honors. Hunt chose Miss Ross because her father, William W. Ross, was a pioneer. He was a pharmacist in Tombstone during the hectic 1880s.

Several reminders of the *USS Arizona* are on Arizona soil. The 20-ton anchor rests on a memorial east of the capitol building. The

This "Sock the Japs" parade sign encouraged Tucson residents to buy war bonds.

The Bushmasters cross a stream during training in Panama.

World War II cartoon by Bill Mauldin.

silver setting is now on permanent display in the west wing of the capitol.

Another kind of trophy from Pearl Harbor was exhibited on Central Avenue in Phoenix for two days in 1943. A two-man Japanese submarine was on tour to promote the sale of bonds. Phoenicians bought about $20,000 in war bonds and stamps to get an inside glimpse of the 81-foot torpedo boat.

2. ARIZONA MEN AND WOMEN SERVED ON MANY WAR FRONTS

Some 30,000 Arizona men and several hundred women did military service during World War II. More than 1,600 were killed in action.

The Arizona National Guard was ordered into active service in 1940 before war broke out. Organized as the 158th Infantry Regiment of the 45th Division, the Guardsmen did duty in Panama during 1942. While there, they were trained in jungle warfare and took the name "Bushmasters," the name of a deadly jungle snake. The 158th was transferred to the Southwest Pacific in 1943. The Bushmasters fought their way through the islands to the Philippines. They landed in Yokahama, Japan in October 1945, two months after the atomic bombs were dropped on Hiroshima and Nagasaki.

Bill Mauldin was one of Arizona's most famous GIs* of World War II. An excellent

*GI: a nickname describing enlisted men. The initials stand for "Government Issue."

art student at Phoenix Union High School from 1935 to 1937, Mauldin went overseas to North Africa as a cartoonist for the 45th Division. He created two characters named Willie and Joe to show the war through the eyes of the common soldier. His cartoons, titled "Up

In 1945 Howard Pyle (right) was sent to the Pacific war front by the Valley Bank to interview Arizona men in the service. His taped recordings were broadcast over radio station KTAR. Here he tells Walter Bimson, the bank's president, about his experiences.

Front with Mauldin," appeared in the GI newspaper, *Stars and Stripes*. They were also syndicated in 130 civilian newspapers. Sergeant Mauldin was awarded the Legion of Merit by General Joseph McNarney. The general described him as "the best-known and the most popular" soldier in the Mediterranean theater of war. After the war, Mauldin became one of the country's best cartoonists.

3. THOUSANDS OF PILOTS AND OTHER MILITARY PERSONNEL WERE TRAINED IN ARIZONA

Arizona, like all the states, was deeply involved in a united effort to win the war. Besides furnishing manpower and buying war bonds, Arizona was able to make other important contributions. The state's copper and cotton were much in demand. Near perfect flying weather made Arizona an ideal location for air bases.

Civilian Pilot Training. Even before Pearl Harbor, civilian aviation schools in Arizona were handling primary flight training for the Army. Hundreds of flyers were turned out by the Ryan School of Aeronautics in Tucson and Southwest Airways in the Phoenix area.

The latter eventually had three schools—Thunderbird No. 1 (Glendale), Thunderbird No. 2 (Scottsdale), and Falcon Field at Mesa. Southwest Airways was started in 1940 by Leland Hayward, a Hollywood actors' agent and movie director. Stockholders in the company included air-minded stars Jimmy Stewart, Henry Fonda, Cary Grant, and Brian Aherne. Southwest trained men from other countries—Great Britain and China in particular—as well as Americans.

Davis-Monthan. In 1940 the Tucson Municipal Airport was designated a U. S. Army air base. The old name Davis-Monthan was restored. During World War II Davis-Monthan was the largest heavy bomber training base in the United States. Nearly 2,000 ten-man bomber crews were trained to fly and fight in B-24 Liberators.

Luke Field was built in the spring and summer of 1941 on desert land donated by the City of Phoenix. Clouds of dust from construction work greeted the first student pilots who arrived in June 1941. Before long, however, Luke Field was the largest single-engine flying school in the United States. More than 12,000 fighter pilots graduated from its advanced training courses during World War II. The pilots also received training at the Gila Bend Gunnery Range.

Douglas Army Air Field was another base built on land donated by a community. Douglas Field was built in 1942 on grazing land. The first class, which arrived in November of that year, included a large number of Chinese cadets. In 1944 the Douglas base became a B-25 Mitchell Bomber school. Training was also given in night flying and AT-9 pursuit aircraft.

Williams Air Force Base was activated in 1941. In the beginning it was known as Mesa Military Airport and then Higley Field. Pilot training began in 1942. By the end of the year Williams became the only base to utilize the P-38 Lightning fighter plane as a trainer. This plane was replaced by the AT-16 in 1943. Two years later, fighter and gunnery schools were

The AT-6 was the primary advanced training aircraft at Luke Field during World War II. In this photo, Chinese pilots of the first foreign graduating class fly over Luke Field in March, 1942.

established at Williams. Both the P-47 Thunderbolt and P-51 Mustang were used. In 1946, after the war was over, Williams became the nation's first jet training base. Pilots learned to fly the F-80 Shooting Star, America's first jet combat plane.

Other bases. Many other air fields were built in Arizona during World War II. Kingman, Yuma, and Marana army air bases gave preliminary flight training. The Navy also availed itself of Arizona's excellent flying weather. Love Field at Prescott was used. Other towns with Navy training facilities were Cottonwood, Williams, St. Johns, Thatcher, Phoenix, Tempe, and Nogales.

The statistics are astounding. According to Department of War records, there were 145,000 Americans who trained in Arizona between 1939 and 1945. This figure includes 61,300 pilots. In addition, there were 3,100 Chinese and 135 British airmen. One reporter said humorously, "A red-tailed desert hawk had to look twice before he went upstairs to stretch his wings."

Not all the soldiers stationed in Arizona were in the air force. Thousands of men were trained in desert warfare at Camp Hyder near Yuma and Camp Horn near Wickenburg. Black soldiers were trained at Fort Huachuca. At that time the armed forces were still racially segregated.

4. ARIZONA MINORITY GROUPS MADE A GOOD RECORD DURING WORLD WAR II

Indians. Arizona Indians played an active part in winning the war. The most famous Indian hero was Ira H. Hayes, a Pima. He was one of six marines who raised the American flag on Mount Suribachi on Iwo Jima. About half of the 3,600 Navajos in the armed services were in the Signal Corps. Navajo signalmen were used in the Pacific to send and receive messages in their native language. The Japanese were never able to "break the code."

World War II brought a big change in Navajo life. Thousands of Navajos were recruited for work in war plants, shipyards, railroads, and mines. They were the principal source of labor supply at the Navajo Ordnance Depot west of Flagstaff. The government built the huge plant in 1942 for the storage and maintenance of ammunition. Two Indian villages, housing more than 4,500 natives, were constructed at the gates of the depot. Besides Navajos, some Hopis and Havasupais worked at the plant.

Papago Indians register for the draft in 1940.

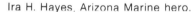
Ira H. Hayes, Arizona Marine hero.

Blacks. Black soldiers were trained at Fort Huachuca. The all-Black 25th Infantry Regiment, long-stationed at Fort Huachuca, was absorbed into the 93rd Division during World War II. After the 93rd departed for the Pacific in 1943, the 92nd Infantry Divison arrived at the fort. It was trained and assigned to the European theater of war. A contingent of Black troops from Fort Huachuca were assigned to guard vital points along Highway 66 for a time. The highway was an important link in the military transportation. The Black soldiers used the American Legion building in Williams as a barracks.

The Blacks were an important source of agricultural labor during the war. They were recruited in Texas, Louisiana, and other southern states. Trainloads of them were brought in as migrant workers. Later, families joined the adult male workers. During the 1940s the Black population of Arizona increased from nearly 15,000 to 26,000, or about 66 per cent.

318

ARIZONA'S

FIRM IN THE GRIP OF PUBLIC CONFIDENCE

Civic Pride
Political Prowess
Religious Sincerity

Let Us
Be Fearless
But Fair!

NEGRO JOURNAL

— OF THE PEOPLE — BY THE PEOPLE — FOR THE PEOPLE —

Vol. II—No. 17 　　TUCSON, ARIZONA, FRIDAY, NOVEMBER 5, 1943 　　Price Five Cents

HUACHUCA SENDS 1500 FOR PARADE

ARMISTICE DAY EDITION

WELCOME!

Remember Pearl

Non-Commissioned Officer Serves In Army 28 Years

DAVIS-MONTHAN FIELD, Tucson, Arizona — Master Sergeant Frank Holder has served in the United States Army 31 years, and for the last 28 years, he has been a non-commissioned offic-

Highlighting Tucson's Armistice Day Parade will be a galaxy of Huachuca military might and talent when the kick-off note is given to march Thursday morning.

Leading the parade will be the 92nd Division one hundred piece band, followed by 1500 troops in full parade regalia.

Charles Young Post

The Charles Young Post No. 36 of the American Legion in this parade with a patriotic float and a marching unit.

Directories

Post Commanders from every Camp in this area will be on

The *Negro Journal* proudly announced that 92nd Division Black soldiers would take part in a November 11, 1943 parade in Tucson.

The 92nd Division in Italy, 1944.

Mexican-Americans. World War II gave Mexican-Americans a chance to show their patriotism. They served throughout the war in all branches of the service. Epimenio Rubi was the first Winslow, Arizona, man to lose his life in the war. He was among the heroic defenders of Bataan in the Philippines in 1942.

Many Mexican-Americans served on the Italian front as part of the 88th Infantry Division, called the "Blue Devils." Sergeant Manuel Mendoza of Tempe, who was called "the Arizona Kid," won the Distinquished Service Cross for heroism. Lieutenant Mauri-

cio Aragon of Avondale was an officer in the division.

Pfc. Silvestre Herrera of Phoenix was the eighth Mexican-American to be awarded the Congressional Medal of Honor in World War II. Herrera was with the 36th Infantry Division in Europe. On March 15, 1945, his platoon was stopped by heavy German machine gun fire near Mertzwiller. The whole area was heavily mined but Herrera made a one-man assault on two different gun emplacements.

He captured eight German soldiers at the first position. In attacking the second machine gun, Herrera stepped on a mine and had both feet blown off. Despite the pain and loss of blood, he pinned down the Germans with accurate rifle fire. Meanwhile, his fellow soldiers skirted the mine field and rushed in from the flank to capture the enemy gunners.

To welcome him home, a "Herrera Day" was proclaimed for August 24, 1945, by Governor Sidney Osborn. The proud people of Phoenix raised a fund to provide their hero with a home. The Mexican government awarded Herrera, who was born in Chihuahua, the highest decoration given to foreigners—the Military Medal of Merit.

Silvestre Herrera

Mexican-Americans. World War II gave Mexican-Americans a chance to show their patriotism. They served throughout the war in all branches of the service. Epimenio Rubi was the first Winslow, Arizona, man to lose his life in the war. He was among the heroic defenders of Bataan in the Philippines in 1942.

Many Mexican-Americans served on the Italian front as part of the 88th Infantry Division, called the "Blue Devils." Sergeant Manuel Mendoza of Tempe, who was called "the Arizona Kid," won the Distinquished Service Cross for heroism. Lieutenant Mauri-

cio Aragon of Avondale was an officer in the division.

Pfc. Silvestre Herrera of Phoenix was the eighth Mexican-American to be awarded the Congressional Medal of Honor in World War II. Herrera was with the 36th Infantry Division in Europe. On March 15, 1945, his platoon was stopped by heavy German machine gun fire near Mertzwiller. The whole area was heavily mined but Herrera made a one-man assault on two different gun emplacements.

He captured eight German soldiers at the first position. In attacking the second machine gun, Herrera stepped on a mine and had both feet blown off. Despite the pain and loss of blood, he pinned down the Germans with accurate rifle fire. Meanwhile, his fellow soldiers skirted the mine field and rushed in from the flank to capture the enemy gunners.

To welcome him home, a "Herrera Day" was proclaimed for August 24, 1945, by Governor Sidney Osborn. The proud people of Phoenix raised a fund to provide their hero with a home. The Mexican government awarded Herrera, who was born in Chihuahua, the highest decoration given to foreigners—the Military Medal of Merit.

Silvestre Herrera

319

5. WORLD WAR II DEFENSE CONTRACTS GAVE MANUFACTURING ITS FIRST BIG BOOST IN ARIZONA

Arizona's economy underwent sweeping changes during World War II. The military bases brought millions of dollars into the state. The federal government encouraged Arizona cotton farmers to double their long-staple cotton acreage as an act of wartime patriotism. World War II gave a big boost to the older copper producing districts: Bisbee-Douglas, Clifton-Morenci, Ray-Superior, Globe-Miami, Ajo, and Jerome.

But the most dramatic change was the growth of manufacturing. The war incubated an industry which became Arizona's number one source of income in the post-war period. Perhaps more important, manufacturing gave the state a well-balanced economy.

Most of the new factories were in the Phoenix area. The Garrett Corporation led the way. It began making airplane components for B-17 bombers. Garrett's AiResearch plant near Sky Harbor was used after 1951 to manufacture gas turbine engines.

Goodyear Aircraft Corporation made complicated flight decks for the Navy's giant four-engine flying boat, known as the Coronado. The company hired up to 7,500 people at its Litchfield plant. Goodyear returned to

Aerial view of the Reynolds Metal Company plant in west Phoenix.

Litchfield in the late 1940s to produce specialized airplane wing assemblies. Later, radar equipment and guided missile parts were manufactured.

Alcoa (Aluminum Company of America) operated the world's largest aluminum plant in West Phoenix. After the war Alcoa sold the plant to the Reynolds Corporation.

Allison Steel, an older Phoenix-area company, made portable bridges during the war.

There was a critical housing shortage in Phoenix during World War II. Many defense plant workers had trouble finding places to live. In 1943 the government started building 800 temporary homes north of the big Alcoa plant. Another 200 homes were added to the Frank Luke Housing Project in east Phoenix for AiResearch employees.

Goodyear Aircraft workers, Mary Salazar and Roxie Barrett, set rivets in the aileron section of a PB2Y flying boat wing in 1943. The factory superintendent at Litchfield and a visiting navy officer watch.

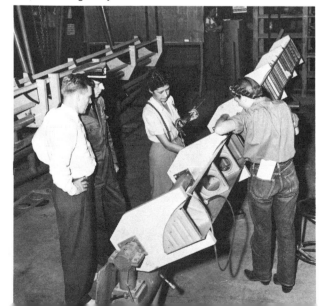

6. THE RELOCATION OF JAPANESE-AMERICANS WAS A SERIOUS MISTAKE AND A SAD EXPERIENCE

The bombing of Pearl Harbor was followed by a wave of anti-Japanese hysteria on the West Coast. Wild rumors—later proven to be untrue—were circulated. Japanese-Americans in Hawaii were accused of having helped the

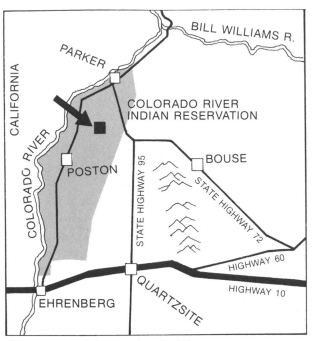

Japanese relocation centers in Arizona.

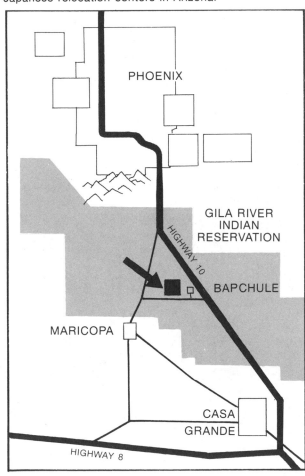

attackers. Nearly all Japanese-Americans became objects of scorn. What is now known about their loyalty was not known then.

President Roosevelt yielded to widespread feelings of fear and suspicion. He took action to prevent race riots and possible acts of disloyalty. The War Department was authorized in 1942 to remove all persons of Japanese ancestry from military areas on the West Coast. The evacuation zone extended inland into Arizona. Japanese living north of U.S. Highway 60 were relocated. This highway runs through Phoenix, Mesa and Globe.

Most of Arizona's approximately 600 Japanese-Americans were not directly affected by the removal order. Nor were those in Hawaii removed. But about 112,000—nearly two-thirds of whom were American-born Japanese, called *Nisei*—were relocated.

In the name of "military necessity," their civil liberties were violated. The Japanese-Americans, most of whom lived in California, also wound up losing most of their property. They were moved away from their homes, farms, and small businesses with only what they could carry. Their destination was one of eight camps in semi-desert areas in the West or two camps in Arkansas. They were interned in these camps from 1942 to 1945.

Japanese-Americans from California unload their baggage at the Poston war relocation camp.

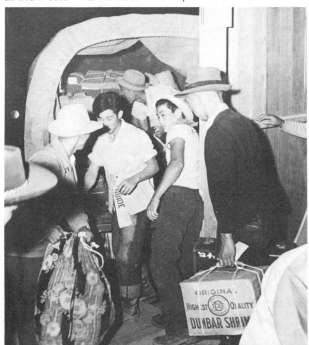

Arizona camps. Two of the 10 relocation centers were on Indian reservations in Arizona. The Gila River Relocation Center was built on land leased from the Pima and Maricopa Indians near Sacaton. The other camp was near Poston on the Colorado River Reservation south of Parker. More than 30,000 Japanese-Americans were confined in these two new desert cities.

The relocation centers were not like the Nazi concentration camps of Germany where the Jews and others were mistreated. There were fences, guard posts, and soldiers ever present—that much is true. But the Japanese were not beaten, starved, or tortured. In fact, the War Relocation Authority (WRA) staff was, for the most part, sympathetic and helpful to the evacuees.

The camps consisted of wooden barracks grouped into blocks. Each block included a mess hall, recreation hall, and a combination washroom-toilet-laundry building. For the family-oriented Japanese it was not home. It was communal living even though each barrack was partitioned with one family to a room. Furniture was made out of crates and scrap lumber.

The Japanese found the Gila soil to their liking. They dug irrigation canals and produced tons of vegetables. The Gila camp members formed the Rivers Cooperative and got a license from the Arizona Corporation Commis-

Evacuees of Japanese ancestry arrive at the Poston war relocation camp.

Japanese-American children enjoy a card game at the Poston camp.

Gila River Relocation Center at Rivers, Arizona.

Japanese-American farmers feed dairy cattle at the Gila River Relocation Center.

sion. The cooperative sold vegetables and shared the profits. The food produced by the Japanese-Americans contributed to the United States war effort.

Japanese laborers also worked outside the Gila camp. They surfaced miles of the state's access roads and repaired bridges.

Attitude of the Arizona state government. The Japanese had long endured discrimination in California. They faced it again in Arizona. In the beginning, Governor Osborn protested against the use of Arizona as a "dumping ground" for "enemy aliens." Osborn later signed a law passed by the legislature that would discourage Japanese from settling in Arizona. The law forbade the selling of anything to persons "whose movements are restricted by law"—meaning the Japanese-Americans—except under certain conditions.

Before a seller could do business with the Japanese-Americans he had to advertise his intentions three times in the newspapers. Documents on the sale had to be filed with the governor. The Arizona law was so restrictive, said a Chicago newspaper, that "a dentist can not pull a Jap's tooth without advertising the fact."

Tsutomu Ikeda of Mesa challenged the law. It was declared unconstitutional by both the Maricopa County Superior Court and Arizona Supreme Court. The law also violated the Civil Rights Act of 1870. This act guaranteed all United States citizens the privilege of owning property and making contracts.

The attitude of Arizona's government began to change after U. S. Army Inspector General Virgil L. Petersen came to Phoenix in 1943. He reminded state officials that hostile acts toward Japanese-Americans might result in retaliation against American boys in Japanese prisoner-of-war camps. Before leaving Phoenix, Petersen praised the "outstanding cooperation" of Arizona's leading citizens.

Education at the camps. The Arizona State Board of Education did its best to provide the Japanese with teachers and school administrators. The Gila camp was fortunate in being close to Arizona State at Tempe. Faculty members from Tempe conducted college classes and supervised the training of Japanese teachers. The Arizona curriculum was followed in the camp schools. Public libraries and private individuals donated books. In 1944, eight Arizona schools sent delegates to a Girls League convention at the Gila Center. American Legion awards were made to outstanding Japanese students.

Arizona newspapers were usually friendly toward the Japanese-Americans. "Remember," the *Arizona Republic* reminded its readers, "we are fighting the militarists in Japan and not the Nisei." The *Arizona Daily Star* said the Japanese had cooperated and Arizonans should do the same "so that we will not be ashamed of ourselves when the war is over."

Camps closed. The West Coast was reopened to people of Japanese ancestry in January 1945. The relocation camps were phased out. More than half the evacuees returned to their former homes. The others scattered over the country. In many cases, those who returned to California found their homes and stores vandalized. It was not unusual for their property to be in the hands of another owner. Later the U. S. government paid the evacuees for property losses. But they

Soldiers in the Japanese-American 442nd combat team do bayonet practice at Camp Shelby, Mississippi.

got only a small percentage of the actual value of their property. There was no way, of course, that they could be compensated for the injustice and humiliation they experienced.

The uprooting of the Japanese-Americans proved to be unnecessary. Their loyalty and combat record during World War II were admirable. In fact, the 442nd Regiment, made up entirely of Japanese-Americans, won more decorations fighting in Europe than any unit in the United States army. Their motto was "Go for Broke."

7. PRISONER-OF-WAR CAMPS WERE LOCATED IN ARIZONA

Many German and Italian prisoners of war were brought to the United States to remain until the end of the war. Two camps for Germans were set up in Arizona. Papago POW Camp at 64th Street and Oak in East Phoenix was the largest. About 4,000 officers and men were held there at one time. Another smaller German camp was built at Yuma. There were temporary camps around the state for German prisoners farmed out to work in forests, on irrigation projects, or in cotton fields. The one big Italian POW colony was near Florence.

The POWs at Papago were mainly captured sailors and submarine personnel. They were shipped to desert Arizona so they would not be near familiar seaport surroundings. Jurgen Wattenberg, navigation officer of the famous battleship *Graf Spee*, was there, for example.

For the most part, the Papago POWs were young and the cream of the German manhood. They were also hard-core Nazis. The worst ones were not moved by horror films of German concentration camps. These films were shown to break their morale. Some of the POWs made anti-Semitic pro-German propaganda leaflets. They tossed the leaflets out of the trucks which carried them to work details.

Some captured German soldiers at the Pagago POW camp.

Tunnel through which German POWs escaped from the Papago prison camp in 1944.

Phoenix school children started a fad of painting POW letters on their sweatshirts. This practice was soon stopped by teachers and parents. It was explained that a boy anywhere near adult size might be mistaken for an escaped prisoner and be shot.

There were many escapes from the Papago prison camp. The "*great escape*" came on Christmas eve, 1944. Sixty men got out of the compound through a tunnel that took months to dig. Soon after arriving at the camp the POWs discovered a blind spot. They strung a clothesline over the blind area and kept it full of blankets for airing. With small coal shovels, cups, and screwdrivers the POWs dug a hole 20 feet deep. Then a 400-foot tunnel was excavated under the Salt River Project's Crosscut

Papago POW camp in East Phoenix.

Canal. Dirt was hauled out in a little wooden cart and flushed down toilets or scattered carefully around the camp.

The escape night was rainy and cold. Three men quickly gave themselves up to get out of the weather. Two surrendered to a Tempe housewife and one to a pumping attendant on the Salt River. The next day Civil Air Patrol planes searched the desert for the POWs. Bloodhounds were brought in from the state prison. Gradually most of the prisoners were rounded up as they tried to reach the Mexican border. Two crossed into Mexico and were captured at Nogales, Sonora. Captain Wattenberg was the last escapee to be picked up. For 35 days he hid out in a cave north of Phoenix. When he ventured into downtown Phoenix on January 28 and asked for directions, his accent betrayed him. A policeman returned Wattenberg to the prison camp. A little over three months after his capture, Germany surrendered on May 8, 1945.

Governor Hunt poses for a picture beside his automobile in 1912.

20

STATE GOVERNMENT AND POLITICS: 1912-1948

Until after World War II Arizona was a one-party state. A two-party system—where either party can win and assume responsibility for governing—was a long time coming.

The Democrats usually controlled the territorial legislature, which began in 1864. The Democrats elected 41 of 52 delegates to the constitutional convention in 1910. And the Democrats won every statewide office in the first election of 1911.

The Democratic Party had a majority in the state legislature continuously from 1912 to 1966—except for a narrow loss of the state senate to the Republicans in 1920.

Democrats also occupied the governor's chair almost without interruption. Republican Thomas E. Campbell won a close race for governor in 1918. And he rode to victory in 1920 on the coattails of Republican presidential candidate Warren G. Harding. But the only other Democratic defeat in the 1920s, 1930s, and 1940s was a loss to one-term Republican Governor John C. Phillips in 1928. Phillips was swept into office with Republican Herbert Hoover's big presidential landslide victory over Al Smith.

In a one-party state there was little party loyalty. With nothing to fear from a weak Republican minority, the Democratic legislators usually divided into factions instead of cooperating with the governor. During the first half century of statehood, the big economic interests had far greater influence with the legislature than did the governor.

The lawmakers listened to the copper corporations, railroads, and big ranch owners. The people didn't complain. Their jobs depended on the prosperity of the mines and agriculture. Manufacturing did not become Arizona's leading industry until after World War II.

It did not matter how popular or capable a governor might be. And his political party made little difference. The framers of the Arizona Constitution intended for the legislative branch to be the most powerful. In the words of one political writer: "The legislature regards the governor, whatever his party affiliation, as a foolish nincompoop who was written into the Constitution by mistake."

KEY CONCEPTS

1. Governor George W. P. Hunt was Arizona's first state governor.

2. Governor Campbell offered many ideas to improve state government.

3. The Colorado River controversy was a big problem for Governor Phillips.

4. Dr. B. B. Moeur was the depression governor.

5. Stanford was a great judge but did not enjoy being governor.

6. Governor Jones cooperated with the Roosevelt administration.

7. Sidney P. Osborn is rated one of Arizona's best governors.

327

1. GEORGE W. P. HUNT WAS ARIZONA'S FIRST STATE GOVERNOR.

George W. P. Hunt, the first governor, is sometimes called "George VII" because he served seven terms off and on. A self-made man and a life-long Democrat, Hunt was born in 1859 at Huntsville, Missouri, a town founded by his grandfather. His family's wealth in land and slaves was largely lost as a result of the Civil War. As a boy George had little opportunity for schooling. All his life he had trouble with grammar.

At age 18 he left home to seek his fortune in the Colorado gold fields. Unsuccessful as a prospector, Hunt drifted across New Mexico into the White Mountains of eastern Arizona. In October 1881, he walked into the town of Globe wearing overalls and leading his burro. Globe was then a rough, booming mining town.

Governor George W. P. Hunt

Hunt took a job as waiter in Pascoe's restaurant and was later employed at a variety of other odd jobs. He worked his way up the ladder from delivery boy to president of the Old Dominion Commercial Company. This company operated a large general store and bank in Globe. By 1900 Hunt was one of the most prosperous men in the territory.

Early political career. Hunt's political career began with his election to the territorial legislature in 1892. Among the laws he authored was a bill offering a $5,000 reward for the capture of the notorious Apache Kid. Hunt got Arizona's first compulsory school attendance law passed in 1899 and an anti-gambling bill in 1907. He grew in stature during seven terms in the legislature. In 1910 Hunt was chosen president of the constitutional convention. His efforts to get the constitution ratified by the voters launched him into statewide politicking and the governor's chair.

Though a well-to-do man, Hunt identified himself politically with organized labor and the common man. The masses understood his simple, direct manner of speaking and were not bothered by his unpolished English.

Hunt was a shrewd politician and a good judge of people. He maintained his power in politics by careful attention to the needs of the voters. As governor he traveled over the state by automobile. He would sit in the back-seat and study the files he kept on the people

Governor Hunt speaks to a crowd in Casa Grande, 1913.

The first Arizona state senate, 1912.

in each county and town. On the return trip to Phoenix he brought the files up to date. Facts to be remembered for the next visit were jotted down.

Hunt's troubles with the legislature. Hunt never figured out how to get his way with the legislature. The legislature was always in the hands of the Democrats but there was no party loyalty. As early as 1913 Hunt branded the lawmakers as a "reactionary" and "do nothing" group. He was especially irked because the lawmakers passed a penal code over his veto. This code, which was later approved by the voters in 1914, provided for capital punishment. It also set up a Board of Pardons and Paroles. The governor could not grant a pardon, reprieve, or commutation without the approval of this board.*

*A *pardon* is the legal (though not moral) forgiveness of a sentence.

A *reprieve* is the official postponement of a sentence, usually because of the discovery of new evidence.

A test case arose in 1915. Hunt gave an unconditional pardon, without the board's approval, to a convicted murderer. Hunt's friend, Warden Robert B. Sims, refused to release the convict from the state prison. Much to Hunt's disgust, the Arizona Supreme Court upheld the penal code and the board's power over pardons.

By the end of Hunt's first term a pattern of conflict developed between the governor and the legislature that would continue during most of the state's history.

The 1914 election. The *Democrats* again swept the state. Hunt defeated Republican Ralph Cameron, Arizona's last territorial delegate to Congress. Hunt had 25,226 votes, Cameron, 17,602; Progressive candidate George U. Young, 5,206; and Socialist J. R. Barnette, 2,973.

A *commutation* is the reduction of a sentence or fine.

A *parole* is the freeing of a prisoner on the condition that he will report from time to time to a parole officer and behave himself.

Governor Hunt leans against the Tempe bridge in 1913. Convict labor was used on this project.

Several important referendums and initiatives which Hunt supported were passed by the voters in 1914. A controversial *"80 per cent" referendum* was approved. This law, aimed mainly at Mexican-American aliens, provided that corporations with five or more employees must certify that at least 80 percent were U. S. citizens. In 1915 the U. S. Supreme Court declared the 80 percent law unconstitutional.

The voters in 1914 also approved an *anti-blacklist* referendum*. An *old-age pension measure* passed but was ruled unconstitutional by the Arizona Supreme Court in 1916.

A *prohibition initiative*, which the people got on the ballot by petition, was approved. This law made Arizona a "dry" state. Liquor dealers filed a suit. They argued that the dry law violated the 14th amendment of the U. S. Constitution. The dealers said the dry law deprived them of property without due process of law. But the federal court saw it a different way. The prohibition law was upheld.

On New Year's Eve of December 31, 1914, thousands of Arizonans gathered in the

---

*A *blacklist* contains the names of certain workers who are denied a job by any employer who has the list. Union organizers used to be blacklisted.

streets, saloons, and churches. Some were out for a last fling. Others wished to usher in prohibition with rejoiceful prayer.

Hunt's second term. Hunt was inaugurated for the second time on January 4, 1915. Again he had troubles with the Democratic legislature. At that time the legislature had only one regular session in a two-year term. But Hunt frequently called them into special session. His proposal to abolish the state senate and create a unicameral (one house) legislature did not win him any friends.

During the World War I era, 1914-1918, Arizona experienced labor unrest, especially in the copper mines. Governor Hunt sympathized with the miners, particularly the Mexican laborers, who were paid lower wages. Hunt worked with both sides, however, to settle several strikes. In October 1915, he sent National Guard troops to the Clifton-Morenci area to prevent violence. He also issued a public call for relief contributions to aid the families of strikers. Eventually a settlement was negotiated by two U. S. Department of Labor conciliators.

"I feel nothing less than elated by the outcome," Hunt said.

The 1916 election dispute. Hunt was elected in 1911, 1914, 1916, 1922, 1924, 1926,

MARKETS
NEW YORK CITY.
Silver 49⅝

The Bisbee Daily Review

MEMBER ASSOCIATED PRESS

WEATHER
FOR ARIZONA
Local Showers in the
North Portion.

VOL. 17. 130.   BISBEE, ARIZONA, WEDNESDAY MORNING, NOVEMBER 4, 1914.   PRICE 5 CENTS

PROHIBITION WAVE SWEEPS ARIZONA IN LINE WITH DRYS
Governor Hunt Is Re-elected In Tight Race

COCHISE COUNTY PROBABLY DRY; NO DEFINITE RETURNS OBTAINABLE BUT PARTIAL COUNT KILLS MOST HOPES

Saloon Men Of This County And Rest Of State Concede Defeat—Hunt Will Carry Cochise Heavily—Others Give Rays Of Light To Several Republicans And Progressives Who Have Fighting Chances Of Nosing Out Ahead

The early returns from the whole of the state indicate two great landslides. From the appearance of the vote in the large centers of Arizona at an early hour this morning the state will go dry by a substantial vote. Goevrnor Hunt democratic candidate and incumbent has an easy lead in nearly all districts, and is gaining is the larger cities count

For State Mine Inspector	
Bolin, G. H	254
Stallings, R. L.	29
Woodman, Parker	69
Hipple, P. J.	29
Briggs, Frank	25

For Supervisor	
V. M. Johnson	292
John Rock	255
J. M. Sparks	296
John E. Kenney	50
Jacob Scheerer	55
C. L. Cummins	69

GERMAN GUNBOATS MEET BRITISH; ENGLAND HAS SEVERAL LESS CRUISERS

Rumor Persists That German Fleet Has Come Out Into The Open Sea—Five German Boats Run Onto English Fleet, Defeat Them Sink Two Ships And Drive Third Into Shelter—British Sub-Marine Goes To Bottom—Character Is Little Changed On Front

DOVER, Nov. 3 A report has been circulated that the German fleet has come out from its base. It is also reported from Dunkirk that many battleships and four cruisers have put to sea from Kiel

GERMAN FLEET HAS NEW SUCCESSES

GERMANS GIVE UP COAST ATTACKS.
LONDON, Nov. 3. That the German army has abandoned the attempt to back its way along the Belgian coast to Calais is accepted opinion...

In 1914 the voters favored prohibition. They also reelected Governor Hunt.

Arizona became a dry state in 1915. Happy prohibition leaders rode the wagon in a Phoenix parade.

Law officers at Clifton pouring gallons of Kentucky whiskey on the ground after Arizona became a dry state in 1915.

and 1930. But he had a close call in 1916. The Republican candidate, Thomas E. Campbell, appeared to be the winner by 30 votes—27,976 to 27,946. Campbell was inaugurated on New Year's Day, 1917.

But Hunt refused to vacate the governor's office and demanded a recount. When Superior Court Judge R. C. Stanford ruled against him, Hunt appealed to the Arizona Supreme Court. He got a favorable decision. The higher

court threw out the ballots of voters who marked an "X" for a straight Democratic ticket and then put another "X" beside the name of Campbell in the Republican column. It was clear that these voters had intended to vote for all Democrats except Hunt. But they did not use the correct procedure to vote a split ticket.

Though disappointed, Campbell gracefully moved out of the capitol. He had served a year

331

Sign on Stone Avenue in Tucson in 1916. Arizona women were urged to vote against Democratic Party officeholders —President Wilson, U.S. Senator Ashurst, and Congressman Carl Hayden. Male voters in Arizona gave women the privilege of voting in 1912, eight years before the U.S. Constitution was amended to allow all women in the nation to vote.

as governor without pay. Hunt finished out the term.

Copper strikes in 1917. While the election dispute was being solved in 1917, the United States entered World War I. Arizona was once again plagued by trouble in the mines. A copper strike at Jerome appeared to be settled. A federal conciliator—former AF of L (American Federation of Labor) president John McBride, who was then a resident of Phoenix—worked out an agreement between labor and the mine owners.

But then the radical Industrial Workers of the World, better known as IWWs or Wobblies, staged another strike. The citizens of Jerome rounded up some 67 of the Wobblies and shipped them to Needles, California, in cattle cars.

When the labor trouble spread, Hunt was asked by President Woodrow Wilson to serve as mediator at Globe. Federal troops, which had been requested by "Governor" Campbell, were maintaining order there. While Hunt was involved in his hopeless task at Globe, trouble erupted at Bisbee.

Cochise County Sheriff Harry C. Wheeler and the Bisbee Citizens Protective League deported nearly 1,400 IWWs to New Mexico. The state legislature passed a resolution condemning the IWWs as radicals. But Hunt was

in sympathy with the deportees. He believed that their rights had been violated. Some of the Governor's enemies called him "G. Wobbly P. Hunt."

Back in the governor's chair in 1918, Hunt tried to show his patriotic attitude toward the war. He rode in a Liberty Loan parade and bought $5,000 worth of bonds. When his picture was taken with a marine, he said he would gladly enlist if the Marine Corps would take a 59-year-old man. Hunt sometimes pointed to his Sons of the American Revolution button to emphasize his Americanism. He even took up knitting as a patriotic duty.

Minister to Siam. Hunt chose not to run in 1918. He was appointed minister to Siam by President Woodrow Wilson. At first he found this exotic job interesting. But after his wife and daughter returned to Arizona's dry climate, Hunt was bored. He traveled and looked for souvenirs. Much of his time was spent sending hundreds of postcards to his friends in Arizona.

Hunt was elected governor again in 1922, 1924, and 1926. During these terms he continued to fight for progressive reforms. He worked for the abolition of capital punishment, even though the people voted for it in 1918 by a big margin of two to one. Hunt said "legalized killing" must go. He compared hanging to the "burning of witches." Hunt never changed his personal views on this issue. He served for awhile as president of the Anti-Capital Punishment Society of America.

Hunt also worked for modernized prisons, minimum wage laws, improved highways, and a bigger share of Colorado River water for Arizona.

Many of the reforms that Hunt proposed were defeated or ignored by the legislature. Hunt did a lot of fighting with the lawmakers. It angered him to see the legislature controlled by the big economic interests—copper corporations, railroads, and cattlemen. Part of the problem was the Arizona Constitution which Hunt helped to write. This document gave most of the power of state government to the

Bisbee citizens watch as a trainload of IWWs departs for New Mexico on July 12, 1917.

El Mosquito, a Spanish language newspaper in Tucson supported Hunt for governor in 1922.

legislature—very little to the governor. Hunt tried in vain to reorganize the boards and agencies so he could exercise some authority over them.

National attention was focused on Governor Hunt in 1924. To stop the spread of hoof and mouth disease, he put an embargo on cattle from California. That was in April. He also ordered motorists and trains from California stopped at the Colorado River.

All travelers had to pass through corrugated iron disinfecting stations. While they took showers, their clothes were sprayed. Their autos and baggage were steamed. Railroad cars were fumigated. No passenger could get off the train in Arizona without a certificate from the Arizona Board of Health. Hunt stationed the Arizona National Guard at disinfection stations to enforce the embargo. California newspapers called it "Hunt's Folly." Finally, after about four months, Governor Hunt lifted the embargo.

Final years. Hunt was defeated by Republican John C. Phillips in 1928. Restless in retirement, he took a leisurely trip around the world. Hunt returned to Phoenix in time to

Colorado River bridge at Yuma in 1924. All travelers from California were stopped. Their clothes and vehicles were fumigated.

Governor Thomas E. Campbell

win his seventh and last term in 1930. Two years later he was defeated in the Democratic primary by Benjamin B. Moeur, a Tempe doctor. After a second primary defeat by Moeur in 1934, Hunt did the unforgivable, by his code. He supported the Republican candidate.

The "Old Roman," as the completely bald Hunt was called, died on December 24, 1934. He was buried beside his wife on a hill in Papago Park in East Phoenix.

2. GOVERNOR CAMPBELL OFFERED MANY IDEAS TO IMPROVE STATE GOVERNMENT

Arizona's second governor was Thomas Edward Campbell. He was the first Republican, the first native son, and the first Catholic to hold the office. Born in 1878 at Fort Whipple, where his father was stationed with the U. S. Army, Campbell grew up in Prescott. He was a member of Prescott High School's first

graduating class in 1893. After attending St. Mary's College in Moraga, California, Campbell worked in the Prescott and Jerome post offices. Eventually he became involved in mine promotion and cattle raising. But he was destined to spend most of his time in politics.

Campbell was elected to the 21st territorial legislature in 1900. He next served as assessor of Yavapai County. In 1914 he won a seat on the first state tax commission. Campbell was the only Republican elected to a statewide office that year.

In 1916 he almost unseated Governor Hunt. This election was historic because it was the closest race for governor in Arizona history. It also led to each of the contestants serving part of the term in the governor's chair. Campbell was an attractive candidate— with "charisma," as they say today. He was young, able, and energetic. Even Governor Hunt conceded that Campbell was "a fine, prepossessing gentleman, and a good campaigner who presented a striking appearance in his ten gallon hat."

In the 1916 campaign Campbell hit hard at the extravagance of Hunt's administration. He claimed the governor sided with labor against capital and used state jobs to build a political machine. He suggested that Hunt should give more attention to the state's schools and spend less time at the penitentiary.

Hunt was quick to defend his reforms at the Florence prison, including the use of convicts on roads and other public works projects. *Dunbar's Weekly* and other Democratic newspapers called Campbell's economy proposals "pure bunk." It was a hard-fought campaign. The results could not have been much closer. It took the courts a year to decide that Hunt was the winner.

After giving up the governor's chair, Campbell left for Washington, D. C. He worked a few months in the Food Administration under Herbert Hoover and then took a job in the Treasury Department.

Election of 1918. Campbell returned to Arizona and defeated Democrat Fred T. Colter, Hunt's choice for governor. It was another close election—25,927 to 25,588. The campaign created little interest. People were more concerned with the Fourth Liberty Loan Drive, the end of World War I, and the flu epidemic. Campbell considered his victory a tribute to the uncompromising stand he took as temporary governor against the radical IWWs in 1917.

Campbell was reelected in 1920. He defeated Democrat Mit Simms 37,060 to 31,385. It was a rare year for Republicans. Warren G. Harding was elected president in a landslide and helped carry Arizona Republican candidates to victory. Ralph Cameron upset Democrat U.S. Senator Marcus Smith. The Republicans also won a 10 to 9 majority in the state senate. This was the only time between 1912 and 1966 when the Republicans

The 1916 campaign for governor was hard fought. "Galloping George" Hunt toured the state with other Democrats. This ad was for a rally in Clifton. "Traveling Tom" Campbell also conducted an active campaign.

Democratic Rally

Princess Theatre
Clifton, Tues., Oct. 24

COME AND HEAR

Hon. Carl Hayden   Hon. G. W. P. Hunt
Hon. Wiley E. Jones   Hon. Chas. R. Howe
Hon. Sidney P. Osborn

NATIONAL AND STATE ISSUES

Free Picture Show Starts 7:30 p. m.
Speeches Begin 8:30 p. m. Sharp

Meeting will Conclude with
FREE DANCE
Everybody Welcome

Former President Roosevelt campaigns in Arizona for Republican candidates, 1916.

had a majority in either house of the state legislature. Arizona was a one-party Democratic state until the 1960s.

Campbell made the operation of the state land department a major issue in the 1920 campaign. He charged the department with fraud in state school land leases. By the 1910 Enabling Act the federal government gave Arizona four sections of every township* to use in supporting schools. The state was leasing some land to individuals for 3 to 10 cents an acre. These persons then sub-leased the land for one to 10 dollars an acre. Other state land was being sold for $3 an acre and resold by real estate firms for $35 an acre.

"The main issue in this campaign," Campbell said, "is whether these lands shall continue to be turned over to the land grabbers."

Unfortunately for the people and the schools, much of the state school land was still not leased for its real value as late as the 1950s.

township: a survey unit containing 36 sections, or 36 square miles

Legislative acts. Several important actions were taken by the legislatures during Campbell's two terms in office. The 4th legislature in 1920 ratified the 19th amendment, giving women the right to vote. Arizona women, of course, already had the suffrage.

One of the most significant laws passed by the 5th legislature was the *Workmen's Compensation Act of 1921.* Under this law, employees would contribute to a fund administered by an Industrial Commission. Workers injured on the job were to be compensated for damages and given medical treatment. Families of workmen killed in the performance of their duties were given benefits. The law was declared unconstitutional, however, by the Arizona Supreme Court. It did not become effective until passed again with changes by the legislature in 1925.

Governor Campbell hoped to reorganize state government to bring order out of chaos. There were 50 independent boards, agencies, bureaus, departments, and commissions which answered to no one. Campbell wanted to consolidate all of them into a few

Governor Thomas Campbell welcoming the Arizona men of the 158th Infantry home from the war. He met the train at El Paso on May 1, 1919.

departments. Each department would be headed by one administrator appointed by and responsible to the governor. Campbell also proposed a budget system coordinated by the governor. The way things were, not much planning was done. Every agency went separately to the legislature for money.

Campbell proposed a second reorganization plan involving constitutional changes that would have to be voted on by the people. He would abolish all elective state offices except governor and auditor who would have four-year terms. All executive duties would be assigned to eight reorganized departments. The department heads would meet with the governor—just like the president's cabinet operates.

To give his plans a good start, Campbell invited ex-Governor Frank O. Lowden of Illinois to address the legislature on that state's recent reorganization. Lowden's address was well-received. But there were opponents who said Campbell's plans were too revolutionary. *The Messenger*, a Democratic weekly in Phoenix, said Arizona would be "transformed from a democracy into a kingdom." It was argued that a governor with so much authority could build up a political machine.

Campbell's reorganization program was defeated by the Democratic House. The Senate passed it by a vote of 10 Republicans to 8 Democrats, one Democrat being absent.

The 1922 campaign was a Campbell-Hunt rematch. Each accused the other of spending excessive state funds and of touring the state too much while in office—hence the nicknames, "Traveling Tom" and "Galloping George." Hunt brought in well-known outsiders—William Jennings Bryan and William Gibbs McAdoo—to speak in his behalf. He won easily by a vote of 37,310 to 30,599.

In 1923 Campbell was given two important jobs by President Harding. As a friend of President Obregon of Mexico, Campbell worked behind the scenes to help restore diplomatic relations with that country. He then headed a fact-finding commission to study federal recla-

mation projects. From 1930 to 1933 he was chairman of the U. S. Civil Service Commission by appointment of President Hoover. He ran as a token candidate for governor in 1936 when Arizona was overwhelmingly Democratic. Campbell died in 1944.

3. THE COLORADO RIVER CONTROVERSY WAS A BIG PROBLEM FOR GOVERNOR PHILLIPS

John C. Phillips was the second Republican to interrupt Hunt's long tenure in office. Born in Illinois in 1870, he grew up on a farm and studied law. Nearly penniless when he came to Arizona in 1898, Phillips worked as a stone mason on the capitol building.

Another of his jobs was remembered by Sidney Osborn, the governor of Arizona in the

Governor John C. Phillips

1940s. Osborn said that one of his lasting childhood impressions was of Mr. Phillips peddling apricots to Osborn's mother.

Though a man of strong character, "Honest John" Phillips was not a handsome man. He often joked about how he was once voted the "homeliest man in Maricopa County" at the territorial fair.

Phillips was a successful politician. He was defeated only once in ten tries for public office. A territorial probate judge, he was elected to the Superior Court after statehood. He also served in both houses of the legislature, being the only Republican elected to the Senate in 1922.

In 1928 he rode the coattails of Herbert Hoover to victory over Governor Hunt. His victory was remarkable considering that there were twice as many Democrats as Republicans in the state. Phillips was governor for only two years. His administration was mainly concerned with the Colorado River controversy.

Background on the Colorado River controversy. Arizona is one of seven states

drained by the Colorado River. In 1922, representatives of these states met at Santa Fe. They agreed that a dam should be built on the Colorado River to prevent flooding of the Imperial Valley in California.

Another agreement, called the Colorado River (or Santa Fe) Compact, provided for a division of Colorado River water between the upper basin and the lower basin states. This compact was submitted to the seven state legislatures for ratification. All signed except one. The Arizona legislature and Governor Hunt feared that Arizona would not get its fair share of water. The compact did not specify how the lower basin states—California, Arizona, and Nevada—would divide their 7,500,000 acre feet* of water.

Swing-Johnson Bill. Congress decided to go ahead without Arizona's approval. Late in 1928 the Swing-Johnson Bill was passed. This law authorized a high dam on the Colorado River. Congress then set aside $165,000,000 to build Boulder Dam. The authors of the Swing-Johnson Bill suggested that California be

Yuma, like the Imperial Valley in California, was in danger of flooding before Hoover Dam was built. This 1916 photo shows Yuma's power plant under water.

*An *acre foot* is enough water to cover an acre of ground a foot deep.

While controversy raged over Boulder (Hoover) Dam, ex-President Calvin Coolidge dedicated the dam named after him. Governor Phillips is seated to the right of Coolidge in this photo.

guaranteed 4,400,000 acre feet of water. Arizona would get 2,800,000 and Nevada 300,000 acre feet. California and Arizona would split any surplus water in excess of 7,500,000 acre feet.

Governor Phillips appointed a Colorado River Commission. But no agreement could be reached with California. In 1930 Arizona asked the U. S. Supreme Court to stop construction on the dam until Arizona's rights were guaranteed. The court refused and upheld the constitutionality of the Swing-Johnson Bill in 1931. Arizona still held out and did not sign the Santa Fe Compact until 1944.

Election of 1930. Hunt returned to the political wars to defeat Phillips in 1930. He won his seventh and last term. Conducting his most vigorous campaign, Hunt traveled 25,000 miles by automobile. A politician in those days was expected to make personal contact with all the voters.

The depression into which the country was moving became an issue. Running on a plat-form of "Back to Prosperity with Hunt," he proposed a highway building program to relieve unemployment. Hunt also promised old age pensions, free textbooks, and a $4 per day minimum wage for state employees.

Phillips reminded voters that he had erased the state debt which Hunt left him in 1929. The Phillips administration also created two important agencies—a Bureau of Criminal Investigation and a State Examiner's office to check on money spent by different departments.

When the votes were counted, Hunt had 48,875 to 46,231 for Governor Phillips.

4. DOCTOR B. B. MOEUR WAS THE DEPRESSION GOVERNOR

"I punched cows from the time I was six years old until I was twenty," said Governor Benjamin B. Moeur. Born in Tennessee, he was raised in south Texas where his father was a doctor and also in the cattle business.

Governor Benjamin B. Moeur

The young Moeur followed in his father's footsteps. After graduation from medical school in 1896, he took a job at the Copper Queen Hospital in Bisbee. A few months later he bought a horse and buggy and moved to the then small town of Tempe in the Salt River Valley.

A country doctor, Moeur reached his patients by buggy or on horseback. He once rode across the Salt River Canyon in a cement bucket attached to a cable. It was the quickest way to reach a patient north of the Roosevelt dam site. Moeur was civic-minded. He served on the Tempe board of education and was also a delegate to the constitutional convention in 1910.

Election of 1932. "High taxes" and "reckless public spending" led Moeur to run for governor in 1932. He conducted a vigorous campaign, shouting his demand for economy all over the state. He won the primary with a 35 percent plurality.* Governor Hunt, who

*A *plurality* is more votes than any other candidate receives. A *majority* is more than half.

ran 5,000 votes behind and in second place, was furious. Beaten by a small town doctor? Hunt referred to Moeur as an "atheist" who "was in the KKK." He gave Moeur little support against the Republican nominee for governor, J. C. Kinney. The latter was chairman of the Pima Country Board of Supervisors. Moeur defeated Kinney 75,314 to 42,202. Arizona was becoming more and more a one-party Democratic state.

By the end of his first term in office, Governor Moeur was able to claim that he had reduced state expenses by about one-third. Property taxes were cut. But new taxes were levied by the legislature on sales, income, and tobacco. A tax was put on liquor, wine, and beer after the 18th "prohibition" amendment was repealed.

The most exciting event of Moeur's first term was the "Colorado River Affair." The national spotlight was focused on Governor Moeur in 1934 when he tried to stop a Los Angeles utilities company from building a diversion dam on the Colorado River at Parker. His purpose was to keep California from getting any more water until Arizona was guaranteed 2,800,000 acre feet a year.

In March, Moeur sent a squad of national guardsmen to patrol the dam site. Unfortunately, the soldiers tried to reconnoiter the site in a couple of antique steamboats—the *Julia B* and the *Nellie T*. The boats got entangled in a cable and the "desert sailors" had to be rescued by the "enemy" Californians. Newspapers naturally took great delight in poking fun at the "Arizona navy" and its "battleships."

Nothing further happened until November when the Six Companies—which earlier built Boulder Dam—started a trestle bridge from the California side of the river. On November 10 Governor Moeur declared martial law. He sent a force of 40 infantrymen and 20 machine gunners to the river "front." To avoid trouble, Secretary of Interior Harold Ickes halted all construction at the dam site. The "battle" was transferred to the courts. The U. S. Supreme

Arizona Democrats met with presidential candidate Franklin D. Roosevelt at the Greenway Ranch in September, 1932. Clockwise from left are F. A. McKinney, Senator Carl Hayden, Major Oscar F. Temple, Governor Hunt, Roosevelt, B. B. Moeur, and Congressman Lewis W. Douglas.

Mrs. Isabella Greenway represented Arizona in the U.S. House from 1933 to 1937. She is the only women ever elected to Congress from Arizona. She was chosen at a special election after Congressman Lewis Douglas resigned to become director of the budget.

Court issued an injunction. Arizona was ordered not to interfere with the construction of Parker Dam.

Work then went ahead. The dam was completed in 1938. If Boulder was the world's tallest dam, Parker was the deepest. Excavation crews had to dig down 233 feet before reaching bedrock.

Moeur won a second term in 1934. Ex-Governor Hunt made a final bid for the office but ran third in the Democratic primary. Moeur received 34,792 votes; Judge R. C. Stanford, 29,088; Hunt, 27,849; and James Minotto, 4,448. Bitter in defeat, Hunt endorsed Thomas Maddock, his friend and the Republican nominee. Moeur ran a quiet campaign, standing on the record of his first term. He easily won the general election with 61,355 votes to 39,242 for Maddock.

Moeur devoted most of his second term to depression problems. He concentrated on getting federal funds and New Deal projects for Arizona. To assist him, Moeur sent an "ambassador" to Washington whose salary was paid by the state.

Using the slogan "Arizona needs Moeur (more)," Moeur ran for a third term in 1936. He lost to R. C. Stanford in the Democratic primary. Moeur died in Tempe a short time after leaving office.

5. STANFORD WAS A GREAT JUDGE BUT DID NOT ENJOY BEING GOVERNOR

Rawghlie Clement Stanford was born in Buffalo Gap, Texas, the son of a cattleman. His family came to Arizona and homesteaded in Phoenix when Rawghlie was a small child. He attended the Creighton one-room rural school. Rejected for the Rough Riders in 1898, Stanford joined the infantry in 1899 and fought in the Philippines. Then came a variety of jobs. He was a good cowboy and sometimes rode broncs in rodeos. Stanford worked in the smelter at Jerome. He operated a mule-pulled scraper in the construction of the Arizona Eastern Railroad. For awhile he was employed at the Old Dominion mine at Globe.

Stanford took up the study of law. It was not necessary in those days to attend college to be an attorney. He passed the bar examination and practiced law in Tombstone before settling down in Phoenix. A capable lawyer, he was elected Maricopa County Superior Court judge in 1914.

Stanford's famous Superior Court decisions. He gained unexpected publicity as the presiding judge in the 1916 Hunt-Campbell election contest. Judge Stanford believed until his death that Campbell had won the election.

In another important case, Stanford won the plaudits of organized labor. He fined the Arizona Eastern Railroad for violating the state's "70-car Limit Law." This law was a referendum passed by the voters in 1912. Convinced that long trains were dangerous to railroad workers, the people voted to limit freight trains to 70 cars and passenger trains

Governor Rawghlie C. Stanford

to 14. Stanford's decision was upheld by the Arizona Supreme Court. But the U. S. Supreme Court, in 1945, declared the law unconstitutional. The higher court held that only Congress can regulate interstate commerce.

Stanford was the Democratic state chairman in the late 1920s. He was defeated in Democratic primaries for the U. S. Senate in 1920 and for governor in 1934. But in 1936 he beat Governor Moeur in the primary. He criticized Moeur's sales tax as a device to remove the tax burden from mine corporations and put it on the backs of the common people.

The Republican nominee, Thomas E. Campbell, picked up some of Moeur's arguments. Campbell asked how Stanford was going to build a promised four-lane highway between Phoenix and Tucson and another between Kingman and Boulder Dam and at the same time reduce state spending and taxes.

In 1936 neither party had much money to spend on advertising—including the use of the radio, which had become an important media for contacting voters.

Stanford's big victory—87,678 votes to 36,114 for Campbell—served to mark the decline of the Republican Party in Arizona. Stanford said in his inaugural address that there were really three parties in Arizona in the 1930s: Democratic Party number one, Democratic Party number two, and the Republican Party.

Once in office, Stanford was besieged by hundreds of jobseekers. He insisted on talking to each one personally. But there were just not enough state jobs for all his supporters. It also hurt him to replace excellent Democratic employees at the state hospital and state prison with his own Democrats. This patronage problem caused him not to run for reelection and to get out of politics for awhile.

Some of Stanford's recommendations to the legislature in 1937—police radios in highway patrol cars and a cooling system for the capitol—indicated life-style changes taking place in Arizona in the late 1930s. The 13th state legislature set up a new Board of Social Security and Public Welfare to handle New Deal federal assistance programs. A law was passed permitting newspapers to keep their news sources secret. Unfair sales practices— such as selling below cost to drive out competition—were outlawed.

Stanford returned to the practice of law. In 1942, however, he was elected to the Arizona Supreme Court. He participated in a thousand cases before his retirement in 1955. He died in 1963 at the age of 85.

6. GOVERNOR JONES COOPERATED WITH THE ROOSEVELT ADMINISTRATION

In a one-party state only the primary election means anything. That was true in Arizona in 1938. Five Democrats vied for the chance to oppose the one sacrificial Republican, Jerrie Lee.

Robert T. Jones, like most governors, rode horseback in parades. This one was in Tucson.

C. M. Zander—a long-time member of the Hunt political machine who was known as "the little general"—appeared to be the front runner. But he was killed in a plane crash at Benson while campaigning. The winner of the primary, with only 34 per cent of the vote, was Robert Taylor Jones. He was trailed by Secretary of State James H. Kerby, Sidney P. Osborn, and Andrew Bettwy. The latter was "the cowboy candidate for governor" who favored legalized gambling.

As a young man in his native Tennessee, Jones worked on a surveying crew, becoming a civil engineer the hard way. He had a construction job on the Panama Canal before coming to Arizona in 1909 to build a roadbed for the Southern Pacific. Settling in Superior, Jones opened a drugstore. He eventually had stores in Mesa, Tucson, and Phoenix. Jones was elected to the state senate, first from Pinal and then from Maricopa County.

After winning the Democratic primary nomination for governor, Jones did little campaigning. No one seriously gave the Republican Lee a chance. There were more than 155,000 registered Democrats in 1938 and only about 20,000 Republicans. Jones won easily with 80,350 votes to 32,122 for Jerrie Lee.

Jones was a one-term governor. But he was able to fulfill a campaign promise to bring economy to state government. The penitentiary at Florence, for example, was operated at lower cost, even though there were about 200 more inmates. The property tax rate was reduced.

By working with the Roosevelt administration in Washington, Jones was able to put the nation's first statewide food stamp program for the needy in operation. During his administration Arizona users were permitted to buy 18 percent of the electricity generated at Boulder Dam.

Governor Jones also cooperated with President Roosevelt in building up our national defense. Working with the citizens of Bisbee, he was able to secure a larger water supply for Fort Huachuca. He also began putting the Arizona National Guard—armed with new automatic Garand rifles—on a wartime footing.

Jones was defeated in the 1940 Democratic primary by Sidney P. Osborn. Another incumbent, U. S. Senator William Fountain Ashurst, was upset in the primary. After more than 28 years in the Senate, Ashurst was defeated by Ernest W. McFarland, a Pinal County Superior Court judge from Florence.

Jones returned to private business. He later took a federal job. For two years he was head of the Office of Price Stabilization in Phoenix.

7. SIDNEY P. OSBORN IS RATED ONE OF ARIZONA'S BEST GOVERNORS

Sidney P. Osborn—Arizona's only governor to be elected four consecutive terms—was always proud to say, "My roots are deep in Arizona." His father and uncle were pages in the first territorial legislature at Prescott in 1864. His grandfather was one of the founders of Phoenix.

Osborn was born in Phoenix in 1884. He attended the old Central School. Anticipating a career in politics, he wrote "Sidney P. Osborn, Governor of Arizona" in one of his sixth grade textbooks. After graduating from Phoenix Union High School, Osborn went to

Governor Sidney P. Osborn

Washington, D. C. He worked as secretary to John F. Wilson, Arizona's delegate to Congress.

Returning to Phoenix, the young Osborn worked as a capitol reporter for the *Phoenix Sun* and later for the *Arizona Democrat*. He was the youngest delegate at the 1910 constitutional convention. After statehood, Osborn was Arizona's first secretary of state. He gave up that office in 1918 to run for governor. In that year and again in 1924 and 1938 Osborn was defeated in the Democratic primary. In 1934 he lost to Senator Ashurst in a try for the U. S. Senate. In between defeats, Osborn raised cotton near Higley for a few years, published *Dunbar's Weekly*, and was appointed collector of internal revenue for Arizona.

Finally, Osborn was elected governor in 1940. He defeated Governor Jones in the primary and Republican Jerrie Lee in the general election. He was reelected in 1942, 1944, and 1946. Osborn's persistence paid off. With a broad knowledge of Arizona's government and people, he became one of the state's best governors.

Arizona signs the Colorado River Compact. The highlight of Osborn's career was the untangling of the Colorado River problem. Arizona had not yet signed the 1922 Colorado River (Santa Fe) Compact. Osborn asked the legislature to ratify it. He explained that the Swing-Johnson Bill of 1928 provided that only states which signed the compact could take water from the Colorado River.

Osborn, like most of Arizona's governors, usually found the lawmakers reluctant to act. The 16th legislature, however, ratified the compact in 1944 within a week after the Governor's request. Money was appropriated to speed up planning for using 2,800,000 acre feet of Colorado River water.

The Robles filibuster*. The votes on these bills came after a 22-hour filibustering speech by Pima County Representative Frank G. Robles. The 32-year-old Tucson service station operator repeated nearly all the arguments against the Colorado River Compact that had been uttered during the previous 22 years. His speech was the longest in the history of the state. No purpose was served, but the proponents of the bill kindly promised him all the time he wanted. They relieved him during the night and brought him coffee and sandwiches. Near collapse, Robles left the hall at 8:16 a.m., saying, "Thank you for bearing with me and staying up with me all night. I can not bear to stay for the vote."

Ground water problem. Governor Osborn tried hard to get the legislature to pass an effective law to regulate the pumping of ground water. A Geological Survey report—covering the five-year period from 1939 to 1944—showed that Arizona's ground water reservoirs were being emptied at an alarming rate. In some areas nearly three times as much water was pumped as could be replaced by rainfall.

---

*A *filibuster* is a long speech by a legislator who wants to stop a bill from passing.

The overpumping was most observable during World War II. In the early 1940s Arizona experienced new industrial development—both in agriculture and manufacturing. One of the greatest migrations of people in the history of the world came to Arizona and other western states. Economic expansion brought new demands for more water. Arizona had a choice: close the door to progress or pump water from below the ground that can not be restored. In a few years the ground water table dropped from just below the surface to several hundred feet in some areas.

The *Ground Water Act of 1945* did nothing to lessen the rate of depletion. It simply required all persons operating wells to file a report with the state land commissioner.

The *Ground Water Act of 1948* was not much better. One disappointed legislator said it was "as weak as restaurant soup and should have been sent from the Senate with crutches." No new wells could be drilled in "critical areas," but no limit was placed on wells already overpumping. A Geological Survey report showed that the amount of water pumped continued to increase—from 3,250,000 acre feet a year in 1949 to 4,800,000 acre feet in 1953.

Osborn's successes. Osborn was more successful with the legislature on other matters. The 15th legislature in 1941 created a new Board of Health. The 16th was the one which ratified the Colorado River Compact. The 17th created a Board of Regents for the universities in 1945. The 18th, which met in one regular and seven special sessions—a total of 200 days—established the Interstate Stream Commission. The 18th also put state and county employees on a classified civil service system. A retirement system for state employees was another achievement of the 18th.

Governor Osborn got some legislative action by giving his views to the people in radio speeches. He would ask the voters to bring pressure on their representatives. His repeated landslide victories on election day had some influence on the legislature too.

Governor Osborn is greeted by the governor of Sonora on Cinco de Mayo day in 1941, in Nogales, Sonora.

The Democratic Party reached its apex of power in the wartime elections of 1942 and 1944. About 87 per cent of the voters were registered Democrats. In 1944 Governor Osborn got 100,220 votes to only 27,261 for Republican Jerrie Lee, who didn't bother to campaign. Osborn confined his electioneering to radio speeches and letters. His backers urged the Democrats to "Vote 'er straight."

There were no oldtime rallies, parades, or oratorical debates in the 1940s. Osborn's opponents in 1946 labelled him a "Phantom Governor." It was true that he had muscular atrophy in his right arm and leg. This condition kept him from making an extensive tour of the state. But he was able to be at his desk every day.

"Right-to-work" amendment. In 1946 the public was more interested in ballot propositions than candidates. The spotlight was focused on the so-called "right-to-work" constitutional amendment.

The backers of this initiative measure claimed that it would merely permit persons to work without joining a labor union. Bruce Brockett, the Republican nominee for governor, said that if the "right-to-work" amendment passed, the unions could still strike, picket, boycott, and have collective bargaining*.

Collective bargaining is a process in which the workers have a spokesman to talk to the employer for higher pay and better working conditions.

But organized labor was fighting mad. The amendment was called the "right-to-starve" bill. Labor leaders argued that passage of the amendment would deal a death blow to labor unions and reduce laborers to a state of "peonage." Governor Osborn, in a rare campaign appearance, referred to the measure as an insult to the intelligence of Arizona voters.

At the polls, the voters separated the issues from the candidates. The "right-to-work" amendment was approved in every county except Gila by a large vote—61,875 to 49,557. Osborn was elected to a fourth term. He received 73,595 votes to 48,867 for Brockett.

Last years in office. Governor Osborn did not complete his fourth term. He was slowly dying of incurable creeping paralysis (amyotrophic lateral schlerosis). During his last years he asked a Phoenix radio broadcaster and future governor, Jack Williams, to read his State of the State messages to the legislature. In December 1947, he suffered a physical collapse as the result of long hours of negotiation in which he tried to bring an end to the Salt River Valley lettuce shed strike.

The CIO Fresh Fruit and Vegetable Workers Union demanded a 17½ cents an hour wage increase. They were picketing sheds along Grand Avenue in the Alhambra district. Fighting broke out when non-union workers tried to cross the picket lines. The Governor made a personal visit to the lines. He said the National Guard would be called out if violence erupted. After a shed near Tolleson was destroyed by fire, Maricopa County Sheriff Cal Boies asked Governor Osborn for help. The Guard was then sent to restore order.

Despite increasing weakness, the Governor stayed on the job. He called three special sessions of the legislature in 1948 to work on a ground water code. When his speech completely failed, he communicated with his secretary by pointing at letters on an alphabetical chart with a pencil held in his mouth. He refused to resign. Osborn died in May 1948. Secretary of State Dan Garvey took over the governor's duties.

UNIT SEVEN

ARIZONA SINCE WORLD WAR II

The world has discovered Arizona—its marvelous climates, natural resources, and scenic wonders. By the 1970s Arizona was the fastest-growing state. From a population of 500,000 in 1940 it grew and grew. By the bicentennial year 1976, there were about 2,250,000 people living in Arizona.

Air conditioning has made year-around living comfortable, even in the hottest areas. The ever-smiling sun was once a barrier to civilization. Now it attracts retirees, millions of tourists, and clean-air industries. Since World War II, manufacturing has become Arizona's number one source of income.

The minority groups have made progress. The Indians, once called "the vanishing Americans," are instead multiplying in number. Black Americans won many civil rights—beginning with the desegregation of schools in 1954. Mexican-Americans have made great strides in improving their standard of living.

Arizona, once solidly Democratic, emerged as a two-party state following World War II. By the 1970s nominees of both parties had a chance to win statewide offices. The Republicans had a slight advantage in Maricopa County. Democrats had a big majority in Tucson and Pima County, the second largest population area.

President Harry Truman waves as he leaves the White House for his inauguration in 1949. Seated with him are Speaker of the House John McCormack of Massachusetts and Senator Carl Hayden of Arizona. Hayden was the president pro tempore of the Senate.

21

STATE GOVERNMENT AND POLITICS SINCE 1948

In the first quarter century after World War II, the Democrats and Republicans occupied the governor's chair about an equal amount of time. Five Democratic governors were elected: Osborn, Garvey, McFarland, Goddard, and Castro. The Republican governors were Pyle, Fannin, and Williams.

The Democrats had a majority in the legislature until 1967. The party was usually divided into factions, however. It was not uncommon for conservative Democrats to join with Republicans to form a majority coalition. In 1966 a federal court reapportioned the legislature on the basis of "one-man, one-vote." Control of the legislature then passed from the more Democratic rural counties to Maricopa County. By the 1960s Maricopa had become both heavily populated and Republican oriented.

The two-party system began emerging in Arizona after World War II. New industries attracted thousands of people to Arizona's dry-air climate. Many of the new residents came from Republican states. Aggressive campaigns by several outstanding Republican candidates in the 1950s also gave the Republican Party a boost.

Victories by Governor Howard Pyle, U. S. Senator Barry Goldwater, Congressman John J. Rhodes, and Governor Paul Fannin created a bandwagon effect. Many conservative Democrats identified with the new image of Republican success.

The Democratic Party in Arizona reached its zenith of power in the elections of 1942 and 1944. More than 87 per cent of the voters were then registered as Democrats. The popularity of Republican President Dwight Eisenhower in the 1950s helped to narrow the gap. The percentage of Democrats fell to 65.9 percent in 1960 and 54.2 in 1970.

KEY CONCEPTS
1. Mild-mannered Dan E. Garvey was a one-term governor.
2. Republican Howard Pyle worked for reforms and helped to create the two-party system in Arizona.
3. Ernest W. McFarland brought a lot of political experience to the governor's office.
4. Paul Fannin discovered that an Arizona governor does not have much power.
5. Sam Goddard and the 27th legislature overcame differences to enact some important laws.
6. Jack Williams worked with the state's first Republican legislatures to modernize state government.
7. Raul Castro became Arizona's first Mexican-American governor.
8. Secretary of State Wesley Bolin became the 15th governor.
9. Bruce Babbitt was elected governor in 1978.

349

POLITICA
of State Legislatures, Top Statew

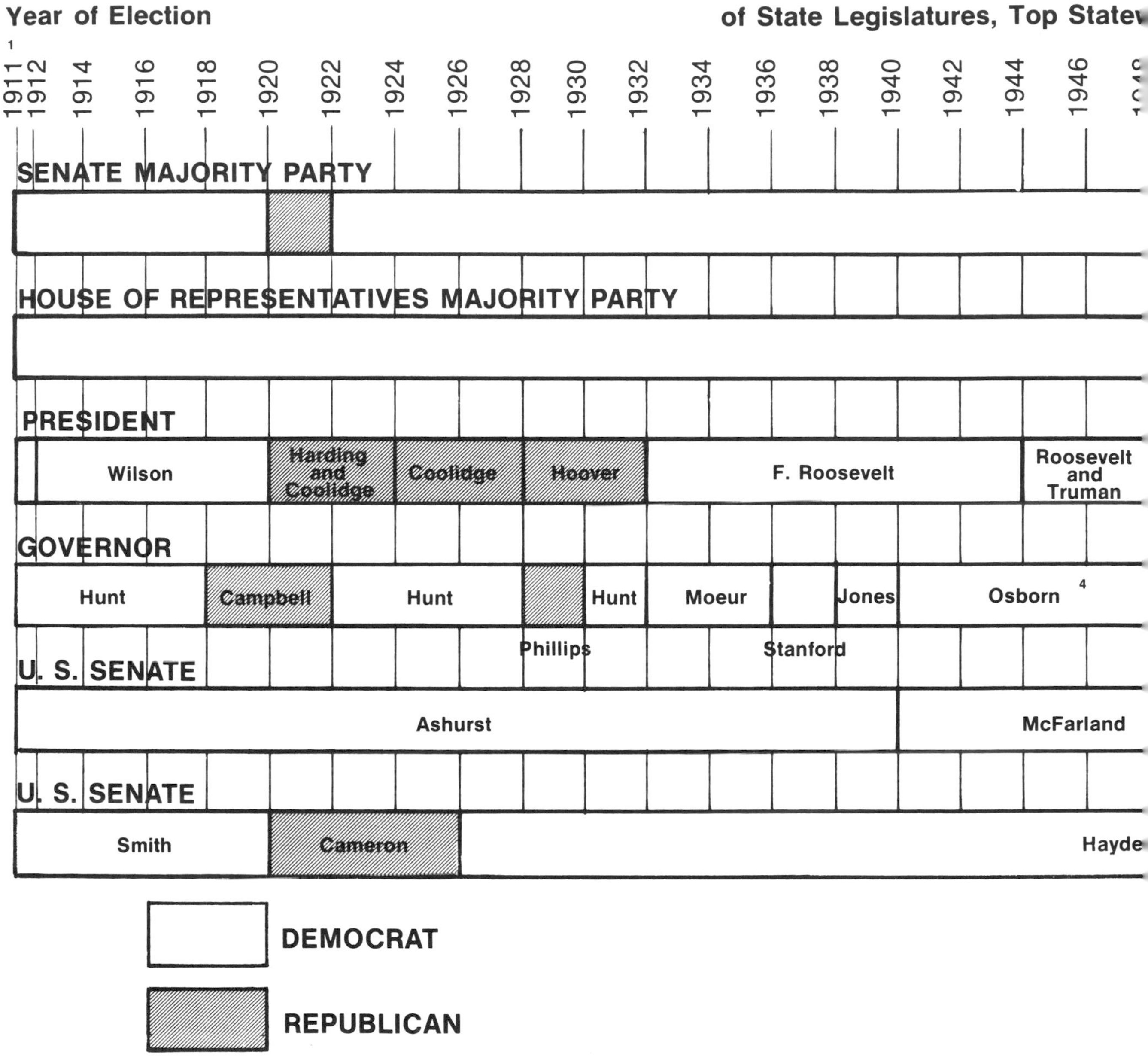
Year of Election
1911[1]
1912
1914
1916
1918
1920
1922
1924
1926
1928
1930
1932
1934
1936
1938
1940
1942
1944
1946
SENATE MAJORITY PARTY
HOUSE OF REPRESENTATIVES MAJORITY PARTY
PRESIDENT
Wilson
Harding and Coolidge
Coolidge
Hoover
F. Roosevelt
Roosevelt and Truman
GOVERNOR
Hunt
Campbell
Hunt
Hunt
Moeur
Jones
Osborn [4]
Phillips
Stanford
U. S. SENATE
Ashurst
McFarland
U. S. SENATE
Smith
Cameron
Hayde
DEMOCRAT
REPUBLICAN

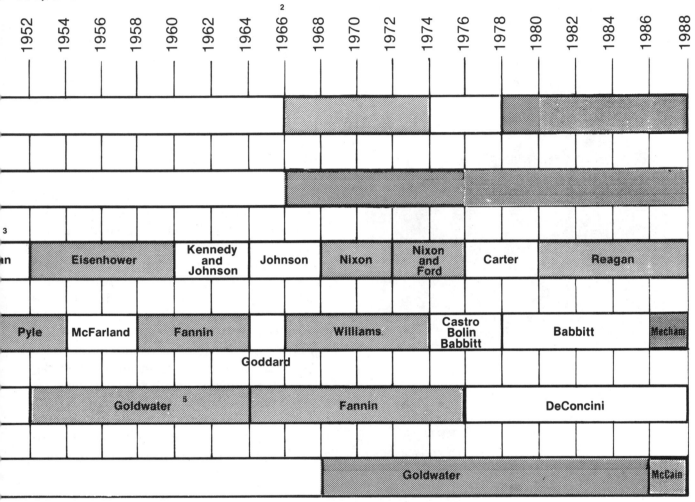

¹Arizona's first election for state and national officers was in 1911.

²Legislature reapportioned by the courts.

³Arizona voted for every winning candidate for president until 1960.

⁴Osborn died in office in May, 1948. He was replaced by Secretary of State Garvey.

⁵Goldwater ran for President of the United States in 1964, giving up his seat in the U. S. Senate.

⁶Hayden served a total of 57 years in the U.S. House and Senate, longer than any other person in American history. He was elected to the House in 1911 and took office in 1912.

Governor Dan Garvey

1. MILD-MANNERED DAN E. GARVEY WAS A ONE-TERM GOVERNOR

Secretary of State Dan E. Garvey was "acting governor" from May 1948, when Governor Osborn died, until November 22, 1948. He could not be sworn in as governor until the people approved a succession amendment to the constitution. This was done at the regular election in November.

Early career. A native of Vicksburg, Mississippi, Garvey came west in 1909 when Arizona was still a territory. He worked as an accountant for the old Randolph Railroad Company. In the early 1930s he went broke in the automobile business in Tucson. His political career began with a term on the Tucson city council. After two terms as Pima County treasurer, he was appointed city treasurer of Tucson. In 1939 he became assistant to Secretary of State Harry M. Moore in Phoenix. Moore died in 1942 and Garvey was appointed to complete the term. He was elected twice to the office on his own.

Election of 1948. When Garvey ran for governor in 1948 he was opposed by six Democrats. He made only one speech—to announce his candidacy. A mild-mannered and polite gentleman, Garvey had little taste for the rough-and-tumble public controversy that delighted Osborn. Stressing his "experience" and "personal integrity," Garvey relied mainly on newspaper advertising. He won the Democratic primary with a plurality of only 28 percent. But even at that percentage he had nearly 10,000 more votes than his closest rival, Congressman Richard F. Harless.

Garvey's Republican opponent, Bruce Brockett, called for an end to the one-party system. "It's time for a change," he said, and hammered away at the "tax and spend" policy of the Democratic state administration. Brockett said Arizona's per capita* tax bill was the fourth highest in the nation. The per capita income of Arizona residents was only 34th in the country. Governor Garvey did little campaigning. It wasn't necessary because Arizona was still a one-party state. He won easily—104,008 votes to 70,419 for Brockett.

The Democratic candidate for secretary of state, Wesley Bolin, was also elected. Bolin was to be chosen secretary of state 13 consecutive times before leaving that office.

The 1948 election was the first in which Arizona Indians were allowed to vote. Another first was recorded when Arizona elected its two congressmen from districts rather than as representatives-at-large. John R. Murdock was returned to Congress from District I, which then consisted of Maricopa County. Ex-University of Arizona football player Harold A. "Porque" Patten won in District 2, the rest of the state.

Per capita means for each person.

Some important laws. Governor Garvey raised a few eyebrows in 1949 by asking the 19th legislature to abolish dog racing. Arizona was one of only five states which permitted dog tracks. During 1947 they operated 279 days. The lawmakers compromised the issue. Both dog and horse racing were limited to 120 days a year in Maricopa and thirty days in other counties. The legislature also created a racing commission to regulate the horses.

Garvey was pleased when the legislature created a permanent home for the Arizona Children's Colony. It was located on state land at Randolph, five miles south of Coolidge.

Governor Dan Garvey (left), President Harry Truman, and U.S. Senator Ernest McFarland at a train whistle stop in Arizona during the 1948 campaign.

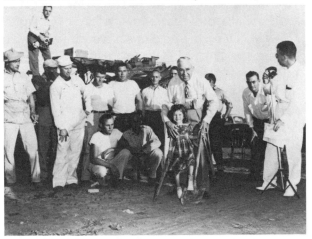

Governor Garvey, with shovel, breaks ground to begin construction of the children's colony at Randolph.

The Governor took part in ground breaking ceremonies in January 1950. The colony was in operation two years later with space for 300 children.

Election of 1950. Governor Garvey sought reelection in 1950 and was again opposed by a flock of Democrats in the primary. The winner this time was Mrs. Ana Frohmiller—the state's first woman candidate for governor. Mrs. Frohmiller had been elected state auditor twelve straight times. An article in *Collier's* magazine referred to her as the "watchdog of the Arizona treasury." She promised more economy and efficiency in government if elected governor. Mrs. Frohmiller won the Democratic nomination with a plurality of 29 percent. Governor Garvey, Richard Harless, Jim Smith, Ralph Watkins, and Howard Sprouse split the rest of the votes.

Mrs. Frohmiller ran against J. Howard Pyle, a popular radio announcer, in the general election. She used the slogan "Experience, not an experiment" to stress the point that her Republican opponent had never held public office. Pyle overcame an overwhelming nine to two Democratic registration advantage to win by a slim margin—99,109 to 96,118. Before the election he barnstormed the state with his campaign manager, Phoenix City Councilman Barry Goldwater.

Despite Pyle's victory, Arizona was still a one-party Democratic state in 1950. The Democrats won every seat in the State Senate and 61 of 72 House seats. Democratic candidates also won all but six offices in the fourteen county courthouses.

Garvey finished his term as governor and was later appointed state examiner.

2. REPUBLICAN HOWARD PYLE WORKED FOR REFORMS AND HELPED TO CREATE A TWO-PARTY SYSTEM IN ARIZONA

J. Howard Pyle was born in Sheridan, Wyoming, in 1906. His father was a minister and moved from church to church in the Midwest. During his boyhood days Pyle worked at odd jobs and considered becoming a mechanic. By the time the family got to Arizona in 1925, however, Pyle had become a good vocalist. Four years later he started working for KTAR radio.

His "Arizona Highlights" program made him the state's "best known voice." NBC radio annually broadcast his description of the Easter sunrise at the Grand Canyon. During World War II Pyle went to the Pacific as a war correspondent. He was on the battleship *Missouri* when the Japanese signed surrender terms.

Following his surprise election victory in 1950, Pyle said, "I was elected because I was not a politician and I had no aspirations to become a politician." Though a Republican, he tried to work in harmony with the Democratic legislature. If Pyle had a scapegoat to blame for Arizona's problems, it was not the Democratic Party. He often attacked the "special interests," especially the mine companies.

Governor Howard Pyle

Pyle gave tax reform high priority. He thought that the school district property tax was unfair. In 1950 the richest school district in Arizona had 375 times more taxable property behind each student than did the poorest district. The Governor proposed school district *tax equalization.* In other words, let the state take over a bigger share of the school financing burden. That way the tax load could be spread out equally over the whole state. But when the legislature submitted an equalization measure to the voters in 1953, it was defeated.

Pyle also made proposals for the reorganization of Arizona's outmoded state government. For greater efficiency, he thought that some 115 independent boards and agencies should be grouped into a few departments. Only a Department of Law was established during his administration, however. A Department of Finance law was passed, but the Arizona Supreme Court declared it unconstitutional on a technicality.

School integration law. Pyle cooperated with the 20th legislature and could be proud of some accomplishments. In the field of civil rights, for example, a bill was passed permitting school districts to ban segregation in elementary schools. This act was three years ahead of the 1954 U. S. Supreme Court decision that outlawed segregation.

The integration bill was managed on the floor by Frank Robles, a Mexican-American from Tucson. It was strongly supported by two Black representatives from Phoenix, Hayzel Daniels and Carl Sims. After Pyle signed the law, Daniels and Sims gave him credit for taking the "initial step toward full and complete integration of all school children."

Election of 1952. In a 1952 radio broadcast to the voters, Pyle announced for reelection. He listed four results of his soft-line approach to the legislature: 1) a $4.5 million surplus in the state treasury, 2) elimination of most of the state's debts, 3) appropriation of $5 million for new buildings and repairs at the state's institutions, 4) and much needed salary increases for state and county offices.

President Dwight Eisenhower and Governor Pyle. After leaving the governor's office, Pyle worked in the White House as an administrative assistant. He later headed the National Safety Council.

Pyle was easily reelected. 1952 was a big year for Republicans in Arizona. The presence of Pyle and popular presidential candidate Dwight D. Eisenhower on the ticket helped other Republican candidates. Mesa lawyer John J. Rhodes upset Congressman John R. Murdock of Tempe. In a close contest, Barry Goldwater unseated U. S. Senator Ernest McFarland, the majority leader in the Senate. McFarland probably lost many conservative Democrat votes because of his close association with the liberal Truman administration.

In 1952 the Republicans also picked up legislative seats. They won 30 of 80 House seats compared to 11 of 72 in the previous legislature. Four Republicans won seats in the 19-member Senate, where the party had not been represented for several years.

Legislature reapportioned. Pyle led a successful drive in 1953 to reapportion the legislature. He said "the House was becoming too large and unwieldy and the Senate was too tightly controlled by the mining interests under the old system." At a special election in 1953 the people approved a reapportionment referendum submitted by the legislature. The Senate was increased from 19 to 28 members, two from each county. The House was

set at 80. It had been increasing in size as the state's population grew.

The new plan for apportioning legislators lasted for a dozen years. In 1966 the courts ordered both houses reapportioned on the basis of "one man, one vote." Instead of each county, large or small, having two state senators, each senator now represents about the same number of people.

Need for a groundwater code. Perhaps the biggest disappointment of Pyle's second term was the legislature's failure to pass a strong groundwater code. Dwindling water supplies was one of the state's major problems. As cotton prices rose, farmers cultivated more land. The amount of irrigated land in Arizona rose from one million acres in 1949 to 1,300,000 acres in 1953.

During the same period, the annual volume of underground water that was pumped increased from 3,250,000 acre feet to 4,800,000. Underground water was being used which had been stored up over thousands of years. But Pyle, like Osborn, did not succeed in getting a law passed that would stop the excessive pumping.

Raid on Short Creek. Governor Pyle was defeated in 1954 by Ernest McFarland who made a political comeback. Pyle's failure to win a third term was due in part to a moonlight raid of 89 officers on the polygamous community of Short Creek, located north of the Grand Canyon.

"Here is a community," Pyle explained in a historic radio broadcast, "unalterably dedicated to the wicked theory that every maturing girl should be forced into bondage of multiple wifehoods with men of all ages for the sole purpose of producing more children."

The raid, on July 26, 1953, cost Pyle votes— particularly among Mormons. They did not question the law against polygamy which Pyle was enforcing. Nor did the Mormons approve the practices of the Short Creek cult. But many resented the overdramatized manner in which the polygamists were arrested and brought to trial.

Governor Pyle was honored at a testimonial dinner in Phoenix before he left office. President Eisenhower sent a telegram in which he credited Pyle with "revitalizing" the two-party system in Arizona.

Pyle was interviewed as he left the governor's office for the last time in January 1955. He listed the extension of social security coverage to state employees, including teachers, as one of his main accomplishments.

3. ERNEST W. McFARLAND BROUGHT A LOT OF POLITICAL EXPERIENCE TO THE GOVERNOR'S OFFICE

Ernest McFarland came to the governor's office with a solid background in education and political experience. A former Oklahoma schoolteacher and a World War I navy veteran, he graduated from Stanford law school. McFarland practiced law in Pinal County where he was elected county attorney and judge of the superior court. When in private

Governor Ernest W. McFarland

practice he specialized in water law. One of his most exciting experiences, however, was as defense lawyer for Winnie Ruth Judd, the notorious trunk murderess. He saved her from the gas chamber by proving insanity.

In the 1940 Democratic primary, Judge McFarland upset William Fountain Ashurst who had represented Arizona in the U. S. Senate since statehood in 1912. After two six-year terms as U. S. Senator, McFarland was defeated by Barry Goldwater in 1952. Out of public office for two years, McFarland unseated Pyle in 1954 and took over the governor's chair.

There was little Democratic party loyalty. The legislature elected in 1954 was 80 percent Democratic. Governor McFarland appealed to party loyalty for support of the party platform. The liberal-inclined Governor soon discovered, however, that the conservative wing of his party had a majority in both houses. The newly-apportioned 28-member Senate—two from each county—was rural-oriented. Maricopa and Pima counties had 70 percent of the people but neither was represented in the the three top Senate leadership positions.

Accomplishments. Even with a huge Democratic majority in both the 22nd and 23rd legislatures, McFarland had only limited success in getting laws passed during his two terms as governor.

He got annual state aid for schools increased from $115 to $157.50 per pupil in average daily attendance. But rich and poor districts got the same amount per student.

Welfare aid was increased. A state office building in Tucson and the football stadium at Arizona State in Tempe were completed. Money was appropriated to remodel the capitol.

State and county employees were given a five-day week. A State Parks and Recreation Board was created. The state laws were recoded. The state sales tax on goods sold to the federal government was removed. A "use tax" was passed.

A two percent sales tax on goods sold to the federal government was removed for a special reason. The Sperry Rand Company would not build a plant in Arizona if it had to pay the sales tax. Sperry Rand officials said the tax would make it impossible for them to compete for federal business with companies in states that didn't have the tax. So the tax was repealed. McFarland proudly put the bringing of Sperry Rand to Phoenix near the top of his achievements in public office.

The "use tax" replaced the repealed tax on sales to the federal government. The use tax was levied on automobiles and other goods which Arizona residents bought outside the state. The use tax made it easier for local car dealers and other businessmen—who have to charge the Arizona sales tax—to compete with out-of-state businesses.

The new tax laws were included in a revised code of laws. A code commission had spent months weeding out a 43-year accumulation of laws. The 5,143 pages of revised laws were adopted on January 7, 1956, after 54 people—each reading a different section of the code—read simultaneously for two hours. They were fulfilling a legal but ridiculous requirement. Every bill—in this case the entire revised code—must be given a full reading before the final vote.

Capitol remodeled. In July, 1957, work began on remodeling of the old capitol and construction of two new detached wings for the House and Senate. Earlier in the year controversy over a capitol building program drew national attention. Neither McFarland nor the legislature would endorse a 20-story United Nations-type of building which was recommended by the state planning and building commission. The skyscraper was designed by a group of Arizona architects at a cost of $155,000 to the taxpayers. Frank Lloyd Wright described the proposed 20-story capitol as "a telephone pole, and a derby hat on the pole, and two wastebaskets for the legislature."

Wright voluntarily submitted his own design which he wanted built in Papago Park

Governor McFarland (right) and Democratic presidential candidate Adlai Stevenson campaign with Mexican sombreros in 1956.

in East Phoenix. His capitol would have three separate single-level buildings for the governor, legislature and supreme court. A six-sided copper canopy, supported on native onyx pillars, would link the separated buildings together. The canopy would have holes for fountains to spout through from below and sunlight to filter in from above.

Wright's critics referred to his design as a "glorified tent," a "Siamese temple," and the "Teahouse of the August Moon." *Life* magazine simply called it "weird." Some observers said it would be a great tourist attraction but not very practical. The governor, legislature, and supreme court would be housed "in oriental splendor in a pagoda-like edifice on the rim of Papago Park"—nine miles away from the other state officers and agencies on the old capitol grounds.

McFarland and the legislature agreed that neither the skyscraper nor the Wright design would meet the government's real needs and the taxpayers' purse. So the old capitol was remodeled and wings were added.

Name of Arizona State changed. The 23rd legislature had some excitement in the 1958 session. An estimated 2,000 college students from Tempe came *en masse* to the capitol. They antagonized the legislature by hanging popular Senator Harold Giss of Yuma in effigy.

Actually the Senator's intentions were good. Realizing that Arizona State College had grown to university status, he had introduced a bill changing the name to "Tempe University." The argument against "Arizona State University"—which the students wanted—was that this name would be confused with "University of Arizona" at Tucson.

After the capitol demonstration, the college administration advised the students not to create any more bad feelings in the legislature. The students then took a more positive approach. With the help of the Phoenix Junior Chamber of Commerce (Jaycees) and other groups, they circulated petitions to get an initiative on the ballot. In November, 1958, the voters endorsed a name change to "Arizona State University" by a margin of 151,135 to 78,693. The students had a good practical lesson in democracy.

McFarland's later career. After two terms as governor, McFarland ran for his old U. S. Senate seat in 1958. After a bitterly-fought campaign he was again defeated by Senator Goldwater. But McFarland was not finished with politics. In 1964 he was elected to the Arizona Supreme Court and became chief justice in 1968. No other Arizonan has served in a top office in three different branches of government: U. S. Senator (legislature), governor (executive), and Arizona Supreme Court (judiciary).

4. PAUL FANNIN DISCOVERED THAT AN ARIZONA GOVERNOR DOES NOT HAVE MUCH POWER

Paul Fannin was only 10 months old in 1907 when his family left Kentucky. The Fannins settled on a five-acre dairy ranch near downtown Phoenix. A boyhood friend of Barry Goldwater, Fannin graduated from Phoenix Union High School in 1925. He attended the University of Arizona for two

Governor Paul J. Fannin

years. Transferring to Stanford, he earned a degree in economics.

With his formal education finished, Fannin joined his brother Ernest in operating the family business at Five Points in West Phoenix. From wagons and buggies they branched out into hardware, farm equipment, and commercial fertilizer. During the 1930s depression they installed their own butane gas plant. While other businesses were failing, the Fannin company prospered, selling bottled gas and gas appliances all over the state. The Fannin brothers were well-to-do when they sold the company in 1956. Too young to retire, Paul Fannin ran for governor—his first try for public office—in 1958.

Election of 1958. Although somewhat shy, Fannin impressed voters with his sincerity and a deep faith in Arizona's future. Considering his inexperience, few people gave him much of a chance. While the Goldwater-McFarland race for U. S. Senate got most of the publicity, Fannin moved quietly around the state shaking hands. He concentrated on two main themes: bringing more industry to Arizona and "a sound business administration." His billboards and newspaper ads described him as a "good citizen" and "a man you would welcome into your home."

Fannin defeated Robert Morrison, the attorney general, by a vote of 160,136 to 130,329. The size of his victory surprised almost everyone. Republicans Goldwater and Congressman Rhodes were also winners. But the Democrats won nearly every other office—including 55 of 80 House seats and 18 of 19 in the Senate.

Cooperation with the Democratic legislature. Fannin was destined to serve six years in the governor's office surrounded by Democrats. Catching on quickly to the political facts of life, he learned to compromise. He gave credit to the other fellow in order to get the job done.

For decades, Arizona's leaders of both political parties fought for the Central Arizona Project. The 1963 Supreme Court decision made the CAP possible. Cartoon by Reg Manning.

Political leaders of both parties smile after the U.S. Supreme Court upheld Arizona's water rights in 1963. Left to right: Congressman John J. Rhodes, U.S. Senator

Barry Goldwater, Governor Paul Fannin, Congressman Morris Udall, U.S. Senator Carl Hayden, and Secretary of Interior Stewart Udall.

Governor Fannin with Vonda Kay Van Dyke (Miss Arizona and Miss America of 1964) and Governor Luis Encinas of Sonora.

An early result of Fannin's strategy of cooperating with the legislature was the School Finance Act of 1959. More state aid—$180 instead of $157.50 per pupil—was given to school districts. This school aid bill was a compromise. Fannin wanted more state aid. And he preferred giving most of the money to poorer school districts in order to equalize educational opportunities. He had to be satisfied with the law that passed.

Some important laws. *Traffic safety* was high on Governor Fannin's list of priorities. In 1959 Arizona had 514 deaths on the highways. Fannin recommended a mandatory Motor Vehicle Inspection Law which the legislature passed in 1962. The law was unpopular with the public. And the Highway Patrol objected to official inspection of automobiles by service stations and private garages. The law was later repealed.

The junior college system was created by the legislature in 1962. The lawmakers set aside $2 million for new colleges in Cochise, Pinal, and Yuma counties. Eastern Arizona at Thatcher became a part of the state system of junior colleges.

A medical college for Arizona was also established in 1962. The location of the school was a political hot potato. Both the University of Arizona and Arizona State University

wanted it. The board of regents voted in favor of the Tucson site—the U of A.

Coalition legislature. In his third term—during 1963 and 1964—Fannin worked with an unusual legislature. The 32 Republicans in the House joined with 16 conservative Democrats to form a coalition majority. They elected Democrat W. B. Barkley of Glendale as Speaker of the House. This coalition passed many of Governor Fannin's recommendations for laws. But the Democratic Senate defeated or tabled most of the Governor's program.

Arizona's water rights upheld. A great historic event in 1963 gave Arizonans reason to cheer. Arizona won its long court battle with California. The U. S. Supreme Court clarified the question of how the first 7,500,000 acre feet of Colorado River water should be divided among lower basin states. California got 4,400,000 acre feet—not the 5,362,000 requested. Arizona was to have 2,800,000 acre feet of water and Nevada 300,000.

The most important part of the decision, as far as Arizona was concerned, had to do with tributary streams of the Colorado. California's lawyers argued that a million acre

Senator Barry Goldwater (right) and his running mate, Congressman William Miller of New York. They were nominated at the 1964 Republican convention.

feet of Gila River water should be counted as part of Arizona's 2,800,000 acre feet of Colorado River water. But the U. S. Supreme Court held that each tributary—including the Gila River in Arizona and New Mexico—was for the sole use of the states through which it passed.

Arizona members of Congress, of both political parties, hailed the Supreme Court's decision as a victory for the state. Arizona had proved its right to water for the Central Arizona Project (CAP). The U. S. Senate had twice approved the CAP. But the U. S. House Interior Committee rejected the CAP until Arizona could prove that it was legally entitled to the water. The Supreme Court removed any doubt. It was 1968, however, before the CAP bill was passed and sent to President Lyndon Johnson for signing.

Racial demonstration. Two events gave the 26th legislature some excitement in 1964—a civil rights demonstration at the capitol and an impeachment trial.

Near the end of March, Congress of Racial Equality (CORE) demonstrators demanded that the Senate pass an anti-segregation public accommodations bill. The CORE people were mainly young Blacks of high school or college age. They entered the Senate building singing "Freedom" and "We Shall Overcome."

During the second week, some 120 Arizona Highway Patrolmen were called in. The demonstrators, who had formed a shoulder to shoulder barrier around the Senate chamber, were forced to leave. They had made their point. A year later, the next legislature passed a civil rights act.

Impeachment trials. Two members of the Corporation Commission were impeached by the House of Representatives. Democrats Eddie Williams and Jack Buzard were accused of taking bribes. William Rehnquist, a Phoenix lawyer, was employed by the House to handle the prosecution. The Senate, sitting in judgment like a jury, cleared the commissioners of all charges. Rehnquist was later an

Clovis Campbell served in the state legislature from 1962 to 1972. He was the first Black elected to the State Senate.

assistant U.S. attorney general. Former President Richard Nixon appointed him to the U.S. Supreme Court.

Fannin gave up the governor's office. Governor Fannin gave up a chance for a fourth term. In 1964 he ran for the U.S. Senate, winning the seat which Barry Goldwater vacated. Goldwater was the 1964 Republican nominee for President. He was the only Arizonan ever nominated for that high office.

In his six years as governor, Fannin did not feel he had enough power to accomplish the things that needed to be done. Arizona had a 19th century government to deal with 20th century problems. The state was changing from a slow-moving era to a new age of rapid growth, industry, sprawl, freeways, and mammoth universities. But the governor's office had less power than in 1912.

Through the years the legislature had created dozens of independent agencies over which the governor had little authority. Fannin was disappointed that the legislature refused to set up a department of finance to give the governor some control over the budget. As it was, he simply compiled the budget from requests sent in by the agencies and passed them on to the legislature.

Fannin considered the junior college system his greatest accomplishment as governor.

Governor Samuel P. Goddard, Jr.

5. SAM GODDARD AND THE 27th LEGISLATURE OVERCAME DIFFERENCES TO ENACT SOME IMPORTANT LAWS

Sam Goddard was the first governor elected from the "new migration" of people who settled in Arizona after World War II. Born in Clayton, Missouri, he graduated from Harvard in 1941. After service in the air force he moved his family to Tucson. Vigorous and ambitious, he rose to the rank of brigadier general in the air force reserve and earned a law degree at the University of Arizona. He practiced law and was an executive in the Niles Radio Corporation. Active in civic affairs, Goddard was honored as "Tucson's man of the year" in 1959.

Election of 1964. Goddard won the Democratic nomination four consecutive times, beginning in 1962. But he was elected governor only once. Governor Fannin defeated him in 1962. Jack Williams bested him in 1966 and 1968. Goddard won in 1964 over Republican Richard Kleindienst. Later, Kleindienst became U.S. Attorney General in the cabinet of President Nixon.

In 1964 the voters passed an important school tax equalization referendum. It authorized the legislature to grant extra state aid to poor school districts. Accordingly, the new legislature which convened in 1965 enacted Goddard's "Fair Share Program."

The Fair Share Program provided $14 million to needy school districts the first year. The money was raised from "fair share taxes"—including increases in the tobacco tax, state income tax, and the sales tax collected by restaurants. To get the Fair Share Program and other bills he wanted, Goddard held the legislature for 199 days—one regular and four special sessions.

The 27th legislature. Like previous governors, Goddard learned that the legislature really runs the state government. To complicate matters, the Governor was a liberal, while the 27th legislature was conservative.

In the 80-member House, a coalition majority of 35 Republicans and 18 conservative Democrats was organized. This coalition elected Jack Gilbert, a Cochise County conservative Democrat, as Speaker of the House.

The 28-member Senate had only two Republicans. It was controlled by Democrats from the rural counties. Clarence Carpenter of Gila County was reelected to a sixth term as president of the Senate.

Despite their differences in political philosophy, Governor Goddard and the 27th legislature made a good record. The Fair Share Program was a good beginning for school tax equalization.

Department of Finance. Governor Goddard called the 27th a "momentous legislature." He was especially pleased with a budget control bill. This bill created the Department of Finance under the governor's direction.

"This measure has been before every legislature in some form for the past 30 years," Goddard said. "It has been a part of the program of every governor of the past 50 years."

The budget control law gave the governor a meaningful role in budget control for the first time. The governor was given his own skilled staff. He could investigate the spending of each state agency on a year-round basis. In addition, the governor had power to trim requests before handing the total budget to the legislature. The new law also provided the legislature with a full-time budget analyst to check on state agencies.

The Civil Rights Act of 1965. This law was passed by the 27th legislature. The act made it illegal to discriminate in places catering to the general public. Included were restaurants, rooming houses with five or more rentals, and places for entertainment, amusement, or recreation. A Civil Rights Commission was set up. It had seven members appointed by the governor. No more than four could be from the same political party. The commission was given responsibility for working with public and private groups to eliminate "discrimination based on race, color, religion, sex, national origin, or ancestry."

Special bonding election. Goddard proposed a new method of financing state construction projects. Instead of "pay as you go," his approach would be "go now and pay later." He wanted the state debt limit raised from $350,000 to $100 million. *General obligation bonds* would be sold to raise money for construction. The bonds would be paid off with tax revenue over a long period of time. It was only right, Goddard thought, that future generations should help pay for facilities that they will be using.

The bonding proposal set off a statewide debate. The Governor's chief opponent on the bonding issue was House Speaker Jack Gilbert. Newspapers in the state were split. At a special election in 1965, the voters rejected the bonding and debt limit proposals by more than a 4 to 1 margin.

Revenue bonds, however, are legal in Arizona. They are sold to raise money for construction that will pay for itself. College dormitories and the Coliseum in Phoenix are examples of facilities built with money raised by the sale of revenue bonds.

Liquor department scandal. During Goddard's administration, ten liquor agents were charged with padding their expense accounts. Nine legislators or former legislators were indicted by grand juries. They were accused of taking bribes to help people get scarce liquor licenses from John Duncan, superintendent of the liquor department. There were few convictions. But the Governor was forced into asking the popular Duncan to resign. Jack Sheik, a former FBI agent from Tucson, was appointed superintendent.

Legislature reapportioned. The legislature was reapportioned in 1966 following a series of court decisions. In *Baker vs. Carr* and *Reynolds vs. Sims* the U.S. Supreme Court ruled that every state legislator must

Sam Goddard's wife Judy sings a "Go Goddard" jingle during the 1962 campaign. The future governor and son Bill listen approvingly.

represent about an equal number of people. These court rulings were based on the "one-man, one-vote principle."

The 27th legislature could not agree on a method to realign district boundaries. So a three-man federal court panel did the job. The federal judges divided the state into eight districts and apportioned 30 senators and 60 representatives according to population. Maricopa County was designated as District 8 and given half the members: 15 senators and 30 representatives. Pima County was District 7 with 6 senators and 12 representatives. The remaining 12 counties made up six districts.

The Congressional districts were also redivided.

Election of 1966. Reapportionment resulted in some important "firsts" in the 1966 election. For the first time in the state's history, the Republicans elected a majority in both houses of the legislature—33 to 27 in the House and 16 to 14 in the Senate. The 14

Democrats in the Senate included the first Black (Clovis Campbell) and the first Chinese-American (Wing Ong) to serve in that body.

Governor Goddard won a bitterly-fought Democratic primary in 1966. He defeated House Speaker Jack Gilbert and Pima County Attorney Norman Green. The latter thought Goddard had moved too slowly in cleaning out the liquor department.

In the general election, Governor Goddard lost to Jack Williams, a radio executive and former mayor of Phoenix. Goddard carried nine of the 14 counties but lost Maricopa—which then had 55.4 percent of the state's registered voters — by about 37,000 votes. Statewide, it was Goddard with 174,904 to 203,438 for Williams. In 1968 Goddard was again defeated by Williams in a fourth try for the governorship.

6. JACK WILLIAMS WORKED WITH THE STATE'S FIRST REPUBLICAN LEGISLATURES TO MODERNIZE STATE GOVERNMENT

Jack Williams was born in Los Angeles in 1909. He lived his first four years on the west coast of Mexico where his father was a superintendent for Wells-Fargo. During the Mexican revolution of 1913, Jack and his mother were placed on a government troop train that carried them and other American refugees from Guaymas to Nogales. His father later escaped to California on a Mexican gunboat. Wells Fargo then sent him to Phoenix.

At the age of six, Jack William's right eye was removed because of a malignant tumor. The socket would not hold a glass eye. Avoiding other children who made cruel jokes about his appearance, the young Williams became a recluse and an avid reader. He was a student at Phoenix Union High School when his father died. To help his mother, Jack got a job handling freight at the Union Depot before and after school. Coming out of his shell, he made the PUHS football squad as a substitute. He

Governor Jack Williams

joined the debate team and won the state oratorical contest. While at Phoenix Junior College he wrote newspaper publicity for the college and started working for KOY radio.

As a radio man, Williams covered the state capitol. He knew all of Arizona's governors. From 1945 to 1948 Williams was chosen by the ailing Governor Osborn to read his "State of the State" messages to the legislature. KOY encouraged Williams to be active in community work. He was elected to the Phoenix elementary school board and the city council. In 1955 Williams was elected mayor of Phoenix. In that job he experienced all the problems of trying to keep pace with Arizona's fantastic growth. The city's boundaries were expanded and the population grew from 155,000 to 520,000 in four years time.

In 1966 Williams was elected to the first of three terms as governor — two 2-year and one 4-year term. A Republican, he unseated Democratic Governor Goddard. The Republicans also won a majority in both houses of the reapportioned 28th legislature.

The 28th was different from previous Arizona legislatures. Not only was it more Republican but also more urban and younger. It was not beholden to the big economic interests that had dominated the Senate and resisted change in the past. Committed to action and reform, the adrenalin-charged 28th legislature set a dizzying pace. It enacted most of Governor Williams's 1967 program.

A central purchasing agency was set up under the Department of Finance. The idea was to save money by buying on a wholesale basis for all state agencies.

The School Finance Act of 1967 transferred an estimated $66 million in school costs from the elementary and high school districts to the state.

A center for the mentally retarded was established in Tucson.

The state liquor department was revamped to separate licensing from enforcement. A three-man State Liquor Board was created with power to issue, suspend, or revoke licenses. The narcotics division was transferred to the attorney general and later to the Department of Public Safety.

Reorganization of state government. When the 28th reconvened in 1968, Williams suggested that the legislators overhaul Arizona's "19th century governmental buggy." Reorganization became an ongoing thing in the Williams administration. He succeeded in modernizing the government. When he took over in 1967, the duties of the governor were largely ceremonial. He had little control over the almost-independent state agencies.

Williams and the Republican legislature succeeded in grouping most of the agencies into "super departments." Each department is headed by a director appointed by the governor. Some of the reorganization was done by constitutional amendments approved by the voters in the form of referendums.

Other changes were made by statutes (laws) passed by the legislature. In 1972, for example, the 30th legislature combined eight large state agencies—including the Welfare Department—into the Department of Economic Security (DES).

The reorganization and modernization of state government was perhaps Williams's greatest achievement in office.

Prison reform. Governor Williams was proud of his record in prison reform. Prior to his administration the state got by with the corrections system established in territorial days. There was a prison for adults at Florence and a boys' industrial school at Fort Grant.

"Today," Williams told the legislature in 1973, "we have the Arizona Girls' School... two correctional conservation centers—one at Alpine for boys and one at Safford for men. Community treatment centers have been established in Phoenix and Tucson." Arrested alcoholics were sent to these treatment centers rather than to jail.

The legislature approved the Governor's request for an intermediate prison to relieve crowded conditions at Florence. This prison was eventually built at Tucson. Residents of

Former Secretary of Interior Rogers C.B. Morton (left) and Governor Jack Williams set off the first dynamite blast near the Colorado River to begin construction of the Central Arizona Project in May, 1973.

south Phoenix objected to having it placed on a site selected in that area.

Williams was concerned about the large number of violent crimes. He asked for a reinstatement of capital punishment which had been suspended as a result of a U.S. Supreme Court decision. A House-Senate compromise in 1973 resulted in a law restoring the death penalty for aggravated murders.

Recall attempt. Governor Williams signed a farm labor bill in 1972 which led to a movement to recall him. The State Agricultural Labor Relations Act permitted farm labor employers to obtain a 10-day court injunction against a strike at harvest time. The law also required a secret ballot election before a union could speak as the bargaining agent for any group of farm workers in the state. Cesar Chavez, head of the United Farm Workers (UFW) didn't like the law. He said

it would prevent farm workers from organizing effective unions to bargain with growers.

Chavez's followers protested the farm labor bill. They circulated petitions to recall Governor Williams. Nearly 103,000 valid signatures were needed—25 per cent of the number of people who voted for governor in the most recent election. Petitions with about 176,000 names were finally filed, but more than half were thrown out. Why? Many of the signers were not registered voters. Some people signed more than once. Other signatures were unreadable. Further, the attorney general ruled that 26,651 names had to be eliminated because they were on petitions circulated by voter registrars. The courts later overruled the attorney general's opinion. By that time, however, Williams had finished his term.

New executive building. Williams was the last governor to occupy an office in the old capitol. In October 1974, he moved to a plush, walnut-paneled gubernatorial suite on the ninth floor of the new executive wing.

"I have given my successor modernized government and modernized offices," Williams said.

Williams was shy for a politician. Not a headline seeker, he did not get much publicity for some impressive programs. In this category were government reorganization and increased state aid for schools. He also formed the Indian Development District of Arizona (IDDA). Some $50 million was spent on furthering economic development on Indian reservations.

Williams was proud of Arizona's growth. He seemed more pleased with the creation of 250,000 new jobs by private enterprise than anything state government did while he was governor. Manufacturing employment increased 103 percent. Governor Williams thought the best way to help laborers, farm workers, and minority groups was to hold down taxes and create a favorable climate for industry, business, and commerce.

7. RAUL CASTRO BECAME ARIZONA'S FIRST MEXICAN-AMERICAN GOVERNOR

Raul H. Castro, Arizona's 14th governor, started life as the son of a poor copper miner in Mexico. One of the youngest of 14 children, he was born at Cananea, Sonora, in 1916. His family lived in a hut about the size of the average American living room. For him, winning the governor's office was the American dream come true.

When Castro was still a boy, the family moved to Douglas, Arizona. There his father was employed by Phelps Dodge. Raul graduated from Douglas High School with honors. He then worked his way through college at Flagstaff and was an undefeated middleweight on the boxing team. In 1939, he graduated from college and became a naturalized American citizen.

During World War II Castro worked in the U.S. Foreign Service at Agua Prieta, Sonora. After the war he earned a law degree at the University of Arizona. Later Castro was elected county attorney and then a superior court judge in Pima County. For a while he was the juvenile court judge.

In 1964, Castro was appointed by President Lyndon Johnson to serve as U.S. Ambassador to El Salvador. He was later transferred to Bolivia. In 1970, Castro was the Democratic nominee for governor but lost to Governor Jack Williams.

Election of 1974. Four years later Castro ran again. His slogan, "This man is a leader," helped to create the image of a self-made, tough-talking lawyer and diplomat. This time Castro won. He squeaked by the Republican nominee, Russ Williams, in a photo finish. The switch of the usually-Republican Navajo voters to Castro was the margin of victory.

Two other new faces joined the ranks of Democratic officeholders in 1974. Bruce Babbitt, then a 35-year-old Phoenix lawyer, was elected attorney general. Carolyn Warner was an easy winner for superintendent of public instruction. The legislature was split—a Democratic Senate and a Republican House. The 1974 election made it clear that either party could win in Arizona.

Governor Castro faced a severe test of leadership. Why? For one reason, he won by a narrow margin. Then the legislature was divided. And the country was in a mild recession in 1975.

Castro had one big advantage. He was the first governor to benefit by the streamlining of state government. He appointed the heads of new super departments. These bureau chiefs had to answer directly to the governor on budget and other matters.

Castro did his part to help the state's economy. He cut $20 million from the proposed budget. Each state agency was ordered to cut spending 5 per cent.

Anti-crime bills did best in the legislature during Castro's first two years in office. A statewide grand jury law was passed. The legislature approved a four-county border narcotics strike force.

Governor Raul H. Castro

More anti-crime bills were passed after the bombing murder of Don Bolles, a Phoenix newspaper reporter. A mandatory five-year minimum prison sentence was set for crimes committed with guns or explosives. The criminal code was changed to make it easier to prosecute land fraud cases. And the monopoly on dog tracks in Arizona was broken up.

Castro resigned. In October, 1977, Governor Castro was appointed ambassador to Argentina by President Carter. Castro resigned the office of governor to accept the diplomatic post.

Castro's four-year term was completed by Secretary of State Bolin and Attorney General Bruce Babbitt.

8. SECRETARY OF STATE WESLEY BOLIN BECAME ARIZONA'S 15th GOVERNOR.

Bolin took the oath of office after Castro resigned. A conservative Democrat, Governor Bolin would have felt at home in either the Democrat or Republican party.

Bolin was born in Missouri in 1908. His family moved to Phoenix when he was seven. As a boy, Bolin worked on the family farm on West McDowell Road. He also sold newspapers and caddied for golfers.

As a young man, Bolin opened a dry-cleaning business. Then in 1938 he was elected constable in West Phoenix. Four years later he was appointed justice of the peace.

In 1948 Bolin was elected secretary of state. In that job he was kept busy as the state's official greeter. Bolin was often seen riding a horse in parades. He attended many service club meetings and gave much time to the Boy Scouts.

Bolin was popular. He was elected secretary of state thirteen times.

As governor, Bolin found that prison overcrowding was one of Arizona's big problems in the 1970s. He appointed a new head for the Department of Corrections and asked the legislature to plan a new prison. Bolin said that the prisoners should be put to work. He thought that much of the violence at the prison in Florence was due to idleness.

Bolin died on March 4, 1978. He served a little over four months as governor. The secretary of state, Rose Mofford, could not become governor. She was appointed by Bolin. Only an elected official could take over the governor's office.

Attorney General Bruce Babbitt was next in line. He took the oath as governor and completed Castro's term.

9. BRUCE BABBITT WAS ELECTED GOVERNOR IN 1978.

Early career. Bruce Babbitt's ancestors were Arizona pioneers. The Babbitts were merchants and ranchers in northern Arizona.

Babbitt graduated from Notre Dame University where he was student body president. Later Babbitt earned a master's degree in geology at the University of Newcastle in England. Then came law school at Harvard.

Babbitt practiced law in Phoenix before running for attorney general. In that office

Governor Wesley Bolin

he was tough on consumer frauds. He prosecuted the major milk and bread companies for price-fixing. The courts ordered the companies to refund money to customers.

The legislature was in session when Babbitt became governor. He continued Bolin's efforts to get more money for prisons and mentally retarded children.

Election of 1978. Babbitt, a Democrat, ran for governor in 1978. In the general election he coasted to an easy victory. He defeated the conservative Republican nominee, Phoenix car dealer Evan Mecham.

Except for the governor's race, however, the voters were in a conservative mood in 1978. As in other states, the voters were demanding lower property taxes. The Republicans won both houses of the state legislature. They won 42 of 60 House seats. This was the largest Republican majority in Arizona history.

The voters in 1978 approved a referendum to limit state spending to 7 per cent of the total personal income in Arizona.

Babbitt's style. The Arizona constitution gave most of the power of state government to the legislature. Babbitt was not satisfied with this arrangement. He tried to strengthen the executive branch. For example, Babbitt used the veto more than any previous governor.

Another key to the Babbitt administration was his policy in dealing with the "super chiefs." (These are the heads of big departments.) The Governor took care to select directors who would make things happen. He also organized the super chiefs and other administrative leaders into a cabinet. Regular cabinet meetings were scheduled.

Babbitt constantly interacted with the people of Arizona. He participated in ceremonies and public events in all parts of the state. He was always on the go. Babbitt quickly became a national figure. He was appointed to a special commission to investigate the Three Mile Island nuclear accident in Pennsylvania.

A "triangle" of water accomplish-

Governor Bruce Babbitt, 1982.

ments. Babbitt was reelected in 1982 by a wide margin. He was in office nearly nine years —longer than any other governor except Hunt. Babbitt learned to work with the Republican legislature and the powerful House majority leader, Burton Barr.

The greatest achievement of the Babbitt administration was the *Groundwater Management Act* of 1980. This law limits the pumping of groundwater. It forces conservation in "water short" areas. The counties of Maricopa, Pinal, Pima, and the Prescott part of Yavapai County fit this description. The law also created the *Department of Water Resources*. The goal of this department is to reduce pumping by the year 2020 to the amount of rainwater that goes back into the groundwater reservoirs.

Another landmark water law was the *Environmental Quality Act* if 1986. It was passed to stop pollution of groundwater. Polluters are now held responsible for cleaning up their hazardous wastes.

Babbitt appointed a committee that worked out "Plan 6" to complete the Central Arizona Project. This plan was a federal state agreement to finance the building or improvement of several dams in the Salt River Valley area. These dams will provide water storage, flood control, and recreation. This plan became necessary after President Jimmy Carter removed Orme Dam on the Verde River from the Central Arizona Project in 1977.

Troubles for Babbitt. Babbitt's most difficult days came in 1983 during the copper strike at Clifton and Morenci. The governor sent highway patrolmen and the National Guard to prevent violence. The labor unions, always supportive of Babbitt in the past, thought he was taking the side of the Phelps Dodge Company.

Babbitt regained some labor union favor in 1986. How? He personally mediated a contract dispute between mine unions and the Magma Copper Company.

A prepaid state health insurance plan for poor people brought out the worst and best in Governor Babbitt. The counties had always been responsible for providing free medical care for the needy. By the 1980s, many counties could not afford this care. No federal money was available because Arizona was the only state that chose not to be in the federal Medicaid program.

The legislature created an alternative to Medicaid. It was called AHCCCS (Arizona Health Care Cost Containment System). This "Arizona Experiment" qualified for some federal funds. Prepaid health insurance covered medical expenses for people below a certain income level.

AHCCCS failed at first. Why? One cause was Babbitt's "hands-off" policy of turning programs over to professionals—a private management company in the case of AHCCCS. Huge cost overruns were a problem. Many doctors and hospitals were not paid on time. AHCCCS began to work, however, when the state took over management. Babbitt then appointed an experienced director.

Babbitt's influence on the Arizona court system. While governor, Babbitt appointed 52 superior court judges, 13 judges to the Court of Appeals, and one judge on the State Supreme Court. The typical appointee was young, a liberal, and a Democrat. A lot of these judges will be in the court system for many years.

The most famous judge appointed by Babbitt, however, was a Republican—Sandra Day O'Connor—to the Court of Appeals. She was later made the first woman justice in the United States Supreme Court by President Ronald Reagan.

Democratic candidate for president. During his last three years in office, Babbitt spent much time out of state. He decided to run for president after the Democratic nominee, Walter Mondale, was defeated badly by President Reagan in 1984.

Babbitt joined several national groups of Democrats interested in changing and reforming the party. In speeches all over the country, he said: "Democrats have gotten lazy and rigid" in their beliefs.

Babbitt tried to create the image of "a western man of action." He rode across Iowa in the annual bicycle trek and skied in New Hampshire. These are the first states to choose delegates to the national conventions. Did Babbitt win the Democratic nomination in 1988?

10. EVAN MECHAM WAS ELECTED GOVERNOR ON HIS FIFTH TRY.

Life before politics. Evan Mecham, a Mormon, grew up on a farm in Utah. World War II brought him to Arizona for fighter pilot training at Williams and other air force bases. Mecham was shot down over Germany and put in a prisoner-of-war camp.

After the war Mecham married his high school sweetheart. They had seven children. He opened automobile dealerships, first in Ajo and then in Glendale.

Try, try again. Mecham served one term in the state senate. He then ran unsuccessfully for the U.S. Senate, losing to Senator Carl Hayden. Mecham ran for governor in 1964, 1974, 1978, 1982, and 1986. The fifth time was a charm. He finally won. A strong conservative, Mecham was for less government and lower taxes. He explained his ideas in a book called *Come Back America*.

Election as governor in 1986. Political experts expected Democrat Bill Schulz to replace Babbitt as governor. A multimillionaire, Schulz almost upset Barry Goldwater in the 1980 U.S. Senate race. For two years Schulz studied other state governments and prepared himself to be Arizona's governor. To everyone's surprise, he withdrew from the race because of his daughter's illness. Carolyn Warner, the superintendent of public instruction, then filed for governor and won the Democratic nomination.

Burton Barr, the House majority leader, seemed to be the choice of Republicans. President Reagan invited Barr to the White House and encouraged him to run. Barry Goldwater endorsed him. Barr was a World War II combat hero and the legislative problem solver for twenty years. How could he lose?

Few observers considered Evan Mecham a serious challenger to Barr. A four-time loser, Mecham did not file until a few months before the primary. He had only a fraction of the campaign money available to Barr. How could he win?

Mecham succeeded in painting Barr as a "wheeler-dealer" and a tool of the special interests. He mailed tabloid newspapers to every Republican voter. Headlines like "Barr's Record Exposed" grabbed attention. Barr did not answer the charges against him. Why not? Campaign advisers told him, incorrectly, that he was well ahead of Mecham in the polls. The result was an upset. Mecham got 54 per cent of the votes in the Republican primary. He carried 11 of the 15 counties, including Maricopa and Pima.

The general election turned out to be a three-way race when Schulz filed as an Inde-

Governor Evan Mecham at a teenage press conference in Benson, Arizona.

pendent. Democratic party leaders were furious. They later blamed Schulz for splitting the Democratic vote and causing Warner's defeat. Mecham won with a 40 per cent plurality.

Mecham's first acts as governor. The Arizona government cannot spend more than it takes in. Revenue to pay for the 1986-1987 Babbitt budget, however, had been overestimated. To solve this problem, Governor Mecham called a special session of the Republican legislature in January 1987. This body cut the budget by $157 million.

The national spotlight fell on Mecham when he cancelled the Martin Luther King, Jr. holiday for Arizona. Babbitt had ordered the holiday by proclamation after the legislature voted against it. But the attorney general ruled that only the legislature or the people could create a paid holiday for state employees.

Mecham suggested that the legislature submit the King holiday to the people in the form of a referendum. Black leaders, however, wanted the legislature to make the holiday legal. How was this issue settled?

Daphne Walters (right) was crowned "Miss LEAP 1970" with Lupe Cruz (left) as runnerup. LEAP (Leadership and Education for the Advancement of Phoenix) was started in the 1960s to help needy people of all races and ethnic groups.

22

ARIZONA'S MINORITIES SINCE WORLD WAR II

Minorities are the groups which have not melted into the general American majority. They are usually identified by race, religion, or national culture. Arizona is one of the few states that can boost of three large ethnic minorities—Indians, Mexican-Americans, and Black Americans. These groups make up one-fourth of the state's population.

For many generations Arizona's ethnic minorities suffered more unemployment, poorer housing, more school dropouts, and a higher disease rate than the rest of the population. Since World War II minority groups nationwide have become more conscious of inequalities and injustices. They have demanded changes—more political, social, and economic opportunities. The goal is to narrow the gap between their real life and the "American dream."

Laws and court decisions have brought great changes in the lives of minorities. Arizona Indians were given the right to vote in 1948. Several tribes have been paid for land wrongfully taken from them in earlier times. School segregation was outlawed in 1954. Federal poverty programs and job training have raised living standards for many people.

The minority groups are getting involved in the political process. Indians, Blacks, and Mexican-Americans are serving in the state legislature. A Mexican-American, Raul Castro, was elected governor in 1974.

KEY CONCEPTS

1. Arizona Indians are constantly undergoing cultural changes.
2. The Mexican-Americans are the largest cultural minority in Arizona.
3. Black Americans gained important civil rights in the 1950s and 1960s.

22

1. ARIZONA INDIANS ARE CONSTANTLY UNDERGOING CULTURAL CHANGES

Who is an Indian? According to anthropologists*, the Indian is a descendant of the natives who lived in America when Columbus arrived in 1492. Not every Indian, of course, is a full-blood. Most Indians identify with a "tribe." A tribe usually has its own language, customs, and reservation.

Arizona is Indian country. Arizona has more Indians, tribes, and reservations than any other state. The reservations contain nearly 20 million acres—more than a quarter of the state's land area. By the mid-1970s about 120,000 Indians were living on the reservations. Another 25,000 were off the reservations.

*anthropologists: specialists who study human beings.

Arizona Indian reservations. In 1986, the Papago tribal name was changed to Tohono O'Odham, meaning *desert people.*

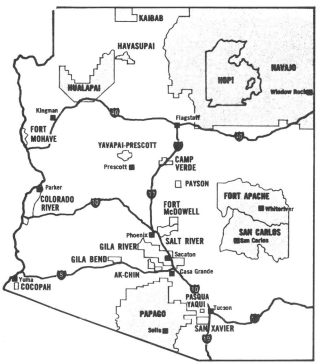

The Arizona Indian population has been increasing three times faster than that of the country as a whole. But the proportion of Indians to Arizona's total population is declining. This change is a result of the large in-migration of non-Indians from other states. In 1890 Arizona's population was 34 percent Indian. In 1970 it was only 5.4 percent Indian.

Cultural groups. The Bureau of Indain Affairs (BIA) classifies Arizona's Indians today into these main cultural groups: 1) *Athapascan* tribes—Navajos and Apaches; 2) *Pueblo* Indians — Hopis and Tewas; 3) *Desert Rancheria* tribes—Pimas and Papagos; 4) *Yuman* tribes — Yumas, Maricopas, Mo-

Apache cowboys. Cattle raising has been one of the biggest sources of income for the Apaches.

Navajo picking cantaloupes near Phoenix.

374

Representative Benjamin Hanley

State Senator Arthur J. Hubbard Sr.

Representative Daniel Peaches

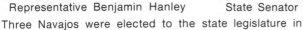

Three Navajos were elected to the state legislature in 1976 from District 3.

haves, Chemehuevis, and Cocopahs; 5) and *Plateau Rancheria* tribes — Havasupais, Hualapais, Yavapais, and Paiutes.

Yaquis. The Yaquis were given tribal status as Native Americans by an act of Congress in 1978. Now they can receive health care and other federal benefits.

The Yaquis immigrated to the United States in the early 1900s to escape persecution by the Mexican government. They settled in several places in Arizona and worked mainly as field hands. The largest group squatted on land northwest of Tucson in 1921.

Pascua Village became well-known for Easter ceremonies. The Yaqui Easter pageant combines Christianity with the Yaqui concept of the eternal struggle between Good and Evil. Pascua Village has been surrounded by motels, a drive-in theater, and other businesses. In the 1970s some of the Yaquis began moving to New Pascua — 202 acres of land given to them by the U.S. government on the edge of the Papago reservation.

There are other Yaqui settlements in Arizona. Guadalupe is along I-10 between Phoenix and Tempe. Other Yaquis live in the Phoenix area and at Barrio Libre in South Tucson.

Indian stereotype. In real life the Indian scarcely resembles the stereotype* created by western movies and television shows. His vocabulary is not limited to "ugh," "kemo sabe," and "many pony soldiers die." There is no one language that all Indians use. In fact, at least 17 different Indian languages are spoken in Arizona today. In addition, there are many dialects and regional variations.

The vitality of Indian languages is illustrated in the story about a Pima girl. She graduated from the St. John's Indian High School at Laveen and applied for a job as telephone operator in Phoenix. One question on the application blank was: "In what foreign languages are you proficient?" The Pima girl neatly wrote "English" on the blank.

Life styles of the Indian tribes are as different as their languages and cultures. Many ancient social and religious customs are still practiced. But the Indians all share one thing in common. Their geographical and

---

*A *stereotype* is a fixed pattern that doesn't vary.

375

Apache girl becomes a woman in this puberty ceremony. Many Indian religious customs are still practiced on the reservations.

Pima Indian children listen to Mrs. Anna Moore Shaw read from her book, *Pima Indian Legends*.

Maxine Norris, Miss Papago of 1973, was chosen Miss Indian America. Unlike some Indians today, she prefers to live on the reservation.

social isolation is disappearing rapidly. All the Indians, to some degree, have accepted the white man's "things"—clothing styles, canned goods, and pickup trucks, for examples.

Taxes. Indians who earn an income are required to pay federal income and Social Security taxes like other Americans. They pay property taxes, however, only on property owned off the reservation—not on the reservation itself.

Voting. In 1948 Indians were given the right to vote in Arizona. They now vote in local, state, and federal elections. For years the Arizona law required that all voters be able to read and write English. Many Indians could not vote because of this law. In 1970, however, the U.S. Supreme Court declared the Arizona language requirement unconstitutional.

The urban Indian. Arizona's town and city Indian population has been doubling every 10 years. In search of a higher economic standard of living, reservation Indians often follow a "step migration" into the city. From reservation communities such as Window Rock, San Carlos, Sacaton, or Sells, they move into reservation border towns. Winslow, near the Navajo reservation, was 14 percent Indian in 1970. Examples of other border reservation towns are Show Low with a 6.4 percent Indian population, Coolidge with 4 percent, and Ajo 9 percent. The next step is the big urban center. In 1970 Phoenix had nearly 6,000 Indians. There were 2,500 Indians in Tucson. About 1,300 lived in Flagstaff.

The greatest hope of Indians is to develop the reservation lands so young people will not want to leave. Federal and state agencies have been working with tribal leaders to bring in industries and businesses that create jobs on the reservation.

The BIA, for example, has promoted industrial parks on or near the Gila River, San Carlos, Navajo, San Xavier, and Colorado River reservations. Industries in these parks get special tax advantages and 25-year leases on the land they use.

Large numbers of Indians, however, continue to go to the cities. Many have trouble finding jobs, even after they take part in training programs sponsored by the BIA and other agencies. Lack of education is often the reason. There is discrimination because of cultural differences too.

The following open letter was written by a Papago to the *Tucson Citizen* newspaper.

Hopi teenagers in a Hotevilla summer music class.

The letter reveals one Indian's frustration in the white society:

"I am a Papago Indian very proud to be one, and what I want to say I hope you'll understand for I don't know much about the so-called English grammar. The main problem I'm concerned with is unemployment for Papago Indians.

"Some of the problems I have in keeping a job I will discuss... The people I worked with were all non-Indians... They criticized the way I dressed. A great many Papagos disapprove of the white shirt and necktie bit... They criticized how quiet I was... They criticized how rude I was not to say: good morning, good afternoon, hi, goodbye, etc. to every one of them..."

Navajo boys at boarding school.

Homes on the Navajo Reservation. The old-style hogan on the left can still be seen on the reservation today.

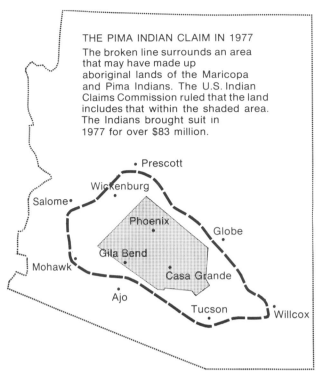

THE PIMA INDIAN CLAIM IN 1977
The broken line surrounds an area
that may have made up
aboriginal lands of the Maricopa
and Pima Indians. The U.S. Indian
Claims Commission ruled that the land
includes that within the shaded area.
The Indians brought suit in
1977 for over $83 million.

Pima Indian Claim

Edwin Nequatewa, a Hopi, picking grapes in his vineyard.

"They criticized how rude it was not to introduce myself to a new person on the job... You know, to the Papago it's quite funny to see people shake hands when introduced. Shaking hands is done only for religious purposes. When meeting a new person a smile shows the person is already accepted as a friend...

"These are some of the reasons I was told to quit my job. So now I'm looking for another, knowing I'll face the same problems in the white society."

Indian land claims. Arizona Indian tribes once occupied more of Arizona than was included in their reservations. Most of the tribes have claimed additional land that was wrongfully taken from them years ago.

The Indians Claims Commission Act, passed by Congress in 1946, made it possible for tribes to sue the federal government. The first Arizona tribes to win claims before the Indian Claims Commission were the Quechans, Hualapais, Havasupais, Southern Paiutes, and Yavapais.

In 1976 the Papagos won a $26 million settlement of their 6.3 million acre claim. It was the largest Indian land settlement in Arizona and the third largest in U.S. history. The claim included all of Pima and Santa Cruz counties. Portions of Yuma, Pinal, Maricopa, and Cochise counties were also claimed. Lawyers for the Papago tribe received 10 percent of the settlement in legal fees.

2. THE MEXICAN-AMERICANS ARE THE LARGEST CULTURAL MINORITY IN ARIZONA

"What do you consider yourself?" That question was asked of nearly 1,500 United States citizens of Mexican origin in Arizona in 1973. A television research team at the University of Arizona was trying to shed some light on the problem of "labels." No issue is more emotional or explosive to many ethnic groups than the problem of what they should be called.

"Mexicano," or "Mexican," got the biggest response in the survey, especially near the border. This name was preferred by 61 percent in Nogales, 47 percent in Tucson and Pinal County, and 44 percent in Phoenix.

"Mexican-American" was second in preference with an average of 31 percent preferring it. The other choices were "American," "American of Mexican Descent," and "Chicano" in that order.

The Mexican-American is caught between two countries, two cultures. He shares the traditions of each, but is not fully accepted by either. Today, more than ever before, the Mexican-American wants to be understood. He would like to be accepted both on his own merit as an individual and as part of an important cultural group within the United States society.

The Mexican-Americans are the largest cultural minority in the United States. Census takers now record them in the same category with "whites." But it is estimated that between 5 and 7 million Mexican-Americans live in the United States. A tenth of the population of the five southwestern states of Arizona, California, New Mexico, Texas, and Colorado have Spanish surnames. In Arizona, it is over 15 percent.

Not all Mexican-Americans are alike, of

International border crossing at Nogales.

course. They are made up of several different races and cultures. Most are *mestizo* — part Spanish and part Indian.

With the exception of the Indians, the Mexican-Americans are the only minority group which has their "old country" next door, rather than across the ocean. The closeness of Mexico makes it easier for them to return to their homeland. Their original culture is reinforced by Mexican films, magazines, newspapers, and Spanish-language programs on American radio and television.

Mexican-American life style. Until World War II there were only two economic classes: the well-to-do and the poor. There was almost no Mexican-American middle class. The prosperous Mexicans usually called themselves "Spanish-Americans." They identified with the Anglos.

The mass of Mexican-Americans usually settled in colonies, or *barrios*. They remained aloof from the Anglo community. This life style was understandable. Most of the Mexi-

can people came to the United States from poor rural areas in Mexico. They had difficulty adjusting to American city life.

For the most part, the Mexican immigrants had little education. Most of them were unskilled and had to take low-paying jobs. Their general health was worse than that of the community as a whole. School attendance for the children was irregular. The poorer people did not participate in politics or civic affairs. This pattern continued into the late 1940s. Up until that time there were almost no Mexican-Americans in the professions except for a handful in Tucson.

World War II was a turning point. The Mexican-American serviceman was treated like any other American. The war also created a civilian labor shortage. Mexican-Americans were needed in jobs formerly held only by Anglos. They now had a chance to work' on equal terms.

The International Union of Mine, Mill and Smelter Workers, CIO, helped Mexican-American miners get equal treatment during World War II. The union hailed three copper companies before the National Labor Relations Board for discriminating against Mexican employees. The Miami, Consolidated, and the International Smelting and Refining com-

Beginning in the 1880s, the Peabody Company hired many Mexicans to work in the copper mine at Johnson, located between Benson and Willcox. On September 16, 1915, the students in Johnson decorated their school to celebrate Mexican Independence Day. The Anglos and a Black student joined their Mexican friends in the project.

Mexican-Americans work in a Salt River Valley onion field.

Cesar Chavez

Former state senator Alfredo Gutierrez, a Democrat from South Phoenix, talks to supporters during his 1976 re-election campaign.

panies classified miners as "Anglo-American Males" and "Other Employees."

An Anglo-American with no experience was paid $6.36 per shift as a "helper." On the other hand, the Mexican with no experience was classified as a "common laborer" and paid only $5.21 per shift. Furthermore, Mexican-American miners in the "Other Employees" category seldom received additional pay for experience. The War Labor Board ordered elimination of the discriminatory wage rates. The Board blamed both the employers and the Unions for having created the unfair system in the past and for continuing it.

After the war, better-paying jobs in the mines and in construction work opened up. More Mexican-Americans began to reach middle class status. Many of them moved out of the *barrios*. Educational goals were raised in the post-war period.

Ups and downs of Mexican immigration. Large numbers of Mexicans entered the United States in 1909 and 1910 during the Mexican revolutionary period. During World War I many temporary workers were brought in to work on farms, railroads, and in the mines. But the peak of permanent Mexican immigration was in the prosperous 1920s. By

1930 Arizona had a Mexican population of 114,000.

During the 1930s depression, however, many returned to Mexico. More than 18,000 left the state between 1930 and 1932. Low-wage farm jobs in Arizona were filled by Anglo migrants from the Mid-West and by unemployed people in the towns. But during World War II there was another manpower shortage. Mexicans were again welcomed.

The federal bracero (manual worker) program was born in 1942 and lasted until 1964. In an agreement with the government of Mexico, the United States guaranteed certain living and working conditions for Mexican field workers. The peak of the *bracero* contract labor program was reached in the late 1950s. At that time there were many farm labor camps in Arizona's agricultural areas.

The *bracero* program offered a legal way for Mexicans to work in the United States. But Mexicans continued to sneak across the border for temporary work. By entering illegally, Mexican laborers and their employers could avoid the regulations. They saved time, money, and inconvenience. *Braceros*

Phoenix police chief Ruben Ortega

Former Vice Mayor Rosendo Gutierrez listens to East High student Cody Williams in 1976. Every year the Phoenix City Council sponsors Youth Government Day at city hall. Each student shadows a city official during the day.

and illegal aliens often worked side by side in the fields.

The *bracero* program was finally ended to protect jobs of domestic workers, many of whom were Mexican-Americans. As late as the 1960s one-fourth of adult Mexican-American males were engaged in unskilled farm labor. Until 1964 they had to compete with the imported *braceros* for jobs.

Illegal aliens remained a problem. In 1975 alone the U.S. Border Patrol detained and returned to Mexico nearly 700,000 illegal immigrants. About 85,000 of these aliens were apprehended in Arizona by 250 border patrolmen and 12 investigators. The U.S. Immigration and Naturalization Service estimated that another 50,000 illegals in Arizona were not caught.

Not all of the illegal immigrants were farm workers. Many found work in urban businesses such as restaurants and hotels. Nearly all the 2,000 illegal aliens picked up in Phoenix, for example, were employed in the city—many in good jobs. Most of the aliens work for cheaper wages. That is why they are hired.

Border patrolmen often feel frustrated. In Tucson, to take one case, they raided several restaurants in the spring of 1976 and deported 45 illegal aliens. The patrolmen returned to the same restaurants two days later. They picked up 22 more illegals, including two deportees from the first raid. Many of the Mexicans, who don't already know the country, pay a border "coyote" to take them safely across the international line and to an area where jobs are available.

La Causa. Mexican-Americans actively seek a better way of life. Today's Mexican-Americans can not be understood without some knowledge of *La Causa* ("The Cause"). *La Causa* means a decent wage, better living conditions, equal opportunity in school and on the job, equality under the law, and political representation. It means dignity and a good self-image for each Mexican-American.

In the 1960s Mexican-Americans began to demand equal opportunities. One of the most militant leaders was Yuma-born Cesar Chavez. His sympathy for Mexican farm workers went back to the depression of the 1930s. The Chavez family lost its farm on the Colorado River when Cesar was about ten. Living in tents, the family followed the crop harvests in California.

As a young man, Cesar Chavez became active in the Community Service Organization (CSO). Working in southern California, he helped Mexicans apply for American citizenship. He conducted voter registration drives.

Then in 1962 Chavez formed the National Farm Workers Association (now the United Farm Workers). Three years later he was involved in the grape pickers strike (*huelga*) at Delano, California. Soon Chavez was urging consumers over the country to boycott grapes and lettuce unless they had the black eagle label of his farm workers union.

Through marches, speeches, and television interviews, Chavez publicized the Mexican-American dream for better pay and improved living conditions. He inspired young Chicanos in Arizona and other states to seek *La Causa* in their own way. Many Mexican-American organizations were formed. The most active college groups in Arizona were MASA (Mexican-American Student Association) and MECHA (Movimiento Estudiantil de Chicanos de Aztlan).

The Mexican-Americans pointed out deficiencies in the educational system. They asked for new courses in Mexican-American culture. Pressure was brought on school boards to hire more Spanish-speaking people. Bilingual education for elementary and high

Sgt. Jimmy Lopez at a hero's ceremony, 1981. Lopez was one of the hostages held in Iran.

schools was a major goal. The high drop-out rate among Mexican-American students was cited to show the need for curriculum changes. Many of the *La Causa* goals were achieved, at least in part.

Political involvement. Mexican-Americans became more active in Arizona politics. By the 1960s the American Coordinating Council of Political Education was active in ten counties. The council backed candidates that would give Mexican-Americans a greater voice in government. In the 1960s and 1970s Mexican-Americans gained more representation in city, county, and state government.

In 1974 Raul Castro was elected the first Mexican-American governor. He brought John Huerta back from a job in Washington, D.C., to head the important Department of Economic Security. Bert Romero was elected state mine inspector. Alfredo Gutierrez was chosen majority leader of the state senate in 1975 and Arizona campaign manager in 1976 for Jimmy Carter.

3. BLACK AMERICANS GAINED IMPORTANT CIVIL RIGHTS IN THE 1950s AND 1960s

Roughly one-tenth of the United States population is Black. As a minority race Black Americans endured 3½ centuries of slavery and segregation. Uprooted from their African culture, they were brought to America in chains.

For generations Black Americans were not only deprived of ancestral culture, but were kept out of the mainstream of American life. On the basis of skin color, Blacks were treated as a separate caste on the bottom rung of society. The Civil War gave them freedom from slavery. But the equality promised in the 13th, 14th, and 15th amendments to the U.S. Constitution came slowly.

Black Americans make up about 3 percent of the population of Arizona. Until World War II the biggest migration of Blacks to Arizona were farm laborers from the southeastern cotton belt states. Since the war the use of more machines in agriculture has decreased the demand for farm workers.

By 1970 more than 80 percent of the 53,344 Blacks in Arizona lived in urban areas. Nearly 33,000 were located in metropolitan Phoenix and over 10,000 in Tucson. More than half— about 30,000 — of all the Blacks in Arizona were inside the city limits of Phoenix.

Residential segregation. In 1960 about 98 percent of Phoenix Blacks lived in the older part of South Phoenix. During the 1960s the Black community spread south from the "inner city" slum across the Salt River toward Baseline Road.

Tucson was also a heavily-segregated city.

But the Black population was not concentrated in one section as in Phoenix. The Tucson Blacks were scattered in pockets. One Black community was in the westernmost part of the city. Two separated Black sections were north of the central business district. Three other clusters of Black residents were south and east of the central business district.

There are two kinds of segregation—*de jure* (by law) and *de facto* (in fact). For nearly a hundred years after the Civil War the South had *de jure* segregation in schools, restaurants, hotels, and public transportation. Many northern cities and parts of the West have had *de facto* segregation.

Most of the low rental public housing in Phoenix, for example, still had *de facto* segre-

Early Black residents in Clifton posed for this picture.

LEGAL SEGREGATION IN THE U.S. ELEMENTARY SCHOOLS
||||| Required Negro-White Segregation

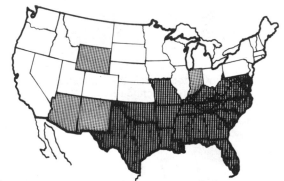

LEGAL SEGREGATION IN THE U. S. SECONDARY SCHOOLS
||||| Required Negro-White Segregation
     Permitted Negro-White Segregation

Segregation in elementary and high schools in 1950.

gation in the 1960s. The City of Phoenix completed the first three housing projects in 1941 with a grant from the U.S. Housing Authority. The Matthew Henson Project was for Blacks, the Marcos de Niza for Mexican-Americans, and the Frank Luke, Jr. Project for Anglos.

By 1968 there were 11 housing projects. Nine of them housed primarily one racial or ethnic group. Four were Black and two Mexican-American. Three were Anglo with less then 6 percent Black residents. The remaining two projects were integrated with Blacks and Mexican-Americans.

There was also *de facto* segregation in privately-owned rentals. In 1962 the Phoenix Urban League reported several cases to the U.S. Commission on Civil Rights which held hearings in Phoenix. Negro airmen at Luke

and Williams fields were unable to find owners of apartments or trailer parks who would rent to Blacks.

Desegregation in housing came mainly after 1968. In that year Congress passed a Civil Rights Act—the fifth since 1957—with an "open housing" provision. Discrimination in the sale or rental of housing was forbidden— except for owner-occupied homes sold directly by the owner. More Blacks began to move into new housing developments and into homes and apartments in previously all-white neighborhoods.

***De jure* segregation in schools.** Every elementary school "shall segregate pupils of the African race from pupils of the Caucasian race"—even if there is only one Black student. That was the Arizona law until 1951. But not all boards of education followed the segregation law to the letter.

There was no "Arizona pattern" on school segregation. Blacks attended mixed schools in Prescott, Williams, Morenci, Hayden, and other towns. Some schools separated Spanish-speaking students. In Douglas, for example, Spanish-speaking and Indian students were not taught in the same classrooms with Anglos. The Black pupils were segregated in another school. Flagstaff segregated both Blacks and Spanish-speaking students in the lower grades, but had one junior high school for students of all races.

Segregated high schools were permitted but not required by state law. If there were 25 or more Black students in a high school, the people could petition the board of education to call an election. If a majority of the people voting were in favor of segregation, a "separate" Black high school had to be provided. The Black high school was supposed to have "equal" facilities to the white high school.

Only two segregated high schools were established — Carver in Phoenix and Casa Grande-Eloy High School. The latter was located in an abandoned dance hall at Eleven Mile Corner, halfway between the two towns.

An all-Black public school near Cashion in Maricopa County, 1932.

A Black soldier who took part in the dedication of a buffalo soldier statue at Fort Huachuca in 1977. Unlike today's Army, the buffalo soldiers were segregated.

In the late 1940s the Casa Grande-Eloy school had 15 Black students and two teachers. The facilities were not "equal" and the cost per pupil was high. The interesting thing is that the white students of Casa Grande High School voted—before the Black school was established—to allow Black students to attend their school.

Phoenix Union High School began segregating Blacks in 1914. Until 1923 the Black students had separate classrooms on the PUHS campus. Then after three years in a frame building on 9th Street and Jefferson, the new Phoenix Colored High School was opened. In 1943 the name was changed to Carver High School. The faculty of Black teachers at Carver was one of the best in the state.

In 1951 the state legislature made a change in the school segregation law. School boards— elementary as well as high school—could decide whether Black pupils would be segregated. In February 1953, however, the 1951 segregation law was ruled unconstitutional by Maricopa County Superior Court Judge Fred C. Struckmeyer, Jr. In a case started by

Mrs. Doris Moten was appointed to head Phoenix Union High School in 1976. She was the first Black woman principal of an integrated high school in Arizona.

three Carver students, the Judge said the legislature could not delegate its power to the school board. In other words, only the legislature had the power to decide that schools are to be segregated.

After Judge Struckmeyer's decision, the Phoenix Union school board voted 3 to 2 to "open" all high schools in the district. During the 1953-1954 school year, 74 Black students enrolled at Phoenix Union. A smaller number of ex-Carver students attended the new South Mountain High School. In March 1954, the school board voted to close down Carver and end segregation in the district.

Two months later the U.S. Supreme Court ruled, in the case of *Brown vs. Board of Education of Topeka,* that segregation in the schools was unconstitutional.

Other forms of segregation were gradually ended in Arizona. Phoenix hospitals permitted Black doctors on their staffs after 1944. Memorial Hospital, which opened that year, was the first to have an interracial policy. In 1950 the first Black was recruited by the National Guard in Phoenix. By 1954 most theaters stopped segregating Black and Indian patrons from the whites.

Eating places strictly discriminated against Blacks before and during World War II. In 1952 the City of Phoenix forbade the Sky Chef Restaurant to discriminate against Blacks at the airport. Lunch counters in dime stores and drug stores began serving Blacks following sit-in demonstrations in Tucson. Walgreen's led the way. After more sit-ins in Tucson in 1960, the Arizona Restaurant Association adopted an open door policy for all races.

A few hotels and motels were still turning away Blacks in the early 1960s. The federal Civil Rights Act of 1964, however, outlawed discrimination in public accommodations. Hotels, motels, restaurants, service stations, and places of amusement were forbidden to refuse service to persons because of race.

23

ECONOMIC GROWTH OF ARIZONA SINCE WORLD WAR II

Phelps Dodge Corporation's New Cornelia open pit copper mine at Ajo, Arizona. Directly behind the pit is the town of Ajo. To the right of the pit are the concentrator, smelter, and shops.

In addition to the "four C's"—copper, cattle, cotton, and citrus—other sources of income have become important in Arizona. In fact, after World War II, manufacturing became the number one producer. And tourism has been called the "unsung hero" of the state's economy. By the late 1970s, almost 60,000 Arizonans were directly employed in the tourism industry. Another 100,000 jobs indirectly depended on tourists and travelers within the state.

Arizona is the fastest growing state in the Union. The population quadrupled between the end of World War II in 1945 and the bicentennial year of 1976. Ideal climate—with the help of air conditioning—attracted not only large numbers of people, but a high percent of skilled workers. A capable labor force has been a major factor in the rapid expansion of clean-air manufacturing in Arizona.

A modern transportation system is another economic advantage that Arizona enjoys. The state is criss-crossed by five U. S. or interstate highways. Ten transcontinental and 30 interstate trucklines give Arizona daily delivery service to other states. Another 40 local trucklines haul everything from delicate electronic equipment to heavy machinery. Two transcontinental railroad lines give Arizona two-day freight service with California and eight-day service with the east coast. Nine interstate airlines serve the state.

Arizona's dramatic economic growth has created a heavy demand on the state's financial institutions. Credit is needed by rapidly expanding business and industry. Home buyers have borrowed enormous amounts of mortgage money. Twelve state banks and three national banks—with a network of over 400 branch offices—and a dozen savings and loan associations have made Arizona a financial center.

Availability of land has been another reason for Arizona's growth—despite the fact that less than 18 percent of the state is privately-owned. A low population density leaves elbow room by the mile. There are planned industrial parks all over the state. New industries that build in these parks have utilities, transportation, and labor available almost immediately. By the mid-1970s some 15 industrial parks had been established by nine Arizona Indian tribes. The labor pool of skilled Indian craftsmen has hardly been touched yet.

Climate, a skilled labor force, transportation, financing, and land are all important factors in Arizona's great economic progress since World War II. Low cost energy and water have been other reasons for Arizona's growth. Future growth depends on the finding of new sources of cheap energy and a wise management of water resources.

KEY CONCEPTS

1. Arizona's fast-growing population has supplied a skilled labor force.
2. Manufacturing is the most rapidly expanding sector of the state's economy.
3. The mining industry is still a big producer of income in Arizona.
4. Agriculture plays an important part in the Arizona economy.
5. Arizona's warm dry climate and scenic wonders attract millions of visitors each year.
6. Metropolitan Phoenix and Tucson are two of the fastest-growing cities in the United States.
7. Arcosanti may be the city of the future.

23

1. ARIZONA'S FAST-GROWING POPULATION HAS SUPPLIED A SKILLED LABOR FORCE

Arizona's population has been growing rapidly. From less than 500,000 in 1940, it grew to 750,000 in 1950. The census takers in 1980 counted 2,717,866 people. The Arizona population projection for the year 2000 is 4½ million. Nearly two-thirds of the state's people came from somewhere else.

Labor force. Arizona's rapid industrial growth since World War II was possible because of a skilled labor pool. Arizona has been successful in attracting young, skilled, and well-educated residents—men and women who quickly find jobs. The median age in Arizona is 26.3 years in comparison to the national median of 27.8.

More than a third of the heads of households in Phoenix and Tucson have at least some college training—double the national average. Only about a third of the heads of households in Phoenix and Tucson do not have a high school education—well under the national average of 45 per cent.

Manufacturing is Arizona's leading industry. Here small gas turbine engines are shown on the final assembly line at AiResearch in Phoenix.

Where Arizonans come from.

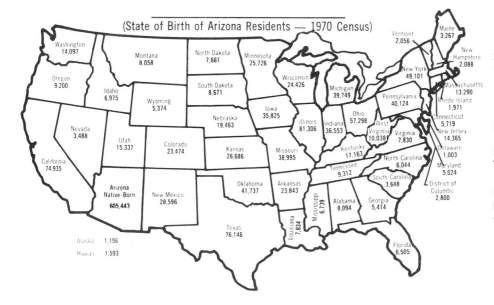

(State of Birth of Arizona Residents — 1970 Census)

State not identified	106,383
Total born in U.S. outside Arizona	1,072,190
Born in U.S. Outlying Area	1,459
Born Abroad (as U.S. Citizens)	11,723
Foreign Born	80,085
Total Migrants to Arizona	1,165,457
Born in Arizona	605,443
Birthplace Unknown	2,528
Total Residents	1,773,428

Assembly line at Motorola's plant in Phoenix.

Meat packing is a major food processing industry in Arizona.

Most of the migrants from other states settled in the "urban oases" of Phoenix and Tucson. But the available labor force in smaller communities has also increased.

2. MANUFACTURING IS THE MOST RAPIDLY EXPANDING SECTOR OF THE STATE'S ECONOMY

The growth of manufacturing in Arizona since World War II has given the state a diversified and well-balanced economy. Manufacturing became Arizona's number one source of income in the 1960s. Since the early 1970s it has supplied over $2 billion annually to the state's economy and employed about a 100,000 people. The Employment Security Commission listed 1,296 manufacturing operations in Arizona in 1972. They made everything from doughnuts to missiles.

The electronics industry provided the breakthrough for large-scale industry in Arizona. Electrical and electronic equipment—ranging from tiny transistors to complex computers—accounts for about one-fifth of the manufacturing. Motorola led the way. Its first plant in Phoenix was built in 1948. Today Motorola is the state's largest single employer. General Electric, in Phoenix since 1956, also hires a lot of workers. Dickson Electronics in Scottsdale and Mesa has done well. Dozens of

Tortillas are cooked, counted, and packaged at the Rosarita Mexican food plant in Mesa.

Sugarbeets being harvested near Tolleson. The beets will be refined into sugar at the Spreckles plant south of Chandler.

391

Cable wires are tested by a Western Electric Company employee at the factory in west Phoenix.

smaller companies are manufacturing electronic parts.

Aerospace and machinery products—including missile and aircraft parts—have been second in importance only to the electronics industry. Hughes Aircraft came to Tucson to produce Falcon missiles in the 1950s. In the same decade, Goodyear Aerospace, AiResearch, and Sperry Flight Systems began manufacturing in the Phoenix area. Lear Jet of Wichita, Kansas, moved some of its airplane manufacturing operations to Tucson in the mid-1970s. Talley Industries in Mesa is another big employer.

Food processing industries employ about a tenth of all manufacturing workers in Arizona. Meat packing firms supply meat products to Arizona markets and the entire country. Cudahy, long active in Arizona, moved its national headquarters to Phoenix in 1967. Swift opened a million-dollar beef processing plant in Tolleson the next year. Besides meat, a wide range of other food products are prepared in Arizona plants. Spreckels Sugar Company has been processing sugar beets near Chandler since 1967. Examples of other food processors are Hayden Flour Mills in Tempe; Rosarita Mexican Foods in Mesa; dairy companies such as Shamrock Foods in Phoenix, Tucson, and Yuma; bakeries; and many others.

Other factories. Many plants in Arizona

manufacture items from Arizona's mines and forests. In this category are the smelters, sawmills, paper mills, cement plants, brick factories, and copper wire mills.

Western Electric Company in Phoenix employs about 2,000 people making telephone cable. Southwest Forest Industries — with plants in Flagstaff, McNary, Snowflake, Eagar, Glendale, and Prescott—manufactures lumber, paper, mouldings, Kachinaboard, wood boxes, corrugated containers, treated poles, and mobile or modular homes.

Many firms in Arizona manufacture textiles. B.V.D. Knitwear in the Hopi Industrial Park near Winslow makes white T-shirts; E. L. Gruber in Glendale and Casa Grande Mills, underwear; Gila River Indian Enterprises, tents; Buckeye Industries, sleepwear; Ari-Togs in Phoenix, women's dresses; and Woods Manufacturing Company in Douglas, shirts.

There are factories scattered all over Arizona. However, by 1970 two-thirds of them were concentrated in the Phoenix metropolitan area. Another 10 per cent were located in Tucson and Pima County.

Inspiration Copper Company's rod plant at Miami, Arizona.

Lumber was Arizona's first major manufactured product. It is still an important source of income.

Southwest Forest Industries' paper mill at Snowflake, Arizona.

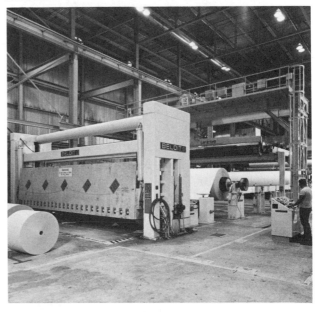

393

Pouring slag from a converter at Phelp Dodge Corporation's New Cornelia copper smelter at Ajo, Arizona.

3. THE MINING INDUSTRY IS SECOND ONLY TO MANUFACTURING AS A GENERATOR OF INCOME

"Copper is King!" Since 1910 Arizona has produced about half the nation's copper. World War II gave a boost to the older copper producing districts: Bisbee-Douglas, Clifton-Morenci, Globe-Miami, Ray-Superior, Ajo, and Jerome. Since the war, mines at San Manuel, Bagdad, Casa Grande, Kingman, and the Tucson area have become major producers.

Nearly all of the modern mines have low-grade copper ore. Most of them are open pit mines operated by large-scale production methods. Explosives are used to blast ore loose. Huge crushers smash four-foot boulders. Gigantic trucks with powerful engines haul up to 235 tons in a single load.

Tucson is now called the "copper capital of the world." About 95 per cent of the state's copper is mined within a 125-mile radius of Tucson. It was not until the 1950s, however, that companies began to mine the Tucson area's low-grade ores. Development came after geologists located a massive ore body that runs along the west bank of the Santa Cruz River.

Pima Mining Company began open pit mining near Twin Buttes south of Tucson in 1952. American Smelting and Refining Company (Asarco) reactivated the old Silver Bell mine northwest of Tucson in 1954. Asarco went into the Twin Buttes area with the Mission mine in 1961. Duval came into the picture in 1959 with its Esperanza mine near Twin Buttes. Duval Sierrita was developed later.

Anaconda Company began mining at Twin Buttes in 1965. Anaconda and Amax—both worldwide companies—combined to form Anamax. The Anamax Company built a new plant to refine copper ore. Instead of smelting, a new chemical and electrolyte process was used. Lots of water is needed for the new process. But water has been a problem for Anamax.

Water problem. By the mid-1970s Anamax was using about 12,000 acre feet of under-

Phelps Dodge Corporation's Morenci open pit copper mine at Morenci, Arizona. It is the largest in Arizona and the second largest open pit copper mine in the U.S.

Phelps Dodge smelter at Morenci.

395

Copper ore trucks are loaded by electric shovel.

A Navajo operates an electric tram. He is hauling uranium ore out of a Kerr-Magee mine in the Lukachukai Mountains on the Navajo Reservation.

A Black Mesa coal mine on the Navajo Reservation.

ground water a year. The company signed a letter of intent to buy 30,000 acre feet a year of Central Arizona Project water when it becomes available. Meanwhile the farmers, pecan growers, and the City of Tucson claim prior rights to the underground water which is being used up at a rapid rate.

Revegetation program. Not only do the mines use water, they also disturb the natural environment. Mining companies are aware of this problem. South of Tucson some land is being reclaimed. After the tailing dumps dry out they are covered with top soil. Native grasses and shrubs are planted. This revegetation helps to control dust and erosion.

Control of air pollution has been another problem for the mines. The companies were ordered by the state to remove most of the sulfur dioxide from smelter stack discharges. In 1974 Kennecott Copper Corporation was given the first smelter operating permit in the state for its Hayden smelter. Sulfur dioxide that used to go up in smoke is now converted into liquid sulfuric acid. Some of this acid is being used to improve agricultural soil that has a high salt content.

Copper mines north of Tucson. In 1956—after eight years preparation and a $100

ASARCO's open pit Sacaton mine northwest of Casa Grande.

Coal from Black Mesa is used at the Navajo generating plant near Page.

million investment—Magma Copper Company began working the giant underground block-caving mine at San Manuel. The San Manuel is the largest underground mine in the United States.

Asarco has two mines in the Casa Grande-Sacaton area. One is underground and the other an open pit that began producing in 1974.

Duval developed the Mineral Park mine near Kingman in 1965.

Other Minerals. No other mineral in Arizona rivals copper. Molybdenum, gold, and silver are mainly by-products of copper or lead-zinc smelting. Molybdenum is used in alloys and such things as the points of spark plugs. Sand and gravel rank third—behind copper and molybdenum—in gross value.

By the mid-1960s there were about 30 uranium mines in Apache, Navajo, Coconino, and Yavapai counties. The largest mine is Westec Corporation's Orphan Lode. The Orphan Lode is located within the boundaries of Grand Canyon National Park. Westec has until 1986 to develop the 20-acre claim. It then becomes the property of the National Park Service.

Employment. By the late 1970s the mining industry provided jobs for approximately 25,000 Arizonans. An estimated 120,000 other persons had jobs that were dependent on mining. Businesses derived nearly a billion dollars a year income from the mines. Manufacturers, the construction industry, gas and electric companies, wholesale concerns, and retail stores all sold goods or services to the mine companies.

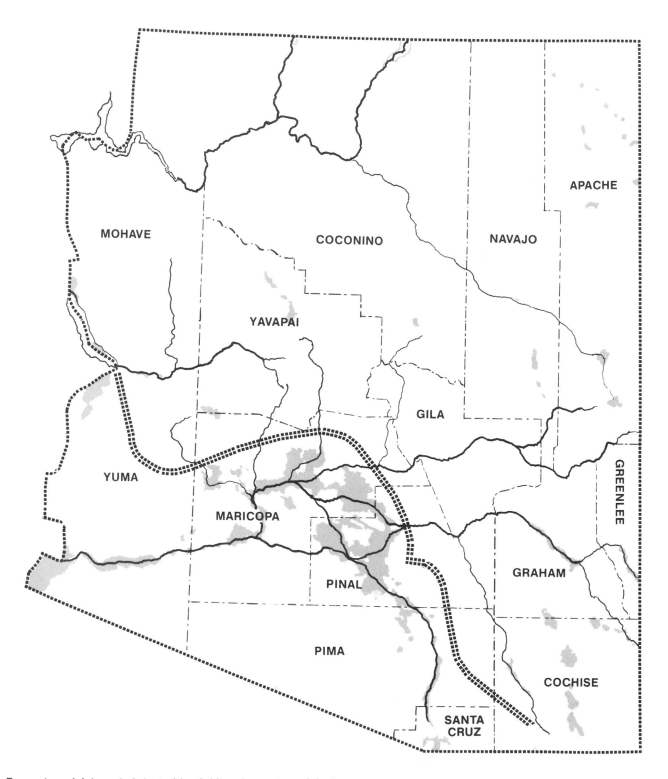

Expansion of Arizona's irrigated land. Line shows the original
route of the Central Arizona Project aqueduct.

4. AGRICULTURE PLAYS AN IMPORTANT PART IN THE ARIZONA ECONOMY

In 1950 agriculture was Arizona's largest basic industry. It employed a labor force of nearly 50,000 people. The amount of irrigated farmland had increased from 200,000 acres in 1900 to 665,000 in 1940 and over a million acres in 1950. Several changes in farming were evident by 1950.

Changes in farming. Farms were larger and more mechanized. Between 1930 and 1945 the average size Arizona farm had increased from 742.7 acres to 2,880.6 acres. The number of tractors doubled. Hired hands tended to live in nearby towns rather than on the farms. The farm labor contractor had appeared on the scene. He organized large groups of workers for seasonal jobs such as melon picking or cotton chopping.

The trend toward bigger farms, use of machinery, and greater efficiency continued. The number of people engaged in agriculture in Arizona was cut in half between 1950 and 1975. Mechanical cotton pickers, for example, gradually replaced thousands of seasonal hand pickers. First used in Arizona on a commercial scale in 1948, a machine could pick as much as 10,000 pounds of cotton in one day. By comparison, a hand picker might average about 200 pounds. At first the machines did not do a clean job of picking. As they were improved, the percent of cotton harvested by mechanical cotton pickers rose from 10 percent in 1950 to most of it by the early 1960s.

The value of Arizona's agricultural production—crops, citrus, and livestock—has continued to increase. Though only about two percent of the state's land area is cultivated, conditions have been favorable. Sunshine and irrigation are an unbeatable combination—if the water doesn't run out! Improved seeds, insecticides, herbicides to control weeds and root rot, fertilizers, and better planting methods have increased production.

Crops consistently yield more per acre in Arizona than in any other state. Cotton, the major crop, is a good example. In the 10 year

Giant chisel on farm near Tempe rips soil to a depth of nearly two feet to permit better water penetration.

Picking cotton by hand near Coolidge in 1948.

Cotton is the principal crop in the Salt River Valley. Machine picking and proper irrigation practices have made it one of the most profitable.

399

A cotton crop near Sahuarita, south of Tucson, is dusted to prevent insect damage.

period, 1965 to 1974, the average yield of cotton per acre in Arizona was 1,008 pounds. The national average was 482 pounds. Arizona's average would have been even higher except for an infestation of pink bollworm in 1967. Two years later, DDT, the primary insecticide used to control bollworms and other insects in cotton, was banned. It took awhile to experiment with other chemicals.

Federal cotton subsidy program. The record number of acres planted in cotton in Arizona was in 1953, the last year of the Korean War. Some 690,000 acres were in cotton that year. The cotton acreage declined to 420,000 acres in 1954 when the federal government imposed controls. Cotton farmers were given subsidies to take land out of cultivation. The idea was to raise prices by cutting production.

Cotton growers actually got bigger yields, however. The government permitted skip row planting to cut down planted acreage. A farmer could plant two or four rows and then skip a row or two, depending on his allotment. With more space, the cotton plants grew larger and filled in the skipped rows. The use of better fertilizer and a new variety of cotton—Acala-44 which was developed by the University of Arizona—increased the yield from 675 pounds per acre in the early 1950s to almost 1,000 pounds in 1955.

Forage, grains, and seeds. Alfalfa has been Arizona's most important forage crop since territorial days. Some of it is used for winter sheep pasture. But most of the alfalfa is cut for hay and fed locally to livestock. Six to eight cuttings a year have been common in Maricopa and Yuma counties.

By the 1960s barley was the principal small grain planted in Arizona. Sometimes it is ratooned with sorghum crops—that is, the seeds for both crops are planted at the same time in June. The sorghum crop matures in the fall and is cut for grain or green forage. The barley then comes up for a winter crop. Grain sorghum does best in Cochise County where the record yield has exceeded six tons per acre.

The high price of wheat in the mid-1970s caused many farmers to shift from cotton to wheat. The average wheat yield on irrigated land in Arizona is 66 bushels per acre. The national average is only 27.4, but most of the wheat fields of the United States are not irrigated.

Arizona grows some crops for seeds. Over 90 percent of the nation's Bermuda grass seed is produced in the Yuma area. Most of the pearl millet seed planted in the Southeastern states comes from Arizona.

Vegetable growing. Lettuce, produced in Arizona since 1913, accounts for more than half of Arizona's vegetable production. Called "Arizona's green gold," it is grown near Yuma, in the Salt River Valley, near Willcox, in the Marana-Red Rock-Maricopa area, at Aguila, and in the Parker-Poston area.

Harvest time varies according to elevation. Yuma lettuce is cut from December into early

Wagon loads of Yuma cantaloupes ready for packing and shipping to markets all over the United States.

Harvesting lettuce near Phoenix.

Sheep grazing on alfalfa in the Salt River Valley.

Wheat is harvested north of Coolidge.

401

Onions are packed by machine on the Lee Wong farms northwest of Phoenix.

Young ladies admire vegetables grown in hydroponic greenhouses near Glendale.

Harvesting citrus in the Salt River Valley.

April. Other areas get two crops a year. Willcox, about 4,000 feet in elevation, harvests fall lettuce in September or October and spring lettuce in June.

A revolution came to the lettuce industry in the 1950s and early 1960s. Great Lakes varieties of lettuce replaced Imperial types. When the lettuce is cut in the fields, it is now boxed in fiberboard cartons instead of wooden crates. It is hauled to vacuum cooling plants. There the lettuce is placed in long tubes for drying and cooling down to just above the freezing point. It is then packed in refrigerated trucks and railroad cars.

About 30 different kinds of vegetables are produced commercially in Arizona. By the 1970s Yuma was the leading cantaloupe-producing area in the Southwest. Arizona's deep orange-colored carrots—high in vitamin A—are raised mainly in the Salt River Valley and in the lower Gila Valley northeast of Yuma. Potatoes are grown mainly at lower elevations in Maricopa County.

Fruit-growing industry. The number of acres in Arizona devoted to citrus trees doubled between 1964 and 1974. Valencia orange trees were planted to supply the need for fresh fruit during the spring season. Valencias do well in the warmer localities of Yuma, Wellton, and in the Salt River Valley. Wind machines have been used effectively to protect trees during the colder winter season. Arizona Valencia oranges are harvested from March to May, before the California oranges are available.

Other varieties of citrus have been grown in Arizona since the late 1880s. Navel oranges are found mainly in the Salt River Valley and are harvested for fresh fruit in November and December. Marsh grapefruit as well as Eureka and Lisbon lemons also do well in Arizona. During the 1960s the Lisbon lemon was found to have advantages in the Yuma area. The Lisbon lemon tree produces heavily in the warm Yuma climate. The lemons can also be harvested at one time, saving harvest costs.

The Medjool date tree does well around

Aerial view of hydroponic units operated by Hydroculture, Inc. near Glendale. Vegetables are grown here in water without soil. This process is called "magic gardening."

Yuma too. It has large fruit with excellent flavor.

A few peaches are grown commercially at elevations above 3,500 feet in southeastern Arizona. Some apples are found in mountains above 4,500 feet.

Cattle Industry. Arizona farmers sell much of their hay and grain to supply cattle feedlots. Before World War II, cattle feeding was only a sideline to the Arizona range cattle industry. Today, it is a separate business. The feedlot operators fatten many cattle from Arizona ranges. But they also import livestock from other states and Mexico. The Arizona

Cattle Feeders Association has its headquarters in Phoenix. It is not part of the Arizona Cattle Growers Association. The cattle growers organization has been one of the most powerful groups in Arizona since territorial days.

Cattlemen face many problems today. The most basic problem is how to get enough land for their livestock. The median age of Arizona ranchers is about 60. That tells the story. Few young people can raise the capital to buy the high-priced land they need to get started in the cattle industry. A few fortunate cattle companies own huge Spanish or Mexican land grants. But most of the cattlemen have to use public grasslands to make a living. Their ranches are often hodgepodges of several different types of land.

Dipping helps to prevent cattle disease.

Cattle grazing on the Coconino National Forest south of Flagstaff.

In the first place, they have to own some patented land to qualify for grazing permits on the federal forest reserves. The ranchers also pay fees to use Taylor grazing lands which are controlled by the Bureau of Land Management in the U. S. Department of Interior. In addition, many Arizona stockmen lease state school lands. Without the federal permits and/or state leases, the typical Arizona cattleman would go out of business.

Livestock disease is still a problem to cattlemen. But it is not as bad as in the early days. Many older Arizona ranchers say that disease prevention is the greatest change in the cattle industry since the 1890s. The modern cowboy—unlike the gun-toting stars of western movies— carries a hypodermic syringe to vaccinate livestock.

Cattlemen find that their operating costs continue to rise. The price tags on good breeding stock, fencing, feed, and other purchases are high. But the price that ranchers get for their beef is uncertain. It depends on the supply and the market. Cattlemen, however, are a self-reliant and hardy lot. They always seem to find a way to stay in business.

A cattle feeding pen in the Salt River Valley.

5. ARIZONA'S CLIMATE AND SCENIC WONDERS ATTRACT MILLIONS OF VISITORS EACH YEAR

The tourist trade is one of Arizona's most important industries. It has been a source of income since territorial days. As early as the 1880s, healthseekers pitched their tents in the desert to take advantage of the dry climate.

Arizona's sun has been the tourist industry's biggest asset since territorial days. The Pilot Knob Hotel in Yuma promised free board to guests on days when the sun didn't shine.

Scottsdale—known nationwide today as the "West's most western town"—was described in 1901 as a place with "thirty-odd tents and a half dozen adobe houses."

Resorts. Well-to-do people relaxed at Castle Hot Springs after it opened in 1896. Other visitors enjoyed Indian Hot Springs, northwest of Safford, where Geronimo and his Apaches soaked in the muds and drank mineralized waters in an earlier time. Many famous people stayed at the San Marcos Hotel built by Dr. A. J. Chandler in 1912. Others preferred Tucson's Arizona Inn operated by Isabella Greenway.

In 1925 the Tucson Tourists Hotel Company began construction of the El Conquistador. Movie stars, politicians, and well-known people from all over the country stayed there. Plush resorts were built in the Phoenix area in the late 1920s and in the 1930s as the desert was being tamed by air conditioning. Among these were the Arizona Biltmore and John C. Lincoln's Camelback Inn. By the mid-1930s there were also more than 60 guest ranches in Arizona.

San Marcos Hotel in Chandler.

An early picture of Camelback Inn, a popular resort in the Phoenix area.

The railroads and airlines have promoted tourism in Arizona. Shortly after the completion of Roosevelt Dam in 1911, the Southern Pacific Railroad included the dam on an excursion tour. The tourists took a train to Globe. From that point they made the trip over the Apache Trail via the dam in Cadillac cars to Phoenix. There they boarded another train. Southern Pacific promoted Arizona. Full-page advertisements appeared in national magazines, including *Sunset* which Southern Pacific owned at the time.

The Union Pacific Railroad opened Grand Canyon Lodge in 1928. The hotel was a stop on the Union Pacific's five-day "motor-bus" tour of southern Utah and northern Arizona. Scenic Airways of Phoenix took thousands of tourists on aerial trips over the canyon beginning in 1928. Northern Arizona was also advertised by the Santa Fe Railroad and Fred Harvey.

Tucson became a tourist mecca. Southern Pacific's Golden State Limited train from Chicago to California and the Sunset Limited from New Orleans and Texas went through Tucson. The Sunshine Climate Club of Tucson was the only group in the state that did effective nationwide advertising in newspapers and magazines before World War II.

Phoenix. During the war Phoenix had a population boom. That is when the motel business began to thrive. During the late 1940s and 1950s the Phoenix Chamber of Commerce hired public relations firms to promote "warm, dry, sunny" Phoenix. The resorts also advertised. In 1949 ten resorts and seven Wickenburg dude ranches offered an eight-day early autumn vacation for $98. The guests split their time between city and ranch. The same year, American Airlines spent $40,000 a month promoting Arizona.

The state government has helped local groups promote tourism. The Arizona State Parks Board maintains scenic and historic

Part of the movie "March or Die," starring Gene Hackman, was filmed in the California sand dunes west of Yuma. About 300 extras were hired in the Yuma area and at the U.S. Marine base at Yuma. The Motion Picture Section of OEPAD promoted the movie industry in Arizona.

John Hance and a party of tourists starting down the Bright Angel Trail at the Grand Canyon in 1902.

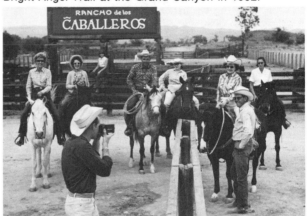

A Wickenburg dude ranch.

These five 1974 *Arizona Highways* special issues included articles and photos on Indian pottery, weaving, and turquoise jewelry.

This 1956 advertisement was designed to attract tourists and new industries to Arizona.

Phoenix civic plaza. Located in the downtown area, it is the site of many large conventions.

sites and provides tourist facilities. In 1954 the legislature created the Arizona Development Board. This agency had the dual function of bringing clean industries to the state and promoting tourism. In 1971 it was reorganized as the Office of Economic Planning and Development (OEPAD). Land use planning is now the main job of OEPAD.

In 1975 Governor Raul Castro took tourist promotion away from OEPAD. He set up an Office of Tourism(OOT), directly under his supervision. OOT concentrates on furnishing stories and photographs to out-of-state media. It is hoped that travel writers will do articles on Arizona. Little money is spent on commercial advertising.

The Arizona Highways magazine has done a most effective job in promoting the state. It was launched in the 1920s by the State Highway Department to present the case of better roads. The magazine soon began to add travel articles. By the late 1930s tourism features occupied most of the space. Raymond Carlson took over as editor in 1938. He put emphasis on photography as a means of displaying the attractions of Arizona. The first four-color pictures and printing were in the July, 1938, issue—a real collector's item.

The Grand Canyon has been the most popular subject of *Arizona Highways*. Between 1925 and 1972, pictures of the canyon appeared on the front cover 25 times. It was the subject of eight special issues. The Navajo Indians have been the second most popular front cover picture subject and the most frequent story topic. The *Arizona Highways* is circulated all over the nation and world. It is the most beautiful and successful publication of its kind.

Greyhound Tower in north Phoenix.

Phoenix Sky Harbor Airport looking northeast.

Tourism statistics. Arizona's transportation and tourism have grown together. By the 1950s the state was no longer a remote area. It was only a few hours by air from any part of the globe.

By the mid-1970s there were more than 2.5 million passengers deplaning at Phoenix Sky Harbor and Tucson International Airport each year. An annual total of more than 7 million automobiles entered the state. Tourists spent an estimated $700 million annually in Arizona for food, lodging, gasoline, recreation, transportation, and other goods and services. Six million people a year were visiting the national parks. About an equal number of visitors were counted at Hoover and Glen Canyon dams.

Modern tourism. By the 1970s "tourism" in Arizona really meant "tourism–travel–hospitality–recreation." The millions who visit Arizona each year include vacationers, business travelers, conventioners, and campers.

Arizona offers a variety of accommodations, from wilderness campsites to luxurious resort hotels. Phoenix, Tucson, Scottsdale, and Yuma all completed major convention centers by the 1970s. Several motel chains and the Greyhound Bus Company maintain their national headquarters in Arizona. Arizona is now a leader in the field of tourism and travel.

6. METROPOLITAN PHOENIX AND TUCSON ARE TWO OF THE FASTEST-GROWING CITIES IN THE UNITED STATES

Phoenix. Between 1940 and 1980 the land area of Phoenix expanded from 9.6 to 325.2 square miles. During that time the population grew from 65,414 to 764,911. National magazines described Phoenix's growth as "miraculous" and "fantastic."

Why the population explosion? World War II set it off. Air bases and wartime industries boosted the population to 90,000. The development of air conditioning was perhaps the main

reason for rapid growth. Right up to the 1930s Phoenix was purgatory in the summer months. All the townspeople who could afford it fled in June and returned in September. Many stores closed for the entire summer. Air conditioning made Phoenix a year-round city.

Phoenix has really grown since 1940. At that time, Thomas Road was on the edge of town. Indian School Road was a country byway. Camelback was strictly a rural road with an odd-shaped mountain at the east end. The town's economy rose and fell with the price of lettuce or cotton. By the 1970s industrial output exceeded farm income.

Phoenix is long out of the adobe age. The tallest buildings between Dallas and Los Angeles are in downtown Phoenix. At its present rate of growth, metropolitan Phoenix

POPULATION GROWTH OF PHOENIX AND MARICOPA COUNTY

As of July 1	Phoenix City Limits	Maricopa County	As of July 1	Phoenix City Limits	Maricopa County
1960 (Census)	439,170	633,510	1971	606,000	1,014,000
1961	452,000	740,000	1972	627,000	1,072,300
1962	468,000	775,000	1973	646,000	1,127,600
1963	483,000	808,000	1974	660,000	1,174,700
1964	494,000	833,000	1975 (Special Census)	669,005	1,207,100
1965	504,000	852,000	1976	673,900	1,238,600
1966	511,000	870,000	1977	690,900	1,305,500
1967	519,000	890,000	1978	716,100	1,435,000
1968	528,000	914,000	1979	752,900	1,479,100
1969	546,000	946,000	1980 (Census)	764,911	1,508,030
1970 (Census)	682,500	971,228			

POPULATION GROWTH OF TUCSON AND PIMA COUNTY

As of July 1	Tucson City Limits	Pima County	As of July 1	Tucson City Limits	Pima County
1960 (Census)	212,892	265,660	1971	269,000	372,600
1961	215,800	280,000	1972	280,000	397,400
1962	218,400	299,000	1973	287,900	416,000
1963	218,500	308,000	1974	293,800	434,400
1964	221,600	310,000	1975 (Special Census)	298,683	442,700
1965	234,600	313,000	1976	293,100	452,500
1966	236,000	318,000	1977	302,300	468,000
1967	241,000	324,000	1978	311,400	502,200
1968	244,000	332,000	1979	319,300	520,300
1969	250,000	345,000	1980 (Census)	330,537	531,263
1970 (Census)	262,933	351,667			

EXPANSION OF THE PHOENIX AND TUCSON INCORPORATED AREAS

As of July 1	Square Miles Phoenix	Tucson	As of July 1	Square Miles Phoenix	Tucson
1960	187.4	70.9	1971	254.9	81.7
1961	189.8	71.0	1972	258.1	84.4
1962	220.2	71.0	1973	269.3	84.5
1963	222.7	71.0	1974	269.3	90.3
1964	222.7	71.7	1975	269.4	91.1
1965	245.7	76.0	1976	276.2	91.1
1966	246.2	76.0	1977	276.6	94.0
1967	247.3	76.0	1978	301.9	96.0
1968	247.6	76.2	1979	325.2	96.4
1969	247.7	77.0	1980	325.2	98.8
1970	247.9	80.0	1981	330.6	101.5

Note: 1975 Special Census figures are for Phoenix only.
Source: U.S. Department of Commerce, Bureau of the Census; Arizona Department of Economic Security, Population Statistics Unit; Phoenix and Tucson City Planning Departments; Valley National Bank Economic Research Department.

may someday be the biggest city in the West. A population of 3 million has been predicted by the year 2000.

Tucson's growth paralleled that of Phoenix. From 8 square miles and a population of 35,752 in 1940, it grew to more than 99 square miles and 330,537 people in 1980. Metropolitan Tucson, of course, was even larger.

Arizona's first shopping center, Broadway Village, was built at Broadway and Country Club in 1939. A year later, the military took over Davis-Monthan air field. The base then stood alone in the desert, far away from the nearest residential area. Beginning in the 1940s, however, the urbanized area began to stretch way beyond the city limits. Land was cheaper and the county had no building code. There was little to stop anyone from sinking a well and a cesspool wherever he bought land. The outlying areas were built up faster than the city annexed them.

Only one-third of the total Tucson urbanized area in 1950 was within the city limits. Much of the uncontrolled growth stretched out along East Speedway. In 1952 Pima County finally adopted a zoning plan—too late to save Speedway from becoming a monument to poor planning.

During the 1950s Tucson's annexations nearly caught up with the fringe building. From less than 10 square miles in 1950 the city

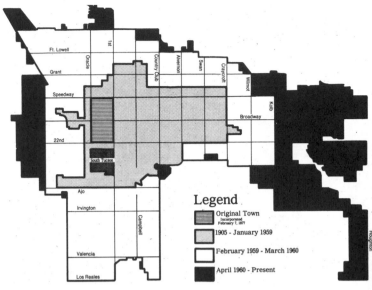

Legend

Original Town
Incorporated
February 7, 1877

1905 - January 1959

February 1959 - March 1960

April 1960 - Present

Growth of Tucson

expanded to nearly 71 square miles in 1960. Growth and annexation continued. During the early 1970s the desert land in southeast Tucson, adjacent to Davis-Monthan, filled up fast.

Tucson, like Phoenix, is a victim of urban sprawl. Everyone wants to live on the outskirts of town. In 1970, Tucson had a population density of only 3,300 per square mile. The Phoenix density—2,350 per square mile—was even lower. By contrast Chicago had 15,126 and Los Angeles 6,073.

Many people came to Arizona seeking wide open spaces. They want single family dwellings with lawns and trees rather than the

Aerial view of Phoenix looking north, 1977.

Downtown Tucson.

crowded, apartment-style of living. But urban sprawl has created some problems. Mass transit systems, for example, are not successful when people are spread out. Dependence on the automobile leads to traffic snarls, freeways, and auto pollution. Freeways divide neighborhoods and force many people to relocate when their homes are taken by eminent domain*.

Urban sprawl also puts a strain on public utilities. During the summer of 1976, for example, Tucson had a water shortage. The city council promoted waterless Wednesdays and encouraged people not to water lawns. When

*Eminent domain is the power of government to buy private property needed for a public purpose.

water rates were raised to force conservation, there was a public outcry.

The council repealed the rate increases. But about 30,000 voters signed petitions to recall four council members who voted to raise rates. Three of the members ran in the recall election and were defeated.

The problem of a fast-dropping underground water table remained unsolved.

7. ARCOSANTI MAY BE THE CITY OF THE FUTURE

Paolo Soleri thinks that urban sprawl uses up too much energy, creates pollution,

412

and wastes the land. He envisions self-contained cities within a single structure. All the facilities would be within walking or elevator distance. Vast open spaces would be left around the cities for agriculture, recreation, and nature.

Soleri studied with Frank Lloyd Wright at Taliesen West. After leaving Wright he gathered his own students around him. He formed the Cosanti Foundation and established a school and community in the desert north of Scottsdale. There he developed a concept called *arcology*—a blending of architecture and ecology.

In the early 1970s Soleri began building Arcosanti. The site is a mesa near Cordes Junction between Phoenix and Flagstaff. When completed Arcosanti will be a 20-story city for 2,500 to 3,500 people. Both land and energy will be conserved. The city will cover only eight or nine acres of the 860 acres that Cosanti Foundation owns. The word Arcosanti is a combination of "arcology" and "cosanti."

Hundreds of students each year work on the model city and attend seminars conducted by Soleri. The students have a chance to experiment with designs that let in the winter sun and shut out the hot rays of summer. The

Students of Paolo Soleri working at Arcosanti. The semi-spherical structures shade the work areas on hot summer afternoons; they utilize the sun's heat during winter months.

Arcosanti will rise high above the Mesa landscape.

413

Bold Abstract designs characterize Soleri's work.

buildings will all be solar-heated.

Eventually the main city will be supplied with heated air from a huge vertical greenhouse. The greenhouse—in which hot air will accumulate as in a closed automobile—will stretch from the bottom of the canyon to the base of Arcosanti. The warm air will be carried in ducts during the winter. It will be vented off in the summer time. The greenhouse will also supply food for Arcosanti.

All Arcosanti roofs are built to catch rainwater to fill cisterns. In the future all sewage and waste materials—except maybe plastics—will be recycled.

Arcosanti will be a *three*-dimensional rather than a sprawling *two*-dimensional city. It may well be the city of the future.

UNIT EIGHT

ARIZONA GOVERNMENT TODAY

State government affects our lives from the cradle to the grave. State law requires that all births be registered. The state partly finances the education of young people in the public schools. School boards, city councils, and county governments get their authority from the Arizona Constitution and from laws passed by the state legislature. The doctor and the lawyer have state licenses. So does the undertaker.

The constitution provides for a check and balance system. The powers of state government are split among the legislative, executive, and judiciary branches. This framework has not changed greatly since statehood. But the functions and size of state government have been enlarged.

As the population grows, people crowd together in large urban areas. Living conditions are far more complex than in pioneer days. Governments at all levels—federal, state, and local—are expected to provide more services.

Highways, schools, health services, parks, law enforcement, courts, and welfare cost money. The annual state budget is over a billion dollars and gets bigger each year. Town, county, and school district budgets also have risen steadily with the population. The property tax will no longer pay the bills. Increased revenues now come from income, sales, gasoline, and other taxes. Federal grants have helped too.

Everyone pays taxes of some kind. This is a good reason to study government. Working people pay out an average of 25 percent of their wages and profits in taxes of all kinds. Unfortunately, however, very few people take any time to see that our elected officials are spending the tax money wisely. As taxpaying citizens we need to be well informed about governments.

There are many other reasons to study government. One of the most important has to do with jobs. Nearly one of five Arizonans works for federal, state, or local government, including school districts.

Arizona State Capitol in Phoenix. The Senate wing is on the left and the House on the right. The Governor's office is on the top floor of the executive wing behind the copper dome.

24

THE LEGISLATIVE BRANCH OF GOVERNMENT

Arizona's Constitution made the legislature the most powerful branch of state government. The main jobs of the legislature are to make laws and appropriate money needed to run state government. Its power comes from "control over the purse strings." The governor puts together a budget. But the legislature finally decides how and how much money will be spent.

The legislative authority in Arizona is split between two houses. The Senate has 30 members. The House of Representatives has 60. The state is divided into legislative districts with about equal population. The boundaries are redrawn after every ten-year census, so the members of each house represent approximately the same number of people.

The legislators are elected to represent the people in their districts. This system is called *representative democracy*. Direct democracy would not be possible in Arizona government. All the voters in the state could not assemble at one place to discuss and vote on bills.

There are alternatives, of course, to the indirect legislative process. More direct methods are *initiative* and *referendum*. By these methods people can get a proposal put on the ballot. The voters then approve or disapprove. Only a small percent of laws, however, are enacted by initiative or referendum. Most laws are made by the legislature.

In deciding laws, legislators appreciate hearing from the people in their districts. They pay close attention to what the voters have to say. Unfortunately, few people know the names of their representatives or how to contact them. Even fewer people take the time to write a letter expressing their opinion on a particular bill. Perhaps a knowledge of the legislature and how it works would encourage more people to get involved. We need good legislators. We also need informed citizens.

KEY CONCEPTS

1. Arizona has a bicameral legislature.
2. Legislative officers direct the lawmaking process.
3. The job of the legislature is to make laws.
4. The voters can make a law or change the constitution through the initiative or referendum.

24

1. ARIZONA HAS A BICAMERAL LEGISLATURE

Arizona is one of 49 states with a bicameral (two-house) legislature. Only Nebraska has the unicameral (one-house) system. The two houses in Arizona are called the Senate and the House of Representatives.

Legislative districts. Arizona is divided into 30 legislative districts with about equal population. The voters in each district elect one state senator and two representatives. More than half the districts are in heavily-populated Maricopa County.

Members of both the Arizona Senate and the House are elected every two years. By contrast, state senators in most other states are elected for four-year terms.

Qualifications for serving in the legislature are listed in Article IV of the Constitution of the State of Arizona. A legislator must be a

Map of Arizona Legislative Districts

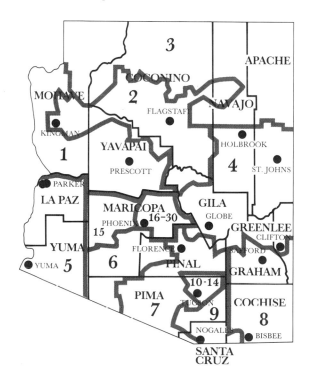

citizen of the United States. He or she must have resided at least three years in the state and one year in the county before election.

An elected legislator who is not 25 years of age must wait until his or her 25th birthday before taking office. That was the case, for example, with Representative Art Hamilton in 1973. The legislature convened on January 8, but he had to wait until January 19 to be sworn in.

No member of the legislature can hold any other state, federal, or local office. There are exceptions. These are justice of the peace, school board trustee, United States court commissioner, or fourth class postmaster.

Legislators cannot be otherwise employed by the State of Arizona or a local government (county, town, or school district). An exception would be a public school teacher.

A legislator can be expelled for "disorderly behavior" by a 2/3rds vote of the members of the house to which he or she was elected. A legislator who is convicted of accepting a bribe also loses his or her seat. Additional punishment for this crime is a fine up to $10,000 or a prison term of up to 10 years.

Salary and expense allowances. The salary of Arizona legislators can be changed only by the voters at an election. The salary is now $15,000 per year. Arizona is different in requiring voter approval of legislative raises. In most states, lawmakers do it themselves.

In addition to the salary, however, the Arizona legislature can vote themselves a daily expense allowance. At present, Maricopa County lawmakers are paid $35 a day. Legislators from the other counties get $60 a day because they have more expenses while away from home. After 120 days of a session, the per diem allowance is cut in half.

Some travel expense reimbursement is also given the legislators. The expense allowances can be changed by the legislature itself.

Getting elected is a big problem. Campaigning for a seat in the legislature takes time and money. Many people who work for wages

Representative Art Hamilton looks on as Former Governor Raul Castro signs a bill.

cannot afford to run or to serve if elected.

An *incumbent* (the person already in office) has an advantage. The voters recognize his or her name. Candidates have to work hard to get this name recognition. In cities and towns they usually go door-to-door and leave campaign literature. In large rural areas the candidates may rely heavily on newspaper and radio advertising. Once elected, the candidate is more

House Majority Leader James B. Ratliff, 1987.

apt to be remembered by the voters.

Candidates for the legislature make use of roadside signs and bumper stickers. They also send letters to the voters, make telephone calls and get press coverage. They speak at clubs and at political rallies.

2. LEGISLATIVE OFFICERS DIRECT THE LAWMAKING PROCESS

Speaker of the House. Each house of the legislature has a presiding officer. The House of Representatives elects the Speaker from among their own members. In practice, the Speaker is chosen by the *majority party.* That is the party with more than half of the members.

The Speaker presides over meetings of the House. He calls on the member he wishes to speak next. The Speaker also appoints members to the committees. This is a real source of power. Legislators know that their effectiveness depends, to a large degree, upon committee assignments. Committee chair positions are especially important.

Committees in the House of Representatives. The most important work of the legislature is done in committees. Each bill is studied by a committee. The committee decides what will be done with the bill

The Arizona House of Representatives has 16 standing committees. They are: agriculture; appropriations; banking and insurance; commerce; counties and municipalities; education; government operations; health and aging; human resources; judiciary; natural resources and energy; public institutions; rules; tourism, professions, and occupations; transportation; and ways and means. Find out what kinds of bills each committee handles.

The House also makes use of *special committees.* They are formed for one particular purpose and then abolished. The most common special committee is a *conference committee.* It is used when the House and Senate have passed different versions of the same bill. A

Carl J. Kunasek, President of the Senate.

conference committee, made up of both senators and representatives, is appointed to work out a compromise.

Interim committees are sometimes appointed to work on important special projects when the legislature is not in session. The interim committee may be one of the standing committees which has been given a special assignment. The interim committee may hold hearings or conduct investigations. It may formulate a bill for the next session of the legislature to consider.

President of the Senate. The presiding officer in the Senate is called the President. He or she is elected by the majority party of that body.

The President of the Senate occupies a powerful position. He or she appoints members to standing, special, and interim committees. As presiding officer, the President recognizes (calls on) senators who wish to speak on the floor.

Committees in the Senate. The Senate has only 10 standing committees: appropriations; commerce and labor; education; finance; government; health, welfare and aging; judiciary; natural resources and agriculture; rules; and transportation.

Floor leaders. Both the House Speaker and the President of the Senate have assistants. They are a *majority floor leader* and a *majority whip.* These are opposed by a *minority floor leader* and a *minority whip* in each house.

What do the floor leaders do? They are the managers of their party's program on the floor of each house. Each floor leader works with a whip. It is the job of the whip to round up votes for bills that the party favors.

In practice, the fate of most bills is decided in the *majority party caucus.* The majority party members in each house meet to decide which bills will be brought out of committee. Those bills will then be debated in a general session. A lot of "horse trading" is done behind the scenes.

3. THE JOB OF THE LEGISLATURE IS TO MAKE LAWS

The legislature has a formal process for doing its work. It starts with the proposal for a law, which is called a bill.

Introduction of a bill. A bill may be introduced by any member of either house. The bill is said to be "introduced" when it is dropped in the *hopper,* a box for new bills. Sometimes a legislator will write "by request" after his or her name. This shows that a bill is being introduced for a private citizen.

The clerk gives each bill a *first reading,* usually by number, title, and sponsor only. The bill is then referred by the presiding officer to one or more standing committees.

Committee work. Each chairperson decides whether the committee will take action on a bill. If it gets on the committee's agenda, it is studied. Arguments for and against the bill are heard at public meetings. *Lobbyists* appear before the committee to speak for the special interests that they represent.

Most bills are killed in committee. That means a bill is not sent to the floor for all the members to debate. It is "tabled" or simply "held for further study" in the committee.

A few bills are returned to the presiding officer. The committee may recommend that a bill "do pass" or "do pass as amended." Also, the committee may decide to return a bill "for consideration" with no recommendation.

Committee of the Whole. After a bill has cleared the committees to which it was assigned, it goes to the *rules committee*. This powerful committee decides whether or not the bill will be sent to the *Committee of the Whole* for debate.

The Committee of the Whole is an informal session of the entire House or Senate acting as one committee. Unlike formal legislative sessions, voting may be done by voice. Each bill is given a *second reading* by number and title along with amendments made by the

standing committees. Conflicts are ironed out. A *simple majority* (more than half of the members present in the Committee of the Whole) may recommend that the bill be taken up in formal session.

The third reading and roll call vote. Next, the bill goes back to the presiding officer

Former Governor Castro addressing the legislature. Note the voting boards above the rostrum. Each member presses "Aye" or "No" button at the desk to cast a vote.

Example of a bill introduced in the Arizona House of Representatives. It was referred to three committees.

How a bill becomes law.

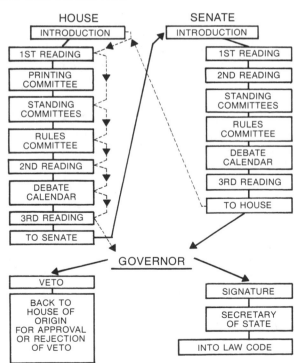

STATE OF ARIZONA

33rd LEGISLATURE

1st REGULAR SESSION

HOUSE

H. B. 2206
Introduced
February 10, 1977

REFERENCE TITLE: motorcycle noise limits

Prefiling date:

Referred on February 10, 1977 to Committees:

Rules

Transportation

Health

Introduced by Representatives Jones, Cajero, Corpstein, Everett, Harelson, Hartdegen, Jordan, Pacheco, Steiner, Thompson, West, Woodward

AN ACT

RELATING TO TRANSPORTATION; PRESCRIBING NOISE LIMITS FOR MOTORCYCLES, AND AMENDING TITLE 28, CHAPTER 6, ARTICLE 15, ARIZONA REVISED STATUTES, BY ADDING SECTION 28-892.01.

```
 1  Be it enacted by the Legislature of the State of Arizona:
 2       Section 1.  Title 28, chapter 6, article 15, Arizona Revised
 3  Statutes, is amended by adding section 28-892.01, to read:
 4       28-892.01.  Motorcycles; noise limits; definition
 5       A.  NO PERSON SHALL OPERATE A MOTORCYCLE OTHER THAN A MOTOR-DRIVEN
 6  CYCLE:
 7       1.  AT ANY TIME OR UNDER ANY CONDITION OF GRADE, ACCELERATION OR
 8  DECELERATION IN SUCH A MANNER AS TO EXCEED A NOISE LIMIT OF EIGHTY-TWO
 9  DBA AT SPEEDS OF FORTY-FIVE MILES PER HOUR OR LESS, OR AS TO EXCEED
10  EIGHTY-SIX DBA AT SPEEDS OF MORE THAN FORTY-FIVE MILES PER HOUR.
11       2.  AT ANY TIME WITHIN A SPEED ZONE OF THIRTY-FIVE MILES PER HOUR
12  OR LESS ON LEVEL STREETS, OR STREETS WITH A GRADE NOT EXCEEDING PLUS OR
13  MINUS ONE PER CENT, AS TO EXCEED A NOISE LIMIT OF SEVENTY-SEVEN DBA.
14       B.  THE DEPARTMENT OF TRANSPORTATION SHALL ADOPT REGULATIONS ESTAB-
15  LISHING THE TEST PROCEDURES AND INSTRUMENTATION TO BE USED IN ENFORCING
16  THIS SECTION.
17       C.  THIS SECTION SHALL NOT BE CONSTRUED TO LIMIT THE ENFORCEMENT
18  OF ANY OTHER PROVISION OF LAW RELATING TO EXHAUST NOISE OF VEHICLES.
19       D.  AS USED IN THIS SECTION, "DBA" MEANS THE MEASUREMENT OF SOUND
20  INTENSITY IN DECIBELS, ON THE A SCALE WHICH IS THEORETICALLY WEIGHTED
21  TOWARD THOSE FREQUENCIES PREDOMINANT IN HUMAN RESPONSE.  AN INCREASE OF
22  TEN DBA, SINCE SUCH UNITS ARE LOGARITHMIC, WOULD BE AN INCREASE OF ONE
23  HUNDRED PER CENT.
```

Former Governor Sam Goddard prepares to sign a bill handed to him by Senator Harold Giss of Yuma, 1965.

and rules committee. They decide "if" and "when" the bill is put on the calendar for a *third reading*.

This time the bill is again read by number and title at a formal session. A roll call vote is taken. The bill is passed if an *absolute majority* vote for it. (That means more than half of all the members eligible to vote.)

The Arizona House of Representatives uses an electric voting machine for roll call votes. When the Speaker calls for a vote, each member pushes a "yes" or "no" button at his or her desk. A light goes on, for all to see, beside the representative's name on a large board in front of the chamber. The entire vote can be taken and recorded in a few seconds.

A passed bill is sent to the other house. There it goes through the same procedure.

Finally, the bill goes to the governor. When both houses of the legislature pass a bill, it goes to the governor for signature or veto. If signed, the bill becomes a law 90 days after the end of the session. A bill can become a law immediately, however, if the *emergency clause* is attached. In this event, the bill must be passed by a 2/3rds vote of all the members and signed by the governor.

Legislative staffs and services. Each house is assisted by a clerical staff, pages, and a sergeant-at-arms.

The *Arizona Legislative Council* is responsible for gathering research information on issues. It also helps legislators put bills in the proper form. The Council consists of six senators and six representatives. It employs a full time professional staff, including lawyers.

The *Joint Legislative Budget Committee* consists of 14 legislators. It includes four members of the appropriations committee from each house. This committee has a staff to analyze the budget needs of the state agencies. The Budget Committee also appoints the auditor general.

The *auditor general* makes sure all state money is spent legally. The auditor must be a certified public accountant. He or she examines the financial records of state agencies, counties, and school districts.

The *Department of Library, Archives, and Public Records* is a legislative service unit. This agency preserves documents of historical importance.

4. THE VOTERS CAN MAKE A LAW OR CHANGE THE CONSTITUTION THROUGH THE INITIATIVE OR REFERENDUM

The Arizona Constitution permits the voters to play a direct role in the lawmaking process.

The initiative is a process by which the people can bypass the legislature. There are several steps. First, a bill is drafted by an individual or a group. The bill, called an *initiative* measure, is given a number by the secretary of state. Then *petitions* are printed and circulated among the voters.

To get an initiative on the ballot, the petitions must be signed by a certain number of voters. For a *law,* 10 percent of the number of people who voted for governor in the most recent election must sign. A *constitutional amendment* takes 15 percent.

The secretary of state publishes a *publicity pamphlet* to explain all the *propositions*

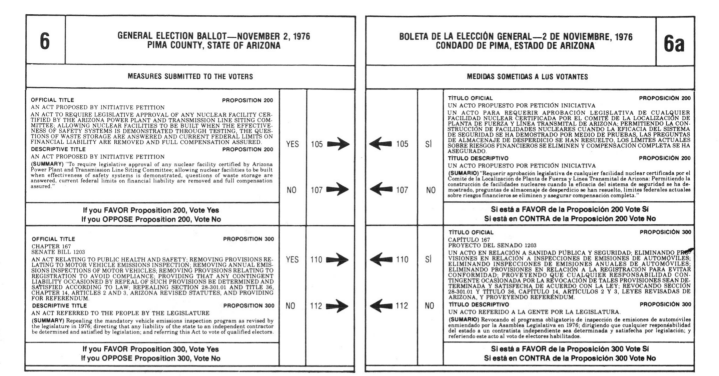

Examples of an initiative and a referendum. Both were defeated.

on the ballot. It takes a majority of the people voting to pass an initiative proposition.

The referendum can be put on the ballot in one of two ways. The legislature may voluntarily put any bill on the ballot for the voters to pass or defeat. That is one way.

The people can also force the legislature to refer a passed bill to the voters. Referendum petitions are circulated. These petitions must contain signatures equal to 5 percent of the number of votes cast for governor at the most recent election.

The completed petitions are filed with the secretary of state. This filing must be done within 90 days after the legislature adjourns. The legislature, of course, can prevent a referendum on a bill by attaching the emergency clause.

Referendum propositions are summarized in the publicity pamphlet along with initiative measures.

Great Seal of the State of Arizona

25

THE EXECUTIVE BRANCH OF GOVERNMENT

The executive branch has a full time job enforcing the laws passed by the legislature. To perform these duties there are elected officials, numerous agencies, and thousands of state employees. They collect taxes, build highways and maintain prisons. They distribute state aid to schools and perform many other needed functions.

There are five elected executive officers: governor, secretary of state, attorney general, treasurer, and superintendent of public instruction. The governor is only the "first among equals." The other officers are not under the governor's control. They are elected independently and may even belong to a different political party. In summary, Arizona has a multiple-executive government. The constitution did not centralize authority in the governor's office.

Unfortunately, a weak executive system has drawbacks. If the governor is to have responsibility for efficient state government, he or she needs authority. In the past, however, the governor has had little control over dozens of state agencies.

Beginning in the 1970s, progress was made in bringing all state governmental services under central direction. At that time many agencies which perform related services were combined into departments. The departments are headed by directors appointed by the governor. Much remains to be done, but the governor today is better able to carry out responsibilities than ever before.

KEY CONCEPTS

1. The governor is the chief executive.
2. In addition to the governor, there are other elected state officers.
3. State government is being gradually reorganized to meet the needs of modern Arizona.
4. Many of the state commissions, boards, and agencies have not been reorganized into line departments.

25

1. THE GOVERNOR IS THE CHIEF EXECUTIVE

The governor is the most important of the five elected executive officers in state government. The others are the secretary of state, attorney general, treasurer, and superintendent of public instruction.

Some experts on government reorganization would like to give the governor power to appoint most of the other executives. A professional person could be appointed to fill each office. The governor then would be held responsible for the efficient operation of the executive branch of state government.

Executive duties of the governor. The Arizona governor wears many hats. As an executive, it is the governor's job to see that all laws passed by the legislature are put into

Governor Evan Mecham, elected 1986.

operation.

Another important executive duty is to appoint about 500 persons to boards, commissions, and as department heads. Some of these people can be replaced whenever the governor feels it necessary. Many others, however, are appointed for a definite term. In that case, the governor has to wait until the term is up before filling the job with a new person.

As an administrator, the governor supervises the day-to-day work of those agencies over which he has authority. In this regard, the governor tries to appoint loyal department directors who will carry out his policies.

There are other duties. The governor is the commander of the Arizona National Guard in peacetime. As a symbol of state government, he appears at all kinds of ceremonies to make speeches and cut ribbons. The governor is also a political leader of his party.

The governor's most important duty is to work with the legislature to get needed laws passed. The governor sets the tone for his legislative program in a *State of the State message* at the beginning of each session. The message outlines the most critical problems which the governor wants corrected by new laws.

The legislature, of course, is not required to consider the governor's suggestions. Usually,

Former Governor Howard Pyle rides in a Mesa parade. As the symbol of state government, a governor is expected to take part in public celebrations.

Governor Babbitt addresses a joint session of the legislature.

however, there is already some prior agreement on which issues need attention. Differences arise over how problems can best be solved.

The governor also is responsible to submit an *annual budget* to the legislature. The budget contains a summary of expected government expenses for the coming year. The lawmakers use this budget in making their appropriations. They do not have to follow it exactly.

Veto power. A bill passed by the legislature becomes a law when the governor signs it. However, if the governor does not like a bill, he can veto it. On appropriations bills only, the governor has the *item* or *selective veto.* That means he can veto any part of it. Few governors have used the veto much. Babbitt, Hunt, and Osborn have been the biggest users.

Special sessions. Another legislative power of the governor is to call the legislature into special session. There is one limitation on this power. The governor is required to list the subjects to be discussed at the special session.

The governor has some judicial powers. The chief executive can grant a *pardon,* a *reprieve,* or a *parole.* He can also *commute* (lessen) a sentence. In each case, however, the governor must first get a recommendation for his action from the Board of Pardons and Paroles.

The governor has sole authority in *extradition*—the return of a fugitive to the state from which he or she has fled.

Finally, the governor can fill vacancies on the State Supreme Court, Court of Appeals, and the Superior Court.

Compensation. In addition to his salary and office staff, the governor has the use of a state car and airplane. He is accompanied by a Department of Public Safety officer.

2. IN ADDITION TO THE GOVERNOR, THERE ARE OTHER ELECTED STATE OFFICERS

The secretary of state is first in line to become governor if the elected governor is is unable to complete his or her term in office. The secretary becomes the *acting governor* if the governor is out of the state. If both of these

Secretary of State Rose Mofford, 1982.

427

executives are gone, the attorney general, treasurer, and superintendent of public instruction take over the governor's chair, in that order.

The secretary of state affixes the *Great Seal of Arizona* to all public documents signed by the governor. The secretary is also the chief elections officer for the entire state. It is the job of this office to prepare the publicity pamphlet. The pamphlet contains summaries of initiative and referendum measures to be placed on the ballot.

Petitions with valid signatures must be filed with the secretary of state by the following: candidates for state office, people filing an initiative or referendum, and political parties seeking recognition.

The secretary's office places the names of qualified candidates on the election ballots. The office also compiles an official canvass of votes cast.

The secretary of state is responsible for the printing and distribution of state laws. The staff also performs many clerical duties. For example, they register lobbyists, issue certificates of trademarks and trade names, and file oaths of office.

The attorney general heads the Department of Law. Next to the governor, the attorney general is probably the most important state executive officer.

Attorney General Bob Corbin, 1982.

The attorney general is the legal adviser for all the state agencies. The elected attorney will write an *advisory opinion* on a legal question for any state officer or county attorney requesting it. This opinion has the effect of law until a court issues an interpretation that is different.

The attorney general supervises all county attorneys who represent the state in superior court cases. The attorney general is not primarily a criminal prosecutor. However, the office handles cases involving antitrust violations and consumer frauds. A *state grand jury* helps in the investigation of these crimes.

The treasurer is in charge of all state funds. It is the job of this officer to receive all state revenue collected by state agencies and to account for money spent. The treasurer is chairman of the *Board of Deposit*. This board chooses the banks in which state funds are deposited.

A referendum was passed by the voters in 1980 which allows the treasurer to serve two consecutive four-year terms. Previously the treasurer could not run for reelection.

The superintendent of public instruction heads the Department of Education. The elected superintendent is the state's educational leader, but has little control over local school districts.

The biggest expenditure in the state budget is for education. The Department of Education apportions the state funds to school districts as directed by the legislature. The department also handles federal funds for schools.

The superintendent's office issues and renews certificates to teachers. The certificate is the teacher's license to teach in Arizona.

Another responsibility of the superintendent's office is to see that the public elementary and secondary schools offer courses required by the state constitution and laws. The superintendent must also carry out programs of the *State Board of Education*. These programs concern vocations, careers, achievement testing for reading and mathematics, driver

Superintendent of Public Instruction C. Diane Bishop, elected 1986.

of student tuition fees. The regents have final authority in approving new courses. They decide what degrees are to be granted and make rules for the universities. They plan for new facilities that are needed at these schools.

The *State Board of Directors for Community Colleges* consists of one appointed member from each of the counties. There are also three *ex officio* members: the superintendent, the director of vocational education, and a member of the Board of Regents.

By 1981 there were nine community college districts in Arizona. Most of these districts have more than one college, campus, or skill center. The community colleges offer a two year program.

Glendale Community College

training, health, and many others. The Superintendent of Public Instruction is an *ex officio* member and the secretary of the State Board of Education.(An *ex officio* member of a board is one who is automatically a member by virtue of the office he or she holds.) The other members are appointed by the governor.

The Superintendent of Public Instruction is also a member of two other boards. The *State Board of Regents* governs the three state universities: University of Arizona at Tucson, Arizona State University at Tempe, and Northern Arizona University at Flagstaff. This board has 10 members. Eight are appointed by the governor for eight-year staggered terms. Both the governor and superintendent are *ex officio* members.

The regents hire the university presidents, deans, and professors. They also set the amount

Term, qualifications, and salaries. The five executive officers of Arizona are elected to four-year terms. To be eligible for office a person must be 25 years of age, a U.S. citizen for 10 years, and a resident of Arizona for five years. The attorney general must also have been eligible to practice law before the Arizona Supreme Court for five years before taking office.

The salaries of executive officers are set by the legislature. Before setting the salaries, the legislature considers the recommendations of the Commission on Salaries for Elected State

429

Officials.

There are other officers who are elected on a statewide basis in Arizona.

The three members of the *Corporation Commission* are elected to six-year staggered terms.

The *state mine inspector* is elected for a two-year term. The inspector must be 30 years of age and have at least seven years practical experience in underground mining. His job is to enforce state health and safety regulations in the mines. The position requires technical knowledge. For that reason, some experts on government think that the mine inspector should be appointed rather than elected. What do you think?

Altogether, there are nine state officers elected from the whole state.

Highway Patrolman

Department of Public Safety helicopter aids an accident victim.

3. STATE GOVERNMENT IS BEING GRADUALLY REORGANIZED TO MEET THE NEEDS OF MODERN ARIZONA

The state constitution gave the governor little power. Executive duties were divided with other elected state officers. The term of office was only two years until 1970. The governor had little authority over the numerous agencies, boards, and councils which the legislature created from time to time. By 1970 there were 176 such agencies.

Reorganization of the state government. The Jack Williams administration (1967–1975) reduced the number of agencies by more than one-third. Many of the agencies were regrouped into superdepartments. The directors of these departments are appointed by the governor. Some serve for a definite term. Others can be removed at the governor's pleasure and are directly responsible to him.

The Department of Public Safety (DPS) was one of the first *line departments* created by the legislature. A line department is one which contains all similar and related activities under one director who answers to the

governor.

The Department of Public Safety is headed by a *director*. He is appointed by the governor for a five-year term. State activities which are related to law enforcement and public safety are grouped in this department.

The *Arizona Highway Patrol* is one of the more important bureaus. The patrol officers provide around-the-clock traffic law enforcement on about 6,000 miles of highway. Their goal is to reduce the number and the severity of traffic accidents.

The *Criminal Investigations Bureau* detects and apprehends illegal drug and narcotics violators. The Investigations Bureau also enforces state liquor laws. It assists sheriffs and local police in investigating major crimes such as murder, rape, arson, auto theft, and white-collar crimes.

The *Criminal Justice Support Bureau* has several important divisions. The *Scientific Analysis Division,* for example, uses modern methods to analyze crimes and identify criminals. The *Aviation Division* includes two main sections. The Air Rescue Section provides helicopter ambulance service for search and rescue. The Flight Operations Section furnishes air transportation for the governor, DPS personnel, legislators, and other state employees.

The Department of Administration was created by the legislature in 1972. The governor appoints a director, with the consent of the Senate. (The governor can also remove a director without cause.) The director appoints an

An employee of the Weights and Measures Division checks a gasoline pump for accuracy.

Bill Wiley, DHS Division of Environmental Services, tests ground water quality near a Phoenix landfill.

assistant director for each division.

Among other duties, the important *Finance Division* assists the governor in preparing the annual budget.

The *Personnel Division* recruits and hires state employees. Workers are given equal pay for equal work, regardless of race, sex, or religion. The Personnel Division also administers fringe benefits programs.

The *Weights and Measures Division* tries to prevent consumers from being cheated when buying things that have to be weighed, counted, or measured. Experts check the accuracy of scales, meters, gasoline pumps, and other devices. Consumer complaints are investigated.

The Department of Health Services was created in 1973. It brings a variety of health related agencies under one director. The director reports to the governor.

The health services include programs to control communicable diseases and to help crippled children. Programs also treat alcohol abuse, drug abuse, and mental disorders. The Department of Health administers the *Arizona State Hospital* and the *Emergency Medical Services* programs.

Bureaus whose main concern is environmental health are grouped in this department. These bureaus work for safe drinking water,

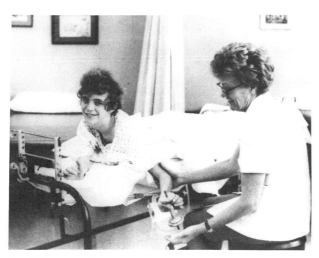

The Division of Family Services, in the Department of Health, provides services for crippled children. This division also administers mobile dental clinics and other health programs.

clean air, and the proper disposal of hazardous wastes. The *Bureau of Vehicular Emissions,* for example, inspects automobiles in Maricopa and Pima counties. The goal is to cut down the amount of air pollutants coming from auto exhaust.

The Department of Economic Security (DES) was created in 1972. Agencies that deal with human services were grouped under its umbrella. The department handles a broad range of programs.

The child welfare services give financial assistance for dependent children. Foster homes are provided for abused, neglected, or abandoned children. Day care centers for younger children have been established so that low-income parents can accept employment.

Federal food stamps are issued to improve the nutrition of people who qualify. A variety of medical and other services are available for the aged, blind, and handicapped who need assistance.

Another important division of DES is job training. Special vocational or on-the-job federal programs are administered by the department. Their purpose is to assist people who can benefit from work experience. These might be veterans, the handicapped, youth, or the unemployed.

The DES has a large budget. Its director serves at the pleasure of the governor.

The Department of Revenue was set up by the legislature in 1973. Some of its duties once were handled by an elected state tax commission. The Department of Revenue now collects the state income, sales, luxury, estate, and use taxes.

The *Division of Property and Special Taxes* works with the county assessors to determine accurate property values. A uniform appraisal of all property is the only way to make certain that every property owner pays a fair amount of taxes.

Property taxes are levied by the state, counties, cities, towns, school districts, and some special districts. Each has to figure a tax rate. The tax rate is the amount of tax that is paid on every $100 of taxable property. The more valuable the property, the bigger the tax bill.

The Department of Transportation also came into being in 1973. A director is advised by a seven-member *Transportation Board,* all appointed by the governor. The department has the responsibility for planning and developing public transportation in the state.

The *Highways Division* builds and maintains state roads. The *Motor Vehicle Division* licenses all motor vehicles and drivers. Another division publishes the *Arizona Highways*

Keeping the highways in good shape is a never-ending job of the Department of Transportation.

Interchange for I-40 and I-17 south of Flagstaff.

magazine. The *Aeronautics Division* improves and develops airports. It regulates aircraft dealers, flying clubs, and commercial flight operators in the state.

The Department of Corrections is headed by a director who serves at the pleasure of the governor. The goal of this department is to protect the public by keeping adult and juvenile offenders in custody. The department tries to rehabilitate law violators for reentry into useful community living.

Maximum security institutions. The Arizona State Prison at Florence is a maximum security institution. It has high walls, armed guards in towers, and cells made of steel. Although there is strict control over inmates at the prison, they have opportunities for recreation and education.

The Alhambra Reception and Treatment Center is also classified as a maximum security institution. It is located on the Arizona State Hospital grounds in East Phoenix. All new adult male prisoners are taken there for fingerprints, photographs, and orientation. They are tested and assigned to a prison. Psychotic prisoners are left at the Alhambra Treatment Center for psychiatric therapy.

Medium security prisons were built to relieve overcrowding at the state prison. There are two facilities in Tucson and one at Perryville. These prisons are enclosed by fences topped with razor wire. The prisoners are

Former State Senator Scott Ulm of Tucson talks to an inmate in the state prison during an inspection tour.

Governor Babbitt breaks ground for a new building at the Adobe Mountain School north of Phoenix. The former director of the Department of Corrections, Ellis C. McDougall, stands at the left.

housed in dormitory rooms rather than in cells. Most of the medium security residents are short-term. Most are adult male first offenders, ages 18 to 25. They have a good chance for rehabilitation.

Minimum security prisons are for nonviolent male prisoners who can live without constant supervision. The men have only a short time left to serve. Fort Grant Training Center and Safford Conservation Center are minimum security institutions. Both of these prisons provide the inmates with work experience and vocational classes taught by Eastern Arizona College teachers.

Women prisoners. Until 1976, female offenders were housed in the prison at Florence. Several temporary facilities then housed the women. Finally, a motel on East Van Buren Street in Phoenix was converted into a prison. For awhile the women were moved from this site to the Perryville prison.

Juvenile institutions. The Adobe Mountain School north of Phoenix is the reception and diagnostic testing center for all juvenile offenders. It is a restricted institution with fences.

The Arizona Youth Center (Catalina Mountain School) north of Tucson is a detention institution for boys. They are given schooling and jobs which teach them responsi-

ble behavior, work ethics, and skills.

A third facility, the Desert Valley Learning Center in Phoenix, has no housing. It offers a program called "Alternative to Incarceration." The boys and girls come to Desert Valley during the day for counseling and job training. They are mainly volunteers from Adobe Mountain who are allowed to live at home.

Community Treatment Centers. The Department of Corrections has community treatment centers, called *halfway houses,* in Phoenix and Tucson. Prisoners readying for release are moved to these centers. They may spend a few days or several months in a home-like atmosphere while preparing for reentry into society.

New prison facilities were created at Douglas, Winslow, Yuma, and Picacho by the legislature in 1983 and 1984.

The Department of Emergency and

Military Affairs is another line department. It is headed by an adjutant general. Unlike the other directors, his term ends six months after the governor's. The adjutant general serves as chief of staff to the governor. He controls the National Guard and the Division of Emergency Services.

The *Division of Emergency Services* is headed by a director who serves at the pleasure of the governor. The director coordinates plans for speedy assistance in event of humanmade or natural catastrophes.

The *State Fire Marshal* is also in the Department of Emergency Services. This official enforces the state fire code with the goal of reducing fire hazards. Fire prevention education is provided for schools, hospitals, industry, and the general public.

4. MANY OF THE STATE COMMISSIONS, BOARDS, AND AGENCIES HAVE NOT BEEN REORGANIZED INTO LINE DEPARTMENTS

As we have seen, the Arizona Constitution did not centralize responsibility for the executive branch in the governor's office. In fact, some officials and agencies are so independent, they are almost like another branch of government. A good example is the Corporation Commission.

Corporation Commission. This board was created by the state constitution. It has three members elected for six-year terms. One member is elected every two years.

The most important duty of the Corporation Commission is to regulate public utilities companies which are not owned by municipalities (cities or towns). The commission must approve rate changes for electric power, natural gas, telegraph, and telephone service. The commission can enforce its decisions by fines.

The Corporation Commission has other duties. It licenses out-of-state and foreign corporations—including land development companies—which wish to do business in Arizona. The commission tries to protect the investing public by stopping the illegal sale of stocks and securities. Investigation of train derailments is an important job of the commission.

The governor and the legislature have almost no control over the Corporation Commission. The people have turned down referendums to make the commissioners appointive rather than elective.

The Industrial Commission has five members appointed by the governor. Each member serves a five-year term. The terms are staggered so that only one member is appointed each year.

The Industrial Commission is responsible for the *Workmen's Compensation Fund*. The commission sees that all employers with three or more workers pay an industrial insurance tax. The money is used to compensate workers injured on the job. The commission has a staff of lawyers and investigators to look into accident reports and claims.

The Industrial Commission also has the responsibility to administer and enforce some labor laws. These laws concern such things as the employment of children, working hours, and equal opportunity employment on the basis of sex or race.

State government is becoming more responsible to the people. The reorganization of many agencies into line departments has increased the power of the governor. He now has control over many agencies which were formerly almost independent of any elected official. A clear line of authority now runs up to the governor, who can be held responsible.

The duties of the administrative agencies are often *quasi* (almost) -*legislative* or *quasi-judicial*. In other words, their decisions are almost like a law passed by the legislature or a court judgment. The decisions of the state agencies directly affect the daily lives and pocket books of every Arizona resident. It is only proper that these agencies should be accountable to officials elected by the people. Until the 1970s they functioned as a "headless fourth branch of government."

A Phoenix municipal court, Judge Alan Hammond presiding.

26

THE JUDICIAL BRANCH OF GOVERNMENT

Each state government has the power to keep peace and order within its boundaries. It exercises this power through all three branches of state government. The legislature passes laws to protect the people. The executive branch enforces these laws. The judicial branch interprets the meaning of the laws and punishes lawbreakers.

The state court system makes up the entire judicial branch. The Arizona Constitution divides the state judicial system into courts of record and courts not of record.

In a *court of record* every word of the proceedings is recorded by a stenographer. There are three levels of this type of court. The *Superior Court* is the lowest court of record. Organized on a county basis, it is the great trial court of the state. Next up the line is the *Court of Appeals*. At the top is the *State Supreme Court*.

The Appeals and the Supreme courts do not have juries. Their main function is to see that no errors were made in cases appealed from the Superior Court.

The *courts not of record* are minor courts. Justice of the Peace courts and municipal courts are in this category. They do not have a court reporter to write down all that is said.

The state's courts, in general, serve several purposes. In criminal cases, they determine the guilt or innocence of persons accused of crimes. *Civil cases* are also settled by the courts. In these civil cases, the courts decide a wide range of disputes between persons. Examples are a claim for damages, a broken contract, a divorce action, or a contested will.

KEY CONCEPTS

1. The Justice of Peace courts are the people's courts.
2. Each incorporated town or city in Arizona has a municipal court.
3. The Superior Court is the great trial court of Arizona.
4. The Court of Appeals was created to relieve the load of the Arizona Supreme Court.
5. The Arizona Supreme Court is the highest state court.
6. Arizona has a merit selection system for filling vacancies on the Supreme Court, the Court of Appeals, and the Superior Court in some counties.

26

1. THE JUSTICE OF THE PEACE COURTS ARE THE PEOPLE'S COURTS

The Justice of the Peace (JP) courts are "courts not of record." They do not need a court reporter to write down everything that is said.

Each county in Arizona is divided into justice precincts by the county board of supervisors. In 1984 there were 84 justices of the peace in Arizona. By county, the number varied from 18 in Maricopa to two each in Graham and Santa Cruz counties. A justice of the peace is elected to a four-year term.

Qualifications. The justice of the peace system goes back to ancient times when a village wise man settled disputes. Modern movies and television, unfortunately, have stereotyped the JP as an old fellow sitting in a rocking chair. While there are no special qualifications for the job, today some justices of the peace are lawyers. A law degree is not required, though it is helpful.

Jurisdiction. The JP courts are minor courts. In other words, they only try cases dealing with minor crimes or lawsuits involving less than $2500.

The JP courts are called the "people's courts." They provide the average person easy access to the judicial system.

Former Justice of the Peace Tim Weeks presiding in an East Phoenix court.

Sample form used in the Justice of Peace Court.

Criminal cases. The only crimes for which a person can be prosecuted in a JP court are lesser *misdemeanors*. These are minor crimes for which the punishment does not exceed a $1,000 fine or six months in the county jail. Examples are petty theft and speeding in excess of 20 mph over the posted limit.

Since 1984, minor traffic violations are classified as *civil offenses,* not crimes. Examples are running a red light or speeding less than 20 mph over the limit.

A person accused of a misdemeanor may demand a jury trial. The six jurors must agree on a verdict—guilty or not guilty.

A JP handles another kind of criminal proceeding too. He or she may conduct a *preliminary hearing* for a person accused of a felony (major crime). A preliminary hearing is held to see if there is enough evidence to hold an accused person for trial in the Superior Court. There is no jury at a preliminary hearing. These hearings are a big job for some JPs

438

whose courts are located in large urban areas.

Civil cases. The amount for which a person can sue in a JP court is set by state law. At present, a JP has *original jurisdiction* in a lawsuit involving less than $500 in money or property. That means the case starts in the JP court.

A JP court also has *concurrent jurisdiction* with the Superior Court in civil suits where the amount involved is between $500 and

$2500. That means the suit can be started in either court.

The party (person, company, or organization) which brings suit against another party is called the *plaintiff*. The party being sued is called the *defendant*.

The plaintiff states his or her claim in a written document called the *complaint*. The defendant replies in a written document called the *answer*. Typical JP civil complaint suits

Steps followed in the Small Claims Division of the JP Court.

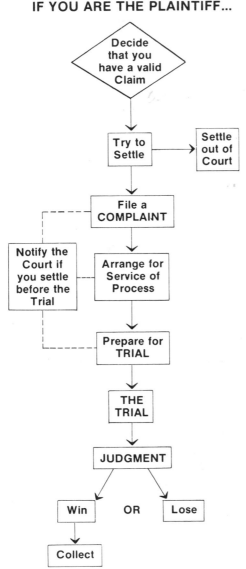

IF YOU ARE THE PLAINTIFF...

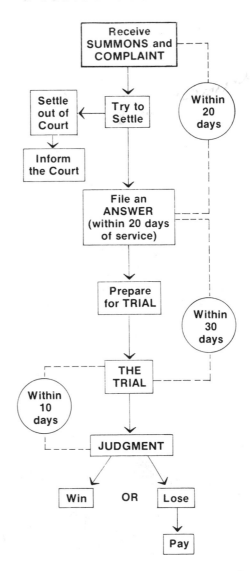

IF YOU ARE THE DEFENDANT...

IN THE JUSTICE COURT

COUNTY OF MARICOPA, STATE OF ARIZONA

_____ PRECINCT

Plaintiff,

vs

Defendant,

No _____

SUMMONS

THE STATE OF ARIZONA TO:

_____
Defendant

_____
Address

You are hereby summoned to appear and defend this action in this court located at

_____ Arizona within twenty (20) days

IF YOU FAIL TO APPEAR AND DEFEND, JUDGMENT BY DEFAULT WILL BE ENTERED AGAINST YOU AS REQUESTED IN THE COMPLAINT

DATED this _____ day of _____, 19 ____

_____
Justice of the Peace

CERTIFICATE OF SERVICE

STATE OF ARIZONA }
                  } ss.
County of Maricopa }

I HEREBY CERTIFY that I received the within Summons and Complaint on the

_____ day of _____, 19 _____, and personally served the same on the

_____ day of _____, 19 _____, at _____ o'clock ____ M, on _____

_____ being the defendant in the Summons and Complaint, by delivering it and

leaving it with _____ personally, in the _____

Precinct, County of Maricopa.

_____
Constable

Sample summons form which constables deliver to defendants.

arise from automobile accidents. The plaintiff sues for the amount of damages (if less than $2,500) done to his or her vehicle. Medical bills for physical injury may be part of the claim, too.

Small Claims Division. Every JP court in Arizona has a Small Claims Division. It provides a simple, speedy method to settle most civil claims under $500. Trials in the Small Claims Division are heard by the JP or a hearing officer. There is no jury. Neither party can be represented by a lawyer without the consent of the other party.

The Small Claims Division makes it possible for working people and small businesses to get speedy justice. They can collect wages or accounts which are legally owed to them.

One of the most common small claims cases deals with landlord-tenant problems. Sometimes a renter fails to pay the rent or breaks the lease in some other way. In this event, the landlord may file a complaint in a JP court to have the renter evicted.

The shoe is sometimes on the other foot. There are cases where renters moving out do not get back their their cleanup deposit. A landlord might keep the deposit, claiming that the rental property was damaged or not cleaned up. The renter may file a civil complaint to get the deposit refunded.

The _decision_ (judgment) of the JP or hearing officer in a small claims case is final. It cannot be appealed to a higher court.

Constables. There is a constable for each justice of the peace court. He or she is elected to a four-year term. A constable's job is to serve legal papers for the JP court, the same way a sheriff serves papers for the Superior Court.

Constables are sworn peace officers. They wear badges, carry guns, and can use handcuffs. They have the power to arrest, but seldom use it. Once a symbol of law and order in the Old West, the constable brought evildoers to justice. Now he spends more time with less glamorous duties.

The constable, for example, delivers _writs of restitution_ to evict renters because of unpaid rent. The constable also serves _writs of execution_. These writs allow the constable to seize personal property. It then may be auctioned to satisfy a debt. Cars are among the main items seized. The value, of course, must be less than $2,500.

2. EACH INCORPORATED TOWN OR CITY IN ARIZONA HAS A MUNICIPAL COURT

The greatest contact of Arizona citizens with the judicial system is in the courts not of record—either the JP or the municipal court.

The _municipal court_ is sometimes called the police court or the city court. The judge in this court is called a _magistrate_. He or she is appointed by the town or city council.

Jurisdiction. The magistrate can hear cases arising out of the violation of town or city ordinances. (An _ordinance_ is a law passed

City Magistrate Eugene K. Mangum started a rehabilitation program for arrested drunk drivers in Phoenix.

Superior Court Judge Lloyd Fernandez of Greenlee County with the Clerk of the Superior Court, Elsie F. Simms.

Maricopa County Superior Court building (center) was completed in 1976.

by a town or city council.) Violations of traffic ordinances bring the largest number of people to municipal court.

3. THE SUPERIOR COURT IS THE GREAT TRIAL COURT OF ARIZONA

Number of judges. Each county has at least one Superior Court judge. As the poplation grows, more judges are added by the county board of supervisors. No county, however, can have more than one Superior Court judge for each 30,000 people. Court hearings are held at the county seat.

In 1981 there were 82 Superior Court judges in Arizona. Maricopa County had 41. Pima, the second largest county, had 17. The three-judge counties were Cochise, Coconino, Pinal, and Yuma. The two-judge counties were Gila, Mohave, Navajo, and Yavapai. The counties with only one judge were Apache, Graham, Greenlee, and Santa Cruz.

Qualifications, selection, term, and salary. A Superior Court judge must be at least 30 years of age. He or she must be an Arizona resident. A judge must have been eligible to practice law in this state for at least five years before taking office.

Superior Court judges in counties with more than 150,000 people are appointed. The governor fills vacancies from recommendations made by the *Commission on Trial Court Appointments*. Only Maricopa and Pima counties have this system.

Superior Court judges in counties with fewer than 150,000 people are elected. They run for office as non-partisan candidates (not as Democrats or Republicans). The governor, however, can appoint a judge to fill a vacancy

441

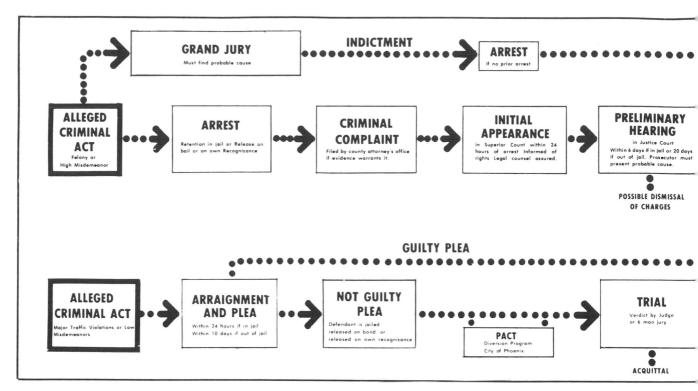

| GRAND JURY
Must find probable cause | | INDICTMENT | ARREST
If no prior arrest | |
| ALLEGED
CRIMINAL
ACT
Felony or
High Misdemeanor | ARREST
Retention in jail or Release on
bail or on own Recognizance | CRIMINAL
COMPLAINT
Filed by county attorney's office
if evidence warrants it. | INITIAL
APPEARANCE
in Superior Court within 24
hours of arrest Informed of
rights Legal counsel assured. | PRELIMINARY
HEARING
in Justice Court
Within 6 days if in jail or 20 days
if out of jail. Prosecutor must
present probable cause. |

POSSIBLE DISMISSAL
OF CHARGES

GUILTY PLEA

| ALLEGED
CRIMINAL ACT
Major Traffic Violations or Low
Misdemeanors | ARRAIGNMENT
AND PLEA
Within 24 hours if in jail
Within 10 days if out of jail | NOT GUILTY
PLEA
Defendant is jailed
released on bond or
released on own recognizance | PACT
Diversion Program
City of Phoenix | TRIAL
Verdict by Judge
or 6 man jury |

ACQUITTAL

How the Legal System Works

Former Superior Court Judge Gordon Farley, Santa Cruz County. The court reporter is making a record of the proceedings.

until the next election.

The term for a Superior Court judge is four years. The salary is paid one-half by the county and one-half by the state.

Jurisdiction. The Superior Court has *exclusive jurisdiction* over civil suits where the amount of controversy is more than $2,500. This means that no other court can try these cases.

The Superior Court also handles all divorce actions and juvenile cases. In the larger counties, one or more Superior Court judges are assigned full time to juvenile court duty. This juvenile court has exclusive jurisdiction over all cases involving delinquent, neglected, and dependent children under the age of 18.

The Superior Court has jurisdiction in all felony trials arising under state law. *Felonies* are major crimes such as murder, robbery, arson, embezzlement, or check forgery. Any state crime for which the punishment exceeds a $1,000 fine and/or imprisonment for more than six months is tried in the Superior Court.

Juries. There are two kinds of juries: grand and petit (trial).

The *grand jury* usually has 12 to 16 members. It holds hearings to determine if there is enough evidence to bring a person to trial. The grand jury's accusation, if there is one, is called

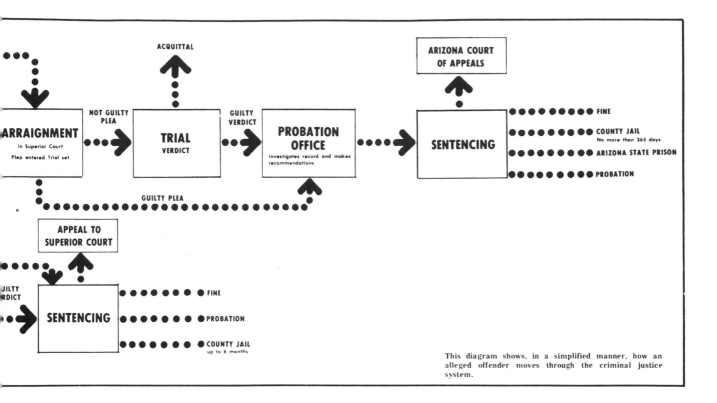

ACQUITTAL

ARIZONA COURT
OF APPEALS

ARRAIGNMENT
in Superior Court
Plea entered Trial set

NOT GUILTY
PLEA

TRIAL
VERDICT

GUILTY
VERDICT

PROBATION
OFFICE
investigates record and makes
recommendations

SENTENCING

● ● ● ● ● ● ● ● ● ● FINE

● ● ● ● ● ● ● ● ● ● COUNTY JAIL
No more than 365 days

● ● ● ● ● ● ● ● ● ● ARIZONA STATE PRISON

● ● ● ● ● ● ● ● ● PROBATION

GUILTY PLEA

APPEAL TO
SUPERIOR COURT

GUILTY
VERDICT

SENTENCING

● ● ● ● ● ● ● FINE

● ● ● ● ● ● ● PROBATION

● ● ● ● ● ● ● COUNTY JAIL
up to 6 months

This diagram shows, in a simplified manner, how an alleged offender moves through the criminal justice system.

a *bill of indictment.* The grand jury, however, is seldom used in Arizona. Most persons suspected of committing a crime are accused by the county attorney. This kind of accusation is called the *information.*

The *petit jury* is the trial jury. It determines the facts in a case. In a criminal trial, the jury decides whether the accused person is guilty or not guilty. In a civil suit, the trial jury decides which party in the suit is right.

Superior Court juries for criminal trials may vary in size. There must be 12 jurors if the maximum sentence for the crime is death or more than 30 years in prison. Other criminal cases have eight jurors. Whatever the number, the *verdict* in a criminal case must be by unanimous vote. A jury which cannot reach a verdict is called a *hung jury.*

In civil cases the Superior Court jury usually has eight members. A *judgment* in a civil suit can be reached by a 3/4ths vote.

How are jurors selected? Their names are drawn from the list of registered voters in the county. For each jury case, a panel of jurors is

sent to the court. The judge and counsel (lawyers) question the people on the panel to determine if any has a bias or prejudice. The judge excuses (dismisses) the persons who might not be impartial. The lawyers can also challenge (reject) other persons on the panel without cause.

Jury duty is an important civic responsibility. The jury and the judge must cooperate to see that justice is done.

Six stages of a jury trial. Once the jury has been sworn, the trial begins. There are six stages: (1) Each counsel gives an opening statement. The lawyers for the plaintiff and the defendant tell the jury what they will try to prove in the case.

(2) The plaintiff's lawyer calls witnesses to prove the plaintiff's case. (3) The defendant's lawyer calls witnesses to disprove the plaintiff's argument and to establish the defendant's case. (4) The plaintiff may call witnesses to rebut new matter brought out by the defendant's witnesses.

(5) The lawyers present summaries to the

jury. (6) The judge charges the jury, explaining the laws related to the case. The jurors are told to consider only the evidence.

Miranda Case. One Maricopa County Superior Court case in 1963 resulted in a famous U.S. Supreme Court decision three years later. Ernesto Miranda was convicted on both robbery and kidnap-rape charges. Miranda claimed he was denied a lawyer at the time of his arrest and at the preliminary hearing.

While Miranda was in prison at Florence, John J. Flynn, a well-known Phoenix criminal lawyer, argued his case before the U.S. Supreme Court. In the *Miranda vs. Arizona* decision, the high court upheld the 5th and 6th amendment rights of accused persons. Suspects have the right to remain silent and the right to have an attorney present when interrogated (asked questions).

The U.S. Supreme Court also overturned Miranda's conviction. The court said he was not advised of his rights at the time of his arrest. Miranda was released from prison. Later, however, he was retried and convicted for his 1963 crimes on new evidence. Paroled after a few years in prison, he was stabbed to death in a Phoenix bar in 1976.

The Miranda decision forced every police officer in the nation to advise every suspect of his rights at the time of an arrest.

4. THE COURT OF APPEALS WAS CREATED TO RELIEVE THE LOAD OF THE ARIZONA SUPREME COURT

The Court of Appeals was created in 1964. As court business increased, new judges were appointed. There are now 18 judges in all. They are divided in six courts, with three judges each.

Jurisdiction. The Appeals Court judges can review all cases appealed from the Superior Court. There is one exception. Any case in which the accused has been sentenced to death or life imprisonment, may be appealed directly to the Arizona Supreme Court.

The Court of Appeals can also review awards made by the Industrial Commission to workers injured on the job.

Two divisions. The Court of Appeals is split into two divisions. Judges of Division 1 have offices at the State Capitol in Phoenix. Judges in Division 2 are located in the state government building in Tucson.

Because of the heavy work load, Division 1 has four courts, each with three judges. These courts are classified as departments A, B, C, and D. The number of appeals judges in Division 1 was increased from 9 to 12 in 1982. The new department was added to concentrate on civil appeals cases.

Miranda card.

YOU HAVE THE RIGHT TO REMAIN SILENT.

80-119D
REV. 9-77

ANYTHING YOU SAY CAN BE USED AGAINST YOU IN A COURT OF LAW.

YOU HAVE THE RIGHT TO THE PRESENCE OF AN ATTORNEY TO ASSIST YOU PRIOR TO QUESTIONING, AND TO BE WITH YOU DURING QUESTIONING, IF YOU SO DESIRE.

IF YOU CANNOT AFFORD AN ATTORNEY YOU HAVE THE RIGHT TO HAVE AN ATTORNEY APPOINTED FOR YOU PRIOR TO QUESTIONING.

DO YOU UNDERSTAND THESE RIGHTS?

DATE   DR#   OFF. INITIALS

Judges of the Court of Appeals, Division 2 at Tucson, 1982. Left to right: James D. Hathaway, Lawrence Howard, and Benjamin C. Birdsall.

President Reagan, Chief Justice Warren Burger, and Justice Sandra D. O'Connor of Phoenix. Appointed to the U.S. Supreme Court by Reagan, Justice O'Connor is the only woman ever to serve on the highest court in the nation.

Division 1 of the Court of Appeals serves these counties: Apache, Coconino, Maricopa, Mohave, Navajo, Yavapai, and Yuma. Eight of twelve judges must be appointed from heavily-populated Maricopa County.

Mrs. Sandra O'Connor of Phoenix was a Division 1 Court of Appeals judge. She resigned in 1981 to accept an appointment on the U.S. Supreme Court. Appointed by President Ronald Reagan, Judge O'Connor became the first woman to serve on the highest court in the nation.

The six judges in Division 2 at Tucson now serve seven counties: Cochise, Gila, Graham, Greenlee, Pima, Pinal, and Santa Cruz. Four of the six judges in Division 2 must be residents of Pima County.

How appointed, term, and qualifications. Judges of the Court of Appeals are appointed by the governor to a six-year term. Recommendations are made to the governor by the *Commission on Appellate Court Appointments.*

A Court of Appeals judge must have the same qualifications as judges of the Superior Court.

5. THE ARIZONA SUPREME COURT IS THE HIGHEST STATE COURT

The Arizona Supreme Court has five justices. They are appointed by the governor for six-year terms. The justices elect one of their members as the presiding chief justice. The Supreme Court holds sessions at the State Capitol building in Phoenix.

Qualifications. A justice taking office must have been an Arizona resident for 10 years. He or she must have been eligible to practice law in the state for the same period of time. Arizona Supreme Court justices usually have had experience as Superior Court judges. However, that is not a constitutional qualification.

Jurisdiction. The Arizona Supreme Court has *final jurisdiction* in cases appealed from lower state courts. An exception would be one like the Miranda case where a United States constitutional question is involved. In that event, the U.S. Supreme Court would have final jurisdiction.

The Arizona Supreme Court gets some difficult cases from the Superior Court. A 1976 case involving water rights illustrates the point. The case arose out of a groundwater shortage problem in the Santa Cruz Valley south of Tucson. Too much water was being pumped. The water was needed by the City of Tucson, by several copper mining companies, and by farmers.

The Farmers' Investment Company (FICO) filed suit in the Pima County Superior Court in 1969. FICO's "prior rights" to the water for irrigation were recognized, but the case was appealed.

The Arizona Supreme Court then upheld the lower court's decision by a 4 to 1 vote. The City of Tucson and the mine companies were ordered to cut down the amount of water that they pumped from the Santa Cruz basin.

The Supreme Court's ruling was based on the *doctrine of prior appropriation.* The court explained, however, that the legislature could decide what economic interests were most important to Arizona. The legislature might, by law, give the cities or mines first priority to use scarce water. This part of the Supreme Court's decision gave some hope to the people of

Supreme Court of Arizona, 1982. Left to right: James Duke Cameron, Justice; Frank X. Gordon, Jr., Vice Chief Justice; William A. Holohan, Chief Justice; Jack D. H. Hays, Justice; and Stanley G. Feldman, Justice.

Tucson who must solve a water shortage problem.

The Arizona Supreme Court makes decisions by majority vote of the five justices. All majority opinions have to be in writing. No jury is used.

6. ARIZONA HAS A MERIT SELECTION SYSTEM FOR FILLING VACANCIES ON THE STATE SUPREME COURT, THE COURT OF APPEALS, AND THE SUPERIOR COURTS IN SOME COUNTIES

In 1974 the voters of Arizona passed a constitutional amendment to start a merit selection system for judges.

Appellate courts. Judges of the Supreme Court and the Court of Appeals are no longer elected. When a vacancy occurs, the governor appoints a new judge. The appointment is made from a list of names recommended by the nonpartisan *Commission on Appellate Court Appointments.*

The Chief Justice of the Arizona Supreme Court is the chairperson of this commission.

Pima County judicial election ballot.

Other commission members are three attorneys nominated by the State Bar Association and five public members—all appointed by the governor.

Ability, not political party, is the basis for the selection of judges. For example, Governor Bruce Babbitt, a Democrat, appointed Sandra O'Connor, a Republican, to the Court of Appeals.

Trial judges. Superior Court judges in counties of more than 150,000 people (Maricopa and Pima) are also on the merit system. Each of these two counties has a commission on trial court appointments. These commissions recommend nominees for Superior Court vacancies to the governor.

Superior Court judges are still elected in the counties with fewer than 150,000 people. However, these smaller counties may choose to select judges by the merit system. The voters would have to approve the change at an election.

Retention as judge or removal from office. After a judge is appointed on the basis of merit, he or she completes the term of office. The judge's name is then placed on the ballot at election time. There are no opposing candidates. The voters simply decide if the judge should stay in office another term. Most judges are retained in office. A few are removed and replaced with new appointees of the governor.

A Phoenix fireman hangs on.

27

LOCAL GOVERNMENTS

A local government is one that serves the people in a political subdivision of a state. The principal subdivisions are the counties, cities, towns, and single-purpose districts. The school district is the most common type of single-purpose district.

There are more than 3,000 counties in the United States. Arizona is divided into large counties. Santa Cruz County, the smallest, is bigger than the state of Rhode Island. Coconino County, the largest, is bigger than Massachusetts, New Jersey, and Delaware combined. It is the second largest county in the United States.

One town or city in each county is the *county seat*. A *courthouse* in the county seat is the center of most activities of county government. Judges and other county officers perform their duties at the courthouse. Additional buildings for office space and courtrooms are needed in the heavily-populated counties.

People who live in towns and cities are served by both a county and a municipal government. This includes 80 percent of the Arizona population. These urban communities range in size from small villages to large metropolitan cities like Phoenix and Tucson. Much of the work of municipal government is done at the town or *city hall*.

As the population of a town or city increases, so do the demands for services. There is a greater need for improved streets, traffic regulation, fire and police protection, sewers, garbage pickup, recreational facilities, and other services. The success of city or town government depends on how well it can improve the needed services.

KEY CONCEPTS

1. County government provides many services.
2. Town or city government is close to the people.
3. There are three kinds of special districts in Arizona: councils of governments (COGS), single-purpose non-school districts, and school districts.

27

1. COUNTY GOVERNMENTS PROVIDE MANY SERVICES

The counties of Arizona are political subdivision of the state. They bring government closer to the people. County officials administer many state laws. They collect taxes, conduct elections, maintain jails, hold court, and provide medical care for the poor. People outside of towns are given county sheriff's protection, county roads, and other services.

County officers. Each county in Arizona has the same elected officers. The state constitution provides for an assessor, county attorney, recorder, sheriff, superintendent of schools, treasurer, and a board of supervisors.

To hold county office a person must be 18

Yuma County Board of Supervisors, 1982. Left to right: J. R. "Sandy" Sanders, Robert W. Kennerly, Chairman R. Pete Woodard, Charyl J. Stanley, and Ray Moore.

years of age, a citizen, a qualified voter of the county, and able to read and write English. All of the elected county officers serve four-year terms. They are elected in presidential election years—1980, 1984, 1988, and so on.

Board of Supervisors. Before 1972 every county was divided into three supervisor districts. The state legislature changed the law to provide for a five-member board for counties that have more than 200,000 people—namely Maricopa and Pima. The other counties may elect five supervisors only if the voters of the county give approval at an election.

In 1980 Coconino and Yuma counties voted to have five supervisors. The two counties had to be redistricted since each supervisor is elected from a district. The change from three to five supervisors gave Coconino an all-Indian district. Its first Navajo supervisor — Louis Yellowman, a Tuba City educator — was elected. One of the new supervisors elected in Yuma County was Ray Moore. He was the first Black elected official in Yuma County.

Duties. The board's most important duties are related to finance. The supervisors approve the annual county budget. They set the county property tax rate after the county's other revenues are estimated. Revenues from the state reduce the amount of money that has to be raised by the county property tax. The county receives, for example, a share of the state sales, auto lieu, and gasoline taxes.

County manager. It is common practice for a board of supervisors to appoint a professional person as county manager. The manager ad-

Arizona Counties and County Seats

ministers the day-to-day details of county government. Maricopa was the first county in Arizona to employ a county manager for this purpose.

The Maricopa County manager now directs about two dozen departments. Pima County has a similar organization. Most of the less-populated counties also have either a manager or an *administrator* to supervise county services.

Other county officers. The *assessor* figures the market value of most real property in the county. The assessor, however, does not appraise railroads, producing mines, utilities, or telephone and telegraph property. That is done by a division of the Arizona Department of Revenue.

The assessor gives partial exemption from property taxes to certain widows and disabled veterans who qualify under state law.

One of the assessor's main duties is to register all motor vehicles in the county. The assessor also issues license plates and collects the *state auto lieu tax* at the same time. The auto lieu tax is really a personal property tax. It is based on the value and age of the vehicle.

The *county attorney* must be a lawyer. The attorney and his or her assistants prosecute persons accused of violating state laws. The county attorney also represents the county in civil and criminal suits. He or she serves as legal advisor to other county officials and public school districts. The attorney is the highest paid elected county official.

The *sheriff* and deputies are responsible for law enforcement outside incorporated towns and cities in the county. They make arrests and gather evidence used in court trials. They serve subpoenas to witnesses for the Superior Court.

The sheriff is in charge of the county jail. He transports convicted criminals to prison. The sheriff sells personal property on which taxes are delinquent. He heads search and rescue operations. In the jargon of the Old West, he can still form a *posse* of citizens in times of emergency. The sheriff is the second-

The sheriff has been an important county officer since territorial days. In this photo, the well-known Yavapai County sheriff, George C. Ruffner, is shown relaxing in 1897.

Maricopa County search and rescue mission.

highest paid county official.

The *recorder* keeps a record of all property deeds, mortgages, and other legal documents. The recorder must maintain an indexing system so that any record can be easily located.

The recorder's second major duty is to register voters. Deputy registrars are appointed to get this job done. An up-to-date list of voters in the county is kept in the recorder's office.

The *school superintendent* must have a valid teacher's certificate to hold office. It is the duty of the county superintendent to see that all rules and regulations of the state board of education are carried out.

451

The superintendent is the official accountant and record keeper for public schools in the county. The superintendent's office pays all school district salaries and expenses with county warrants. Banks cash these warrants as if they were checks.

Clerks in the superintendent's office make a record of teacher certificates. The superintendent also fills vacancies that occur on school boards in the county.

The *treasurer* collects property taxes for the county. He or she also collects them for the state as well as for school districts, cities, towns, and special districts within the county.

The treasurer pays out money to banks which turn in county warrants that they have cashed. Another duty of the treasurer is to invest county and school funds in banks as directed by the board of supervisors.

The *clerk of the Superior Court* is another elected county officer. But this position was created by state law, not by the constitution. The clerk keeps a record of all Superior Court

The second of Pinal County's three courthouses still houses some county offices. It also provides an eye-pleasing scene in downtown Florence.

cases filed in the county. Another important duty of the clerk's office is to issue marriage licenses.

County services. Collecting taxes, running elections and providing health services are some traditional county services. Others are keeping public records, building roads and protecting people from crimes.

As the population grows, more is demanded of county government. Today, counties provide a variety of services. Included are parks and recreation, airports, libraries, street lighting, garbage collection, sewage facilities such as Pima County's Ina Road plant, and others.

What is the present status of county

Child in emergency room of Maricopa County General Hospital.

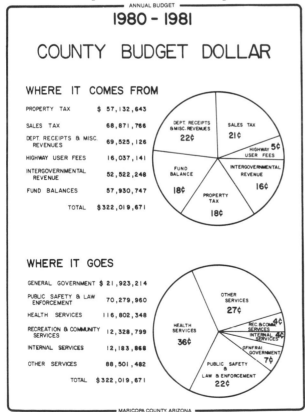

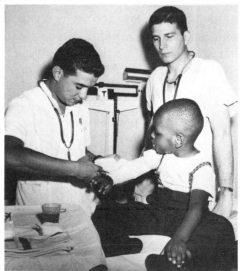

Yavapai County Recorder's office about 1900.

government? Arizona's first 14 counties were created by the territorial legislature back in horse and buggy days. The county courthouses brought government closer to the people in rural areas.

The fifteenth county was formed by voters in Yuma County in May, 1982. The northern part of that county was to be split off to form the new county. The name and county seat were to be decided at the November, 1982 election.

Through the years, county governments have been treated as branches of state government. They have been saddled with expenses that should be paid by the state. For example, counties must pay most of the cost of the criminal justice system—law enforcement, courts, and jails. Health care for poor people has been a heavy county burden. (An indigent health care bill passed by the legislature in 1981 will provide more state and federal funds.) Counties also have to pay the employer's contribution to the State Retirement System for school employees.

County governments have had little decision-making power. They have to seek legislative approval for nearly every change. This situation is unfortunate because Arizona is one of the fastest growing states. It has many modern problems that call for solutions. Dozens of bills are introduced at every legislative session to deal with county problems. This process is slow. It creates a delay in meeting county responsibilities for new services.

Some political scientists favor *home rule* county government. Under the home rule plan, county governments would be organized under a local *charter* approved by the voters. This system would give the county powers to govern itself. The county supervisors would have more flexibility in dealing with problems. The board could take action without first going to the legislature to get power to act.

2. TOWN OR CITY GOVERNMENT IS CLOSE TO THE PEOPLE

Services. Town or city government directly affects the lives of people. The local government furnishes water, maintains streets, and develops parks. It provides police and fire protection, collects trash, and performs many other services.

In many places these basic services are taken for granted. People now are expecting local government to do more to improve the quality of life. Such projects include urban renewal, a civic center, a zoo, and beautified streets with trees and sidewalks. Libraries, sports arenas, programs for the young and elderly and many more municipal services are becoming realities.

The magic numbers in Arizona municipal government. A *town* with 1,500 people may incorporate. When the population reaches 3,000, a town may choose to call itself a *city*. A town or city with 3,500 people may draw up a *charter* (constitution) and adopt home rule government.

"General law" towns or cities. From the legal point of view, there are two types of municipalities in Arizona: "general law" and "home rule."

General law towns get their powers from laws passed by the state legislature and from the Constitution of Arizona. One state law outlines a simple mayor-council form of government. The only elected officials are the members of the town council.

Towns with fewer than 1,500 people elect

five council members at large for two-year terms. The council selects one of its members to act as mayor. The salary paid to these people is small and cannot exceed a maximum amount set by state law. The council appoints other people as needed to run the town. Typical town jobs are the police chief, fire chief, magistrate, attorney, public works director, and clerk. The jobs and duties vary from town to town.

Towns with more than 1,500 people may elect seven council members, including the

Rhinos at the Phoenix zoo.

Youth members of a drama workshop, sponsored by Glendale Parks and Recreation Department, learn a movement.

mayor. They may also incorporate.

There are a few incorporated towns with a population of less than 1,500. The reason is that an earlier state law required only 500 for incorporation. Examples are Duncan, Fredonia, Hayden, Patagonia, Wellton, and Winkelman.

Why incorporate? As a *municipal corporation,* the town or city has legal rights. It can sue or be sued in the courts. It can make contracts and own property. By incorporating, a town can get a share of the state sales tax and other revenues. Federal grants-in-aid also provide some money for street improvement, sidewalks, sewers, parks, poverty programs, tree planting, or airport construction.

Guadalupe, a town with about 4,500 people southeast of Phoenix on Interstate 10, is a good example of a town that underwent changes after it incorporated in 1975. Guadalupe had a first year budget of $386,000 without a town property tax. Federal funds were used for the town's first grass-covered park, a fire station, and new fire hydrants. A library, town hall, and a youth club were also built.

New town ordinances were passed by the seven-member Guadalupe council. One regulation, for example, restricted mobile homes to certain sections of the town. County zoning and building regulations had been ignored before Guadalupe was incorporated. The new town government also provides better garbage pickup than the county had been able to furnish.

There are two ways a town can incorporate. The county board of supervisors must verify that one or the other of these methods has been followed. One way is for 2/3rds of the qualified voters in the town to sign a petition asking for incorporation. Another way is for the majority of people voting at an election to favor incorporation.

Options. In incorporated towns or cities, the council and mayor may be elected at large for two-year terms, but there are options. A few towns and cities now elect council members from districts, called *wards.* The

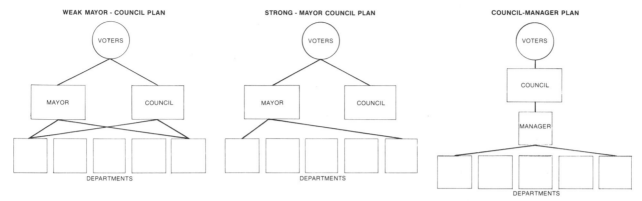

WEAK MAYOR - COUNCIL PLAN

STRONG - MAYOR COUNCIL PLAN

COUNCIL-MANAGER PLAN

Types of city government

length of the term can be changed too. For example, about 50 Arizona towns and cities elect council members to overlapping four-year terms.

"Home rule" charter cities. The Arizona Constitution permits any city with 3,500 or more people to adopt its own "home rule" charter. The charter must be approved by a majority of voters at an election and by the governor. The charter is the city's constitution. However, it must not conflict with any state law or the Arizona Constitution.

There are 16 charter cities in Arizona. Tombstone was given home rule in 1881 during territorial days. The other cities and the dates they got their charters approved are: Phoenix (1913), Yuma (1914), Nogales (1926), Tucson (1929), Glendale and Winslow (1957), Flagstaff and Prescott (1958), Avondale (1959), Scottsdale (1961), Tempe (1964), Chandler (1965), Mesa (1967), Casa Grande (1975), and Peoria (1983).

A "home rule" city can have the form of government that best serves its needs. This freedom to choose makes sense because all cities and their problems are not the same. Most charter cities, however, have the council-manager form of government.

Types of town or city government. There are three main types of government used in Arizona's towns and cities. They are the weak mayor-council plan, the strong mayor-council plan, and the council-manager

City charter of Scottsdale, (first page).

City of Scottsdale
CITY CHARTER
Scottsdale, Arizona

ARTICLE 1 — Incorporation, Form of Government, Powers and Boundaries

Section 1 — Incorporation

The inhabitants of the City of Scottsdale, within the corporate limits as now established or as hereafter established in the manner provided by law, shall continue to be a municipal body politic and corporate in perpetuity, under the name of the "City of Scottsdale."

Section 2 — Form of Government

The municipal government provided by this charter shall be known as the COUNCIL MANAGER FORM GOVERNMENT. Pursuant to its provisions and subject only to the limitations imposed by the state constitution and by this charter, all powers of the City shall be vested in an elective council, hereinafter referred to as "the council," which shall enact local legislation, adopt budgets, determine policies and appoint the city manager and such other officers deemed necessary and proper for the orderly government and administration of the affairs of the City, as prescribed by the constitution and applicable laws, and ordinances hereafter adopted by the City. All powers of the City shall be exercised in the manner prescribed by this charter, or if the manner be not prescribed, then in such manner as may be prescribed by ordinance.

Section 3 — Powers of City

The City shall have all the powers granted to municipal corporations and to cities by the constitution and laws of this state and by this charter,

plan.

The *weak mayor-council plan* is most common in Arizona. The mayor is only the first

455

among equals in the council. He or she presides over meetings. The whole council is the executive head. When a manager is hired, the weak mayor-council plan becomes the council-manager plan.

With a few changes, the weak mayor-council system can also operate like the commission form of government used in other states. The council in Marana, for example, is organized like a commission. Each council person is responsible for a specific government function. The Marana council chooses one of its members to be mayor.

The *strong mayor-council plan* gives the mayor more authority. He or she does more than preside over the council. The strong mayor is the administrative head of city departments and can make decisions promptly. There is a clear line of responsibility in the strong mayor-council system.

Nogales is an example of a city which has a strong mayor-council system. The council, known in Nogales as the board of aldermen, sets policy. The mayor presides over the board but is also the administrator. As an example of his authority, he can fire city officials. These officials include an administrative assistant, police chief, fire chief, finance director, superintendent of streets, attorney, engineer, magi-

strate, and planning director.

The *council-manager plan* is the most popular type of government in towns and cities that can afford it. The mayor and council make policy. They adopt the budget and enact local laws, called ordinances. One of their most important jobs is to hire or to remove the manager.

The manager is in charge of day-by-day administrative details of city government. His or her directions come from the mayor and council. The manager, however, has control over the departments.

Phoenix charter government. In October, 1913, the people of Phoenix voted nearly two to one for a charter. The charter made Phoenix one of the first cities in the nation to adopt the council-manager form of government. At first the council was called a commission.

Unfortunately, Phoenix city government was bad for the first 35 years. It was corrupt and inefficient. Political favoritism was common. Campaign contributors were rewarded with city business. The position of city manager was treated as a political plum. Twenty-four different men served as manager between 1914 and 1950.

The way was paved for a new start in 1947. Mayor Ray Busey appointed a Charter Revision Committee of 40 citizens. This committee proposed a charter amendment. It was approved by the voters in 1948. The name "commission" was changed to "council" and a new system of government was started.

The charter amendment specified that the nonpartisan council should select a manager on the basis of his or her experience and training in city government. The manager was given power to appoint most employees of the city. For manager, the new council selected Ray W. Wilson, an experienced assistant manager in Kansas City. Wilson held the job for 11 years.

In the decades after 1950, Phoenix did more than just change—it exploded! From a city of less than 17 square miles, it expanded to more than 330 square miles by 1981. During the

Joel Valdez, Tucson City Manager.

Phoenix City Council, 1985.

Mayor Terry Goddard of Phoenix.

Phoenix has about 2,700 miles of sewer lines.

Many elderly people are in need of transportation. The Human Resources Department, City of Phoenix, helps by providing rides to adult centers, nutrition sites, the county hospital, and to other health and social service agencies.

Phoenix policemen search a suspect as a police helicopter hovers overhead.

Garbage collection is an important city service.

same time, the population grew from about 100,000 to 800,000. In keeping up with this growth, city government naturally became more complex.

Every city service became a big operation. Nearly a million people must be provided with police and fire protection. About 3,000 miles of streets have to be maintained and traffic regulated. Thousands of tons of garbage are collected twice a week. Parks and libraries are provided. The city's Sky Harbor Airport serves thousands of passengers every day. The list goes on. City residents have come to expect a lot from city government.

Like other Arizona cities, Phoenix is concerned with more than the traditional services. Social and economic problems get a lot of attention. The Phoenix *Human Relations Department,* for example, works to end all discrimination on the basis of race, religion, national origin, and sex.

The *Human Resources Department* provides many city services to help low income people. Programs have ranged from Head Start for preschool children to a hot lunch service for senior citizens.

New Method of representation. In 1983 Phoenix voters began electing eight city councilors from wards. The city had been divided into eight districts, each with about equal population. Previously, the council had only six members, all elected at large. Now the mayor is the only city official elected at large.

3. THERE ARE THREE KINDS OF SPECIAL DISTRICTS IN ARIZONA: COUNCILS OF GOVERNMENTS (COGs), SINGLE-PURPOSE NON-SCHOOL DISTRICTS, AND SCHOOL DISTRICTS

Voluntary regional councils of government (COGs). The cities, towns, and counties of Arizona have formed regional councils of government. These COGs bring together representatives to plan and work together on a regional basis. There is a need for this type

of planning.

The rapid growth of Phoenix, Tucson, and other urban areas in Arizona has created problems. These problems have no geographical boundaries. Only by cooperative effort can they be solved. It would be ridiculous, for example, for one community to attack the air pollution program alone. And no matter where homes are built—in a city, in a suburb, or in an outlying county area—certain services are demanded.

Planning by regional councils of government is often needed to provide water, proper sewage disposal, police and fire protection, and transportation. Gone are the days when a city or county could plan a major road, flood control project, or sewer system and ignore the plans of neighboring areas.

One of the best examples of intercity cooperation is the metropolitan Phoenix sewage treatment center. It all started in 1958 when Phoenix and Glendale joined to construct a disposal plant at 91st Avenue and the Salt River.

In 1966 Scottsdale, Tempe, and Mesa were hooked into the Phoenix-Glendale sewer system. All three of these cities had outgrown local facilities. They were discharging effluent through one or more of their neighboring communities. The 91st Avenue sewage plant now serves other cities too. Peoria, Youngtown, and Sun City are part of the system.

MAG (Maricopa Association of Governments) and PAG (Pima Association of Governments) were formed in 1967. Other COGs have been formed by local governments in the following areas: Gila-Pinal counties, Mohave-Yuma-La Paz counties, Apache-Coconino-Navajo-Yavapai counties, and Cochise-Graham-Greenlee-Santa Cruz counties.

Special districts. Arizona state law permits the formation of single-purpose districts. The best known one is the Salt River Project. It supplies water and electricity for both homes and farms.

Another important district is the Central Arizona Water Conservation District. An

The Phoenix 91st Avenue sewage disposal plant. It is also used by other cities and towns in the Phoenix area.

elected board contracts with the Secretary of Interior for Central Arizona Project (CAP) water from the Colorado River. Among the people elected to this board in 1980 were two former governors, Howard Pyle and Jack Williams. Another well-known member elected was Stewart Udall, a former Arizona Conressman and Secretary of the Interior.

Other districts have been formed for fire prevention, flood control, and sanitation.

School districts make up the largest category of single-purpose districts. There are over 200 elementary and high school districts in Arizona. Each of these districts elects a board of education. There are usually three members, but union and county districts have five.

The board of education adopts budgets and employs school personnel. Another duty of the board is to establish policies on such things as curriculum and discipline. The details of running the schools are left to administrators.

Advantages of special districts. One advantage of special districts is the elimination of party politics. School board elections are nonpartisan.

Another advantage is that the boundaries of a special district do not have to coincide with the boundaries of a town or county. A special district also has its own taxing power or source of revenue. It does not have to compete for a share of a county or town budget.

459

Some Arizona voters at their polling place.

28

THE ELECTION PROCESS AND POLITICAL PARTIES

An election is democracy in action! It is the most effective way we can influence our government. We have the privilege of voting for people who will govern us the way we want to be governed.

Every vote counts! It is wrong to say, "My vote won't make any difference." There are many good examples to illustrate how one vote at each polling place decided the outcome of an election. Even more important, voting is a means by which every citizen can get involved in government. Without elections we have no democracy.

The simplest election is by a "show of hands" or a "yea" or "no" voice vote. These methods may work in a small group. They are not suitable, however, where hundreds or millions of people are involved. Why not? In the first place, it would be impossible to assemble all the voters in one place. Secondly, every voter is entitled to vote secretly.

The election process begins with the nomination of candidates. In Arizona each political party chooses its candidates at a primary election. Candidates who win the primary election are called *nominees*. They represent the party in the general election. The winners in the general election take office a short time later.

Arizona has had elections since 1864. In that year the territorial government was organized. The voters elected members of the legislature and sent Charles D. Poston to Washington, D.C., as delegate to Congress.

As new counties were created and new towns were started, the number of elective offices increased. Today there are hundreds of jobs filled by the elective process.

KEY CONCEPTS

1. Voting is one way a citizen can become involved in the political process.
2. Three types of elections in Arizona are the direct primary, the general election, and special elections.
3. A political party is organized to gain control of government through the election of its candidates to public office.
4. Campaigning for office usually takes time and money.
5. Like people in other states, Arizona voters elect representatives and senators to serve in Congress.

28

1. VOTING IS ONE WAY A CITIZEN
CAN BECOME INVOLVED IN THE
POLITICAL PROCESS

Why vote? Voting at elections is democracy in action. It is the means by which we choose people to run our government for us. Without elections we would have no representative democracy.

Who can vote in Arizona? To vote you must be a citizen of the United States. You must be 18 years of age. You must be a resident of the state for at least 50 days before the next election. You must be able to write your name or make your mark. (Knowing how to read and write English is no longer required for voting.)

Convicts and insane persons are denied the privilege of voting. An ex-convict, however, can vote if his or her civil rights have been restored by a court.

Before a person can vote, he or she must be *registered*. The voter fills out a card giving name, address, political party, and other information.

People who qualify may register with the county recorder. This officer also has part-time deputies who sign up voters at home or in

In this cartoon the people of Arizona are being encouraged by the Secretary of State's office to register to vote.

shopping centers. A justice of the peace can register voters too. There is no charge for this service.

Most people register as either Democrat or Republican. A voter, however, may choose to be a member of a minor party. Some voters belong to no party and register as "Independent."

Where and how do you vote? Each county is divided into voting *precincts*. Each precinct has a *polling place* where people vote. The polling place may be a schoolroom, a church, or some other convenient place.

Election officials are appointed by the board of supervisors for each precinct polling place. The officials cannot all be members of the same political party. They make certain that each voter has previously registered. After the voter signs the poll book, the official gives him or her a ballot. The officials are the inspector, marshal, two judges, and at least two clerks for each precinct.

Most voting in Arizona is done on the *Votomatic*. The voter is given a computer card which is inserted into a holder. The holder shows the names of all candidates in the election. Voters use a stylus to punch holes in the card opposite the names of candidates of their choice. Use of the Votomatic speeds up the counting of ballots. After the polling places close, the ballot cards are taken to a computer and quickly tabulated electronically.

Some people have to vote by *absentee ballot*. A voter may not be able to go to the polling place on election day. He or she may be disabled or away from home. Under these or other legal conditions, the voter applies to the county recorder for an absentee ballot. This can be done as early as 90 days preceding the Saturday before an election. A ballot is later sent to the voter's home.

Absentee ballots are not counted until after the polls close on election day. Every vote is important. In 1980, for example, U.S. Senator Barry Goldwater got a big majority of the absentee ballot votes. Without them he would have been defeated by his opponent.

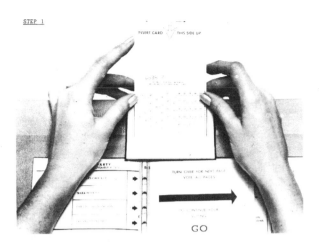

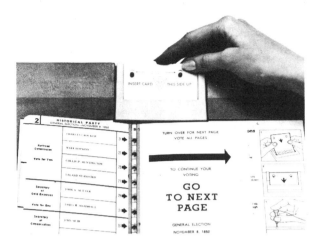

STEP 1

Using both hands, slide the ballot card all the way into the Vote Recorder.

STEP 2

Be sure the two holes at the top of the card fit over the **two red pins** on the Vote Recorder.

STEP 3

To vote, hold the Punch straight up and push down through the card for each of your choices. Vote all pages. **Use the punch provided. Do not use pen or pencil.**

Instructions for voting on the Votomatic. The board of supervisors of each county has the duty of holding and supervising elections.

STEP 4

After voting, slide the card out of the Vote Recorder and place it under the flap in the write-in envelope. **If you make a mistake, ask for another ballot.**

2. **THREE TYPES OF ELECTIONS IN ARIZONA ARE THE DIRECT PRIMARY, THE GENERAL ELECTION, AND THE SPECIAL ELECTION**

Direct primary. In Arizona, any qualified person may run for office. His or her name is gotten on the primary election ballot by *petition*. Only registered voters in the candidate's political party may sign the petition. These voters must also live within the area served by the office. For example, if it is a county office, they must live in the county.

The direct primary is used to select the people to run for each party. A Democrat runs against other Democrats. A Republican runs against other Republicans. The winner for each party is said to be nominated and is called the *nominee*. Each party tries to have a nominee for every office.

To win a primary, a candidate must have a *plurality*—that is, more votes than any other person.

Arizona has the *closed primary*. That means you can vote only for persons of your party. Voters who are registered "Independent" cannot vote in the Democratic or Republican primaries. They can vote in the general election, however.

The primary election in Arizona is held in September, eight weeks before the general election.

General election. The general election is held on the first Tuesday after the first Monday in November. Voters decide who will win each public office.

The party nominee for an office runs against the nominees of other parties. Each nominee's name is placed on the ballot along with his or her political party.

The *office column ballot* is the type used in Arizona. The names of all the party nominees for an office are listed together under the name of that office. The party names are rotated from office to office. In that way, no party has an advantage in the placement of candidates on the ballot.

The office column ballot discourages *straight ticket voting*. If a voter wants to vote for candidates of only one party, it can be done. However, it is necessary to vote for each candidate separately. The voter cannot automatically vote for every candidate of a particular party by making only one mark.

Many voters in Arizona vote a *split ticket*. They vote for candidates of more than one political party. These voters say they are voting for the best candidate rather than the party.

Split ticket voting was obvious in the 1980 election, for example. The Republican candidate for President, Ronald Reagan, defeated

Congressman Morris K. Udall of Tucson was first elected to the U.S. House of Representatives in 1961. He filled the seat vacated by his brother, Stewart Udall, who was appointed Secretary of Interior by President John F. Kennedy.

Congressman Bob Stump was first elected to the U.S. House of Representatives from District 3 as a Democrat. In 1981 he changed his registration to Republican.

464

his Democratic opponent by a landslide. Reagan carried every county except Greenlee. Democrats, on the other hand, won two of the four Congressional seats. Liberal Democrat Morris Udall was reelected in District 2. Conservative Democrat Bob Stump won in District 3. There were thousands of voters in these districts who voted Republican for President. Then they switched to vote Democratic for Representative in Congress.

Special election. A special election has to be called to fill a vacancy in Congress. For instance, in 1961 a special election was held in District 2 when Stewart Udall resigned. He was appointed Secretary of Interior by President John Kennedy. His brother, Morris Udall, won the special election.

The *recall* is another kind of special election. The recall has been used mainly at the local level. Voters have replaced unsatisfactory school board members or city council members with new people.

Bond elections are also usually held between general elections. The voters are asked to approve the selling of bonds to finance school construction, roads, parks, sewers, or other projects. Voter approval is needed because the bonds have to be paid later with tax money.

3. A POLITICAL PARTY IS ORGANIZED TO GAIN CONTROL OF GOVERNMENT THROUGH THE ELECTION OF ITS CANDIDATES TO PUBLIC OFFICE

Political parties play an important role in representative government. In general, the parties give voters a choice on issues and candidates. Most voters identify with a political party even though they may not strictly follow party recommendations.

Two-party system. In Arizona, political parties are defined in state election laws. "Existing parties" are those which received at least five percent of the votes in the last general election.

The Democratic and Republican parties have been Arizona's two main political parties.

However, the two-party system did not emerge in this state until after World War II. Until then, Arizona was considered a one-party Democratic state. It was not until 1966, for example, that the Republican Party first controlled both houses of the state legislature.

The Republican rise was due to several factors. Migration of new residents from other states brought Republicans. Attractive candidates in the 1950s and 1960s, and skillful state party chairmen brought in Republican votes.

Minor parties can get on the ballot by filing petitions with the secretary of state. The petitions must be signed by a percentage of qualified voters. These must equal two percent of the number who voted for governor in the last general election. In 1980, for instance, the Libertarian Party was on the ballot with candidates for several offices.

Political party organization. Political parties are organized by steps from the precinct up to the national level. There are more than 1,400 precincts in Arizona. Each major party is permitted to elect at least one *committeeperson* in each precinct. These precinct workers are elected at the party primary in September. Their job is to work for party candidates and get people to vote.

All the precinct committeepersons are members of a *county committee*. Some also serve on the *state committee*. Each party has a *state chairperson* who heads the executive committee. He or she tries to build up party registration and raise funds. The chairperson also persuades electable party members to run for office, and develops campaign strategy.

Each party has its own method for choosing delegates to a *national convention* which nominates candidates for president and vice president. Each party also has a *national committee* made up of one man and one woman from each state.

4. CAMPAIGNING TAKES TIME AND MONEY

How do you campaign for office? Candidates usually try to personally meet as many voters as possible. They shake hands, put up signs, and advertise wherever they can. Personal appearances at clubs, rallies, and on television or radio give the candidate visibility. The candidate may send letters to voters. Friends may put bumper stickers on their cars or make telephone calls to get out the voters on election day. Sometimes a newspaper will endorse a candidate. That often helps.

While the candidates are campaigning to win votes, the party leaders and committees are also busy. They ask party members for contributions. They also publicize the candidates and work to get out the vote.

There are state and federal laws which limit the amount of money that a person or organization may give to a campaign. Candidates for state office are required to turn in a list of their expenses to the Secretary of State. They must also show from where they got their campaign money. Candidates for county offices must file an expense report with the Board of Supervisors.

5. REPRESENTATIVES AND SENATORS ARE ELECTED TO SERVE IN CONGRESS

The United States Congress has two branches: the Senate and the House of Representatives.

The *U.S. Senate* has 100 members. The term of office is six years. Approximately one-third of the senators are elected every two years.

Each state, large or small, elects two U.S. Senators. Arizona voters, for example, re-elected Senator Barry Goldwater in 1974 and again in 1980. Senator DeConcini was elected in 1976 and again in 1982.

Representation in the *U.S. House of Representatives* is based on population. The size of the House is frozen at 435. After each census, which is taken every 10 years, the 435 seats are reapportioned among the states. Arizona, a fast-growing state, has been gaining seats.

Once the number of seats is determined, the Arizona legislature must divide the state into *congressional districts*. Each district is supposed to contain about the same number of people.

In the 1960s Arizona had three U.S. Representatives, usually called Congressmen. In the 1970s there were four. By 1980 Arizona's population was large enough for the state to have five Congressmen. Jim McNulty, a Democrat from Bisbee, was elected in 1982 as the first U.S. Representative in the new district number five.

Can you name the five congressmen by district today?

Congressional Districts of Arizona

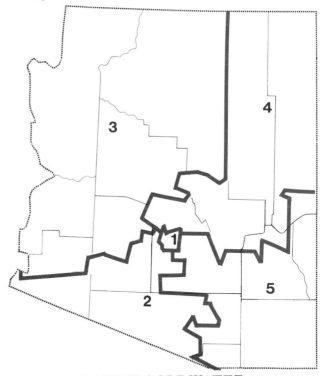

BARRY GOLDWATER

A native Arizonan, Barry Goldwater was born in Phoenix on January 1, 1909, when Arizona was still a territory. An energetic and talented youngster, Barry loved sports and the great Arizona outdoors. After his freshman year at Phoenix Union High School, Barry's father sent him to Staunton

U.S. Senator John McCain, Republican.

U.S. Senator Dennis DeConcini, Democrat.

Military Academy in Virginia. He graduated there as the "outstanding cadet."

Goldwater then enrolled at the University of Arizona. But when his father died, Barry dropped school. He was needed in the family's department store in Phoenix. Goldwater also joined the Army Reserve and learned to fly. He pursued his hobby of ham radio. He traveled to the back country to photograph Arizona's scenery, the Navajos, and the Hopis. (See picture on page 17, top.)

During World War II, Goldwater joined the Army Air Force and later rose to the rank of general in the reserve.

In 1949, he was elected to the Phoenix City Council. In 1952, Goldwater was elected to the U.S. Senate. This was a great achievement for a Republican in what was then an overwhelmingly Democratic state. He became known nationally as "Mr. Conservative." He was outspoken against big government and big labor.

Goldwater did not run for the Senate in 1964. He was nominated for president by the Republican National Convention. His chances were less than good. The country was not about to choose a third president in the span of twelve months. Lyndon Johnson, who became president when John Kennedy was shot, won all but six states.

Governor Paul Fannin, Goldwater's close

friend, won the vacant Senate seat in 1964. Goldwater returned to the U.S. Senate in 1968, when Senator Carl Hayden retired. For the first time, Arizona had two Republican senators.

Goldwater retired in 1986, after 30 years (five terms) in the Senate. He ended his career as chairman of the Armed Services Committee. His proudest achievemement was a law to reorganize the Department of Defense. This law was named in his honor.

Barry Goldwater.

467

Joggers running down Central Avenue in Phoenix.

UNIT NINE

LIVING IN ARIZONA TODAY

As the nation's fastest growing state, Arizona provides a variety of opportunities for its residents. The state is rich in cultural heritage. A wide range of cultural events are available for watching and participation. Arizona is a fun place to live.

New business and industry attract people to Arizona. They come to take advantage of the economic prosperity that accompanies growth. There is a wide choice of job types for people of all ages.

Rapid growth has resulted in many problems for Arizona. Cities and counties are forced to provide services for more people. The additional buildings draw upon our limited water and energy resources. Air pollution increases from automobile and industrial waste. Many tourists and winter residents who once came for the healthy climate are finding conditions similar to their own states.

You are a very important part of Arizona's future. Your active community participation will help guide the future. Your interest in community and cultural affairs will help preserve our unique heritage.

As citizens of Arizona, we are responsible to help solve its problems. By joining together with neighbors and other community members, we can help preserve our rich heritage. By solving our problems now, we can have better lives in the future.

Indian cowboys at a Prescott rodeo.

29

ARIZONA'S HERITAGE TODAY

The first Europeans and Americans came to Arizona looking for precious metals. Only a few struck it rich. Most of the early explorers and pioneers were repulsed by the burning sun and the vast empty spaces. Arizona grew slowly at first.

Today, Arizona is the nation's fastest growing state. People come in swarms. They are lured by the warm climate and open spaces. The hot sun, once a curse, has been tamed by air conditioning.

The public philosophy has been "grow as much as you can, as fast as you can." Arizona's government and businessmen have encouraged people and industry to come. The state has much to offer to outside investors. An ideal climate, a skilled labor pool, land, and a growing market for goods—all of these factors attract new manufacturing industries to Arizona.

New industries have broadened the economic base. The state is no longer solely a producer of raw materials—copper, cotton, and cattle. Manufacturing is now the leading industry.

Growth means prosperity and the good life. New people and new industries mean better business for merchants, more housing construction, and a greater variety of jobs. As Arizona grows, people have a wider choice of occupations, schools, recreation, and entertainment.

Rapid growth also brings many problems. Urban planning experts say that growth must be controlled—maybe even limited in some areas. Otherwise it will destroy the open spaces and clean air that brought people to Arizona in the first place.

When urban sprawl is uncontained, it takes over and destroys pollen-free desert vegetation. It results in traffic congestion, air pollution, a strain on water and energy sources, and the decay of inner cities. These problems threaten the "high quality" environment and life style that most people want.

KEY CONCEPTS

1. Arizonans have many opportunities and challenges.
2. Urbanization has resulted in many problems for Arizona cities.
3. Urbanized Arizona has achieved a new high in cultural tradition.
4. Arizona's rich heritage is being preserved.
5. You are a part of Arizona's heritage.

1. ARIZONANS HAVE OPPORTUNITIES AND CHALLENGES

The schools have kept pace with business and industry. Arizona's school system has grown along with the population. The three tax-supported universities rank among the best in the nation. They are trying hard to meet the "now" needs of students. But they are also developing outstanding research facilities.

For a long time the University of Arizona has been known worldwide for its agricultural experiments. Today the U of A is a leader in optical sciences. It is one of only a few schools which offer advanced degrees in this field. The optical sciences professors have been involved in the lunar, Mars, and other space programs.

Arizona State University's College of

Engineering has one of the best computer centers in the country. The School of Forestry at Northern Arizona University also has a national reputation for excellence. Each of Arizona's universities affords many opportunities to both undergraduate and graduate students.

The only four-year private college now operating in Arizona is Grand Canyon College in Phoenix. It is sponsored by the Southern Baptists. Another private school, the American Graduate School of International Management in Glendale, enjoys a global reputation. Students come from all over the world to study economics, languages, and other subjects.

A two-year community college system provides a wide range of educational opportunities for high school graduates. In addition to liberal arts subjects, the community colleges offer many vocational and technical courses.

Part of the University of Arizona campus at Tucson.

Livability, recreation, and tourism. Arizona's varied climate and geography give the state a *high "livability index."* An abundance of recreational and cultural opportunities brings happiness to local residents and tourists. Thanks to good weather, the percentage of Arizonans who take part in *outdoor fun* is well above the national average.

People get out-of-doors to camp, hike, or swim. There are thousands of hunters and fishermen in the state. Skiing is a popular pastime—both on water and on the snowy slopes. Many Arizonans are rock hounds, sightseers, or just plain sun worshippers who enjoy the leisure of relaxing in a chaise or hammock.

Within the state's 114,000 square miles there is an amazing *variety of terrain, climate, and scenery* for travelers to enjoy. The Grand Canyon, the national forests, the national monuments, and the state parks draw tourists like magnets.

On almost any weekend hundreds of Arizonans head for the lakes or tall timber. Many take their trailers, truck-campers, and boats. There are more pleasure boats per capita in Arizona than in any other state—and also plenty of man-made lakes on which to go boating.

In keeping with the state's *western tradition,* there are dozens of horseback riding

Family outing on the Verde River.

Water skiing on Lake Powell.

Snow Bowl near Flagstaff.

Big Surf in Tempe.

Camping on shore of Lake Apache northeast of Phoenix.

stables. Many communities stage annual rodeos and parades. During rodeo season people are encouraged to dress in western clothes. Tourists get a taste of the Old West by visiting

Shooting the rapids of the Colorado River.

Mayor Margaret Hance in the driver's seat during a Phoenix rodeo parade.

Tombstone, Old Tucson, the "ghost town" of Jerome, an Indian ceremonial, or one of the many museums in the state.

Many out-of-state visitors, of course, see only the big cities. They fly into Phoenix Sky Harbor or Tucson International Airport.

Their time is often spent at *conventions* in the civic centers. These conventions are becoming big business. A boon to the tourist industry, they give the state an opportunity for a good, clean source of income.

Professional and college spectator sports give the avid sports fan plenty of action in Arizona. The state has great baseball weather. A half dozen major league teams hold spring training here. The "Cactus League" exhibition games are well-attended. A full summer season of minor league ball follows. The Phoenix Giants and the Tucson Toros are in the AAA Pacific Coast League.

College baseball in Arizona is the best in the country. Both ASU and the U of A have won the national championship. These universities are now in the Pacific-10 Conference and field good athletic teams in all sports. NAU is in the Big Sky Conference. Grand Canyon

A young baseball player learns from Arizona State stars in a program sponsored by the Salt River Project.

Phoenix Suns star, Walt Davis, in action.

Pro golfer Johnny Miller watches Bob Hope ham it up.

College excels in small college baseball and basketball.

The Phoenix Suns basketball team brought Arizona its first glory in a major league sport in 1976. The Suns got to the finals in the National Basketball Association (NBA) playoffs.

In 1981 Governor Bruce Babbitt appointed a committee of citizens to study the desirability of securing a National Football League (NFL) franchise for Phoenix. Professional golf tournaments can be seen in Arizona during the winter. The Phoenix and Tucson Open events are on the PGA (Professional Golf Association) circuit. Top golf stars compete.

Arizona sports fans have the opportunity to watch some of the best athletes in the country.

Maintaining a water supply is a great challenge for Arizona. The maxim, "Arizona grows where water flows," is as true today as it was in pioneer days.

Arizona's rapid growth since World War II has been costly. The state has been *over-drafting its groundwater* bank account. At present about two-thirds of all water used in

An earth fissure east of Mesa. Cracks such as this one are caused by overpumping of groundwater.

Water can be saved by lining canals with concrete.

As water becomes scarce, desert landscaping becomes more popular. Desert plants survive on natural rainfall.

Arizona is pumped from the ground. The amount pumped now exceeds the natural recharge from rain and snow by 2½ million acre feet per year.

The groundwater level is going down and down. In some areas of the state, land subsidence* is a problem. Furthermore, the quality of pumped water is not as good as it was in previous times. The salinity (salt) content has been increasing over the years.

To keep on growing, Arizona must conserve water, prevent waste, and find *new sources of water*. Effluent from sewage plants is in demand by mines and farmers. Eventually, a cheap means of desalting ocean water will provide some water. In the future it may be necessary to divert fresh water from agriculture to home and industrial uses. In addition, fresh water may have to be imported from other states.

The *Central Arizona Project* will enable Arizona to use its full share of Colorado River water. The CAP will bring water to the counties of Maricopa, Pinal, and Pima. The new surface water will reduce but not eliminate the groundwater overdraft in these counties.

The CAP water will be taken from Lake Havasu above Parker Dam on the Colorado.

*Subsidence: sinking

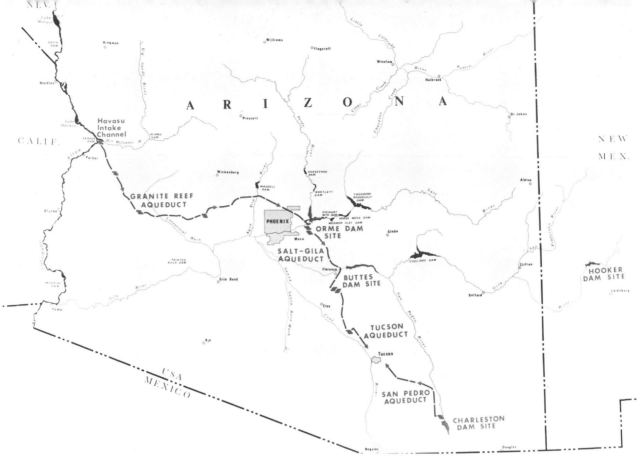

Map of the Central Arizona Project before 1977. In that year, President Carter deleted the Orme and Charleston dams in Arizona. Hooker Dam in New Mexico was also cut.

The beginning of the Central Arizona Project on the Colorado River.

Huge rotary rock boring machine used in the Buckskin Mountain Tunnel of the CAP.

Part of the Granite Reef Aqueduct under construction. The dike was designed to protect northern Phoenix metropolitan areas from flooding.

The water will be lifted by pumps to the inlet portal of the 6½ mile Buckskin Mountain Tunnel. From the tunnel it will flow over the concrete-lined Granite Reef Aqueduct to central Arizona.

Two more aqueducts—the Salt-Gila and the Tucson—will take part of the Colorado water to the fast-growing Tucson metropolitan area.

Arizona's growth and progress in the future depends to a great extent on an ample supply of good water.

Providing energy at a reasonable cost is another top priority for Arizona. Low cost energy helped Arizona to grow. For many years most of the energy came from two sources: hydroelectric plants in Arizona and the natural gas fields of Texas and other states.

Geothermal well near Chandler in the early 1970s.

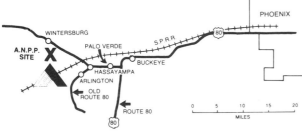

Map showing Palo Verde nuclear project.

Artists's drawing of the Palo Verde nuclear generating plant as it will look in 1986.

Large *thermal electric generating plants* have been built to supply the growing demand for electricity. But thermal plants have drawbacks. Oil and natural gas fuels are becoming scarce and costly. Coal-fired steam generators pollute the air. Nuclear energy is the cheapest fuel, though many people still wonder if it is safe. The Arizona (Palo Verde) Nuclear Power Project—the first nuclear generating plant in the state—will be completed west of Buckeye by 1986.

Arizona's *natural gas* is piped in from Texas, New Mexico, and other states. In the 1970s natural gas supplied about 40 percent of the state's total energy. But there was a shortage. During peak use periods the big industrial customers had to be cut off. In the future, industries and homes may have to replace natural gas with other sources of energy.

More and more *coal* may be used to replace natural gas. Arizona has an estimated two billion tons of coal reserves. Black Mesa coal on the Navajo Reservation is of higher quality than other coal found in the state. It is being used at the huge Navajo Generating Station near Page.

The Mohave Power Plant across the river from Bullhead City also burns the coal from Black Mesa. Coal for the Mohave plant is pulverized and mixed with water to form a

Navajo generating station near Page.

Night view of Kyrene generating plant near Tempe.

This solar-heated home in Flagstaff has a rock-bin storage system. Common river rocks soak up the sun's energy during the day and radiate it back at night.

slurry. It is then pumped nearly 300 miles across northern Arizona through a pipeline.

As Arizona grows, so does its need for electricity. At present, nuclear energy is the most economical source of electric power to replace fossil fuels. More research is needed to make *solar energy* practical for general use. The problem is to learn how to store heat from sunshine for a long period of time and at a low cost. The use of geothermal power—hot steam in the interior of the earth — also has possibilities for the future.

Challenges for the future. By 1980 the population of Arizona had skyrocketed to about 2.7 million. It is estimated that the state will have 4½ million people by the year 2000. Businesses, families, and individuals will continue moving to Arizona because of the high quality of life in the "Sun Belt."

POPULATION OF ARIZONA COMMUNITIES – 1980 CENSUS

Community/County	Population	Community/County	Population
Ahwatukee / Maricopa	4,382	Marana / Pima	1,674
Ajo / Pima	5,189	McNary / Apache	475
Apache Junction / Pinal	9,935	Mesa / Maricopa	152,453
Apache Wells / Maricopa	1,736	Miami / Gila	2,716
Arizona City / Pinal	825	Moenkopi / Coconino	679
Arizona Sun Sites / Cochise	852	Morenci / Greenlee	2,736
Avondale / Maricopa	8,134	Nogales / Santa Cruz	15,683
Bagdad / Yavapai	2,349	Oracle / Pinal	2,484
Benson / Cochise	4,190	Oraibi / Navajo	636
Bisbee / Cochise	7,154	Oro Valley / Pima	1,489
Buckeye / Maricopa	3,434	Page / Coconino	4,907
Bullhead City-Riviera / Mohave	10,363	Paradise Valley / Maricopa	10,832
Bylas / Graham	1,175	Parker / Yuma	2,542
Camp Verde / Yavapai	1,125	Patagonia / Santa Cruz	980
Carefree / Maricopa	986	Payson / Gila	5,068
Casa Grande / Pinal	14,971	Peoria / Maricopa	12,251
Cashion / Maricopa	3,014	Phoenix / Maricopa	789,704
Catalina / Pima	2,749	Pima / Graham	1,599
Cave Creek / Maricopa	1,589	Pinetop / Navajo	1,527
Central Heights-Midland City / Gila	2,791	Pirtleville / Cochise	1,425
Chandler / Maricopa	29,673	Polacca / Navajo	989
Chinle / Apache	2,815	Prescott / Yavapai	20,055
Chino Valley / Yavapai	2,858	Prescott Valley / Yavapai	2,284
Clarkdale / Yavapai	1,512	Sacaton / Pinal	1,951
Claypool / Gila	2,362	Safford / Graham	7,010
Clifton / Greenlee	4,245	Saint Johns / Apache	3,343
Coolidge / Pinal	6,851	San Carlos / Gila	2,668
Cottonwood / Yavapai	4,550	San Luis / Yuma	1,946
Davis-Monthan AFB / Pima	6,279	San Manuel / Pinal	5,443
Douglas / Cochise	13,058	Scottsdale / Maricopa	88,364
Dreamland Villa-Velda Rose / Maricopa	5,921	Sedona / Yavapai & Coconino	5,368
Dudleyville / Pinal	1,205	Seligman / Yavapai	510
Duncan / Greenlee	603	Sells / Pima	1,864
Eagar / Apache	2,791	Show Low / Navajo	4,298
El Mirage / Maricopa	4,307	Shungopavi / Navajo	505
Eloy / Pinal	6,240	Sierra Vista / Cochise	25,968
Flagstaff / Coconino	34,641	Snowflake / Navajo	3,510
Florence / Pinal	3,391	Somerton / Yuma	5,761
Fort Defiance / Apache	3,431	South Tucson / Pima	6,554
Fort Huachuca / Cochise[1]	10,506	Springerville / Apache	1,452
Fountain Hills / Maricopa	2,771	Stargo / Greenlee	1,038
Fredonia / Coconino	1,040	Sun City / Maricopa	40,664
Ganado / Apache	816	Sun City West / Maricopa[2]	3,741
Gila Bend / Maricopa	1,585	Sun Lakes / Maricopa	1,944
Gilbert / Maricopa	5,717	Superior / Pinal	4,600
Glendale / Maricopa	96,988	Surprise / Maricopa	3,723
Globe / Gila	6,708	Taylor / Navajo	1,915
Goodyear / Maricopa	2,747	Tempe / Maricopa	106,743
Grand Canyon / Coconino	1,348	Thatcher / Graham	3,374
Green Valley / Pima	7,999	Tolleson / Maricopa	4,433
Guadalupe / Maricopa	4,506	Tombstone / Cochise	1,632
Hayden / Gila	1,205	Tuba City / Coconino	5,045
Holbrook / Navajo	5,785	Tucson / Pima	330,537
Hotevilla / Navajo	680	Tucson Estates / Pima	2,814
Huachuca City / Cochise	1,661	Valencia / Maricopa	907
Jerome / Yavapai	420	Wellton / Yuma	911
Kayenta / Navajo	3,345	Whiteriver / Navajo	3,385
Keams Canyon / Navajo	233	Wickenburg / Maricopa	3,535
Kearny / Pinal	2,646	Willcox / Cochise	3,243
Kingman / Mohave	9,257	Williams / Coconino	2,266
Lake Havasu City / Mohave	15,737	Williams AFB / Maricopa	3,435
Lakeside / Navajo	1,333	Window Rock / Apache	2,230
Litchfield Park / Maricopa	3,657	Winkelman / Gila	1,060
Luke AFB / Maricopa	4,515	Winslow / Navajo	7,921
Mammoth / Pinal	1,906	Youngtown / Maricopa	2,254
Many Farms / Apache	1,364	Yuma / Yuma	42,433
		Yuma Proving Ground / Yuma	1,098

1. Included in Sierra Vista.
2. Preliminary census count: Provisional 'final' is 2,762 (under review by Correct Count Committee).
Source: U.S. Department of Commerce, Bureau of the Census; Arizona Department of Economic Security, Population Statistics Unit.

Population of Arizona communities in 1980.

We have great challenges in the years ahead. We must continue to develop a strong economy that will provide jobs for the growing population. At the same time, we must be sure that the state's natural beauty is preserved. A balance between economic development and environmental protection must be achieved.

Looking forward to the 21st century, Governor Raul Castro said in 1977:

"We have to pay special attention to the supply and demand for energy and water in Arizona. Conservation and efficient management of our resources must play a role in the process.

"We must strive to enhance the dignity of the individual," Castro said, "while guaranteeing equality of opportunity to all our citizens — regardless of race, sex, or ethnic heritage."

"We must work to create conditions that maximize individual growth and cultural diversity. The path ahead is one of excitement, challenge, and renewal of faith in ourselves."

2. URBANIZATION HAS RESULTED IN MANY PROBLEMS FOR ARIZONA CITIES

Urbanization is the movement of people to the cities. A great deal of urbanization is taking place in Arizona. About three-fourths of the state's residents live in the Phoenix or Tucson metropolitan areas.

A majority of the remaining fourth of the people live in smaller cities like Flagstaff, Prescott, Kingman, Winslow, Yuma, Casa Grande, Sierra Vista, Nogales, Douglas, Globe, Safford, Clifton, and others. Arizona has a small rural population.

Suburbanization. Today much of the new growth is taking place in *suburbs*. The once-isolated farm towns of Tempe, Scottsdale, and Glendale have expanded to the city limits of Phoenix. These cities—along with

Suburban Scottsdale is part of metropolitan Phoenix. This residential area along the Cross Cut Canal was formerly used for agriculture.

Metro Center shopping mall in suburban northwest Phoenix.

fast growing Mesa and about a dozen smaller places—are part of a complex "super community" known as "greater Phoenix."

Each of the component cities has its own local government and shopping centers. Some have developed their own civic centers too. But the whole Phoenix metropolitan area has a degree of unity in social and economic life.

Urban sprawl. The spread of suburbs has taken over some of Arizona's best farm lands and open spaces. The building of interstate highways has added to this problem. In the 1970s an average of over 4,000 acres a year were taken out of cultivation in the Phoenix area alone.

When urban sprawl closes in on a farm, the market value and taxes go up. A farmer usually decides to sell to housing developers. Senator Barry Goldwater analyzed the problem faced by farmers and ranchers:

"A farmer can keep his land in production," Goldwater said, "until his taxes get so high on his land that he can not make a profit. And the major factor in high taxation is urban growth."

Norman Cousins, a well-known writer and editor who once lived in Patagonia, dramatized his opposition to urban sprawl. He said that the real effects of what is happening to farm land can best be viewed from the air. High up, the new subdivisions look like spreading cancer cells under a microscope.

Most city planners want to stop "cancerous" urban sprawl. One way is for cities to buy up farms and desert land and establish *green belts*. The green belts would be wide enough to prevent new satellite cities from being built too close to the older cities.

Another way to stop urban sprawl is to change zoning laws to allow more high rise dwellings in the inner city. California's "Williamson Act of 1965" might also work in Arizona. This law gives a tax break to any farmer who signs a contract not to develop his land for 10 years.

There is still building room left inside the city limits of most urban areas. Vacant land, which already has streets and utilities, was leapfrogged as people rushed to cheaper lots

Urban sprawl is gradually taking over Arizona's open spaces.

in the suburbs. A Tucson city planner estimated in the early 1970s that the vacant land in that city could accommodate 140,000 to 200,000 more people. One problem is that 99 percent of new homes are built by developers who prefer the large tracts of land found in suburbs.

In stopping urban sprawl, city planners offer a word of caution. Problems arise when the population density of inner cities is increased too much. For one thing, the crime rate usually goes up when more people are concentrated in a smaller area. Also, there never seems to be enough parking spaces in high rise building districts. Noise pollution is also a major problem.

Urban transportation problems. City dwellers in Arizona depend on the automobile for transportation. It is the only way that most people can get to where they are going.

The automobile, however, presents many problems. Urban areas in Arizona do not have an adequate system of freeways to move the traffic. During rush hours the grid system of east-west and north-south streets is often

Traffic on the Black Canyon freeway in Phoenix.

Air pollution over Phoenix in the early 1970s.

Night view of Superstition Freeway and pedestrian overpass in Tempe.

I-17 freeway in Phoenix with Grand Avenue interchange in center.

overcrowded. Auto emissions are also the greatest source of air pollution.

Arizona cities do not have subways, elevated trains, or monorails. The urban areas are too spread out for rapid transit systems to operate efficiently. Phoenix and Tucson have bus systems but lose money on them. City of Phoenix bus routes to Glendale, Scottsdale, Tempe, and Mesa also operate at a loss. These intercity routes have to be subsidized by the local governments of the suburban cities which want the bus service.

Some Arizona cities have tried new kinds of transit systems. Glendale, for example, started a *dial-a-ride* service in 1975. People phone in for an air-conditioned minibus to pick them up. The customers are given door-to-door service. The minibus is like a taxi except that the driver detours along the way to pick up and deliver other passengers.

For most people in Arizona, private cars are still the most convenient form of transportation. They are ready where and when needed. The driver can stop where he pleases. Sooner or later, however, cities must build more freeways or stop urban sprawl.

The Glendale Dial-A-Ride service offers door-to-door bus service for city residents. It is used in large part by senior citizens.

In 1975 a Phoenix city planner said, "If we have low density, we will sprawl. Freeways are a must. Low density and freeways go together like ham and eggs."

Mass transit systems will never replace many automobiles unless growth is stopped at the present edges of the cities. New population would then have to be added to the urban areas already developed.

3. URBANIZED ARIZONA HAS ACHIEVED A NEW HIGH IN CULTURAL TRADITION

Urbanization has brought many cultural changes to Arizona. Just as the population has increased, so too has interest in the fine arts. Today Arizonans can enjoy live symphonies, rock concerts, or oldtime fiddling. Many communities have art exhibits, legitimate theater, dance programs, and band concerts. The heritage of Indian and Mexican culture is preserved in arts and crafts centers, festivals, and ceremonials.

Arizona architecture reflects the changes brought by urbanization. The new high-rise buildings in Phoenix and Tucson are fresh and clean in design and sturdy in construction. Many of the newer buildings combine the better features of earlier Spanish and Indian architecture with modern designs.

Arts and Crafts Center on the Gila River Indian Reservation near Interstate-10 south of Phoenix.

Western Savings building in north Phoenix.

Modern church architecture is shown in this Phoenix church.

486

Scottsdale City Hall, designed by Bennie M. Gonzales.

Grady Gammage Auditorium on the Arizona State University campus at Tempe.

The contrast between modern and Spanish-style architecture is shown in this view of downtown Phoenix.

The College of Architecture building at the University of Arizona combines a shaded Spanish-style patio with modern freestanding pillars to support the roof. Another example is the Scottsdale Civic Center designed by Bennie M. Gonzales. A native Arizonan, Gonzales put a love for vast space and panoramic views into his award-winning design.

The opening of Arizona State University's Grady Gammage Auditorium in 1964 marked a new era in cultural growth. Designed by Frank Lloyd Wright, the auditorium is the site of many excellent theatrical and musical productions.

Art. Urbanization has increased the number and variety of *artists* in Arizona. The state is a natural center for Indian art. Navajo painters and Hopi silversmiths have been especially outstanding. Some native painters have learned to blend traditional Indian and modern styles.

Navajo rug weaver.

487

Painting by the Navajo artist, Quiney Tahoma.

Hopi silversmith, Eldon Siewiyumptewa, at work.

Numerous galleries in the major cities exhibit and sell original paintings, sculpture, ceramics, jewelry, weavings, and glass work. Scottsdale is nationally known as the home of hundreds of artists. Many other cities and towns have fine arts associations which sponsor arts and crafts shows. Yuma's annual Southwest Invitational, begun in 1965, is but one example.

Among the good *collections of paintings* in Arizona are those at the state universities in Tucson and Tempe, the Phoenix Art Museum, and the Tucson Museum of Art. There are also many private collections.

Music, like the other fine arts, got its greatest boost with the influx of people into Arizona after World War II. An important role in the state's musical growth has been played by the universities, community colleges, schools, National Federation of Music Clubs, churches, and civic groups.

The greatest concentration of music activities has naturally been in the metropolitan areas of Phoenix and Tucson. Each city has had a symphony orchestra since the 1920s. For years the Phoenix Symphony performed in the Phoenix Union High School Auditorium. Since the early 1970s concerts have been played at the beautiful Symphony Hall at the Phoenix Civic Plaza.

Among the better-known local singing

Ted DeGrazia, a famous Arizona artist, paints a mural.

Phoenix Symphony Orchestra

groups are the Tucson Boys Chorus and the Orpheus Club in Phoenix. Both have received standing ovations after performances in Europe. People in Phoenix and Tucson who appreciate music also have many opportunities to hear nationally famous concert soloists and musical groups.

Local festivals have promoted music along with the other arts. Since 1951, for example, the Tucson Festival Society has presented ethnic programs. The annual San Xavier Fiesta and the Fiesta of La Placita highlight the colorful songs, dances, and customs of Indian and Mexican people.

Flagstaff is fast becoming a fine arts cultural center. The Shrine of the Ages Choir has a national reputation for singing at Easter sunrise services at the Grand Canyon. The Flagstaff Symphony draws many musicians from NAU and surrounding towns. The annual Flagstaff Festival, which was started in 1966, has grown into a summer of great music, dance, theater, and film classics. Big name artists, such as opera star Roberta Peters in 1975, have attracted large audiences. The Flagstaff Festival has received grants from the National Endowment for the Arts, a federal agency.

Funds from the National Endowment for the Arts are distributed in Arizona by the *Arizona Commission on the Arts and Human-*

ities. This commission was created by the state legislature in 1967. It assists community groups that sponsor arts and crafts events. The commission is trying to make the arts more widely available to all Arizonans. Grants are given for projects of black and Mexican-American groups, on the Indian reservations, and in small towns. The symphonies and other arts and crafts groups also receive funds.

Arizona's theater heritage can be traced back to territorial days. The mining camps and frontier towns were visited by traveling entertainers. By the late 1920s both Phoenix and Tucson had little theaters. The Phoenix Little Theater produced its first play in 1921

Music Hall at the Tucson Community Center seats 2,400

489

Apache crown dancer.

in a barn donated by the Dwight B. Heard family. Since World War II many school, college, and community drama groups have been organized. Amateur plays and musicals are presented in beautiful theaters and auditoriums all over the state.

Professional stars from Hollywood and Broadway have performed in plays and musicals at the Sombrero Playhouse in Phoenix, Grady Gammage Auditorium, and the Phoenix Celebrity Theater. The Celebrity Theater is one of the most successful "in-the-round" theaters in America. Tucson's Arizona Civic Theater, organized in 1967, also presents off-Broadway plays. Since 1971 the Civic has used the Tucson Community Center theater.

The dance has been an important fine art to Arizona's Indians for a long time. But dance never attracted strong interest in Arizona until the 1960s. The state's first civic ballet was organized in Tucson in 1965.

As prosperity continues and leisure time is available, the arts and literature will flourish in Arizona. Eventually, the great novel, play, or musical will be written that catches the full spirit of Arizona's heritage.

4. ARIZONA'S RICH HERITAGE IS BEING PRESERVED

A study of the past would be impossible without written records or the possessions of people who came before us. We can study Arizona's rich heritage because many written records and artifacts have been preserved. Take the early Indians, for example. Much can be learned about them from the diaries of Spanish explorers and missionaries.

Modern archaeologists also have helped to piece together the story. They use scientific detective methods to study Indian ruins that are unearthed. Unfortunately, much of what happened in Arizona's past can never be known because no records were kept.

Research in Arizona history also is complicated because many valuable documents have been lost or destroyed. Other records are scattered over the world. Many of the sources outside the state, however, are being put on microfilm for use here.

Arizona has several large collections of family papers, old newspapers, diaries, letters, government records, photographs, and other materials. These collections can be used by serious students of Arizona history.

The *Arizona Historical Society* in Tucson has been Arizona's official repository for historical materials since 1884. Besides a huge library, the Society also maintains a museum. The whole scope of Arizona history is featured in colorful dioramas and displays of early memorabilia.

The *three state universities* also have extensive collections of historical records. The *Arizona Department of Library and Archives* at the capitol in Phoenix houses the official government records of the territory and state.

Many materials and artifacts on Indians can be found at the Museum of Northern Arizona at Flagstaff, the Arizona State Museum in Tucson, the Heard Museum in Phoenix, and The Amerind Foundation at Dragoon.

There are dozens of local museums and historical societies throughout the state. They usually feature the possessions and photographs of early-day families.

Another way to preserve history is through publication. Arizona is fortunate in having several good historical journals. *Arizona and the West* has been published quarterly by the University of Arizona since 1959. The *Journal of Arizona History* was

A blacksmith at Pioneer Arizona, a living history museum located north of Phoenix.

Pipe Spring National Monument north of the Grand Canyon in Mohave County. Pioneer Mormon cattle raisers built the Pipe Spring fort, called Windsor Castle, in the 1870s.

The Hubbell Trading Post on the Navajo Reservation is an example of a national historic site.

started a year later by the Arizona Historical Society. The *Kiva* is a quarterly journal devoted mainly to research studies in archaeology. Newspapers and magazines, including the *Arizona Highways*, print historical articles too.

National Historical Sites. A special effort has been made to preserve Arizona's historic buildings and sites. The idea is that once these historic remains are gone, they cannot be replaced. The U. S. Congress helped by passing the National Historic Preservation Act in 1966. By this law the U. S. Department of Interior can pay 50 percent of the cost of preserving sites listed in the National Register of Historic Places. The state pays the other half.

Sites in Arizona are recommended for the National Register by the Arizona Historic Sites Review Committee. The members of this group are also on the Historical Advisory Committee appointed by the governor.

Every county in Arizona has some National Register sites. Cochise County was given two more in July, 1976, when the Gadsden Hotel and The Grand Theater in Douglas became sites number 132 and 133. Other sites all over the state are being added from time to time. The State Parks Board has surveyed hundreds of sites for future consideration.

Some cities like Mesa have identified their own local sites with historical plaques.

5. YOU ARE A PART OF ARIZONA'S HERITAGE

Our study of Arizona's past gives us an appreciation for the lives and achievements of people who made the state what it is today. Contributions to Arizona's heritage have been made by people of *many different races and origins*: Indians, Spaniards, Mexicans, Orientals, Blacks, and Anglo-Americans.

Men and women in *all walks of life* have played important roles on the stage of Arizona history. There were fur trappers, soldiers, Indian leaders, merchants, miners, ranchers, farmers, politicians, scientists, teachers, religious leaders, housewives, artists, industrialists, and many others.

Arizona's history has been shaped by *outside influences* too. Wars, the Great Depression, the population explosion, and many other national or world events have made a great impact on Arizona affairs. New inventions—the automobile, airplane, radio, television, and air conditioning—have changed our life styles significantly.

Our study of Arizona's past makes us aware of *values* held by people who settled and built the state. The pioneers had dreams and visions for a better way of life. But they were practical, self-reliant, hard-working, and resourceful. While they greatly respected individual freedom, the pioneers also believed in cooperation and sacrificing for the common good. They put a high value on education and on service to the community.

We all share, to varying degrees, in the *material aspects* of Arizona's heritage. Highways, schools, and churches have been built for us. Parks and recreation areas were established where we can enjoy ourselves. State and local governments strive to protect our property and perform other needed services. In learning what Arizona's past generations have accomplished, we gain courage and inspiration to make the state an even better place in which to live.

Yes, we are a part of history too. A knowledge of the past makes it easier to understand our present problems. We gain a better *perspective* to make decisions for the future. We should all remember the Indian who never got lost because he always looked back to see where he had been.

ACKNOWLEDGMENTS AND PICTURE CREDITS

During thirty years of study and research of Arizona's heritage, the author has been indebted to many people for their assistance and encouragement. Much gratitude is due the individuals and institutions which made available primary sources, records, monographs, and reference works. The special collections staffs at the state's three universities, the Arizona Historical Society and the Arizona State Museum in Tucson, the Phoenix Public Library, and the Sharlot Hall Museum in Prescott have been especially helpful. The University of Arizona Press, which has published three of the author's books, was most cooperative in sharing many maps and photographs for this text.

Appreciation is expressed to Gibbs M. and Catherine Smith of Peregrine Smith, Inc. They saw the need for a textbook and encouraged the author to write it. Richard Firmage edited and designed the book. Goff Dowding did some of the maps and drawings. Jean Paulson assisted with editing. Bernard Adams helped with paste ups.

Heather Hatch, photo curator at the Arizona Historical Society, worked with the author for six months in locating relevant illustrations. Her professional advice was invaluable. Susan Luebbermann, staff photographer at the Arizona Historical Society, also deserves special commendation.

The numerous photographs and maps in *Arizona's Heritage* are a credit to the following people who helped in one way or another:

Tom Ambrose, Bruce Babbitt, Louis J. Battan, Sylvia Bender, Kay Benedict, Rob Boley, Wesley Bolin, John L. Bolles, Russ Boshart, Linda Bossom, Margaret S. Bret Harte, Sidney B. Brinckerhoff, Storm Bryant, Don Bufkin, Jeanne Burt, Clovis Campbell, Ethel Carey, Governor Raul Castro, Pierce Chamberlain, Jerry B. Chilton, Glenn O. Clark, June Clark, Charles C. Colley, Marguerite Cooley, Hal Coss, Lynn Cressan, Edette Datus, Don Davis, Lori Davisson, Senator Dennis DeConcini, Bud DeWald, Larry Doerschlag, Richard A. Duff, Mrs. Lynn Earley, and Ron Elias.

Senator Paul Fannin, Robert Fisher, Jerry Flynn, John Foster, Walter S. Fruland, Timothy W. Fuller, Governor Sam Goddard, Senator Barry Goldwater, Rosa Gomez, Bennie Gonzales, Carol Goodman, Max Guthrie, Marjorie M. Hackett, Robert P. Hale, Pat Hallickson, Representative Ben Hanley, Kathleen D. Harlan, Joseph A. Hatch, Emil W. Haury, O. C. Havens, Glenn Haynes, Pat Henry, Mrs. Charles W. Herbert, Karen Hoffman, Alice Holmes, Richard I. Hopper, State Senator Arthur J. Hubbard, Sr., and Don Hutchinson.

John W. Irwin, Grace Jarboe, Duncan Jennings, Larry and Dorothy Jorgenson, Charles O. Kemper, Carol Kirk, Bill Kleinz, Thomas W. Korff, John A. Kuehn, David P. Kurrasch, Helen C. Land, Jerry Landis, Cleve Langston, Mervin W. Larson, Barbara LeGrande, C. H. Lockhart, Austin Long, Lt. Donald Lowe, and Ken Lucas.

Daniel Mahar, Ray Manley, John Mark, Cyd Martin, Larry A. May, Warren McArthur, Carla McClain, Ken McClure, Judge Ernest McFarland, Ross W. McLachlan, Bety McMahon, Linda Miller, Doris Moten, Clyde Murray, Ivan Murray, Shelby Myer, Bruce Naegeli, Tad Nichols, and Arthur Olivas.

Representative Daniel Peaches, Dave Perry, Linda Pederson, Susan Peters, Mrs. H. B. Peterson, Sue Peterson, Thomas H. Peterson, Don Phillips, Andrew Poggenpohl, Don Powell, Tom Preston, Governor J. Howard Pyle, Cheryl Rexford, Congressman John J. Rhodes, Les Rhuart, Jim Richardson, A. Tracy Row, Congressman Eldon Rudd, Al Ruland, and Ted Rushton.

Mark Sanders, Donald B. Sayner, M. P. Scanlon, Allan Schmidt, Walter Schuck, Elizabeth Shaw, Robert Shelton, Bill Sizer, Dana M. Slaymaker, Wilma Smallwood, Winn W. Smiley, Tom Smylie, Susie Sato, Lyle K. Sowls, Arthur Springer, Kathleen Stanley, Marvin A. Stokes, Dick Stuart, Congressman Bob Stump, and Bob Sullivan.

Steve Talley, Helga Teiwes, Jim Thomas, Margaret H. Thomas, Don Thompson, Ed Toliver, Marshall Townsend, Congressman Morris Udall, Jean Updike, Peter Urban, Martin Vanacour, and Jay Van Orden.

Gordon Wagner, Lewis Wayne Walker, Bob Wallace, Carolyn Warner, Margo Warren, Justice of the Peace Tim Weeks, Dave Weiser, Richard R. Willey, Chris Williams, Cody Williams, Governor Jack Williams, Jo Williams, Travis Williams, Marjorie Wilson, George W. Worley, Judy Wright, Ray Wyatt, Herbert Yazhe, and John York.

Additional people who provided pictures for the 1983 edition were: Neta J. Bowman, S. Alan Cook, Lola Dunaway, Judge Lloyd Fernandez, Elizabeth Urwin Fritz, Sue Glawe, Sandy Johnson, Joe Madrigal, Ruben Ortega, Stephanie Ostrom, Oscar C. Palmer, Sr., Judge Cecil B. Patterson, Jr., Bob Rink, Don Stevenson, and Carol Taylor.

The specific pictures used in this book are credited below. The author and publisher also wish to thank the people who offered pictures that could not be used for lack of space.

Letters besides the numbers designate position on the page: L (left side), R (right side), T (top), M (middle), and B (bottom).

Arizona Department of Economic Security, 382L.
Arizona Department of Economic Planning and Devel-

494

INDEX

Cárdenas, Captain García López de, 69-70
Carleton, Colonel (later General) James H., 157-60, 161
Carpenter, Clarence, 362
Carranza, President Venustiano (Mexico), 272, 273
Carrier, Dr. Willis, 309
Carson, Kit, 123, 127, 159
Carter, President Jimmy, 368, 370, 383, 423, 478
Carver High School, 385-87
Casa Grande, city of, 194, 204, 210, 280, 385-86, 393, 397, 455, 482
Casa Grande Monument, 51-52
Castro, Governor Raul, 367-68, 373, 383, 421, 482
Catholic Church, 61. *See also* missionaries
Cattle industry: Spanish period, 78-81, 85, 98, 100; Mexican, 108-13, 133; territorial, 191, 195, 235-38, 253, 254-55; branding, 237-38; cowboys, 112-13, 226-27, 238, 404; hoof and mouth disease, 333; since World War II, 403-404. *See also* 27-28, 30, 36, 38, 39, 41, 127, 302-303
Cenozoic Age, 12, 14-15
Central Arizona Project (CAP), 359, 361, 458-59, 477-79
Central School (Phoenix), 276
Centralists, 107
Census: 1860, 148, 225; 1864, 167-68; 1870, 165, 225; 1880, 165, 225; 1890, 225; 1900, 225, 253; 1910, 225. *See also* population
Chacón, Augustine, 255
Chambers, Major Reed, 275
Chandler, city of, 50, 210, 243, 276, 279, 284, 391, 392, 405-406, 455, 480, 482
Chandler, Dr. A. J., 242, 405
Charles III, King, 85, 92, 98
Chavez, Cesar, 366, 381, 382-83
Chauncey, Tom, 426
Check and balance system, 415
Chichilticale, 68
Children's Colony, 353
Chinese, 211, 212, 229, 273-74
Chinle, 14, 210
Chiricahua Apaches: See Indians, Apaches
Chiricahua Mountains, 15, 19, 33, 150, 159
Chivington, Major J. M., 157
Church, William, 234
Cíbola, Seven Cities of, 63, 67, 68
Cisco Kid, 290-91
City manager, 456
City government: See town or city government
Civil Rights Act, U. S. (1964), 387
Civil Rights Act, U. S. (1968), 385
Civil Rights Commission, 363
Civil rights law of 1965, Arizona, 363
Civil service system, 345
Civilian Conservation Corps (CCC), 301-303, 306
Civil Air Patrol, 325
Civilian Pilot Training (WWII), 316
Civil War, 147, 152, 154-62
Clanton, M. E., 241
Clark, Charles M., 224
Clark, John, 239
Clarkdale, town of, 58, 482

Clerk of the Superior Court, 452
Cleveland, President Grover, 174, 233
Clifton, town of, 204, 210, 219, 233, 234, 244-45, 274, 331, 384, 482
Climate, 14, 22-24, 347, 389. *See also* climate chart, 23
Clum, John P., 186-87, 224
Clothing in territorial days, 214
Cochise, 159, 184, 187
Code of laws, 168-69, 329, 357, 371
Collective bargaining, 346
Collier, John, 307
Colossal Cave, 302
Coloradas, Mangas, 159, 239
Colorado City, 149
Colorado Plateau, 14-15, 16-18
Colorado River: toad, 36; Patayan Indians, 59-60; Alarcon, 68; Oñate, 73; Kino, 81; Sedelmayr, 82; Yuma crossing, 86, 127-28, 129, 210; Yumas, 91; Anza crosses, 92, 93; missions, 95-96; Romero expedition, 107; fur trappers, 120, 121, 123; Sitgreaves expedition, 141; Anglo settlements, 165; Laguna Dam, 253; shooting rapids, 197, 475. *See also* Grand Canyon, Central Arizona Project
Colorado River Affair, 340-41
Colorado River (Santa Fe) Compact, 338, 345
Colorado River controversy, 332, 338-39, 359, 360-61
Colorado Volunteers, 157-58
Colquhoun, James, 234, 245
Colyer, Vincent, 183-84
Comaduran, Antonio, 129
Committee of the Whole, 421
Committees, legislative, 419-21
Community colleges, 360, 361, 429, 472
Commutation, 329
Concho, 210, 239
Conde, Governor Alejo García, 101
Conde, General Pedro García, 132, 133
Condon, Dr. Daniel J., 314
Confederate Territory of Arizona, 155, 156-58
Congress, town of, 201, 211, 233, 253
Congressional districts: map, 467
Congressmen, 464-65, 466-67
Conlan, Congressman, 369, 371
Conquistadores, 61, 66
Constitution, Arizona, 262-66, 332-33
Constitutional Convention, 262-66, 332-33, 344
Convict labor, 330, 335
Cook, Charles H., 184, 220
Cook, Nathan, 140
Cooke, Captain Philip St. George, 126, 128-29
Cooke's wagon road, 128, 131, 143
Coolers, evaporative, 24, 308, 309
Coolidge, city of, 51, 376, 399, 401, 482
Coolidge, President Calvin, 285, 339
CORE (Congress of Racial Equality), 361
Coronado, Francisco, 67-71, 73
Corporation Commission, 430, 435. *See also* 361
Correctional institutions, 365-66, 433-34
Cortés, Hernán, 61, 62, 63, 72
Coues, Elliott, 170
Councils of Government (COGs), 458

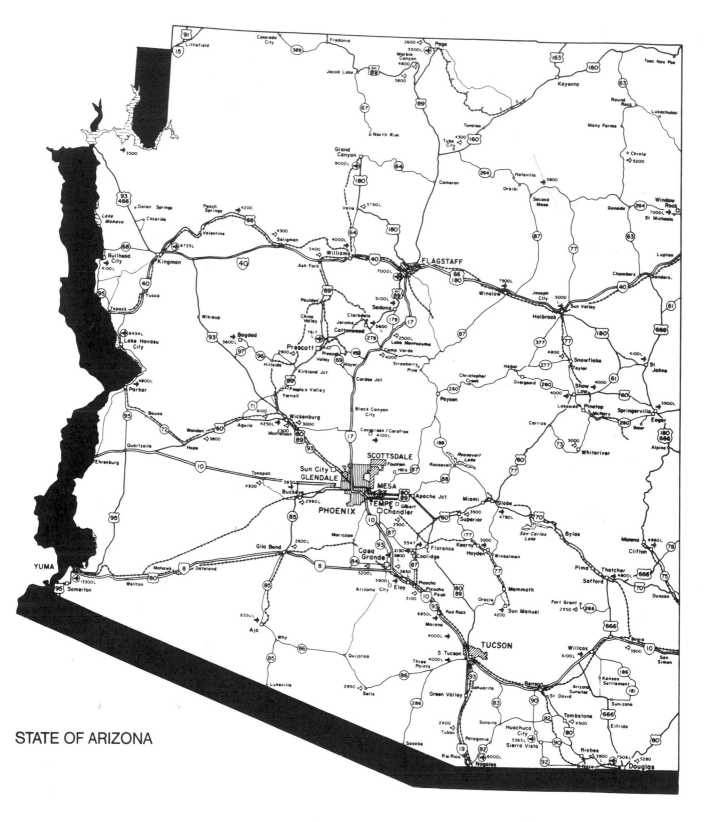

STATE OF ARIZONA

```
0   10  20  30  40  50
        MILES
```

SOURCES: "ARIZONA ROAD MAP" ARIZONA STATE
HIGHWAY COMMISSION, 1973; FLIGHT GUIDE,
AIRPORT AND FREQUENCY MANUAL, VOL. I,
AIRGUIDE PUBLICATIONS, LONG BEACH, 1973.

REVISED INFORMATION SUPPLIED BY ARIZONA
DEPARTMENT OF TRANSPORTATION, DECEMBER 1981

Arizona Counties and County Seats

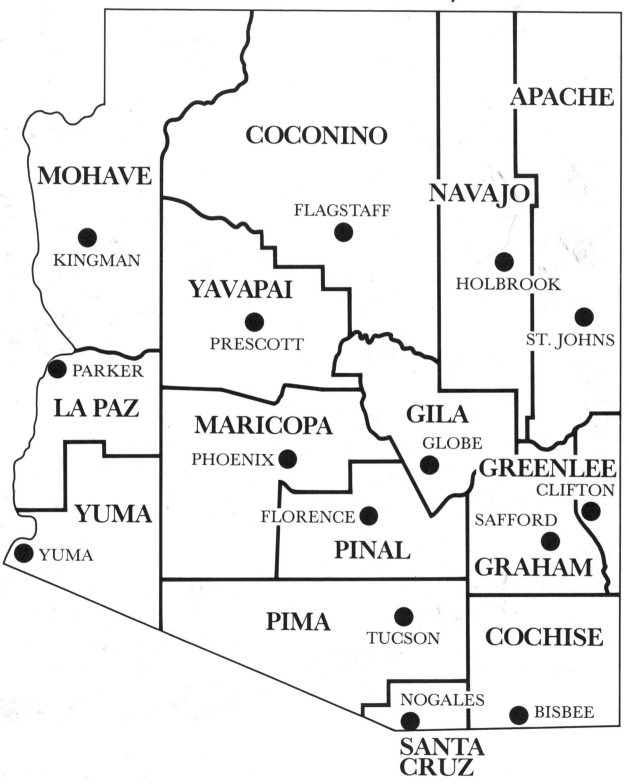